Crafting Trade and Investment Accords for Sustainable Development

Crafting Trade and Investment Accords for Sustainable Development

Athena's Treaties

MARIE-CLAIRE CORDONIER SEGGER

OXFORD
UNIVERSITY PRESS

OXFORD
UNIVERSITY PRESS

Great Clarendon Street, Oxford, OX2 6DP,
United Kingdom

Oxford University Press is a department of the University of Oxford. It furthers the University's objective of excellence in research, scholarship, and education by publishing worldwide. Oxford is a registered trade mark of Oxford University Press in the UK and in certain other countries

First Edition published in 2021
Impression: 1

Published in the United States of America by Oxford University Press
198 Madison Avenue, New York, NY 10016, United States of America

British Library Cataloguing in Publication Data
Data available

Library of Congress Control Number: 2020953018

ISBN 978–0–19–883134–1

DOI: 10.1093/oso/9780198831341.001.0001

Printed and bound by
CPI Group (UK) Ltd, Croydon, CR0 4YY

Foreword

Professor Thomas Cottier

For all too long, the fields of international trade and investment, environmental and human rights law evolved in isolation, dealt with by separate epistemic communities. It is only recently that these fields are finding a common roof in international law for sustainable development, and are exposed to mutual interaction and debate. This volume makes a substantial contribution to this process. It is motivated by the concern that poorly regulated economic activities and normative contradictions are contributing substantially to global challenges such as climate change and the collapse of ecological systems, as well as to rising poverty and disrespect for human rights. It is motivated by the need for in-depth analysis with a view to bring about greater coherence, interaction, and integration among these fields of international law in future international agreements.

Professor Marie-Claire Cordonier Segger, senior director of the Centre for International Sustainable Development Law and Leverhulme Trust visiting professor at the University of Cambridge, also a full professor of international law in Canada, is a pioneer and one of the world's leading legal scholars in interfacing trade, investment, and sustainable development. In the initial pages of this volume, she notes that if the ancient Greek goddess Athena, patroness of justice, wisdom, and the crafts, were to consider the current state of globalization, she would be deeply concerned, perhaps even horrified. She likely would induce oracles changing our minds and perceptions. This book is an invitation to do so and to choose a different path, extended to the thousands of decision-makers, advisors, and academics whose efforts shape our potential for success in international, regional, and bilateral trade, investment, and sustainable development endeavours. It is a call for sound scientific assessment, legal scholarship and analysis; for reasoned legal dialogue and drafting; for careful and creative legal drafting; for coherent and consistent implementation and compliance; and for peaceful, rational settlement of disputes.

The author's extensive law and policy research is international in scope and grounded in a profoundly humanist, interactional understanding of the law which views legal principles and rules as both shaping and being shaped by political, economic, and social compromise. She proposes a series of tailored legal solutions to the challenges wrought by globalization which, rather than closing borders and building walls, require the careful crafting and negotiation of more effective, sophisticated international accords that integrate social and environmental considerations into economic development endeavours. In her view, by carefully identifying environmental and social concerns, then crafting and weaving appropriate provisions into trade and investment treaties, the accords themselves become more likely to succeed over the long term, in essence—more sustainable.

Through carefully researched legal scholarship, the author defends the need for deeper international collaboration, tracing interactional regimes that extend across nationalist views and borders and seeking to achieve common goals of integrated economic and social progress and environmental protection. Her objective is to explore innovative ways to extend relationships among communities and States through a well-crafted, just, and more sustainable globalization. Her work is both analytical and aspirational. It makes a profound contribution to the dialogue and process of bringing about normative coherence with a view to produce the public goods required to meet the challenges of our times. I truly recommend the volume to you.

Preface

Professor Stephen J Toope

Over the last fifty years or so, we have seen extensive international environmental treaty-making. Many multilateral environmental accords (MEAs) contain provisions to secure sustainable development in different ways across diverse fields. Parallel to these MEAs, new international economic treaties are also being negotiated. In principle, as this volume argues, environmental and social priorities should be considered fully in economic development decision-making, and in international trade law and policy as part of that economic decision-making. While not well-documented before now, more and more trade and investment accords address the global Sustainable Development Goals of the United Nations. Yet, comparatively little robust scholarly legal analysis exists on how trade and investment rules affect a State's potential for sustainable development, and how economic treaties might foster rather than frustrate sustainable development.

Building on years of careful comparative legal research and several edited scholarly collections, this volume addresses these gaps. The author argues that in many countries, treaty decision-makers, negotiators, and their advisors are finding innovative ways to integrate environmental and social considerations into a new generation of trade and investment agreements, particularly in regional economic accords. Through this integration, international trade and investment law could be better positioned to contribute to sustainable development. In particular, Professor Cordonier Segger examines three key tensions, which States can address by adopting measures to integrate environmental and social development priorities into the economic rules of trade and investment treaties themselves. These tensions, the author suggests, are interlinked, as each has the potential to build economic law while, at the same time, explicitly or implicitly promoting the many facets of sustainable development. Further, the author proposes, procedural innovations such as impact assessments can assist in identifying, ex-ante, potential social, and environmental effects of a new economic treaty. Through a transparent, inclusive engagement process and reasoned debate, carefully crafted compromises can lead to policy coherence, rather than exacerbating social and economic marginalization, degradation, and conflict. By acknowledging and effectively addressing these tensions, international society and domestic citizenry can shape economic law to further sustainable development. In today's anxious world, these findings also have profound significance for areas well beyond the realm of economic law and policy.

The volume explores the interactions between specialities in international law and, more fundamentally, the essential interactions that inform and lead to the creation of international law. Elsewhere, Professor Jutta Brunnée and I have developed an interactional account of legitimacy and legality in international law. We offer a framework for analysis by bringing together the concepts of shared understandings of actors and criteria of legality that build legitimacy in law. Law is then further supported by continuing practices of legality or is undermined if those practices degrade. Applying this framework, this volume builds on an understanding of international law as inherently interactional. It demonstrates that without these forms of social interaction, particularly shared understandings of the actors involved, bringing together the lex specialis of international economic, human rights and environmental law is most difficult. However, shared understandings, when connected with the instantiation of criteria of legality, allow for dialogues across specialties and disciplines. Within this framework, as the volume demonstrates, legitimacy exists because of the will and understanding of the Parties even while addressing global challenges from different fields and experiences.

It is a pleasure to commend this volume to readers from many audiences. The book offers valuable insights in many dimensions. The study of innovations in treaty negotiation can provide useful advice for the future crafting of trade agreements that take sustainable development seriously, for the interpretation of trade treaties and also for the continuing WTO negotiations. It can also provide those participating in treaty negotiations with essential lessons as to how inclusive treaty agreements can be created and implemented when there are multiple—and often competing—identities, constituencies and interests involved. The lessons of this volume will appeal to those working as officials and analysts in international, environmental and development-related institutions, where the issues it addresses arise on a near-daily basis. For academics, professors and students alike, this volume poses and answers deeply challenging questions that lie at various intersections amongst environmental law, sustainable development, international economics and international political economy. Practicing lawyers and attorneys, those working in positions as environmental advisors and those consulting with governments, will find that the volume offers fresh analytical perspectives on difficult law and policy issues, as well as an assessment of the ways in which they can be addressed now and in the future. Finally, civil society organizations and foundations, notably those prodding us to meet the world's sustainable development goals, will find that this volume offers unique insight into process and law. It also points to where their efforts may best be deployed during treaty negotiations and to fill in the gaps of existing treaty regimes.

This volume brings the voice of justice and wisdom from antiquity to modernity through the lens of international law both as an appropriate continuation and in a distinctly novel manner. It offers a fitting tribute to Athena, and to all the voices for future generations that continue to strive— across all disciplines and professions— to build a better world to leave our children and grandchildren.

Acknowledgements

This volume is the result of nearly twenty years of legal research and comparative inquiry, with sincere thanks and acknowledgement due to key mentors, including my former Dean and current Vice-Chancellor Professor Stephen Toope, Professor Sir Christopher Greenwood and Professor Markus Gehring at the University of Cambridge; Professor Armand de Mestral, Professor Richard Janda, Professor Francois Crepeau and Professor Andrea Bjorklund at McGill University; Professor Daniel C Esty at Yale University; and especially Professor Vaughan Lowe, Professor Dan Sarooshi, Professor Christopher McCrudden and Professor Catherine Redgwell who supervised and guided the original international law doctoral research at the University of Oxford which laid the foundations for this volume, as well as Professor Thomas Cottier and Professor Rodrigo Polanco at the World Trade Institute in the University of Bern; and also Dr Ashfaq Khalfan, valued friend and Chair of the Centre for International Sustainable Development Law (CISDL) Board of Governors, along with all my CISDL colleagues. In addition, I am deeply grateful to David Runnalls, Aaron Cosbey and the late Konrad von Moltke at the International Institute for Sustainable Development (IISD) whose insights and knowledge shaped this work; to Ricardo Melendez-Ortiz whose mentorship and guidance at the International Centre for Trade and Sustainable Development (ICTSD) also significantly strengthened this research; and to Bill Loris, Irene Khan, Paul Crowley, Dr Tom McInerney, Dr Dave Sadoff, Robert Buergenthal, Dr Ilaria Bottigliero, Erwin van der Borght, Dr Fabiano Andrade de Correa, Yolando Saito and other colleagues with whom I was privileged to collaborate at the International Development Law Organization (IDLO). I must especially deeply thank and recognize the invaluable research and drafting assistance of Emily Morison, Blessing Ajayi, Sebastien Jodoin, Patrick Reynaud, Oliver Taherzadeh and Rodrigo Mella, among others, without whose brilliance, long hours of revision and research assistance this volume could not exist. Finally, I must recognize the invaluable support and guidance provided by the late Hon Judge Charles D Gonthier, first Chair of the CISDL Board of Governors, and the late HE Judge CG Weeramantry, Patron of the CISDL, both of whom are deeply missed.

Sincere thanks are also due to Jack McNichol, Vijay Chandrasekaran, also originally John Louth, from Oxford University Press and their partners, for all their assistance and support in the publication process.

Finally, this volume is dedicated to Nico Cordonier Gehring and Jona Cordonier Gehring, two very prominent voices of the future generations that depend on all our efforts towards sustainable development for their survival.

Table of Contents

Table of Treaties & Statutes

1. INTERNATIONAL TREATIES

Table of Bilateral and Regional Economic Agreements

Table of Multilateral Treaties

Table of Further International Treaties

Table of Cases

1. INTERNATIONAL COURT OF JUSTICE

2. WORLD TRADE ORGANIZATION APPELLATE BODY AND PANEL

3. INTERNATIONAL TRIBUNAL ON THE LAW OF THE SEA

4. EUROPEAN COURT OF JUSTICE

5. REGIONAL COURTS

6. INTERNATIONAL ARBITRATIONS

List of Abbreviations

AA	association agreement
AB	Appellate Body
ABS	access and benefit sharing
ACCTS	Agreement on Climate Change, Trade and Sustainability
ACP	African, Caribbean and Pacific
ASIL	American Society of International Law
BITs	bilateral investment treaties
BSTC	Bilateral Scientific and Technical Commission
CAMPOCOOP	National Confederation of Farming Cooperatives Representing Small Farmers
CARIFORUM	Caribbean Forum
CCAEC	Canada-Chile Agreement on Environmental Cooperation
CEC	Commission for Environmental Co-operation
CES	European Confederation of Trade Unions
CETA	Comprehensive Economic and Trade Agreement
CIPMA	Center for Environmental Investigation and Planning
CISDL	Centre for International Sustainable Development Law
CITES	Convention on International Trade in Endangered Species of Wild Fauna and Flora
CONAF	National Forest Corporation
CSR	corporate social responsibility
CTD	Committee on Trade and Development
CTE	Committee on Trade and Environment
CUP	Cambridge University Press
CUT	Chilean Central Workers' Union
DFAIT	Canadian Department of Foreign Affairs and International Trade
DIRECON	Chilean Office of International Economic Relations
DSB	dispute settlement body
DSM	dispute settlement mechanism
EAs	environmental assessment
EC	European Commission
EIA	environmental impact assessment
EMIT	Environmental Measures and International Trade
EPA	economic partnership agreements
ER	environmental review
ESA	Eastern and South Africa
EU	European Union
EZZ	exclusive economic zone
FAO	Food and Agriculture Association
FDI	Foreign Direct Investment
FLEGT	Forest Law Enforcement Governance and Trade
FTA	free trade agreement
FTAA	Free Trade Agreement of the Americas

GATS	General Agreement on Trade in Services
GATT	General Agreement on Tariffs and Trade
GDP	gross domestic product
GHG	greenhouse gases
GMOs	genetically modified organisms
GNI	gross national income
IA	impact assessment
IADB	Inter-American Development Bank
IAEG-SDGs	Inter-Agency and Expert Group on SDG Indicators
ICESCR	International Covenant on Economic, Social and Cultural Rights
ICSID	International Centre for the Settlement of Investment Disputes
ICTSD	International Centre for Trade and Sustainable Development
IDPM	Institute for Development Policy and Management
IISD	International Institute for Sustainable Development
ILA	International Law Association
ILO	International Labour Organization
ITC	International Trade Centre
IUCN	International Union for Conservation of Nature and Natural Resources
IUU	illegal, unreported and unregulated
JPAC	Joint Public Advisory Committee
JPOI	Johannesburg Plan of Implementation
LDCs	least developed countries
LMOs	living modified organisms
M&E measures	mitigation and enhancement measures
MEA	multilateral environmental agreement
MEBF	Mercosur-EU Business Forum
MFN	most-favoured nation
MoU	Memorandum of Understanding
NAAEC	North American Agreement on Environmental Cooperation
NACEC	North American Commission for Environmental Cooperation
NAFTA	North American Free Trade Agreement
NALCA	North American Labour Cooperation Agreement
NAO	National Administrative Offices
OAS	Organization of American States
ODA	official development assistance
OECD	Organisation for Economic Co-operation and Development
OUP	Oxford University Press
POPs	persistent organic pollutants
PPMs	processing and production methods
PRTR	pollutant release and transfer register
REDD	reduction of emissions from deforestation and forest degradation
RFMOs	Regional Fisheries Management Organizations
RTAs	regional trade agreements
SDGs	Sustainable Development Goals
SIA	sustainability impact assessment
SICE	OAS Foreign Trade Information System
SIECA	Secretariat for Central American Economic Integration
SMEs	small and medium-sized enterprises
SNASPE	National System of State Protected Wild Areas
SPS Agreement	Agreement on the Application of Sanitary and Phytosanitary Measures

TBT	technical barriers to trade
TPA	Trade Promotion Agreement
TPP	Trans-Pacific Partnership
TPRM	Trade Policy Review Mechanism
TRIMS	Agreement on Trade-Related Investment Measures
TRIPS	Agreement on Trade-Related Aspects of Intellectual Property Rights
TPRM	Trade Policy Review Mechanism
UK	United Kingdom
UN	United Nations
UN CBD	United Nations Convention on Biological Diversity
UNCED	1992 UN Conference on Environment and Development
UN CESCR	UN Committee on Economic, Social and Cultural Rights
UNCITRAL	UN Commission on International Trade Law
UNCLOS	UN Convention on the Law of the Seas
UNCSD	United Nations Conference on Sustainable Development
UNCTAD	UN Conference on Trade and Development
UNECOSOC	UN Economic and Social Council
UNEP	UN Environment Programme
UN FCCC	UN Framework Convention on Climate Change
UN GA	UN General Assembly
UNHRC	UN Human Rights Council
US	United States
USMCA	United States of America, the United Mexican States, and Canada Agreement
USTR	United States Trade Representative
VCLT	Vienna Convention on the Law of Treaties
WHO	World Health Organization
WIPO	World Intellectual Property Organization
WSSD	World Summit on Sustainable Development
WTO	World Trade Organization

SECTION ONE
INTRODUCTION

1
Introduction

In a time of deadly global pandemics, dangerous climate change and financial instability, global cooperation has never been more important. Nonetheless, forces of populism and intolerance are seriously questioning the value of collaborative relationships across borders; confidence in the rules that govern international trade and investment flows, and our global economy, is eroding. Critics such as Naomi Klein and demagogues such as Donald Trump seek to dismantle the economic, environmental and social ties between communities and nations, and resist globalization. Their concerns are not new—indeed, the herald Hermes, ancient Greek patron of travellers, trade and commerce, was also known as the God of Thieves.[1] However, if Athena, Greek goddess of justice, wisdom and the crafts were consulted, she would likely advise more careful crafting of our economic agreements—calling for reasoned negotiations based on scholarship, on law and sustainability expertise. All those committed to international cooperation would be challenged to extend their thinking beyond facile mercantilism or false *noblesse oblige* charity, and to develop more intricate, balanced economic regimes that can promote sustainable justice across and among generations. This volume represents an effort in legal scholarship towards trade and investment rules which foster rather than frustrate the world's sustainable development goals—to contribute to the drafting of Athena's treaties.

The pressing need to ensure that the relations between countries, both in terms of international affairs and treaty-making, as well as cooperation for development, advance environmental, social and economic priorities in an integrated manner is reflected in the consensus of over 190 States in the 2002 World Summit on Sustainable Development (WSSD) and over 200 States in the 2012 UN Conference on Sustainable Development, with the resulting adoption of the world's Sustainable Development Goals (SDGs) in 2015, and also in the decisions of international tribunals.[2] These global SDGs were adopted to replace the UN Millennium Development Goals, and offer a clear agenda for sustainable development worldwide. Comprising seventeen overarching and aspirational universal objectives that all countries, peoples and communities seek to achieve by 2030, they encompass 169 time-bound targets and a detailed set of evolving indicators. The SDGs address the key priorities of all nations for sustainable development today—from ending poverty and stopping hunger (SDGs 1 and 2); to securing quality education, good health and gender equality (SDGs 3, 4 and 5); to providing access to clean water and sanitation, and affordable and clean energy (SDGs 6 and 7); to enabling decent work and economic growth, innovation,

[1] DA Leeming, *The World of Myth* (3rd edn, Oxford, OUP 2018).

[2] Johannesburg Declaration and Johannesburg Plan of Implementation (JPOI), Report of the World Summit on Sustainable Development, 4 September 2002, UN Doc A/CONF.199/20; Report of the United Nations Conference on Sustainable Development, July 2012, UN Doc A/CONF.216/16; *Transforming our World: the 2030 Agenda for Sustainable Development*, GA Res 70A/1, UNGAOR, 70th Sess, 25–27 September 2015, UN Doc E/15/16301 (2015) 1. See also, for instance, *In the Arbitration Regarding the Iron Rhine (Ijzeren Rijn) Railway (Belgium v. Netherlands)* Arbitral Award of 24 May 2005, <http://www.pca-cpa.org/showfile.asp?fil_id=377> accessed 16 December 2020, 58–59.

Crafting Trade and Investment Accords for Sustainable Development. Marie-Claire Cordonier Segger, Oxford University Press.
 DOI: 10.1093/oso/9780198831341.003.0001

industry and infrastructure and sustainable cities and communities (SDGs 8, 9 and 11); to promoting sustainable consumption and production, action on climate change and the protection of life below water and life on land (SDGs 12, 13, 14 and 15); to reducing inequalities and ensuring peace, justice and strong institutions (SDGs 10 and 16); to engaging international partnerships, including through trade, investment and financing, which can support achievement of all the goals (SDG 17). Taken together, these SDGs offer an entire suite of a government's legislative and policy agenda, representing the responsibilities of nearly all ministries and authorities in one way or another. There are also many binding international treaties among nations, supported by programmes of international agencies and organizations, and in many cases also by international financial facilities, with mandates related to each SDG and its targets.[3] Indeed, in recent decades, there has been extensive international treaty-making on the protection of the environment, and in many of the multilateral, regional and bilateral environmental accords State Parties also seek to secure sustainable development in different ways across diverse fields.[4] Such agreements are extremely important, but do not represent the full extent of binding international treaties on sustainable development. In addition to further covenants, accords and declarations on universal human rights, the elimination of discrimination against women, children's rights, indigenous peoples' rights and other key social aspects of sustainable development, many international

[3] MC Cordonier Segger and E Mrema, (eds), 'The SDGs: Contributions of International Law, Policy and Governance—Series of Issue Briefs' (CISDL and UNEP, Nairobi and Montreal, 2016) <https://www.cisdl.org/publications/> accessed 16 December 2020.. See also United Nations Department of Economic and Social Affairs—Sustainable Development, Sustainable Development Goals Knowledge Platform <https://sdgs.un.org/goals > accessed 16 December 2020. See 'Pandemic Recovery, the SDGs and the Law', Online lecture and Distinguished experts panel, 4 November 2020, <https://www.cisdl.org/2020/10/17/online-leverhulme-lecture-distinguished-experts-dialogue-pandemic-recovery-the-sdgs-and-the-law/> accessed 04 April 2021.

See also 'Natural Resources, the Sustainable Development Goals and the Law', Online Leverhulme lecture and Distinguished experts panel, 17 March 2021, <https://www.cisdl.org/2021/02/20/online-leverhulme-lecture-distinguished-experts-dialogue-natural-resources-the-sustainable-development-goals-and-international-law/ > accessed 04 April 2021.

And see University of Oxford All Souls College Event Records 'International Law and the Sustainable Development Goals: Shaping the Rules for our Common future' 2 November 2017, noting that 'SDGs and their targets can be found in the object and purpose of many important international treaties in the field of sustainable development. While many SDGs in principle and many targets in concrete terms already form part of international legal obligations of states, the SDGs have been received by legal practitioners as much more than a simple policy document. The SDGs are shaping the application and interpretation of sustainable development as a concept and perhaps interstitial norm, arguably more than even the Rio Declaration Principles. Although designed as a set of country-level goals, the SDGs are already shaping the rules for our common future at the international level.'<https://www.law.ox.ac.uk/events/international-law-and-sustainable-development-goals-shaping-rules-our-common-future > accessed 16 December 2020. See also the records of the American Society of International Law (ASIL) and George Washington University School of Law conference on 'Sustainable Development and International Law: Fragmentation, disconnects and the challenge of international policy coherence in meeting the SDGs' (25–26 June 2020) noting that: 'public international law norms are relevant to a wide range of the [SDGs]. Yet there is a systemic failure to connect the two spheres and a dearth of literature on the interaction between public international law and the policy and political frameworks that underpin development … yet another example of the fragmentation of international law exemplifying the challenge of international policy coherence: the same countries are parties to core international treaties and participants in international development (whether as donors or partners) and yet engage in development activities without a systematic assessment of which international norms apply even in sectors where international treaties clearly govern.' <https://asil.virtualeventsolutions.com/session/sustainable-development-and-international-law-fragmentation-disconnects-and-the-challenge-of-international-policy-coherence-in-meeting-the-sdgs/> accessed 16 December 2020.

[4] P Sands and J Peel, *Principles of International Environmental Law* (4th edn, Cambridge, CUP 2018) 217–229; MC Cordonier Segger and A Harrington, 'Environment & Sustainable Development' in S Chesterman, DM Malone and S Villalpando (eds), *The Oxford Handbook of United Nations Treaties* (Oxford, OUP 2019); P Birnie, A Boyle and C Redgwell, *International Law & the Environment* (Oxford, OUP 2009) 106–114; S Atapattu, *Emerging Principles of International Environmental Law* (Ardsley, Transnational 2006) 140–145; D Hunter, J Salzman and D Zaelke, *International Environmental Law and Policy* (New York, Foundation Press 2002) 19, 923.

economic agreements are also being negotiated, adopted and implemented. In a growing number of these treaty regimes, Parties also seek to address sustainable development, including in the World Trade Organization (WTO)[5] and a growing body of regional and bilateral economic agreements, including Regional Trade Agreements (RTAs).[6] As the WTO Appellate Body noted, in the 1998 *US-Shrimp* dispute:

> The preamble of the *WTO Agreement* – which informs not only the GATT 1994, but also the other covered agreements – explicitly acknowledges 'the objective of sustainable development'... This concept has been generally accepted as integrating economic and social development and environmental protection.[7]

There may be sound policy reasons for these trends in international trade and investment law. Indeed, in principle, environmental and social priorities can be considered an integral part of economic development decision-making, and the crafting of international trade and investment treaties are important economic decisions. The plans of Costa Rica, Fiji, Iceland, New Zealand and Norway to negotiate an Agreement on Climate Change, Trade and Sustainability (ACCTS);[8] the growing momentum of the European New Green Deal and the European Commission's ongoing negotiations to 'modernize' existing bilateral and region-to-region trade, economic partnership and association agreements;[9] and the United

5 G Sampson, *The WTO and Sustainable Development* (Tokyo, UNU Press 2005); M Gehring and MC Cordonier Segger (eds), *Sustainable Development in World Trade Law* (Alphen aan de Rijn, Kluwer Law International 2005) 129–152, based on early research for this book; S Alam, *Sustainable Development and Free Trade: Institutional Approaches* (New York, Routledge 2008). See also Agreement Establishing the World Trade Organization, 15 April 1994, *The Legal Texts: The Results of the Uruguay Round of Multilateral Trade Negotiations* 4 (1999) 1867 UNTS 154, 33 ILM 1144 (1994) (WTO Agreement), <http://www.wto.org/english/tratop_e/envir_e/sust_dev_e.htm>. WTO, 'Mainstreaming Trade to Attain the Sustainable Development Goals' (October 2018), <http://www.wto.org/english/res_e/booksp_e/sdg_e.pdf> accessed 15 July 2019; M Chi, 'Sustainable Development Provisions in Investment Treaties' (United Nations Social Commission for Asia and the Pacific, October 2018), <http://www.unescap.org/sites/default/files/Sustainable%20Development%20Provisions%20in%20Investment%20Treaties.pdf> accessed 15 July 2019.

6 See MC Cordonier Segger, 'Inspiration for Integration: Interpreting International Trade and Investment Accords for Sustainable Development' (2017) 3(1) Canadian Journal of Comparative and Contemporary Law 159 and MC Cordonier Segger, 'Sustainable Development in Regional Trade Agreements' in L Bartels and F Ortino (eds), *Regional Trade Agreements and the WTO Legal System* (Oxford, OUP 2006) 313–340, sharing early findings from research for this book.

7 WTO, *United States: Import Prohibition of Certain Shrimp and Shrimp Products—Report of the Panel* (15 May 1998) WT/DS58/R; WTO, *United States: Import Prohibition of Certain Shrimp and Shrimp Products—Report of the Appellate Body* (6 November 1998) Doc.WT/DS58/AB/R, 123, Note 107.

8 According to the Joint Leaders' Statement on the launch of the 'Agreement on Climate Change, Trade and Sustainability' Initiative (25 September 2019), the 'ACCTS aims to bring together some of the inter-related elements of the climate change, trade and sustainable development agendas. The nature of the climate and environmental challenges our world is facing demands this coherency. The ACCTS will address trade policy, rules and architecture in order to achieve the goals of the Paris agreement and facilitate increased trade contributing to sustainable development. The signatories to the ACCTS will seek to address these in a transparent and coherent manner. The ACCTS will include measures such as the removal of tariffs on environmental goods and the establishment of new and binding commitments for environmental services; establishment of disciplines to eliminate harmful fossil fuel subsidies; and development of guidelines to inform the development and implementation of voluntary eco-labelling programmes and mechanisms. This treaty-level instrument will be open to other countries to accede to in the future if they are able to meet its obligations.' <https://www.beehive.govt.nz/sites/default/files/2019-09/ACCTS%20joint%20leaders%20statement.pdf> accessed 16 December 2020; see also the new initiative launched by New Zealand with Costa Rica, Fiji, Iceland and Norway—the Agreement on Climate Change, Trade and Sustainability (ACCTS), 25 September 2019, <https://www.mfat.govt.nz/en/trade/free-trade-agreements/climate/agreement-on-climate-change-trade-and-sustainability-accts-negotiations/> accessed 16 December 2020.

9 Communication from the Commission to the European Parliament, the European Council, the Council, the European Economic and Social Committee and the Committee of the Regions, 'The European Green Deal', COM/2019/

Kingdom's trade and investment negotiation aims;[10] in addition to debates on economic measures to stimulate recovery from the impacts of the global COVID-19 pandemic,[11] simply underscore the pressing importance of such intersections. However, there remains comparatively little legal scholarly analysis on how trade and financial flows can affect a country's potential to meet its sustainable development goals and targets, and how trade and investment treaty rules could foster rather than frustrate sustainability.[12]

This volume addresses these gaps. The book focuses on pressing questions such as how could new trade and investment agreements promote more sustainable development, rather than increasing the negative social and environmental impacts of economic growth? Are States currently attempting to integrate social and environmental considerations into trade and investment policies for the purpose of incentivizing more sustainable development, and if so, how is the integration operationalized in trade and investment treaties themselves? What specific measures are being adopted by States in the WTO, and in bilateral or regional trade and investment agreements, and what are their implications for the global Sustainable Development Goals?

The book argues that governments are seeking innovative ways to integrate environmental and social considerations into economic agreements and their implementation, particularly through experiments in bilateral and regional trade and investment agreements, and that through this integration, international economic law can be better positioned to contribute to sustainable development. It is intended to provide guidance and, at the least, insights for decision-makers, negotiators, scholars and stakeholders interested in policy, law and governance related to trade and investment, climate change, biodiversity protection and the environment, human rights, equity and social development and sustainability in general; those willing to consider new approaches which take commitments to sustainable development seriously.

640 final, <https://eur-lex.europa.eu/legal-content/EN/TXT/?qid=1588580774040&uri=CELEX:52019DC0640> accessed 16 December 2020; see also <https://ec.europa.eu/info/strategy/priorities-2019-2024/european-green-deal_en>;<https://ec.europa.eu/trade/policy/countries-and-regions/negotiations-and-agreements/> accessed 16 December 2020; European Commission, Overview of FTA and Other Trade Negotiations (Brussels, August 2020).

[10] UK Parliament Lords Select Committee, 'International Trade Secretary Discusses Possible Free Trade Agreements', 21 July 2020, <https://committees.parliament.uk/committee/448/eu-international-agreements-subcommittee/news/115294/international-trade-secretary-discusses-possible-free-trade-agreements/> accessed 16 December 2020.

[11] See MC Cordonier Segger, F Crepeau, A Harrington, FK Phillips and N Ramanujam, 'Human Rights, the Sustainable Development Goals and the Law" 15 May 2020 (Montreal, CISDL 2020) <https://www.cisdl.org/2020/04/19/human-rights-the-sustainable-development-goals-the-law-international-legal-symposium/> accessed 16 December 2020; C Hepburn, B O'Callaghan, N Stern, J Stiglitz and D Zenghelis, 'Will COVID-19 Fiscal Recovery Packages Accelerate or Retard Progress on Climate Change?', Oxford Smith School of Enterprise and the Environment Working Paper No 20-02, 4 May 2020, <https://www.smithschool.ox.ac.uk/publications/wpapers/workingpaper20-02.pdf> accessed 16 December 2020 (forthcoming in the Oxford Review of Economic Policy 36(S1)); UN Global Compact, 'Over 150 Global Corporations Urge World Leaders for Net-Zero Recovery from COVID-19', 18 May 2020, <https://ungc-communications-assets.s3.amazonaws.com/docs/publications/recover-better-statement.pdf> accessed 16 December 2020.

[12] A Boyle and D Freestone, *International Law and Sustainable Development* (Oxford, OUP 1999) 10 identified trade as an area where scope for integration or conflict remains. A decade later, HC Bugge and C Voigt (eds), *Sustainable Development in International and National Law* (Groningen, Europa 2009) 271–295 called for new research on sustainable development in trade law. See also Birnie, Boyle and Redgwell (n 4) 117, which identifies international trade as an area with 'significant scope for improvement' for integration of environmental considerations. See further V Lowe, *International Law* (Oxford, OUP 2009) 4.

2

International Trade, Investment and Sustainability

2.1 Potential Negative Effects of Trade and Investment on Sustainable Development

There is no guarantee of free trade or investment in international law—it is every State's sovereign decision to permit trade with another State, to set the terms of trade and investment and to govern investments from other States.[1] The current world trading system is governed by national economic authorities that regulate trade and investment in accordance with the principles and disciplines set out in the agreements of the World Trade Organization (WTO), the UN Commission on International Trade Law (UNCITRAL), the UN Conference on Trade and Development (UNCTAD), the International Centre for the Settlement of Investment Disputes (ICSID) and in an increasingly complex web of hundreds of regional and bilateral trade and investment agreements.[2]

The terms agreed in the global institutions and regional accords may serve to reduce barriers to trade and investment, encouraging economic growth.[3] However, there is concern that absent due care, trade and investment promotion could lead to unnecessarily destructive impacts on the environment and on social cohesion.[4] Critics warn that the type of economic growth stimulated by a trade or investment agreement may harm both social and environmental sustainability.[5] In certain circumstances, studies show, trade liberalization under the WTO or regional and bilateral trade and investment agreements

[1] A Lowenfeld, *International Economic Law* (Oxford, OUP 2002) 30, 45–67; M Trebilcock and R Howse, *The Regulation of International Trade* (New York, Routledge 2005) 20–23; JH Jackson, 'The Evolution of the World Trading System', in D Bethlehem and others, *The Oxford Handbook of International Trade Law* (Oxford, OUP 2009) 36–37.

[2] As at July 2019, there were 473 RTA notifications, with 294 in force: WTO, 'Regional Trade Agreements: Scope of RTAs', <https://rtais.wto.org/UI/PublicMaintainRTAHome.aspx> accessed 16 December 2020; JA Crawford and RV Fiorentino, *The Changing Landscapes of Regional Trade Agreements* (Geneva, WTO 2005) 3; J Mathis, *Regional Trade Agreements in the GATT / WTO* (The Hague, TMC Asser 2002); M Gehring, J Hepburn and MC Cordonier Segger, *World Trade Law in Practice* (London, Globe 2006) 12; VD Do and W Watson, 'Economic Analysis of Regional Trade Agreements' in L Bartels and F Ortino (eds), *Regional Trade Agreements and the WTO Legal System* (Oxford, OUP 2006) 8; RE Baldwin, 'Multilateralising Regionalism: Spaghetti Bowls as Building Blocs on the Path to Global Free Trade', NBER Working Paper No W12545, October 2006; M Gehring and MC Cordonier Segger, *Sustainable Development in World Trade Law* (Alphen aan de Rijn, Kluwer Law International 2005); MC Cordonier Segger, M Gehring and A Newcombe, *Sustainable Development in World Investment Law* (Alphen aan de Rijn, Kluwer Law International 2010).

[3] WTO, *World Trade Report 2008: Trade in a Globalising World* (Geneva, 2008) xiii; UNCTAD, *Trade and Development Report 2005* (2005) 10.

[4] J Cameron, 'What Now? Trade and the Environment' in P Geraint, A Qureshi and H Steiner (eds), *The Legal and Moral Aspects of International Trade* (Routledge, New York 1998) 166–182; J Schott (ed), *The WTO after Seattle* (IIE, Washington 2000); A Taylor, 'The Trade and Environmental Debate' in A Taylor and C Thomas (eds), *Global Trade and Global Social Issues* (London, Routledge 1999) 72–90.

[5] S Matusz and D Tarr, 'Adjusting to Trade Policy Reform' World Bank Policy Research Working Paper No 2142, 1999; NA McCulloch, LA Winters and X Cirera, *Trade Liberalization and Poverty: A Handbook* (London, Centre for Economic and Policy Research 2001).

Crafting Trade and Investment Accords for Sustainable Development. Marie-Claire Cordonier Segger, Oxford University Press.
 DOI: 10.1093/oso/9780198831341.003.0002

could encourage economic growth that undermines social protections,[6] worsens conditions for the rural and urban poor,[7] degrades biological diversity,[8] increases greenhouse gas emissions,[9] augments soil erosion[10] and increases unsafe exposure to toxic pollutants.[11] As UNCTAD and others have noted, in certain circumstances trade and investment agreements can leave the poorest and most vulnerable groups worse off.[12] Leading legal scholars have underlined the potential of new trade and investment rules to pose difficulties for multilateral environment agreements (MEA) implementation, for protection of the environment beyond national jurisdiction, for adoption of regulations to protect domestic environments and for efforts to improve environmental standards,[13] and the

[6] E Mendes and O Mehmet, *Global Governance, Economy and Law: Waiting for Justice* (London, Routledge 2003) 67–115; T Evans, 'Trading Human Rights' in A Taylor and C Thomas (eds), *Global Trade and Global Social Issues* (London, Routledge 1999) 46–47; B Johnson (ed), *Who Pays the Price?* (Island Press, Washington 1994); R Howse and M Mutua, 'Protecting Human Rights in a Global Economy: Challenges for the World Trade Organization' in ICHRDD, *Rights and Democracy* (Montreal, 2000); P Ranjan, 'International Trade and Human Rights: Conflicting Obligations' in T Cottier, J Pauwelyn and E Bürgi (eds), *Human Rights and International Trade* (Oxford, OUP 2005) 311; R Howse, 'Human Rights in the WTO: Whose Rights, What Humanity?' (2002) 13 European Journal of International Law 651–659; R Labonté, 'Trade, Investment and Public Health: Compiling the Evidence, Assembling the Arguments' (2019) 15 Global Health 1; F Humbert, 'The WTO and Child Labour: Implications for the Debate on International Constitutionalism' in H Gött (ed), *Labour Standards in International Economic Law* (Cham, Springer, 2018) 93.

[7] T Collier and D Dollar, *Globalization, Growth and Poverty* (Oxford, OUP 2002); T Collier and J Gunning, *Trade Shocks in Developing Countries* (Oxford, Clarendon 1999); J Jackson, W Davey and A Sykes, *Legal Problems of International Economic Relations* (3rd edn, West, St Paul 1995) 278–279; R Bhala, 'Clarifying the Trade-Labor Link' (1998) 37(1) Columbia Journal of Transnational Law 30–31; R Ferguson, *The Right to Food and the World Trade Organization's Rules on Agriculture: Conflicting, Compatible, or Complementary?* (Leiden, Brill 2018).

[8] UN CBD Secretariat, 'The Impact of Trade Liberalization on Agricultural Biological Diversity', CBD Technical Series No 16 (Montreal, 2006); PM Vitousek and others, 'Human Appropriation of the Products of Photosynthesis' (1986) 36 BioScience 368, BL Turner and others (eds), *The Earth as Transformed by Human Action: Global and Regional Changes in the Biosphere over the Past 300 Years.* (Cambridge, CUP 1990); B Kjellen, *A New Diplomacy for Sustainable Development: The Challenge of Global Change* (Routledge, New York 2008); EU Petersmann, 'Taking Human Dignity, Poverty and Empowerment of Individuals More Seriously' (2002) 13 European Journal of International Law 845–851.

[9] O Endresen and E Sørgaard, 'Emissions from International Sea Transportation and Environmental Impact' (2003) 108 Journal of Geophysical Research D17, 4560. See also B Chambers, 'International Trade Law and the Kyoto Protocol: Potential Incompatibilities' in B Chambers (ed), *Inter-linkages: The Kyoto Protocol and the International Trade and Investment Regimes* (Tokyo, UNU 2001); Y Li and CN Hewitt, 'The Effect of Trade between China and the UK on National and Global Carbon Dioxide Emissions' (2008) 36 Energy Policy 1907; NH Stern and others, *The Stern Review: The Economics of Climate Change* (HM Treasury 2006) <http://webarchive.nationalarchives.gov.uk/+/http:/www.hm-treasury.gov.uk/sternreview_index.htm> accessed 16 December 2020.

[10] S Oeter, 'Trade, Agriculture and Sustainability in Land Use' in M Gehring and MC Cordonier Segger (eds), *Sustainable Development in World Trade Law* (The Hague, Kluwer Law International 2005) 327–353; EB Barbier, 'The Economic Determinants of Land Degradation in Developing Countries' (1997) 352(1356) Philosophical Transactions of the Royal Society B: Biological Sciences 891–899; K Arrow and others, 'Economic Growth, Carrying Capacity, and the Environment' (1996) 1 Environment and Development Economics 104–110.

[11] S Williams and CR Shumway, 'Trade Liberalization and Agricultural Chemical Use: United States and Mexico' (2000) 82(1) American Journal of Agricultural Economics 183–199; S Dasgupta and others, 'Agricultural Trade, Development and Toxic Risk' (2002) 30 World Development 1401.

[12] UNCTAD, *Developing Countries in World Trade* (Washington, 2002) 51–83; UNCTAD, *Policy Coherence, Development Strategies and Integration into the World Economy* (Washington, 2004) 43–69. See also S Rose-Ackerman and J Tobin, 'Do BITs Benefit Developing Countries?' in C Rogers and RP Alford (eds), *The Future of Investment Arbitration* (Oxford, OUP 2009) 131–143.

[13] P Birnie, A Boyle and C Redgwell, *International Law & the Environment* (Oxford, OUP 2009) 753–810. See also J Scott, 'International Trade and Environmental Governance: Relating Rules (and Standards) in the EU and the WTO' (2004) 15(2) European Journal of International Law 307–354; S Baughen, *International Trade and the Protection of the Environment* (London, Routledge Cavendish 2007); C Robb, *International Environmental Law Reports* vol 2, Trade and Environment (Cambridge, CUP 2001); E Vranes, *Trade and the Environment: Fundamental Issues in International Law, WTO Law and Legal Theory* (Oxford, OUP 2009) 90–94; see also A Eliason, 'Using the WTO to Facilitate the Paris Agreement: A Tripartite Approach' (Society of International Economic Law, Sixth Biennial Global Conference, July 2018), specifically that: 'certain types of climate change mitigation measures may require violating WTO rules'.

United Nations Environment Programme (UNEP) has expressed similar concerns, also linking particular environmental problems to growth in volume of certain trade or investment flows.[14]

These concerns can affect States' willingness to cooperate in multilateral trade and investment negotiations. In the WTO, debates on such issues have led to deadlocked negotiations,[15] trade disputes,[16] even violent public protests characterized by self-immolations.[17] At the regional and bilateral levels, challenges related to effects on the environment and development may mean trade negotiations falter,[18] and are abandoned.[19] The uncertainties surrounding impacts can generate instability for governments, the private sector and others engaged in trade and investment.[20] Rather than *promoting sustainable development through trade and investment*, global, regional and bilateral economic agreements can appear to limit environment and social development regulations, causing treaty implementation difficulties in developing and developed countries alike.[21]

14 UNEP, *Trade Liberalisation and the Environment: Lessons learned from Bangladesh, Chile, India, Philippines, Romania and Uganda*, Synthesis Report of Country Studies (Geneva, 1999); UNEP, *Environment and Trade—A Handbook* (Geneva, 2000); UNEP and WTO, *Trade and Climate Change* (Geneva, 2009). See also section on trade instruments, Report of the Secretary General, 30 November 2018, UN Doc UNGA/73/419 'Gaps in International Environmental Law and Environment-Related Instruments: Towards a Global Pact for the Environment', <https://wedocs.unep.org/bitstream/handle/20.500.11822/27070/SGGaps.pdf?sequence=3&isAllowed=y> accessed 16 December 2020, 30.

15 T Collier, 'Why the WTO is Deadlocked: And What Can Be Done about It' (2006) 29 World Economy 1423–1449; A Narlikar, *Deadlocks in Multilateral Negotiations: Causes and Solutions* (Cambridge, CUP 2010); G Sampson and B Chambers, *Trade, Environment and the Millennium* (Tokyo, UNU 2000); S Vaughan, 'World Trade Organization Gridlock and Alternative Regimes to Pursue an International Social Cause' in J Kirton and P Hajnal (eds), *Sustainability, Civil Society and International Governance* (Aldershot, Ashgate 2006) 261–278.

16 E Brown Weiss, J Jackson and N Bernasconi-Osterwalder, *Reconciling Environment and Trade* (Leiden, Martinus Nijhoff 2008) 3–4, 27–38; J Pauwelyn, 'Human Rights in WTO Dispute Settlement' in Cottier, Pauwelyn and Bürgi (n 6) 205–231.

17 'WTO Trade Talks collapse in Mexico' *China Daily* (15 September 2003) <http://www.chinadaily.com.cn/en/doc/2003-09/15/content_264077.htm> accessed 16 December 2020; 'The WTO Stalemate: One Very Big No' *Z-Magazine* (November 2003) <http://www.zcommunications.org/the-wto-stalemate-one-very-big-no-by-site-administrator> accessed 16 December 2020; 'Curfew in Effect as Seattle Struggles to Control WTO Protests' *CNN US* (30 November 1999) <http://articles.cnn.com/1999-11-30/us/9911_30_wto.04_1_protesters-wto-state-of-civil-emergency?_s=PM:US> accessed 16 December 2020.

18 A Estevadeordal, M Shearer and K Suominen, 'Multilateralizing RTAs in the Americas: State of Play and Ways Forward' in R Baldwin and P Low (eds), *Multilateralising Regionalism: Challenges for the Global Trading System* (Cambridge, CUP 2009) 427. By way of a recent example, the environment was one source of opposition to the Comprehensive Economic and Trade Agreement (CETA) from the Belgian region of Wallonia, which delayed conclusion of the deal until 2018; see P Magnette (President of Wallonia) 'Wallonia Blocked a Harmful EU Trade Deal—But We Don't Share Trump's Dreams' op-ed to *The Guardian* (18 November 2016), who states citizens 'wonder if it is reasonable to import beef from the other side of the Atlantic when we are at the same time supposed to be fighting global warming'. In addition, observers have noted that efforts to initiate talks on a Canada-China trade agreement failed due to Canadian Prime Minister Justin Trudeau's insistence on including environmental and social provisions in an eventual deal: A Ballingall, 'Trudeau Fails To Come Back from China with the Trade Talks He Wanted', *The Toronto Star* (7 December 2017).

19 'Ecuador Rules Out FTA with US', 24 January 2008, <http://www.bilaterals.org/spip.php?article11000> accessed 16 December 2020.

20 A Ades and HB Chua, 'Thy Neighbours Curse: Regional Instability and Economic Growth' (1997) 2(3) Journal of Economic Growth 279; D Rodrik, 'Policy Uncertainty and Private Investment in Developing Countries' (1991) 36(2) Journal of Development Economics 229; R Wacziarg and KH Welch, 'Trade Liberalization and Growth: New Evidence' (2008) The World Bank Economic Review 22, 187.

21 WJ Davey, 'Has the WTO Dispute Settlement System Exceeded its Authority?' (2001) 4(1) Journal of International Economic Law 79; C Deere, *The Implementation Game* (Oxford, OUP 2008); D Zaleke and T Higdon, 'The Role of Compliance in the Rule of Law, Good Governance and Sustainable Development' (2006) 3(5) Journal for European Environmental and Planning Law 376;

2.2 Impact Assessments of Trade and Investment Treaties

For countries involved in trade and investment negotiations, and all those who may be affected by less positive impacts of economic agreements, it is important to identify which concerns are simply fears, and which concerns may raise significant impacts. States, regional bodies and international organizations have commissioned scientific studies and assessments to model and analyse the potential environmental and social impacts of economic liberalization.[22] Some now require *ex-ante* and *ex-post* impact assessments to identify potential effects of new liberalization commitments, and to suggest mitigation or flanking measures.[23] For instance, the original 1994 North American Free Trade Agreement (NAFTA)[24] including its Chapter 11 on investment was studied *ex-post* by the trilateral North American Commission for Environmental Cooperation of United States, Canada and Mexico, which found that NAFTA-related environmental threats are most serious in sectors of the economy where regulators are unprepared for an increasing scale of production stimulated by trade and investment liberalization such as base metals, petroleum and transportation.[25]

The *NAFTA Effects* study was conceived nearly 20 years ago. Since then, trade and investment impact assessment practices have evolved, but two principal modes of assessment are still used by States, each identifying a different set of impacts from economic liberalization. As one approach, several 'Environmental Impact Assessment' (EIA) and 'Environmental Review' (ER) approaches are based on the venerable *NAFTA Effects* technique. They focus on predicting potential *environmental* effects of the *economic changes* resulting from a specific economic treaty in the specific country undertaking the assessment, and are used by Canada and by the United States among others during trade and investment negotiations with other countries.[26] As another example, the US-Peru Trade Promotion Agreement (TPA) between Peru and the US in 2006 was preceded by the US-Peru Environmental Review (ER) in 2005, and this *ex-ante* review projected several potential environmental impacts.[27]

As an alternative method, the Sustainability Impact Assessment (SIA) developed by the European Union involves an independent assessment of the broader impacts of economic treaties on all the Parties' potential for *sustainable development*.[28] These approaches use integrated or SIA methods to analyse economic liberalization scenarios, sector by sector, to determine their likely effects on selected social, economic and environmental indicators.

[22] European Commission, *Handbook for Trade Sustainability Impact Assessment* (2nd edn, Luxembourg, 2016) <https://trade.ec.europa.eu/doclib/docs/2016/april/tradoc_154464.PDF> accessed 16 December 2020; C George, C Kirkpatrick and S Scrieciu, *Final Global Overview Trade SIA: Inception and Mid-Term Reports* (Manchester, Institute for Development Policy & Management 2006); UNEP, *Reference Manual for the Integrated Assessment of Trade-Related Policies* (Geneva, 2001); UNCSD, *Indicators of Sustainable Development: Framework and Methodologies* (New York, 1999).

[23] See Annex 1 for Table of Sustainability Impact Assessments, Environmental and Labour Reviews, and Environmental and Labour Assessments of Trade and Investment Agreements.

[24] Entered into force 1 January 1994.

[25] North American Commission for Environmental Cooperation, *Potential NAFTA Effects: Claims and Arguments 1991-1994* (Montreal, 1996).

[26] General Council—Preparations for the 1999 Ministerial Conference—Trade and Sustainable Development—Communication from the United States (6 August 1999) WT/GC/W/304 99-3364; General Council—Preparations for the 1999 Ministerial Conference—Canadian Approach to Trade and Environment in the New WTO Round-Communication from Canada (12 October 1999) WT/GC/W/358 99-4298 <http://docsonline.wto.org> accessed 16 December 2020.

[27] The US-Peru Trade Promotion Agreement was adopted 12 April 2006); USTR 'Interim Environmental Review United States-Andean Free Trade Agreement' (2005) <http://www.ustr.gov/sites/default/files/perinter.pdf> accessed 16 December 2020.

[28] European Commission (n 22).

The European Commission (EC) then responds to the study, which is carried out by a third party, with a position paper. As one example, when the EU and Mexico sought to modernize the trade aspect of their Global Agreement which governs trade in goods and services between the Parties, a full SIA was carried out by July 2019, leading to a European Commission SIA Position Paper in January 2020 on how the agreement could minimize or mitigate any social, environmental or economic harms from the accord, and enhance any benefits for sustainable development.[29]

Many impact assessments of both main types and more have been carried out in recent decades by the EU, the US, Canada and others, analysing the potential impacts of many new regional trade and investment agreements, and several rounds of WTO trade negotiations. Over 110 new regional and bilateral economic agreements have been negotiated over recent decades with explicit commitments on sustainable development, many preceded by some form of assessment.[30]

It is crucial, while negotiating, implementing and interpreting today's trade and investment agreements, to be aware of potential social and environmental effects. This is important both in order to engage institutions and stakeholders who can inform the accord itself, enhancing positive and avoiding or mitigating negative impacts, and also to develop a better-crafted, more politically stable treaty that is more likely to be implemented in a sustainable manner. Taken together, such impact assessments at the very least can provide a valuable source of data. In this volume, from a survey of the challenges outlined in environmental reviews and sustainability impact assessments, building on existing secondary literature, three main tensions are identified with regards to the potential social, environmental and other impacts of economic agreements. The first tension refers to ways that trade and investment treaty rules may constrain legitimate new law and policy measures intended to foster sustainable development, with a focus on measures for the implementation of multilaterally agreed treaties that contribute to the achievement of the world's Sustainable Development Goals. The second tension refers to the way that changes in trade and investment rules can exacerbate pre-existing sustainable development problems at the domestic level, without strengthening corresponding laws and policies that could prevent or mitigate impacts. The third tension involves the escalation or propagation—through trade and investment liberalization—of obsolete, polluting or inappropriate technologies and industries, rather than enhancement of more socially and ecologically sound goods and services that can support sustainable development.

2.3 Measures to Address Sustainability Impacts of Trade and Investment Treaties

Given continuing concern about the impacts of economic liberalization, and more than three decades of experience with increasingly sophisticated impact assessment practices, it

[29] European Commission, 'Sustainability Impact Assessment in Support of Negotiations for the Modernisation of the Trade Part of the Global Agreement with Mexico', 17 September 2019, <https://trade.ec.europa.eu/doclib/docs/2020/january/tradoc_158558.pdf> accessed 16 December 2020; European Commission, European Commission Services' Position Paper on the Sustainability Impact Assessment in Support of Negotiations for the Modernisation of the Trade Part of the Global Agreement with Mexico, January 2020, <https://trade.ec.europa.eu/doclib/docs/2020/january/tradoc_158559.pdf> accessed 16 December 2020.

[30] See Annex 1.

is a good moment to take stock. Specifically, it is time to assess whether, and how, States are addressing sustainability concerns that emerge from assessments of international economic agreements, including in the treaties themselves.

There may be many different options to address sustainability concerns. These can include the adoption of diverse domestic legal, economic or policy 'flanking measures' to mitigate impacts of increased trade and investment flows, but also international measures *within the trade and investment agreements themselves* to address the most significant challenges. The latter – as binding international treaty instruments – are the focus of this volume. States have reaffirmed that international trade and investment flows can and should support sustainable development in numerous 'soft law' declarations and processes, reflecting global policy objectives.[31] This conviction has begun to be reflected in international trade and investment negotiations and in the resulting treaty regimes. As WTO members noted in the 2001 WTO Doha Declaration:

> We strongly reaffirm our commitment to the objective of sustainable development, as stated in the Preamble to the Marrakesh Agreement. We are convinced that the aims of upholding and safeguarding an open and non-discriminatory multilateral trading system, and acting for ... the promotion of sustainable development can and must be mutually supportive. We take note of the efforts by members to conduct national environmental assessments of trade policies on a voluntary basis.[32]

This commitment to sustainable development as an objective, as is further discussed in this volume, has been debated in WTO negotiations and committees, reflected in decisions of the WTO Panel and Appellate Body, was the subject of inquiries in the WTO Trade Policy Review Mechanism (TPRM), and was raised in negotiations of the WTO Doha 'Development Round'.[33] Consensus remains elusive to date.[34]

[31] 'Soft law' describes high level declarations of intent, consensus declarations agreed by States, technical standards, codes of conduct and guidelines that are not aligned with the classical sources of law defined in the Statute of the International Court of Justice at art 38. One nuanced understanding of 'soft law' suggests that in certain circumstances, such declarations can still give rise to legitimate expectations among States. See 1945 Statute of the International Court of Justice TS 993; (1945) 39 American Journal of International Law Supplement 215, art 38; For discussion, see G Simpson, 'The Situation on the International Legal Theory Front: The Power of Rules and the Rule of Power' (2000) 11(2) European Journal of International Law 439–464; JHH Weiler and AL Paulus, 'The Structure of Change in International Law or is There a Hierarchy of Norms in International Law?' (1997) 8(4) European Journal of International Law 545–565; U Fastenrath, 'Relative Normativity in International Law' (1993) 4 European Journal of International Law 305–340; T Gruchalla-Wesierski, 'A Framework for Understanding Soft Law' (1984–1985) 30 McGill Law Journal 37; M Bothe, 'Legal and Non-Legal Norms—a Meaningful Distinction in International Relations?' (1980) 11 Netherlands Yearbook of International Law 65; I Seidl-Hohenveldern, 'International Economic Soft Law' (1980) 163 Rec des Cours 164; J Gold, 'Strengthening the Soft International Law of Exchange Arrangements' (1983) 77 American Journal of International Law 443. But see CM Chinkin, 'The Challenge of Soft Law: Development and Change in International Law' (1989) 38 International and Comparative Law Quarterly 850 and H Hillgenberg, 'A Fresh Look at Soft Law' (1999) 10(3) European Journal of International Law 499–515.

[32] Doha WTO Ministerial 2001: Ministerial Declaration, WT/MIN(01)/DEC/1, para 6.

[33] For the 2001 Doha Round, see C Kirkpatrick, C George and S Scrieciu, *Sustainability Impact Assessment of Proposed WTO Negotiations Final Global Overview Trade SIA of the Doha Development Agenda: Final Report* (Manchester, IDPM 2006) 60; C George and C Kirkpatrick, *Sustainability Impact Assessment of Proposed Doha Agenda Assessment of Individual Trade Measures: Preliminary Overview* (Manchester, IARC 2003) 10–15; for proposed 2000 'Millennium Round', see C Kirkpatrick, N Lee and O Morrissey, *Sustainability Impact Assessment Study WTO New Round: Phase One Report* (Manchester, IDPM 1999); and see C Kirkpatrick and N Lee, *Sustainability Impact Assessment Study WTO New Round: Phase Two Report* (Manchester, IDPM 1999) <https://trade.ec.europa.eu/doclib/docs/2005/february/tradoc_111192.pdf> accessed 16 December 2020. For debates in WTO negotiations and committees, and sustainable development in decisions of the WTO Panel and Appellate Body, see Chapter 12.1. For TPRM inquiries, see Chapter 14.

[34] WTO Annual Report 2011, 16.

Studies of the lowest common denominator at the WTO present only a partial view of measures taken by States to address sustainability concerns linked to trade and investment liberalization, particularly given challenges that arose in the WTO 'Doha Round' negotiations.[35] A new generation of regional and bilateral trade and investment treaties are being negotiated among developed and developing country Parties. These accords appear discriminatory by nature, designed to grant certain trade preferences and in some cases also investment protections to the Parties to each arrangement.[36] In 2019, 473 'regional trade agreements' had been notified to the WTO, with at least 294 in force.[37] Over fifty further trade and investment treaty negotiations were ongoing in the Americas alone.[38] Beyond debates on the venerable 1994 NAFTA and its successor, the United States of America, the United Mexican States, and Canada (USMCA),[39] in addition to certain European studies, this growing collection of regional and bilateral economic treaties and their impact assessments are only beginning to be analysed in law and economics.[40] Most studies address the relationship *between* the WTO and regional trade agreements,[41] and whether bilateral and regional trade treaties provide 'stumbling blocks' or 'building blocks' for global trade liberalization.[42] However, like the WTO, the bilateral and regional economic treaties do not simply have an impact on global trade liberalization, or economic growth. They may also have significant positive or negative implications for social development and for the environment.

Trade agreements can contribute towards sustainable development by serving as a conduit for the transfer of green or environmentally sound technologies to partner countries. These technologies have the capacity to significantly improve environmental performance when compared with other technologies. However, these transfers should not just be structured as transfers of intellectual property or capital equipment, but as transfers of know-how and capacity building.[43]

[35] See n 33.

[36] JN Bhagwati, P Krishna and A Panagariya (eds), *Trading Blocs: Alternative Approaches to Analyzing Preferential Trade Agreements* (Boston, MIT Press 1999); A Krueger, 'Free Trade Agreements versus Customs Unions', NBER Working Paper No 5084, 1995; CA Cooper and BF Massell, 'Toward a General Theory of Customs Unions for Developing Countries' (1965) 73(5) Journal of Political Economy 461; BA Balassa, *The Theory of Economic Integration* (London, Allen and Unwin 1961); SY Kim, ED Mansfield and HV Milner, 'Regional Trade Governance' in TA Börzel and T Risse (eds), *The Oxford Handbook of Comparative Regionalism* (Oxford, OUP 2016); BA Melo Araujo, 'Setting the Rules of the Game: The Rise (and Fall) of Mega-Regionals, Deep Integration and the Role of the WTO' (2017) 21(2) UCLA Journal of International Law & Foreign Affairs 101.

[37] See WTO (n 2); see also R Baldwin and P Low, *Multilateralising Regionalism: Challenges for the Global Trading System* (Cambridge, CUP 2009).

[38] Organisation of American States, Foreign Trade Information System (OAS SICE) <http://www.sice.oas.org/tpd_e.asp> accessed 16 December 2020.

[39] Agreement between the United States of America, the United Mexican States and Canada 12/13/19 Text—not yet ratified by Canada, <https://ustr.gov/trade-agreements/free-trade-agreements/united-states-mexico-canada-agreement/agreement-between> accessed 13 March 2020. See also P Vieira, 'Canada Begins USMCA Ratification Process That Won't Necessarily Be Smooth Sailing: Trudeau will likely have to strike a deal with opposition parties, which have been critical of some elements of the trade deal', *Wall Street Journal* (27 January 2020).

[40] Bartels and Ortino (n 2); Mathis (n 2); OECD, *Environment and Regional Trade Agreements* (Paris, 2007); P Konz (ed), *Trade, Environment and Sustainable Development: Views from Sub-Saharan Africa and Latin America* (Tokyo and Geneva, UNU/IAS & ICTSD 2000) 235, 251–261; I Martínez-Zarzoso, 'Assessing the Effectiveness of Environmental Provisions in Regional Trade Agreements: An Empirical Analysis', OECD Trade and Environment Working Paper No 2018/02 <https://www.oecd-ilibrary.org/docserver/5ffc615c-en.pdf?expires=1566501248&id=id&accname=guest&checksum=938FDC8D16D076AE97B59C9A540B5354> accessed 21 August 2019.

[41] Bartels and Ortino (n 2); Baldwin and Low (n 37).

[42] Baldwin (n 2); Bhagwati, Krishna and Panagariya (n 36).

[43] ILA, *Sustainable Development and The Green Economy in International Trade Law* (ILA, 2018).

Certain economic law scholars have argued that States can be innovative with regional and bilateral accords, testing new trade and investment law provisions which (if proven useful) may eventually be proposed in WTO negotiations, or in future economic treaties.[44] Indeed, new regional and bilateral economic agreements:

> can also be used by some countries as a vehicle for promoting deeper integration of their economies than is presently available through the WTO, particularly for issues which are not fully dealt with multilaterally, such as investment … environment and labour standards.[45]

If this is the case, it is time for an exploration of how States commit to sustainable development in global, regional and bilateral economic treaties, and the implications of this commitment. In regional and bilateral agreements, where echoes of the global trade debates resonate, deeper economic liberalization is under negotiation for areas such as services, government procurement and investment. Many countries also now recognize a joint resolution 'to promote sustainable development' in the free trade or international investment agreements that they negotiate,[46] and are seeking new models for their trade and investment treaty negotiations which respond more directly to their efforts to achieve the global Sustainable Development Goals (SDGs) for their people. In the EU's trade and investment accords, States have been even more emphatic, pledging, for instance:

> to commit, in the recognition that sustainable development is an overarching objective, to the development of international trade in such a way as to contribute to the objective of sustainable development and strive to ensure that this objective is integrated and reflected at every level of the Parties' trade relationship.[47]

The EU has embarked on efforts to 'modernize' its economic treaties with key countries, including Mexico, and is conducting sustainability impact assessments as part of this process. There is a need for all actors—from governments to industry to academia and civil society—to carefully consider what these treaty commitments to sustainable development actually mean, and by which provisions Parties can seek to deliver upon them in their trade and investment treaties. But it is very difficult to do so.

Part of the problem is conceptual. There is a growing body of scholarly work examining international law on sustainable development, much of which has been published in the recent decades.[48] But it is not straightforward to find one accepted universal legal definition

[44] Bartels and Ortino (n 2) 2; Bhagwati, Krishna and Panagariya (n 36); Jackson, Davey and Sykes (n 7).

[45] WTO Secretariat, 'The Changing Landscape of RTAs' (2003) Regional Trade Agreements and the WTO Seminar, <http://www.wto.org/english/tratop_e/region_e/sem_nov03_e/boonekamp_paper_e.doc> accessed 16 December 2020, 23.

[46] See, e.g., Agreement establishing an association between the European Community and its Member States, of the one part, and the Republic of Chile, of the other part (EU-Chile Association Agreement), signed 18 November 2002, entered into force 1 February 2003 [2002] OJ L 352.

[47] European Union-Korea Free Trade Agreement (6 October 2010), art 1.1.2(g).

[48] HC Bugge and C Voigt (eds), *Sustainable Development in International and National Law* (Groningen, Europa 2009); D French, *International Law and Policy on Sustainable Development* (Manchester, Juris 2005) 168–209; N Schrijver and F Weiss, *International Law and Sustainable Development: Principles and Practice* (Lieden, Martinus Nijhoff 2004); MC Cordonier Segger and CG Weeramantry (eds), *Sustainable Justice* (Lieden, Martinus Nijhoff

for sustainable development that is appropriate for all cultures and regions of the world,[49] across all environmental and development problems,[50] for all treaty regimes.[51] This is not necessarily due to a lack of scientific clarity on what it means to use a resource in a way that is *sustainable*, but might also be linked to differing expectations of what is meant by *development*. Like other important global objectives such as peace, democracy and human rights, a commitment to sustainable development takes on new meanings in different contexts. In several prominent MEAs, the Parties have developed particularized commitments to sustainable development.[52] For instance, in the 1992 UN Framework Convention on Climate Change (UN FCCC), countries arguably recognized a right to sustainable development, and the meaning of this commitment has been debated in the UN FCCC Conference of the Parties and in scholarly literature.[53] In addition to the MEAs, in accords such as the International Treaty on Plant Genetic Resources for Food and Agriculture of the Food and Agriculture Organization (FAO 'Seed Treaty'), the specific legal and policy mechanisms by which States plan to secure sustainable development and use of food and agriculture are actually detailed by the Parties in a specific treaty provision, article 6.[54] However, the meaning of a commitment to sustainable development in a trade and investment treaty is only now being investigated.

Gaps in policy and scholarly understanding may be due to a lingering lack of clarity in the precise legal character of State commitments to sustainable development. Some judges and legal scholars maintain that sustainable development should be characterized as an emerging principle of customary law itself.[55] Others have proposed that it be recognized as

2005); MC Cordonier Segger and A Khalfan, *Sustainable Development Law: Principles, Practices and Prospects* (Oxford, OUP 2004); A Boyle and D Freestone, *International Law and Sustainable Development* (OUP 1999); Food and Agriculture Organization (FAO), *Law and Sustainable Development since Rio* (Rome, FAO 2002); P Sands, 'International Law in the Field of Sustainable Development: Emerging Legal Principles' in W. Lang (ed), *Sustainable Development and International Law* (Oxford, OUP 1999); D Ginthers, M Denters and P de Waart (eds), *Sustainable Development and Global Governance* (Boston, Kluwer 1995); M McGoldrick, 'Sustainable Development: The Challenge to International Law' (1994) Review of European Community and International Environmental Law 3.

49 *Case Concerning the Gabčíkovo-Nagymaros Project* (Hungary/Slovakia) (Separate Opinion of Vice President Weeramantry) [1997] ICJ Rep 7; HP Glenn, *Legal Traditions of the World* (5th edn, Oxford, OUP 2015).

50 C Echevarria, D Brooks and G Peeling, 'Mining and Stakeholders' Involvement: Addressing Social Sustainability Changes' in MC Cordonier Segger and M Leichner Reynal (eds), *Beyond the Barricades: The Americas Trade and Sustainable Development Agenda* (England, Ashgate 2005) 97; NO Keohane and SM Olmstead, *Markets and the Environment* (Connecticut, Island Press 2007) 190–198. See also G Handl, 'Environmental Protection and Development in Third World Countries: Common Destiny-Common Responsibility' (1987–1988) 20 New York University Journal of International Law and Politics 603.

51 Schrijver and Weiss (n 48) xi–ix; Boyle and Freestone (n 48) 19–26; MC Cordonier Segger, 'Sustainable Development in International Law' in D Armstrong (ed), *Routledge Handbook of International Law* (New York, Routledge 2009) 355, 359–371.

52 Birnie, Boyle and Redgwell (n 13) 57–58.

53 See, e.g., Decision 1/CP.8 Delhi Ministerial Declaration on Climate Change and Sustainable Development FCCC/CP/2002/7/Add.1; A Najam and others, 'Integrating Sustainable Development into the 4th Assessment of the Intergovernmental Panel on Climate Change' (2003) Climate Policy 168, 169; B Metza and others, 'Towards an Equitable Global Climate Change Regime: Compatibility with Article 2 of the Climate Change Convention and the Link with Sustainable Development' (2002) 2(2) Climate Policy 211–230; M Munasinghe and R Swart, *Primer on Climate Change and Sustainable Development: Facts, Policy Analysis and Applications* (Cambridge, CUP 2005).

54 Adopted 3 November 2001, entered into force 31 March 2004; HD Cooper, 'The International Treaty on Plant and Genetic Resources for Food and Agriculture' (2002) 11 Review of European Community and International Environmental Law 1.

55 *Gabčíkovo-Nagymaros* (n 49) 86; S Atapattu, 'Sustainable Development: Myth or Reality? A Survey of Sustainable Development under International Law and Sri Lankan Law' (2001–2002) 14 Georgetown International Environmental Law Review 265, 268–271.

a right of States.[56] Still others suggest that it could be considered a general principle of international law,[57] or an obligation *erga omnes*.[58] It is also argued that commitments to sustainable development have an 'interstitial' nature, as a form of meta-norm.[59]

It has further been proposed that sustainable development is best characterized as an objective; part of the object and purpose of international treaties—not just for MEAs, but also for treaties on economic, natural resource management and social development issues.[60] From this perspective, while there may not be one single principle of sustainable development, there is an emerging body of *international law in the field of sustainable development*, as noted in the 1992 Agenda 21 and affirmed in the 2002 Johannesburg Plan of Implementation (JPOI), which explicitly highlights over thirty international treaties on sustainable development, *including international economic agreements*.[61] In this volume, rather than canvassing these well-trodden debates in great detail, the latter approach is adopted with certain caveats, in order to focus on how State commitments to sustainable development are actually being addressed in the most recent decades of international economic law and practice.

As a first caveat, this volume builds on an understanding of sustainable development as an objective that is firmly rooted in the concept of human *development*.[62] In this light, sustainable development refers to a commitment to more socially equitable and environmentally sound development that can last over the long term.[63] This is a different focus than, for instance, a call to protect ecosystems and the millions of other species with which humanity shares this Earth, an important related commitment with its own intrinsic value.[64] The

[56] A Boyle, 'The Environmental Jurisprudence of the Law of the Sea' (2007) 22(3) International Journal of Marine and Coastal Law 369; *Pulp Mills on the River Uruguay (Argentina v. Uruguay), Provisional Measures*, Order of 13 July 2006, [2006] ICJ Rep 133 (General List No 135, 67).

[57] C Voigt, *Sustainable Development as a Principle of International Law* (Danvers, Brill 2009).

[58] P Sands and J Peel, *Principles of International Environmental Law* (Cambridge, CUP 2018) 254.

[59] V Lowe, 'The Politics of Law-Making: Are the Method and Character of Norm Creation Changing?' in M Byers (ed), *The Role of Law in International Politics: Essays in International Relations and International Law* (Oxford, OUP 2000) 214–215; V Lowe, 'Sustainable Development and Unsustainable Arguments' in Boyle and Freestone (n 48) 19–28.

[60] Boyle and Freestone (n 48) 17–18; Cordonier Segger and Khalfan (n 48) 46–50; M Gehring and MC Cordonier Segger (eds), *Sustainable Development in World Trade Law* (The Hague, Kluwer Law International 2005) 3–7; Birnie, Boyle and Redgwell (n 13) 126–127; P Sands, 'International Law in the Field of Sustainable Development' (1994) 65 British Yearbook of International Law 303; MC Cordonier Segger with HE Judge CG Weeramantry (eds), *Sustainable Development Principles in the Decisions of International Courts and Tribunals: 1992-2012* (London, Routledge 2017); E Hush, 'Where No Man Has Gone before: The Future of Sustainable Development in the Comprehensive Economic and Trade Agreement and New Generation Free Trade Agreements' (2018) 43 Columbia Journal of Environmental Law 93.

[61] See also Boyle and Freestone (n 48) 17–18; Cordonier Segger and Khalfan (n 48).

[62] See World Commission on Environment and Development, *Our Common Future* (Oxford, OUP 1987) ix; N Schrijver, 'Development—The Neglected Dimension in the Post-Rio International Law of Sustainable Development' in Bugge and Voigt (n 48) 233–250; Cordonier Segger and Khalfan (n 48) 15–45; S Anand and A Sen, 'Human Development and Economic Sustainability' (2000) 28(12) World Development 2029–2049. This view is not without detractors, see, e.g., GD Meyers and SC Muller, 'The Ethical Implications, Political Ramifications and Practical Limitations of Adopting Sustainable Development as National and International Policy' (1996) 4 Buffalo Environmental Law Journal 1; A Geisinger, 'Sustainable Development and the Domination of Nature: Spreading the Seed of the Western Ideology of Nature' (1999) 27 British Columbia Environmental Affairs Law Review 43.

[63] EB Weiss, *In Fairness to Future Generations: International Law, Common Patrimony and Intergenerational Equity* (New York, Transnational 1989) 17–26.

[64] These extend beyond the 'anthropocentric' needs ofhuman beings. See P Taylor, *Respect for Nature* (Princeton, Princeton University Press 1986); S Emmenegger and A Tschentscher, 'Taking Nature's Rights Seriously: The Long Way to Biocentrism in Environmental Law' (1993–1994) 6 Georgetown International Environmental Law Review 545; D French and LJ Kotzé (eds), *Sustainable Development Goals: Law, Theory and Implementation* (Cheltenham, Edward Elgar 2018).

view, hardly controversial, is that environmental ministries and laws are not alone in promoting sustainable development—economic institutions are also responsible.[65] Indeed, the United Nations Economic and Social Council (ECOSOC), alongside other development institutions and economic ministries, was tasked in 1987 by the UN General Assembly (GA) with a reorientation of social and economic policy toward more sustainable development.[66] As the UN GA noted, 'while seeking to remedy existing environmental problems, it is imperative to influence the sources of those problems in human activity, and economic activity in particular, and thus to provide for sustainable development'.[67] This concept of sustainable development was further elaborated in the 1992 United Nations Conference on Environment and Development (UNCED, or Rio Earth Summit), the 1997 New York General Assembly Special Session on Sustainable Development, the 2002 Johannesburg World Summit on Sustainable Development (WSSD), and the 2012 Rio United Nations Conference on Sustainable Development (UNCSD, or Rio+20).[68] Countries, and international bodies, grapple with guidance to ensure that post-COVID-19 pandemic economic stimulus efforts can help, rather than hinder, sustainable development efforts. As such, this volume adopts a theory of sustainable development which recognizes that political, economic and legal systems are created by human processes, and shape the opportunities and capabilities of human societies into the future, as well as affecting ecological and other systems.

Second, while sustainable development may well be recognized as part of the 'object or purpose' of certain treaties including economic agreements,[69] the concept may also play an 'interstitial' role in treaty negotiations and legal decision-making, as outlined by Professor Vaughan Lowe.[70] A characterization as 'object and purpose' does not preclude States from adopting operational provisions to deliver on their shared purpose, nor from recognizing further *principles of international law on sustainable development* in order to achieve their object and purpose.[71] As such, this volume considers how, where States commit to sustainable development as an objective, its interstitial normative character may encourage States to reflect related principles in their treaty-making, particularly a principle that environmental concerns should be integrated into economic decision-making, including trade and investment policy.

A third caveat is that this volume focuses on the meaning of a commitment to *sustainable development* in international economic law.[72] This require a consideration of both

[65] Lowe (n 7); D Esty, *Greening the GATT* (Washington, IIE 1994).

[66] Report of the World Commission on Environment and Development, UN General Assembly Resolution 42/187.

[67] Ibid.

[68] See Bartels and Ortino (n 2), see also n 47.

[69] HG Ruse-Khan, 'A Real Partnership for Development? Sustainable Development as Treaty Objective in European Economic Agreement Partnerships and beyond' (2010) 13(1) Journal of International Economic Law 139; X Wang and J Ashton, 'Equity and Climate: In Principle and Practice' in *Beyond Kyoto: Advancing the International Effort against Climate Change* (Washington, Pew Foundation 2003); Gehring and Cordonier Segger (n 60).

[70] V Lowe, 'The Politics of Law-Making: Are the Method and Character of Norm Creation Changing?' in M Byers (ed), *The Role of Law in International Politics: Essays in International Relations and International Law* (Oxford, OUP 2000) 214–215. See also Lowe (n 59) 27.

[71] MC Cordonier Segger, 'International Law on Sustainable Development' in Bugge and Voigt (n 48); Cordonier Segger and Khalfan (n 48) 97.

[72] Gehring and Cordonier Segger (n 2); G Sampson, *The WTO and Sustainable Development* (Tokyo, UNU Press 2005); French (n 48).

international trade law, such as the agreements of the World Trade Organization, and also the myriad bilateral, regional and even region-to-region or supra-regional economic agreements some of which cover mainly liberalization of trade in goods and services; some of which also cover intellectual property, sanitary and phytosanitary measures, trade-related investment measures or even broader investment disciplines as well; some of which cover mainly investment liberalization and may be negotiated in the context of early trade accords involving the same Parties; and some of which extend to liberalize additional economic relationships.[73] For ease of reference, in this volume, these other bilateral, regional and further accords are mainly referred to as 'economic agreements' or 'trade and investment agreements.'

As a fourth caveat briefly mentioned above, in current trade and investment law literature examining bilateral and regional treaties, there is still very little consideration of sustainable development tensions and related innovations. Instead, legal literature has largely been divided into sharply delineated studies on trade and environment,[74] trade and human/labour rights,[75] or trade and development.[76] Regional studies on the NAFTA or the USMCA explore trade and labour issues,[77] or trade and environment linkages,[78] keeping them in separate silos. Others examine Europe's regional accords with developing countries, but focus on their economic development ramifications,[79] or compare mechanisms used in the agreements to promote human rights.[80] And a limited inter-governmental review compares how

[73] See early research for this volume in M Gehring, J Hepburn and MC Cordonier Segger, *World Trade Law in Practice* (London, Globe 2006) 12; Baldwin (n 2); Gehring and Cordonier Segger (n 2); Cordonier Segger, Gehring and Newcombe (n 2).

[74] Trebilcock and Howse (n 1) 507–555; D Bodansky and J Lawrence, 'Trade and Environment' in Bethlehem, McRae, Neufeld and van Damme (n 1); J Cameron, P Demaret and D Geradin (eds), *Trade and Environment: The Search for Balance* (London, Cameron & May 1994); Vranes (n 13); Esty (n 65).

[75] Trebilcock and Howse (n 1) 557–588; G Marceau, 'Trade and Labour' in Bethlehem, McRae, Neufeld and van Damme (n 1) 539–570; Cottier, Pauwelyn and Bürgi (n 6) 199; B Hepple, *Labour Laws and Global Trade* (Oxford, Hart 2005); OECD, *International Trade and Core Labour Standards*, Policy Brief (October 2000); D Puga and D Trefler, 'Wake up and Smell the Ginseng: International Trade and the Rise of Incremental Innovation in Low-Wage Countries' (2010) 91(1) Journal of Development Economics 64; HM Wolffgang and W Feuerhake, 'Core Labour Standards in World Trade Law: The Necessity for Incorporation of Core Labour Standards in the World Trade Organization' (2002) 36(5) Journal of World Trade 883.

[76] C Thomas and J Trachtman (eds), *Developing Countries in the WTO Legal System* (Oxford, OUP 2009); H Katrak and R Strange (eds), *The WTO and Developing Countries* (Basingstoke, Palgrave Macmillan 2004); SE Rolland, 'Developing Country Coalitions at the WTO: In Search of Legal Support' (2007) 48 Harvard International Law Journal 483, 511. EK Kessie, 'Developing Countries in the World Trade Organisation' (1999) 22 World Competition 83; RE Baldwin, J McLaren and A Panagariya, *Regulatory Protectionism, Developing Nations, and a Two-Tier World Trade System* (Washington, Brookings Trade Forum 2000).

[77] S Charnovitz, 'The Labor Dimension of the Emerging Free Trade Area of the America' in P Alston (ed), *Labour Rights as Human Rights* (Oxford, OUP 2005).

[78] O Saunders, 'NAFTA and the North American Agreement on Environmental Cooperation: A New Model for International Collaboration on Trade and the Environment', (1994) 5 Colorado Journal of International Environmental Law and Policy 273; Esty (n 65); S Richardson, 'Sovereignty, Trade, and the Environment-The North American Agreement on Environmental Cooperation', (1998) 24 Canada-United States Law Journal 183; J Kirton, 'The Commission for Environmental Cooperation and Canada-U.S. Environmental Governance in the NAFTA Era' (1997) 27 American Review of Canadian Studies 459; BR Copeland and MS Scott, 'Trade, Growth and the Environment', National Bureau of Economic Research Working Paper No 9823, 2003; A Tyc, 'Workers' Rights and Transatlantic Trade Relations: The TTIP and Beyond' (2017) 2 Economic and Labour Relations Review 113; JS Vogt, 'The Evolution of Labor Rights and Trade—A Transatlantic Comparison and Lessons for the Transatlantic Trade and Investment Partnership' (2015) 18(4) Journal of International Economic Law 827.

[79] DK Brown, AV Deardorff and RM Stern, 'Some Economic Effects of the Free Trade Agreement between Tunisia and the European Union' in RM Stern (ed), *Globalization and International Trade Policies* (Singapore, World Scientific Publishing 2009) 343; GM Caporale and others 'On the Bilateral Trade Effects of Free Trade Agreements between the EU-15 and the CEEC-4 Countries' (2009) 145 Revue of World Economics 189.

[80] EU Petersmann, 'The WTO and Regional Trade Agreements as Competing Fora for Constitutional Reforms: Trade and Human Rights' in Bartels and Ortino (n 2) 281–312; EM Hafner-Burton, 'Trading Human Rights: How Preferential Trade Agreements Influence Government Repression' (2005) 59 International

bilateral or regional trade and investment treaties address environmental concerns.[81] But such studies can be descriptive, containing very little legal analysis or mention of the impact assessment findings themselves, and constrained from drawing out implications for broader international economic law-making, or proposing improvements for sustainable development. While some interesting papers have been published,[82] many do not fully analyse new global perspectives on sustainable development, or take into account the most important international legal and policy debates, such as the outcomes of the 2002 WSSD, the 2012 UNCSD and the 2015 adoption of the global Sustainable Development Goals (SDGs).[83] There remains little clarity as to what is meant by a sustainable development commitment in a trade or investment treaty, and the means by which States can contribute to realizing sustainable development in international economic law. This volume focuses on that gap.

Of course, and as a final caveat, among those who have published work in this area, some neo-liberal and other scholars have suggested that trade has very little effect on sustainable development, and that trade disciplines have no link to – and therefore cannot interfere with – legitimate measures aimed at ensuring that development is more sustainable.[84] Others, as mentioned above, maintain that trade and investment are automatically good for sustainability,[85] or that the impacts are perennially negative.[86] However, it is more likely that trade and investment are neither automatically good nor bad for sustainable development. A more nuanced perspective reflects compromises agreed in the 1992 Agenda 21,[87] the 2002 JPOI,[88] the 2012 UNCSD Outcomes and the world's SDGs,[89] where it was recognized that changes in

Organisation 593; L Bartels, 'Human Rights and Sustainable Development Obligations in EU Free Trade Agreements' (2013) 40(4) Legal Issues of Economic Integration 297; SY Kim, ED Mansfield and HV Milner, *Regional Trade Governance* (Oxford, OUP 2016); K Milewics and others, 'Beyond Trade: The Expanding Scope of the Nontrade Agenda in Trade Agreements' (2016) 62(4) Journal of Conflict Resolution 743.

[81] OECD (n 40).

[82] M Pallemarts, 'International Law and Sustainable Development: Any Progress in Johannesburg?' (2003) 12 Review of European Community and International Environmental Law 1; SJ Scherr and RJ Gregg, 'Johannesburg and Beyond: The 2002 World Summit on Sustainable Development and the Rise of Partnerships' (2005–2006) 18 Georgetown International Environmental Law Review 425. Literature in recent years has started to investigate links between trade and sustainable development. See S Schacherer, 'The CETA Investment Chapter and Sustainable Development: Interpretive Issues' in MM Mbengue and S Schachere (eds), *Foreign Investment Under the Comprehensive Economic and Trade Agreement (CETA)* (Switzerland, Springer 2019); J Orbie and others, 'Promoting Sustainable Development or Legitimising Free Trade? Civil Society Mechanisms in EU Trade Agreements' (2016) 1(4) Third World Thematics: A TWQ Journal 526; Heinrich Wohlmeyer and Theodore Quendler (eds), *The WTO, Agriculture and Sustainable Development* (London, Routledge 2017); Bartels (n 78).

[83] MC Cordonier Segger, 'Inspiration for Integration: Interpreting International Trade and Investment Accords for Sustainable Development' (2017) 3(1) Canadian Journal of Comparative and Contemporary Law 159 based on early research for this volume; M Gehring, S Stephenson and MC Cordonier Segger, 'Sustainability Impact Assessments as Inputs and as Interpretative Aids in International Investment Law' (2016) 17 Journal of World Investment and Trade 155.

[84] See R Muradian and J Martinez-Alier, 'Trade and the Environment: From a 'Southern' Perspective' (2001) 36 Ecological Economics 281.

[85] W Weber, 'Competing Political Visions: WTO Governance and Green Politics' (2001) 1 Global Environmental Politics 92; DI Stern, 'The Rise and Fall of the Environmental Kuznets Curve' (2004) 32 World Development 1419; DI Stern, 'The Environmental Kuznets Curve After 25 Years' (2017) 19(1) Journal of Bioeconomics 7.

[86] I Ropke, 'Trade, Development and Sustainability—A Critical Assessment of the 'Free Trade Dogma' (1994) 9 Ecological Economics 13; S Giljum and N Eisenmenger, 'North-South Trade and the Distribution of Environmental Goods and Burdens: A Biophysical Perspective' (2004) 13(1) Journal of Environment Development 73.

[87] See United Nations Conference on the Environment and Development, *Agenda 21*, 2.1–2.22

[88] United Nations, 'Johannesburg Plan of Implementation' (2002) 84–101.

[89] United Nations, 'The Future We Want' (2012). See also A Cosbey, 'New Views of Trade and Sustainable Development: Using Sen's Conception of Development to Re-examine the Debates' Thematic Research Paper, TIPS/IISD Trade Knowledge Network Workshop (Geneva, ICTSD 2003) 1; D Runnalls, 'Shall We Dance: What the North Needs to do to Fully Engage the South in the Trade and Sustainable Development Debate' (Winnipeg, International Institute for Sustainable Development 1997).

trade and investment patterns may have both positive and negative effects on a country's potential for sustainable development. The key is to uncover under what circumstances, and in accordance with what provisions with what interpretive weight, economic law levers are more likely to foster sustainable development. This approach is adopted in the volume.

2.4 Insights on International Economic Law and Sustainability

The global call in the 2002 JPOI[90] and the 2015 SDGs[91] for trade and investment liberalization that actively contributes to sustainable development is important, and worthy of serious legal study that extends beyond brilliant but brief policy papers.[92] A growing number of State-level scientific and policy assessments review the potential sustainability impacts of trade and investment agreements.[93] But there remains little legal analysis of the rules governing global and regional trade and investment, in terms of how to best address related environmental and social concerns in an integrated manner.[94] There exists very little comparative legal analysis of States' efforts to identify and address the potential impacts of economic treaties on the environment and social development, or to include binding provisions that will contribute to sustainable development in treaties.[95] This research holds potential, if only to indicate whether the outcomes of impact assessments do affect negotiations for new trade and investment treaties, how the issues identified are addressed in final treaty texts, and what might be their interpretive weight.

Focusing mainly on the decades after 1992, from the 1992 Rio Earth Summit to the 2002 WSSD to the 2012 UNCSD and beyond, the period during which the 1994 WTO Agreements, the 1994 NAFTA, the 2019 USMCA entered into force, the European Union's new economic partnership agreements and trade agreements for sustainable development were negotiated, along with a new generation of regional and bilateral economic agreements, and the global Sustainable Development Goals were adopted, this volume seeks to bridge the gap. Given discussions on the new Agreement on Climate Change, Trade and Sustainability (ACCTS) between Costa Rica, Fiji, Iceland, New Zealand and Norway,[96] other important efforts such as the European New Green Deal and the European Commission's agenda to modernize its regional and bilateral economic agreements[97] and the UK's plans

[90] Johannesburg Declaration and Johannesburg Plan of Implementation (JPOI), Report of the World Summit on Sustainable Development, 4 September 2002, UN Doc A/CONF.199/20 47, 92, 97, 99.

[91] *Transforming our World: The 2030 Agenda for Sustainable Development*, GA Res 70A/1, UNGAOR, Seventieth Session, 25–27 September 2015, UN Doc E/15/16301 (2015) 1; SDG 16.3, 16.6, 16.b; SDG 17.5, 17.7, 17.10, 17.11, 17.12. 17.14.

[92] See, e.g., IISD, *A Sustainable Development Roadmap for the WTO* (Winnipeg, Trade and Investment Program IISD, 2009); ICTSD, *Trade, Climate Change and Sustainable Development* (Geneva, 2010); Cosbey (n 89).

[93] C Kirkpatrick and N Lee, *Sustainable Development in a Developing World: Integrating Socio-Economic Appraisal and Environmental Assessment* (Cheltenham, Edward Elgar 1997).

[94] To survey the diverse Impact Assessment techniques, in a paper based on early research for this volume, see M Gehring and MC Cordonier Segger, 'Sustainable Development through Process in World Trade Law' in Gehring and Cordonier Segger (n 60) 189–213.

[95] V Lowe, 'Preface' in Cordonier Segger, Gehring and Newcombe (n 2) 99.

[96] Joint Leaders' Statement on the launch of the 'Agreement on Climate Change, Trade and Sustainability' Initiative (25 September 2019), n 8.

[97] European Commission, 'The European Green Deal', Communication from the Commission to the European Parliament, the European Council, the Council, the European Economic and Social Committee and the Committee of the Regions COM/2019/640, n 9.

for further trade and investment negotiations,[98] as well as crucial debates on economic measures to stimulate recovery from the impacts of the global COVID-19 pandemic,[99] innovative legal research and analysis may be critically important as a foundation for expert advice and informed dialogue among all stakeholders grounded in fresh law, policy and sustainability knowledge and insights.

[98] UK Parliament Lords Select Committee, 'International Trade Secretary Discusses Possible Free Trade Agreements', 21 July 2020, n 10.

[99] See MC Cordonier Segger, F Crepeau, A Harrington, FK Phillips and N Ramanujam, 'Human Rights, the Sustainable Development Goals and the Law', Montreal, Centre for International Sustainable Development Law (CISDL), 15 May 2020, <https://www.cisdl.org/2020/04/19/human-rights-the-sustainable-development-goals-the-law-international-legal-symposium/> accessed 16 December 2020; C Hepburn, B O'Callaghan, N Stern, J Stiglitz and D Zenghelis, 'Will COVID-19 Fiscal Recovery Packages Accelerate or Retard Progress on Climate Change?' Oxford Smith School of Enterprise and the Environment Working Paper No 20-02, 4 May 2020 <https://www.smithschool.ox.ac.uk/publications/wpapers/workingpaper20-02.pdf> accessed 16 December 2020 (forthcoming in the Oxford Review of Economic Policy 36(S1)); UN Global Compact, 'Over 150 Global Corporations Urge World Leaders for Net-Zero Recovery from COVID-19' (New York, 2020) <https://ungc-communications-assets.s3.amazonaws.com/docs/publications/recover-better-statement.pdf> accessed 16 December 2020.

3

Advancing Trade and Investment Rules for the World's Sustainable Development Goals (SDGs)

To explore the meaning of commitments to sustainable development, including alignment with the UN's Sustainable Development Goals (SDGs), in the World Trade Organization (WTO) and in bilateral and regional economic agreements, this volume is guided by four objectives. First, through an analytical review of over 90 recent impact assessments (IAs), it identifies the principal sustainability concerns associated with trade and investment agreements, highlighting three main points of tension. Second, the volume examines how commitments to integrate environmental and social concerns into economic development[1] have been characterized in international trade law and policy, analysing the challenges of addressing these tensions at the global level in the WTO, and critiquing efforts in the WTO to date. Third, it identifies the main approaches to addressing these tensions from across over 110 bilateral and regional economic agreements that contain references to sustainable development, analysing the sustainable development-related provisions from selected accords using a typology based on their normative functions, taking into account how different provisions might be interpreted under the Vienna Convention on the Law of Treaties (VCLT). Fourth and finally, building on analysis of how existing bilateral and regional trade and investment agreements can contribute to the global SDGs, the volume suggests elements of more integrated procedural and substantive approaches that could help resolve key points of tension related to sustainable development in the WTO and bilateral and regional economic agreements.

The methods adopted for this volume include legal research and textual analysis of trade and investment treaties, in light of the *travaux préparatoires*[2] and relevant dispute settlement decisions. In particular, the volume analyses and draws lessons from recent procedural innovations, and provisions on sustainable development in bilateral and regional economic agreements. It considers their interpretation and potential as models for future trade and investment treaties, including the proposed Agreement on Climate Change, Trade and Sustainability (ACCTS), especially where these accords extend beyond WTO

[1] 'Rio Declaration on Environment and Development' Report of the UN Conference on Environment and Development, 13 June 1992, UN Doc A/CONF.151/26 (Vol I).

[2] See R Jennings and A Watts, *Oppenheim's International Law* (9th edn, Oxford, OUP 1992) 1277, which defines *travaux préparatoires* as 'the record of the negotiations preceding the conclusion of a treaty, the minutes of the plenary meetings and of committees of the Conference which adopted a treaty, and so on'. According to the VCLT (signed 23 May 1969, entered into force 27 January 1980) 1155 UNTS 331, art 32, the *travaux préparatoires* can be used as a supplementary means of interpreting treaties. And see P Daillier and A Pellet, *Droit International Public* (7th edn, Paris, LGDJ 2002), 262, which surveys several International Court of Justice cases, noting that 'an evolution can be traced for some years now tending to accord greater weight to travaux préparatoires'. In 'Young Loan Arbitration' (Belgium, the French Republic, Swiss Confederation, United Kingdom and United States of America/ Federal Republic of Germany) 59, 194, it was stressed that *travaux* are usually 'material set down in writing-and thereby actually available at a later date ... A further prerequisite if material is to be considered as a component of travaux préparatoires is that it was actually accessible and known to all the original parties.' The sustainable impact assessments (SIAs) and EAs referenced herein fulfil these conditions.

Crafting Trade and Investment Accords for Sustainable Development. Marie-Claire Cordonier Segger, Oxford University Press.
 DOI: 10.1093/oso/9780198831341.003.0003

rules in a manner relevant to the implementation of existing obligations, and to innovations in the design of future international instruments.

Research undertaken for this volume included a review of secondary literature and 'soft law' declarations on sustainable development. trade and investment, in order to understand the current state of global policy debates and identify common threads. This also involved reviewing the outcomes of over 90 *ex-ante* and *ex-post* impact assessments conducted or commissioned by States. In light of this literature and the concerns raised in the impact assessments, it was possible to identify three key normative tensions with respect to sustainable development in economic agreements, and briefly investigate European experience with the integration principle in addressing these tensions.

The volume also builds on a comparative analysis of relevant global trade and investment treaty provisions on sustainable development, supplemented with reference to the *travaux préparatoires* and subsequent relevant treaty practice. This involved analysing the main WTO treaties for provisions related to sustainable development, and also reviewing the documented debates on sustainable development in the Uruguay Round negotiations prior to the adoption of the WTO Agreements (when the issue was first raised), as well as subsequent debates in the WTO General Council, the Committee on Trade and Environment (CTE) and the Committee on Trade and Development (CTD), including the records of the WTO Ministerial Meetings over several decades. It further involved review, based mainly on secondary legal literature, of over twenty WTO disputes related to sustainable development in the WTO. Out of these disputes, six that most clearly addressed sustainable development issues were selected for closer analysis. Further, by analysing the formal responses of more than forty States to specific questions related to sustainable development in WTO Trade Policy Reviews over several dates, it becomes clearer how, over recent decades, States have debated or sought to address the key tensions identified in the review of the impact assessments. By focusing on emerging points of consensus, and also on key areas where agreement on measures to address sustainable development tensions has been stymied in the WTO 2001 Doha 'Development Round' of negotiations, more nuanced findings are induced.

In recent decades, States have concluded over 470 bilateral and regional trade agreements[3] and even more investment treaties, many of which explicitly address sustainable development concerns. As noted above, with the possible exception of the EU and the 1994 North American Free Trade Agreement (NAFTA) which was updated by the 2019 United States of America, the United Mexican States and Canada Agreement (USMCA), sustainable development elements of these trade and investment accords have been poorly documented in legal scholarship. This book focuses especially on the bilateral and regional economic agreements signed with countries of the Americas that explicitly mention sustainable development. As such, it takes into account a comparative analytical survey of over 110 trade and investment treaties that have been negotiated since the 1992 Earth Summit, most involving countries of the Americas and their developed country trading partners, along with several others which also explicitly mention sustainable development even though they do not

[3] As at July 2019, there were 473 RTA notifications, with 294 in force: WTO, 'Regional Trade Agreements: Scope of RTAs', <https://rtais.wto.org/UI/PublicMaintainRTAHome.aspx> accessed 1 August 2019; for the Americas, see Organization of American States, Foreign Trade Information System (OAS SICE), <http://www.sice.oas.org/> accessed 1 August 2019 for international economic agreement texts.

directly engage Parties from North America, Central America, South America, the Andes or the Caribbean. Research involved the study and analysis of the original regional and bilateral economic treaty texts in Spanish and English, as well as the *travaux préparatoires* to these treaties. By analysing over 90 environmental assessments, environmental reviews, human rights reviews and sustainability impact assessments commissioned and conducted by States during and after the negotiations of WTO rounds and the regional or bilateral economic agreements, many of which could be considered *travaux* in themselves, key concerns were traced and initial conclusions formed. In order to compare and distinguish the most relevant provisions and how they address the three key tensions identified by the impact assessments, the volume offers a classification system (typology). This typology draws on different 'integration' functions to identify and characterize the principal 'innovations'—the treaty provisions that actually seek to address potential social and environmental impacts of liberalization of trade and investment.[4] The typology serves as a tool for more meaningful comparisons between trade and investment agreements, demonstrating how States address sustainable development concerns in the text of the trade and investment treaties, identifying normative functions of the different types of measures, considering how the innovative provisions might be interpreted and linking the measures to the overall objective of sustainable development. The typology also assists in drawing out the implications of the research findings.

The assessment reviews reveal that the actual scope and relevance of sustainable development issues raised by each bilateral and regional economic agreements varies, in some cases considerably, depending on the economic relationship that exists between the Parties prior to the agreement, and the sectors in which economic growth is expected to be stimulated by increased trade and investment flows. As such, selected case studies of experiences under existing treaties are provided to illustrate and complete the research, as these permitted a more robust substantive legal understanding of the specific provisions and their effects. The case studies are not chosen randomly, but for their value as models. Successive rounds of negotiations for large international trade and investment agreements, including the Cotonou Agreement between the European Union and the African, Caribbean and Pacific (ACP) countries, the Free Trade Agreement of the Americas (FTAA), the Trans-Pacific Partnership (TPP), also for the Agreement on Climate Change, Trade and Sustainability (ACCTS) launched in 2019, inform the relevance of this inquiry. While the economic gains may appear significant,[5] attempts to negotiate strict trade and investment disciplines among such disparate groups of States remain elusive, whether for thirty-four countries of the Americas, eleven countries of the Pacific Rim, or 105 countries of the ACP and the EU.[6] It is possible that the coalition of six trade-dependent, sustainable development oriented allies of the ACCTS fares better. Sustainable development concerns are often directly raised

[4] Gratitude is owed to Professors Dan Sarooshi and Christopher McCrudden for recommending to develop such a 'typology' or classification system for the measures used by States in these agreements.

[5] In 2018, the trade volume between the EU and ACP was valued at EUR 169 billion, with the EU importing EUR 84.6 billion from the ACPs and exporting EUR 84.8 billion, <https://webgate.ec.europa.eu/isdb_results/factsheets/region/details_acp-total-african-caribbean-and-pacific-countries_en.pdf> accessed 18 July 2019. According to WTO 'International Trade Statistics 2010', trade volume within the FTAA zone represented an amount in excess of US$ 1,132 billion during negotiations in 2009.

[6] Cotonou involves 78 ACP countries and the 14 to 15 member States of the EU depending on the UK's brexit. FTAA includes all of the countries of the Americas save Cuba, so 34 countries. TPP includes 12 countries of the Pacific Rim, less the US, which withdrew, so 11 countries.

by States and stakeholders in the negotiations of these attempted treaties, and in some cases, failures to address them effectively undermines the accords.[7]

The case studies provide examples of the two prevalent models, offering insights into how sustainable development concerns can be addressed in bilateral and regional economic agreements. First, the US and Canada most often negotiate free trade agreements with third Parties that include sustainable development commitments and the experience of design and negotiation for the US-Chile FTA[8] provides a case study for this approach, supplemented with insights from the drafting of the US-Peru TPA,[9] the Canada-Peru FTA[10] and the Chile-New Zealand-Singapore-Brunei Darussalam TPS-EPA,[11] among other relevant agreements. Second, the EU often negotiates 'Association Agreements' (AA) or 'Economic Partnership Agreements' (EPA) with trade and investment partners, and these increasingly include sustainability commitments. The experience of design and negotiation of the European Union-Chile AA,[12] supplemented by examination of the EU-Colombia Peru FTA,[13] the EU-CARIFORUM EPA,[14] the EU-Central America EPA[15] and other similar accords, provides a second set of case studies.

Environmental and social issues concerns can be raised by the negotiations for both treaties, although much depends on the significance of the economic relationship between the Parties. The US-Chile FTA, for instance, eliminated tariffs on 90 per cent of US exports to Chile and 95 per cent of Chilean exports to the US; in 2004 it also covered US$ 1.17 billion of Chilean exports to the US, mainly in natural resources and processed goods based on natural resources.[16] In 2001, as the agreement was being advanced, EU-Chile trade was worth EUR 6,140 billion, mainly in manufactured goods, raw materials, agricultural products and beverages and tobacco and more than EUR 10,412 billion was invested by Europeans in Chile, mainly in mining, agriculture and energy.[17] As discussed below, rapid

[7] See, e.g., Economic Partnership Agreements, Secretariat of the Africa Caribbean and Pacific Group of States, where the 79 ACP countries note that their EPA general objectives are 'sustainable development of the ACP States, their smooth and gradual integration in the world market, and eradication of poverty' and specific objectives include 'enhancing sustainable growth ... ' <http://www.acpsec.org/en/epa/note_on_epa.htm> accessed 1 August 2019. See also the Third Draft FTAA Text, Chapter 1 Institutional Issues, which resolves in draft form that the 34 Parties are 'determined to better protect the environment and promote sustainable development ...', <http://www.ftaa-alca.org/FTAADraft03/ChapterI_e.asp> accessed 1 August 2019.

[8] Chile-US Free Trade Agreement (adopted 2003, entered into force 1 January 2004), <https://ustr.gov/trade-agreements/free-trade-agreements/chile-fta> accessed 16 December 2020.

[9] US-Peru Trade Promotion Agreement (adopted 12 April 2006); USTR 'Interim Environmental Review United States-Andean Free Trade Agreement' (2005) <http://www.ustr.gov/sites/default/files/perinter.pdf> accessed 16 December 2020.

[10] Signed 29 May 2008, entered into force 1 August 2009.

[11] Signed 18 July 2005 and by Brunei on 2 August 2005; entry into force 1 May 2006 for New Zealand and Singapore; Brunei deposited an instrument of provisional application on 12 May and the Trans-Pacific Agreement has provisionally applied to Brunei since 12 June 2006; entry into force on 8 November 2006 for Chile: < <https://www.mfat.govt.nz/en/trade/free-trade-agreements/free-trade-agreements-in-force/p4/> accessed 16 December 2020.

[12] Agreement establishing an association between the European Community and its Member States, on the one part, and the Republic of Chile, on the other part (EU-Chile Association Agreement), signed 18 November 2002, entered into force 1 February 2003 [2002] OJ L 352.

[13] Signed 30 March 2010, not yet in force.

[14] Signed 15 October 2008, provisionally entered into force 29 December 2008.

[15] Initialled 22 March 2011, not yet signed.

[16] See Office of the United States Trade Representative, 'The US-Chile Free Trade Agreement', June 2004, <https://ustr.gov/about-us/policy-offices/press-office/fact-sheets/archives/2004/june/-us-chile-free-trade-agreement-early-record-suc> accessed 16 December 2020.

[17] European Union-Chile Association Agreement Trade and Investment Background Information, EU Bilateral Trade Relations Division, September 2001, <http://europa.eu.int/comm/trade/bilateral/chl.htm> accessed 16 December 2020.

and unsound economic growth in these sectors risks considerable environmental and social harm especially for the most vulnerable and marginalized groups in Chile, while ecologically sound and socially justice development in the same areas might have exponential benefits.

The sets of case study treaties analysed in this volume, like the ACCTS, link developing and developed country Parties. Many of the treaties examined link several developing countries with their largest trade and investment partners: the US and the EU respectively. As sustainable development is a concern for many developing countries, this offers a timely and relevant perspective for any lessons learned. Both sets of treaties also remain significant as precedents for potential large-scale negotiations, either for future rounds of the EU-ACP (Cotonou) Agreement and other agreements in Latin America,[18] for the various evolving trade relationships across the Americas,[19] or even for the ACCTS. Further, all Parties to the case study treaties are members of the WTO. The treaties analysed bind the Parties to 'deeper' liberalization than in the WTO, making significant new liberalization commitments in areas such as services, government procurement and investment, allowing innovations identified to provide useful implications for WTO negotiations.[20] Of additional interest, in each set of treaties the Parties characterize their sustainable development commitments in distinct ways, allowing a comparison of how the provisions of the treaty might be interpreted in light of differing characterizations.

As such, the present Section One introduces the volume by setting out the academic context of this book, laying out the objectives and central arguments and describing the legal research methodology selected. It explains why the case study treaties were chosen, acknowledging important data sources that benefited the research and analysis. It also shows the structure of the work, and describes how it is based on legal theories, dispute settlement solutions and evidence of provisions that have been adopted to date, extending past simple comparisons of environmental measures or human rights concerns into an intensive analysis of how a trade and investment accord could actually be crafted to promote achievement of the world's SDGs.

Section Two provides an articulation of the potential material impacts of changes in trade and investment rules on the environment and on social development, especially in developing countries, based on a cross-cutting analysis of the potential material impacts identified in recent trade and investment reviews and assessments commissioned or carried out by States.[21] A table, annexed to the volume, provides a list of over 90 sustainability impact assessment reports, environmental and labour assessments and other reviews (Annex 1). Taking these material impacts into account, three normative impacts or 'key points of tension' are identified for sustainable development in trade and investment agreements.

Section Three of the volume then argues that it is not desirable to simply 'let the impacts fall where they may' onto developing country Parties to economic agreements and considers both legal and policy rationales for seeking less harmful alternatives. In this respect,

[18] A Panagariya, 'EU Preferential Trade Arrangements and Developing Countries.' (2002) 25 World Economy 1415.

[19] Indeed, Chilean, US and Canadian negotiators referred directly to their experience with the Chile-US Agreement when negotiating the FTAA. See O Rosales, 'Chile-US Free Trade Agreement: Lessons and Best Practices', paper presented at the American Chamber of Commerce, Washington, 28 April 2003.

[20] UNCTAD, *Multilateralism and Regionalism: The New Interface* (New York and Geneva, UNCTAD 2005) 1–2.

[21] For initial background on regulatory aspects of impact assessments, see C Kirkpatrick and D Parker (eds), *Regulatory Impact Assessment: Towards better Regulation* (Cheltenham, Edward Elgar 2007).

an emerging customary legal principle of integration is explored, focusing on its implications for economic decision-making, and this part discusses how this principle may influence the interpretation of bilateral and regional economic agreements to address the three key points of tension identified. In this context, European experiences with the principle of integration is advanced with respect to their relevance for trade and investment law that can contribute to sustainable development. Further, given four decades of consensus in the UN and other processes, including myriad 'soft law' commitments to sustainable development through trade and investment, this section also argues that States have a good faith, legitimate expectation that if informed, Parties to trade and investment agreements will seek ways to mitigate or prevent environmental and social damage from their treaties. In essence, the section highlights why, should States accept sustainable development as part of the 'object and purpose' of trade and investment treaties, this commitment should be reflected in different types of operational provisions, briefly also touching on how such mechanisms can be interpreted in light of the integration principle under the VCLT.[22] A table, annexed to the volume, provides a brief analytical survey of sustainable development measures included in over 110 bilateral and regional economic agreements (Annex 2).

Section Four summarizes the evidence from the survey of sustainable development-related negotiations and practices in the WTO over several decades, in light of decisions of the WTO Panel and Appellate Body in disputes related to sustainable development, and responses of WTO members in the Trade Policy Review Mechanism (TPRM) in discussions on their commitments to sustainable development. From this analysis, and building on other works of the author, this book explains that State commitments to sustainable development may best be characterized in WTO law as part of the 'object and purpose' of the WTO Agreements, while highlighting that this alone has not been enough to address the three tensions underlined earlier in the volume. A table, annexed to the volume, provides quotations and analysis of several selected WTO members' replies to TPRM questions, analysing how the members characterize their own commitments to sustainable development in trade policy (Annex 3).

Section Five then examines two principal alternative approaches to sustainable development adopted in experiences of crafting bilateral and regional economic agreements, based on the typology of provisions and representative case study accords, demonstrating how those bilateral and regional economic agreements which explicitly aim to promote sustainable development have tried to address the points of tension related to integration identified in Sections 2 and 3 and found them unresolved at the global level in Section Four. This analysis highlights the normative functions of the provisions identified and how they may be interpreted in light of an integration principle, revealing how certain provisions may contribute to sustainable development as a 'purpose' of the treaty itself, and could serve to integrate social and environmental concerns into trade and investment law. This section also discusses the 'integration' processes used by the State Parties during the negotiations of these treaties, returning to the impact assessments themselves, and considering how the legal and regulatory aspects of impact assessments and economic agreements might be improved in light of the findings.

[22] VCLT (n 2).

Sections Six and Seven consider how trade and investment treaty innovations and experiences might advance the SDGs, based on international scoping research. The book concludes by drawing together the implications of the findings in light of the analysis, proposing a new approach to sustainability impact assessment, and to sustainable development, for the design and negotiation of bilateral and regional economic agreements, including the ACCTS. It discusses how the findings could lead to new approaches for crafting international trade and investment accords and in future regional trade and investment agreements, as well as the broader agenda to deliver the SDGs through changes in international economic law.

In essence, this volume explores the nature of the legal provisions that States are starting to use in bilateral and regional economic agreements to reconcile and integrate environmental, social and economic development norms, and makes recommendations for how such measures might be taken into account in the WTO and future bilateral and regional accords, including the ACCTS negotiations. The book offers a contribution to the study of international law on sustainable development.

SECTION TWO

ENVIRONMENTAL AND SOCIAL IMPACTS OF TRADE AND INVESTMENT AGREEMENTS

4

Trade and Investment Treaties and their Impacts

Changes in trade and investment rules can have adverse impacts on the environment and on social development, especially in developing countries. Based on a cross-cutting analysis of material and normative effects identified through several decades of impact assessments (IAs) of trade and investment agreements by States and international organizations, the chapters in this section raise concerns about negotiating new bilateral, regional and global economic agreements which can lead to such adverse impacts. In light of more than three decades of global and regional 'soft law' commitments by States to harness trade and investment flows in order to foster rather than frustrate sustainable development, such concerns are worth careful consideration. In this regard, three key points of tension are identified in the next chapter, which provide a framework for the analysis of sustainable development-related innovations in global and regional economic agreements in the following chapters.

Liberal and neo-liberal theorists argue that increases in international trade and investment flows, by supporting economic growth, will automatically prove positive for both social development and the environment.[1] An 'Environmental Kuznets Curve' has been hypothesized, whereby increases in trade and investment volumes in sectors of comparative advantage lead to increases in individual wealth and social development, which then (after a delay) lead citizens to require better environmental quality and standards, which then (after a further delay), may result in tougher codes and gradual improvements or even restoration of the environment.[2] From this point of view, it would be unnecessary for trade and investment agreements to be concerned with sustainable development and other issues, as environmental and developmental benefits would simply flow naturally from economic liberalization.[3] And indeed, as mentioned earlier in this book, many positive effects of trade and investment law and policy may be possible, particularly if carefully tailored to support

[1] See R Muradian and J Martinez-Alier, 'Trade and the Environment: From a "Southern" Perspective' (2001) 36 Ecological Economics 281; W Weber, 'Competing Political Visions: WTO Governance and Green Politics' (2001) 1 Global Environmental Politics 92; DI Stern, 'The Rise and Fall of the Environmental Kuznets Curve' (2004) 32 World Development 1419; I Ropke, 'Trade, Development and Sustainability—A Critical Assessment of the 'Free Trade Dogma' (1994) 9 Ecological Economics 13; S Giljum and N Eisenmenger, 'North-South Trade and the Distribution of Environmental Goods and Burdens: A Biophysical Perspective' (2004) 13 Journal of Environment Development 73; R Hudec, *Developing Countries in the GATT Legal System* (London, Gower 1987) 1–22; B Balassa, *New Directions in the World Economy* (New York, NYU Press 1989) 20–32; J Bagwhati and R Hudec (eds), *Fair Trade and Harmonization: Prerequisites for Free Trade?* (Cambridge, MIT Press 1996) 3–14; K Mathis, 'Sustainable Development, Economic Growth and Environmental Regulation' in Klaus Mathis and Bruce R Huber (eds), *Environmental Law and Economics* (Cham, Switzerland, Springer 2017).

[2] G Grossman and A Krueger, 'Economic Growth and the Environment' (1995) 110(2) Quarterly Journal of Economics 353; S Dasgupta, B Laplante, H Wang and D Wheeler. 'Confronting the Environmental Kuznets Curve' (2002) 16(1) Journal of Economic Perspectives' 147; S Shaw, 'Business and the Environment: Is there More to the Story?' (2005) 40 Business Economics 40. For policy influence, see *The Economist*, 'Issues 2000' 30 September 2000 (Campaign point of George W Bush: Don't link Trade to the Environment); DI Stern, 'The Environmental Kuznets Curve After 25 Years' (2017) 19(1) Journal of Bioeconomics 7.

[3] Stern (n 1); H Nordström and S Vaughan, *Trade and Environment* (Special Studies 4, Geneva, WTO 1999) 47–58.

Crafting Trade and Investment Accords for Sustainable Development. Marie-Claire Cordonier Segger, Oxford University Press. © Marie-Claire Cordonier Segger 2021. DOI: 10.1093/oso/9780198831341.003.0004

sustainable development. However, the theory that these benefits will accrue automatically over time as income levels rise has been convincingly critiqued: certain environmental impacts are irreversible, the gains of trade do not always accrue to those who are exposed to resulting pollution, and wealthiest societies continue to generate the highest levels of waste without being forced to live in it.[4] Also, the costs of repairing certain types of environmental damage can be far higher than the economic benefits obtained through growth, trade or increased investment, just as the costs of preventing environmental damage are often much lower than later restoration costs.[5] Increased trade and investment in certain natural resources may even lead to conflict and governance challenges that leave a country worse off than before.[6]

In order to better understand the risks, Canada, the US and the EU, among others, have begun to use impact assessment techniques to identify potential negative environmental and social effects of trade agreements, mainly prior to concluding trade negotiations. Over 110 of these assessments have been carried out, and many could be considered to form part of the *travaux préparatoires* for the trade and investment treaties.[7]

One type of assessment which was introduced in the first chapters of this book is used mainly by the EU, pursuant to a 2002 Communication of the European Commission (EC),[8] the related guidelines and a handbook.[9] The EC (DG-Trade) commissions a sustainability impact assessment (SIA) of each new international economic agreement that is being contemplated. These SIAs are undertaken both before and during a trade and investment agreement negotiation, and aim to identify the potential economic, social and environmental impacts of the resulting agreement.[10] The SIAs, including the EU-Chile SIA and other such processes, are carried out under broad conception of sustainable development, whereby scenarios of outcomes are anticipated, then available economic and scientific data is surveyed to analyse the potential economic, social and environmental effects of a new trade and investment agreement.[11] They examine impacts both in Europe and in developing country trading partners, often making particular efforts to uncover the potential impacts in the less-developed partner country.

[4] Ibid; Stern (n 3); Selin Özokcu and Özlem Özdemir, 'Economic Growth, Energy and Environmental Kuznets Curve' (2017) 72 Renewable and Sustainable Energy Reviews 639.

[5] TEEB, *The Economics of Ecosystems and Biodiversity: Mainstreaming the Economics of Nature: A Synthesis of the Approach, Conclusions and Recommendations of TEEB* (2010) 7.

[6] P Collier, *The Bottom Billion: Why the Poorest Countries are Failing and What Can Be Done About It* (Oxford, OUP 2007) 40; P Collier, *The Plundered Planet: How to Reconcile Prosperity with Nature* (Oxford, OUP 2010) 38; MG Desta, 'Competition for Natural Resources and International Investment Law: Analysis from the Perspective of Africa' in Z Yihdego, Melaku Geboye Desta and Fikremarkos Merso (eds), *Ethiopian Yearbook of International Law 2016* (Cham, Switzerland, Springer 2017).

[7] See Chapter 3, n 2 for a discussion of the Vienna Convention on the Law of Treaties (VCLT) rules for *travaux préparatoires*.

[8] Commission (EC), 'Communication from the Commission on Impact Assessment' COM (2002)276 final, 5 June 2002.

[9] EC, *Handbook for Trade Sustainability Impact Assessment* (2nd edn, Brussels, 2018) <https://trade.ec.europa.eu/doclib/docs/2016/april/tradoc_154464.PDF> accessed 16 December 2020.

[10] See Section Four of this volume.

[11] See Annex 1, SIAs 1.1–1.14; and see European Commission, Handbook for Trade Sustainability Impact Assessment (Brussels, 2006); C George, C Kirkpatrick and S Scrieciu, *Final Global Overview Trade SIA: Inception and Mid-Term Reports* (Manchester, Institute for Development Policy & Management 2006); UNEP, *Reference Manual for the Integrated Assessment of Trade-Related Policies* (Geneva, 2001); UNCSD, *Indicators of Sustainable Development: Framework and Methodologies* (New York, 1999).

The second type of assessment involves an environmental review (ER).[12] These are carried out by the US in accordance with an Executive Order[13] and by Canada as mandated by Cabinet Directive,[14] prior to the conclusion of a new regional trade or investment treaty. For instance, the US-Chile ER was carried out before the conclusion of the US-Chile Free Trade Agreement.[15] Such reviews, known as environmental assessments (EAs) in Canada, involve an investigation by a government inter-agency task force with opportunity for public comment; they focus on potential physical and regulatory effects of the economic growth predicted from the trade agreement on the environment.[16] The North American reviews are usually limited in scope, addressing only impacts within the country's territory, though global impacts can be taken into account.

Increases in trade and investment flows and changes in economic rules may not be uniquely positive, nor even simply neutral for the environment or for development in the countries of trading partners. In this section, the growing body of trade and investment impact assessment reports are canvassed to reveal concerns about direct physical impacts on economic, social development and environmental conditions from economic changes predicted from trade and investment treaty implementation.[17] The review of these material effects assists in identifying three key tensions which highlight potential normative effects of these agreements on a country's regulations related to sustainable development.

[12] See Environmental Assessments and Reviews documented in Annex 1, 2.1–2.1.17 and 3.1–3.20.

[13] US Trade Act of 2002 s 2102(b)(11)(D–E), s 2102(c)(4), Executive Orders 13277 (2002) and 13141 (1999). J Salzmann 'Executive Order 13.141 and the Environmental Review of Trade Agreements' (2001) 95 American Journal of International Law 368.

[14] Government of Canada, *The Cabinet Directive on the Environmental Assessment of Policy, Plan and Program Proposals: Guidelines for Implementing the Cabinet Directive* (Privy Council Office and Canadian Environmental Assessment Agency, Ottawa 2010) <https://www.canada.ca/content/dam/ceaa-acee/documents/strategic-environmental-assessment/cabinet-directive-environmental-assessment-policy-plan-program-proposals/cabinet_directive_on_environmental_assessment_of_policy_plan_and_program_proposals.pdf> accessed 16 December 2020.

[15] USTR, *Interim Environmental Review of the US-Chile FTA* (Washington, 2001); USTR, *Final Environmental Review of the US-Chile FTA* (Washington, 2003), <https://ustr.gov/sites/default/files/chilefinal.pdf> accessed 16 December 2020.

[16] USTR, *Guidelines for Implementation of Executive Order 13141: Environmental Review of Trade Agreements* (Washington, 2000), <http://www.ustr.gov/sites/default/files/guidelines%20for%2013141.pdf> accessed 16 December 2020; Canadian Environmental Impact Assessment Agency Guidance Materials, <http://www.ceaa.gc.ca/default.asp?lang=En&n=DACB19EE-1> accessed 16 December 2020.

[17] See S Richardson, 'A "Critique" of the EU's WTO Sustainability Impact Assessment Study and Recommendations for Phase III' (Gland, Switzerland, WWF-European Policy Office 2000); OECD 'Methodologies for Environmental and Trade Reviews' (Paris, 1994); C Deere and D Esty (eds), *Greening the Americas: NAFTA's Lessons for Hemispheric Trade* (Boston, MIT Press 2002).

5

Material Impacts of Trade and Investment on Sustainable Development

Based on a survey of the concerns raised in recent impact assessments (IAs), in this chapter a few illustrative examples are uncovered which can help explain the potential material impacts of increased trade and investment on economic, social and environmental conditions that can affect a country's potential for sustainable development.

5.1 Material Impacts Identified in Sustainability Impact Assessments (SIAs) of Trade and Investment Agreements

According to World Trade Organization (WTO) estimates, in the last completed round of global trade negotiations, the 1994 Uruguay Round, concessions were negotiated covering over US$ 1.6 trillion of trade in industrial and agricultural products alone.[1] The proposed 2001 Doha Round of WTO negotiations were calculated to be worth many times this amount,[2] and were projected to lead to many positive gains in terms of economic growth.[3] However, according to IAs commissioned by the European Commission (EC), absent mitigating measures, economic changes wrought by the proposed Doha round of international trade negotiations were also projected to lead to significant social and environmental impacts, especially in developing countries.[4]

These material impacts, sometimes called 'scale effects', are not universally positive. As has been noted in several assessments over time, important socio-economic impacts can be triggered by changes in trade patterns. On the social side, these can include the loss of jobs and the lowering of wages in vulnerable sectors of developed and developing country economies, such as agriculture and manufacturing, when trade and investment flows result in production moving to different regions or countries.[5] Further social impacts that have also

[1] WTO, 'Developing Countries and the Uruguay Round: An Overview' Note by the Secretariat, 10 November 1994, <http://www.wto.org/english/docs_e/legal_e/ldc2_512.htm>, Annexes 1, 2.

[2] For example, trade liberalization in natural resources which has been advocated at the WTO could involve US$ 452 billion in exports annually from oil-producing regions. See WTO, *The Trade Situation in 2009-2010* (Geneva, 2010) 26.

[3] See, e.g., Doha WTO Ministerial 2001: Ministerial Declaration, WT/MIN(01)/DEC/1, para 1.

[4] For 2001 Doha Round, see C Kirkpatrick, C George and S Scrieciu, *Sustainability Impact Assessment of Proposed WTO Negotiations Final Global Overview Trade SIA of the Doha Development Agenda: Final Report* (Manchester, IDPM 2006) 60; and C George and C Kirkpatrick, *Sustainability Impact Assessment of Proposed Doha Agenda Assessment of Individual Trade Measures: Preliminary Overview* (Manchester, IARC 2003) 10–15; for proposed 2000 'Millennium Round', see C Kirkpatrick, N Lee and O Morrissey, *Sustainability Impact Assessment Study WTO New Round: Phase One Report* (Manchester, IDPM 1999); and see C Kirkpatrick and N Lee, *Sustainability Impact Assessment Study WTO New Round: Phase Two Report* (Manchester, IDPM 1999).

[5] A Maltais, M Nilsson, A Persson and L Segnestam, *Sustainability Impact Assessment of WTO Negotiations in the Major Food Crops Sector: Final Report* (Stockholm, SEI 2002) 149–156; O Morrissey, DW te Velde and I Gillson, *Sustainability Impact Assessment of Proposed WTO Negotiations for the Agriculture Sector Study: Final Report* (London, IARC and ODI 2004) 1–8; O Morrissey and DW te Velde, *Sustainability Impact Assessment of*

Crafting Trade and Investment Accords for Sustainable Development. Marie-Claire Cordonier Segger, Oxford University Press. © Marie-Claire Cordonier Segger 2021. DOI: 10.1093/oso/9780198831341.003.0005

been raised in assessments include increases in health risks, for instance due to increases in production in manufacturing and agricultural export industries with high chemical exposure, low protections from infectious diseases or unsafe and unhealthy working conditions.[6]

Direct environmental impacts identified in assessments include increased risks to biological diversity due to the conversion of native forests to plantations,[7] loss of marine ecosystems due to increases in the exploitation of fisheries[8] and increases in land and water degradation due to higher circulation or unsafe disposal of chemicals and wastes generated through increased production.[9] Such concerns have been raised by non-governmental organizations and in secondary literature.[10] Trade and investment impact assessments

Proposed WTO Negotiations Sector Study for Market Access: Final Report (London, IARC and ODI, 2003) 21, 43, 80; JL Clarke, SJ Evenett and KR Gray, *Sustainability Impact Assessment of Proposed WTO Negotiations Sector Study for Competition: Final Report* (Manchester, IARC and others 2003) 59–60; Kirkpatrick, George and Scrieciu (n 4) 20.

[6] C George, C Kirkpatrick and S Scrieciu, *Final Global Overview Trade SIA: Inception and Mid-Term Reports* (Institute for Development Policy & Management, Manchester 2006); Morrissey and te Velde (n 5) 51; Morrissey, te Velde and Gillson (n 5) 13.

[7] George and Kirkpatrick (n 4) 4, 63; M Katila and M Simula, *Sustainability Impact Assessment of Proposed WTO Negotiations for the Forest Sector Study: Final Report* (Helsinki, IARC and others 2005) 41.

[8] Kirkpatrick, George and Scrieciu (n 4) 67; George and Kirkpatrick (n 4) 83; U, Kleih, P Greenhalgh and A Marter, *Sustainability Impact Assessment of Proposed WTO Negotiations for the Fisheries Sector Study: Final Report* (London, IARC and NRI 2006) 5–13; J Arkell and M Johnson, *Sustainability Impact Assessment of Proposed WTO Negotiations for the Distribution Services Study: Mid-Term Report* (London, IARC and ITSP 2004)33.

[9] Kirkpatrick, George and Scrieciu (n 4) 64; George and Kirkpatrick (n 4) 26; R Bisset, D Flint, C Kirkpatrick, D Mitlin and K Westlake, *Sustainability Impact Assessment of Proposed WTO Negotiations Sector Study for Environmental Services: Final Report* (Manchester, IARC and others 2003) 58.

[10] See T Collier and D Dollar, *Globalization, Growth and Poverty* (Oxford OUP 2002); T Collier and J Gunning, *Trade Shocks in Developing Countries* (Oxford, Clarendon 1999); J Jackson, W Davey and A Sykes, *Legal Problems of International Economic Relations* (3rd edn, West, St Paul 1995) 278–279; R Bhala, 'Clarifying the Trade-Labor Link' (1998) 37(1) Columbia Journal of Transnational Law 30–31; UN CBD Secretariat, 'The Impact of Trade Liberalization on Agricultural Biological Diversity' CBD Technical Series No 16 (UN CBD, Montreal 2006); PM Vitousek and others, 'Human Appropriation of the Products of Photosynthesis' (1986) 36 BioScience 368, BL Turner and others (eds), *The Earth as Transformed by Human Action: Global and Regional Changes in the Biosphere over the Past 300 Years* (Cambridge, CUP 1990); B Kjellen, *A New Diplomacy for Sustainable Development: The Challenge of Global Change* (New York, Routledge 2008); EU Petersmann, 'Taking Human Dignity, Poverty and Empowerment of Individuals More Seriously' (2002) 13 European Journal of International Law 845–851; O Endresen and E Sørgaard, 'Emissions from International Sea Transportation and Environmental Impact' (2003) 108 Journal of Geophysical Research, D17, 4560; B Chambers, 'International Trade Law and the Kyoto Protocol: Potential Incompatibilities' in B Chambers (ed), *Inter-linkages: The Kyoto Protocol and the International Trade and Investment Regimes* (Tokyo, UNU 2001); Y Li and CN Hewitt, 'The Effect of Trade between China and the UK on National and Global Carbon Dioxide Emissions' (2008) 36 Energy Policy 1907; NH Stern and others, *The Stern Review: The Economics of Climate Change* (2006) HM Treasury, <http://webarchive.nationalarchives.gov.uk/+/http:/www.hm-treasury.gov.uk/sternreview_index.htm>; S Oeter, 'Trade, Agriculture and Sustainability in Land Use' in M Gehring and MC Cordonier Segger (eds), *Sustainable Development in World Trade Law* (The Hague, Kluwer Law International 2005) 327–353; EB Barbier, 'The Economic Determinants of Land Degradation in Developing Countries' (1997) 352(1356) Philosophical Transactions of the Royal Society B: Biological Sciences 891–899; K Arrow and others, 'Economic Growth, Carrying Capacity, and the Environment' (1996) 1 Environment and Development Economics 104–110; S Williams and CR Shumway, 'Trade Liberalization and Agricultural Chemical Use: United States and Mexico' (2000) 82(1) American Journal of Agricultural Economics 183–199; S Dasgupta and others, 'Agricultural Trade, Development and Toxic Risk' (2002) 30 World Development 1401; UNCTAD, *Developing Countries in World Trade* (Washington, 2002) 51–83; UNCTAD, *Policy Coherence, Development Strategies and Integration into the World Economy* (Washington, 2004) 43–69; UNCTAD Trade and Development Reports, <http://www.unctad.org/templates/Page.asp?intItemID=2508>; See also S Rose-Ackerman and J Tobin, 'Do BITs Benefit Developing Countries?' in C Rogers and R P. Alford (eds), *The Future of Investment Arbitration* (Oxford, OUP 2009) 131–143; P Birnie, A Boyle and C Redgwell, *International Law & the Environment* (Oxford, OUP 2009) 753–810; J Scott, 'International Trade and Environmental Governance: Relating Rules (and Standards) in the EU and the WTO' (2004) 15 European Journal of International Law 307–354; S Baughen, *International Trade and the Protection of the Environment* (London, Routledge Cavendish 2007); C Robb, *Trade and Environment* International Environmental Law Reports 2 (Cambridge, CUP 2001); E Vranes, *Trade and the Environment: Fundamental Issues in International Law, WTO Law and Legal Theory* (Oxford, OUP 2009) 90–94; UNEP, *Trade Liberalisation and the Environment: Lessons learned from Bangladesh, Chile, India, Philippines,*

provide new data, based on economic modelling of scenarios that are likely to result from WTO trade negotiations, related scientific studies and concerns raised in stakeholder consultations.[11]

Regional and bilateral economic agreements can also be important in stimulating economic growth through trade liberalization. The EU-Chile AA is significant for both Europe and Chile, though given the comparative sizes of the economies, the new trade and investment resulting from the agreement was considered most important for Chile.[12] Concerns about potential environmental and social impacts of rapid and unsound economic growth in many sensitive sectors were raised in the EU SIA of the EU-Chile AA. Such concerns have also been raised in further SIAs commissioned by the EU prior to the conclusion of economic cooperation agreements with strong trade liberalization components, including the EU-Central America AA SIA,[13] the EU-Andean AA SIA,[14] the EU-Mercosur AA SIA,[15] and the EU-India AA SIA,[16] among others.[17]

SIAs can be used to model and anticipate potential economic, social and environmental impacts of a new trade or investment agreement. With comparative review, a complex picture emerges. In terms of direct economic impacts, as has also been recognized in economics literature,[18] not all sectors of economies actually benefit from a new trade or investment agreement. According to the EU-Chile SIA, the EU-Chile AA was expected to increase overall employment and lead to a reduction in prices relative to wages, with the benefits to employment being widely distributed across most sectors over the medium to long term, leading to net economic gains from the EU-Chile AA that would be relatively

Romania and Uganda, Synthesis Report of Country Studies (Geneva, 1999); UNEP, *Environment and Trade-A Handbook* (Geneva, 2000); UNEP and WTO, *Trade and Climate Change* (Geneva, 2009).

[11] C George, 'Sustainable Development and Global Governance' (2007) 16 Journal of Environment and Development 102; C George and C Kirkpatrick, 'Trade and Development: Assessing the Impact of Trade Liberalization on Sustainable Development' (2004) 38 Journal of World Trade 441.

[12] See Office of the United States Trade Representative, 'The US-Chile Free Trade Agreement', June 2004, <https://ustr.gov/about-us/policy-offices/press-office/fact-sheets/archives/2004/june/-us-chile-free-trade-agreement-early-record-suc> accessed 16 December 2020; European Union-Chile Association Agreement Trade and Investment Background Information, EU Bilateral Trade Relations Division (September 2001), <http://europa.eu.int/comm/trade/bilateral/chl.htm>.

[13] ECORYS, *Trade Sustainability Impact Assessment of the Association Agreement to be negotiated between the EU and Central America: Draft Final Report* (Rotterdam, July 2009) [EU-Central America SIA] 42–43, 60 with regard to losses in different sectors, 45–47 with regard to increases in poverty.

[14] Development Solutions, *EU-Andean Trade Sustainability Impact Assessment: Draft Final Report* (Brussels, July 2009) [EU-Andean SIA] 91 with regard to output reduction and employment loss in Peru's machinery and equipment sectors, and Ecuador's automotive sector, 120 with regard to decreases in financial, insurance, business and recreation services.

[15] IARC, *Trade Sustainability Impact Assessment (SIA) of the Association Agreement under Negotiation between the European Community and Mercosur: Final Overview Report Trade SIA EU-Mercosur* (Manchester, March 2009) [EU-Mercosur SIA] 48 with regard to manufacturing, metals, textiles and other sectors, especially for Paraguay.

[16] PricewaterhouseCoopers, *Sustainability Impact Assessment of the EU-ACP Economic Partnership Agreements: Key Findings, Recommendations and Lessons Learned* (Paris, May 2007) [EU-ACP SIA] 16.

[17] ECORYS, CUTS and CENTAD, *Trade Sustainability Impact Assessment for the FTA between the EU and the Republic of India: Final Report* (Rotterdam, May 2009) [EU-India SIA] 20; Emerging Markets Group and Development Solutions, *Trade Sustainability Impact Assessment of the Negotiations of a Partnership and Cooperation Agreement between the EU and China: Final Report* (Brussels, Emerging Markets Group 2008) [EU-China SIA] 13–14; IBM Belgium, *Trade Sustainability Impact Assessment of the EU-Korea FTA: Final Report* (Brussels, June 2008) [EU-Korea SIA] 257–258; ECORYS, *Trade Sustainability Impact Assessment of the FTA between the EU and ASEAN: Final Report* (Rotterdam, May 2009) [EU-Asean SIA] xviii–xx.

[18] A Subramaniam and S-J Wei, 'The WTO Promotes Trade, Strongly but Unevenly' (2007) 71 Journal of International Economics 151; DA Irwin, *Free Trade Under Fire* (4th edn, Princeton, Princeton University Press 2015).

modest in both Chile and the EU.[19] However, the EU-Chile AA was also expected to reinforce existing negative economic trends in Chile.[20] The treaty was predicted to lead to increased demand and economic restructuring in favour of resource-intensive sectors in which Chile has a comparative advantage, such as processed foods, agriculture, wood, pulp and paper and chemicals, as well as certain services, with increased foreign direct investment expected in such sectors. However, Chile could also lose employment in steel, motor vehicles and other machinery sectors, especially faced with highly skilled and technologically advanced competition from the EU.[21] The IA essentially identified both potential positive and negative economic impacts. It predicted that without the adoption of mitigating or 'flanking measures' at domestic or international levels to offset the negative impacts, the accord would only result in very small economic gains. Similar 'trade-offs' leading to negative, as well as positive, economic impacts of trade have been identified in other SIAs prior to the conclusion of new trade agreements.[22] For instance, in the EU-Andean SIA, concerns were raised with regard to potential losses in Peru's machinery and equipment sectors; Ecuador's automotive sector; and negative growth among the Andean countries' financial, insurance, business and recreation services.[23]

The social impacts of new economic agreements were also predicted to be mixed, in certain circumstances. Reflecting the concerns raised in economics and human rights literature,[24] SIAs note that trade agreements may also lead to important social impacts, if measures are not also adopted to mitigate problems and to promote social development.[25] Indeed, a growing body of SIAs identify the potential for both positive and negative social impacts from new trade and investment agreements.[26] For instance, as a result of the

[19] Planistat, *Sustainable Impact Assessment (SIA) of the Trade Aspects of Negotiations for an Association Agreement between the European Communities and Chile* (Santiago 2002) 12–13.

[20] Ibid 12.

[21] Ibid.

[22] EU-Central America SIA (n 13) 42–43, 60 with regard to losses in different sectors, 45–47 with regard to increases in poverty; EU-Mercosur SIA (n 15) 48 with regard to manufacturing, metals, textiles and other sectors, especially for Paraguay; EU-ACP SIA (n 16) 61–62 with regard to severe potential economic and fiscal damage (loss of government revenue) caused by removing certain agro-industry tariffs in Western Africa, also rural poverty; EU-India SIA (n 17) 284–285; EU-China SIA (n 17) 80–82; EU-Korea SIA (n 17) 26–27; EU-ASEAN SIA (n 17) 2.

[23] EU-Andean SIA (n 14) 91 with regard to output reduction and employment loss in Peru's machinery and equipment sectors and Ecuador's automotive sector, 120 with regard to decreases in financial, insurance, business and recreation services.

[24] See E Mendes and O Mehmet, *Global Governance, Economy and Law: Waiting for Justice* (London, Routledge 2003) 67–115; T Evans, 'Trading Human Rights' in A Taylor and C Thomas (eds), *Global Trade and Global Social Issues* (London, Routledge 1999) 46–47; B Johnson (ed), *Who Pays the Price?* (Washington, Island Press 1994); R Howse and M Mutua, 'Protecting Human Rights in a Global Economy: Challenges for the World Trade Organization' in ICHRDD, *Rights and Democracy* (Montreal 2000); P Ranjan, 'International Trade and Human Rights: Conflicting Obligations' in T Cottier, J Pauwelyn and E Burgi (eds), *Human Rights and International Trade* (Oxford, OUP 2005) 311; R Howse, 'Human Rights in the WTO: Whose Rights, What Humanity?' (2002) 13 European Journal of International Law 651–659; J Pauwelyn, 'Human Rights in WTO Dispute Settlement' in T Cottier, J Pauwelyn and E Burgi (eds), *Human Rights and International Trade* (Oxford, OUP 2005) 205–231; JD Taillant, 'A Rights-Based Approach to Development', Presentation to the World Social Forum on Globalization and Human Dignity, Porto Alegre, 2 March 2002; G Shaffer, 'Retooling Trade Agreements for Social Inclusion' (2019) 2019 University of Illinois Law Review 1; see also United Nations, Office of the High Commissioner of Human Rights, 'UN experts voice concern over adverse impact of free trade and investment agreements on human rights', 2 June 2015, <https://www.ohchr.org/EN/NewsEvents/Pages/DisplayNews.aspx?NewsID=16031&LangID=E> accessed 22 August 2019.

[25] As discussed in the rest of this volume.

[26] EU-Central America SIA (n 13) 56–58 with regard to labour, health, indigenous peoples, migration; EU-Andean SIA (n 14) 120–121 with regard to health, education, poverty, workers rights; EU-Mercosur SIA (n 15) 96–97 with regard to poverty, social exclusion, gender, labour standards; EU-ACP SIA (n 16) 11–15 with regard to social impacts of infrastructure, competition from Europeans and loss of tariff revenues; EU-India SIA (n 17) 201,

EU-Chile AA, increases in total employment and a reduction in prices relative to wages were predicted, improving social conditions for Chileans overall.[27] However, the EU-Chile SIA also suggested that the EU-Chile AA could exacerbate pre-existing social instabilities in Chile, which has a dual economy plagued by gaps in effective regulation and secure land titles.[28] These problems were seen as especially serious in rural areas, where negative outcomes—reductions in the creation of new jobs and loss of existing employment—were expected. Essentially the economic agreement could mean that poverty would worsen for Chile's most vulnerable rural populations.[29] For instance, in agriculture, the expansion of agro-industries that export flowers to Europe had led to higher numbers of temporary workers.[30] Temporary workers were, in certain instances, paid by piece rate with no social security benefits, unions, health or employment insurance, and lower wages.[31] The EU-Chile AA, by stimulating these industries through improvements in market access and resulting increases in exports of these products to Europe, was predicted to increase the number of people working without a social safety net.[32]

Similarly, as noted in many SIAs, new trade and investment agreements could bring about negative impacts on human health.[33] In the case of the EU-Chile AA, increases in transportation with related air pollution, in forest product processing with related effluents, in mining and metals processing with related land and water pollution, in coal-based energy generation with related air emissions, and in commercial agriculture and aquaculture with related chemical pollution, could all negatively affect the health of workers and communities.[34] As such, while employment might increase overall due to the treaty, the agreement could also generate negative social impacts, including gendered impacts.[35] For instance, as the EU-Chile SIA noted, Chile's success in fruit exports has led to the creation of jobs in the processed food sector. It was estimated that 70 per cent of temporary workers in the fruit export sector are women in fruit-packing plants exposed to significant health-related hazards due to the use of chemical fertilizers, pesticides and herbicides.[36] If trade increases and more female workers are exposed to these conditions, the social effects can include lost income due to illness, long-term health complications, children with birth defects and disruption of families due to disabilities.[37] Especially where agricultural exports are a key sector of the economy, similar gendered health impacts due to increases in uses of pesticides among vulnerable groups have been raised in other SIAs.[38] Concerns about

206, 278 with regard to employment, trade, agriculture; EU-China SIA (n 17) 12, 131–132 with regard to the environment, health labour and housing; EU-Korea SIA (n 17) 23; EU-ASEAN SIA (n 17) 28–29.

[27] Planistat, *Sustainable Impact Assessment (SIA) of the Trade Aspects of Negotiations for an Association Agreement between the European Communities and Chile* (Santiago, 2002) [EU-Chile SIA] 12.

[28] Ibid 187–190.

[29] Ibid 13.

[30] Ibid 188.

[31] Ibid.

[32] Ibid.

[33] EU-Central America SIA (n 13) 56–57 with regard to health of rural poor and migratory workers; EU-Andean SIA (n 14) 79–84, 92 with regard to reductions in availability of medicines due to Intellectual Property Rights protections, 120–121 with regard to workers' rights and vulnerable groups; EU-Mercosur SIA (n 15) 53 with regard to effects of industrialization on health and 72 with regard to decline in quality of health care.

[34] EU-Chile SIA (n 27) 13.

[35] Ibid 188.

[36] Ibid.

[37] Ibid.

[38] EU-Mercosur SIA (n 15) 53 with regard to gender impacts; EU-ACP SIA n 16) 60, 68 with regard to the need for strong social regulations to protect women in agricultural processing, also tourism in the Caribbean.

increased effects of pesticides among vulnerable migrant workers, particularly women, were similarly raised in the SIAs of the negotiations for the EU-Central America Economic Cooperation Agreement and the EU-Andean Association Agreement.[39]

In addition, as emphasized in the SIA, the EU-Chile AA had potential to exacerbate existing inequalities in terms of practical rights and access to social and economic opportunities.[40] For small farming communities, artisanal fishing communities and forest-based indigenous peoples such as the Mapuche Peoples in Chile, already precarious conditions were predicted to further decline as a result of growth occasioned by the disciplines imposed by the economic liberalization treaty.[41] For instance, rapid increases in the areas of land being exploited for commercial forestry could lead to encroachments upon the lands of vulnerable forest-based indigenous peoples.[42] If investments in the mechanisation of mining and other industries increase, new technologies could actually generate loss of jobs.[43] New investments and growth would also increase demand for energy, and if this led to further hydro-electric development that imposed forced resettlement, severe socio-cultural and economic impacts could be predicted for indigenous peoples whose ancestral ties with specific landscapes would be broken, risking loss of language, livelihood and identity and the potential to be deprived of unique and valuable traditional knowledge and cultural heritage.[44] Similar potential increases have been identified, in terms of negative social impacts for vulnerable groups affected by changes in natural resources sectors, across other SIAs of new regional or bilateral economic agreements.[45] In an additional illustrative example, concerns were raised about the potential social and environmental effects on indigenous peoples of increases in mining activities in Ecuador, in the EU-Andean SIA.[46]

The impacts of new trade and investment agreements on the environment are often negative and absent flanking measures, many SIAs found, important environmental impacts could be predicted from increases in trade and investment flows, or changes in the structure of key sectors.[47] As noted in the EU-Chile SIA, while the EU-Chile AA might indeed lead to the introduction of new techniques and cleaner technologies, absent new collaborations, the increases in the scale of resource exploitation and cumulative effects of pollution were likely to outweigh any benefits for Chile's air, water and land quality.[48] Increases in mining and the processing of metals can generate greater and cumulative air, water and land

[39] EU-Central America SIA (n 13) 55–57 with regard to pesticides and migratory workers; EU-Andean SIA (n 14) 84 with regard to health impacts of pesticides and chemicals on women, 120–121.

[40] EU-Chile SIA (n 27) 12.

[41] Ibid.

[42] Ibid.

[43] Ibid 217.

[44] Ibid 129.

[45] EU-Central America SIA (n 13) 75 with regard to pressures of agriculture on lands of indigenous peoples and rural poor; EU-Mercosur SIA (n 15) 29–31 with regard to effects of expansion of the agricultural frontier on indigenous peoples, also feminization of rural poverty; EU-ACP SIA (n 16) 71–74 with regard to need for stronger social and environmental laws governing investment in natural resources, e.g. the petroleum sector in Nigeria.

[46] EU-Andean SIA (n 14) 81 with regard to extractive industries conflicts with indigenous peoples, 107–108 with regard to copper mining on lands of indigenous peoples in Mirador and Junin, Ecuador.

[47] EU-Central America SIA (n 13) 63–65, also 77–80 with regard to atmosphere, land use, biodiversity, environmental quality, fresh and waste water, deforestation; EU-Andean SIA (n 14) 84–86, also 120–121 with regard to natural resources, environmental quality and biodiversity; EU-Mercosur SIA (n 15) 97, with regard to greenhouse gases (GHGs), water pollution, deforestation and biodiversity loss; EU-ACP SIA (n 16) 11 with regard to increases in pollution, 13 with regard to infrastructure development, 55 with regard to transboundary environmental impacts of industrial and tourism increases, 60 with regard to agro-industry development; EU-India SIA (n 17) 18 with regard to GHGs, use of fertilizers and water quality; EU-China SIA (n 17) 9–13; EU-Korea SIA (n 17) 17–22.

[48] EU-Chile SIA (n 27) 12.

pollution in local areas, including vulnerable ecosystems and the communities that depend on them, and are already at risk.[49] Not all tailings ponds and other hazardous wastes strategies were being correctly implemented in Chile, the assessment noted, and the addition of further waste could compound existing problems.[50] Pollution from chemical and non-ferrous metals industries was already placing significant pressures on the environment, and despite voluntary engagements and new regulations, the increases in the scale of the problems ('scale effects') were predicted to outweigh any improvements in pollution control.[51]

Further, as highlighted in the SIA, land and water quality could be negatively affected by intensification of commercial agriculture, leading to soil salinization and erosion, and increases in chemical residues through over-use of pesticides and herbicides.[52] Increases in energy demand was also predicted to lead to greater air emissions, and as natural gas was already in short supply in Chile, there were concerns that the increasing energy demand could spark reintroduction of coal-generated electricity or even petcoke (a very polluting fuel resulting from oil refining), with related increases in toxic emissions, acid rains, greenhouse gases and corrosion of buildings.[53] Fauna and flora biodiversity, both for the species and their habitats, was also seen to be at risk of being impacted by further hydroelectric development to meet the demand for higher amounts of energy.[54] Where energy demand was predicted to rise, similar concerns were raised in other recent SIAs.[55] For instance, as highlighted in the EU-Mercosur SIA, natural gas exploitation may increase due to the new economic agreement, with negative impacts on carbon emissions.[56]

Continued survival of natural resource stocks such as fisheries was seen as dependent on the effective enforcement of sustainable management practices. As discussed in the EU-Chile SIA, in the Chilean and European fishing industries, mechanization had already increased pressure on fish stocks, and threats to stocks existed due to over-fishing and the environmental impacts of low-technology operators.[57] The increased demand brought about by the tariff reductions, coupled with increased fishing in certain areas due to secure facilities access, was seen as likely to increase the incentives to evade established quotas.[58] Competitive pressures brought about by increased investment in the industry, either by domestic or EU owners, absent policies, were predicted to have a similar effect.[59] The cumulative effects of fishing increases encouraged by the EU-Chile AA were seen as potentially leading to thresholds being reached for some fish stocks.[60] Further, as noted in the SIA, if the increased economic cooperation led to uncontrolled growth in the aquaculture sector (which is exempt from quotas), there was also a risk of damage to the local marine environment, for instance due to increases in toxic pesticides and marine mammal

[49] Ibid 13–14.
[50] Ibid 13–14.
[51] Ibid 48.
[52] Ibid; see also EU-Andean SIA (n 14) 84.
[53] Ibid.
[54] Ibid.
[55] EU-Central America SIA (n 13) 61; EU-Andean SIA (n 14) 21, 126; EU-ACP SIA (n 16) 68; EU-India SIA (n 17) 18; EU-China SIA (n 17) 27–28; EU-Korea SIA (n 17) 94–95; EU-ASEAN SIA (n 17) 37–38.
[56] EU-Mercosur SIA (n 15) 141 with regard to increases in demand for fossil fuels, including natural gas, in both Europe and the Mercosur, especially in Associate Partners such as Venezuela and Chile.
[57] EU-Chile SIA (n 27) 195.
[58] Ibid.
[59] Ibid.
[60] Ibid.

exclusion technologies used in salmon-farming.[61] Similar concerns have been raised in further SIAs where fisheries are an important resource.[62] For example, concerns that the economic agreement might exacerbate existing problems with over-fishing were raised in the EU-Korea SIA.[63]

Further concerns have also been identified for the forestry sector. Chile's forestry sector had grown at a rate of 9 per cent annually in the decade prior to the economic agreement negotiations, with approximately 61 per cent of output for export.[64] Pulp and paper were a main source of foreign exchange, with Japan and Europe as important destinations.[65] Increases in production in this sector, as liberalization eased controls and tariffs, were found to risk serious negative impacts on land quality and biodiversity and, as most of the output of this sector was destined for intermediate consumption of export-oriented manufacturing industries, further concerns were raised that absent stringent waste controls, increases in production would also lead to higher levels of water and air pollution. Increased production in pulp mills can generate increases in fumes and effluents.[66] In SIAs of other agreements where forests were an important resource in the trading partner country, such as the EU-Andean SIA and the EU-Mercosur SIA, similar concerns arose.[67] It was noted that absent effective conservation and restoration policies, laws and programmes, constant unsustainable exploitation levels, facilitated by trade and investment liberalization, could eventually lead to the disappearance of the native forest resources entirely.[68]

Tourism is often seen as a milder and more sustainable outcome of closer economic ties, especially if opportunities open for eco-tourism and other related services. However, as also signalled in the EU-Chile SIA, uncontrolled tourism growth in Chile's unique and fragile ecosystems of the Region of the Lakes and Araucanía were raised as a concern, due to the possibility of biodiversity and habitat degradation from over-exploitation.[69] Fragile ecosystems could also be negatively impacted or even destroyed by the introduction of alien species from increases in trade, as was raised in other SIAs, for instance the SIA of the EU-Andean EPA,[70] and the SIA of the EU-ACP EPA with the Caribbean.[71] In addition, Chile's urban development was plagued by planning and land management problems; and the SIA raised concerns that increased urbanization would also lead to greater pressure on sanitation, waste disposal and other infrastructure.[72] Similar concerns have been signalled where

61 Ibid 207.

62 EU-Andean SIA (n 14) 75–78; EU-Mercosur SIA (n 15) 145; EU-ACP SIA (n 16) 66–67; EU-India SIA (n 17) 227–228; EU-China SIA (n 17) 146–147; EU-ASEAN SIA (n 17) 11.

63 EU-Korea SIA (n 17) 96, which notes over-fishing as a significant sustainable development issue linked to expansions of trade.

64 Ibid 90.

65 Ibid 92.

66 EU-Chile SIA (n 27) 195–196.

67 EU-Central America SIA (n 13) 57–59; EU-Andean SIA (n 14) 47, 84–85; EU-Mercosur SIA (n 15) 145; IARC, *Trade Sustainability Impact Assessment (SIA) of the Association Agreement under Negotiation between the European Community and Mercosur: Forest Sector Study* (Manchester, June 2007) 53–68; EU-ACP SIA (n 16) 68 with regard to impacts of tourism increases on biodiversity; EU-India SIA (n 17) 44–45, 91; EU-China SIA (n 17) 29, 38; EU-ASEAN SIA (n 17) 38.

68 M Shimamoto, F Ubukata and Y Seki, 'Forest Sustainability and the Free Trade of Forest Products: Cases from South-East Asia' (2004) 50 Ecological Economics 23.

69 EU-Chile SIA (n 27) 20.

70 EU-Andean SIA (n 14) 52 with regard to effects in The Galapagos.

71 EU-ACP SIA (n 16) 68 with regard to Caribbean tourism; EU-Central America SIA (n 13) 62; EU-Mercosur SIA (n 15) 32–37, 43, 97; EU-India SIA (n 17) 279.

72 EU-Chile SIA (n 27) 205–206.

urbanization is an important trend in the developing country trading partner, for example in the EU-India SIA,[73] the EU-ACP SIA[74] and others.[75]

5.2 Material Impacts raised in Environmental Assessments of Trade Agreements

North American assessments and reviews are carried out directly by government agencies, often with a rather narrow scope. These reviews focus mainly on potential domestic environmental impacts, although the reports can also signal certain broader concerns.[76] For instance, in the Canadian environmental assessment of the Uruguay Round of global (WTO) trade negotiations, concerns were raised about potential physical impacts from global trade liberalization in key sectors.[77] According to the Canadian Department of Foreign Affairs and International Trade (DFAIT), there were concerns that WTO Doha Round negotiations might lead to reductions of tariffs that resulted in increases in production for environmentally sensitive chemicals, fertilizers, fish and fish products, non-ferrous metals and forest products.[78] Increases in chemicals production may entail environmental and health risks for workers and the environment,[79] increases in fertilizer production and use can be linked to degradation of soil and water resources,[80] and there were concerns that increases in extraction and trade in non-ferrous metals can lead to pollution and unsafe disposal.[81] Increases in the harvesting and trade in forest products, for instance, from the fragile boreal forests of Canada's north or the ancient temperate rainforests of Canada's west coast, might lead to over-exploitation of forest ecosystems,[82] while increases in harvesting of fish and fish products, for instance east coast cod fisheries or farmed/wild west coast salmon,

[73] EU-India SIA (n 17) 39 signals challenges of inequalities in access to drinking water and sanitation infrastructure among urban poor, 42 signals high levels of exposure to particulate matter in urban air pollution, 43–46, 164–165, further details current urban problems of waste management and municipal infrastructure which may be exacerbated by unplanned urban growth occasioned by increases in trade.

[74] EU-ACP SIA (n 16) 17, 81 suggests that absent mitigating measures, increased trade may strain existing urban infrastructure in terms of: transportation infrastructure, existing technology and capacity to handle waste (including hazardous waste), capacity to deliver, treat and/or recycle water, and capacity to maintain healthy urban infrastructure, to develop industrial zones and to provide basic services to residents and migrant workers.

[75] EU-Central America SIA (n 13) 60; EU-Andean SIA (n 14) 35–39, 44–45; EU-Mercosur SIA, (n 15) 29–31, 46, 145; EU-China SIA (n 17) 12; EU-Korea SIA (n 17) 88; EU-ASEAN SIA (n 17) 8,11.

[76] See, e.g., DFAIT, 'Final Environmental Assessment of the Government Procurement Chapter to be added to the Canada-Chile Free Trade Agreement' (December 2006) <http://www.international.gc.ca/trade-agreements-accords-commerciaux/agr-acc/chile-chili/report-chile-final.aspx?lang=en> [Canada-Chile EIA] accessed 16 December 2020; USTR, *Final Environmental Review of the US-Chile FTA* (Washington, 2003) https://ustr.gov/sites/default/files/chilefinal.pdf accessed 16 December 2020 [US-Chile Final ER].

[77] DFAIT, 'Retrospective Analysis of the 1994 Canadian Environmental Review' (November 1999).

[78] Committee on Trade and Environment, Initial Environmental Assessment—Trade Negotiations in the World Trade Organizations—Submission by Canada (24 January 2003) W/CTE/W/221 03-0432, 15 [Canada-WTO EA] concluded that as most trade is already governed by the North American Free Trade Agreement (NAFTA), overall effects were likely minimal for Canada, but noted cumulative and local effects of certain increases could still be important for particular environments. Studies of the NAFTA have underlined this concern, see, e.g., North American Commission for Environmental Cooperation (NACEC), *Potential NAFTA Effects: Claims and Arguments 1991-1994* (Montreal, 1996).

[79] Canada-WTO EA (n 78) paras 9–25.

[80] Ibid.

[81] Ibid.

[82] Ibid.

might lead to degradation of marine ecosystems.[83] Similar potential environmental impacts of changes in trade volumes and patterns have been identified in other environmental assessments of WTO trade negotiations.[84]

Environmental assessments and reviews of the US plans for new trade and investment treaties have signalled related concerns.[85] Material environmental impacts of increases in trade volumes were raised in the interim and final reports of the US-Chile ER of the 2003 US-Chile FTA, especially in the interim report during the negotiations.[86] The Chilean Office of International Economic Relations (DIRECON) of the Ministry of Foreign Relations have also commissioned reviews, for instance with the School of Engineering of the University of Chile, that raise concerns of environmental impacts.[87]

The US-Chile Final ER noted that Chile's economy is heavily dependent on exports from natural resource sectors, including mining and metals processing, forestry products, fisheries and agriculture.[88] If the trade and investment agreement opened additional US market access for Chilean products, the resulting pressures could stimulate increased exploitation of fisheries and forestry resources.[89] Without appropriate controls, such increases can lead to higher levels of pollution and greater encroachment on the habitat of wildlife and endangered species. King crab fisheries provided one example.[90] In coastal Chilean waters between 48 and 56 degrees southern latitudes, the ER noted, dolphins and sea lions have been killed in great numbers to provide bait for the king crab fishery. One study estimated that in the three years between 1976 and 1979, approximately 8,900 dolphins, primarily of two species (*Cephalorhynchus commersoni* and *Lagenorhynchus australis*) were killed for use as king crab bait.[91] Expansion of the fishery, with no other source of bait, risked simply increasing these killings. Similar potential environmental impacts on fisheries from changes in trade volumes and patterns have been identified in other environmental assessments of new trade and investment agreement negotiations.[92]

A second example raised in the review process involved effects on biodiversity from the new trade and investment agreement, including reductions of Chilean forest biodiversity due to the clearing of the land for plantations of introduced species. Further increases in production were seen as likely to affect the viability of Chile's native forests, generate further soil degradation and increase pesticide and herbicide use.[93] Biological diversity could also be affected by the expansion of monocultures. Conversion of native forest to

83 Ibid.
84 See, e.g., Kirkpatrick, George and Scrieciu (n 4).
85 See Annex 1.2.
86 USTR, *Interim Environmental Review of the US-Chile FTA* (Washington, 2001) [Interim US-Chile ER]; Overall, as the economic changes directly attributable to the accord itself in the US were minimal, the reviews conclude that overall environmental impacts could be low. However, concerns raised during the process help to explain linkages between trade, the environment and development.
87 M Matus and E Rossi, 'Trade and the Environment in the FTAA: A Chilean Perspective' in C Deere and D Esty (eds), *Greening the Americas: NAFTA's Lessons for Hemispheric Trade* (Boston, MIT Press 2002) 259; Interviews with E Rossi, Director General of Trade, Environment and Sustainable Development, International Affairs Ministry, Government of Chile (Santiago, March 2007) [Rossi Interview].
88 US-Chile Final ER (n 76) 16.
89 Ibid 20–22.
90 Matus and Rossi (n 87); Rossi Interview (n 87).
91 JA Iriarte, P Feinsinger and FM Jaksic, 'Trends in Wildlife Use and Trade in Chile' (1997) 81 Biological Conservation 9.
92 See, e.g., USTR, *Interim Environmental Review United States-Korea Free Trade Agreement* (Washington, 2006) 16; DFAIT, 'Initial Environmental Assessment of the Canada-Panama Free Trade Agreement' (28 February 2009)
93 Rossi Interview (n 87).

plantation-style forests, it was argued, would lead to habitat destruction, affecting and possibly causing the irreversible loss of endangered plant and wildlife species.[94] As noted in the ER, losses were already affecting three endangered tree species unique to the coastal range of Chileang Regions VII and VIII.[95] Such impacts could become more severe, as exploitation of the forests for export increases under the trade and investment agreement.

Given the ecological similarities between Chile and the US west coast, concerns were also raised about the risks of invasive species.[96] Invasive species are typically introduced into a country through pathways such as vehicles, people and goods, and can have severe impacts on the environment and the economy.[97] As noted in the Interim ER, an example of an invasive species introduced from one Party to the other was the yellow starthistle, *Centaurea solstitialis*, which originated in Eurasia but was introduced to California by way of alfalfa imported from Chile in the nineteenth century, infesting an estimated 23 million acres in the US to the detriment of both wildlife and livestock.[98] When trade-related shipping traffic increases between the US and Chile, the spread of such invasive organisms may also increase via the ships (in ballast water, as fouling organisms on hulls, in cargo or in packaging material). Further, the ER flagged concerns about increases in illegal trade in endangered species due to a reduction in monitoring occasioned by the trade liberalization measures, which could place increased pressure on fragile ecosystems.[99] Similar potential environmental impacts on biodiversity from changes in trade volumes and patterns have been identified in other environmental assessments and reviews of new free trade and investment agreement negotiations.[100]

Changes in agricultural development occasioned by a free trade treaty can also lead to social impacts such as health risks, due to increased use of pesticides and other toxic substances.[101] Indeed, the US-Chile FTA was seen as likely to facilitate increased trade in such chemicals.[102] But as noted in the IA, levels of awareness of safe use of pesticides were not high in Chile at the time of the negotiations, especially among Chile's agricultural workers and small-scale farmers, so higher levels of use were seen as leading to corresponding increases in health risks.[103] Essentially, the change in scale of the enterprise, due to a new free trade agreement such as the US-Chile FTA, may place increased pressure on sensitive ecosystems, due to increases in the generation, transport and storage of waste and pollution, and in the use of pesticides and other dangerous chemicals. Similar potential impacts were identified in other EAs of new trade and investment agreements.[104] Such concerns could

[94] US-Chile Final ER (n 76) 22.

[95] A Lara and T Veblen, 'Forest Plantations in Chile: A Successful Model?' in A Mather (ed), *Afforestation: Policies, Planning and Process* (London, Belhaven Press 1993).

[96] US-Chile Final ER (n 76) 23–24.

[97] Ibid; see also C Shine, N Williams and L Gruendling 'A Guide to Designing Legal and Institutional Frameworks on Alien Invasive Species', Environmental Policy and Law Paper No 40, IUCN Environmental Law Centre (2000).

[98] Interim US-Chile ER (n 86) 28, citing B Mullin and others, 'Invasive Plant Species', Council for Agricultural Science and Technology Issue Paper 13 (2000). See also M Arroyo and others, 'Plant Invasions in Chile: Present Patterns and Future Predictions' in H Mooney and R Hobbs (eds), *Invasive Species in a Changing World* (Washington, Island Press 2000).

[99] Interim US-Chile ER (n 86) 41–45.

[100] See, e.g., USTR, *Final Environmental Review of the United States-CAFTA Free Trade Agreement* (Washington, 2003) <http://www.ustr.gov/sites/default/files/CAFTA%20interim%20review.pdf> 15, 23; accessed 16 December 2020

[101] Interim US-Chile ER (n 86) 38–40.

[102] Ibid.

[103] Ibid 41–45.

[104] See, e.g., EU-Korea SIA (n 17) 88–89.

be addressed in different ways, either by identification of mitigating domestic measures, or through the provisions in the trade and investment agreements themselves, as examined in later chapters of this volume.

5.3 Summary of Potential Negative Social and Environmental Material Impacts

This brief review has highlighted material economic, social and environmental concerns documented in European SIAs such as the EU-Chile SIA, and in North American ERs such as for the US-Chile. Of course, impacts of new global or regional trade or investment agreements are all negative. Indeed, as noted by Professor John H Jackson and others, there are surely many positive effects, or one would beg the question as to why such treaties are concluded by States at all.[105] States find many positive economic and other effects of a trade and investment agreement, not least in the way that it signals closer ties between countries or a region, and there can also be potential for high economic benefits for economic interests that can successfully externalize social and environmental costs of increases in opportunities, even if it simply means that these costs are covered by taxpayers for them.[106]

Even a brief comparative survey of assessments indicates that negative social and environmental impacts may be either caused or exacerbated by a wide variety of provisions in a trade and investment accord. In some cases, each tariff line that is reduced or eliminated might even lead to a distinct impact. The assessments also demonstrate that material impacts are specific to the character of actual relationships between the Parties, as well as existing social and environmental conditions in the sectors stimulated by the new trade and investment agreement, and the new treaty's potential to promote different kinds of development, including increases in the scale or character of the trade transport routes themselves, or increases in actual production and consumption of the industry sectors which seek to benefit. For instance, as Chile and the US conduct a great deal of trade by ship, an increase in investments in shipping, leading to more cargo ships travelling between the US and Chile, raises concerns about invasive species carried by ballast water. In contrast, as the Chilean cut flower industry has high exports to Europe, increases in trade of, and investments in, cut flowers between Chile and Europe raises concerns about health effects of pesticide residues on workers without access to adequate social safety nets. Another instance of this can be seen in the final impact assessment of the UK-Japan Comprehensive Economic Partnership, which found that an overall net increase in production for trade between the world's 3rd (Japan) and 5th (UK) largest economies as a result of the trade agreement will likely increase waste output, leading to negative environmental impacts unless effective mitigation measures are put in place.[107]

105 M Gehring, J Hepburn and MC Cordonier Segger, *World Trade Law in Practice* (London, Globe 2006) 12.

106 NAFTA (n 78); DFAIT, 'Initial Environmental Assessment of the Canada-Korea Free Trade Agreement' (16 November 2007) 1 notes 'there is a strong correlation between open markets, economic development and enhanced environmental protection'; G Sampson, *The WTO and Sustainable Development* (Tokyo, UNU 2005) 262; P Konz (ed), *Trade, Environment and Sustainabe Development: Views from Sub-Saharan Africa and Latin America* (Tokyo and Geneva, UNU/IAS and ICTSD 2000) 211, 229.

107 Department for International Trade, 'Final Impact Assessment of the Agreement between the United Kingdom of Great Britain and Northern Ireland and Japan for a Comprehensive Economic Partnership' (DIT, London, 2021) https://assets.publishing.service.gov.uk/government/uploads/system/uploads/attachment_ data/file/965154/UK-Japan-impact-assessment-comprehensive-economic-parternship.pdf accessed 26 March 2021.

The motivations and methods of different States to analyse the potential for distinct impacts also vary greatly, and different impacts also receive greater or lesser attention depending on the indicators and methods of assessment.[108] For instance, the US ER simply did not examine the effects of deforestation and related soil degradation on land rights or on forced migration of indigenous peoples with attendant socio-cultural risks of identity loss, or the gendered health effects of increased use of chemicals to prepare products for export. It focuses only on narrow environmental issues that could be linked directly to the increased trade or investment generated by the new trade and investment liberalization under the agreement, and the officials examined mainly on impacts projected to occur within the territory of the US. The SIA, considering an agreement with the same country, did examine these issues, and demonstrates deep concerns about the social and environmental effects, absent mitigating measures being set in place.

In the context of this volume, though, the comparative analysis of over 110 recent IAs does demonstrate that social and environmental impacts of liberalization under trade and investment agreements are not always certain to be positive. In essence, absent specific measures, many aspects of increases or changes in trade and investment flows have the potential to generate important and damaging impacts, damage that a country's policy and regulatory framework, scientific and technological knowledge or even simple infrastructure may not be prepared to easily address or avoid. The next question is to consider how States are seeking to mitigate such impacts, including the necessary policy and legal dimensions.

[108] See UNEP and CBD (2003), 'The Impact of Trade Liberalisation on Agricultural Biological Diversity: A Synthesis of Assessment Frameworks', UNEP/CBD/COP/7/INF/15, United Nations, Kuala Lumpur, 1–2.

6

Normative Intersections of Trade, Investment and Sustainability Measures

Potential physical, material impacts from new trade and investment agreements can be traced to deeper normative tensions, particularly if negative effects cause deeper concern, or are greatly exacerbated by existing gaps in policy and regulatory frameworks of partner countries with whom trade and investment ties are being strengthened. Concerns that are raised in impact assessments (IAs) and reviews echo the sustainable development issues that are documented in scholarly literature, in terms of both environment and social development concerns about trade and investment liberalization. Indeed, three key normative impacts, or 'tensions' can be identified between the demands of trade and investment agreements that focus mainly on economic growth, and the corresponding effects on regulations for the environment and for social development, including the efforts of States to comply with obligations in other international treaties related to the environment and human rights. These tensions are explained briefly below, then further specific detail is provided in other chapters of this volume.

6.1 Tension One: Constraining Legitimate Measures on Sustainable Development, including International Treaty Implementation Measures

The first normative tension of focus in this volume is raised by the concern that new trade and investment liberalization obligations of non-discrimination and most-favoured nation (MFN) treatment for 'like products' or for 'investments in like circumstances' could prevent States from effectively enacting trade- or investment-related measures to prevent unsustainable development.[1] In over one hundred impact assessments (IAs) and environment reviews (ERs) surveyed, concerns were raised that the application of the new economic rules, absent appropriate exceptions, could be interpreted to constrain States from regulating to prevent environmental or social harm, or lead to trade or investment law tribunals disallowing legitimate environmental and social measures.

This tension includes situations when the rules of a trade and investment agreement might limit State efforts to implement trade and investment law obligations agreed in MEAs and

[1] Infra; see also PricewaterhouseCoopers, *Sustainability Impact Assessment of the EU-ACP Economic Partnership Agreements: Key Findings, Recommendations and Lessons Learned* (Paris, May 2007) [EU-ACP SIA] 183–186; Development Solutions, *EU-Andean Trade Sustainability Impact Assessment: Draft Final Report* (Brussels, July 2009) [EU-Andean SIA] 42–57.

Crafting Trade and Investment Accords for Sustainable Development. Marie-Claire Cordonier Segger, Oxford University Press. © Marie-Claire Cordonier Segger 2021. DOI: 10.1093/oso/9780198831341.003.0006

other treaties related to sustainable development,[2] affecting the effectiveness of these treaty regimes.[3]

This tension also arises from the potential that the adoption of legitimate new domestic environment and social development laws and measures by regulators may be constrained or weakened when the provisions of a trade and investment agreement influence the process of law-making.[4] In essence, the concern is that agreed trade and investment disciplines will reduce the ability or flexibility of national governments to regulate to achieve the Sustainable Development Goals (SDGs), including by preventing or constraining the implementation of other international obligations to protect or restore the environment, to respect human rights or to promote development.[5] The disciplines may also affect the scope of new regulations indirectly, when interpreted by vested economic interests to prevent or negotiate changes to domestic laws (so-called 'regulatory chill').[6] Indeed, a related concern is that certain investment rules, incorporated in the economic treaties, are found to provide new mechanisms to allow other Parties and their investors to challenge measures related

[2] Trade and environment, also trade and human rights literature, emphasizes concerns that trade agreements may constrain efforts to ensure more sustainable use of natural resources agreed in MEAs, and prevent efforts to secure internationally recognized human rights. See E Neumayer, 'Trade Measures in Multilateral Environmental Agreements and WTO Rules: Potential for Conflict, Scope for Reconciliation' (2000) 55 Aussenwirtschaft 1, 2; A Cosbey, 'NAFTA's Chapter 11 and the Environment', Discussion Paper for the CEC's Public Workshop on NAFTA's Chapter 11, 6 (2003), <https://www.iisd.org/publications/naftas-chapter-11-and-environment-discussion-paper-cecs-public-workshop-naftas-chapter> accessed 16 December 2020; G Marceau, 'Conflicts of Norms and Conflicts of Jurisdictions: The Relationship between the WTO Agreement and MEAs and other Treaties' (2001) 35 Journal of World Trade 1081; P Birnie, A Boyle and C Redgwell, *International Law & the Environment* (Oxford, OUP 2009) 754, 766–769, 778–787; E Vranes, *Trade and the Environment: Fundamental Issues in International Law, WTO Law and Legal Theory* (Oxford, OUP 2009) 172–183, 319–350; P Konz (ed), *Trade, Environment and Sustainable Development: Views from Sub-Saharan Africa and Latin America* (Tokyo and Geneva, UNU/IAS and ICTSD 2000) 115–147; P Ranjan, 'International Trade and Human Rights: Conflicting Obligations' in T Cottier, J Pauwelyn and E Burgi, *Human Rights and International Trade* (Oxford, OUP 2005) 311; R Howse, 'Human Rights in the WTO: Whose Rights, What Humanity?' (2002) 13 European Journal of International Law 651–659; S Walker, 'Human Rights Impact Assessments of Trade-Related Policies' in M Gehring and MC Cordonier Segger (eds), *Sustainable Development in World Trade Law* (The Hague, Kluwer Law International 2005) 217–256; X Fuentes, 'International Law-Making in the Field of Sustainable Development: Unequal Competition between Development and the Environment' in N Schrijver and F Weiss (eds), *International Law and Sustainable Development: Principles and Practice* (Leiden, Martinus Nijhoff 2004) 7, 8; P-M Dupuy and JE Vinuales, *International Environmental Law* (Cambridge, CUP 2018).

[3] WB Chambers, 'Towards an Improved Understanding of the Legal Effectiveness of International Environmental Treaties' (2004) 14 Georgetown International Environmental Law Review 501–532.

[4] J Bohanes and N Lockhard, 'Standard of Review', D Bodansky and J Lawrence, 'Trade and Environment' and H Nottage, 'Trade and Development' in D Bethlehem and others (eds), *The Oxford Handbook of International Trade Law* (Oxford, OUP 2009); S Vaughan, 'Understanding the Environmental Effects of Trade: Some Lessons from NAFTA' in JJ Kirton and VW Maclaren (eds), *Linking Trade, Environment, and Social Cohesion* (Aldershot, Ashgate, 2002) 225, 236–237.

[5] M Trebilcock and R Howse, *The Regulation of International Trade* (New York, Routledge 2005) 471–587; Bethlehem and others (n 4) 596; Birnie, Boyle and Redgwell (n 2) 778–787; D French, *International Law and Policy on Sustainable Development* (Manchester, Juris 2005) 198–212; S Baughen, *International Trade and the Protection of the Environment* (London, Routledge Cavendish 2007); N Schrijver and F Weiss, *International Law and Sustainable Development: Principles and Practice* (Lieden, Martinus Nijhoff 2004) 159–270; G Sampson, *The WTO and Sustainable Development* (Tokyo, UNU 2005); Konz (n 2); G Sampson and WB Chambers, *Trade, Environment and the Millennium* (2nd edn, Tokyo, UNU 2002); C Thomas and JP Trachtman (eds), *Developing Countries in the WTO Legal System* (Oxford, OUP 2009); R Sarkar, *International Development Law: Rule of Law, Human Rights & Global Finance* (Oxford, OUP 2009); M Grosz, *Sustainable Waste Trade under WTO Law* (Leiden, Martinus Nijhoff 2011); CJ Cortes, *GATT, WTO and the Regulation of International Trade Textiles* (Aldershot, Ashgate, 1997); MR Chertow and DC Esty (eds), *Thinking Ecologically: The Next Generation of Environmental Policy* (New Haven and London, Yale, 1997); M Stilwell, 'Trade and Environment in the Context of Sustainable Development' in Gehring and Cordonier Segger (n 2) 27, 70–71.

[6] Cosbey (n 2); E Neumayer, 'Do Countries Fail to Raise Environmental Standards? An Evaluation of Policy Options Addressing 'Regulatory Chill' (2001) 4 International Journal of Sustainable Development 231.

to sustainable development in arbitral proceedings that are closed to the public.[7] The need to secure regulatory flexibility can be especially important for developing countries.[8] The types of measures that might be disallowed by trade and investment disciplines include adoption of import restraints against products or services that do not comply with domestic norms, or labelling, packaging and recycling regulations affecting imported as well as domestic products, or barriers to export restrictions to secure sustainable use of natural resources.[9] This is both an environmental and a social concern; regulators choosing levels of health protection may be constrained by commitments not to discriminate between dangerous substances.[10]

As indicated in the actual assessments surveyed, the potential effects of trade and investment disciplines on sustainable development can depend on many factors. But where laws are needed to secure sustainable development domestically or to comply with other international obligations related to key SDGs for a country, this normative tension emerges.

The challenge is that international obligations related to trade and investment, the environment and social development may overlap when they regulate the same subject matter.[11] The potential for overlap has grown as the host of issues covered by international treaty law has expanded.[12] For sustainable development, overlaps between economic law and social development measures are relevant. As highlighted by the World Commission on the Social Dimension of Globalization, trade and investment rules may limit the effectiveness of labour and social standards.[13] Further, as noted in a joint World Health Organization (WHO) and World Trade Organization (WTO) study, there are still challenges in coherence between health and trade laws at national and international levels.[14] In a missive to the Third Ministerial Conference of the WTO, the United Nations Committee on Economic, Social and Cultural Rights (CESCR) urged the WTO to 'undertake a review of the full range of international trade and investment policies and rules in order to ensure that these are consistent with existing treaties, legislation and policies designed to protect and promote all human rights'.[15]

[7] Ibid; see also N Beransconi-Osterwalder, 'Transparency and Amicus Curiae in ICSID Arbitrations' in MC Cordonier Segger, M Gehring and A Newcombe, *Sustainable Development in World Investment Law* (Alphen aan de Rijn, Kluwer Law International 2010) 191–207.

[8] R Sarkar, *International Development Law: Rule of Law, Human Rights & Global Finance* (Oxford, OUP 2009) 432–453.

[9] Birnie, Boyle and Redgwell (n 2) 778–787; Bodansky and Lawrence (n 4) 518–528; AE Appleton, 'Environmental Labelling Schemes Revisited: WTO Law and Developing Country Implications' in Sampson and Chambers (n 5).

[10] C Button, *The Power to Protect: Trade, Health and Uncertainty in the WTO* (Oxford, Hart 2004) 193–212.

[11] F Francioni, 'Environment, Human Rights and the Limits of Free Trade' in F Francioni (ed), *Environment, Human Rights and International Trade* (Oxford, Hart 2001) 2–3; Proceedings of the WTO High Level Symposium on Trade and Environment, Geneva, 15–16 March 1999; Proceedings of the WTO High Level Symposium on Trade and Development, Geneva, 17–18 March 1999.

[12] Convention on International Trade in Endangered Species of Wild Fauna and Flora (adopted 3 March 1973, entered into force 1 July 1975) 993 UNTS 243 (CITES); D Brack (ed), *Trade and Environment: Conflict or Compatibility?* (London, Earthscan 1998) 323.

[13] World Commission on the Social Dimension of Globalization, *A Fair Globalization: Creating Opportunities for All* (Geneva, International Labour Office 2004) <http://www.ilo.org/public/english/wcsdg/docs/report.pdf> accessed 16 December 2020.

[14] WTO and WHO, *WTO Agreements and Public Health: A Joint Study between the WHO and the WTO Secretariat* (Geneva, 2002) <http://www.wto.org/english/res_e/booksp_e/who_wto_e.pdf> accessed 16 December 2020.

[15] UN CESCR, The Substantive Issues Arising in the Implementation of the International Covenant on Economic, Social and Cultural Rights: Statement of the United Nations Committee on Economic, Social and Cultural Rights to the Third Ministerial Conference of the World Trade Organization, 26 November 1999, UN Doc E/C.12/1999/9, 2.

Similar overlaps have been identified between international trade and investment rules, and the specific trade and investment measures agreed in MEAs.[16] As the WTO has noted, while in general MEAs 'are to be encouraged', its Committee on Trade and Development (CTE) 'has wrestled with the issue of how to address the trade provisions which several of these agreements contain'.[17] While considered essential to avoid 'free riders' for an environmental regime, trade bans (or border tax adjustments for high greenhouse gas intensity products) could be found to be incompatible with economic law 'most favoured nation treatment' and non-discrimination obligations.[18] These obligations do not permit trading partners to limit or treat differently a product from one country while permitting entry of a like product from another country—if the product is the same, or 'like', the general rule is that it should be treated the same, even if the processing and production methods (PPMs) used to create it were different (i.e. one uses techniques with low environmental impact or health risk, while the other does not).[19] In several important MEAs, States have agreed on specific trade obligations that serve both environmental and also sustainable development objectives, or sought to use market-based instruments to achieve their MEA obligations.[20] Links between WTO rules and the intellectual property and traditional knowledge benefit-sharing rules of other treaties on sustainable development, such as the FAO Seed Treaty, have also been raised as problematic.[21] Where the State seeks to undertake such measures in order to comply with their obligations under international treaties on the environment, human rights or sustainable development, but is constrained or blocked by concerns that the measures will be disallowed under trade or investment liberalization disciplines, these types of tension arise.

It has been argued that there has never been a WTO dispute on a measure taken pursuant to such treaties.[22] However, though direct conflicts of obligations may be rarely argued in WTO cases, the need to meet social and environmental objectives of other treaties has

[16] See Neumayer (n 2) 2; A Cosbey, 'New Views of Trade and Sustainable Development: Using Sen's Conception of Development to Re-examine the Debates' Thematic Research Paper, TIPS/IISD Trade Knowledge Network Workshop (Geneva, ICTSD 2003) 6; Marceau (n 2); Birnie, Boyle and Redgwell (n 2) 754, 766–769, 778–787; Vranes (n 2) 172–183, 319–350; Konz (n 2) 115–147; P Ranjan, 'International Trade and Human Rights: Conflicting Obligations' in Cottier, Pauwelyn and Burgi (n 2) 311; Howse (n 2) 651–659; Walker (n 2) 217–256; Fuentes (n 2) 7, 8. See also Brack (n 12) 331–334; Chambers (n 3); D Brack, 'Reconciling the GATT and Multilateral Environmental Agreements with Trade Provisions: The Latest Debate' (1997) 6 Review of European Community and International Environmental Law 112; R Tarasofsky, 'Ensuring Compatibility between Multilateral Environmental Agreements and GATT/WTO' (1996) 7 Yearbook of International Environment Law 52; R Tarasofsky and M Stilwell, *Towards Coherent Environmental and Economic Governance: Legal and Practical Approaches to MEA-WTO Linkages* (Gland, WWF/CIEL 2001).

[17] WTO Secretariat, *Trade and Environment at the WTO* (Geneva, 2004) 36.

[18] Andrew L Stoler, 'The Doha Round Negotiations on the MEA-WTO Interface: Shared Perceptions or Ulterior Motives?' (International Bar Association Conference, Auckland, New Zealand, 2004) 1–2. OECD, *Trade Measures in Multilateral Environmental Agreements* (Paris, 1999); see also Tarasofsky (n 16); Tarasofsky and Stilwell (n 16); Birnie, Boyle and Redgwell (n 2) 754.

[19] WTO Secretariat (n 17) 49–50; Trebilcock and Howse (n 5) 49, 83; Bodansky and Lawrence (n 4) 525. See also A R Ziegler and D Sifonios, 'The Assessment of Environmental Risks and the Regulation of Process and Production Methods (PPMs) in International Trade Law' in M Ambrus, R Rayfuse and W Werner (eds), *Risk and the Regulation of Uncertainty in International Law* (Oxford, OUP 2017).

[20] See D Brack, 'Environmental Treaties and Trade: Multilateral Environmental Agreements and the Multilateral Trading System' in Sampson and Chambers (n 5); WTO Committee on Trade and Environment Special Session—Matrix on Trade Measures pursuant to Selected Multilateral Environmental Agreements—WT/CTE/W/161/Rev.4, TN/TE/S/5/Rev.2, 14 March 2007 (07-1070); Sampson (n 5) 130.

[21] WB Chambers, *Interlinkages and the Effectiveness of Multilateral Environmental Agreements* (Tokyo, UNU 2008) 199–234; see also International Treaty on Plant Genetic Resources for Food and Agriculture of the Food and Agriculture Organization (adopted 3 November 2001, entered into force 31 March 2004).

[22] See, e.g., WTO Secretariat (n 17); see also Neumayer (n 2) 2.

actually been raised numerous times by Parties to trade and investment disputes.[23] In one particularly stark example, a WTO Panel was called to examine Chile's decision to close its ports to the trans-shipment of European Community (Spanish) trawlers' swordfish harvests in the *Chile-Swordfish Case*, a decision that Chile claimed was being taken in part due to legitimate sustainability concerns,[24] just as the International Tribunal on the Law of the Sea was asked by Chile to consider the actions of European Community (Spanish) fishing fleets in relation to their obligations under the United Nations Convention on the Law of the Seas, a claim that was said to concern the sustainability of the fisheries being exploited.[25] The decision to advance claims in competing forums with compulsory jurisdiction agreed in the two treaty regimes could have led to extremely awkward normative conflicts,[26] as recognized by many at the time. In the particular instance, both cases were suspended through an agreement on scientific cooperation and sustainable use of the fishery between the Parties to the dispute.[27] The experience left the matter of how two sets of treaty obligations might overlap, each with a binding forum for dispute settlement, open for further debate.

New treaties that make explicit commitments to sustainable development contain trade- and investment-related measures which appear *prima facie* to run contrary to trade and investment disciplines in some bilateral and regional treaties, as well as in the WTO. Concerns are being raised, especially in environment, development and human rights scholarship and policy debates, that implementation of these measures, which can be crucial to stop 'free-riders' from weakening the sustainable development regime effectiveness, is being constrained by the rules agreed in trade and investment treaties.

First, however, it must be noted that overlaps of rules are not always conflicts. As explained by Professor Joost Pauwelyn, international trade and investment treaties may aim to regulate the same subject matter, or might be applied to the same subject matter as other treaties.[28] In such situations, often the obligations will simply accrue. However, obligations might also conflict. As Pauwelyn notes:

> Norms of international law, whatever their function, may interact in two ways. They either (i) accumulate, or (ii) conflict. If two norms do not conflict, they necessarily accumulate

[23] See E Brown Weiss, J Jackson and N Bernasconi-Osterwalder (eds), *Reconciling Environment and Trade* (2nd edn, Leiden, Martinus Nijhoff 2008), including with regard to the *US-Shrimp* and *EC-Biotech* disputes discussed in Chapter 4.

[24] *Case Concerning the Conservation and Sustainable Exploitation of Swordfish Stocks in the South-Eastern Pacific Ocean (Chile v. European Community)* (Order of 20 December 2000) Case No 7.

[25] Adopted 10 December 1982, entered into force 16 November 1994, 1833 UNTS 3, 21 ILM 1245 [UNCLOS].

[26] *Case Concerning the Conservation and Sustainable Exploitation of Swordfish Stocks in the South-Eastern Pacific Ocean* (n 24); M Orellana, 'The Swordfish Dispute between the EU and Chile at the ITLOS and the WTO' (2002) 71 Nordic Journal of International Law 55; M Gehring, 'Sustainable Development Angles to the Swordfish Dispute' (2001) 5(7) Bridges Journal 13. A Bilateral Scientific and Technical Commission (BSTC) on the Swordfish Stocks in the South-East Pacific was eventually established, with a joint scientific evaluation of the swordfish stocks leading to a multilateral framework for sustainable development of the resource; see M Orellana, 'The EU and Chile Suspend the Swordfish Case Proceedings at the WTO and the International Tribunal of the Law of the Sea' (2001) 60 American Society of International Law Insights <http://www.asil.org/insights/insigh60.htm> accessed 16 December 2020; L Murphy, 'EC and Chile Reach Agreement on 10-Year Swordfish Dispute' [2001] International Fisheries Bulletin No 4 >; and see EU@UN, 'EU and Chile Settle WTO/ ITLOS Swordfish Dispute' (24 January 2001) <http://www.eu-un.europa.eu/articles/en/article_2230_en.htm> accessed 16 December 2020.

[27] Gehring (n 26).

[28] J Pauwelyn, *Conflict of Norms in Public International Law: How WTO Law Relates to Other Rules of International Law* (Cambridge, CUP 2003); Brack (n 20).

(and vice versa). Two norms accumulate when they can be applied together and without contradiction in all circumstances. Two norms conflict when this is not the case.[29]

In terms of normative intersections, as Pauwelyn notes, conflicts can occur between a command and an opposing command, between a command and a prohibition, between a prohibition and a permission, and between a command and an exemption.[30] When a direct conflict occurs between permission versus prohibition, as Pauwelyn explains, it may be resolved by a Party simply not exercising its rights under one treaty. While mutually agreed, such an outcome may not adequately balance or respect the objectives of both regimes.

A conflict can occur either between Parties to both conflicting treaties, or between Parties to one treaty that are not all Parties to a second one. States that are all Parties to both conflicting accords might be able to negotiate a solution in the context of one treaty or the other.[31] The problem becomes more acute, however, where the Parties to one treaty are not Parties to the other. If a trade or investment measure is challenged, a tribunal would be expected to apply the rules in article 30 of the Vienna Convention on the Law of Treaties (VCLT).[32] These rules include interpreting the respective provisions in light of the overall object and purpose of the treaties in question.[33] First, if there are conflicts clauses in one of the treaties, establishing a subordinate relationship, the other will take precedence. Second, if all Parties to one treaty have ratified the new one later, the doctrine of *lex posterior derogat priori* would likely apply, whereby the treaty which is later in time prevails among the Parties to both.[34] Pauwelyn rightly criticizes this outcome, noting that treaties are 'continuously confirmed, implemented, adapted and expanded, for example by means of judicial decisions, interpretations, new norms, and the accession of new States'.[35] Dr W Bradnee Chambers adds that while the intent of article 30 may be for Parties 'with multiple memberships in international agreements' to 'interpret the interactive effect and implications of these agreements on the basis of a full knowledge'... 'in practice, this is far from the reality. National and international agendas for multilateral political negotiations have become overwhelmed with the number and the range of international treaties, agreements and unsettled disputes'.[36] The doctrine of *lex specialibus non derogant* may assist in finding a more reasonable interpretation, essentially holding that the rules which are more specific to a particular treaty matter will govern, rather than the more general principles. However, as noted by the International Law Commission's Study Group on Treaty Fragmentation,[37] it is not always straightforward to understand which set of rules is, indeed, the most specialized when complex treaty instruments overlap. Traditional conflict rules may result in one legal

[29] Pauwelyn (n 28) 161.

[30] As Pauwelyn observes, in the WTO *EC-Tariff Preferences* case 88, 100–103, the Appellate Body appears to interpret the notion of conflict broadly. J Pauwelyn, 'The World Trade Organization' in R Huesa Vinaixa and K Wellens, *L'influence des sources sur l'unite et la fragmentation du droit international*, Travaux du Seminaire tenu a Palma, les 20-21 Mai 2005 (Brussels, Bruylant 2006) 227.

[31] Pauwelyn (n 28) 422.

[32] Signed 23 May 1969, entered into force 27 January 1980, 1155 UNTS 331, art 30.

[33] I Buffard and K Zemanek, 'The Object and Purpose of a Treaty: An Enigma?' (1998) 3 Austrian Review of International and European Law 311; A Aust, *Modern Treaty Law and Practice* (Cambridge, CUP 2000); R Gardiner, *Treaty Interpretation* (2nd edn, Oxford, OUP 2015).

[34] Gardiner (n 33).

[35] Pauwelyn (n 28) 545.

[36] Chambers (n 21) 50–51.

[37] ILC (2006) A/CN.4/L.682, finalized by Martti Koskenniemi, 36.

norm rendering invalid applications of the rights granted in, or obligations provided by, the other treaty.[38] Should neither a negotiated solution nor a deferential interpretation by a tribunal be possible, States bound to fulfil their obligations under one treaty must break their obligations under the other, and can be held responsible for the (unwilling) breach.[39] This is not necessarily the optimal solution for sustainable development, particularly if the result weakens efforts to address serious and pressing global challenges such as climate change.

In the practice of SIAs to date, the EU does not yet conduct separate assessments of potential 'regulatory effects', instead considering law and policy issues as an aspect of each type of impact analysed. The EU-Chile SIA did not, for instance, directly address the potential impacts of the EU-Chile AA on either Party's ability to fulfil their international commitments, and neither have many other SIAs to date. The EU-Mercosur SIA did briefly consider effects on abilities of Parties to comply with key principles reflected in the Rio Declaration[40] (without clearly defining their normative effects or status in international law). For instance, in its Sector Study for Agriculture, the EU-Mercosur SIA noted potential conflicts with Rio Principle 8 which recognizes a need to reduce and eliminate unsustainable patterns of consumption,[41] and with Rio Principle 9 which advocates the need to enhance technology transfer.[42]

In the 2020 Draft EU-Mercosur Agreement, States appear to be more permissive, providing a less robust framework to address sustainable development issues in comparison to other recent EU FTAS. For example, in the Draft EU-Mercosur Agreement, Parties miss an opportunity to ensure that compliance with climate change obligations in the Paris Agreement can be reviewed by the dispute settlement mechanism, instead simply providing for specific dialogue. Such less stringent requirements, as compared to other more recent EU economic agreements, may be due to the lengthy negotiations, which in 2021 had not fully concluded, given that certain provisions reflect much earlier EU FTAs.[43]

Environmental reviews and assessments of trade and investment agreements, however, have addressed this tension with greater attention. In the 1994 Canadian EA of the WTO Uruguay Round commitments,[44] Canadians raised concerns that the WTO Agreement on Trade Related Intellectual Property Rights (TRIPS) obligations to ensure a high level of intellectual property protection could increase the cost of environmentally sound technologies through licensing fees, and thereby prevent Canada from ensuring technology transfer to developing countries in accordance with commitments in, for instance, the UN Framework Convention on Climate Change (UN FCCC).[45] Similarly, concerns were raised that WTO TRIPS obligations requiring States to provide for patent protection on plant

38 Pauwelyn (n 30).

39 ibid

40 IARC, *Trade Sustainability Impact Assessment (SIA) of the Association Agreement under Negotiation between the European Community and Mercosur: Final Overview Report Trade SIA EU-Mercosur* (Manchester, March 2009) [EU-Mercosur SIA] 85.

41 'Rio Declaration on Environment and Development (Annex 2)', *Report of the UN Conference on Environment and Development, 13 June 1992*, UN Doc A/CONF.151/26 (Vol I).

42 EU-Mercosur SIA (n 40) 85.

43 Markus W Gehring, Christian Delev and Freedom Kai Phillips, 'Assessing EU FTA environmental obligations: putting the Draft EU-MERCOSUR trade agreement into perspective—Draft Analysis for the European Climate Foundation' (CISDL nd); James Harrison and Sophia Paulini, 'The Trade and Sustainable Development Chapter in the EU-Mercosur Association Agreement: Is it fit for purpose?' (ClientEarth 2020).

44 A later review claimed that all such concerns were either groundless or had not yet been proven. DFAIT, 'Retrospective Analysis of the 1994 Canadian Environmental Review' (November 1999).

45 ICTSD and ISD, *Climate Change, Technology Transfer and Intellectual Property Rights* (Geneva, 2008) 3.

varieties might block realization of United Nations Convention on Biological Diversity (CBD) commitments to respect the traditional knowledge, innovation and practices of indigenous peoples.[46] International legal scholars have highlighted these concerns, noting in particular that in spite of tailored provisions in the CBD, trade and investment treaty obligations could allow Parties to enforce compulsory jurisdiction of the WTO to defend patents which violate CBD principles.[47] Similar concerns about overlaps between international commitments to encourage the sustainable use of biodiversity, and international trade law obligations to open borders to goods and services which result in increases in biodiversity and habitat degradation have been raised in other ERs.[48]

The US-Chile environmental review examined possible impacts of the Chile-US Free Trade Agreement (FTA) on US international obligations.[49] Problems were raised with regard to potential conflicts between treaties, and these provide a useful illustration of the types of obligations that might be affected by trade and investment treaty obligations.[50] For instance, in the 1989 Basel Convention on the Control of Transboundary Movements of Hazardous Wastes and their Disposal,[51] 183 countries and the EU agree on trade measures to prevent developed country Parties (or States with which they trade) from risking that their hazardous wastes become subject to illegal disposal in the territories of developing country Parties, but also to allow for safe, sustainable recycling and reuse.[52] A concern was raised in the US-Chile ER process that the proposed US-Chile FTA might lead to the shipping of hazardous wastes from the United States to Chile, where proper disposal might not be possible, in violation of certain obligations in the Basel Convention. The US had signed the Basel Convention in 1990, and the Senate gave its consent for ratification in 1992, but ratification has not been forthcoming. However, Chile is a Party to the Basel Convention and is therefore not permitted to export or import hazardous waste from a non-Party, such as the US.[53] The Basel Convention seeks to minimize the transboundary movement of hazardous waste and requires that Parties manage their hazardous waste in an environmentally sound manner. Its trade measures are crucial to the effectiveness of the Convention, by ensuring that transboundary movement of hazardous waste is adequately controlled and that the gains of this control, such as sustainable re-processing and use of such wastes, are not undermined.[54] As a Party to the Basel Convention, Chile cannot trade in covered wastes with non-Parties in the absence of a bilateral, multilateral, or regional agreement regarding the transboundary movement of hazardous waste. At the time of the negotiations, the US

[46] B Dhar, 'The Convention on Biological Diversity and the TRIPS Agreement: Compatibility or Conflict?' in C Bellmann, G Dutfield and R Meléndez-Ortiz (eds), *Trading in Knowledge: Development Perspectives on TRIPS, Trade and Sustainability* (London, Earthscan and ICTSD 2003).

[47] Birnie, Boyle and Redgwell (n 2) 801–807; I Walden, 'Intellectual Property Rights and Biodiversity' in M Bowman and C Redgwell (eds), *International Law & the Conservation of Biological Diversity* (London, Kluwer Law International 1996) 178.

[48] See, e.g., IBM Belgium, *Trade Sustainability Impact Assessment of the EU-Korea FTA: Final Report* (Brussels, June 2008) [EU-Korea SIA] 25–26.

[49] USTR, *Interim Environmental Review of the US-Chile FTA* (Washington, 2001) [Interim US-Chile ER].

[50] R Newfarmer, *Trade, Doha and Development: A Window into the Issues* (Washington, The World Bank 2005), with regard to the relationship between the Chile-US FTA and obligations under TRIPS.

[51] Adopted 22 March 1989, entered into force 5 May 1992, 1673 UNTS 57.

[52] Ibid 330. See also Trebilcock and Howse (n 5) 471–587; Birnie, Boyle and Redgwell (n 2) 778–787; French (n 5) 198–212; Baughen (n 5). See further P-M Dupuy and JE Viuales, *International Environmental Law* (Cambridge, CUP 2018).

[53] Basel Convention (n 51), art 4(5).

[54] OECD, 'Trade Measures in the Basel Convention on the Control of Transboundary Movements of Hazardous Wastes and their Disposal' (27 May 1998) COM/ENV/TD(97)41/FINAL.

and Chile did not have such an accord. If Chile traded with other Basel Convention Parties as agreed, but refused to trade with the US, it would *prima facie* discriminate against US wastes. While US policy of the times dictated that the US does not ship hazardous waste to non- Organisation for Economic Co-operation and Development (OECD) countries, Chile had recently joined the OECD. Should a US firm wish to export wastes to Chile for treatment or disposal, the US would be able to require Chile to accept imports (or permit exports) under the non-discrimination obligations of the US-Chile FTA. In effect, the concern was that the FTA could make full implementation of Chile's obligations under the treaty more difficult, and might even be used to convince Chile to violate their Basel Convention restrictions in order to live up to its trade non-discrimination obligations. Concerns about overlaps between international commitments to encourage less polluting disposal of hazardous wastes, and international trade obligations, have been raised in other assessments as well.[55] Further, the Chile-US EA raised concerns about increases in persistent organic pollutants (POPs), the chemical substances that persist in the environment, bio-accumulate through the food chain, and pose a risk of causing adverse effects to human health and the environment, an issue important to sustainable development.[56] Faced with growing evidence of long-range transport of these substances to regions where they have never been used or produced and consequent threats to the global environment, States initiated urgent global action to reduce and eliminate releases of these chemicals, resulting in the 2001 Stockholm Convention on Persistent Organic Pollutants (Stockholm POPs Convention).[57] Chile is a Party to the Stockholm POPs Convention, which requires participating countries to reduce and/or eliminate the production and use of key internationally produced POPs used as pesticides or industrial chemicals.[58] The Stockholm POPs Convention contains strict provisions to prevent and control the release of certain POPs, including those unintentionally produced as by-products to industrial and other processes.[59] Under article 3, Parties agree to ban imports of listed substances, except if the import is from another Party and is destined for environmentally sound disposal, or in the case of other limited exemptions, in order to ensure that all use and disposal of POPs existing or produced within the Parties are subject to its restrictions. The United States signed the Stockholm POPs Convention in 2001, but has not ratified, and at the time of negotiations on the trade agreement, exported a wide variety of pesticide products to Chile. In 2000, the total value of this trade exceeded US$ 12 million.[60] Should a US firm wish to continue exporting POPs to Chile, the concern was raised that Chile's efforts to comply with its obligations under the Stockholm POPs

[55] DFAIT, 'Initial Environmental Assessment of the Canada-Korea Free Trade Agreement' (16 November 2007) [Canada-Korea EA] 31 for hazardous e-waste; USTR *Interim Environmental Review United States-Thailand Free Trade Agreement* (Washington, 2005) 4.

[56] L Nizzetto and others, 'Past. Present, and Future Controls on levels of Persistent Organic Pollutants in the Global Environment' (2010) 44 Environmental Science and Technology 6526.

[57] Stockholm Convention on Persistent Organic Pollutants (adopted 22 May 2001, entered into force 17 May 2004) (2001) 40 ILM 532; see JA Mintz, 'Two Cheers for Global POPs: A Summary and Assessment of the Stockholm Convention on Persistent Organic Pollutants' (2001–2002) 14 Georgetown Environmental Law Review 319.

[58] The Agreement initially targets 12 POPs, which include: aldrin, chlordane, DDT, dieldrin, endrin, heptachlor, hexachlorobenzene, mirex, toxaphene, polychlorinated biphenyls (PCBs), dioxins and furans.

[59] See n 56.

[60] USTR, *Final Environmental Review of the US-Chile FTA* (USTR, Washington 2003) <https://ustr.gov/sites/default/files/chilefinal.pdf> accessed 16 December 2020 [US-Chile Final ER]. See also C Vanden Bilcke, 'The Stockholm Convention on Persistent Organic Pollutants' (2002) 11(3) Review of European Community and International Environmental Law 328–342.

Convention not to import POPs from the US would conflict with its obligations under the FTA for non-discrimination between POPs from the US (a non-Party with which trade is not permitted) and POPs from Parties to the Stockholm POPs Convention (with which trade is permitted). At the very least, the new trade and investment agreement risked undermining Chile's attempts to live up to its commitments to reduce the spread of dangerous persistent organic pollutants. Similar concerns about normative overlaps between international commitments to slow the spread of POPs, and to respect international trade and investment liberalization commitments, have been raised in other assessments as well.[61]

A further example is possible, concerning social and environmental measures to protect human health, other species and also access to markets for agricultural products. Many trade and investment treaties contain provisions to discipline the use of sanitary and phytosanitary measures, covering the same subject as the health- and environment-related provisions of the 2001 Cartagena Protocol on Biosafety to the CBD.[62] Here, the issue is not one of a ban. Rather, the Protocol focuses on safe use of potentially risky new biotechnology[63] and expressly *permits* States to use the precautionary approach when determining whether and how to permit the import of living modified organisms (LMOs).[64] In the Preamble of the Protocol, States recognize a potential overlap with trade disciplines, stating 'that trade and environment agreements should be mutually supportive with a view to achieving sustainable development'.[65] In the treaty, Parties then noted that on one hand, the treaty shall not be interpreted as implying a change in the rights and obligations of a Party under any existing agreements, while also recognizing, on the other hand, that this recital is not meant to subordinate the Protocol to other international agreements.[66]

The procedures agreed in the Protocol require both risk assessment and risk management.[67] In the Protocol, and in Annex III which contains guidelines for risk assessments under the Cartagena Protocol on Biosafety,[68] Parties agree that State Parties can make their own determinations of risk based on the principle of the precautionary approach, whereby their decision concerning the importation of a living modified organism can be condition on the Party's need to protect the environment or on health concerns.[69] In particular, the

[61] See, e.g., USTR, *Interim Environmental Review U.S.-Andean Free Trade Agreement* (February 2005) <https://ustr.gov/sites/default/files/perinter.pdf> accessed 16 December 2020, 33–34; DFAIT, 'Initial Environmental Assessment of the Canada-India Foreign Investment Promotion and Protection Agreement' (25 June 2007) <https://www.international.gc.ca/trade-agreements-accords-commerciaux/agr-acc/india-inde/finalEA-FIPA-EEfinale.aspx?lang=eng> accessed 16 December 2020, 10.

[62] Cartagena Protocol on Biosafety to the United Nations Convention on Biological Diversity (adopted 29 January 2000, entered into force 11 September 2003) 39 ILM 1027, art 1.These concerns have been documented further in legal academic literature, see, e.g., M Pollack and GC Shaffer, *When Cooperation Fails: The International Law and Politics of Genetically Modified Foods* (Oxford: OUP, 2009); L Bodiguel and M Cardwell (eds), *The Regulation of Genetically Modified Organisms: Comparative Approaches* (Oxford, OUP, 2010).

[63] United Nations Convention on Biological Diversity (UNCBD) (opened for signature 5 June 1992, entered into force 29 December 1993) 1760 UNTS 79, 143, arts 1, 2, 19.

[64] Rio Principle 15 reads: 'In order to protect the environment, the precautionary approach shall be widely applied by States according to their capabilities. Where there are threats of serious or irreversible damage, lack of full scientific certainty shall not be used as a reason for postponing cost-effective measures to prevent environmental degradation.' United Nations Conference on the Environment and Development, Agenda 21, 15.

[65] Cartagena Protocol (n 62) Preamble. F Pythoud and UP Thomas, 'The Cartagena Protocol on Biosafety' in PG LePrestre (ed), *Governing Global Biodiversity: The Evolution and Implementation of the Convention on Biological Diversity* (Ashgate, Aldershot 2002) 39; Bodiguel and Cardwell (n 62).

[66] Cartagena Protocol (n 62) Preamble, best described as the normative equivalent of a 'stalemate'.

[67] Ibid, arts 15, 16.

[68] Ibid Annex III.

[69] IUCN, *An Explanatory Guide to the Cartagena Protocol on Biosafety* (IUCN and FIELD, Cambridge 2003) 340.

Cartagena Protocol on Biosafety states that: '[l]ack of scientific knowledge or scientific consensus should not necessarily be interpreted as indicating a particular level of risk, an absence of risk, or an acceptable risk.'[70] Inclusion of precaution in the Cartagena Protocol on Biosafety was not without controversy, as debates continue about what the principle actually means, and whether or not it is a principle of customary international law.[71] But in the Cartagena Protocol on Biosafety, provisions on precaution allow importing Parties to shift the burden of compiling evidence on the safety of an LMO to the exporter, who often has access to more information about the LMO that they seek permission to export.[72] This 'permissive norm' appears to overlap with sanitary and phytosanitary (SPS) provisions in the Chile-US FTA that require SPS standards to be based on sound science.[73] Indeed, the SPS provisions could be used to restrict measures aimed at controlling trade in LMOs, such as in the case of regulations to ensure food safety,[74] or regulations to protect nature in the importing country from uncertain risks related to the testing of LMOs or other unsafe releases of LMOs into the environment.[75] Under a trade agreement, should it be established that a product containing LMOs is a 'like product' to one that does not contain LMOs, and that the SPS measure discriminates between the two products, the burden of proof to defend a trade restriction falls on the Party seeking to constrain the imports. This Party is required to defend its measure by demonstrating that the rules fall within certain exceptions, for instance that it is transparent, science-based and necessary for the protection of human, animal and plant health.[76] Occasions in which a 'precautionary approach' can be used may be limited to provisional measures, which must be reviewed periodically.[77] If Chile tried to design regulations to implement the provisions of the Cartagena Protocol on Biosafety which explicitly permit a decision to restrict imports to be taken on the basis of precaution, as is permitted by the Protocol, the adoption of the precautionary regulations could be constrained by the provisions of the Chile-US FTA which require all restrictions to be science-based. The US is not a signatory to the Cartagena Protocol, and is committed to the development and exportation of biotechnology, including through incentivizing trade and investment in LMOs. The EU has ratified the Cartagena Protocol and has adopted highly precautionary policies, including in trade and investment relationships. Agricultural products which cannot be certified as LMO-free can be barred from European markets. Chile became a signatory to the Cartagena Protocol in 2000, but during the US trade negotiations, was still considering ratification. Chile was debating its options in terms of implementing

[70] Cartagena Protocol (n 62) Annex III, 4.

[71] MC Cordonier Segger and M Gehring, 'Precaution, Health and the World Trade Organization: Moving Toward Sustainable Development' (2003) 29 Queen's Law Journal 133; A Trouwborst, 'The Precautionary Principle in General International Law: Combating the Babylonian Confusion' (2007) 16 Review of European Community and International Environmental Law 185; T Treves, 'Environmental Impact Assessment and the Precautionary Approach: Why Are International Courts and Tribunals Reluctant to Consider Them as General Principles of Law?' in M Andenas and others, *General Principles and the Coherence of International Law* (Leiden, Brill 2019).

[72] Cartagena Protocol (n 62) art 15(2).

[73] Chile-US FTA (adopted 2003, entered into force 1 January 2004), art 6.1–6.4.

[74] Agreement on the Application of Sanitary and Phytosanitary Measures (adopted 15 April 1994, entered into force 1 January 1995) 1867 UNTS 493, Annex A.

[75] Ibid. Annex A:1.

[76] Ibid. art 5.7.; see also discussion of *Biotech* case at Chapter 3.1.

[77] In the *Hormones* dispute, the Appellate Body did not take a position on the status of the precautionary principle in international law, noting that it is reflected, *inter alia*, in the SPS Agreement, art 5.7, but does not override the SPS Agreement, art 5.1, 5.2. WTO, *EC Measures Concerning Meat and Meat Products (Hormones)* (13 February 1998) WT/DS26/AB/R and WT/DS48/AB/R.

legislation, so the potential regulatory effects of closer trade and investment relationships with both the US and the EU were particularly relevant. Could the US-Chile FTA be affecting Chile's ability to ratify and implement the Cartagena Protocol, as a matter of international regulatory chill? It certainly seems possible. The trade agreement text reaffirms the WTO SPS Agreement in its entirety, importing the challenges mentioned above. As noted in the US-Chile ER, the US-Chile bilateral SPS Committee established by the accord provides Parties with the opportunity to raise concerns about specific SPS measures. These might include challenges, therefore, to each Party's SPS standards. Both Parties anticipated that implementation of the US-Chile FTA SPS would increase the level of trade and investment between them.[78] The Committee could be used to bring pressure to bear upon regulators, requiring at a minimum resources to be expended in each instance to legally defend their proposed measures. In particular, articles 2.2 and 5.1 of the WTO SPS Agreement require a sanitary or phytosanitary measure to be based on scientific principles and an appropriate risk assessment.[79] While the State is permitted under article 5.7 of the WTO SPS Agreement to provisionally adopt SPS measures on the basis of available pertinent information if relevant scientific evidence is insufficient, there is an ongoing obligation to continue to seek additional information and to review the measure in a reasonable period of time.[80] The concern would be that the US-Chile FTA, by reinforcing the requirement that Parties make only science-based judgements in SPS matters, could be weakening Chilean rights and abilities to take decisions based on precaution. Further, while the US-Chile FTA makes clear that the desire to further harmonize SPS rules preserves the right of the Parties to impose a requirement more stringent than an international standard, it emphasizes that a scientific justification will be required for such decisions, as well. One solution would be for the Cartagena Protocol to be recognized as an international standard for LMOs, but it is not clear that this interpretation would be accepted.[81] The problem raises the concern that the burden of proof would fall upon the Party seeking to protect health and the environment under the Cartagena Protocol to justify their policy and regulatory choices based only on a scientific risk assessment (rather than also on precaution, as permitted in the Protocol).

A final example looks beyond conflicts between treaties, towards other aspects of this tension relating to the potential constraining effects of a new trade and investment agreement on the enactment of measures for sustainability. In particular, many bilateral and regional economic agreements cover more than just trade—they include investment chapters granting protections to investors in order to encourage increases in investments in the territory of Parties.[82] The tension exists between maintaining policy flexibility for regulators, and securing protections for investors such as certainty, predictability and respect for acquired rights.[83] As noted earlier in this book, the inclusion of investment provisions in trade and investment agreements might increase foreign direct investment (FDI), by fostering an enabling environment and strengthening the credibility and security of government commitments to investors. However, sceptics continue to question the actual influence of

[78] Chilean DIRECON Statement, US-Chile Final ER (n 60).
[79] SPS Agreement (n 74).
[80] Ibid.
[81] A Negi, 'World Trade Organisation and the EC Biotech Case: Procedural and Substantive Issues' (2007) 44 International Studies 1.
[82] Cordonier Segger, Gehring and Newcombe (n 7).
[83] ibid.

investment agreements on FDI decisions, and express deep concern about the potential loss of control over domestic policy and legal flexibility to incentivize investments and financial flows for sustainable development.[84] As noted by Professor Andrew Newcombe, efforts to maintain regulatory space for the sustainable development of natural resources can be stymied by strict investment rules.[85] As the 2003 World Investment Report highlights:

> For developing countries, the most important challenge in future [investment rules] is to strike a balance between the potential contribution of such agreements to increasing FDI flows and the preservation of the ability to pursue development oriented FDI policies that allow them to benefit more from them—that is, the right to regulate in the public interest. This requires maintaining sufficient policy space to give governments the flexibility to use such policies within the framework of the obligations established by the IIAs to which they are parties. The tension this creates is obvious . . .[86]

Governments can use a number of economic instruments in order to promote the sustainable development of natural resources, including spending, taxation, controls and penalties.[87] Disciplines on investment measures in economic agreements, if wide exceptions are not agreed for spending (subsidies and grants) and for taxation measures, could greatly reduce, or even constrain, this regulatory space.[88] Key pressure points for sustainable development involve investment measures to encourage sustainable use of natural resources. Several principal cases related to sustainable development in international investment tribunals have arisen out of failed or nationalized natural resource concessions or large power infrastructure projects. As Newcombe and other eminent jurists have noted, investment treaties have been used to challenge who would bear the costs for environmental impact assessments requirements for failed chemical production plants (*Maffezini v. Spain*),[89] for reclamation requirements for mines (*Glamis v. United States*),[90] for black economic empowerment ownership requirements for mining properties (*XYZ v. South Africa*),[91] for prohibitions on the use or transport of certain fuel additives (*Ethyl Corporation v. Canada, Methanex v. United States*),[92] for verification of records relating to reporting requirements (*Pope & Talbot Inc. v. The Government of Canada*),[93] for land use zoning (*MTD Equity Sdn.*

[84] K von Moltke, 'The FTAA in the Graveyard of Economic Negotiations' in MC Cordonier Segger and M Leichner Reynal (eds), *Beyond the Barricades: The Americas Trade and Sustainable Development Agenda* (Farnham, Ashgate 2005) 141; H Mann, K von Moltke, A Cosbey, LE Peterson, *IISD Model International Agreement on Investment for Sustainable Development-Negotiators' Handbook* (Winnipeg, 2005).

[85] A Newcombe, 'Report for Natural Resources Canada on Issues Related to 'General Exceptions' in Future Trade/Investment Agreements' (10 August 2007). See also MC Cordonier Segger, 'From Protest to Proposal: Options for an Americas Investment Regime?' in Cordonier Segger and Leichner Reynal (n 84) 145–165; F Baetens, 'Combating Climate Change Through the Promotion of Green Investment: From Kyoto to Paris Without Regime-Specific Dispute Settlement' in Kate Miles (ed), *Research Handbook on Environment and Investment Law* (Cheltenham, UK and Northampton, MA, USA, Edward Elgar 2019).

[86] United Nations Conference on Trade and Development, *World Investment Report 2003* (New York and Geneva, 2003) xvii.

[87] N Schrijver, *Sovereignty over Natural Resources: Balancing Rights and Duties* (Cambridge CUP 1997); S Alam, J Hossain Bhuiyan and J Razzaque (eds), *International Natural Resources Law, Investment and Sustainability* (London, Routledge 2017).

[88] Ibid.

[89] Damages, but not for EIA, using MFN to select a preferable forum under Chile-Spain BIT (Award, 13 November 2000).

[90] *Lis pendens.*

[91] *Lis pendens.*

[92] Ethyl settled, Methanex dismissed (Final Award, 3 August 2005).

[93] Damages (Award 31 May 2002).

Bhd. & MTD Chile S.A. v. Chile),[94] for the phase-out of agro-chemicals (*Chemtura Corp v. Canada*),[95] and for taxes on the hydrocarbon industry (*EnCana Corporation v. Republic of Ecuador, Occidental Exploration and Production Company v. The Republic of Ecuador*).[96] This last, for instance, raises concerns that tribunals will not defer to public policy or regulatory objectives in deciding whether investments are in 'like circumstances'. In *Occidental*, the tribunal found that oil exporters, as exporters, were in 'like circumstances' to other exporters such as exporters of flowers, minerals and seafood products that received VAT refunds. It is possible that oil exporters would also be found to be in 'like circumstances' to exporters of sustainable energy that benefit from measures to phase out fossil fuels. Decisions such as this highlight divergences in investment treaty jurisprudence on the meaning of 'like circumstances'.[97] Such cases have included claims relating to breaches of national treatment, minimum standards of treatment and the requirement to pay compensation for indirect (regulatory) expropriation.[98]

Claims of indirect expropriation have been particularly controversial. As argued by one international expert, if a:

> [G]overnment measure is undertaken for a clear public welfare purpose (such as health and safety, environment, public morals or order, etc.), and is non-discriminatory, but has the effect of harming a ... foreign investor, under what circumstances can that measure be held to be an indirect expropriation, for which the government must pay compensation? The concern is obvious: ... taxpayers should not be paying investors to alter behaviour that is contrary to the public interest. A secondary concern is that regulators who are held liable for their impacts on investors will not regulate to the extent that they should (the regulatory chill argument).[99]

While the EU-Mercosur SIA notes that negotiations concerned only fairly minimalist potential investment provisions,[100] many concerns were raised in the Interim US-Chile environmental review process regarding the proposals for an extensive investment chapter in the US-Chile FTA, and its potential to constrain domestic regulations for the sustainable use of natural resources.[101] As recognized in the review, the US Trade Act notes concerns with substantive investment protections such as expropriation, fair and equitable treatment and full protection and security, explaining: 'protections must be balanced so that they do not come at the expense of making US Federal, State, and local laws and regulations more vulnerable to successful challenges by foreign investors than by similarly situated US investors.'[102]

National treatment obligations prohibit discrimination between similarly situated investments based on the nationality of the owners.[103] However, sustainable development

[94] Damages (Award, 25 May 2004).

[95] *Lis pendens.*

[96] Dismissed, no jurisdiction (Award, 3 February 2006), Damages (Final Award, 1 July 2004).

[97] Ibid

[98] A Newcombe, 'Sustainable Development and Investment Treaty Law (2007) 8 Journal of World Investment & Trade 357; Q Ren, *Public Interests in International Investment Law: Balancing Protection for Investor and Environment* (Cambridge, Cambridge Scholars Publishing 2018).

[99] Cosbey (n 2).

[100] EU-Mercosur SIA (n 40) 96.

[101] Interim US-Chile ER (n 49) 35–36 .

[102] Ibid 35–36

[103] Ibid 64–65.

measures may need to treat large new investments differently than small investments, or apply more stringent operating conditions to investments located in a wetlands areas than investments located in less ecologically sensitive areas.[104] Foreign investors may even be treated differently than domestic investors because, for instance, the foreign investors lack assets to cover potential liability associated with potentially unsustainable activities, or seek to establish operations in an area which has already reached the limit of its carrying capacity.[105] This can result in differences in treatment between a foreign owned investment and a domestically owned investment in the same sector or activity.

Provisions on performance requirements also raise concerns, as environmental measures that require the use of a given product or the transfer of a particular technology to other users for environmental purposes could be constrained by the trade or investment treaty.[106] For instance, investors were required to provide pollution control technology information to the Administrator of the US Environmental Protection Agency to comply with the US Clean Air Act, but these conditions might be characterized as performance requirements being imposed on an investor in exchange for performance incentives.[107] New Chilean programmes that provide advantages to investors conducting research and development on renewable energy could also be disciplined, if a tribunal found that they discriminated between appropriate technologies.[108]

As noted in the US-Chile environmental review, expropriation and compensation provisions set conditions under which governments may expropriate a foreign investment and set terms for calculating and paying compensation to foreign investors.[109] Challenges might be brought by investors to influence new regulatory measures under debate, that is, for the purposes of regulatory chill. Further, while investor–state dispute settlement procedures permit challenges to public policies and regulations, many trade and investment treaties do not guarantee public access to this dispute settlement process.[110] Indeed, Parties to the North American Free Trade Agreement (NAFTA) Chapter Eleven on Investment were eventually required to issue an Interpretive Statement to underline that 'nothing in the NAFTA ... imposes a general duty of confidentiality ... [or] ... precludes the Parties from providing public access to documents submitted to, or issued by, a Chapter Eleven tribunal.'[111] As also noted in the US-Chile ER, there are further concerns about the scope and content of a minimum standard of treatment.[112] These provisions can be seen to require Parties to provide to foreign investors 'fair and equitable treatment' and 'full protection and

[104] A Newcombe, 'Sustainable Development and Investment Treaty Law, (2007) 8 Journal of World Investment & Trade 357.

[105] Ibid.

[106] Interim US-Chile ER (n 49) 65–66.

[107] Ibid 65.

[108] Ibid.

[109] Ibid 67.

[110] Ibid. See also R Polanco, 'Third-Party Rights and Transparency in Foreign Investment International Arbitration' (2010) Revista de Derecho Económico, Año XLVII, No 75, Chile; D Euler, M Gehring and M Scherer (eds), *Transparency in International Investment Arbitration: A Guide to the UNCITRAL Rules on Transparency in Treaty-Based Investor-State Arbitration* (Cambridge, CUP 2015); AK Bjorklund, 'Sustainable Development and International Investment Law' in Kate Miles (ed), *Research Handbook on Environment and Investment Law* (Cheltenham, UK and Northampton, MA, USA Edward Elgar 2019).

[111] NAFTA FTC, 'Notes of Interpretation of Certain Chapter 11 Provisions' (July 31, 2001). Such Interpretive Statements, under VCLT (n 32) art 31(3)(a), can be taken into account together with the context, in the interpretation of a treaty, Gardiner (n 33); *International Arbitration under Chapter 11 of the NAFTA and the UNCITRAL Arbitration Rules, Methanex v. USA (Merits)*, Award of 3 August 2005 (2005) 44 ILM 1345, 1345 paras 18–21.

[112] Interim US-Chile ER (n 49) 67.

security,' which some consider to be in addition to the normal customary legal standard. This obligation has been interpreted expansively in certain awards.[113] Essentially, the environmental review flagged concerns that investment liberalization commitments would encourage Parties to weaken or reduce the domestic standards to encourage investment in its territory, leading to negative consequences for the environment and for development.[114]

In addressing this tension, it is not automatic that States will successfully develop the 'mutually supportive' relationships between trade and investment priorities, and the environmental and social concerns that are integral to sustainable development.[115] The potential is that a new trade and investment law commitment will generate difficult-to-resolve overlaps between obligations, constraining or disciplining the implementation of trade- or investment-related measures for sustainable development. Domestic adoption of new laws and regulations can also be constrained, as per concerns raised in the assessments discussed above. This normative tension, if successfully addressed in a trade and investment treaty at any level, might strengthen its potential to support sustainable development.

6.2 Tension Two: Constraining Enforcement of Domestic Laws Addressing Social and Environmental Problems

A second tension which becomes apparent from trade and investment impact assessments conducted to date involves concerns that through the new treaty rules, there will be increased incentives for trade and investment led economic growth which can exacerbate environmental and social problems that already exist at the domestic level due to lack of adequate enforcement of the law.[116] As discussed above and in many assessments, often negative impacts of trade or investment flows are due to a lack of domestic capacity to enforce adequate domestic environmental and social regulations, or even simply a lack of domestic human and financial resources to address known challenges, especially in developing countries.[117] These pre-existing domestic challenges can be exacerbated by the economic growth that occurs due to the increases in scale and scope of trade and investment occasioned by a new treaty. Absent specific provisions to the contrary, new trade and investment disciplines

[113] Ibid.

[114] Ibid 66–68.

[115] Johannesburg Declaration and Johannesburg Plan of Implementation (JPOI), *Report of the World Summit on Sustainable Development*, 4 September 2002, UN Doc A/CONF.199/20, 15.

[116] These concerns are also well-documented in trade and environment, and trade and social development literature. Key concerns include the 'scale effects' whereby there are increases in pollution due to rising production, packaging and transport for trade, increases in depletion of natural resources to supply international markets, or increases in low-wage unskilled employment with poor working conditions and little respect for workers' rights from growth of certain types of industries. See SK Sell, 'Corporations, Seeds, and Intellectual Property Rights Governance' in Jennifer Clapp and Doris A Fuchs (eds), *Corporate Power in Global Agrifood Governance* (Massachusetts, MIT Press 2009); United Nations Conference on Trade and Development, *World Investment Report 2003* (New York and Geneva, 2003) xvii; N Schrijver, *Sovereignty over Natural Resources: Balancing Rights and Duties* (Cambridge, CUP 1997); IT Odumosu-Ayanu, 'Local Communities, Environment and Development: The Case of Oil and Gas Investment in Africa' in K Miles (ed), *Research Handbook on Environment and Investment Law* (Cheltenham, UK and Northampton, MA, USA, Edward Elgar 2019); S Alam, 'Trade, Investment and Biodiversity Conservation' in Elisa Morgera and Jona Razzaque (eds), Biodiversity and Nature Protection Law (Vol III, Cheltenham Edward Elgar 2017).

[117] Infra. As will be explored later: in what specific instances could *new parallel sustainable development cooperation*, including through capacity-building, new financial resources, or even the joint implementation of new cooperative measures between trading partners, actually *compensate* for other social and environmental impacts of trade?

may fail to support domestic laws and policies that otherwise seek to achieve internationally agreed sustainable development objectives.

Such effects, generated by the second 'tension', are perhaps better described as normative constraints, rather than conflicts. The impact of the new trade and investment rules is not to forbid the strengthening of regulations. Rather, it simply further constrains the implementation of regulations that could otherwise deliver on the sustainable development objectives of the other treaties making them more difficult to adopt, enforce or monitor.[118] For instance if, under a new trade or investment agreement, weak enforcement of social or environmental laws can lower costs of production, securing advantages for domestic firms, the expanded market access occasioned by the accord indirectly undermines the effectiveness of laws on sustainable development in the partner countries.[119] The concern is that trade and investment flows will shape the rules governing patterns and processes of production in ways that negatively affect resource uses and potential for sustainable development.[120] In the impact assessments and associated literature, this is sometimes called a 'structural' or 'indirect effect' of a trade and investment agreement.[121]

As the scope of regulation expands to address new international challenges, it is not surprising that trade and investment regimes might constrain the flexibility of States to rigorously enforce their own social or environmental laws for sustainable development. Indeed, certain measures may exist to protect domestic industries without broader social or environmental gains, and in these instances, the new economic regimes, with their rules and dispute settlement bodies, provide a logical place for legal questions to be raised.[122] The tension occurs when developing country States with existing challenges in enforcing their laws risk further weakening domestic standards and regulations on sustainable development, in order to take advantage of new market access occasioned by an economic accord. Such an effect becomes more perverse if, in the same trade and investment agreement, the Parties actually commit to promote sustainable development. The normative tension is not simply the constraint, but rather, as has been raised in several impact assessments, the way the trade and investment agreement appears to *do nothing* to support the Parties' sustainable developed objectives, even where opportunities arise.[123]

From experience to date with different assessments, there are several examples which illustrate some of the ways that new economic agreements may influence domestic regulations on sustainable development. For instance, in the 1994 Canadian EA of the WTO

118 RE Hudec, 'GATT/WTO Constraints on National Regulation: Requiem for an 'Aim and Effects Test' (1998) 32 International Lawyer 619; Birnie, Boyle and Redgwell (n 2) 754.

119 Neumayer (n 2).

120 North American Commission for Environmental Cooperation (NACEC), *Potential NAFTA Effects: Claims and Arguments 1991-1994* (Montreal, 1996) 13–18.

121 Ibid 3.

122 D van den Bossche, *The Law and Policy of the WTO: Text, Cases and Materials* (Cambridge, CUP 2005) 19–24; RE Hudec, 'The New WTO Dispute Settlement Procedure: An Overview of the First Three Years' (1999) 8 Minnesota Journal of Global Trade 1, 3–15; JE Vinuales, 'Foreign Investment and the Environment in International Law: Current Trends' in K Miles (ed), *Research Handbook on Environment and Investment Law* (Cheltenham, UK and Northampton, MA, USA Edward Elgar 2019).

123 See Canada-Korea EA (n 55) 33 for concerns about effects on investment regulations; or EU-Andean SIA (n 1) 124 for concerns about trade not supporting improved labour regulations. JR Paul, 'Free Trade, Regulatory Competition, and the Autonomous Market Fallacy' (1994) 1 Columbia Journal of European Law 29, 29–32; RE Baldwin, J McLaren and A Panagariya, *Regulatory Protectionism, Developing Nations, and a Two-Tier World Trade System* (Washington, Brookings Trade Forum 2000); OECD, *Environment and Regional Trade Agreements* (Paris 2007); P Sands and J Peel, *Principles of International Environmental Law* (4th edn, Cambridge, CUP 2018).

Uruguay Round,[124] Canadians expressed concern that MFN obligations might challenge Canadian regulations for the management and sustainable use of international fisheries, leading to weaker enforcement of fisheries and oceans management laws and regulations[125]– this could affect Canadian efforts to designate and maintain marine protected areas (an important target under SDG 14 life below water), or to establish and enforce quotas to preserve the fishing stocks. Concerns were also raised that the WTO Agreement on the Application of Sanitary and Phytosanitary Measures (SPS Agreement) could constrain Canada's ability to enforce high levels of sanitary and phytosanitary protection, that Canadian standards might be lowered to harmonize with less stringent international standards, and that efforts to prevent the entry of pests could be constrained by the need to be consistent with the SPS Agreement, leading for instance, to beetle and other infestations in Canadian forests.[126] Concerns were also raised that the WTO Agreement on Trade-Related Investment Measures (TRIMS), which requires national treatment and prohibits trade-related investment measures that restrict and distort trade such as quantitative restrictions, might constrain application of Canadian policies to encourage more sustainable investments.[127] Concerns were further expressed that the WTO Subsidies Agreement could prevent Canada from adequately funding environmental initiatives.[128]

Similar concerns were raised in the EU-Mercosur SIA that the EU-Mercosur AA could accelerate economic growth in both the EU and Mercosur in a manner that drives increases in consumption and associated wastes rather than helping to reduce these patterns.[129] Concerns were also raised that the EU-Mercosur AA might encourage a movement of capital out of high value-added industrial production and into lower value-added agricultural production.[130] This could inhibit the transfer of green technologies rather than enhancing this transfer in the Parties' countries, an important target under SDG 17 global partnership.[131]

Recommendations from the EU-Mercosur SIA include the use of a multifaceted approach in the implementation and enforcement of sustainability provisions, which could include the combination of specific dialogue mechanisms, dispute settlement mechanisms and targeted ex-post monitoring processes.[132]

Three examples can be provided in relation to this normative tension from across existing experiences of impact assessments. In these areas, without cooperation, domestic ability to enforce laws on sustainable development are at risk of being weakened by a new trade and investment agreement.

A first example relates to government procurement rules that could, with appropriate parallel collaboration, support policies and laws for sustainable social development. Many trade and investment liberalization agreements contain provisions to open government

124 See DFAIT (n 44).
125 Ibid 31.
126 Ibid 22.
127 Ibid 28–29.
128 Ibid 30.
129 EU-Mercosur SIA (n 40).
130 Ibid
131 Ibid
132 James Harrison and Sophia Paulini, 'The Trade and Sustainable Development Chapter in the EU-Mercosur Association Agreement: Is it fit for purpose?' (ClientEarth 2020); London School of Economics, 'Sustainability Impact Assessment in Support of the Association Agreement Negotiations between the European Union and Mercosur' (Draft Final Report) (London School of Economics 2020).

procurement bidding processes, extending beyond the minimal commitments of the WTO in this area.[133] Procurement decisions, however, can be linked to the delivery of specific social and environmental priorities, such as the targeting of employment for groups that face discrimination in the labour market, support for small and medium sized enterprises, or 'green procurement' programmes.[134] As they are administratively straightforward and affect consumption directly, the UN now highlights such instruments as potential tools for sustainable development.[135] Most public procurement 'social linkage' schemes involve either a price preference for goods or services that meet certain social criteria,[136] or a specification of a product's social or environmental attributes.[137] Public procurement 'social linkage' policies are often the result of a domestic political and legal process, and are maintained for a mix of reasons.[138] Such reasons have led States to enact rules which ensure that procurement supports their commitment to the social and environmental elements of sustainable development. For example, social measures can give preference to companies which employ workers from disadvantaged ethnic or racial groups or have an excellent record in workers' health and safety, or to comply with compensation agreements for forcibly resettled indigenous peoples, contributing directly to progressive realization of important social or economic rights.[139] However, such programmes may have trade or investment implications. Parties to the International Covenant on Economic, Social and Cultural Rights (ICESCR) guarantee that the Covenant rights will be 'exercised without discrimination of any kind as to race, colour, sex, language, religion, political or other opinion, national or social origin, property, birth or other status'.[140] Rights covered by this obligation include article 6 obligations to 'recognize the right to work' and to 'take appropriate steps to safeguard this right'.[141] In addition, it is detailed that Parties commit to achieving the full realization of this right through 'technical and vocational guidance and training programmes, policies and techniques to achieve steady economic, social and cultural development and full and productive employment under conditions safeguarding fundamental political and economic freedoms to the individual'.[142] Under article 7, Parties also commit to 'women being guaranteed conditions of work not inferior to those enjoyed by men, with equal pay for equal work'... and 'safe and healthy working conditions'.[143]

133 CM Dent, 'Freer Trade, More Regulation? Commercial Regulatory Provisions in Asia-Pacific Free Trade Agreements' (2010) 14 Competition and Change 48, 51–52.

134 UNEP, 'Green Procurement Initiative' <http://www.uneptie.org/pc/sustain/policies/green-proc.htm> accessed 16 December 2020.

135 See 'Latin America and Caribbean Meetings on Sustainable Consumption and Production' (2003) 8(3) UNCSD Update On-Line 4.

136 For example, a certain company can be granted pre-award preference, in spite of higher costs, because they employ racially discriminated minorities, women or indigenous peoples.

137 For example, criteria can ensure that all equipment must meet a certain workplace safety standard.

138 C McCrudden, 'International Economic Law and Human Rights: A Framework for Discussion of the Legality of "Selective Purchasing" Laws under the WTO Government Procurement Agreement' (1999) 2 Journal of International Economic Law 3; C Cravero, 'Socially Responsible Public Procurement and Set-Asides: A Comparative Analysis of the US, Canada and the EU' (2019) 8 Arctic Review on Law and Politics 174.

139 See McCrudden (n 138).

140 International Covenant on Economic, Social and Cultural Rights (adopted 16 December 1966, entered into force 3 January 1976) GA Res 2200A (XXI), UN Doc A/6316 (1966), 993 UNTS 3.

141 Ibid, art 6.1.

142 Ibid, art 6.2.

143 Ibid, art 7(a), 7(b).

In order to respect, protect and fulfil these social and economic rights, as part of the domestic measures that a State sets in place in accordance with the ICESCR regime,[144] governments may enact public procurement policies that require a domestic-level independent certification that the employer respects fundamental rights at work, or safety and health standards,[145] and similar policies are often adopted to promote green procurement. Independent certification saves under-resourced purchasing officers from being required to undertake expensive verification and auditing procedures, but might only be available in certain countries. Indeed, several international social development programmes have provided capacity-building to assist governments to establish such programmes through new domestic laws and policies.[146]

However, in trade and investment agreements, public procurement provisions can lay out strict directions for tendering procedures, and non-discrimination obligations may limit the use of usual procurement measures to ensure that contractors can deliver social priorities or have good social records. For example, it is not clear in economic law provisions that lay out the procedures to bid for tenders, that non-economic factors can even be taken into consideration by the tendering authority in pre-award or post-award criteria for public procurement contracts.[147] In particular, if a trade and investment agreement restricts procurement decisions to price alone, it would effectively constrain the use of socially sustainable regulatory measures, as well as measures for green procurement.

As noted in the Interim US-Chile ER, the US-Chile FTA seeks to ensure non-discrimination, transparency, predictability and accountability in the government procurement process. To this end, concerns were raised in the environmental review process that the procedural requirements with respect to tenders, qualification of suppliers, advertisement to bid, bid challenge procedures and the awarding of contracts would require public authorities to award contracts to the fully capable tender that is the lowest price or the most advantageous based on certain restricted evaluation criteria enumerated in the tender documentation. Requirements of domestic content or licensing of technology could be prohibited, and technical specifications could be limited to performance rather than design. Particular concerns included that the definition of 'technical specification' may not accommodate labelling requirements and process and production methods (such as low carbon intensity, or lack of child labour), blocking agencies from ensuring that public procurement purchases products that meet environmental or social objectives.[148] Strict requirements

[144] According to the CESCR, the obligation to fulfil further contains duties 'to provide, promote and facilitate' the realization of the rights in the Covenant on the part of the State: UN CESCR, *General Comment No 14: The Right to the Highest Attainable Standard of Health*, UN Doc E/C.12/2000/4; UN CESCR, General Comment No 16: The Equal Right of Men and Women to the Enjoyment of All Economic, Social and Cultural Rights (art 3), UN Doc E/C.12/2005/3; The General Comments are available at <https://digitallibrary.un.org/record/425041?ln=en> accessed 16 December 2020.

[145] Peru (Ley No 27070 que modifica el artículo 44 de la Ley No 26850, Ley de Contrataciones y Adquisiciones del Estado. 19-III-1999), Brazil ('lei da obtenção' Lei n 8.666 de 21 de Junho de 1993), Ecuador (Ley de Contratación Pública. 22-II-2001), Costa Rica (Ley 7.494 Contratación Administrativa. 08-VI-1995); Case C-513/99 *Concordia Bus Finland Oy Ab v Helsingin kaupunki and HKL-Bussiliikenne* [2002] ECR I-07213 (*Helsinki Corcordia Bus Case*).

[146] International Labour Organization (ILO), <http://www.un.org/esa/sustdev/sdissues/consumption/MikeShone.pdf> accessed 16 December 2020; C McCrudden, 'Social Aspects in Sustainable Public Procurement', United Nations Division on Economic and Social Affairs discussion forum, <http://www.un.org/esa/sustdev/sdissues/consumption/ChristopherMcCrudden.pdf> accessed 16 December 2020; UNEP, 'Green Procurement Initiative' <http://www.uneptie.org/pc/sustain/policies/green-proc.htm> accessed 16 December 2020.

[147] On the contract, procurement provisions might instead state that the negotiation disciplines shall be applied in those procedures in which *price* is the determining element in the award.

[148] US-Chile Interim ER (n 49) 11, 29.

such as these could limit the Parties' ability to ensure that public spending supports sustainable development priorities, particularly if domestic capacity was weak in this area from the outset. The EU-Chile SIA raises such social and economic concerns regarding liberalization of government procurement. In particular: '… government procurement has been widely used as a tool for domestic policy … In developing countries it is used as tool for industrial and social policy, with government procurement expenditures being used to develop infant or strategic industries, and to support employment growth, small firm development or regional growth.'[149]

A related concern, also noted in the EU-Chile SIA, was that liberalization could also have a social impact on the use of procurement to support development of small and medium-sized enterprises, or in the implementation of government efforts to promote regional and local development, concessions that can be crucial for national stability or for indigenous peoples' rights.[150] It seemed highly unlikely the economic gains from government procurement liberalization could immediately be secured by the fiscal system and redistributed to support these goals.[151] Liberalization of government procurement remained a contentious point,[152] and changes that impose disciplines were seen, in assessments, as at risk of weakening domestic scope for enforcement of green or social procurement laws.[153]

In a second example, the 1997 Montreal Protocol on Substances that Deplete the Ozone Layer[154] to the 1985 Vienna Convention for the Protection of the Ozone Layer[155] has 191 Parties which in the treaty, adopted trade and investment measures that prevent Parties from trading with certain non-Parties in goods that either contain or *were produced using* prohibited ozone-depleting substances.[156] Methyl bromide is a dangerous ozone-depleting chemical that was highlighted in the ER. Both Chile and the United States are committed to phase out methyl bromide production under the Montreal Protocol. Agreed accelerated phase-out schedules required developed States to eliminate production and import by 2005 and developing States by 2015. However, methyl bromide use for pre-shipment and quarantine plays a key role in controlling agricultural pests, and at the time of the trade and investment accord negotiations, was required by sanitary and phytosanitary standards for Chilean grapes, citrus fruits, peaches, nectarines, plums and other fruit, which had to be fumigated for export to the US. More sustainable alternatives to the chemical exist and could be developed, but at the time of the trade negotiations, were more costly. Chile had a longer period for phase-out, and the US-Chile FTA appeared likely to stimulate competition between US and Chilean growers, with US authorities not included in efforts to enforce phase-out

149 Planistat, *Sustainable Impact Assessment (SIA) of the Trade Aspects of Negotiations for an Association Agreement between the European Communities and Chile* (Santiago, 2002) [EU-Chile SIA] 137.

150 Ibid 116.

151 Ibid

152 See C McCrudden 'Using Public Procurement to Achieve Social Outcomes' 28(4) Natural Resources Forum 257; M Shone, 'Social Dimensions of Public Procurement: An ILO Perspective', Presentation at the Second Expert Meeting on Sustainable Public Procurement, Kifissia, Greece, 2003, <http://www.un.org/esa/sustdev/sdissues/consumption/MikeShone.pdf> accessed 16 December 2020.

153 EU-Mercosur SIA (n 40) 138.

154 D Brack, *RIIA Montreal Protocol Study* (London, Earthscan 1996); Montreal Protocol on Substances that Deplete the Ozone Layer (adopted 16 September 1987, entered into force 1 January 1989) 1522 UNTS 3, arts 2 and 4; Basel Convention (n 51) arts 3–6, 8–9; O Yoshida, 'The Montreal Protocol and the International Trade Law Regime of the WTO/GATT' in Osamu Yoshida, *The International Legal Régime for the Protection of the Stratospheric Ozone Layer* (2nd revised edn, Leiden, Brill 2019).

155 Montreal Protocol (n 154).

156 Brack (n 12) 329–330.

regulations, and growers further delaying the switch to the more expensive but sustainable alternatives. Simultaneously, as bilateral trade in agricultural commodities which require pre-treatment and quarantine use of methyl bromide was due to increase under the US-Chile FTA, this would raise total US-Chilean levels.[157] As certain limited production and import of methyl bromide may be permitted under the Protocol after the phase-out date for 'critical uses', exemptions could be sought. The concern raised in the 2001 US-Chile ER process, therefore, was not that the new Free Trade Agreement might require the US to violate its obligations under the Montreal Protocol. Nor was it that the treaty could, in practice, lead the US to surpass its limits. Rather, the concern was that the trade and investment treaty would indirectly encourage competition between the Chilean growers that were permitted to use the ozone-depleting substances and the US growers that were being required to pay for the development of more sustainable but expensive alternatives. This would generate pressure to weaken US laws, undermining efforts to achieve the Montreal Protocol phase-out objectives. And indeed, during the US-Chile trade and investment agreement negotiations, the US Clean Air Act was amended through section 764 of the 1999 Omnibus Consolidated and Emergency Supplemental Appropriations Act to allow the US government to exempt the production and importation of methyl bromide for critical uses, including pre-treatment and quarantine uses. These exemptions were extended each year in the Montreal Protocol, by special request from the US government, which continued seeking to increase the amount of methyl bromide that its producers are permitted to use.[158] Again in this example, the concern involves indirect effects of the treaty that appeared likely to weaken and perhaps even sabotage regulatory efforts to advance multilaterally agreed health and environment priorities in both Parties to the treaty.

Third, as emphasized in the EU-Central America SIA among others, the opportunities opened by new trade regulations, absent cooperation to vitiate this indirect effect, might have severe social impacts for vulnerable groups in natural resources sectors.[159] Indeed, the SIA raised concerns that the EU-Chile AA might exacerbate existing inequalities by weakening enforcement of regulations governing land use for the most vulnerable people.[160] For small farming communities, artisanal fishing communities and forest-based indigenous peoples, already precarious conditions could decline further, as pressure on natural resources leads to lack of respect for existing regulations.[161] For instance, rapid increases in the areas of land being exploited for commercial forestry in areas where land tenure laws are not always evenly enforced could lead to encroachments upon the lands of vulnerable indigenous peoples.[162] Concerns were also raised in the EU-Andean SIA as to the potential social and environmental effects on indigenous peoples of changes in investment laws that

[157] According to the National Commission for the Environment of Chile, the amounts used fluctuate, but had already increased from 393.6 metric tonnes in 1996 to 536.9 in 1998.

[158] Despite commitments to eliminate production and use of the methyl bromide in industrial nations by 2005, the US government submitted a request to further increase US exemptions to 9400 tons at the 16th Conference of Parties to the Montreal Protocol on 29 November 2004 in Prague. See PANNA, 'US Muscles Montreal Protocol on MB Limits' (2004) <http://www.panna.org/legacy/panups/panup_20041210.dv.html> accessed 16 December 2020

[159] ECORYS, *Trade Sustainability Impact Assessment of the Association Agreement to be negotiated between the EU and Central America: Draft Final Report* (Rotterdam, July 2009) [EU-Central America SIA] 75 with regard to pressures of agriculture on lands of indigenous peoples and rural poor; EU-Mercosur SIA (n 40) 29–31 with regard to effects of expansion of the agricultural frontier on indigenous peoples, also feminization of rural poverty.

[160] EU-Chile SIA (n 149) 12.

[161] Ibid.

[162] Ibid

increase mining activities in Ecuador.[163] Further, if industrial activities and mining were to increase demand for energy, and this led to further hydro-electric development that is unable to respect existing human rights laws and imposes forced resettlement, severe social impacts for indigenous peoples could result.[164]

These concerns, which a new trade and investment agreement may not support, and perhaps would even constrain or render more difficult to implement, domestic social and environmental standards and regulations related to trade and investment, are the second normative tension that can be identified in both the scholarly and legal literature, and also across the experiences of actual impact assessments.

6.3 Tension Three: Providing Incentives for Unsustainable Trade and Investment

The third and perhaps most challenging tension that can be identified involves concerns that application of trade rules for liberalization will inadvertently support *unsustainable growth* in obsolete technologies and sectors.[165] Essentially, in spite of State intentions to avoid expansion of these unsustainable sectors, as expressed in other treaties on sustainable development issues, it becomes clear through assessments that a trade and investment agreement may encourage the wrong *kind* of growth. In existing legal and economic literature, one environmental aspect of this problem has been called the 'pollution haven' hypothesis.[166] For sustainable development, this tension relates to situations where a new trade and investment agreement unintentionally encourages unsustainable economic growth in the sensitive zones, obsolete technologies or even entire economic sectors that States are seeking to phase out, often through international agreements. Examples could include economic liberalization agreements that, without offering more sustainable alternatives, offer to expand investment in the exploration and exploitation of fossil fuels,[167] to increase trade and investment flows towards certain hazardous chemicals and other domestically prohibited goods that are being multilaterally phased out,[168] to boost volumes of illegally

[163] EU-Andean SIA (n 1) 81 with regard to extractive industries' conflicts with indigenous peoples, 107–108 with regard to copper mining on lands of indigenous peoples in Mirador and Junin, Ecuador.

[164] Ibid 129.

[165] K Miles, 'International Investment Law and Climate Change: Issues in the Transition to a Low Carbon World', Society of International Economic Law Inaugural Conference, Geneva, 15–17 July 2008, 1–4; see also R Muradian and J Martinez-Alier, 'Trade and the Environment: From a 'Southern' Perspective' (2001) 36 Ecological Economics 281, 284; E von Weizsacker and others, 'Factor Five: Transforming the Global Economy through 80% Improvements in Resource Productivity' (London, Earthscan 2009) 274–275. See generally J Barry and R Eckersley (eds), *The State and Global Ecological Crisis* (Cambridge, MA, MIT Press 2005); P Bartelmus, *Environment, Growth and Development: The Concepts and Strategies of Sustainability* (Florence, KY, Routledge 1994); Chertow and Esty (n 6); MC Cordonier Segger, 'Inspiration for Integration: Interpreting International Trade and Investment Accords for Sustainable Development' (2017) 3 Canada Journal Comparative and Contemporary Law 159.

[166] GS Eskeland and AE Harrison, 'Moving to Greener Pastures? Multinationals and the Pollution Haven Hypothesis' (2003) 70 Journal of Development Economics 1. For a useful review of different perspectives on the pollution haven hypothesis, see MS Taylor, 'Unbundling the Pollution Haven Hypothesis' (2004) 4 Advances in Economic Analysis & Policy 1.

[167] RU Ayres and EH Ayres, *Crossing the Energy Divide: Moving from Fossil Fuel Dependence to a Clean Energy Future* (US, First Printing 2009); TA Boden, G Marland and RJ Andres, *Global, Regional, and National Fossil-Fuel CO_2 Emissions* (Tennessee, Carbon Dioxide Information Analysis Center 2009); United Nations Framework Convention on Climate Change (UNFCCC) (opened for signature 4 June 1992, entered into force 21 March 1994) 1771 UNTS 107.

[168] H Selin, *Global Governance of Hazardous Chemicals: Challenges of Multilevel Management* (Cambridge, MA, MIT Press 2010); O Morgenstern and others, 'The World Avoided by the Montreal Protocol' (2008) 35 Geophysical

harvested timber and ivory,[169] or to lead to a rise in products made with child labour, or services which exploit or traffick children.[170]

In one practical example highlighted in both the EU-Chile SIA and the Interim US-Chile ER, at the time of negotiations, there was growing controversy surrounding the enforcement of regulations and encouragement of trade and investment in the Chilean forest sector, due in part to a lack of adequate legal mechanisms to ensure proper enforcement in Chile.[171] The cutting of three types of trees was prohibited altogether in Chile: alerce, araucaria and cypress of the Guaitecas.[172] One of Chile's existing forestry laws, DFL 701 of 1974, required all native forest landowners to file a forest management plan with the National Forest Corporation (CONAF), a non-profit institution owned by the State, before cutting down any trees. CONAF would have 120 days to accept or reject the plan. Since the passage of the 1994 Environmental Framework Law, the timber industry was also required to complete environmental impact studies when they submitted proposals for large-scale timber operations. However, in 1995, Banco Nacional de Aguas (BNA) reported that the CONAF had an extremely scant annual budget of US$ 2.5 million and only 75 people with 30 vehicles to patrol 14 million hectares of native forest and protect it from illegal cuttings.[173] The concern was that the measures and means of implementation to ensure sustainable development laws related to forestry were inadequate in Chile, and as such, any increases in timber production encouraged by the trade treaty would lead to further violations of the law, and any new laws intended to strengthen protection could be considered measures to restrict foreign investment or to reduce the value of foreign investments, requiring compensation.[174] Given the low level of resources available, these laws or measures would be unlikely to be adopted if they were potentially subject to challenge under the Chile-US FTA's investment provisions, even though they are badly needed. Similarly, the EU-Chile SIA noted that Chilean regulations affecting the forestry sector have difficulties balancing a mandate to both promote economic forestry development and conserve native forests in a National System of State Protected Wild Areas (SNASPE), especially since

Research Letters 1; D Kaniaru (ed), *The Montreal Protocol: Celebrating 20 Years of Environmental Progress* (London, UNEP 2008); Montreal Protocol (n 154); Stockholm Convention on Persistent Organic Pollutants (adopted 22 May 2001, entered into force 17 May 2004) (2001) 40 ILM 532; Basel Convention (n 51); Convention to Ban the Importation in Forum Islands Countries of Hazardous Wastes and Radioactive Wastes and to Control the Transboundary Movement and Management of Hazardous Wastes within the South Pacific Region (adopted 16 September 1995, entered into force 21 October 2001) 2161 UNTS (Waigani Convention).

169 T Gehring, 'When Arguments Prevail Over Power: The CITES Procedure for the Listing of Endangered Species' (2008) 8 Global Environmental Politics 123; MJ Smith and others, 'Assessing the Impacts of International Trade on CITES-Listed Species: Current practices and opportunities for scientific research' (2010) 144 Biological Conservation 82; CITES (n 12); Convention to Ban the Importation in Forum Islands Countries of Hazardous Wastes and Radioactive Wastes and to Control the Transboundary Movement and Management of Hazardous Wastes within the South Pacific Region (adopted 16 September 1995, entered into force 21 October 2001) 2161 UNTS (Waigani Convention).

170 R Bhala, 'Clarifying the Trade-Labor Link' (1998) 37(1) Columbia Journal of Transnational Law 30; S Polaski, 'Protecting Labor Rights through Trade Agreements' (2004) 10 University of California Davis Journal of International Law 13; ILO, *Worst Forms of Child Labour Convention*, 17 June 1999, C182, <http://www.unhcr.org/refworld/docid/3ddb6e0c4.html> accessed 8 November 2011; UN General Assembly, Convention on the Rights of the Child, 20 November 1989, United Nations, Treaty Series, vol 1577, 3, <http://www.unhcr.org/refworld/docid/3ae6b38f0.html> accessed 8 November 2011; BM Araujo, 'Labour Provisions in EU and US Mega-regional Trade Agreements: Rhetoric and Reality (2018) 67 International & Comparative Law Quarterly 233.

171 Interim US-Chile ER (n 49).; EU-Chile SIA (n 147) 91–100.

172 Interim US-Chile ER (n 49).

173 Ibid.

174 Ibid.

the economic success of the industry is closely linked to the extension of industrial plantations.[175] From 1974 onwards, the Chilean government promoted forest plantations through a direct subsidy to producers.[176] In this context, the development of the forestry sector has been distorted by a government policy that gave preference in awarding subsidies to large plantation landowners. A new Law on Native Forests was under discussion since 1995 in Chilean Congress, and was finally passed in August 2007 after perhaps one of the longest revision processes in Chilean legislative history.[177] The amendments provided incentives to protect fragile lands and areas under desertification, and to adopt more sustainable logging practices.[178] Given the limited resources of the Chilean forest authorities, however, a non-discrimination requirement to extend such subsidies to new foreign investors would likely bankrupt the system.

Similar concerns emerged in the SIA of the EU-CARIFORUM EPA, and in the SIA of the EU-Central American AA. In the case of the EU-CARIFORUM SIA, the concern was expressed that social and environmental issues linked to increased transportation linked to the economic agreement could be expected to increase with the volume of goods transported.[179] The means of transport promoted was key, with land transport particularly affecting adjacent populations and habitats.[180] Similarly, in the EU-Central American SIA, the concern was expressed that increased land use for fruits, vegetables and nuts would encourage unsustainable levels of land conversion for agricultural purposes and threats to biodiversity.[181] Specifically, the SIA of this economic agreement anticipated pressure on forested areas due to competing land use for vegetables, fruits and nuts and biofuels.[182] The SIA also noted that if increased forestry activity was not 'flanked by adequate addressing of illegal logging and wood processing, the ultimate impacts of trade liberalisation may be negative for land and water quality, biodiversity and natural resources use'.[183]

Similar examples were found in the US-Andean ER, and in the Canada-Peru-Colombia EA. In the US-Peru ER, the potential increased deforestation was linked to illegal clearing for timber and agricultural production (especially coffee and timber for export), causing a loss of biodiversity, including for instance in species of migratory birds.[184] Similarly, the ER noted concerns regarding loss of biodiversity linked to an increase in foreign investment for natural gas exploitation. The proposed Camisea Natural Gas Pipeline in the Peruvian Amazon was cited as a project that might have significant negative effects if the FTA facilitated a relaxation in rules governing foreign investment.[185] Prior to the Canada-Korea FTA, the concern was expressed that opening for exports in bituminous coal (Canada's top export to Korea) would encourage increased mining activities in Canada, leading to impacts on carbon emissions and sensitive ecosystems, as well as pollution of local water supplies and

175 Ibid.
176 Ibid.
177 See Sara Kerosky, 'Chile's Senate Passes Native Forest Law', *The Santiago Times* (19 August 2007).
178 Ibid.
179 EU-ACP SIA (n 1) 179.
180 Ibid. See also OECD, *Freight and the Environment: Effects of Trade Liberalization and the Transport Sector Reforms* (Paris, 1997).
181 EU-Central America SIA (n 159) 26.
182 Ibid 62.
183 Ibid 62–63.
184 USTR 'Interim Environmental Review United States-Andean Free Trade Agreement' (2005) <http://www.ustr.gov/sites/default/files/perinter.pdf> accessed 16 December 202021–22.
185 Ibid 29–31.

contamination of soils.[186] Similarly, an increase in Canadian exports of measuring equipment and controllers, without increased implementation of environmentally conscious manufacturing, was anticipated to risk a negative impact on the environment through 'the use of hazardous materials, water waste, energy use and airborne pollutants'.[187]

In each of these instances, the key normative tension is that the provisions of the economic agreement, by granting market access, liberalizing constraints and encouraging investment, appeared to encourage an unsustainable industry in its more harmful practices.

The evidence of the experiences with such assessments and the growing body of secondary literature suggests that increases in economic activities from trade and investment flows that are stimulated by liberalization agreements may, absent any mitigating measures, lead to negative material and normative environmental and social consequences.[188] Three key tensions are identified between the economic development aspect of an economic agreement, and potential environmental and social impacts.

The first tension involves situations in which new trade and investment liberalization obligations constrain the adoption of new regulations to meet international commitments on sustainable development. The concern is that application of economic rules, absent appropriate exceptions, may prevent States from regulating effectively to prevent environmental or social harm, leading to unsustainable development. For instance, as noted above, several assessments identified concerns that trade and investment disciplines such as non-discrimination without taking PPMs in account in the determination of like-products or without considering sustainability aspects of whether investors were in like-circumstances, or restricting the use of trade bans and rules to sunset investments, would constrain the adoption of laws and standards to stop natural resources from being depleted, to control the import of unknown living modified organisms, or to phase out chemicals that harm human health. The assessments were also identifying concerns that the liberalization of investment rules would lead regulators to lower standards related to the environment, labour and sustainable development, in order to attract investment.

The second tension involves pre-existing social and environmental challenges that can be indirectly exacerbated by the economic growth due to changes in trade and investment flows occasioned by a new treaty. In these situations, the main problem is often lack of domestic capacity to enact and enforce adequate environmental and social regulations that exist to achieve sustainable development, or lack of human and financial resources to address problems. For instance, as noted above, several impact assessments identified concerns that due to trade and investment liberalization, tariff reductions could increase low-wage employment for women in unsafe conditions where social security laws are not always enforced, increase unsafe disposal of hazardous waste where pollution laws can be weak, or by opening forest areas for increased exploitation, lead to marginalization for indigenous peoples in already precarious situations where property rights and land use planning laws are not universally respected.

The third and most challenging tension involves situations in which economic agreements risk encouraging economic development in sensitive zones, obsolete technologies or

[186] Canada-Korea EA (n 55) 21–22.

[187] Ibid 23.

[188] See, e.g., UNEP and CBD (2003), 'The Impact of Trade Liberalisation on Agricultural Biological Diversity: A Synthesis of Assessment Frameworks', UNEP/CBD/COP/7/INF/15, United Nations, Kuala Lumpur, 1–2; see also Table 1.2.

economic sectors that States have multilaterally agreed to phase out. For instance, as noted above, assessments have signalled concerns about trade and investment agreements that may lead to increased investment and trade in fossil fuels, in illegally logged timber, in agricultural practices that utterly deplete soils, in fisheries that threaten fragile fish stocks and in obsolete chemicals and other goods that threaten health or public safety.

In conclusion, analysis of the outcomes of several decades of assessments, together with scientific and legal literature, demonstrates that absent mitigating measures, new trade and investment agreements may lead to serious material and normative impacts on the environment and on social development. Three key normative tensions in the relationship between trade and investment rules, risk constraining the Parties' efforts and capacities to achieve their sustainable development goals. If it is possible, through wiser, more careful crafting of the treaties themselves, to prevent such impacts from 'falling where they may' onto the fragile ecosystems and vulnerable populations of developing country trading partners, surely this is a just objective for treaty-makers, implementers and interpreters to pursue, in the interest of future generations.

SECTION THREE

INTEGRATION OF ENVIRONMENTAL AND SOCIAL CONSIDERATIONS INTO TRADE AND INVESTMENT AGREEMENTS

7

International Legal Reasons for Countries to Address Environmental and Social Impacts of Trade and Investment Agreements

In earlier chapters, potential environmental and social impacts of trade and investment liberalization agreements have been outlined, and together with scientific and legal literature, the evidence demonstrates that absent mitigating measures, new economic treaties risked causing or contributing to serious material and normative impacts on the environment and on social development. As the particularized examples demonstrated, potential and actual impacts depend on the specifics of each accord, pre-existing economic relationships of the trade and investment partners, the types of industries and sectors that are stimulated by the economic agreement, the effectiveness of existing measures and other diverse factors. However, taken together the body of sustainability impact assessment carried out and commissioned by States over the past two decades do raise concerns about the potential effects of new global trade and investment disciplines, and regional or bilateral economic agreements. Three key normative tensions were identified in terms of the ways that trade and investment law might frustrate the sustainable development goals of countries if nothing was done to avert such outcomes. In the next part of this book, the international policy and 'soft law' reasons that such impacts should not simply be left to 'fall where they may' onto the fragile ecosystems and vulnerable populations of developing country trading partners will be canvassed. First, however, it is important to consider whether there are also international 'hard law' considerations of relevance—both in terms of customary legal principles, and the interpretation of treaty obligations.

This first part considers whether States are legally bound to address the sustainability impacts of trade and investment liberalization—at least to prevent harm, and potentially also to actually integrate environmental and social development considerations in order to strengthen and enhance the contribution of increased trade and investment flows towards achieving countries' global Sustainable Development Goals (SDGs). It discusses customary and interstitial norms, and whether international law requires States to integrate significant environmental and social considerations into economic development plans, including into the negotiations of new trade and investment agreements, taking into account *pacta sunt servanda*—canonist Cardinal Hostiensis' thirteenth-century rule that promises must be kept, which in civil law systems, includes an assumption of good faith. The next chapter then discusses the relevant EU 'integration principle' experiences, and suggests an approach which, taking into account the rules of the Vienna Convention on the Law of Treaties (VCLT) on the interpretation of treaty obligations that appear to violate customary norms, offers options for how States may be addressing the tensions identified above within the texts of their trade and investment treaties, through careful crafting over time. Finally,

Crafting Trade and Investment Accords for Sustainable Development. Marie-Claire Cordonier Segger, Oxford University Press.
 DOI: 10.1093/oso/9780198831341.003.0007

a chapter discusses the policy considerations and 'soft law' rationales which might support considering whether such an approach has global relevance.

7.1 Sustainable Development as an Interstitial Norm

The question of whether there are any legal obligations for States to promote sustainable development through trade and investment is more complex than it appears at first. As noted in the introduction to this book and elsewhere, the legal status of State commitments to sustainable development has been debated in scholarly literature for two decades.[1] Certain States, academics and non-governmental organizations argued that the obligation to develop sustainably is a new and emerging (or even accepted) customary principle of international law, binding upon all but a few persistently objecting States.[2] However, as Professor Gunter Handl bluntly stated in 1990, '[n]ormative uncertainty, coupled with the absence of justiciable standards for review, strongly suggest that there is as yet no international legal obligation that development must be sustainable'[3] and that as such 'decisions on what constitutes sustainability rest primarily with individual governments'.[4] As Professor Vaughan Lowe notes wryly, 'the argument that sustainable development is a norm of customary international law, binding on and directing the conduct of states, and which can be applied by tribunals, is not sustainable'.[5] It is not novel to conclude that States have not yet accepted a customary legal obligation to always develop sustainably.[6] Indeed, a search for evidence of one single agreed customary norm that 'all development must be sustainable' may

[1] P Birnie, A Boyle and C Redgwell, *International Law & the Environment* (Oxford, OUP 2009) 116–118. See also P Sands, 'International Law in the Field of Sustainable Development: Emerging Legal Principles' in W Lang (ed), *Sustainable Development and International Law* (Oxford, OUP 1999); D Ginthers, M Denters and P de Waart (eds), *Sustainable Development and Good Governance* (Dordrecht, Kluwer Academic Publishers 1995); UNCSD, 'Sustainable Development: The Challenge to International Law. Report of a Consultation held at Windsor 27 to 29 April 1993' (1993) 2(4) Review of European Community and International Environmental Law 1; P Sands, 'International Law in the Field of Sustainable Development' (1994) 65 British Yearbook of International Law 303; RE Kim, 'The Nexus between International Law and the Sustainable Development Goals' (2016) 25(1) Review of European Community and International Environmental Law 15; Report of the UN Secretary General, 'Gaps in International Environmental Law and Environment-Related Instruments: Towards a Global Pact for the Environment', 3 December 2018, UN Doc A/73/419 (advance edition).

[2] D Hunter, D Zaelke and J Salzman, *International Environmental Law and Policy* (New York, Foundation Press 2001) 210; A Kiss and D Shelton *International Environmental Law* (2nd edn, New York, Transnational Publishers 1994) 51; P Sands and J Peel, *Principles of International Environmental Law* (4th edn, Cambridge, CUP 2018); W Lang (ed), *Sustainable Development and International Law* (Martinus Nijhoff, London 1995); S Atapattu, *Emerging Principles of International Environmental Law* (Transnational, New York 2006); HC Bugge '1987-2007: "Our Common Future" Revisited' in HC Bugge and C Voigt (eds), *Sustainable Development in International and National Law* (Groingen, Europa 2009) 20. But see A Boyle and D Freestone, *International Law and Sustainable Development* (Oxford OUP 1999) 6; Birnie, Boyle and Redgwell, (n 1) 116–118, 126–127; MC Cordonier Segger, 'Inspiration for Integration: Interpreting International Trade and Investment Accords for Sustainable Development' (2017) 3 Canadian Journal of Comparative and Contemporary Law 159; MC Cordonier Segger with HE Judge CG Weeramantry (eds), *Sustainable Development Principles in the Decisions of International Courts and Tribunals: 1992-2012* (London, Routledge 2017).

[3] See G Handl, 'Environmental Security and Global Change: The Challenge to International Law' (1990) 1 Yearbook of International Environmental Law 25 rejecting the possibility that sustainable development is a peremptory norm of international law; see also G Handl, 'The Legal Mandate of Multilateral Development Banks as Agents for Change towards Sustainable Development' (1998) 92 American Journal of International Law 641.

[4] Boyle and Freestone (n 2) 16.

[5] V Lowe, 'Sustainable Development and Unsustainable Arguments' in Boyle and Freestone (n 2) 30.

[6] Birnie, Boyle and Redgwell (n 1) 125–127. This chapter builds on early work for this volume published in MC Cordonier Segger, Sustainable Development in International Law' in D Armstrong (ed), *Routledge Handbook of International Law* (New York, Routledge 2009) and other fora.

actually be a chase in the wrong direction. As observed by His Excellency, the late Justice CJ Weeramantry in his extraordinary Separate Opinion in the *Gabcikovo-Nagymaros Case*,[7] there is 'wide and general acceptance by the global community' of sustainable development. As has been canvassed elsewhere in academic literature, the concept has become legally relevant, informing tribunals and treaties, particularly in its procedural dimensions.[8] Professor Lowe has further argued that State commitments to sustainable development might engage a certain interstitial normativity, acting 'upon other legal rules and principles – a legal concept exercising a kind of interstitial normativity, pushing and pulling the boundaries of true primary norms when they threaten to overlap or conflict with each other'.[9] As Lowe observes, there is:

> an immense gravitational pull exerted by concepts such as sustainable development, regardless of their standing as rules or principles of *lex lata*. That is plain when they are used by judges as modifiers; but it is also true when they are used in the same way by States as they negotiate (either with other States, or within their own governmental apparatus) on ways of reconciling conflicting principles.[10]

Taking this interstitial character into account, the global commitment to sustainable development might still engender further normative consequences for States' economic development planning, including in their negotiations of trade and investment agreements. As an interstitial norm which can play a role in importing a 'group of congruent norms',[11] the broadly held commitment to promote sustainable development—particularly as reflected in the global Sustainable Development Goals—may 'push or pull' States to use and apply certain international practices *and even other emerging customary principles*, to guide the future development and implementation of treaty regimes. Such further principles *for* sustainable development may be recognized as customary rules, binding on all States that have not persistently objected.[12] From this perspective, it is important to consider which, of such principles, could be most relevant to economic agreements.

[7] *Case Concerning the Gabčíkovo-Nagymaros Project (Hungary/Slovakia)* (Separate Opinion of Vice President Weeramantry) [1997] ICJ 7.

[8] Birnie, Boyle and Redgwell (n 1); E Kentin, 'Sustainable Development in International Investment Dispute Settlement' in N Schrijver and F Weiss (eds), *International Law and Sustainable Development: Principles and Practice* (Martinus Nijhoff, Leiden 2004) 309; MC Cordonier Segger, 'Charles Doherty Gonthier: 1928-2009: Un hommage, A Tribute: Sustainability, Global Justice, and the Law: Contributions of the Hon. Justice Charles Doherty Gonthier' (2010) 55 McGill Law Journal 337. See also MC Cordonier Segger and CG Weeramantry (eds), *Sustainable Development in International Courts and Tribunals* (Abingdon, Routledge 2019).

[9] Lowe (n 5) 31; V Lowe, 'The Politics of Law-Making: Are the Method and Character of Norm Creation Changing?' in M Byers (ed), *The Role of Law in International Politics: Essays in International Relations and International Law* (Oxford, OUP 2000) 214–215.

[10] Lowe (n 5) 35.

[11] Ibid 26.

[12] MC Cordonier Segger and A Khalfan, *Sustainable Development Law: Principles, Practices and Prospects* (Oxford, OUP 2004) 47–50. Widespread adoption of such principles in the 1992 Rio Treaties, might even support a contention that certain principles are already gaining this level of recognition. The practical implications of such recognitions, given the nearly universal membership of these treaties, might be minimal. But it does not discount the value of examining these principles themselves, particularly if they could also be relevant to international economic law and policy.

7.2 Integration as an International Customary Norm of Relevance to Trade, Investment and Sustainable Development

The process of crystallizing principles of international law related to sustainable development has been complex and is not yet complete. The most important undertakings ran parallel to key global policy-making events. In the 1987 Annex on Legal Principles to the Brundtland Report, the World Commission on Environment and Development (WCED) called for the international adoption of legal principles to promote sustainable development. The Commission presented a considered legal analysis, commentary and clear normative proposals for a series of twenty-two legal principles.[13] In article 7, the experts recommended recognition of the principle that the conservation of natural resources and the environment shall be treated as an integral part of the planning and implementation of development activities.[14] The 1992 Rio Declaration echoed many of the Principles recommended by the Brundtland Report, and was followed by the Report of the Expert Group Meeting on Identification of Principles of International Law for Sustainable Development, commissioned by the UN Division for Sustainable Development in accordance with a request of States at the UN Conference on Sustainable Development (UNCSD) Second Session in 1994.[15] This Report identified nineteen principles and concepts of international law for sustainable development in the context of international legal instruments of that time, though it was not exhaustive. In 1997, in light of the recommendations of the Report, States noted in the Programme of Action for Further Implementation of Agenda 21 that: 'While some progress has been made in implementing [UNCED] commitments through a variety of international legal instruments, much remains to be done to embody the Rio principles more firmly in law and practice.'[16]

Building on these processes, in 2002 at its seventieth Conference in New Delhi India, the International Law Association's (ILA's) Committee on the Legal Aspects of Sustainable Development released a Declaration on Principles of International Law relating to Sustainable Development.[17] This Declaration notes that 'sustainable development is now widely accepted as a global objective and that the concept has been amply recognized in various international and national legal instruments, including treaty law and jurisprudence at international and national levels …' and then outlines seven principles of international law on sustainable development.[18] Analysis of the principles highlighted in the New Delhi Declaration can be found elsewhere, documenting both relevance and options for

[13] WCED, *Brundtland Report's Legal Experts Group Recommendations* (1987) 65.

[14] Ibid.

[15] Division for Sustainable Development, 'Report of the Expert Group Meeting on Identification of Principles of International Law for Sustainable Development' (Geneva, 26–28 September 1995), Background Paper for the UNCSD New York, 18 April–3 May 1996.

[16] The UN General Assembly Special Session (GASS) also noted that: 'Progress has been made in incorporating the principles contained in the Rio Declaration on Environment and Development – including the principle of common but differentiated responsibilities, which embodies the important concept of and basis for international partnership; the precautionary principle; the polluter pays principle; and the environmental impact assessment principle – in a variety of international and national legal instruments.' Programme for the Further Implementation of Agenda 21, UNGA Res S-19/2, 19 September 1997, UN Doc A/Res/S-19/2 14.

[17] ILA, *Report of the Expert Group on Identification of Principles of International Law for Sustainable Development* (London, 1995); ILA, *Report of the Sixty-Second Conference* (Seoul, 1987) 1–11, 409–87; N Schrijver and F Weiss, 'Editorial Introduction' (2002) 2 International Environmental Agreements 105.

[18] ILA, *Report of the Expert Group* (n 17).

international legal status.[19] However, among these seven principles identified in the New Delhi Declaration reappears the duty to integrate environmental and social considerations into economic decision-making.[20] This builds on Principle 4 of the Rio Declaration, which states that:

> In order to achieve sustainable development, environmental protection shall constitute an integral part of the development process and cannot be considered in isolation from it.[21]

If one customary international rule *named* a 'sustainable development principle' were to be recognized, Principle 4 of the Rio Declaration seems a likely candidate, given its first five words. However, as the New Delhi Declaration recommends, this norm could also simply be described as the 'integration principle'. The ILA New Delhi Declaration emphasizes recent developments in soft law, such as the need to give equal weight to the social and human rights pillar of sustainable development, essentially advocating an integration principle which requires States to take social and human rights, as well as environmental protection, into account in the development process.[22] Indeed, this integration principle, as argued below, may be considered an emerging customary norm in itself, particularly in key regions of the world.

As noted in the 1903 *Gentini* case, a principle 'expresses a general truth, which guides our action, serves as a theoretical basis for the various acts of our life, and the application of which to reality produces a given consequence'.[23] Further, as argued by Professor Martii Koskenniemi more recently, when 'States enter an agreement, or when some behaviour is understood to turn from habit into custom, the assumption is that something that was loose and disputed crystallizes into something that is fixed and no longer negotiable'.[24] Customary principles, if recognized, can establish obligations for all States except those that have persistently objected to a practice and its legal consequences.[25]

19 Ibid 1–152, 699–706; D French, *International Law and Policy on Sustainable Development* (Manchester, Juris 2005) 20. See also Cordonier Segger and Khalfan (n 12) 95–191; MC Cordonier Segger, 'International Law on Sustainable Development' in Bugge and Voigt (n 2); MC Cordonier Segger, 'Sustainable Development in International Law' in Armstrong (n 6). See also <http:www.cisdl.org> accessed 16 December 2020 for notes on how each principle has been reflected in international treaty law on sustainable development over several decades; Nico Schrijver, 'Advancements in the Principles of International Law on Sustainable Development' in Cordonier Segger and Weeramantry (n 2).

20 MC Cordonier Segger, 'International Law on Sustainable Development' in Bugge and Voigt (n 2).

21 'Rio Declaration on Environment and Development (Annex 2)', Report of the UN Conference on Environment and Development, 13 June 1992, UN Doc A/CONF.151/26 (Vol I) Principle 4.

22 Cordonier Segger and Khalfan (n 12) 102–109. This principle is fast becoming recognized as a rule of customary international law. See United Nations Convention on Biological Diversity (opened for signature 5 June 1992, entered into force 29 December 1993) 1760 UNTS 79, 143, art 6; Cartagena Protocol on Biosafety to the United Nations Convention on Biological Diversity (adopted 29 January 2000, entered into force 11 September 2003) 39 ILM 1027, Preamble, art 2.4–2.5; International Treaty on Plant Genetic Resources for Food and Agriculture of the Food and Agriculture Organization (adopted 3 November 2001, entered into force 31 March 2004), Preamble, art 5.1. See also, e.g., North American Free Trade Agreement (adopted 17 December 1992, entered into force 1 January 1994) Can. T.S. 1994 No 2, 32 ILM 289 (NAFTA) arts 103, 104, 104.1, 1114, 2101. See also S Jodoin, 'The Principle of Integration and Interrelationship in International Sustainable Development Law', in A Usha (ed), *Environmental Law: Principles and Governance* (Hyderabad, India, ICFAI University Press 2008) 83.

23 *Gentini Case* (*Italy v. Venezuela*) (1903) 10 RIAA 551, 556; as cited in B Cheng, *General Principles of Law as Applied by International Courts and Tribunals* (Cambridge CUP, 2006) 24; also cited in Sands and Peel (n 2) 233.

24 M Koskenniemi, 'What is International Law For?' in M Evans (ed), *International Law* (3rd edn, Oxford, OUP 2010) 69.

25 M Shaw, *International Law* (6th edn, Cambridge, CUP 2008) 68–88.

According to article 38(1)(b) of the Statute of the ICJ: 'The Court, whose function is to decide in accordance with international law such disputes as are submitted to it, shall apply ... international custom, as evidence of a general practice accepted as law.'[26] These rules of international custom can be derived from the consistent conduct of States acting in the belief that international law requires them to so act, and jurists, to prove an international customary principle, must show State practice by demonstrating the widespread repetition by States of similar international acts over time.[27] Such acts must be taken by a significant number of States, and not be rejected by too many others with an interest in the matter.[28] The ICJ has stated that: 'it might be that, even without the passage of any considerable period of time, a very widespread and representative participation in the convention might suffice of itself, provided this included States whose interest were specifically affected.'[29] The bar to rapidly transform a broadly practised principle into one accepted as customary law, as set by the ICJ in the *North Sea Continental Shelf* cases, is relatively high:

> an indispensable requirement would be that within the period in question, short though it might be, state practice, including that of states whose interests are specially affected, should have been both extensive and virtually uniform in the sense of the provision invoked; and should moreover have occurred in such a way as to show a general recognition that a rule of law or legal obligation is involved.[30]

The ICJ has also found that it is sufficient that the conduct of States should, in general, be consistent with a customary principle, and that instances of inconsistent conduct have been generally treated as breaches of the rule rather than indications of a new rule having emerged.[31] If a norm has been accepted as a principle of customary international law, the international acts that follow the rule should occur out of sense of legal obligation. As noted by ICJ in the *North Sea Continental Shelf* cases: 'The need for such a belief, i.e. the existence of a subjective element, is implicit in the very notion of the *opinio juris sive necessitates*.'[32] Further, if a norm that is enshrined in a treaty is still followed in the practices of non-Parties, it can, provided that there is *opinio juris*, lead to the evolution of a customary rule which will be applicable between states that are not Party to the treaty and between Parties and non-Parties, even before the treaty has entered into force.[33] However, as was demonstrated in the *Anglo-Norwegian Fisheries Case* at the ICJ, a State can avoid being bound by a customary rule if it persistently objects to that rule.[34]

[26] Article 38(1)(b) of the Statute of the ICJ T.S. 993; (1945) 39 American Journal of International Law Supplement 215; see also Shaw (n 25).

[27] H Thirlway, 'The Sources of International Law' in Evans (n 24) 121–127.

[28] A D'Amato, *The Concept of Custom in International Law* (Cornell University Press, Ithaca 1971); M Akehurst, 'Custom as a Source of International Law' (1974–1975) 47 British Yearbook of International Law 1; MH Mendelson, 'The Formation of Customary International Law' (1999) 272 Recueil des Cours de l'Académie de Droit International 9, 155; ILC, 'Report on the Work of the Seventieth Session', 30 April–1 June and 2 July–10 August 2018, UN Doc A/73/10.

[29] *North Sea Continental Shelf (Federal Republic of Germany v. Denmark; Federal Republic of Germany v. Netherlands)* (Judgement) [1969] ICJ 3.

[30] Ibid 43.

[31] *Case Concerning Military and Paramilitary Activities in and against Nicaragua (Nicaragua v. United States of America)* (Judgement) General List No 70 [1986] ICJ 14 186.

[32] *North Sea Continental Shelf* (n 29) 44.

[33] H Thirlway, 'The Law and Procedure of the International Court of Justice' (1990) 60 British Yearbook of International Law 1, 87.

[34] *Fisheries Case (United Kingdom v. Norway)* (Judgment) General List No 5 [1951] ICJ 131, 138–139.

Before discussing general State practice and *opinio juris*, a further 'precondition' should also be addressed. To prove the existence of a norm of customary law, there is a need to show that State practice and *opinio juris* has been extensive and virtually uniform *in the sense of the provision invoked*. This element relates to the requirement that a principle must have the 'fundamentally norm-creating character such as could be regarded as forming the basis of a general rule'.[35] Several eminent legal scholars have been critical of whether such a precondition is needed at all in the context of treaties and custom.[36] However others, such as Professor Hans Kelsen, have noted that an international legal norm, whether derived from an international treaty or international customary law, should be understood in reference to its function.[37] In international law, as Kelsen explains, most norms have one of four functions. Either they impose an obligation on States to do something, as a command (prescriptive norms); or they impose an obligation on States not to do something, as a prohibition (prohibitive norms).[38] They can also grant a right to a State not to do something, as an exemption (exempting norms), or grant a right to a State to do something, as a permission (permissive norms).[39]

Indeed, if 'integration' were proposed as a principle of customary law, there would need to be some clarity as to what the commitment actually prescribes, prohibits, exempts or permits States to do. Like a prohibition against armed attack, or a permission for each State to control an exclusive economic zone 200 miles from their coast, a commitment to integrate should normatively require or permit States to take (or not take) certain actions. A customary principle should be specific – or at least normative enough to form the basis of a claim against a State.[40]

Could a requirement to 'integrate social and environmental considerations into economic decision-making' be emerging as a customary rule? International courts and tribunals have not been silent on these matters, over the years. Certain guidance can be found in the often-quoted decision of the ICJ in the *Gabcikovo-Nagymaros Case*. In that case, faced with the question as to whether one Party could compel another to continue building a dam in accordance with a treaty, in spite of concerns about the impacts of the project and the damage to their shared Danube River watercourse, the majority stated that:

> Throughout the ages, mankind has, for economic and other reasons, constantly interfered with nature. In the past, this was often done without consideration of the effects upon the environment. Owing to new scientific insights and to a growing awareness of the risks for mankind – for present and future generations – of pursuit of such interventions at an unconsidered and unabated pace, new norms and standards have been developed, set forth in a great number of instruments during the last two decades. Such new norms have to be taken into consideration, and such new standards given proper weight, not only when

[35] Ibid 63.

[36] R Baxter, 'Treaties and Custom' (1970) 129 Recueil des Cours 62 where Professor Baxter argues that the notion of norm-creating rules was redundant: 'if a rule does pass into international law, it is norm-creating ...' See also ME Villiger, *Customary International Law and Treaties* (Leiden, Martinus Nijhoff 1985) 190–202. But see R Jennings, 'What is International Law and How Do We Tell It When We See It?' (1981) 37 Schweizerisches Jahrbuch für Internationales Recht 59–88.

[37] H Kelsen, *Theorie Generale des Normes* (Paris, Presses Universitaires de France 1996) 1.

[38] Ibid.

[39] Ibid.

[40] Lowe (n 5).

> States contemplate new activities but also when continuing with activities begun in the past. This *need to reconcile economic development with protection of the environment* is aptly expressed in the concept of sustainable development. For the purposes of the present case, this means that *the Parties together should look afresh at the effects on the environment* of the operation of the Gabcíkovo power plant. In particular they *must find a satisfactory solution* for the volume of water to be released into the old bed of the Danube and into the side-arms on both sides of the river.[41]

Perhaps only procedural requirements were imposed on the Parties, where they are required to 'look afresh' at the effects.[42] Indeed, it has been argued that the word 'concept' was carefully chosen by the majority to defer recognition of custom.[43] However, it can also be argued that the Court ordered the Parties to integrate environmental protection into their development project by requiring them, after their assessment, to also 'find a satisfactory solution'. From this view, the Court applied a nascent *principle of integration*, a requirement to reconcile economic development with the protection of the environment, addressing the environmental aspects of the project as an integral part of their economic endeavour *in order to achieve an objective*—sustainable development.

A careful reading of the 2005 *Iron Rhine (Belgium v. Netherlands)* Award of the Arbitral Tribunal struck under the auspices of the Permanent Court of Arbitration can lend support to this view.[44] The Tribunal found that there is 'considerable debate as to what ... constitutes "rules" or "principles"; what is "soft law"; and which environmental treaty law or principles have contributed to the development of customary international law'.[45] It further states that: '... [t]he emerging principles, whatever their current status, make reference to conservation, management, notions of prevention and of sustainable development, and protection for future generations ... '.[46] But as the Tribunal then explains:

> Today, both international and EC law require *the integration of appropriate environmental measures in the design and implementation of economic development activities.* Principle 4 of the Rio Declaration on Environment and Development, adopted in 1992 which reflects this trend, provides that '*environmental protection shall constitute an integral part of the development process and cannot be considered in isolation from it.*' Importantly, *these emerging principles now integrate environmental protection into the development process.* Environmental law and the law on development stand not as alternatives but as mutually reinforcing, integral concepts, which require that where development may cause significant harm to the environment there is a duty to prevent, *or at least mitigate*, such harm ...This duty, in the opinion of the Tribunal, has now become a principle of general international law.[47]

41 *Case Concerning the Gabčíkovo-Nagymaros Project* (n 7) 140 (emphasis added).

42 P Sands, 'International Courts and the Concept of Sustainable Development' (1999) 3 Yearbook of United Nations Law 390, 391–394.

43 Lowe (n 5).

44 *In the Arbitration Regarding the Iron Rhine (Ijzeren Rijn) Railway (Belgium v. Netherlands)*, Arbitral Award of 24 May 2005, <http://www.pca-cpa.org/showfile.asp?fil_id=377> accessed 16 December 2020, paras 58–59.

45 Ibid para 58.

46 Ibid.

47 Ibid paras 58–59 (emphasis added).

It may be that the Court only meant that the 'duty to prevent ... such harm' is an accepted principle. But it is equally possible that an emerging principle of integration has been further recognized. As explained by the Tribunal: 'This principle applies not only in autonomous activities but also in activities undertaken in implementation of specific treaties between the Parties.'[48] And as further noted:

> The reactivation of the Iron Rhine railway cannot be viewed in isolation from the environmental protection measures necessitated by the intended use of the railway line. These measures *are to be fully integrated* into the project and its costs.[49]

This suggests that the 'duty to integrate appropriate environmental measures in the design and implementation of economic development activities' as recognized by the Tribunal, could be recognized as a principle of customary law. Such a duty might be weak, but it is normative. It is both corollary *and extension* of the established duty that 'where development may cause significant harm to the environment, there is a duty to prevent, or at least mitigate, such harm'.[50]

This customary principle of integration, as highlighted in the 1972 Stockholm Declaration at Principles 12 and 13, analysed in the 1987 Brundtland Report's Legal Experts Group Recommendations at article 7 on planning and implementation of development activities,[51] and further recognized in Principle 4 of the Rio Declaration, might be characterized as *lex ferenda*, an emerging customary norm.

For economic law, such a principle is relevant to cases where the 'development process' or 'economic decision-making' consists of the negotiation of trade and investment agreements, and also to activities undertaken in implementation of specific economic treaties. While the application of such a customary principle may suggest that this norm is only relevant in a transboundary context, it is important to note that ecological systems are globally and regionally inter-related in complex ways that science and technology have only begun to explore.[52] Finally, the principle surely has its limits. 'Constituting an integral part' is not the same as 'becoming a trump card' or 'receiving a blank cheque'.

Indeed, another case at the ICJ suggests an outer boundary for this integration principle, also linked directly to sustainable development. Positive claims based on a State's 'sovereign right to implement sustainable economic development projects' were used by States in the 2006 *Pulp Mills Case*.[53] The ICJ notes that in pleadings on Provisional Measures in this case, Uruguay maintained that 'the provisional measures sought by Argentina would ... therefore irreparably prejudice Uruguay's sovereign right to implement sustainable economic development projects in its own territory'.[54] Concern for this right appears in the ICJ's reasoning in its initial Order with Regards to Provisional Measures, where the Court found that:

[48] *Iron Rhine* (n 44) 58–59 (emphasis added).
[49] Ibid 223 (emphasis added).
[50] Birnie, Boyle and Redgwell (n 1) 137–152; Sands and Peel (n 2) 241–246.
[51] Stockholm Declaration, UN Conference on the Human Environment, 16 June 1972, UN Doc A/Conf 48/14/Rev.1, (1972) 11 ILM 1461 12, 13; *Brundtland Report's Legal Experts Group Recommendations* (n 13) 65.
[52] TEEB, *The Economics of Ecosystems and Biodiversity: Mainstreaming the Economics of Nature: A Synthesis of the Approach, Conclusions and Recommendations of TEEB* (2010).
[53] *Case Concerning Pulp Mills on the River Uruguay (Argentina v. Uruguay), Provisional Measures*, Order of 13 July 2006 [2006] ICJ Rep 133.
[54] Ibid.

> … the present case highlights the importance of *the need to ensure environmental protection of shared natural resources while allowing for sustainable economic development* … it is in particular necessary to bear in mind the reliance of the Parties on the quality of the water of the River Uruguay for their livelihood and economic development … from this point of view account must be taken of the need to safeguard *the continued conservation of the river environment and the rights of economic development* of the riparian States …[55]

In the ICJ's final judgment on the Uruguay *Pulp Mills Case*, this perspective is reinforced:

> … Regarding Article 27, it is the view of the Court that its formulation reflects not only the need to reconcile the varied interests of riparian States in a transboundary context and in particular in the use of a shared natural resource, but also *the need to strike a balance between the use of the waters and the protection of the river consistent with the objective of sustainable development* … The Court wishes to add that such utilization could not be considered to be equitable and reasonable if the interests of the other riparian State in the shared resource and the environmental protection of the latter were not taken into account. Consequently, it is the opinion of the Court that Article 27 embodies this *interconnectedness between equitable and reasonable utilization of a shared resource and the balance between economic development and environmental protection that is the essence of sustainable development.*[56]

Principle 21 of the 1972 Stockholm Declaration, which was re-affirmed in Principle 2 of the Rio Declaration, recognizes that:

> States have, in accordance with the Charter of the United Nations and the principles of international law, the sovereign right to exploit their own resources pursuant to their own environmental and developmental policies, and the responsibility to ensure that activities within their jurisdiction or control do not cause damage to the environment of other States or of areas beyond the limits of national jurisdiction.

As noted by Professor Nicolas Schrijver and others, this principle of sovereignty over natural resources is well recognized in international law.[57] Indeed, a right to sustainable use of natural resources, held by indigenous peoples against their own countries, and by States against other States, appears to be gaining further recognition in, for instance, recent decisions of regional human rights tribunals.[58] This right to sustainable development, based

[55] Ibid 80 (emphasis added).

[56] Ibid 177–178 (emphasis added).

[57] 'Permanent Sovereignty over Natural Resources of Developing Countries', 18 December 1972, UN Doc A/Res/3016 (XXVII) 1. See N Schrijver, *Sovereignty over Natural Resources: Balancing Rights and Duties* (Cambridge, CUP 1997). See also *Case Concerning East Timor (Portugal v. Australia)* (Judgment, Dissenting Opinion of Judge Weeramantry) General List No 84 [1995] ICJ Rep 90, 197–200; *Case Concerning the Fisheries Jurisdiction (United Kingdom of Great Britain and Northern Ireland v. Iceland)* (Merits, Dissenting Opinion of Judge Petrel) General List No 55 [1974] ICJ Rep 3, 161; *Case Concerning the Barcelona Traction, Light and Power Company, Limited (New Application: 1962) (Belgium v. Spain)* (Second Phase, Separate Opinion of Judge Jessup) General List No 50 [1970] ICJ Rep 3, 165–167; S van Wyk, *The Impact of Climate Change Law on the Principle of State Sovereignty Over Natural Resources* (Nomos, Verlag 2017). See International Law Association (2020)., Sustainable Development and The Green Economy in International Trade Law

[58] See Inter-American Court of Human Rights, *Case of the Sawhoyamaxa Community (Paraguay)* (2006) 137–141; Inter-American Court of Human Rights, *Case of the Saramaka Peoples (Suriname)* (2007) 93–95, 122, 129–132; African Commission on Human and Peoples' Rights, *Case of the Social and Economic Rights Action Center*

on the principle of sovereignty and the duty to prevent activities within their control from causing damage outside their jurisdiction, provides the outer boundaries of the integration principle. It engages part of the social development dimension of sustainable development, which is of great importance to developing countries, as noted in the 2002 Johannesburg Plan of Implementation (JPOI) and the 2015 SDGs.

This emerging customary 'integration' principle does not provide a panacea in the process of treaty-making.[59] States can decide to deviate from customary norms in their treaties, in accordance with the maxim *pacta sunct servanda*, in all but a few instances.[60] It remains disputed, in international law, whether the emergence of a new customary rule would lead to the revision of an earlier treaty that contradicts the norm.[61] But under the VCLT, a customary norm of integration is relevant for the *interpretation* of international economic treaties by tribunals and dispute settlement bodies,[62] or as is more common in this field, by a sustainable development regulator seeking to understand the limits of their discretion. According to article 31(3)(c) of the VCLT, a treaty shall be interpreted in good faith, in accordance with the ordinary meaning to be given to its terms in their context, and in the light of its object and purpose, and there shall be taken into account, together with the context, 'any relevant rules of international law applicable in the relations between the Parties'.[63]

and the Center for Economic and Social Rights v. Nigeria (2002) 96 American Journal of International Law 937, 47 Journal of African Law 126 52.

59 Birnie, Boyle and Redgwell (n 1) 118; See Agenda 21, Annex 2 Report of the UN Conference on Environment and Development, 13 June 1992, UN Doc A/CONF.151/26 (Vol I) Ch 39; French (n 19).

60 For instance, a treaty that deviates from *jus cogens* preremptory norms is invalid. See H Thirlway, 'The Structure of International Legal Obligation' in Evans (n 24) 137–138; T Hillier, *Sourcebook on Public International Law* (London, Cavendish Publishing 1998) 74. See also *Anglo-Norwegian Fisheries case* [1951] ICJ Rep.

61 Hillier (n 60) 65: 'Customary Law and Treaty have equal authority. However, if there is a conflict between the two it is the treaty that prevails.' See also *Wimbledon Case* [1923] PCIJ Rep, Ser A, No 1.

62 J Pauwelyn, *Conflicts of Norms in Public International Law: How WTO Law Relates to Other Rules of International Law* (Cambridge, CUP 2003) 137–143. But see N Kontou, *The Termination and Revision of Treaties in the Light of New Customary Law* (Oxford, OUP 1994) 145–147.

63 Vienna Convention on the Law of Treaties (signed 23 May 1969, entered into force 27 January 1980) 1155 UNTS 331, art 31(3)(c). See Pauwelyn (n 62) 241; J-M Grossen, *Les Presomptions en Droit International Public* (Neuchatel, 1954), 114–117; 115–117 where it is argued that customary norms are included among relevant rules of international law applicable in the relations between the Parties. See also I Sinclair, *The Vienna Convention on the Law of Treaties* (Manchester, Manchester University Press 1984) 119 who suggests that art 32(3)(c) may be taken to include not only the general rules of international law but also treaty obligations existing for the Parties, as followed in *Al-Adsani v. United Kingdom* (App no 35763/97) (2001) 123 ILR 24, 55. And see P Sands, 'Treaty, Custom and Cross-Fertilization of International Law' (1998) 10 Yale Human Rights and Development Law Journal 3, 11–12, who notes that while these norms are relevant, the treaty being interpreted retains a primary role and 'there is no question of a customary norm displacing the treaty norm, either partly or wholly'. See further D French, 'Treaty Interpretation and the Incorporation of Extraneous Legal Rules' (2006) 55 International & Comparative Law Quarterly 281; R Gardiner, *Treaty Interpretation* (2nd edn, Oxford, OUP 2015) 332–334: 'That article 31(3)(c) may have a useful role in handling such potential conflicts has been considered in academic study, in the work of the ILC and in some instances ... invoked in ... rulings of courts and tribunals ... A particular issue in the realm of treaty implementation is what account is to be taken of developments in international law, particularly the striking emergence of new specialist fields such as environmental law and human rights law ... the Court did give a clear indication that developments in environmental law were to be taken into account, and did so quite clearly in a context of treaty interpretation'; *Case concerning the Gabcikovo-Nagymaros Project* (n 7) 140; *Advisory Opinion on Legal Consequences for States of the Continued Presence of South Africa in Namibia (South West Africa), notwithstanding Security Council Resolution 276* (1970) [1971] ICJ Rep 16, 31, para 53 'an international instruments has to be interpreted and applied within the framework of the entire legal system prevailing at the time of the interpretation'; *Iron Rhine* (n 44) 58 'an evolutive interpretation, which would ensure an application of the treaty that would be effective in terms of its object and purpose will be preferred to a strict application of the intertemporal rule'. See too ILC Fifty-Eighth Session, 'Report of the Study Group on Fragmentation of International Law: Difficulties arising from the Diversification and Expansion of International Law' finalized by M Koskenniemi, 13 April 2006 A/CN.4/L.682 206-44; ILC Further Report, 18 July 2006 A/CN.4/L.702; ILC Report on its Fifty-Eighth Session (2006) UNGA OR 61 SS 10 (A/61/10) 400-423.

While the integration rule may not trump a clear obligation 'not to integrate', the regulator or treaty interpreter may, for instance, appeal to this rule in order to interpret obligations that cause the tensions discussed above in the survey of assessment findings and concerns.

In the light of this legal analysis, further policy rationales and also the experiences of the European Union with this integration principle are worthy of examination. The next chapters briefly review, in the context of extensive literature, how the integration principle has been applied by the EU in its trade, investment and economic decision-making in accordance with the EU's agreed sustainable development objective, and whether there are important additional policy and 'soft law' rationales for addressing social and environmental concerns in trade and investment treaties internationally.

8

Integration as a Principle of European Law, and its Relevance to the Negotiation of Trade and Investment Agreements

The European Union (EU) is one of the main trading partners in many impact assessments and economic agreements with developing countries and regionally, and the European approach to integration is instructive.[1] The European experience offers elements of a response to the key tensions identified earlier in this volume.

Sustainable development is recognized as an objective of the EU.[2] A principle of 'integration' is enshrined in article 6 of the Treaty Establishing a European Community (EC Treaty) (now reflected in article 11 of the Treaty on the Functioning of the European Union (the Lisbon Treaty)), which states that:

> environmental protection requirements must be integrated into the definition and implementation of the Community policies and activities referred to in Article 3 EC, in particular with a view to promoting sustainable development.[3]

At the European level, it is a recognized principle that environmental considerations must be integrated into Community policies and activities, including those that concern economic decisions such as those relating to trade, investment and development. While a full discussion of European legal intricacies is not necessary for this volume, it can be noted that the 'integration principle' is not new to Europe. Originally reflected in former article 130r(2) of the EU Treaty, the principle of integration has, as Professor Marc Pallemaerts argued, been 'given far greater prominence and a clear finality by virtue of being directly linked to the promotion of sustainable development'.[4] In Europe, 'environmental integration is the

[1] M Pallemaerts, M Herodes and C Adelle, 'Does the EU Sustainable Development Strategy contribute to Environmental Policy Integration', EPIGOV Paper No 9, Ecologic-Institute for International and European Environmental Policy, Berlin (2007), 'Experimentalist Environmental Governance in the EU: Complex Challenges, Recursive Policy-Making, International Implications', Berlin Conference on the Human Dimensions of Global Environmental Change, 22–23 February 2006, Berlin, Germany.

[2] The Treaty of the European Union, as amended by the Treaty of Amsterdam, recognizes ' … the following objectives: … to achieve balanced and sustainable development'. Article 2 further mandates the Community to, *inter alia*, 'promote a harmonious, balance and sustainable development of economic activities'. See M Pallemaerts, 'The EU and Sustainable Development: An Ambiguous Relationship' in M Pallemaerts and A Azmanova (eds), *The European Union and Sustainable Development: Internal and External Dimensions* (Brussels, VUB Press 2006) 24; Presidency Conclusions, Rhodes European Council, 2–3 December 1988, Annex 1, para 1: 'Sustainable development must be one of the overriding objectives of all Community policies.'

[3] Consolidated Version of the Treaty establishing the European Community [2002] OJ C 325/01 (EC Treaty), art 6; see also Consolidated Version of the Treaty on the Functioning of the European Union [2012] OJ C 306/49 (Lisbon Treaty), art 11.

[4] M Pallemaerts, *The European Union and Sustainable Development: Internal and External Dimensions* (Brussels, IES 2006) 25.

Crafting Trade and Investment Accords for Sustainable Development. Marie-Claire Cordonier Segger, Oxford University Press. © Marie-Claire Cordonier Segger 2021. DOI: 10.1093/oso/9780198831341.003.0008

main means of promoting sustainable development …'[5] As the European Commission (EC) originally noted:

> Most of our environmental problems have their origins in current practices in sectors such as agriculture, transport, energy and industry and we must look to these areas for their solution … A credible response to the legal obligation of the Treaty requires that the Community equips itself with the necessary tools. Adherence to the integration requirement is in principle subject to judicial control by the European Court of Justice …'[6]

Further, the EU has undertaken this integration in EU external relations, including for new economic agreements, giving weight to the social dimension. In the EC Strategy for Integrating Environment into EU Policies,[7] the Commission notes ' … the importance of the integration principle in the Treaty', further stating:

> The real challenge facing the Community is to find a way of developing action which meets all of its objectives in an integrated way. This is the challenge of sustainable development, a concept too often perceived as purely environmental, but which brings together concerns for social and economic development alongside protection of the environment.[8]

The Lisbon Treaty (formerly known as article 3 of the EC Treaty) lists many areas of competence for the European Community, including commercial policy.[9] To secure integration in these areas, the 'Cardiff Process'[10] involved designing new sustainable development strategies intended to 'mainstream' environmental considerations into different sectors of the European economy such as fisheries,[11] energy,[12] and transportation.[13] An early EC Communication on integration highlighted the need to 'develop strategies in respect

[5] Ibid.

[6] Commission Communication, 'Partnership for Integration: A Strategy for Integrating Environment into EU Policies' COM(98) 333 final.

[7] Ibid.

[8] Communication from the Commission to the European Council of 27 May 1998, '*A* Partnership For Integration: A Strategy for Integrating *the* Environment into EU Policies' (Cardiff—June 1998) (COM(98) 333—not published in the Official Journal) (emphasis added).

[9] In art 3 of the EC Treaty, this includes '(b) a common commercial policy; (r) a policy in the sphere of development cooperation; (s) the association of the overseas countries and territories in order to increase trade and promote jointly economic and social development;… ' In Article 177, the Community's policy on the development cooperation objective is 'to foster the sustainable economic and social development of the developing countries'.

[10] Commission Working Document, 'From Cardiff to Helsinki and beyond: Report to the European Council on integrating environmental concerns and sustainable development into Community policies' SEC(1999) 1942, 24 November 1999; Commission Communication, 'Integrating Environmental Considerations into other Policy Areas-a Stocktaking of the Cardiff Process' COM(2004) 394 final.

[11] 'Elements of a Strategy for the Integration of Environmental Protection Requirements into the Common Fisheries Policy' COM(2001) 143. See K Van den Bossche and N van der Burgt, 'Integrating Environmental Concerns into the European Common Fisheries Policy' in M Pallemaerts and A Azmanova (eds), *The European Union and Sustainable Development: Internal and External Dimensions* (Brussels, VUB Press 2006) 237. See also C Coffey, *Integrating Environment into the Common Fisheries Policy* (London Institute for European Environmental Policy 2000) 5.

[12] Council Resolution, Strategy for Integrating Environmental Aspects and Sustainable Development into Energy Policy 30 April 2001; Commission Communication, 'Strengthening Environmental Integration within Community Energy Policy (Brussels— October 1998) COM(98) 571 '; A Hadfield, 'The Role of Energy Policy in Sustainable Development: Greening the Environment and Security Energy Supply' in M Pallemaerts and A Azmanova (eds), *The European Union and Sustainable Development: Internal and External Dimensions* (Brussels, VUB Press 2006) 217.

[13] Commission Staff Working Paper, 'Integrating Environment and Sustainable Development into Energy and Transport Policies: Review Report 2011 and Implementation of Strategies' SEC(2001) 502, Brussels.

of . . . development and trade policies' as an 'area which should be given early attention'.[14] As such, by 1999 the Commission recognized a direct link between the integration principle, the objective of sustainable development for international economic agreements, especially the system of international trade law, and the use of sustainability assessments as a tool to achieve this integration. The Commission particularly highlighted the challenges faced by developing countries in the trade liberalization context.[15]

In 2000, a strategy was proposed for integrating environmental issues with economic policy,[16] and the Commission began conducting impact assessments.[17] In the EU, in accordance with the Directive on Environmental Impact Assessment, it may be required to conduct such assessments for the elaboration of Community policies and plans, as treaty negotiation instruments represent plans that could affect the environment.[18] The principle of integration has been interpreted by the European Court of Justice (ECJ) in scoping Members legal obligations to undertake impact assessment.[19] In the 2010 *Wallonia* cases the Advocate General of the ECJ noted that:

> the environmental assessment of legislative measures . . . requires the contracting parties to endeavour to ensure that environmental, including health, concerns are *considered and integrated* to the extent appropriate in the preparation of their proposals for policies and legislation that are likely to have significant effects on the environment, including health. The aim in this context is . . . *to integrate the environment into the considerations in some form or other . . .*[20]

As noted by the Court in *Wallonia*, 'Significant effects on the environment can therefore be taken fully into account only if they are assessed in the case of all preparatory measures which may result in projects subsequently implemented having such effects'.[21]

Beyond the Cardiff Process, the EC interpretation of this integration principle has evolved over the past decade. This can be traced through various strategies, communications of the EC, decisions of the European Council, as well as binding directives and regulations, each with a place in European law and policy.[22]

14 Commission Communication, 'Partnership for Integration: A Strategy for Integrating Environment into EU Policies' COM(98) 333 final.

15 Commission Working Paper, 'Mainstreaming of Environmental Policy', submitted to the Cologne European Council SEC(1999) 777.

16 Commission Communication, 'Bringing Our Needs and Responsibilities Together-Integrating Environmental Issues with Economic Policy' COM(2000) 576, 20.

17 Directive 2001/42/EC of the European Parliament and of the Council of 27 June 2001, art 1. See also European Commission, *Handbook for Trade Sustainability Impact Assessment* (Brussels 2006).

18 Directive 2001/42/EC of the European Parliament and of the Council of 27 June 2001 on the Assessment of the Effects of Certain Plans and Programmes on the Environment [2001] OJ L 197, 30, arts 2(a), 3(1) to (5).The instructions to negotiate EU trade treaties are (1) subject to preparation by an authority at the regional level, and (2) required by administrative provisions once European negotiating instructions have been issued. They are also likely to have significant environmental effects, as discussed in Chapter 2.

19 Directive 91/414/EEC Case T 229/04 *Sweden v. Commission of the European Communities* [2007] ECR II-02437.

20 Opinion of Advocate General Kokott delivered on 4 March 2010, *Terre Wallonne ASBL (C-105/09) and Inter-Environnement Wallonie ASBL (C-110/09) v. Région wallonne* [2010] ECR I-05611 [ECJ *Wallonia* Case]; Council Decision 2008/871/EC of 20 October 2008 on the approval, on behalf of the European Community, of the Protocol on Strategic Environmental Assessment to the 1991 UN/ECE Espoo Convention on Environmental Impact Assessment in a Transboundary Context [2008] OJ L 308, 33) (emphasis added).

21 ECJ *Wallonia* Case (n 20) 35.

22 G de Burca, 'The Constitutional Challenge of New Governance in the European Union', University College London: Current Legal Problems Series, November 2002.

First, integration covers environmental, social and economic effects, and is clearly linked to sustainable development. In the launch of the 2001 Sustainable Development Strategy for Europe (SDS),[23] the operational aspects of integration were highlighted and the Council was asked 'to finalise and further develop sector strategies for integrating environment into all relevant Community policy areas . . .'[24] However, the principle of integration was extended in the final approved SDS, with recognition that it is 'based on the principle that the economic, social and environmental effects of all policies should be examined in a coordinated way and taken into account in decision-making'.[25] The Commission recommended that 'careful assessment of the full effects of a policy proposal must include estimates of its economic, environmental and social impacts inside and outside the EU'.[26] The final SDS calls for mechanisms in the Commission's action plan for better regulation, which is mainly internal, 'to ensure that all major policy proposals include a sustainability impact assessment covering their potential economic, social and environmental consequences'.[27] However, one year later in 2002, the EU also adopted a Global Partnership for Sustainable Development Strategy, with a prominent call to take environmental sustainability *systematically into account* when economic and social policies were being agreed in external relations:

> Sustainable long-term economic development is compatible with environmental sustainability. To ensure this, environmental sustainability needs to be taken systematically into account in formulating economic and social policies.[28]

The Strategy further highlights that some EC development cooperation policies 'already have a fully integrated approach to sustainable development . . . In many cases, however, environmental considerations could be analysed more systematically.'[29]

SIAs were identified by the EU as a procedural way to implement the integration principle in trade law and policy.[30] Indeed, in the EC's 2002 Communication on Impact Assessment,[31] it was made clear that impact assessments would be required for negotiating guidelines for international agreements that have an economic, social or environmental impact.[32] The Commission sought to base its decisions on sound analysis of potential impacts,

[23] See Presidency Conclusions—Göteborg, 15 and 16 June 2001 SN 200/1/01 REV 1. See also Commission Communication, 'A Sustainable Europe for a Better World: A European Union Strategy for Sustainable Development' COM(2001) 264 final.

[24] See Presidency Conclusions—Göteborg (n 23) 32.

[25] Ibid 22.

[26] See Commission Communication, 'A Sustainable Europe' (n 23) 6, noting that: 'The Commission will submit an action plan to improve regulation to the Laeken European Council in December. This will include mechanisms to ensure that all major legislative proposals include an assessment of the potential economic, environmental and social benefits and costs of action or lack of action, both inside and outside the EU. The Council and Parliament should amend legislative proposals in the same spirit.'

[27] See Presidency Conclusions—Göteborg (n 23) 24.

[28] Commission Communication, 'Integrating environment and sustainable development into economic and development co-operation policy—Elements of a comprehensive strategy' COM(2000) 264 final.

[29] Ibid.

[30] Regulation (EC) No 2493/2000 of the European Parliament and of the Council of 7 November 2000 on measures to promote the full integration of the environmental dimension in the development process of developing countries, [2000] OJ L 288; Commission Communication, 'Towards a global partnership for sustainable development' COM(2002) 82 final; Commission Communication, 'Integrating environment and sustainable development' (n 28).

[31] Commission Communication, 'On Impact Assessment' COM(2002) 276 final.

[32] See Commission Communication, SEC(2001) 1197 for a definition of such measures. See also Better Regulation Action Plan, COM (2002)278.

and a balanced appraisal of available policy instruments.[33] The Commission argued that by doing this, it was 'delivering on its Göteborg commitments to implement sustainable development and to establish a tool for sustainable impact assessment'.[34]

This sustainability impact assessment policy dovetailed with the EC's Framework for the External Dimension of Sustainable Development,[35] with respect to the world economy,[36] which reports:

> Developing countries can be integrated into the world economy through trade and regional economic integration ... negotiations in this area should take full account of the needs of developing countries and of the objective of sustainable development ... the EC has initiated an environment and sustainability review of the [World Trade Organization (WTO) Millennium Round] ...'[37]

In this Framework, several practical measures are underlined as tools for integration to achieve sustainable development. Europe's Generalized System of Preferences (GSP), which allows for additional preferential treatment for countries that respect minimum social and environmental standards, is mentioned with approval.[38] The Communication on public procurement, which integrates a chapter on the environment and on social issues, is highlighted.[39] And Protocol 10 to the Lomé IV Convention is emphasized as the first formal international agreement acknowledging the need for forest-certification systems for trade in tropical wood, based on internationally harmonized criteria and indicators.[40] As the Strategy notes:

> To be conducive to sustainable development, the regulatory framework should preserve the ability of host countries to regulate transparently and in a non-discriminatory way, the activity of the investors, foreign and domestic alike, on their respective territory and to pursue a stable business climate. This is particularly important to developing countries. In this respect, traditional provisions on special and differential treatment, such as exemptions and exceptions, or longer transitional periods, for developing countries may no longer suffice. Rather, the environment and sustainable development should be built into the regulations so that they can be implemented and applied by all countries.[41]

This policy direction was strengthened after the 2002 World Summit on Sustainable Development (WSSD). In the 2006 Renewed Sustainable Development Strategy (RSDS), the Council recognized 'the principle that sustainable development is to be integrated into policy-making at all levels'.[42] In this RSDS, the EU further commits to 'promote sustainable

33 Commission Communication, 'Impact Assessment' (n 31).

34 ibid

35 See also C Bretherton and J Vogler, *The European Union as a Global Actor* (London, Routledge 1999) 83.

36 Article 177 of the EC Treaty specifies that the EC development cooperation policy shall foster 'the smooth and gradual integration of developing countries into the world economy'.

37 Commission Communication, 'Integrating environment and sustainable development' (n 28).

38 Regulations (EC) Nos 3281/94 and 1256/96 and Commission Communication, 'Special incentive arrangements concerning labour rights and environmental protection' COM(97) 534/4.

39 Commission Communication, 'Public Procurement in the European Union' COM(98)143final.

40 Agreement Amending the Fourth ACP-EC Convention of Lomé (Signed 4 November 1995) ACP-CE 2163/95, Protocol 10.

41 Commission Communication, 'Integrating environment and sustainable development' (n 28).

42 EU RSDS as adopted by the European Council on 15/16 June 2006, 10.

development in the context of the WTO negotiations'.[43] And the Council further mandated that:

> ... all EU institutions should ensure that major policy decisions are based on proposals that have undergone high quality Impact Assessment (IA), assessing in a balanced way the social, environmental and economic dimensions of sustainable development and taking into account the external dimension of sustainable development and the costs of inaction.[44]

EU law and policy has continued to develop in this direction. The Council in December 2009 further confirmed that '[s]ustainable development remains a fundamental objective of the European Union under the Lisbon Treaty'. In its 2009 Review of the RSDS, the Presidency also re-affirmed that the SDS will 'continue to provide a longterm vision and constitute the overarching policy framework for all Union policies and strategies'. A related report highlights that: 'The EU has also made progress in mainstreaming the SDS agenda into its external policies, for example through Sustainability Impact Assessments carried out in the context of the preparation of Free Trade Agreements ...' In the EU's 2009 regulation on its generalized system of preferences at article 2, an exception is granted to guarantee special market access for goods and services from developing countries which demonstrate 'sustainable development and good governance'.[45] Article 8 defines this commitment to sustainable development as, *inter alia*, having 'ratified and effectively implemented all the conventions listed in Annex III', having provided 'an undertaking to maintain the ratification of the conventions and their implementing legislation and measures',[46] and accepting 'regular monitoring and review of its implementation record in accordance with the implementation provisions of the conventions it has ratified'.[47]

Certain lessons can be drawn from the experience of European law and policy in using the integration principle links between sustainable development and international economic law and policies. It is clear that sustainable development is a confirmed treaty objective of the EU. To achieve this objective, it is a well-recognized principle of European Law that environmental protection requirements must be integrated into the definition and implementation of the Union's policies and activities, in particular with a view to promoting sustainable development. This principle was enshrined in article 6 of the EC Treaty, and is now found in article 11 of the Lisbon Treaty, and has been given effect through many EU measures and regulations.[48] In the European context, the normative function of the principle, and how it operates, does not actually seem so impossible.

The principle is applied in process and substance to the external relations of the EU, and is relevant to the interpretation of the EU's economic policy and trade or investment agreements. At first, the EU was only required to integrate environmental considerations into

43 Ibid.

44 Ibid 11.

45 Council Regulation (EC) No 732/2008 of 22 July 2008 applying a scheme of generalised tariff preferences for the period from 1 January 2009 to 31 December 2011 and amending Regulations (EC) No 552/97, (EC) No 1933/2006 and Commission Regulations (EC) No 1100/2006 and (EC) No 964/2007 [2008] OJ L 211, The actual effect of this provision is limited, due to most countries already being tariff free under the terms of the Lomé Convention.

46 Ibid.

47 Ibid.

48 EC Treaty (n 3); Lisbon Treaty (n 3); Pallemaerts, Herodes and Adelle (n 1).

its policies and actions, and this remains the focus of the Treaty provisions themselves. However, in practice over the past decade since the 2002 WSSD shaped the external dimensions of their SDS, the EU has increasingly emphasized that both environmental *and social* considerations must be identified and taken into account. This point has been re-affirmed in 2002, 2006, 2007 and 2009, by both the Commission and Council, in numerous strategies, communications and even regulations.[49] Furthermore, the EU SDS and other related policies identify sustainability impact assessment as a main procedural instrument for integration. Such sustainability impact assessments are required for all international negotiations that might have economic, environmental or social impacts, such as new trade or investment liberalization agreements. The measures in the EU's economic agreements may be interpreted in light of their commitment to integrate social and environmental dimensions into trade. The EU has sought exceptions and exemptions from trade and investment rules to provide regulatory flexibility and accommodate environment and social development interests. Recently, the EU is going further, committing through cooperation and trade incentives such as the GSP to promote improved environment and social standards for trading partners,[50] and even negotiating new instruments to enhance trade and investment in more sustainable goods and services.[51] Taken as a whole, these developments appear encouraging.

However, in light of the key tensions discussed in Section 2, it must be noted that current EU policies stop short of *requiring* the EC to actually mitigate the negative environmental impacts identified in sustainability impact assessments, a position that appears less than fully respectful of the integration principle laid out in global policy debates, and in the *Iron Rhine* decision. The sustainability impact assessment process must identify potential impacts, and the EC is obliged to report on what will be done in a position paper. But in the way that article 11 of the Lisbon Treaty has been interpreted, the EU does not, at present, *require* substantive measures be taken to ensure that negative environmental and social impacts are actually mitigated, or even significantly reduced. As noted in the EU communication on impact assessment: 'Impact Assessment is an aid to decision-making, not a substitute for political judgment.'[52] At present, '[a]n impact assessment will not necessarily generate clearcut conclusions or recommendations. It does, however, provide an important input by informing decision-makers of the consequences of policy choices.'[53] As such, it seems that the EU is bound to conduct an *ex-ante* assessment of a new trade agreement, examining both impacts in Europe and in the trading partner, and also to explain what measures are being taken to address environmental and social challenges that have been identified in the

49 Current Sustainable Development Strategy (2006): European Council DOC 10917/06; Commission Communication, 'Review of the EU Sustainable Development Strategy' COM(2009) 400; Commission Communication, 'On the Review of the Sustainable Development Strategy-A Platform for Action' COM(2005) 658 final; Commission Communication, 'Draft Declaration on Guiding Principles for Sustainable Development' COM(2005) 218 final; Commission Communication, 'The 2005 Review of the EU Sustainable Development Strategy: Initial Stocktaking and Future Orientations' COM(2005) 37.

50 EC Regulations No 3281/94 and 1256/96 and Commission Communication COM(97) 534/4 (n 31).

51 Agreement Amending the Fourth ACP-EC Convention of Lomé (n 40) Protocol 10; see also European Commission, *Trade, Growth and World Affairs: Trade Policy as a Core Component of EUs 2020 Strategy*, November 2010, <https://eur-lex.europa.eu/LexUriServ/LexUriServ.do?uri=COM:2010:0612:FIN:EN:PDF> accessed 16 December 2020.

52 Commission Communication 'On Impact Assessment' (n 31).

53 Ibid.

assessment.[54] But it is not required to mitigate the social or environmental problems that the change in trade rules occasioned by the accord might cause.

Is integration only procedural in the EU after all, or are there also substantive mechanisms, at least for international economic law and policy, provisions that can be adopted in a trade or investment treaty to accommodate relevant environmental and social concerns? What can the European law and policy experience with integration tell us about how that the three tensions identified earlier in this volume may be addressed in international economic agreements? Current European experience does offer certain insights vis-à-vis integration of environmental and social concerns to address the tensions occasioned by new economic liberalization rules.

First, in the European context, guided by a binding integration principle, increases in the scale or scope of trade and investment flows are not meant to cause direct material environmental damage through increases in unsustainable economic development activities, and this principle is slowly extending to social development in practice. Nor are direct normative impacts that encourage disallowing or 'chilling' environment and social development laws and measures expected. Rather, European law and related policies require the EC to conduct sustainability impact assessments, attempt to provide exceptions and exemptions in trade agreements, and call for measures to ensure that economic accords, environmental protection and social development objectives are mutually supportive, contributing to the world's SDGs.

Second, in the context of the integration principle, economic policies and agreements are not intended to create incentives for trade and investment led economic growth that will add to serious environmental and social problems which already exist at the domestic level. Rather, at least in European law and related policies, there is an emphasis on the need for development cooperation, for technical assistance and for international dialogue to ensure that trade and investment disciplines can achieve sustainable development objectives and will strengthen related social and environmental standards and laws in each sector.

Third, in the context of an integration principle, evolving trade and investment policies and treaties are not intended to encourage unsustainable growth in highly polluting or exploitative sectors, or stimulate—through pollution havens and other developments—they are not intended to promote the relocation or spread of obsolete, unsustainable industries that are being phased out of most developed country economies. Rather, European law and policy calls for increased trade and investment in cleaner low-carbon technologies, in environmental goods and services and in sustainably managed natural resources such as forest products. Indeed, the European GSP regulations provide direct market access incentives aimed specifically at encouraging sustainable development and good governance in developing countries.

Such steps appear to move beyond procedural questions of impact assessment or policy coherence and into substantive legal measures to encourage sustainable development through trade rules and investment incentives granting market access and encouraging

[54] Ibid, noting that: 'Sometimes the impact assessment may point towards a preferred basic approach and the optimal policy instrument early in the process. Subsequent analysis will then focus on improving the effectiveness of the proposal in terms of changes introduced to key design parameters or stringency levels. It may also identify accompanying measures to maximize positive and minimize negative impacts. The reasons for the most preferred policy option will be clearly outlined in the Impact Assessment Report. Alternative instruments that meet the same set of policy objective(s) should always be considered at an early stage in the preparation of policy proposals.'

financial flows.[55] This suggests that rather than imposing external standards on developing country partners through sanctions, the EU may be taking initial steps to link the ratification and implementation of multilaterally negotiated accords on environment, human rights and other aspects of sustainable development with the trade preferences and investment incentives granted. At the very least, the European experience suggests that this form of integration is by no means impossible, and indeed, may suggest a starting point or initial elements for a more balanced approach to international economic law and policy, one in which both policy and legal principles are approaching alignment.

[55] See, in preparation, Commission Communication, 'Developing countries, international trade and sustainable development: the function of the Community's generalized system of preferences (GSP) for the ten-year period from 2006 to 2015' COM(2004) 461 final.

9

Policy and 'Soft Law' Rationales for Addressing Social and Environmental Concerns in Trade and Investment Treaties

While European practice offers some ideas, the argument that States have customary or other obligations, in international law, to proactively integrate social and environmental considerations into trade and investment treaty negotiations and practices for sustainable development, is in the process of being made. As discussed above, should such contentions be accepted, there are several ways that a regulator or tribunal could interpret, in accordance with the Vienna Convention on the Law of Treaties (VCLT), the wide diversity of provisions found today in trade and investment agreements which might, in light of an integration principle, address the concerns, tensions and problematic social and environmental outcomes identified in the initial impact assessments discussed above. Emerging international legal principles and specific European regional policy and practice experiences notwithstanding, there may also be further reasons that States are starting to address the key tensions in trade and investment negotiations from a sustainable development policy perspective. In particular, this chapter further considers the international policy arguments in the equation. It explores whether, as mentioned previously, the physical and related normative impacts of trade and investment law should simply be left to 'fall where they may', onto those with the weakest negotiating positions, or the most vulnerable populations and environments in the new economic agreements, or whether there are sound international policy and legal reasons that States are seeking ways to avoid these impacts, by integrating social and environmental measures into their trade and investment agreements.

By analysing international policy debates linking sustainable development with trade and investment, it is possible to clarify inter-actional imperatives to respond to the risks of negative social and environmental impacts from trade and investment agreements in developing countries. Given the weight of 'soft law' on this topic, developing countries and those concerned about human rights and the environment worldwide may have a legitimate expectation that trade and investment partners—especially those with the greatest knowledge, capacity and resources to do so—shall help to identify and mitigate such impacts. Policy and soft law rationales exist for not simply dismissing these concerns, nor consigning them to a bewilderingly complex European particularity, but rather, exploring whether the integration principle may have global relevance. In essence, the focus is on the last part of the 'why', before the book advances to consider the 'what' and the 'how'.

Crafting Trade and Investment Accords for Sustainable Development. Marie-Claire Cordonier Segger, Oxford University Press. © Marie-Claire Cordonier Segger 2021. DOI: 10.1093/oso/9780198831341.003.0009

9.1 Not Leaving Negative Impacts of Trade Liberalization to 'Roll Downhill' onto the Most Vulnerable

One response to concerns regarding impacts of economic treaties, as advocated by neo-liberal economic and legal scholars, would be to simply let burdens fall where they may.[1] From this view, sovereign States negotiate trade and investment liberalization treaties, and are surely in the best position to decide what risks and impacts are most acceptable to their national interests.[2] Just as the benefits of trade and investment liberalization will accrue to those States most astute in securing them, so should the costs fall upon those less wary.[3] Higher social and environmental standards may be inappropriate to the special circumstances of each State, and could limit the comparative advantages of developing countries in the global economy.[4] Attempts to reflect or integrate social and environmental concerns into trade and investment negotiations, from this perspective, are no more than 'disguised protectionism' and should be rejected or at least addressed separately from 'pure' economic law.[5] The purpose of an economic agreement is to stimulate economic growth through comparative advantage, and any other 'non-trade' issue should be regarded with extreme caution.[6] In the next section, it is argued that this position is no longer realistic, both for the legal reasons mentioned above and for important global policy reasons.

9.2 Policy Rationale for Trade and Investment Liberalization to Support Sustainable Development

Global and regional trade and investment regimes, and the related risks of impacts, have been negotiated over the past decades in parallel with global and regional policy debates on sustainable development. These global policy debates were launched as early as the 1972 Stockholm Conference on the Human Environment,[7] and were informed by the 1987 World Commission on Environment and Development mandate[8] and Report.[9] Through

[1] See M Friedman, *Capitalism as Freedom* (Chicago, University of Chicago Press 1962) 57–58; RA Lawson, 'Economic Freedom and the Well-Being of Nations' in E Chamlee-Wright (ed), *The Annual Proceedings of the Wealth and Well-Being of Nations* (Wisconsin, Beloit College Press 2010) 65, 67–69; J Schultz, 'The Demise of "Green" Protectionism: The WTO Decision on the US Gasoline Rule' (1996–1997) 25 Denver Journal of International Law & Policy 1, 3–5; SJ Everett and J Wiley, 'Resist Green Protectionism-or pay the Price at Copenhagen' in R Baldwin and SJ Everett (eds), *The Collapse of Global Trade, Murky Protectionism and the Crisis: Recommendations for the G20* (London, VoxEU.org and Center for Economic and Policy Research 2009) 93.

[2] See T Cottier and KN Schefer, 'The Relationship between World Trade Organization Law and Regional Law' (1998) 1 Journal of International Economic Law 83, 84–86 for a discussion of *pacta sunt servanda* in the WTO.

[3] Ibid 120–122.

[4] Friedman (n 1) 56–58; Everett and Wiley (n 1) 93–96.

[5] National Foreign Trade Council, *'Enlightened' Environmentalism or Disguised Protectionism? Assessing the Impact of EU Precautionary-Based Standards on Developing Countries* (Washington, National Foreign Trade Council, Inc 2004) iv–vii; MC Cordonier Segger, 'Inspiration for Integration: Interpreting International Trade and Investment Accords for Sustainable Development' (2017) 3 Canadian Journal of Comp & Contemporary Law 159.

[6] RN Cooper. *Environment and Resource Policies for the World Economy* (Washington, Brookings Institution 1994); J Bhagwati, 'Third World Intellectuals and NGOs Statement Against Linkage' (1999), Letter drafted by Bhagwati and signed by several dozen academics, copy on file with author.

[7] 16 June 1972, UN Doc A/Conf 48/14/Rev.1.

[8] 'Process of Preparation of the Environmental Perspective to the Year 2000 and Beyond, Meeting no. 102' UNGA Res 38/161, 19 December 1983, UN Doc A/RES/38/161.

[9] World Commission on the Environment and Development (WCED), *Our Common Future* (1983) para 41.

the 1992 Rio Conference on Environment and Development (UNCED),[10] a series of regional sustainable development summits such as the 1996 Summit of the Americas on Sustainable Development in Santa Cruz de la Sierra, Bolivia,[11] the 1997 United Nations General Assembly Special Session on Sustainable Development to evaluate progress,[12] and a decade later, the 2002 World Summit on Sustainable Development (WSSD),[13] a certain consensus has begun to emerge. This consensus was taken further forward in the 2012 United Nations Conference on Sustainable Development in Brazil, which focused on encouraging 'the green economy in the context of poverty reduction and sustainable development',[14] and also in the 2030 Agenda with commitment to the global Sustainable Development Goals (SDGs). Environmental aspects of these global policy debates are well-documented in the leading international environmental law texts.[15] The debates are also covered in legal literature on development and on human rights,[16] though to a lesser extent, and policy debates were canvassed in Summits such as the 1995 Copenhagen UN Conference on Social Development and the 2002 Monterrey International Conference on Financing for Development.[17] International legal and policy aspects of globalization are also analysed in recent studies of international law in the field of sustainable development.[18] The intent here is not to travel again over well-trodden ground, but simply to underscore that recent decades of trade and investment treaty-making have taken place against a backdrop of broader international policy debates in which States have not been silent on linkages between trade, investment, financial flows and sustainable development.

Through the soft law consensus declarations emerging from these events,[19] it is possible to trace a growing clarification of the linkages between trade, investment and sustainable

[10] 'Rio Declaration on Environment and Development (Annex 2)', Report of the UN Conference on Environment and Development, 13 June 1992, UN Doc A/CONF.151/26 (Vol I).

[11] Santa Cruz de la Sierra, Bolivia (7–8 December 1996).

[12] New York (23–27 June 1997).

[13] 4 September 2002, UN Doc A/CONF.199/20.

[14] See UNGA/10909 Sixty-Fourth Session 23 December 2009, Report of the Second Committee (Economic and Financial) UN Doc A/64/420/Add.1 on Implementation of Agenda 21, the Programme for the Further Implementation of Agenda 21, and Outcomes of the World Summit on Sustainable Development; see also UN CSD Fifth Committee Report UN Doc A/64/600.

[15] P Sands and J Peel, *Principles of International Environmental Law* (4th edn, Cambridge, CUP 2018); P Birnie, A Boyle and C Redgwell, *International Law & the Environment* (Oxford, OUP 2009) 106–208; A Kiss and D Shelton, *International Environmental Law* (3rd edn, Ardsley, Transnational 2004).

[16] See R Sarkar, *International Development Law: Rule of Law, Human Rights & Global Finance* (Oxford, OUP 2009) 257–331 for human rights in the context of global finance; see also O de Schutter, 'Transnational Corporations as Instruments of Human Development' in P Alston and M Robinson, *Human Rights and Development: Towards Mutual Reinforcement* (Oxford, OUP 2005) 403; T Novitz, 'Labour Standards and Trade: Need We Choose Between "Human Rights" and "Sustainable Development"?' in H Gött (ed), *Labour Standards in International Economic Law* (Cham, Switzerland, Springer 2018).

[17] Copenhagen, Denmark (6–12 March 1995).

[18] D Hunter, D Zaelke and J Salzman, *International Environmental Law and Policy* (Foundation Press, New York 2001) 210; Kiss and Shelton (n 15); Sands and Peel (n 15); W Lang (ed), *Sustainable Development and International Law* (London, Martinus Nijhoff 1995); S Atapattu, *Emerging Principles of International Environmental Law* (New York, Transnational 2006); HC Bugge '1987-2007: "Our Common Future" Revisited' in HC Bugge and C Voigt (eds), *Sustainable Development in International and National Law* (Groingen, Europa 2009) 1, 20.

[19] On the nuances of 'soft law', see G Simpson, 'The Situation on the International Legal Theory Front: The Power of Rules and the Rule of Power' (2000) 11 European Journal of International Law 439–464; JHH Weiler and AL Paulus, 'The Structure of Change in International Law or is There a Hierarchy of Norms in International Law?' (1997) 8 European Journal of International Law 545–565; U Fastenrath, 'Relative Normativity in International Law' (1993) 4 European Journal of International Law 305–340; T Gruchalla-Wesierski, 'A Framework for Understanding Soft Law' (1984–1985) 30 McGill Law Journal 37; M Bothe, 'Legal and Non-Legal Norms—a Meaningful Distinction in International Relations?' (1980) 11 Netherlands Yearbook of International Law 65; I Seidl-Hohenveldern, 'International Economic Soft Law' (1980) 163 Rec des Cours 164; J Gold, 'Strengthening the Soft International Law of Exchange Arrangements' (1983) 77 American Journal of International Law 443. But see

development. In particular, there are sound policy justifications for the proposition that negative social and environmental impacts of economic liberalization should *not* simply be left to 'fall where they may' onto the most vulnerable groups of developing country Parties to trade agreements, or kept completely separate from international trade and investment policy.

In the 1972 UN Conference on the Human Environment, [20] by focusing on the need for financial assistance and economic stability, Principles 9 and 10 of the Stockholm Declaration located 'the debate on the environment clearly in the context of the international economy'.[21] States also recognized in Principle 8, that 'economic and social development is essential ... for the improvement of the quality of life',[22] and agreed in Principle 14 on the need for rational planning to reconcile conflicts 'between the needs of development and the need to protect and improve the environment'.[23] The Stockholm Conference also increased impetus for certain multilateral environmental agreements (MEAs) in which Parties adopt specific trade obligations (STOs) as incentives to secure compliance, such as the Montreal Protocol.[24]

After Stockholm, the 1983 World Commission on the Environment and Development (WCED) was given a mandate to discuss trade and investment matters.[25] In its seminal 1987 Report, *Our Common Future*, the WCED called for a 'sustainable world economy'.[26] At that time, the WCED also found that:

> ... these issues have not been taken up systematically by intergovernmental organizations. The mandates of ... GATT and UNCTAD – should include sustainable development. Their activities should reflect concern with the impacts of trading patterns on the environment and the need for more effective instruments to integrate environment and development concerns into international trading arrangements ... [27]

Agreed by consensus in the 1992 UNCED, the 1992 Rio Declaration and Agenda 21 further elaborated the links between trade, investment and sustainable development.[28] At Principle

CM Chinkin, 'The Challenge of Soft Law: Development and Change in International Law' (1989) 38 International and Comparative Law Quarterly 850; H Hillgenberg, 'A Fresh Look at Soft Law' (1999) 10(3) European Journal of International Law 499–515. Certain nuances are discussed in Chapter 2. See also Report of the UN Secretary General, 'Gaps in International Environmental Law and Environment-Related Instruments: Towards a Global Pact for the Environment', 3 December 2018, UN Doc A/73/419 (advance edition). See also Brunnee J and Toope SJ, *Legality and Legitimacy in International Law* (Cambridge, CUP 2010)

20 UN Conference on the Human Environment, 16 June 1972, UN Doc A/Conf 48/14/Rev.1.

21 V Lowe, 'Sustainable Development and Unsustainable Arguments' in A Boyle and D Freestone, *International Law and Sustainable Development* (Oxford, OUP 1999) 253.

22 Stockholm Declaration, UN Conference on the Human Environment, 16 June 1972, UN Doc A/Conf 48/14/Rev.1 (1972) 11 ILM 1461, 8.

23 Ibid 14.

24 Convention on International Trade in Endangered Species of Wild Fauna and Flora (adopted 3 March 1973, entered into force 1 July 1975) 993 UNTS 243; D Brack, *International Trade and the Montreal Protocol* (London, Earthscan 1996); UNEP and IISD, *Environment and Trade: A Handbook* (2nd edn, Winnipeg, 2005), as discussed above.

25 'Process of preparation of the Environmental Perspective to the Year 2000 and Beyond, Meeting no. 102' UNGA Res 38/161, 19 December 1983, UN Doc A/RES/38/161.

26 WCED (n 9) para 41.

27 Ibid, paras 55–56.

28 Report of the UN Conference on Environment and Development, 13 June 1992, UN Doc A/CONF.151/26 (Vol I). See also Experts Group on Environmental Law of the World Commission on Environment and Development, *Environmental Protection and Sustainable Development* (Martinus Nijhoff, London 1987), which was a key input to the 1992 Rio Declaration.

2, States recognized both their sovereign rights to exploit their own resources pursuant to their own environmental and developmental policies, and their responsibility to ensure they do not cause damage to others. Principle 27 calls for 'the further development of international law in the field of sustainable development', and Principle 12 focuses on international trade and investment, calling for a 'supportive and open international economic system that would lead to economic growth and sustainable development'. As discussed in earlier chapters, in Principle 4 States declared that 'in order to achieve sustainable development, environmental protection shall constitute an integral part of the development process and cannot be considered in isolation from it'.[29] The Rio Declaration also highlights the need for procedural innovations such as impact assessment and public participation mechanisms. Agenda 21 calls for further efforts to codify and develop 'international law on sustainable development',[30] and recognizes the need to bring international economic law into accordance with the rest of this international law.[31] Though a section on 'making trade and the environment mutually supportive' is most often cited in academic literature,[32] policy guidance on trade, investment and sustainable development for States is actually found throughout Agenda 21 in diverse sections on social and economic dimensions,[33] conservation and management of resources for development,[34] strengthening the role of major groups,[35] and various means of implementation.[36] By consensus, States affirmed the need for an open, rule-based, non-discriminatory, equitable, secure and transparent multilateral trading system. They reaffirmed the 1972 Stockholm principle that certain social and environmental standards may not be appropriate in all countries. But there is no indication that States intended for developing countries to bear significant risks from negative social and environmental impacts related to trade liberalization. Indeed, the opposite is constantly repeated. Global agendas instead called for the international economy to:

> provide a supportive international climate for achieving environment and development goals through four principal sets of policies: (a) promoting sustainable development through trade; (b) making trade and environment mutually supportive; (c) providing adequate financial resources to developing countries; and (d) encouraging economic policies conducive to environment and development.[37]

In 1992, States highlighted the need for global efforts to build consensus on the intersections of environment, trade and development issues, both through existing international

[29] See especially analysis in Birnie, Boyle and Redgwell (n 15) 116–123.

[30] Report of the UN Conference (n 28); Birnie, Boyle and Redgwell (n 15).

[31] Agenda 21, Annex 2 of the Report of the UN Conference on Environment and Development (n 28) 39.1–39.10.

[32] D Hunter, D Zaelke and J Salzman, *International Environmental Law and Policy* (New York, Foundation Press 2001) 151; Sands and Peel (n 15).

[33] *International co-operation to accelerate sustainable development in developing countries*, poverty, consumption patterns, demographic dynamics, human health, human settlements and *integrating environment and development in decision-making*.

[34] Atmosphere, land resources, deforestation, desertification and drought, mountain ecosystems, sustainable agriculture and rural development, biological diversity, biotechnology, oceans and seas, fresh waters, toxic chemicals, hazardous wastes, solid and sewage wastes and radioactive wastes.

[35] Roles of women, children and youth, indigenous people, non-governmental organizations, local authorities, workers and trade unions, business and industry, science and technology and farmers.

[36] Financing mechanisms, technology transfers, science, education, capacity-building in developing countries, *international institutional arrangements, international legal instruments* and information for decision-making.

[37] Agenda 21 (n 31) 2.3, 2.5–2.43.

forums and in the domestic policy of each country.[38] Indeed, UNCED led to the signing of three international treaties which each aim to achieve sustainable development in different ways, with distinct linkages to international trade policy and law: the 1992 UN Framework Convention on Climate Change (UNFCCC),[39] the 1992 UN Convention on Biological Diversity (UNCBD),[40] and the 1994 UN Convention to Combat Desertification (UNCCD).[41]

UNCED also led to a new UN Commission for Sustainable Development (UNCSD)[42] which reviews implementation of Agenda 21.[43] States expressed concerns about failure to adequately address trade and sustainable development links in the UNCSD Third Session,[44] and UNCSD Eighth Session.[45] In the 1997 New York UN General Assembly Special Session on Sustainable Development (Earth Summit+5) Programme of Further Action to Implement Agenda 21, they laid out a further agenda for trade to support sustainable development, also highlighting the need to 'further strengthen and codify international law related to sustainable development'.[46] States agreed that:

> In order to accelerate economic growth, poverty eradication and environmental protection, particularly in developing countries, there is a need to establish … instruments and structures enabling all countries, in particular developing countries, to benefit from globalization … There should be a balanced and integrated approach to trade and sustainable development, based on a combination of trade liberalization, economic development and environmental protection.'[47]

In the 1997 Programme, both procedural and substantive guidance is found for this 'integrated approach'. The assembled States noted that decisions on further liberalization of trade should take effects on sustainable development into account; and they urged national

[38] Ibid 2.4.

[39] Opened for signature 4 June 1992, entered into force 21 March 1994, 1771 UNTS 107; see, e.g., UNEP, *Climate and Trade Policies in a Post-2012 World* (Geneva, 2000) 22; G Sampson, 'WTO Rules and Climate Change: The Need for Policy Coherence' in WB Chambers (ed), *Interlinkages and the Effectiveness of Multilateral Environmental Agreements* (Tokyo, UNU 2008) 75 where the author notes Kyoto Protocol provisions on measures to enhance energy efficiency, enhance sinks and reservoirs, increase use of new and renewable forms of energy, phase out fiscal incentives in greenhouse gas (GHG)-emitting sectors and promote the application of market instruments.

[40] Opened for signature 5 June 1992, entered into force 29 December 1993, 1760 UNTS 79, 143. See also, e.g., PG LePrestre (ed), *Governing Global Biodiversity: The Evolution and Implementation of the Convention on Biological Diversity* (Aldershot, Ashgate 2002); I Walden, 'Intellectual Property Rights and Biodiversity' in C Redgwell and M Bowman (eds), *International Law and the Conservation of Biological Diversity* (London, Kluwer 1995) 172, 178.

[41] United Nations Convention to Combat Desertification in those Countries Experiencing Serious Drought and/or Desertification, Particularly in Africa (opened for signature 14 October 1994, entered into force 16 December 1996) 1954 UNTS 3; see also, e.g., K Mayrand, 'Integrated Assessment of Trade-Related Policies: Agricultural Trade Liberalisation and the Convention to Combat Desertification' (2006) 24 Impact Assessment and Project Appraisal 311.

[42] See Establishment of the Commission on Sustainable Development, UNESC Res 1993/207, 12 February 1993, UN Doc E/1993/207; Institutional Arrangements to Follow Up the United Nations Conference on Environment and Development, UNGA Res 47/191, 29 January 1993, UN Doc A/RES/47/191 3-5; M McCoy and P McCully, *The Road From Rio: An NGO Action Guide to Environment and Development* (Amsterdam, Utrecht International Books 1993) 45.

[43] McCoy and McCully (n 42); NA Robinson (ed), 'Agenda 21: Earth's Action Plan', IUCN Environmental Policy & Law Paper No 27 (1993) 655.

[44] UNCSD, *UNCSD Report on the Third Session* (1995) Official Records, Supplement No 12, paras 37–40.

[45] UNCSD, *UNCSD Report on the Eighth Session* (1999–2000) Official Records, Supplement No 9, paras 28–34.

[46] Programme for the Further Implementation of Agenda 21, UNGA Res S-19/2, 19 September 1997, UN Doc A/Res/S-19/2 (UNGASS) 109–110.

[47] Ibid para 29.

governments to make every effort to ensure policy coordination on trade, environment and development in support of sustainable development. At no instance did the UN General Assembly (UNGA) suggest that developing countries should simply accept all environmental and social risks from global or regional trade agreements, or allow trade treaties to limit effective implementation of environmental and social accords. Instead, States identified the need for renewed system-wide efforts to ensure greater responsiveness to sustainable development objectives, recommending strengthened cooperation and support for capacity-building in trade, environment and development at both international and national levels, for international cooperation to ensure mutual supportiveness among economic and environmental agreement, and for trade liberalization to be accompanied by new policies for more efficient allocation and use of resources.[48] The UNGA also warned that 'any future agreements on investments should take into account the objectives of sustainable development and, when developing countries are Parties to these agreements, special attention should be given to their needs for investment.'[49]

Responses were uneven, however, and in a 10-year review at the 2002 World Summit on Sustainable Development,[50] States re-focused on means to better *implement* sustainable development commitments. In the 2002 Johannesburg Plan of Implementation (JPOI),[51] States established a broadened institutional architecture for sustainable development,[52] to further implement Agenda 21 and the WSSD outcomes, and to meet emerging sustainable development challenges.[53] In JPOI Chapter XI, economic institutions such as the World Trade Organization (WTO) and regional trade and investment bodies were tasked to enhance their work to realize sustainable development objectives.[54] Rather than repeating the UNCED and the 1997 General Assembly Special Session (UNGASS) texts, the guidance on trade, investment and sustainable development is brief, with a change in tone that strongly focuses the agenda on the social development dimensions of international economic policy. States noted that '[g]lobalization offers opportunities and challenges for sustainable development',[55] identified special challenges of 'poverty, exclusion and inequality within and among societies',[56] emphasized the special difficulties faced by developing countries, and called for globalization to become 'fully inclusive and equitable'.[57] They also emphasized, in addition to calls for the WTO Doha 'Development Round' of trade negotiations to better take development concerns into account, the need to '[s]trengthen regional trade and cooperation agreements … with a view to achieving the objectives of sustainable development'.[58] In Chapter X on Means of

[48] Ibid.

[49] Ibid, para 29(g).

[50] 'Ten-year Review of Progress Achieved in the Implementation of the Outcome of the United Nations Conference on Environment and Development' UNGA Res 55/199, 20 December 2000, UN Doc A/RES/55/199.

[51] Johannesburg Declaration and Johannesburg Plan of Implementation (JPOI), Report of the World Summit on Sustainable Development, 4 September 2002, UN Doc A/CONF.199/20, paras 140–170.

[52] 'Ten-year Review of Progress' (n 51); JPOI (n 51); see also O Anaedu and L-G Engfeldt 'Sustainable Development Governance'; MC Cordonier Segger and M Ivanova, 'Sustainable Development Governance: Take Two', Concept Paper for South African Chair of UNCSD 11, April–May, 2003, on file with author. See Brunnee and Toope (n 19)

[53] 'Follow-up to the World Summit on Sustainable Development and the Future Role of the Commission on Sustainable Development: The Implementation Track' UNESC Rep 2003/2, 21 February 2003, UN Doc E/CN.17/2003/2.

[54] JPOI (n 51) paras 47–48, 51, 151, 154, 155, 158–161.

[55] Ibid, paras 47–52.

[56] Ibid, paras 90–100.

[57] Ibid, paras 90–100.

[58] Ibid, paras 90–100.

Implementation, a detailed agenda for integrating social development and environmental priorities into global and regional trade and investment negotiations was agreed.[59] States, *inter alia*, recognized 'the major role that trade can play in achieving sustainable development and in eradicating poverty'; encouraged 'efforts to promote cooperation on trade, environment and development, including in the field of providing technical assistance to developing countries'; encouraged 'the voluntary use of environmental impact assessments as an important national-level tool to better identify trade, environment and development inter-linkages ... '; further encouraged 'countries and international organizations with experience in this field to provide technical assistance to developing countries for these purposes'; and called for 'further action ... to enhance the benefits, in particular for developing countries ... of trade liberalization' through actions to 'establish and strengthen existing trade and cooperation agreements ... with a view to achieving sustainable development'.[60] While the provisions were hortatory, this guidance has been unanimously negotiated and agreed by States, and as soft law, can be useful in future treaty-making.

In summary, there is scant indication from the 1972 Conference on Human Environment (UNCHE), the 1992 UNCED, the UNCSD deliberations, the 1997 UNGASS, the 2002 WSSD, the 2012 UN CSD,[61] or the 2015 SDGs that the risks and burdens of trade and investment led economic growth should be left to fall upon the most vulnerable in developing country economic partners, or that social and environmental decision-making should be kept separate from trade and investment law. Indeed, the clear opposite is emphasized, though much work remains to be done.

9.3 Legitimate Expectations that States Will Promote Sustainable Development in Trade and Investment Agreements

The 1992 Rio Declaration and other documents are not hard, binding international law: indeed, they are often cited as the quintessential examples of soft law.[62] However, soft law can be relevant to the future development of international law in a more nuanced manner than the hard law found in treaties, established customary rules, or other formal sources recognized in article 38 of the 1946 Statute of the International Court of Justice (ICJ).[63] As legal scholars have convincingly argued, soft law norms and standards can lead to binding obligations upon States through subsequent negotiation of international treaties or eventual recognition as international customary rules.[64] The initial phases of development of new international treaty regimes, and recognition of new legal principles, are often shaped by the inter-actional

59 Ibid, paras 81–136.

60 Ibid, paras 90–100.

61 Rio+20 UN CSD Bureau Co-Chairs, 'The Future We Want' Outcome Document New York, 2012, reaffirms an urgent need to ensure that developing countries, particularly the least developed countries, are able to benefit from the advantages of trade.

62 See n 19 and Chapter 2 on the nuances of soft law. The courts of many countries and regions, including Canada, Chile and the EU, have, however, recognized the precautionary principle in their judgments.

63 (1945) 39 American Journal of International Law Supplement 215; see n 19 and below for analysis.

64 A Boyle, 'Soft Law in International Law-Making' in M Evans, *International Law* (3nd edn, Oxford, OUP 2010) 141–158, which posits the 1992 Rio Declaration as an instrument that both codifies existing international law and seeks to develop new law; Simpson (n 19); Weiler and Paulus (n 19); Fastenrath (n 19); for earlier discussions, see Gruchalla-Wesierski, (n 19). See also JL Charney, 'Compliance with International Soft Law' in D Shelton (ed), *Commitment and Compliance: The Role of Non-Binding International Norms in the International Legal System* (Oxford, OUP 2000) 115–118. See Brunnee and Toope (n 19)

inter-State debates and consensus building that characterizes these soft legal processes.[65] From an inter-actional framework of analysis, the shared understandings of actors, a genuine concern for legitimacy, the practice of trade and investment legality itself as it relates to sustainable development, and the typology of legality criteria including those proposed in this volume, support an inter-actional account of the *lex specialis* governing these intersections. In this sense, soft law declarations may be further relevant. Scholars suggest that in accordance with the doctrine of good faith in international law, very widely supported soft law may generate *legitimate expectations* among other States.[66] Such expectations are not decisive, as they can be rebutted, for instance through explicit statements that a particular standard or principle found in soft law is not applicable in the circumstances at hand,[67] but in this case the preponderance of unanimous consensus statements is convincing. Overall, certain conclusions can be drawn with respect to the three key tensions in the trade, investment and sustainable development relationship that were identified in earlier chapters of this volume.

First, trade and investment policies and agreements are *not* intended to constrain the adoption and enforcement of legitimate new environment and social development measures, nor to make it more inherently difficult to implement economic provisions from other international treaties focused on the SDGs. Rather, the consensus declarations and instruments on these topics are replete with calls for trade and investment policies to mutually support environment and development priorities in a balanced and integrated way for sustainable development,[68] to strengthen sustainable natural resources management,[69] to strengthen and encourage environmental regulations and standards,[70] and to support poverty eradication, including through the realization of human rights enshrined in the International Labour Organization (ILO) Conventions.[71]

Second, trade and investment policies and agreements are *not* expected to create incentives for trade and investment led economic growth that will add to serious environmental and social problems which already exist at the domestic level, and curtail the enforcement of laws intended to support sustainable development, especially in developing countries. Rather, the detailed action plans and other 'soft law' instruments on these topics emphasize and re-emphasize an urgent need for accompanying cooperative measures to increase social and environmental regulatory capacity and provide technical assistance,[72] and for

65 J Brunnee and S Toope, *Legality and Legitimacy in International Law* (Cambridge, CUP 2010) 5–9.

66 Ibid; P Allott, 'The Concept of International Law' (1999) 10(1) European Journal of International Law 31–50; N Krisch, 'International Law in Times of Hegemony: Unequal Power and the Shaping of the International Legal Order' (2005) 16 European Journal of International Law 369–408; M Koskenniemi, 'The Politics of International Law' (1990) 1 European Journal of International Law 4–32; N Krisch, 'The Pluralism of Global Administrative Law' (2006) 17 European Journal of International Law 247–278.

67 Charney (n 64) 115–118 but see P-M Dupuy, 'Soft Law and the International Law of the Environment' (1990–1991) 12 Michigan Journal of International Law 420, 428 and CM Chinkin, 'The Challenge of Soft Law' (1989) 38 The International and Comparative Law Quarterly 850, 859.

68 UNGA Res (n 46) para 29: 'There should be a balanced and integrated approach to trade and sustainable development, based on a combination of trade liberalization, economic development and environmental protection.'

69 Ibid: 'Trade liberalization should be accompanied by environmental and resource management policies in order to realize its full potential contribution to improve environmental protection and the promotion of sustainable development through the more efficient allocation and use of resources.'

70 Report of the Commission on Sustainable Development on the Fourth Session (18 April–3 May 1996) Decision 4/1. Trade, environment and sustainable development: (c) 'Stresses that it would be inappropriate to relax environmental laws, regulations and standards or their enforcement in order to encourage foreign direct investment or to promote exports.'

71 JPOI (n 51) paras 7–13.

72 Report of the Commission on Sustainable Development on the Fourth Session (n 70) Decision 4/1. Trade, environment and sustainable development: 'Recognizes that positive measures, such as improved market access, capacity-building, improved access to finance, and access to and transfer of technology, taking into account the relationship

cooperative measures to generate new and additional financial, human and other resources to address environmental or developmental challenges associated with regional and bilateral economic treaties.[73]

Third, and perhaps most challenging, trade and investment policies and treaties should not serve to encourage *unsustainable growth* in obsolete technologies, goods or economic sectors, or to stimulate, through pollution havens, subsidies and other means, the growth of these sectors. The soft law declarations firmly call for the continued phase-out of such measures.[74] States do not support the imposition of social or environmental standards that are not appropriate for developing countries. Instead, in internationally negotiated treaties, resolutions, standards and guidelines, States are increasingly calling for measures to encourage *increased* trade and investment in more sustainable low-carbon technologies,[75] the sustainable use of genetic resources,[76] more sustainably produced or harvested goods,[77] environmental goods and services,[78] and pesticide-free products.[79]

In summary, there is a convincing international policy rationale for States to undertake measures to prevent, or at least mitigate, the environment and social development impacts of trade and investment agreements, addressing the main tensions identified in this volume. States have repeatedly committed, in consensus declarations of principles,[80] detailed action plans,[81] UN conference debates,[82] solemn resolutions,[83] and international guidelines

between trade-related agreements and technology, are effective instruments for assisting developing countries in meeting multilaterally agreed targets in keeping with the principle of common but differentiated responsibilities.'

[73] 1997 UNGA Special Session on Sustainable Development: 'The multilateral trading system should have the capacity to further integrate environmental considerations and enhance its contribution to sustainable development, without undermining its open, equitable and non-discriminatory character. The special and differential treatment for developing countries, especially the least developed countries, and the other commitments of the Uruguay Round of multilateral trade negotiations should be fully implemented in order to enable those countries to benefit from the international trading system, while conserving the environment.

[74] UN General Assembly, 'The Future We Want', 11 September 2012, UN Doc A/Res/66/288, reaffirms calls for phase out of subsidies that impede the transition to sustainable development, including those on fossil fuels and fisheries, at paras 173 and 225.

[75] JPOI (n 51) para 20, 59; UNCSD, *Report of the Commission on Sustainable Development on the Seventeenth Session* (16 May 2008 and 4–15 May 2009) 12(g)(i); UNFCCC, *Report of the Conference of the Parties on its Seventh Session* (21 January 2002) FCCC/CP/2001/13/Add.1.

[76] UNCBD, *Decision adopted by the Conference of the Parties to the Convention on Biological Diversity at its 10th Meeting* (Nagoya, Japan, 18–29 October 2010) Decision X/1; UNEP, *Environment & Trade: A Handbook* (Geneva, 2000) 55–56; MK Seely and others, 'Creative Problem Solving in Support of Biodiversity Conservation' (2003) 54 Journal of Arid Environments 155.

[77] UNGA Res S-19/2 (n 46) para 29: 'Trade obstacles should be removed with a view to contributing to the achieving of more efficient use of the earth's natural resources in both economic and environmental terms.'

[78] OECD, 'Opening Markets for Environmental Goods and Services' (September 2005) Policy Brief, <http://www.oas.org/dsd/Tool-kit/Documentos/ModuleIIIdoc/Opening%20Markets%20for%20Environmental%20Goods%20and%20Services.pdf > accessed 16 December 2020; Doha WTO Ministerial 2001: Ministerial Declaration, WT/MIN(01)/DEC/1, paras 31–33; ZX Zhang, 'Liberalizing Climate-Friendly Goods and Technologies in the WTO: Product Coverage, Modalities, Challenges and the Way Forward' (2009) 1 UNCTAD Trade and Environment Review 1.

[79] Rotterdam Convention on the Prior Informed Consent Procedure for Certain Hazardous Chemicals and Pesticides in International Trade (adopted 10 September 1998, entered into force 24 February 2004) 2244 UNTS 337, preamble; Stockholm Convention on Persistent Organic Pollutants (adopted 22 May 2001, entered into force 17 May 2004) (2001) 40 ILM 532, preamble; G Fridell, 'Free Trade, Fair Trade and the State' (2010) 15 New Political Economy 457, 457–458.

[80] See, e.g., United Nations Declaration on the Rights of Indigenous Peoples (13 September 2007) UNGA Res 69-295; UNCSD, *Report of the Secretary-General on Trade, Environment and Sustainable Development* (18 April 1996–3 May 1996) E/CN.17/1996/8.

[81] Agenda 21 (n 31); JPOI (n 51).

[82] See, e.g., IISD Reporting Services, 'Summary of the First Prepcom for the UN Conference on Sustainable Development' (21 May 2010) <http://www.iisd.ca/download/pdf/enb2701e.pdf>.

[83] UNGA Res A/RES/S-19/2 (n 46).

and standards,[84] to make increased efforts to ensure that trade and investment can support sustainable development, especially in developing countries. It can be argued that States are justified in forming legitimate expectations on sustainable development in trade negotiations.[85] In this context, it is not credible to maintain that negative social and environmental effects of economic agreements should be simply left to roll downhill onto the weakest Parties to a trade and investment treaty. Rather, the soft law suggests that States agree in practice that where possible in trade and investment agreements, measures can and should be taken. Absent explicit instructions to the contrary, both developed and developing country Parties to trade and investment negotiations should be able to rely on these expectations.

[84] See, e.g., European Commission 'Impact Assessment Guidelines' SEC(2005) 791.
[85] P Allot, *The Health of Nations* (Cambridge, CUP 2002).

10

International Trade and Investment Agreements in Light of the Integration Principle

Given the international legal principles at play, the practical example of the European experiences in both law and policy, and the pressing policy rationale, how can integration translate to the international level? As noted earlier in this volume, and as highlighted by the Tribunal in the *Iron Rhine Award*, Principle 4 of the 1992 Rio Declaration provides that 'environmental protection shall constitute an integral part of the development process and cannot be considered in isolation from it'.[1] Just as States negotiate to secure access to foreign markets through an economic liberalization accord, States may also be seeking to negotiate to ensure trade and investment agreements do not result in the impacts identified in across nearly three decades of assessment experience. This brief chapter concludes with a discussion of how the principle might assist in interpreting the provisions of trade and investment agreements, as a basis for later examination of progress in the World Trade Organization (WTO), and in bilateral and regional economic negotiations which make an explicit commitment to sustainable development.

10.1 Addressing Sustainable Development Tensions in Trade and Investment Agreements through Integration

First, if sustainable development, as a policy objective, is explicitly recognized as part of the 'object and purpose' of a trade and investment agreement, might this recognition help to resolve the tensions outlined above? Sustainable development may be found to be part of the 'object and purpose' of an economic liberalization treaty. In international law, this is relevant in two principal ways. First, it is important for interpretation. Article 31 of the Vienna Convention on the Law of Treaties (VCLT)[2] as a general rule of interpretation, provides at 1 that 'A treaty shall be interpreted in good faith in accordance with the ordinary meaning to be given to the terms of the treaty in their context and in the light of its object and purpose'. And at 2, the Convention further states that: 'The context for the purpose of the interpretation of a treaty shall comprise, in addition to the text, including its preamble and annexes ... '.[3] In essence, the ordinary meaning of the terms of a treaty, in their context

[1] 'Rio Declaration on Environment and Development (Annex 2)', Report of the UN Conference on Environment and Development, 13 June 1992, UN Doc A/CONF.151/26 (Vol I) Principle 4.

[2] Signed 23 May 1969, entered into force 27 January 1980, 1155 UNTS 331.

[3] Note also the relevance of '... (b) any instrument which was made by one or more parties in connection with the conclusion of the treaty and accepted by the other parties as an instrument related to the treaty ... 3(b) any subsequent practice in the application of the treaty which establishes the agreement of the parties regarding its interpretation; ... 4. A special meaning shall be given to a term if it is established that the parties so intended.' Also, art 32 permits recourse to supplementary means of interpretation, including the preparatory work of the treaty and the circumstances of its conclusion. These reflect pre-existing customary international law, applying to treaties concluded before the VCLT and also to non-Parties: *Case Concerning the Territorial Dispute (Libyan Arab Jamahiriya*

Crafting Trade and Investment Accords for Sustainable Development. Marie-Claire Cordonier Segger, Oxford University Press. DOI: 10.1093/oso/9780198831341.003.0010

and taking into account the treaty's *object and purpose*, are taken together to guide a lawyer in understanding the intentions of the Parties, and are the prevailing elements for interpretation.[4] As explained by Professor Richard Gardiner, the 'object and purpose function as a means of shedding light on the ordinary meaning' of a treaty.[5]

This solution is not quite so simple, however. The precise nature and role of the 'object and purpose' of a treaty remains something of an 'enigma' in the law of treaties.[6] The combining of 'object' and 'purpose' in the VCLT has been ascribed in part to an International Law Commission (ILC) member's suggestion in relation to the draft article on *pacta sunt servanda*, that 'the English word "objects" be better rendered in French by the expression "l'objet et la fin"... for the object of an obligation was one thing and its purpose was another'.[7] In French public law, as Buffard and Zemanek explain, a distinction has developed between 'l'objet' of a legal instrument, which means what it does to create a set of rights and obligations, and 'le but' which refers to the reason for establishing 'l'objet'.[8] The term 'object' indicates thus the substantial content of the norm; the provisions, rights and obligations created by the norm. The object of a treaty is 'the instrument for the achievement of the treaty's purpose, and this purpose is, in turn, the general result which the [P]arties want to achieve by the treaty'.[9] As Gardiner notes, while the Preamble provides guidance to discern the object and purpose of a treaty, the whole treaty text and associated matter listed in article 31(2) should be taken into account. An object and purpose can also be discerned by comparing a treaty to others of its type, as the International Court of Justice (ICJ) did in the *Oil Platforms* case by comparing the provisions of the 1955 *Treaty of Amity, Economic Relations and Consular Rights between the United States of America and Iran*, with others of treaties of friendship.[10] This said, as the Appellate Body of the WTO has clarified, 'most treaties have no single, undiluted object and purpose but rather a variety of different, and possibly conflicting, objects and purposes ... This is certainly true of the WTO Agreement'.[11] The purpose of the treaty is, then, legally relevant for interpretation, and there may be more than one.

The object and purpose of a treaty is raised multiple times in the VCLT,[12] serving for instance to determine the incompatibility of a reservation at article 19(c), as a possible characteristic of a multilateral treaty to which reservations require the consent of all Parties at article 20(2), or to characterize the material breach of a treaty at article 60(3)(b) and as part of the general guidance for interpretation at article 31(1).[13] This last point is the most

v. Chad) (Judgment) General List No 83 [1994] ICJ 6; *Kasikili/Sedudu Island (Botswana/Namibia)* (Judgment) General List No 99 [1999] ICJ 1045; *Case Concerning Sovereignty over Pulau Ligitan and Pulau Sipadan (Indonesia v. Malaysia)* (Judgment) General List No 102 [2002] ICJ 625 37–38.

[4] P Reuter, *Introduction to the Law of Treaties* (2nd edn, London, Kegan Paul 1995); RS Aryal, *Interpretation of Treaties: Law and Practice* (New Delhi, Deep & Deep 2003).

[5] R Gardiner, *Treaty Interpretation* (2nd edn, Oxford, OUP 2015).

[6] I Buffard and K Zemanek, 'The Object and Purpose of a Treaty: An Enigma?' (1998) 3 Austrian Review of International and European Law 311; A Aust, *Modern Treaty Law and Practice* (Cambridge, CUP 2000).

[7] [1964] Yearbook of the International Law Commission, vol I, 26; Gardiner (n 5). See also *Reservations to the Genocide Convention Case* [1951] ICJ Rep 15, 23, which actually uses 'l'objet et le but'.

[8] Buffard and Zemanek (n 6) 325–328; Gardiner (n 5).

[9] Buffard and Zemanek (n 6) 326.

[10] *Oil Platforms (Iran v. USA)* [1996-II] ICJ Rep 803, para 27.

[11] WTO, *United States: Import Prohibition of Certain Shrimp and Shrimp Products-Recourse to article 21.5 by Malaysia* (13 October 2000) WT/DS58/17, 17.

[12] VCLT (n 2).

[13] See Buffard and Zemanek (n 6) 320.

important, as it guides the implementation of the agreements, arguably including the further evolution of the treaty regimes themselves.[14]

Taking these explanations of Gardiner, Buffet and Zemaneck into account, it can be noted that sustainable development is a 'purpose' of over thirty treaties which explicitly commit to achieve it in very diverse sectors and ways—those mentioned in this volume and elsewhere in the literature as having been highlighted by States as delivery mechanisms for the 2002 Johannesburg Plan of Implementation (JPOI) and also the 2015 Sustainable Development Goals (SDGs).[15] As just one example, in the FAO Seed Treaty, the Parties establish a Multilateral System for Access and Benefit-Sharing that is meant to provide an efficient, effective and transparent framework to facilitate access to plant genetic resources for food and agriculture, and to share the benefits in a fair and equitable way.[16] As objectives in article 1.1, States agree that the 'objectives of this Treaty are the conservation and *sustainable use of plant genetic resources for food and agriculture* and the fair and equitable sharing of the benefits arising out of their use, in harmony with the Convention on Biological Diversity, *for sustainable agriculture and food security*' (emphasis added).[17] Sustainable use of plant genetic resources for food and agriculture is an 'object' of this international treaty, and overall sustainable agriculture is set as one of two ultimate purposes.[18] Further, though, the Parties include provisions to define what is meant by sustainable use in article 6, committing to develop and maintain legal measures in this respect. Under article 6.1 the Contracting Parties accept a duty. They 'shall develop and maintain appropriate policy and legal measures that promote the sustainable use of plant genetic resources for food and agriculture.'[19] In article 6.2, the Parties then provide a list of specific legal measures meant to explain what they mean by sustainable use of plant genetic resources.[20] These provisions were debated in the treaty negotiations,[21] have been raised in the Conferences of the Parties,[22] and have also been analysed in scholarly legal literature.[23] In this treaty, it is now clear that States can and do focus on 'sustainable use' in one particular context, that of plant genetic resources for food and agriculture. In this specific sector, the Parties pinpointed the meaning

[14] Ibid 333; Gardiner (n 5).

[15] MC Cordonier Segger and A Khalfan, *Sustainable Development Law: Principles, Practices, and Prospects* (Oxford, OUP 2004) 45–50 is based on preliminary research for this volume, and lists the treaties explicitly highlighted as international law in the field of sustainable development in the 2002 World Summit on Sustainable Development (WSSD) JPOI, including those which contain key provisions on sustainable development in addition to other environment, economic or social purposes.

[16] The Multilateral System applies to over 64 major crops and forages. Resources may be obtained from the Multilateral System for utilization and conservation in research, breeding and training. When a commercial product is developed using these resources, equitable contributions are made to the System. The Governing Body sets out conditions for access and benefit-sharing in a 'Material Transfer Agreement'.

[17] International Treaty on Plant Genetic Resources for Food and Agriculture of the Food and Agriculture Organization (adopted 3 November 2001, entered into force 31 March 2004) (FAO Seed Treaty) art 6.

[18] M Lightbourne, 'The FAO Multilateral System for Plant Genetic Resources for Food and Agriculture: Better than Bilateralism?' (2009) 30 Washington University Journal of Law and Policy 465, 507; Matthias Herdegen, *The International Law of Biotechnology: Human Rights, Trade, Patents, Health and the Environment* (Massachusetts, Edward Elgar 2018).

[19] FAO Seed Treaty (n 17) art 6.

[20] Ibid.

[21] S Coupe and R Lewins, *Negotiating the Seed Treaty* (Warwickshire: Practical Action Publishing, 2007); Florian Rabitz, *The Global Governance of Genetic Resources: Institutional Change and Structural Constraints* (London, Routledge 2017).

[22] Report of the Third Session of the Governing Body of the International Treaty on Plant Genetic Resources for Food and Agriculture (Tunis, Tunisia, 1–5 June 2009) IT/GB-3/09/Report.

[23] Lightbourne (n 18).

of sustainable use of the resource, and operationalized their commitment in the treaty by agreeing on a set of legal measures that are required to ensure that this takes place.

As will be shown in the rest of this volume, however, though sustainable development may be recognized in preambles and other provisions as part of the purpose of many economic agreements,[24] such legal clarity has only begun to be sought in the context of trade and investment.[25] Before turning to this matter, it is also important to consider the limits of the 'purposive' approach, noting alternative views that are equally relevant.

10.2 Interpreting Sustainable Development Provisions in Trade and Investment Accords

While a joint intention of the Parties to promote sustainable development may be found in a trade and investment treaty preamble, and may be considered part of the 'object and purpose' of the accord in question, this recognition also has limits. As Gardiner explains, according to the VCLT, though it can shed light on the meaning of a provision within the context of the treaty itself, a broader or different 'object and purpose' does not provide a valid means of challenging a clear operational term.[26] Essentially, if a regulator from the EU or another Party sought to demonstrate that a clear obligation in a trade and investment liberalization accord should be interpreted to accommodate the tensions identified above, in order to integrate environmental and social considerations, reference to a preambular commitment alone may not provide the strongest guidance.[27]

The VCLT, as noted earlier, enshrines customary rules of treaty interpretation. Article 30 governs the application of successive treaties relating to the same subject matter, and may assist in the interpretation of treaty obligations which appear to differ, as discussed at tension one earlier in this volume, from sustainability commitments that are enshrined in other accords.[28] Indeed, the tensions noted above do invoke certain types of conflicts

[24] MC Cordonier Segger. 'Inspiration for Integration: Interpreting International Trade and Investment Accords for Sustainable Development' (2017) 3(1) Canadian Journal of Comparative and Contemporary Law 159; N Schrijver and F Weiss, *International Law and Sustainable Development: Principles and Practice* (Lieden, Martinus Nijhoff 2004); A Boyle and D Freestone (eds), *International Law and Sustainable Development: Past Achievements and Future Challenges* (Oxford, OUP 1999). See also Report of the UN Secretary General, 'Gaps in International Environmental Law and Environment-Related Instruments: Towards a Global Pact for the Environment', 3 December 2018, UN Doc A/73/419 (advance edition). See also Table of Treaties in this volume which lists the Regional Trade Agreements (RTAs) in which States commit to promote sustainable development.

[25] P Birnie, A Boyle and C Redgwell, *International Law & the Environment* (Oxford, OUP 2009) 123–127; G Sampson, *The WTO and Sustainable Development* (Tokyo, UNU 2005) 78–109. Brunnee J and Toope SJ, *Legality and Legitimacy in International Law* (Cambridge, CUP 2010)

[26] See Gardiner (n 5) 74.

[27] Ibid. In *Case Concerning the Arbitral Award of 31 July 1989 (Guinea-Bissau v. Senegal)* [1991] 1CJ Rep 53, 67–72; *Land, Island and Maritime Frontier Dispute (El Salvador v. Honduras)* [1992] ICJ Rep 351, 584, paras 375–376, the ICJ was unwilling to expand its jurisdiction beyond the very specific limits set out in the arbitration agreements, even to accommodate the express object and purpose of the accord it had identified; for cases where the WTO dispute settlement bodies simply interpreted treaty provisions in the context of object and purpose, see WTO, *United States: Import Prohibition of Certain Shrimp and Shrimp Products—Report of the Panel* (15 May 1998) WT/DS58/R; WTO, *United States: Import Prohibition of Certain Shrimp and Shrimp Products—Report of the Appellate Body* (6 November 1998) Doc.WT/DS58/AB/R; WTO, *EC Measures Concerning Meat and Meat Products (Hormones)—Reports of the Appellate Body* (13 February 1998) WT/DS26/AB/R and WT/DS48/AB/R; WTO, *Chile—Price Band System and Safeguard Measures Relating to Certain Agricultural Products—Report of the Appellate Body* (7 May 2007) WT/DS207/AB/R; *European Communities—Measures Affecting the Approval and Marketing of Biotech Products—Reports of the Panel* (29 September 2006) WT/DS291/R/Add.4, WT/DS292/R/Add.4, WT/DS293/R/Add.4.

[28] VCLT (n 2) art 30; see J Pauwelyn, *Conflict of Norms in Public International Law: How WTO Law Relates to Other Rules of International Law* (Cambridge, CUP 2003) 361–385.

among treaties. For instance, there may be a conflict where trade and investment liberalization obligations could constrain effective implementation of other treaty obligations which govern the same subject matter related to sustainable development.

However, in international law, there is a generally accepted presumption against conflicts. As Pauwelyn explains, in theory every new treaty norm is created within the context of pre-existing international law, and the presumption is that this new norm builds upon the existing laws.[29] Not only would an explicit conflict of norms need to be found in treaty text and proven by the claimant to limit an environmental or social measure, but if faced with two possible interpretations, one of which harmonizes the meaning of the norms in question, the treaty will be 'interpreted as producing and as intended to produce effects in accordance with existing law and not in violation of it'.[30]

For a trade and investment tribunal, or as is more likely in this field, for a regulator charged with interpreting a new trade and investment obligation and how it will apply to efforts to secure more sustainable development in their sector of economic law and policy, it is therefore important under VCLT article 31 to look first to other provisions in the trade and investment treaty in question, to see if there is further guidance provided in their ordinary meaning, in the context of the treaty, in light of its object and purpose, that can assist in interpreting the scope and application of problematic obligations. If little guidance appears in the text itself, an analysis might also be conducted under the *lex posteriori* and other rules of the VCLT at article 30. But before applying formal rules, a careful analysis of the other provisions of the trade treaty in question is important, particularly as Parties may have included other provisions that are part of the treaty context and specifically address the tension, not to mention references to further *lex specialis*.[31] A careful search by the regulator may reveal textual solutions in the economic treaty itself. Certain types of provisions that could be present, particularly given Parties' tendency to innovate in economic agreements, may address the 'integration tensions' before a conflict takes place.

From this 'textual' viewpoint, other provisions in the treaty are therefore doubly important. In the examination of the terms of the trade and investment treaty in question, the interpretive rules of the VCLT will be relevant. The customary principle of integration can be taken into account in the interpretation of the terms of the trade and investment agreement itself.[32] A great deal turns on the specific mechanisms agreed by the Parties to the trade

29 See Pauwelyn (n 28) 241; J-M Grossen, *Les Presomptions en Droit International Public* (Paris, Neuchâtel 1954) 114–117.

30 *Right of Passage over Indian Territory* (Preliminary Objections) [1957] ICJ Rep 142.

31 *Threat or Use of Nuclear Weapons* [1996] ICJ Rep 4. See also M Koskenniemi, 'Study on the Function and Scope of the lex specialist rule and the question of self-contained regimes' (ILC(LVI)/SG/FIL/CRD.1 and Add.1) 160; Gardiner (n 5); See Brunnee and Toope (n 25).

32 VCLT (n 2) art 31(3)(c); D French, 'Treaty Interpretation and the Incorporation of Extraneous Legal Rules' (2006) 55 International and Comparative Law Quarterly 281; Gardiner (n 5) 332–334: 'That article 31(3)(c) may have a useful role in handling such potential conflicts has been considered in academic study, in the work of the ILC and in some instances ... invoked in ... rulings of courts and tribunals ... A particular issue in the realm of treaty implementation is what account is to be taken of developments in international law, particularly the striking emergence of new specialist fields such as environmental law and human rights law ... the Court did give a clear indication that developments in environmental law were to be taken into account, and did so quite clearly in a context of treaty interpretation'. See also *Al-Adsani v United Kingdom* (App no 35763/97) (2001) 123 ILR 24: 'The Convention should so far as possible be interpreted in harmony with other rules of international law of which it forms part ...'; *Case Concerning the Gabčíkovo-Nagymaros Project (Hungary/Slovakia)* (Judgment) [1997] ICJ Rep 7, 140; *Advisory Opinion on Legal Consequences for States of the Continued Presence of South Africa in Namibia (South West Africa), notwithstanding Security Council Resolution* [1971] ICJ Rep 16, 31, para 53: 'an international instruments has to be interpreted and applied within the framework of the entire legal system prevailing at the time of the interpretation'; *In the Arbitration Regarding the Iron Rhine (Ijzeren Rijn) Railway (Belgium v. Netherlands),*

accord, and whether these measures include ways to integrate social and environmental priorities in order to prevent or at least mitigate the impacts in question.[33]

In this respect, the tensions become opportunities for the principle of integration to be taken into account in interpreting the treaty. To address the first tension as an opportunity, the regulator can examine the trade and investment treaty in question for provisions that would prevent the economic liberalization rules from constraining the regulatory flexibility of the Parties for social and environmental purposes in the field of sustainable development. To use Kelsen's terms, there may be provisions in the economic liberalization treaty which grant a series of permissions, providing the Parties with exceptions to certain trade and investment disciplines, where it can be shown that the disciplines might unduly constrain measures necessary to achieve other legitimate policy objectives. Should the overall treaty follow overwhelmingly along economic liberalization in its context and structure, this could influence interpretation away from the preferred 'integrated' outcome. However, general and specific exceptions, if found in the operational texts of the treaty, may provide clear exemptions that permit the sustainable development measures to be adopted. Similarly, provisions in the trade and investment treaty itself or its preamble might set out an order of precedence between the trade and investment accord and other treaties. If these provisions seem clear, the regulator would simply look, in good faith, to the context and the treaty object and purpose to confirm their ordinary meaning.[34] The context will include the treaty text, with its preamble and annexes, along with any agreement relating to the treaty, and also any instrument made by one or more Parties.[35] If notes appear in an annex to the accord, clarifying that the treaty will not apply for certain economic sectors, such notes would be considered part of the treaty context, in addition to any further agreements provided in the annexes.[36] There is also the possibility to take into account any subsequent agreement between the Parties regarding the interpretation of the treaty or the application of its provisions, and this might include a subsequent joint statement between the Parties

Arbitral Award of 24 May 2005, 58 <https://pca-cpa.org/en/cases/1/> accessed 16 December 2020 'an evolutive interpretation, which would ensure an application of the treaty that would be effective in terms of its object and purpose will be preferred to a strict application of the intertemporal rule'. See also ILC Fifty-Eighth Session, 'Report of the Study Group on Fragmentation of International Law: Difficulties arising from the Diversification and Expansion of International Law' finalized by M Koskenniemi 13 April 2006 A/CN.4/L.682 206-44; ILC Further Report 18 July 2006 A/CN.4/L.702; ILC Report on its 58th Session (2006) UNGA OR 61 SS 10 (A/61/10) 400–423.

[33] VCLT (n 2) art 31(3)(c). Article 31 of the VCLT permits interpretation to take into account, in addition to context and in light of the object and purpose, at art 31(3)(c) any relevant rules of international law applicable in the relations between the Parties. See Pauwelyn (n 28) 251–256; I Sinclair, *The Vienna Convention on the Law of Treaties* (Manchester, Manchester University Press, 1984) 119 who suggests art 32(3)(c) may be taken to include not only the general rules of international law but also treaty obligations existing for the Parties, and customary law. But see P Sands, 'Treaty, Custom and Cross-Fertilization of International Law' (1998) 10 Yale Human Rights and Development Law Journal 3 11–12, who notes that in the sense of art 31(3)(c), the treaty being interpreted retains a primary role and 'there is no question of a customary norm displacing the treaty norm, either partly or wholly'; See Brunnee and Toope (n 25).

[34] See Gardiner (n 5); see also *Aguas del Tunari v Bolivia* (ICSID ARB/02/03) Award of 21 October 2005, para 21, which notes that the VCLT does not privilege any of these three aspects of the interpretation method; Waldock, Third Report [1964] Yearbook of the International Law Commission, vol II, 7 an early draft art 55-1, which noted the need to interpret the treaty as a whole in good faith.

[35] VCLT (n 2) art 31.2.

[36] Ibid; in connection with the conclusion of the treaty that is accepted by the other Parties as an instrument related to the treaty, see art 31.2(b); if made by all the Parties in connection with the conclusion of the treaty, see art 31.2(a).

clarifying how the trade and investment rules should be interpreted to take customs into account.[37]

To address the second tension as an opportunity, similarly, the regulator may find that there are provisions in the trade and investment agreement to secure environmental and social cooperation, or that such provisions run alongside the trade and investment agreement in a separate accord. In Kelsen's terms, these accords might include permissions or prescriptions to cooperate on key environmental and social problems, as well as mechanisms to investigate situations in which laws appear to be weakened or not enforced, and even in some cases, permissions to provide resources, capacity-building and other support for programmes to address trade- and investment-related environmental and social concerns. Again, VCLT rules will be relevant to interpretation. There may be clearly operational terms of the treaty committing to ensure cooperation on environment, labour or sustainable development matters, and the regulator can consider these in context, and in light of any provisions showing a sustainable development object and purpose. Annexes that are provided can be taken into account as part of this context, as will side agreements which were made between all the Parties in connection with the conclusion of the treaty, and there may also be separate memoranda of agreement which, if they were accepted as related to the trade and investment treaty by the other Parties, can be considered authentic means for interpretation.[38]

Addressing the third set of tensions as opportunities, integrated substantive economic liberalization rules may be included in the trade and investment treaty as well, delivering sustainable development benefits through increases in liberalization in targeted 'sustainable' sectors of the economies, or for certain types of goods or services that meet internationally agreed sustainable development goal. Essentially, in Kelsen's terms, the States would need to include prescriptive provisions that oblige the Parties to liberalize trade in specific economic sectors that they agree will contribute to sustainable development. Again, the regulator might seek integral provisions which agree to promote trade and investment in sustainable goods and services, or to develop new markets, together with annexes, side agreements or separate memoranda of agreement.[39] Such provisions, if the regulator finds them included in the text of the treaty, can assist in avoiding conflicts, and may have greater weight than turning to documents exchanged during trade and investment negotiations as *travaux préparatoires*, including impact assessments in certain instances, as supplementary means of interpretation.[40] From the 'textual' viewpoint, therefore, it is important to

[37] Ibid 31.3(a); see also ILC, 'Yearbook of the International Law Commission (1966-II)' UN Doc A/CN.4/SER.A/1966, 222 para 15.

[38] VCLT (n 2) art 31.2; 31.2(a); 31.2(b); Gardiner (n 5) 265–275.

[39] VCLT (n 2) art 31(3)(a) which, as noted by Gardiner (n 5), includes any subsequent agreements between the Parties as to interpretation or application of its provisions, and at art 31(3)(b) also includes any subsequent practices in the application of the treaty which establish agreement of Parties regarding its interpretation; [1966] Yearbook of the International Law Commission, vol II, 221 para 14: '[A]n agreement as to the interpretation of a provision reached after the conclusion of the treat represents an authentic interpretation by the parties which must be read into the treaty for the purposes of its interpretation'. See also *Kasikili/Sedudu Island (Botswana v Namibia)* [1999] ICJ Rep 1045, 1076, para 49.

[40] VCLT (n 2) art 32, provides for supplementary means of interpretation to which recourse is often had, but which are used to confirm the meaning resulting from the application of art 31, or to determine meaning if the ordinary meeting in context and in light of the object and purpose is either left ambiguous or obscure, as per art 32(a) or leads to a result which is manifestly absurd or unreasonable, as per art 32(b). See Gardiner (n 5).

consider the further provisions of a new economic treaty, particularly inasmuch as they might avoid conflicts of obligations.

A further perspective is also helpful, informed by advances in international relations theory. Few international treaties today are simply contracts among States. As Professors John Ruggie and Stephen Krasner have suggested, to understand the norms found in international treaties and how they are implemented, it is important to analyse the implicit understandings between a broad range of actors in a treaty regime, not only the formal views of States.[41] A 'regime' is an institution that might coalesce or be structured around certain legal rules and certain formal organizations, but goes well beyond them, and develops iteratively.[42] Such regimes, as posited by Professor John Vogler, can be defined as 'sets of implicit or explicit principles, norms, rules and decision-making procedures around which actors' expectations converge in a given area of international relations'.[43] Principles, norms, rules and decision-making procedures are all necessary parts of an inter-actional international treaty regime, which exists to achieve the common object and purpose of States and other international actors.[44]

Regimes, therefore, in international relations theory, can be described as governing specific issue areas in an interactive way.[45] This distinguishes them from broader 'international orders' which imply an authority superintending over a wide range of institutions and issues.[46] As such, regimes are more 'specialised arrangements that pertain to well defined activities, resources or geographical areas and often involve only some subset of the members of international society'.[47] As Vogler observes, the boundaries of a regime are thus determined partly by perceptions of the extent and linkage between issues.

The regime is useful as an analytical construct in this volume, as it calls attention to the way that principles, rules and decision-making procedures develop, interact and evolve in one 'sub-system', focusing on the converging expectations of a group of international actors. As Professors Stephen Toope and Jutta Brunnee suggest, regime analysis can serve the study of international law, drawing on the 'inter-actional' behaviours of legal subjects and rules originally observed by Lon L Fuller.[48] Inter-actional regimes, as they note, can coalesce around international treaty commitments, which evolve and 'deepen' over time through

[41] JG Ruggie, 'International Responses to Technology: Ideas and Trends' (1975) 29 International Organization 557, 557–583. See also JG Ruggie, 'Reconstituting the Global Public Domain-Issues, Actors, and Practices' (2004) 10 European Journal of International Relations 499, 499–531.

[42] JG Ruggie, 'International Responses to Technology: Ideas and Trends' (2004) 10 European Journal of International Relations 557–583. See also Ruggie (n 41) 499–531.

[43] J Vogler, *The Global Commons: Environmental and Technological Governance* (2nd edn, Chichester, John Wiley and Sons 2000) 20–43.

[44] See especially JG Ruggie, 'International Regimes, Transactions and Change: Embedded Liberalism in the Postwar Economic Order' in S Krasner (ed), *International Regimes* (Ithaca, Cornell University Press 1983); see also S Haggard and BA Simmons, 'Theories of International Regimes' (1987) 41 International Organization 491; OS Stokke, 'Regimes as Governance Systems' in OR Young (ed), *Global Governance: Drawing Insights from the Environmental Experience* (Boston, MIT Press 1997) 27–64; See Brunnee and Toope (n 25).

[45] OR Young, *International Cooperation: Building Regimes for Natural Resources and The Environment* (Ithaca, Cornell University Press 1989) as cited in Vogler (n 43) 23; See Brunnee and Toope (n 25).

[46] Vogler (n 43) 20–43.

[47] Young (n 44) 23.

[48] See Brunnee and Toope (n 25) See SJ Toope and J Brunnée, 'International Law and Constructivism: Elements of an Interactional Theory of International Law' (2000) 39 Columbia Journal of Transnational Law 19, 19–74; see also J Brunnée and SJ Toope, 'The Changing Nile Basin Regime: Does Law Matter?' (2002) 43 Harvard International Law Journal 105, 105–159.

interactions between states and non-state actors, shaping and being shaped by the norms and rules, knowledge and networks generated by the regime.[49]

From this perspective, both the 'hard' and 'soft' law between Parties to a treaty (or a series of treaties) evolves with the regime, and involves more than States in its implementation.[50] A regime may start with a legally binding agreement with broad participation but shallow substantive commitments, then deepen in substantive content and engagement of more and better informed actors, leading to greater compliance over time. As such, the emergence, evolution and effects of normative systems can coalesce around a particular object and purpose in international law, reinforced by 'epistemic communities' which share scientific information and data.[51] In certain circumstances, it may be undesirable to negotiate seemingly strong international treaties without first going through a careful, incremental process of regime-building. Without it, formal legal commitments are unlikely to be meaningful; States may simply assent with no intention of complying, or no capacity to comply.[52] As Brunnee and Toope suggest, once a contextual agreement (such as a framework convention) initiates the development of self-reinforcing norms and institutions, regimes can then evolve in the direction of deeper substantive legal commitments. A steady building process, focused on the object and purpose of the treaty, may yield increasingly complex and sophisticated regimes of nearly universal application.[53] For other treaties on sustainable development, such as the 1992 UN Convention on Biological Diversity (UNCBD)[54] and the 1992 UN Framework Convention on Climate Change (UNFCCC),[55] it has been convincingly argued that States established framework agreements which commit to certain common objects and purposes, and a process by which further more detailed and specific protocols are negotiated.[56] In emerging trade and investment regimes, from this perspective, it is possible that while agreed provisions appear likely to generate the tensions discussed above, as the regime continues to evolve, new purposes can be accepted by the Parties, and new operational provisions negotiated to take evolving customary law and policy including commitments to integration, and global Sustainable Development Goals, into account. For instance, even if the WTO Agreements did not originally include sustainable development as part of the purpose, and even if there were WTO Members that had persistently objected to a principle of integration in customary law, the WTO may still be able to evolve as a regime for an eventual acceptance of this objective, taking into account an integration principle in certain areas of its work, and in that context, new obligations may be negotiated within the regime framework.

Whether one departs from a purposive, a textual or a 'regime' perspective, if it is desirable to integrate social and environmental concerns into trade and investment treaties for sustainable development, *either* for sound international policy reasons, *or* out of respect for an

49 See Brunnee and Toope (n 25); See Toope and Brunnée (n 48) 19–74; see also J Brunnée and S J Toope, 'Persuasion and Enforcement: Explaining Compliance with International Law' (2002) XIII Finnish Yearbook of International Law 1, 1–23.

50 D Shelton 'International Law and Relative Normativity' in M Evans (ed), *International Law* (3rd edn, Oxford, OUP 2010) 183. See also Birnie, Boyle and Redgwell (n 25).

51 Shelton (n 50); J Brunnée, 'Coping with Consent: Lawmaking under Multilateral Environmental Agreements' (2002) 15 Leiden Journal of International Law 1, 1–52; A Roberts, *Is International Law International?* (Oxford, OUP 2017); See Brunnee and Toope (n 25).

52 Roberts (n 51) 5–6.

53 Ibid 33–37.

54 Opened for signature 5 June 1992, entered into force 29 December 1993, 1760 UNTS 79, 143 .

55 Opened for signature 4 June 1992, entered into force 21 March 1994, 1771 UNTS 107 .

56 See Brunnee and Toope (n 25); Brunnée (n 51) 37–38.

emerging customary principle of integration, *or* simply to achieve a common objective that is set as an 'object and purpose' of the trade and investment treaty in a new treaty or as a new commitment while a treaty regime evolves, the question remains as to which provisions might best be interpreted as doing so effectively. What obligations can be included as an 'FAO Seed Treaty article 6' to add clarity to a commitment for sustainable development in an international trade and investment treaty? How are States addressing the three key normative tensions identified in the surveys of impact assessments?

Earlier chapters of this volume raised concerns about the sustainability of entering into trade and investment agreements which might lead to serious environmental and social impacts, identifying three key tensions. In this section, it has been argued that in light of two decades of global and regional 'soft law' commitments to sustainable development through trade and investment, States may have legitimate expectations that these key tensions will be addressed. These chapters also argued that given these commitments to sustainable development, particularly if the concept is accepted as part of the 'object and purpose' of trade and investment treaties themselves, or has an interstitial influence on the process of economic treaty negotiations, certain customary norms may be useful to address the tensions. It has argued that the principle of integration, as defined in Principle 4 of the 1992 Rio Declaration and supplemented by social considerations from the 2002 JPOI, is particularly relevant for economic policy-making. It has considered how the principle of integration, in European law and policy, assists to overcome the key normative tensions identified, advancing sustainable development through trade and investment. Noting that notwithstanding its potential interpretive weight as part of the 'object and purpose' of a treaty, a preambular reference alone in a trade and investment treaty may not provide a comprehensive response to these tensions, this part of the book considered further reasons that States may adopt additional textual mechanisms, converting tensions to opportunities for sustainable development, arguing that such mechanisms can be interpreted in light of the integration principle. The volume now turns to whether and how States are addressing these tensions/opportunities in global trade and investment law (the WTO, including its Agreement on Trade-Related Investment Measures (TRIMS)) or failing this, in their regional and bilateral trade and investment arrangements.

SECTION FOUR

WTO PROVISIONS AND PROCESSES ON SUSTAINABLE DEVELOPMENT

11

Development and Environment in Early World Trade Debates

Focusing on the key integration challenges identified earlier in this volume, the upcoming sections analyse current practices in international trade and investment treaties on sustainable development. This current section focuses on how the three tensions in economic liberalization in relation to sustainable development are addressed in World Trade Organization (WTO) law and policy. As such, the following chapters summarize the evidence from a survey of State practice in the WTO. They briefly analyse two decades of WTO negotiations and practices related to sustainable development, including key decisions of the WTO Panel and Appellate Body in recent disputes and WTO member State responses in the Trade Policy Review Mechanism (TPRM). The chapters argue that sustainable development has come to be recognized as part of the 'object and purpose' of the WTO regime, briefly discussing the implications of this. This section also provides a critical perspective on whether State Parties to the WTO have, up to this point, been able to effectively integrate environmental and social considerations into economic law and policy-making in the WTO, in order to achieve sustainable development. It focuses on how the opportunities for integration identified earlier in this volume have been addressed, highlighting the limits of the WTO.

Multilateral trade and investment rules have progressively gained currency in the global economy since the 1930s.[1] Their links to environmental and social development concerns have only been seriously analysed more recently.[2] Economists such as Adam Smith, David Ricardo and John Stuart Mill argued persuasively that countries could benefit economically from free trade and liberalized investment between them, as free trade and investment allows each country to build on its respective comparative advantages.[3] A key moment was the negotiation of a Havana Charter for an International Trade Organization in 1947.[4] The Charter would have added a 'missing leg' to the Bretton Woods Institutions.[5] While

[1] M Trebilcock and R Howse, *The Regulation of International Trade* (New York, Routledge 2005); D Bethlehem and others, *The Oxford Handbook of International Trade Law* (Oxford, OUP 2009); J Mathis, *Regional Trade Agreements in the GATT / WTO* (The Hague, TMC Asser 2002). See also for investment treaties, A Newcombe and L Paradell, *Law and Practice of Investment Treaties* (Chicago, Kluwer Law International 2009).

[2] See G Sampson, *The WTO and Sustainable Development* (Tokyo, UNU 2005); M Gehring and MC Cordonier Segger (eds), *Sustainable Development in World Trade Law* (The Hague, Kluwer Law International 2005); D French, *International Law and Policy on Sustainable Development* (Manchester, Juris 2005).

[3] A Smith, *An Inquiry Into the Nature and Causes of the Wealth of Nations* (1776); Ricardo, *The Principles of Political Economy and Taxation* (1817); D van den Bossche, *The Law and Policy of the WTO: Text, Cases and Materials* (Cambridge, CUP 2005) 19–24. See also V Lowe, *International Law* (Oxford, OUP 2009) 215–226; G Sampson, *The Role of the World Trade Organization in Global Governance* (Tokyo, UNU 2001); J Baylis and S Smith (eds), *The Globalization of World Politics* (Oxford, OUP 2001); M Fujimoto, 'J.S. Mill's Idea of International Trade' in S Senga, M Fujimoto and T Tabuchi (eds), *Ricardo and International Trade* (London, Routledge 2017).

[4] See 'Havana Charter for An International Trade Organization', UN Conference on Trade and Development, Final Act and Related Documents, 24 March 1948, UN Doc E/Conf 2/78 (1948) 46.1.

[5] JH Jackson, *The World Trading System-Law and Policy of International Economic Relations* (2nd edn, Boston, MIT Press 1997).

Crafting Trade and Investment Accords for Sustainable Development. Marie-Claire Cordonier Segger, Oxford University Press. © Marie-Claire Cordonier Segger 2021. DOI: 10.1093/oso/9780198831341.003.0011

environmental concerns were not yet current in international debates, the 1947 trade talks addressed management of natural resources, and also social issues such as labour and development, as well as investment.[6] However, the Charter failed when the US Senate could not ratify it, and instead, the General Agreement on Tariffs and Trade (GATT)[7] was enacted provisionally, focusing narrowly on placing disciplines on the tariffs that countries would apply to trade in goods. These somewhat limited economic rules formed the basis for almost 50 years of trade, with little scope to consider environmental or social issues.[8]

Debates on development, in the GATT, began in a different context from either the discussions on the environment, or on human rights, which focused mainly on labour rights. Certain developing countries, such as Chile, participated in the GATT from 1948.[9] However, from the entire proposed Havana Charter Part III on development priorities, only proposed articles 13 and 14 were modified and included as article XVIII GATT 1947, addressing protection of infant industries and balance of payments.[10] It was not until the Kennedy Round from 1963 to 1967 that changes were made to the GATT, in an attempt to address development concerns.[11] As many newly independent countries acceded to the GATT in 1965, the Contracting Parties adopted Part IV of the GATT on 'Trade and Development'.[12] These guidelines prioritized developed country reductions of trade barriers and tariffs for products of interest to developing countries, but left the main structure of the GATT unchanged, providing only limited accommodations through longer timelines and certain other exceptions.[13] Many developing countries expressed dissatisfaction, and a GATT Committee on Trade and Development (CTD) was established as a forum to debate solutions.[14] In this same period, the United Nations Conference on Trade and Development (UNCTAD) was formed, though it was only modestly able to mitigate the GATT's initial lack of progress in addressing trade and development concerns.[15] However, UNCTAD gained certain prominence by focusing on economic issues of interest to developing countries, hosting debates on the 'New International Economic Order',[16] and in 1968,

[6] P Demaret, 'The Metamorphoses of the GATT: From the Havana Charter to the World Trade Organisation' (1995) 34 Columbia Journal of Transnational Law 123, 126.

[7] Adopted 30 October 1947, provisionally entered into force 1 January 1948, 55 UNTS 194, CTS No 31 (1948).

[8] M Matsushita, TJ Schoenbaum and PC Mavroidis, *The World Trade Organization: Law, Practice, and Policy* (Oxford, OUP 2006) 2; Jackson (n 5) 38.

[9] EK Kessie, 'Developing Countries in the World Trade Organisation' (1999) 22 World Competition 83; RE Baldwin, J McLaren and A Panagariya, *Regulatory Protectionism, Developing Nations, and a Two-Tier World Trade System* (Washington, Brookings Trade Forum 2000); ten of the twenty-three original GATT Contracting Parties were developing countries (Brazil, Burma, China, Ceylon, Chile, Cuba, India, Pakistan, Syria and Lebanon). See also Matsushita, Schoenbaum and Mavroidis (n 8) 765; TN Srinivasan, *Developing Countries and the Multilateral Trading System: From GATT to the Uruguay Round and the Future* (New York, Routledge 2019).

[10] Trebilcock and Howse (n 1) 471–587.

[11] R Bahla, *Modern GATT Law: A Treatise on the General Agreement on Tariffs and Trade* (London, Sweet and Maxwell 2005) 244.

[12] Ibid.

[13] Bethlehem and others (n 1); WTO Secretariat (ed), *Trade, Development and the Environment* (London, Kluwer Law International 2000) 155.

[14] SE Rolland, 'Developing Country Coalitions at the WTO: In Search of Legal Support' (2007) 48 Harvard International Law Journal 483.

[15] Establishment of the United Nations Conference on Trade and Development as an Organ of the General Assembly (adopted 30 December 1964) UNGA Res 1995 (XIX); Matsushita, Schoenbaum and Mavroidis (n 8) 766.

[16] JN Bhagwati, 'The New International Economic Order: The North-South Debate' (1977) MIT Bicentennial Studies.

jointly with the GATT, established an International Trade Centre (ITC) to facilitate trade promotion and market identification for developing countries.[17]

In the 1970s, many GATT members argued that development priorities should be met using development assistance rather than by changes to trade or investment laws, agreeing a target for official development assistance (ODA) levels by developed countries to the poorest countries to reach 0.7 per cent of GDP.[18] Though this target was formally adopted by the UN General Assembly in 1970, and has been consistently reaffirmed, levels have not yet risen above 0.33 per cent.[19] Observing a real lack of progress on ODA commitments, many developing countries focused on trade and investment regimes, with the hope that increased trade and investment flows would bring economic development through productivity gains. While economists and others are convinced that trade-led growth can yield important benefits for a developing country, they also agree that such benefits will not be generated automatically, and are even less likely to be automatically shared equally among economic actors.[20]

Attempts were made in the Tokyo Round from 1973 and 1979 to facilitate development interests through world trade law, resulting in a WTO 'Enabling Clause' on 'Differential and More Favourable Treatment, Reciprocity and Fuller Participation of Developing Countries' which permitted special and differential treatment for developing countries (through, for instance, longer timelines to implement liberalization commitments).[21] A Group of Least Developed Countries (LDCs) was also identified through the UNCTAD, and it begun to serve as a focal point for economic development and technical assistance.[22]

In the 1970s, as discussed earlier in this volume, concerns also began to be raised about whether economic projects were excessively harming the environment, particularly in developed countries.[23] The 'Limits to Growth' Report of the Club of Rome predicted global shortages if future economic development were not redirected to secure less impact on non-renewable natural resources.[24] This was controversial for developing countries, as many planned to focus on the full exploitation of their natural resources, along with the comparative advantage of their cheaper labour, in order to realize economic growth targets.[25] In

17 International Trade Centre, <https://www.intracen.org/> accessed 16 December 2020.

18 Matsushita, Schoenbaum and Mavroidis (n 8) 780.

19 LA Winters, 'Trade Liberalization and Economic Performance: An Overview' (2004) 114(493) Economic Journal F4, F18. Seven countries met the UN target to provide 0.7 per cent of gross national income (GNI) as ODA in 2017 and 2018: OECD, 'Trends and insights on development finance', in *Development Co-operation Profiles* (Paris, 2019) <https://doi.org/10.1787/5e331623-en> accessed 7 September 2019.

20 OECD, 'Trade Facilitation Reforms in the Service of Development' TD/TD/WP(2003)11/FINAL; S Polaski, *Winners and Losers: Impact of the Doha Round on Developing Countries* (Washington, Carnegie Endowment 2006); M Ravallion, 'Looking Beyond Averages in the Trade and Poverty Debate' (2004) World Bank Policy Research Working Paper 346, <http://ideas.repec.org/p/wbk/wbrwps/3461.html>; J Stiglitz and A Charlton, *Fair Trade for All: How Trade Can Promote Development* (Oxford, OUP 2006); DW Te Velde and D Bezemer, 'Regional Integration and Foreign Direct Investment in Developing Countries' (2006) <http://www.odi.org.uk/iedg/Projects/ec_prep2.pdf> accessed 16 December 2020; D Ben-David, H Nordstrom and LA Winters (eds), *Trade, Income Disparity and Poverty* (Special Studies 5, Geneva, WTO 1999). LA Winters, 'Trade and Poverty: Is There a Connection?' in Ben-David, Nordstrom and Winters, ibid; K Siddiqui, 'Globalization, Trade Liberalisation and the Issues of Economic Diversification in the Developing Countries' (2017) 4(4) Journal of Business & Economic Policy 30.

21 M Gehring, 'Sustainable Development in World Trade Law' in HC Bugge and C Voigt (eds), *Sustainable Development in International and National Law* (Groingen, Europa 2009) 271, 728.

22 Ibid.

23 Ibid 279.

24 See DL Meadows and others, *Limits to Growth* (Boston, MIT Press 1972).

25 RN Cooper, *Environment and Resource Policies for the World Economy* (Washington, Brookings Institution 1994).

1971, the Executive Director of the United Nations European Programme (UNEP) urged the GATT Council to strike a new GATT Working Group on Environmental Measures and International Trade (EMIT).[26] While the EMIT Group was created, it did not meet formally for nearly two decades. Instead, in the Tokyo Round of trade negotiations of the late 1970s, additional agreements were adopted, further disciplining the application of technical barriers to trade (TBT), sanitary and phytosanitary standards (SPS) and subsidies, including those which had been set in place to address health, natural resources conservation and environmental concerns.[27] Eventually, in the Brussels GATT Ministerial Conference on 3 December 1990, a group of countries advanced a formal negotiating proposal to consider trade and environment questions in the GATT, underscoring the need to reactivate the 1971 EMIT.[28] The proposal was, however, not adopted at the Ministerial Conference, in part due to scepticism on the part of developing countries and the US regarding such topics in terms of GATT's restricted mandate.[29] However, discussions of environmental concerns continued in subsequent GATT Council meetings.[30]

At the WTO General Council in February 1991, Mexico challenged US measures to prevent the import of tuna fished with dolphin-unfriendly nets in the WTO (the *US-Tuna/Dolphin Case*[31]) and the Ambassador of Brazil (Rubens Ricupero, later WTO Director General and then UNCTAD Secretary General) raised the issue of sustainable development, noting that 'a new dimension – development – had been added to the environment question, which presented the challenge of defining the equation between the two'.[32]

Essentially, the concept of sustainable development was introduced in international trade and investment policy debates as a manner of bridging or 'balancing' environmental concerns with development issues.[33] At the GATT Council in May 1991, during the preparations for the 1992 UN Conference on Environment and Development, several Contracting Parties of the GATT began seeking changes to the GATT Preamble to make explicit reference to sustainable development. According to the Session Report, Austria, speaking on behalf of the countries that had requested re-activation of the 1971 EMIT and a possible GATT contribution to the UNCED process, argued that 'the concept of sustainable development, especially the sustainable management of resources, was an important addition to the objective laid down in the Preamble to the General Agreement of "developing the full use of the resources of the world" ', while also noting that '[e]nvironmental concerns should not, however, lead to unnecessary trade barriers' and that 'the measure with the least trade impact should be used to achieve a given end'.[34] In 1995, Canada added that:

[26] Adverse Trade Effects of Environmental Measures, Communication from UNEP (25 November 1988), GATT Document L/6437, <https://docs.wto.org/gattdocs/q/GG/L6599/6437.PDF> accessed 16 December 2020.

[27] van den Bossche (n 3) 82.

[28] Communication from Austria, Finland, Iceland, Norway, Sweden and Switzerland (3 December 1990) GATT Document MTN.TNC/W/47, <http://www.wto.org/gatt_docs/English/SULPDF/92120048.pdf> accessed 16 December 2020.

[29] Gehring (n 21).

[30] Ibid.

[31] *United States—Restrictions on the Import of Tuna* (1991) GATT BISD 39S/155, (1991) 30 ILM 1594.

[32] Minutes of Meeting held in the Centre William Rappard on 6 February 1991 (5 March 1991) GATT Document C/M/247, <http://www.wto.org/gatt_docs/English/SULPDF/91530241.pdf> accessed 16 December 2020.

[33] P Sands and J Peel, *Principles of International Environmental Law* (4th edn, Cambridge, CUP 2018) 217–229; P Birnie, A Boyle and C Redgwell, *International Law & the Environment* (Oxford, OUP 2009); A Kiss and D Shelton, *International Environmental Law* (3rd edn, New York, Transnational 2004).

[34] Minutes of Meeting held in the Centre William Rappard on 29–30 May 1991 (28 June 1991) GATT Document C/M/250, <http://www.wto.org/gatt_docs/English/SULPDF/91530724.pdf> accessed 16 December 2020.

> The growing public concern to respond to environmental degradation has encouraged Contracting Parties to develop environmental policies more appropriate to sustainable development. The right of Contracting Parties to adopt measures in response to environmental objectives, even where these may impinge on trade, is clearly recognized under GATT rules and in some of the Tokyo Round instruments.[35]

Canada also signalled that Article XX GATT, which provides general exceptions to GATT rules, might be useful in the balancing of environment and trade concerns:

> There is limited jurisprudence respecting the use of the general exceptions provided under Article XX.... It is clear, however, that there is a need for greater clarity respecting their scope of the exceptions ...'[36]

During these debates, developed countries such as Canada focused on the environmental dimension of sustainable development, without fully taking the development dimension into account.[37] Due in part to this, developing countries remained unconvinced.[38] As Peru noted:

> ... sustainable development is a very broad concept and trade issues are only one of its many aspects. We should therefore ask ourselves whether or not this is the right time to devise trade measures in GATT that contribute to the formulation of a comprehensive concept of sustainable development. We believe that it is still too early ...'[39]

After extensive consultations, the 1971 EMIT was finally re-activated at GATT Council on 8 October 1991, not without criticisms from both developed and developing countries. GATT Parties also participated in the UNCED, of course, and in the 1992 Agenda 21, an initial agenda for trade, environment and development issues were laid out, tasking the GATT, the UNCTAD and others to 'elaborate adequate studies for the better understanding of the relationship between trade and environment for the promotion of sustainable development', and to 'promote a dialogue between trade, development and environment communities'.[40]

The GATT Committee on Trade and Development discussed trade, environment and development issues at its Seventy-Fifth Session on 26 July 1993, with presentations by UNCTAD and the ITC.[41] There had been a significant shift in perspectives among the Contracting Parties present. Many may have gained comfort from the UNCED negotiations in which, while committing to sustainable development as an objective, States had also recognized the need to avoid environmental or health standards that actually disguised

35 Trade and Environment, Statement by the Delegation of Canada (2 July 1991) GATT Document Spec(91)38, <http://www.wto.org/gatt_docs/English/SULPDF/92270087.pdf> accessed 16 December 2020.

36 Ibid.

37 Trebilcock and Howse (n 1).

38 H Katrak and R Strange (eds), *The WTO and Developing Countries* (Palgrave Macmillan, Basingstoke 2004).

39 Trade and Environment, Statement by the Delegation of Peru (12 June 1991) GATT Document Spec(91)39, <http://www.wto.org/gatt_docs/English/SULPDF/92270088.pdf> accessed 16 December 2020.

40 Ibid Chapter 2.10.

41 Note on Proceedings of the Seventy-Fifth Session, 26 July 1993 (20 October 1993) GATT Document COM.TD/134, <http://www.wto.org/gatt_docs/English/SULPDF/91730169.pdf> accessed 16 December 2020.

protectionism, and for trade policy that balanced environmental and socio-economic factors.[42] For instance, India:

> underlined the special importance his country attached to the [CTD] work on the UNCED follow-up. Recalling that the primary focus of Agenda 21, Chapter 2 was on achieving sustainable development in developing countries, the representative pointed out that UNCED had recognized that the prescription for achieving this objective might have to be different from that of other countries. For this reason, the UNCED had acknowledged that environmental standards valid for developed countries might have unwarranted social and economic costs in developing countries.[43]

This socio-economic development dimension was also emphasized by other GATT Contracting Parties, such as Mexico. As noted in the 1993 CTD Report:

> Mexico believed that in examining the concept of sustainable development, it was important to take into account the differences between developed and developing countries. While the problems of developed countries were related to high consumption levels, developing countries suffered from poverty, misery and lack of resources. For the latter, the economic development through trade, as well as external and financial flows, were essential to achieve sustainable development.[44] [sic]

Both representatives referred to sustainable development as a policy objective. The Chairman's Report of the CTD noted that:

> Several Committee members recalled that the primary focus of Chapter 2 of Agenda 21 was on *achieving sustainable development in developing countries, an objective which might require different prescriptions* than that of other countries . . .[45]

The EMIT held several meetings in 1992–1993, making submissions to the first and second meetings of the UNCSD on the need for mutual supportiveness between trade and development, and trade and the environment, while UNCTAD and the GATT CTD also became more active on both environment and development aspects of the trade and investment debates.[46]

Labour issues were addressed completely separately, and did not enter significantly into these debates, in part due to the active participation of the International Labour Organization (ILO) which shared many Members with the WTO, and was seen by many WTO members as the proper forum to debate linkages between labour rights, trade policy and where appropriate, investment as well.[47]

42 Agenda 21, Annex 2 of the Report of the UN Conference on Environment and Development, 13 June 1992, UN Doc A/CONF.151/26 (Vol I), Chapter 2.22.

43 Note on Proceedings of the Seventy-Fifth Session (n 41) 14.

44 Ibid 33.

45 Committee on Trade and Development, Report by the Chairman on the follow-up to UNCED in GATT (11 February 1994) GATT Document COM.TD/W/509, <http://www.wto.org/gatt_docs/English/SULPDF/91760062.pdf> accessed 16 December 2020 (emphasis added).

46 See Note on Proceedings of the Seventy-Fifth Session (n 41) UNCTAD presentation.

47 See, e.g., A Panagariya, 'The Return of Labour Standards in the WTO?' *Economic Times* (6 November 1999).

In 1994 in Marrakesh, after nearly a decade of 'Uruguay Round' trade deliberations and negotiations, the GATT 1947 was replaced by the Agreement Establishing the World Trade Organization (WTO Agreement) and its subsequent agreements, one pillar of which remained the GATT treaty.[48] In addition, the GATT dispute settlement system, which was seen as ineffective and inefficient, as reports for controversial cases could not be adopted due to a lack of unanimity, was replaced in the 1994 WTO Agreements by the WTO dispute settlement mechanism ('DSM'). These agreements are briefly described in the Table of Treaties in this volume, with notes on their relevance for sustainable development.

Part of this package was the 1994 WTO Marrakech Decision on Trade and Environment, which echoed Agenda 21 by affirming that 'there should not be, nor need be, any policy contradiction between upholding and safeguarding an open, non-discriminatory and equitable multilateral trading system on the one hand, and acting for the protection of the environment, and the promotion of sustainable development on the other'.[49] This Decision emphasized the 'need for rules to enhance positive interaction between trade and environmental measures, for the promotion of sustainable development, with special consideration to the needs of developing countries, in particular those of the least developed among them' and established a WTO CTE with an agenda of items for deliberations'.[50] At the 1994 Marrakech Conference which adopted the WTO Final Act, Ireland noted:

> The debate has intensified since the [UNCED] endorsed the principle of sustainable development as the guiding force for economic development worldwide. Indeed the 'greening' of trade policies promises to be one of the more complex and politically charged issues to be tackled in the future. At the heart of the issue is how to strike the difficult balance between the drive for greater trade liberalization and the need to counter environmental degradation.[51]

In 1994, therefore, in spite of the sustainable development framework of the 1992 UNCED, the WTO mechanisms to debate environment and development issues were institutionally distinct, responding to what was perceived as the separate interests of different communities.[52] Leading trade law scholarship, inasmuch as it considered the links of trade to environment, to development and to human rights, perpetuated these divisions.[53] And both sets of issues were fairly marginal in the WTO's main trade and economic liberalization agenda.[54] Further, the Uruguay Round 'development' expectations of developing countries for concessions in, for instance, agricultural and textile trade through new WTO

[48] John H Jackson, 'The Birth of the GATT-MTN System: A Constitutional Appraisal' (1980) 12 Law and Policy in International Business 21, 52. See also Trebilcock and Howse (n 1) 27. MW Gehring, MC Cordonier Segger and J Hepburn, *Global Trade Law in Practice* (Globe Business Publishing 2004) 11; See also <https://www.wto.org>.

[49] Ministerial Decision on Trade and Environment (15 April 1994) LT/UR/D-5/8, 33 ILM 1267, preamble <http://docsonline.wto.org> ('Noting: The Rio Declaration on Environment and Development, Agenda 21, and its follow-up in GATT, as reflected in the statement of the Chairman of the Council of Representatives to the CONTRACTING PARTIES at their 48th Session in December 1992 ...').

[50] Ibid.

[51] Ireland, Statement by Mr Charles McCreevy, Minister for Tourism and Trade (13 April 1994) WTO Document MTN.TNC/MIN(94)/ST/52, <http://www.wto.org/gatt_docs/English/SULPDF/92150246.pdf> accessed 16 December 2020.

[52] H Ward, 'Common but Differentiated Debates: Environment, Labor and the WTO' (1996) 45 International Comparative Law Quarterly 592, 595.

[53] Ibid.

[54] Gehring and Cordonier Segger (n 2) 43; Bethlehem and others (n 1).

Agreements were mostly frustrated.[55] Many developing countries found that they had consented to cut certain tariffs (and hence, government revenues) even more deeply than industrialized countries, while also committing to robust implementation of the General Agreement on Trade in Services (GATS)[56] and the Agreement on Trade-Related Aspects of Intellectual Property Rights (TRIPS),[57] which created significant challenges for some governments of developing country.[58] From a regime analysis perspective, at the start of the new WTO, tensions were formed between constituencies interested in trade-led economic growth, constituencies seeking trade to support development, and countries wishing to make links between trade and the environment.

[55] Gehring and Cordonier Segger (n 2).

[56] Adopted 15 April 1994, entered into force 1 January 1995, 1869 UNTS 183.

[57] Adopted 15 April 1994, entered into force 1 January 1995, 1869 UNTS 299; C Bellmann, G Dutfield and R Meléndez-Ortiz, *Trading in Knowledge: Development Perspectives on TRIPS, Trade and Sustainability* (London, Earthscan and ICTSD 2003) Foreword.

[58] C Thomas and J Trachtman (eds), *Developing Countries in the WTO Legal System* (Oxford, OUP 2009).

12

Sustainable Development Provisions in the 1994 GATT/WTO Agreements

A mention of sustainable development was added to the World Trade Organization (WTO) Agreement in 1994, in the Preamble.[1] While the WTO may have accepted sustainable development as an objective of its members, it is not clear that the WTO has successfully integrated either environment or social development concerns into trade policy-making, to date. The preambular sustainable development objective has been interpreted by the WTO dispute settlement mechanism (DSM) and has begun to be reflected in negotiations among States, in the activities of the WTO, and in the trade and investment laws and practices of WTO members.[2] The discussion below considers the three opportunities for integration discussed in Chapter 3, and the implications of attempts to respond to them within the WTO, in two phases. First, it considers the WTO Agreements after the conclusion of the 1992 United Nations Conference on Environment and Development (UNCED) and the 1994 Uruguay Round, and how they are interpreted by the WTO Panel and Appellate Body (AB) in trade disputes, as well as any progress in WTO negotiations with respect to the tensions identified earlier during that period. Second, it considers developments in the WTO Doha Round of trade negotiations that were launched in 2001, directly before the 2002 World Summit on Sustainable Development (WSSD), and how subsequent WTO disputes have addressed these tensions.

12.1 Recognition of a Sustainable Development Objective in the WTO and its Relevance to the General Exceptions at Article XX from 1994–2001

The first opportunity for integration identified in Chapters 2 and 3 of this volume involves the provision of windows, or exemptions, in trade agreements to permit States a certain degree of regulatory flexibility on environmental and social development matters. The WTO Agreements include provisions to prevent trade and investment rules from constraining the regulatory flexibility of the Parties for social and environmental purposes, in the context of their commitments to sustainable development.[3] In the GATT, and the WTO

[1] G Sampson, *The WTO and Sustainable Development* (Tokyo, UNU 2005); M Gehring and MC Cordonier Segger (eds), *Sustainable Development in World Trade Law* (The Hague, Kluwer Law International 2005); S Alam, *Sustainable Development and Free Trade: Institutional Approaches* (New York, Routledge 2008). See also Agreement Establishing the World Trade Organization, 15 April 1994, *The Legal Texts: The Results of the Uruguay Round of Multilateral Trade Negotiations* 4 (1999), 1867 UNTS 154, 33 ILM 1144 (1994) [WTO Agreement]. See WTO <http://www.wto.org/english/tratop_e/envir_e/sust_dev_e.htm> accessed 16 December 2020.

[2] Sampson (n 1) Foreword by WTO Director-General Pascal Lamy vii–xi.

[3] General Agreement on Tariffs and Trade (GATT) (adopted 30 October 1947, provisionally entered into force 1 January 1948) 55 UNTS 194, CTS No 31 (1948), art XX(b)(g); A Green, 'Climate Change, Regulatory Policy and the WTO: How Constraining are Trade Rules?' (2005) 8(1) Journal of International Economic Law 143; Y

Crafting Trade and Investment Accords for Sustainable Development. Marie-Claire Cordonier Segger, Oxford University Press. © Marie-Claire Cordonier Segger 2021. DOI: 10.1093/oso/9780198831341.003.0012

Agreements, as has been well-documented in legal scholarship, States agreed to certain general exceptions at article XX and in other provisions, granting Parties an exception from trade disciplines if certain conditions are met.[4] The WTO dispute settlement mechanism has interpreted these exceptions in light of the WTO's commitment to an objective of sustainable development.

As noted above, the negotiations of the Preamble of the 1994 WTO Agreement were influenced by the outcomes of the 1992 UNCED. The words 'sustainable development' were added to the text of the WTO Agreement Preamble in one of the last negotiating sessions, and this Preamble was highlighted in the 1994 WTO Decision on Trade and Environment which quotes extensively from the Rio Declaration and Agenda 21. The Preamble of the WTO Agreement now states that:

> *Recognizing* that their relations in the field of trade and economic endeavour should be conducted with a view to raising standards of living, ensuring full employment and a large and steadily growing volume of real income and effective demand, and expanding the production of and trade in goods and services, while allowing for the optimal use of the world's resources *in accordance with the objective of sustainable development*, seeking both to protect and preserve the environment and to enhance the means for doing so in a manner consistent with their respective needs and concerns at different levels of economic development ...
>
> *Recognizing* further that there is need for positive efforts designed to ensure that developing countries, and especially the least developed among them, secure a share in the growth in international trade commensurate with the needs of their economic development.[5]

While preambular statements are not formally legally binding in the same way as operational provisions, as discussed earlier in this volume they can play a role in interpretation of a treaty, including in the identification of the treaty's object and purpose.[6] The WTO Preamble brings together and links many concepts. WTO Members link their intentions to raise standards of living and ensure full employment with their plans to expand production and trade in goods and services, but note that they will do this while allowing the optimal use of the world's resources *in accordance with the objective of sustainable development*. They add that this will be done while seeking to protect and preserve the environment, and also to enhance the means of doing so in a way that is consistent with the respective needs and concerns of countries at different levels of development. Sustainable development is set as an objective, to be balanced against other considerations,

Ngangjoh-Hodu, 'Relationship of GATT Article XX Exceptions to other WTO Agreements' (2011) 80 Nordic Journal of International Law 219.

[4] Ibid.

[5] WTO Agreement (n 1) Preamble (emphasis added).

[6] As noted earlier, the Preamble forms part of the context in which the treaty can be interpreted. See Vienna Convention on the Law of Treaties (VCLT) (signed 23 May 1969, entered into force 27 January 1980) 1155 UNTS 331, art 31; M Shaw, *International Law* (6th edn, Cambridge, CUP 2008); G Simpson, 'The Situation on the International Legal Theory Front: The Power of Rules and the Rule of Power' (2000) 11 European Journal of International Law 439; JHH Weiler and AL Paulus, 'The Structure of Change in International Law or is there a Hierarchy of Norms in International Law?' (1997) 8 European Journal of International Law 545; U Fastenrath, 'Relative Normativity in International Law' (1993) 4 European Journal of International Law 305.

in connection with the optimal use of the world's resources and, ambiguously, linked also to improvement of means to protect the environment in appropriate ways for different countries. This Preamble is an expansion of the GATT 1947 Preamble, which referred conclusively to the need for '... developing the full use of the resources of the world ...'[7] It is not completely clear, in the WTO Preamble, whether member States simply intend the optimal use of the world's resources to be carried out in accordance with the objective of sustainable development, or whether they intend all the various elements of their relations in the field of trade and economic endeavour to pursue this objective.[8] The WTO sustainable development objective is also linked indirectly to a recognition that while the States seek to protect and preserve the environment, they also seek to enhance the means for doing so differently.

The references to sustainable development in this Preamble have been interpreted by the WTO DSM. While there is no *stare decisis* in world trade law, WTO Panels and the AB find the *acquis* of past GATT and WTO cases highly persuasive for the purposes of deciding disputes, shaping the views of WTO Members and shedding light on the meaning of treaty provisions.[9] Though several WTO cases are relevant, three particular WTO dispute settlement decisions assist in explaining how the concept of sustainable development may be viewed in WTO law, as it stood in the 1990s: the *US-Gasoline Case*,[10] the *US-Shrimp Case*[11] and the *EC-Tariff Preferences Case*.[12] These cases concerned the interpretation of the article XX exceptions to the WTO Agreements, in light of the preambular commitments on sustainable development.

Article XX of the GATT allows WTO members an exception to WTO disciplines in tightly described circumstances, such as the protection of public health or conservation of exhaustible natural resources. Other exceptions are agreed in GATT articles XII, XIX and XXV,[13] and a further systemic exception involves the recognition of non-reciprocal, special and differential treatment for developing countries, but Article XX is most relevant.[14] It reads, in relevant parts:

> Subject to the requirement that such measures are not applied in a manner which would constitute a means of arbitrary or unjustifiable discrimination between countries where the same conditions prevail, or a disguised restriction on international trade, nothing in this Agreement shall be construed to prevent the adoption or enforcement by any contracting party of measures: ...

7 GATT (n 3).

8 M Boas and J Vevatne, 'Sustainable Development and the World Trade Organisation' in McNeill D and M Boas (eds), *Global Institutions and Development: Framing the World?* (London, Routledge 2004) 98.

9 R Bhala, 'The Myth about Stare Decisis and International Trade Law (Part One of a Trilogy)' (1999) 14 American University International Law Review 845.

10 WTO, *United States—Standards for Reformulated and Conventional Gasoline—Report of the Appellate Body* (29 April 1996) WT/DS2/AB/R.

11 See WTO, *United States: Import Prohibition of Certain Shrimp and Shrimp Products—Report of the Panel* (15 May 1998) WT/DS58/R; see also WTO, *United States: Import Prohibition of Certain Shrimp and Shrimp Products—Report of the Appellate Body* (6 November 1998) DocWT/DS58/AB/R.

12 WTO, *European Communities: Conditions for the Granting of Tariff Preferences to Developing Countries—Report of the Appellate Body* (20 April 2004) WT/DS246/AB/R.

13 V Lowe, *International Law* (Oxford, OUP 2009) 219–220.

14 1979 'Enabling Clause' decision of the GATT Contracting Parties, see *European Communities-Tariff Preferences* (n 12).

(b) necessary to protect human, animal or plant life or health; . . .

(g) relating to the conservation of exhaustible natural resources if such measures are made effective in conjunction with restrictions on domestic production or consumption; . . . [15]

In the General Agreement on Trade in Services (GATS) and the Agreement on Trade-Related Aspects of Intellectual Property Rights (TRIPS), WTO Members made similar commitments.[16] The Canadian Department of Foreign Affairs and International Trade (DFAIT) *Retrospective Analysis of the 1994 Canadian Environmental Review of the WTO* focused on GATT article XX as an important safeguard for a State's ability to secure sustainable development.[17] In these exceptions, however, once a violation of the obligations mentioned above has been established, the burden of proof to defend an environmental or social measure falls upon the WTO member State that is invoking the exception.[18] This burden can be difficult to meet.[19]

The WTO dispute settlement mechanism has relied on the WTO Preamble commitment to sustainable development to interpret the scope and meaning of the GATT general exceptions, for both the substantive 'heads' of exceptions as well as the 'chapeau'.

Tensions around trade and the environment, as mentioned above, first arose in the context of the GATT, prior to the creation of the WTO and the adoption of preambular provisions on a 'sustainable development objective'. In a GATT Panel for the *Tuna-Dolphin dispute*,[20] in which Mexico, as mentioned above, challenged US measures to prevent the import of tuna caught by nets which killed dolphins by blocking trade in tuna, it was found that references to domestic production and consumption meant that a GATT Contracting Party could only adopt restrictions within their own jurisdiction, rather than for the protection of global resources.[21] The Panel also suggested such a measure could only be adopted for the resource in question (tuna), not for other species impacted by the exploitation of the resource (such as dolphins). As the GATT dispute settlement mechanism at that time required decisions of the Panel to be adopted by consensus among the GATT Contracting Parties, and the US and several others were not in agreement with this interpretation of GATT law, the Report of the Panel remained unadopted.[22]

This narrow interpretation of article XX prevailed at the time of WTO signature, as exemplified by the approach of the WTO AB in the *US-Gasoline* dispute. In this dispute, which concerned conditions that the US had imposed on foreign gasoline exporters in relation to fuel standards, the WTO AB decided, relying on the GATT Preamble, that:

[15] GATT (n 3) art XX.

[16] GATS (adopted 15 April 1994, entered into force 1 January 1995) 1869 UNTS 183, art XIV(b); TRIPS (adopted 15 April 1994, entered into force 1 January 1995) 1869 UNTS 299, arts 27.2 and 27.3.

[17] DFAIT, *Retrospective Analysis of the 1994 Canadian Environmental Review-Uruguay Round of Multilateral Trade Negotiations* (Ottawa, 1999).

[18] H Horn, 'The Burden of Proof in Trade Disputes and the Environment' (2011) 62 Journal of Environmental Economics and Management 15.

[19] MT Grando, 'Allocating the Burden of Proof in WTO Disputes: A Critical Analysis' (2006) 9 Journal of International Economic Law 615, 620–624; G Le Moli, PS Vishvanathan and A Aeri, 'Whither the Proof? The Progressive Reversal of the Burden of Proof in Environmental Cases before International Courts and Tribunals' (2017) 8(4) Journal of International Dispute Settlement 644.

[20] *-United States—Restrictions on the Import of Tuna* (1991) GATT BISD 39S/155; (1991) 30 ILM 1594.

[21] Ibid.

[22] For the legal value of unadopted GATT Panel Reports, see D Palmeter and PC Mavroidis, 'The WTO Legal System: Sources of Law' (1998) 92 American Journal of International Law 398, 402, which states that Panels can find useful guidance in the reasoning of unadopted GATT Panel Reports.

> WTO Members have a large measure of autonomy to determine their own policies on the environment (including its relationship with trade), their environmental objectives and the environmental legislation they enact and implement. So far as concerns the WTO, that autonomy is circumscribed only by the need to respect the requirements of the General Agreement and the other covered agreements.[23]

In that 1996 dispute, the AB did not fully underline the importance of a commitment to sustainable development for the interpretation of article XX of the GATT 1994 general exception, but rather, noted that while the WTO permits members to determine their own environmental laws and policies, those laws and policies must be constrained by a respect for WTO disciplines.[24] This decision was critiqued by environmental law scholars at that time, as the dispute settlement body (DSB) appeared to be finding that in spite of the article XX exceptions available for WTO members, States would be held to the WTO disciplines, giving trade law a blanket precedence over environmental law and potentially rendering environmental measures less effective.[25] The decision was encouraged by other international experts, such as Professor Daniel Esty, who argued that:

> Regulations that intentionally discriminate against foreign products may constitute blatant protectionism and should be subject to careful scrutiny. Strict scrutiny should also be applied to requirements that have a disproportionate effect on imported products-perhaps indicating that the 'environmental' standard was surreptitiously designed as a hidden trade barrier.[26]

It was clear, in any event, that there was little integration.

Two years later, in the 1998 *US-Shrimp* dispute, the WTO dispute settlement mechanism adopted a much broader view, through four Panel and AB Reports which provide the clearest expression, to date, of the meaning of State commitments to sustainable development in the WTO Agreements.[27] It is this controversial case which clarified how the exceptions of article XX can create a 'window' in trade law for sustainable resources management and endangered species conservation, in light of the preambular recognition of sustainable development as an objective of the WTO.

The *US-Shrimp* dispute concerned a regulation under the 1973 US Endangered Species Act to protect five different species of endangered sea turtles, requiring that US shrimp trawlers use 'turtle excluder devices' in their nets and prohibiting shrimp imports from States where shrimp harvests affected endangered turtles unless the States in question were certified users of the technologies that protected the sea turtles. India, Malaysia, Pakistan and Thailand, as exporters of shrimp to the US, argued that the embargo on shrimp violated

[23] WTO, *United States Gasoline Dispute* (n 10).

[24] Ibid.

[25] MD Calapai, 'International Trade and Environmental Impact: The WTO Reformulated Gasoline Case' (1996) 3 Environmental Lawyer 209.

[26] D Esty, *Greening the GATT* (Washington, IIE 1994) 234.

[27] R Howse, 'The Appellate Body Rulings in the Shrimp/Turtle Case: A New Legal Baseline for the Trade and Environment Debate' (2002) 27 Columbia Journal of Environmental Law 491; HF Chang, 'Toward A Greener GATT: Environmental Trade Measures and the Shrimp-Turtle Case' (2000) 74 South California Law Review 31; and PC Mavroidis, 'Trade and Environment after the Shrimp-Turtles Litigation' (2000) 34 Journal of World Trade 73.

the most-favoured nation rule of article I:1 and the non-discrimination article XIII:1 of the GATT 1994 as like products from different countries were treated differently based solely on the production method.[28] The complainants also argued a violation of article XI:1 of the GATT 1994 as the US had implemented an embargo which restricted trade.[29] The Panel agreed that the US had violated article XI:1 of the GATT 1994.[30] It then interpreted the scope and nature of article XX.

The US, at the Panel stage of the dispute, seems to have argued that sustainable development was a binding principle of WTO law:

> The United States noted that the World Trade Organization Agreement ('WTO Agreement'), which was the first multilateral trade agreement concluded after the UN Conference on Environment and Development, provided that the rules of trade must not only promote expansion of trade and production, but must do so in a manner that respects the *principle of sustainable development* and protects and preserves the environment. Yet, the complainants claimed that in becoming a Member of the World Trade Organization, the United States had agreed to accept imports of shrimp whose harvest and sale in the US market might mean the extinction from the world of sea turtles for all time.[31]

As such, the US advocated that article XX of the GATT should be interpreted in the light of the Preamble of the WTO Agreement:

> [a]n environmental purpose is fundamental to the application of Article XX, and such a purpose cannot be ignored, especially since the preamble to [the 'WTO Agreement'] acknowledges that the rules of trade should be 'in accordance with the objective of sustainable development', and should seek to 'protect and preserve the environment'.[32]

In its arguments, the US did not refer directly to the related provisions on optimal use of the world's resources, nor to the 'respective needs and concerns at different levels of economic development', from the Preamble of the 1994 WTO Agreements.

The interpretation that the Panel and AB adopted in this dispute departed from the findings of the earlier GATT Panel in the *US-Tuna* dispute.[33] In the *US-Shrimp/Turtle* dispute, the Panel found that the new preambular language of the WTO Agreement influences the interpretation of article XX of the GATT, but highlighted the recognition that the means to enhance environmental protection should be 'in a manner consistent with the [Members'] respective needs and concerns at different levels of economic development'.[34] The Panel further clarified that 'the Preamble endorses the fact that environmental policies must be designed taking into account the situation of each Member, both in terms of its actual needs and in terms of its economic means'.[35] In its reasoning, the Panel highlighted the 1992 Rio Declaration, where it was recognized that all countries could design their own

28 WTO, *United States: Shrimp–Panel Report* (n 11) 161.
29 Ibid 162.
30 Ibid 284.
31 Ibid 146 (emphasis added).
32 Ibid 12.
33 *United States-Restrictions on the Import of Tuna* (n 20).
34 WTO, *United States: Shrimp–Panel Report* (n 11) 7.52.
35 Ibid.

environmental policy and that international cooperation rather than unilateral measures are needed for sustainable development.[36] The measures to protect the endangered turtles were disallowed.

Upon appeal, the AB took a more subtle approach. It found in favour of the US that article XX (g) could be applied to protect turtles. However, the AB did not completely follow the US argument about a binding principle of sustainable development, instead choosing to broaden their interpretation of the term 'exhaustible natural resources' in light of the objective of sustainable development:

> The words of Article XX(g), 'exhaustible natural resources', were actually crafted more than 50 years ago. They must be read by a treaty interpreter in the light of contemporary concerns of the community of nations about the protection and conservation of the environment. While Article XX was not modified in the Uruguay Round, the preamble attached to the *WTO Agreement* shows that the signatories to that Agreement were, in 1994, fully aware of the importance and legitimacy of environmental protection as a goal of national and international policy. The preamble of the *WTO Agreement*—which informs not only the GATT 1994, but also the other covered agreements—explicitly acknowledges 'the *objective of sustainable development*'.[37]

The enclosed legal note,[38] as part of the AB's decision, deserves particular attention. The AB refers to the *objective* of sustainable development, explaining that '[t]his *concept* has been generally accepted as integrating economic *and* social development *and* environmental protection.' (emphasis added). This is remarkable for two reasons, as discussed earlier in this volume. First, the WTO AB recognizes sustainable development as an objective of the WTO. This objective, taking into account discussions of 'object and purpose' of treaties, could likely be best characterized as part of the 'purpose' of the WTO Agreements.[39] Second, the WTO recognizes (in line with the 1997 UN General Assembly (UNGA) Special Session which had just taken place) that this objective refers to the need to integrate all three elements or 'pillars' of sustainable development—social development, economic development and environmental protection. Under the VCLT, as discussed earlier, this could be described as using a preambular provision to shed light on the object and purpose,[40] which then is taken into account in the interpretation of the exceptions.[41]

The decision to characterize the preambular commitment to sustainable development as part of the object and purpose of this treaty was directly relevant to the outcome of the dispute in several ways. First, the WTO AB was willing to adopt a more expansive interpretation of the term 'exhaustible natural resource' in article XX of the GATT. In particular, it was willing to recognize that both living and non-living resources could be 'exhaustible'. In

[36] Ibid.

[37] Note 107 reads 'This concept has been generally accepted as integrating economic and social development and environmental protection': WTO, *United States: Shrimp–Appellate Body Report* (n 11) (emphasis added); See, e.g., G Handl, 'Sustainable Development: General Rules versus Specific Obligations', in W Lang (ed), *Sustainable Development and International Law* (London, Martinus Nijhoff 1995).

[38] WTO, *United States: Shrimp–Appellate Body Report* (n 11) 123.

[39] See earlier discussion at n 7.

[40] VCLT.

[41] VCLT; see also R Gardiner, *Treaty Interpretation* (2nd edn, Oxford, OUP 2015).

order to make this point, the AB turned again to Agenda 21, as well as to other international accords with environmental and sustainable development objectives, for guidance:

> The Convention on Biological Diversity[111][42] uses the concept of 'biological resources'. Agenda 21[112][43] speaks most broadly of 'natural resources' and goes into detailed statements about 'marine living resources'.[44]

In making this finding, the AB also stated:

> Given the recent acknowledgement by the international community of the importance of concerted bilateral or multilateral action to protect living natural resources, and recalling the explicit recognition by WTO Members of the objective of sustainable development in the preamble of the *WTO Agreement*, we believe it is too late in the day to suppose that Article XX(g) of the GATT 1994 may be read as referring only to the conservation of exhaustible mineral or other non-living natural resources.[45]

The AB continued with their interpretation of the Preamble in WTO law:

> We note once more that this language demonstrates recognition by WTO negotiators that optimal use of the world's resources should be made in accordance with the objective of sustainable development. As this preambular language reflects the intentions of negotiators of the *WTO Agreement*, we believe it must add colour, texture and shading to our interpretation of the agreements annexed to the *WTO Agreement*, in this case, the GATT 1994. We have already observed that Article XX(g) of the GATT 1994 is appropriately read with the perspective embodied in the above preamble.[46]

This 'addition of colour, texture and shading' suggests the AB may have understood this sustainable development objective to inform interpretation of all of the annexed WTO agreements. This first AB decision was carefully nuanced but clearly describes sustainable development's part of the object and purpose of this treaty in the sense ascribed by the VCLT at article 31. However, as the AB further insisted:

> In their Decision on Trade and Environment, Ministers expressed their intentions, in part, as follows: ... *Considering* that there should not be, nor need be, any policy contradiction between upholding and safeguarding an open, non-discriminatory and equitable multilateral trading system on the one hand, and acting for the protection of the environment, and the promotion of sustainable development on the other. In this Decision, Ministers took 'note' of the Rio Declaration on Environment and Development,[147][47] Agenda

[42] This footnote 111 reads: 'Done at Rio de Janeiro, 5 June 1992, UNEP/Bio.Div./N7-INC5/4; 31 International Legal Materials 818. We note that India, Malaysia and Pakistan have ratified the Convention on Biological Diversity, and that Thailand and the United States have signed but not ratified the Convention.'

[43] This footnote 112 reads: 'Adopted by the United Nations Conference on Environment and Development, 14 June 1992, UN Doc A/CONF. 151/26/Rev.1. See, for example, para. 17.70, ff.'

[44] WTO, *United States: Shrimp–Appellate Body Report* (n 11) 120.

[45] Ibid 121.

[46] Ibid 153.

[47] Note 147: 'We note that Principle 3 of the [Rio Declaration] states: "The right to development must be fulfilled so as to equitably meet developmental and environmental needs of present and future generations." Principle 4 of

21,[148[48]] and 'its follow-up in the GATT, as reflected in the statement of the Council of Representatives to the CONTRACTING PARTIES at their 48th Session in 1992'.[49]

Of relevance to this volume, the AB cited two specific principles from the Rio Declaration, in particular the principles of sustainable development which were later emphasized, as discussed earlier in this volume, by the Tribunal in *Iron Rhine Arbitration* (the integration of environmental considerations into development decision-making) and by the International Court of Justice (ICJ) in the *Uruguay Pulp Mills Case* (the sovereign right to promote sustainable economic development). The AB interpreted the Preamble using the 1992 Rio Declaration and Agenda 21,[50] and focused specifically on the particular elements of these 'soft law' Declarations which highlight that environmental protection should be integrated with socio-economic development in trade and investment law, while noting that this does not override the rights of States to develop in a sustainable manner.

The chapeau of article XX focuses on the measure and whether it qualifies for an exception (which in this case, it did), but also examines whether the measure was applied in a manner that was non-discriminatory. The US failed to convince the AB that its conservation measure had also been applied in a manner consistent with the chapeau of article XX, as the US had concluded agreements with other WTO members on the protection of sea turtles and was therefore permitting imports of shrimp from those States.[51] After again taking the Preamble into account in interpreting this second chapeau provision, the AB found that the measures had not been applied in a non-discriminatory manner, and thus the US measures to protect the turtles failed to be permitted through the exception of article XX of the GATT.

Echoing the tone of debates in the GATT Council described above, the European Community largely supported the US in this case, arguing for recognition of sustainable development as a principle of international law:

> The European Communities states further that the issues at stake in this dispute concern principles to which it attaches great importance, such as respect for the environment and the functioning of the multilateral trading system. The European Communities is bound by the text of the Treaty Establishing the European Community to ensure a harmonious and balanced development of economic activities with respect for the environment. The *principle of sustainable development, also laid down in the first paragraph of the preamble to the WTO Agreement*, as well as the precautionary principle, play an important role in the

the Rio Declaration on Environment and Development states that: "In order to achieve sustainable development, environmental protection shall constitute an integral part of the development process and cannot be considered in isolation from it." '

48 In the Appellate Body Report (n 11), this footnote 148 reads: 'Agenda 21 is replete with references to the shared view that economic development and the preservation and protection of the environment should be mutually supportive. For example, paragraph 2.3(b) of Agenda 21 states: "The international economy should provide a supportive international climate for achieving environment and development goals by ... [m]aking trade and environment mutually supportive ..." Similarly, paragraph 2.9(d) states that an "objective" of governments should be: "To promote and support policies, domestic and international, that make economic growth and environmental protection mutually supportive." '

49 Ministerial Decision on Trade and Environment (15 April 1994) LT/UR/D-5/8.

50 WTO, *United States: Shrimp–Appellate Body Report* (n 11) 66.

51 Ibid 63.

implementation of all EC policies. The EC position is mirrored in public international law by statements of the International Court of Justice, stressing the significance of respect for the environment.[52]

It is important to note, based on the analysis earlier in this volume, that the European Communities considered itself bound by the European principle of sustainable development and argued that its position was supported by international law. The dispute did not end there. The chapeau reasoning was reaffirmed in the subsequent WTO Panel and AB decisions related to the *US-Shrimp Case*, when Malaysia took recourse to article 21.5 of the WTO Dispute Settlement Understanding,[53] arguing that the follow-up measures taken by the United States did not comply with the recommendations and rulings of the DSB,[54] and lost. In this further dispute, however, the Panel is less nuanced about sustainable development:

> In that framework, assessing first the *object and purpose* of the WTO Agreement, we note that the WTO preamble refers to the notion of 'sustainable development'.[55] This means that in interpreting the terms of the chapeau, we must keep in mind that sustainable development is one of the objectives of the WTO Agreement.[56]

Though both the Panel and the AB reviewed the first AB decision thoroughly during the article 21.5 Recourse disputes, in spite of Malaysia's arguments to the contrary, the sustainable development interpretation was simply reaffirmed. At that point the US measures were saved, as the Panel also found that the US had no obligation to actually conclude an agreement on sea turtle protection, but rather was simply obliged to engage in multilateral negotiations in good faith with Malaysia, in order to satisfy the requirements of the chapeau that a measure be applied in a way that was not discriminatory.[57]

The reasoning of the Panel and the AB in the *US-Shrimp* dispute strongly suggests that sustainable development has been recognized as an objective of the WTO, as part of the object and purpose of the WTO Agreements, and as such has relevance to interpretation of these treaties.[58] Under the VCLT, the AB was willing to interpret the preambular provisions of the WTO Agreements to shed light on the object and purpose of the WTO,[59] and in this case, the sustainable development purpose of the WTO was found to be relevant for the

[52] Ibid 67 (emphasis added).

[53] WTO, *United States: Import Prohibition of Certain Shrimp and Shrimp Products-Recourse to article 21.5 by Malaysia* (13 October 2000) WT/DS58/17.

[54] For an analysis of the decision and its critique by WTO members, see S Shaw and R Schwartz, 'Trade and Environment in the WTO State of Play' (2002) 36 Journal of World Trade 129, 149.

[55] In the Panel Report, this citation reads: '*See* the final texts of the agreements negotiated by Governments at the United Nation Conference on Environment and Development (UNCED), Rio de Janeiro, Brazil, 3-14 June, 1992, specifically the Rio Declaration on Environment and Development (hereafter the "Rio Declaration") and Agenda 21 at www.unep.org; the concept is elaborated in detailed action plans in Agenda 21 so as to put in place development that is sustainable—i.e. that "meets the needs of the present generation without compromising the ability of future generations to meet their own needs". See World Commission on Environment and Development, *Our Common Future* (OUP Oxford 1988).

[56] WTO, *United States: Import Prohibition of Certain Shrimp and Shrimp Products-Recourse to article 21.5 by Malaysia—Panel Report* (15 June 2001) WT/DS58/RW 5.4.

[57] Ibid 6.1.

[58] I Buffard and K Zemanek, 'The Object and Purpose of a Treaty: An Enigma?' (1998) 3 Austrian Review of International and European Law 311, 333; Gardiner (n 41).

[59] See VCLT, art 31.

interpretation of the exceptions,[60] which led to an outcome that was able to interpret the terms of the exception as being broad enough to encompass both non-living and also living natural resources.[61] As trade law scholars have noted, the interpretive value of integration was, in this case, relevant.[62] Subsequent cases have affirmed this view, both in terms of arguments of WTO members, and in terms of Panel reasoning.

In the *European Communities-Tariff Preferences* dispute,[63] which concerned whether the European Communities' scheme of generalized tariff preferences (discussed above), discriminates among developing countries, the European Communities sought to justify its system as a sustainable development policy. India had complained that the European Communities' special preferences for drug arrangements were inconsistent with the most-favoured nation clause (article 1.1 of the GATT 1994) and could not be justified under the *Decision on Differential and More Favourable Treatment, Reciprocity, and Fuller Participation of Developing Countries* (the 'Enabling Clause').[64] Similar provisions exist for environmental protection and labour rights, but were not challenged here. The European Communities argued that because the Enabling Clause was designed to fulfil the objectives of the WTO, it should not be interpreted as an exception to article 1.1 of the GATT but rather as an incentive for developed countries to grant such preferences.[65] The AB found that the objectives of the WTO could be fulfilled through 'general exceptions'. In its finding, the Panel specifically cited the *US-Shrimp* decision with approval, noting that as 'the objective of sustainable development' could be achieved through application of the WTO exceptions, such as article XX (g) of the GATT, it was clear that exceptions could be used to achieve other objectives of WTO law.

A further obligation is relevant to this volume, and was also highlighted by WTO tribunals in the years after the 1994 WTO Agreements were ratified and before the WTO Doha Round was initiated. In particular, a special and differential treatment rule was enshrined in article XXVIII bis of the GATT 1947, which requires that the special needs of developing countries be taken into account. In addition, article XXXVI:8 of the GATT exempts developing countries from the application of reciprocity in trade negotiations. The rule was retained in all WTO Agreements, through the inclusion of special provisions for developing countries and least developed countries.[66] The Preamble of the WTO Agreement also recognizes the special needs of developing countries. In connection with this obligation, India, in *India-Quantitative Restrictions*, invoked the AB's earlier recognition of sustainable development as an objective of the WTO, arguing that:

> Any precipitous action on removal of quantitative restrictions which may undermine the stability of the Indian economy or the reform process itself, cannot only do great harm to

[60] Ibid.

[61] Gardiner (n 41).

[62] See, e.g., T Cottier and M Foltea, 'Constitutional Functions of the WTO and RTAs' in L Bartels and F Ortino (eds), *Regional Trade Agreements and the WTO Legal System* (Oxford, OUP 2006) 51–58.

[63] WTO, *European Communities-Tariff Preferences* (n 12).

[64] *Differential and More Favourable Treatment Reciprocity and Fuller Participation of Developing Countries* (28 November 1979) L/4903, BISD 26S/203.

[65] Ibid 93; a similar argument was made by one dissenting panel member in the Panel Report, WTO, *European Communities: Conditions for the Granting of Tariff Preferences to Developing Countries—Report of the Panel* (1 December 2003) WT/DS246/R.

[66] WTO, *Brazil: Export Financing Programme for Aircraft- Recourse to article 21.5 by Canada—Report of the Panel* (9 May 2000) WT/DS46/RW 6.47.

India, but as well to the foreign investors and major trading partners who have a stake in the sustainable development of the Indian economy.[67]

The Panel did not address the point directly, but stated that:

> At the outset, we recall that the Preamble to the WTO Agreement recognizes both (i) the desirability of expanding international trade in goods and services and (ii) the need for positive efforts designed to ensure that developing countries secure a share in international trade commensurate with the needs of their economic development . . .[68]

Overall, the reasoning of the WTO DSB indicates that sustainable development has been recognized as an objective of WTO law. Legal arguments based on this objective have been made by the Parties, and accepted by the WTO. In light of this 'object and purpose' of sustainable development, the WTO was willing to interpret the exemptions granted in article XX of the GATT more broadly, taking into account other treaties related to the environment and sustainable development. By the late 1990s, the WTO Panel and AB were willing to require the integration of environmental and social considerations in defining exemptions to the obligations of WTO members. However, just as clearly, the Panels and the AB will not lightly accept sustainable development as a 'trump card'. Rather, a solid legal understanding of a sustainable development objective and its underlying principles, applied to specific facts of each case in a reasoned legal argument, is required to make a successful sustainable development argument in the WTO. It appears that with respect to the opportunity to address the first tension identified earlier in this volume, the WTO has made certain limited progress.

12.2 Debates on Cooperation on Environmental and Social Issues in the WTO, and the Potential for Trade and Investment Liberalization to Contribute to More Sustainable Development from 1994–2001

Sustainable development may be recognized as an objective of the WTO, and States may be interpreting the WTO law exceptions in this light. However, two other tensions were identified earlier in this volume, namely the need not to weaken but rather to strengthen domestic environmental and social laws related to trade, and also the way economic liberalization can create incentives to enhance trade and investment in economic sectors that are more sustainable. To address the first, provisions would be needed to secure additional environmental and social cooperation parallel to the trade and investment agreement itself (i.e. inclusion of either permissions to cooperate on key environmental and social problems, or even prescriptions to provide resources, capacity-building and other support for programmes and projects to address, as part of the economic agreement, environmental and social concerns). To address the second, integrated substantive trade and investment

[67] WTO, *India: Quantitative Restrictions on Imports of Agricultural, Textile and Industrial Products-Report of the Panel* (6 April 1999) WT/DS90/R 3.9.

[68] Ibid 7.2.

liberalization rules would need to be agreed which seek to deliver sustainable development benefits through increases in liberalization in targeted sectors of economies, goods or services (i.e. inclusion of prescriptive provisions that oblige the Parties to liberalize trade and investment in specific economic sectors that they agree will contribute to sustainable development). It is not clear that the WTO, between 1994–2001, has enjoyed success in taking up either of these further opportunities for integration.

Part of the challenge involved finding mechanisms themselves. After 1994, international discussions on sustainable development among member States moved from the Committee on Trade and Development (CTD) to the Committee on Trade and Environment (CTE) for a period, and were confined to a particular aspect of the CTE mandate. In the CTE debates on the relationship between the WTO and multilateral environment agreements (MEAs), proposals included:

> to analyse the flexibility of trade principles to accommodate current and emerging environmental policies, to determine whether they prevent the internalization of environmental externalities, and *whether the trade rules contribute to integrated sustainable development policies.* Another suggestion is that the relationship between specific environmental policies and specific WTO Agreements could only be usefully examined on a case by case basis.[69]

Two years later in the 1996 Singapore Ministerial Declaration,[70] the Preamble of the WTO Agreement did not inspire new negotiations on binding rules. Instead, a short note appears at 16 stating that: 'Full implementation of the WTO Agreements will make an important contribution to achieving the objectives of sustainable development'.[71] In this reference, sustainable development objectives were clearly linked to the implementation of the international trade and investment regimes, rather than simply the optimal use of natural resources. However, this expanded recognition of the concept still appears to conceive of sustainable development as though it were an automatic result of economic liberalization.

In the 1998 Geneva Ministerial Conference, there was further movement towards establishing sustainable development as more than a reason for enhanced trade and investment. The preamble of the Ministerial Declaration states, at 4: 'We shall also continue to improve our efforts towards the objectives of sustained economic growth and sustainable development.'[72] Member States formally recognized in negotiated text that sustainable development is not simply related to natural resources, or an automatic result of the liberalization process, but is actually an objective of the WTO itself. The differentiation and link between the objective of sustainable development and the objective of sustained economic growth is also recognized.

During the 1998–1999 'WTO Seattle Round' preparations, several countries sought to strengthen the WTO's sustainable development mandate. The debates, however, revealed fractures in the way that members understood their commitment. They also demonstrated

[69] WTO CTE, 'Report of the Committee on Trade and Environment' (12 November 1996) WT/CTE/1 (emphasis added).

[70] Ministerial Declarations are adopted unanimously and reflect WTO policy: they are not binding on members.

[71] Singapore Ministerial Declaration (18 December 1996) WT/MIN(96)/DEC, 36 ILM 218, <http://www.wto.org/english/thewto_e/minist_e/min96_e/singapore_declaration96_e.pdf> accessed 16 December 2020.

[72] Geneva Ministerial Declaration (20 May 1998) WT/MIN(98)/DEC/1, <http://docsonline.wto.org>.

that in the WTO, developing country members remained unconvinced that the integration of further 'non-trade' issues (addressing social or environmental objectives within the WTO) was either warranted or would support development interests.

On the environmental side, the US proposed measures '[t]o ensure that negotiations contribute to sustainable development, *inter alia,* by promoting free trade in a manner consistent with and supportive of high environmental standards'.[73] Norway proposed 'that trade and environmental policies should be mutually supportive and legally consistent in order to promote the objectives of sustainable development'.[74] Norway equally emphasized:

> Furthermore, the Ministerial Declaration should contain a reference to the objective of sustainable development, including environmental and developmental principles as reflected in the Rio Declaration, in particular the precautionary principle, the polluter pays principle and the right to development.[75]

Along similar lines, the European Communities proposed that '[t]rade and environment policies should play a mutually supportive role in favour of sustainable development'.[76] Cuba offered the following response:

> [t]he Marrakesh Ministerial Decision on Trade and Environment established the close link between trade, the environment and sustainable development. However, in practice, sustainable development is seen by the developing countries as increasingly threatened and unattainable because of the accelerating pace at which trade is being liberalized without properly implementing the results of the Uruguay Round, in particular the provisions on special and differential treatment for the developing countries.[77]

Several States underscored the developmental dimension of sustainable development, and warned that if the needs of developing countries were ignored or undervalued, it would jeopardize developing country support for sustainable development through trade liberalization.[78] Cuba also noted:

[73] See Preparations for the 1999 Ministerial Conference—Trade and Sustainable Development—Communication from the United States (6 August 1999) WT/GC/W/304, 8.

[74] Preparations for the 1999 Ministerial Conference—Trade and Environment—Communication from Norway (30 April 1999) WT/GC/W/176,.

[75] Ibid. Several of these principles are highlighted in the ILA New Delhi Declaration, see Chapter 3.

[76] Preparations for the 1999 Ministerial Conference—EC Approach to Trade and Environment in the New WTO Round—Communication from the European Communities (1 June 1999) WT/GC/W/194,.

[77] Preparations for the 1999 Ministerial Conference—Trade, Environment and Sustainable Development, Paragraph 9(d) of the Geneva Ministerial Declaration—Communication from Cuba (15 November 1999) WT/GC/W/387.

[78] See also the statements: Preparations for the 1999 Ministerial Conference—Contribution to the Preparatory Process—Communication from Kenya (5 July 1999) WT/GC/W/233, <http://docsonline.wto.org> accessed 16 December 2020; The Challenge of Integrating LDCs into the Multilateral Trading System-Communication from Bangladesh (13 July 1999) WT/GC/W/251, <http://docsonline.wto.org> accessed 16 December 2020; Informal Meeting held on 2 December 1998-Statement by Pakistan (17 December 1998) WT/GC/W/126, <http://docsonline.wto.org> accessed 16 December 2020; General Council-Preparations for the 1999 Ministerial Conference—The Future WTO Work Programme (under Paragraph 10 of the Geneva Ministerial Declaration—Statement by the Dominican Republic, Honduras and Pakistan (16 July 1999) WT/GC/W/255, <http://docsonline.wto.org> accessed 16 December 2020; Preparations for the 1999 Ministerial Conference—Negotiations on Agriculture—Communication from Cuba, Dominican Republic, El Salvador, Honduras, Nicaragua and Pakistan (9 April 1999) WT/GC/W/163, http://docsonline.wto.org> accessed 16 December 2020; as referenced in 'Environment' *Bridges Weekly Trade News Digest* (24 November 1999) <https://ictsd.iisd.org/bridges-news/bridges/news/new-issues> accessed 16 December 2020.

> The objectives of economic growth and sustainable development can be achieved simultaneously if the basic principles of Agenda 21 and the 1992 Rio Declaration are respected, above all the principles establishing the indispensable requirement to eradicate poverty and the common responsibility for the environment, but differentiated according to levels of development.[79]

This intervention reveals that Cuba viewed sustainable development as an objective which could be supported, or achieved, through the implementation of several principles related especially to equity and the eradication of poverty, and common but differentiated responsibility, both of which were affirmed by the International Labour Association (ILA) in the New Delhi Declaration.[80]

Social development is not synonymous with labour rights. Developing countries, fearing effects on their comparative advantage of low labour costs, were not willing to support explicit linkages between trade and investment law and labour rights. Indeed, in the Seattle Ministerial preparations, reactions to proposals for links between trade and labour rights were unenthusiastic.[81] The US position, based on a Congressional mandate, proposed the establishment of a WTO Working Group on labour issues.[82] The European Communities proposed a Joint International Labour Organization (ILO)/WTO Standing Forum, outside the WTO institutions. Developing countries described these proposals as veiled protectionist mechanisms sought by developed countries to prevent developing countries' comparative advantage in labour, questioning why certain strong advocates of labour rights in the WTO were not even Parties to most multilateral labour conventions.[83] It was also reaffirmed that at the First WTO Ministerial in Singapore in December 1996, WTO members had agreed that the ILO was the appropriate agency to address trade and labour linkages. For instance, the Group of 15 (G-15) developing countries stated that they 'resolutely oppose any renewed attempt' to raise linkages with labour issues in the WTO.[84]

As such, by 1999, several WTO Members were not yet supportive of integrating social or environmental concerns in trade law, should such mechanisms appear likely to justify further restrictions on access to developed country markets. They were not able to agree on the parameters for debate, in the world trade regime, let alone to support innovative provisions to strengthen cooperation on environmental and social dimensions of trade and investment, or to secure increased liberalization of trade in more sustainable goods or services,

79 Communication from Cuba (n 77).

80 G Kaufmann, *Globalisation and Labour Rights: The Conflict between Core Labour Rights and International Economic Law* (Oxford, Hart 2002) 87; M Burianski, C Negri and M Ulbrich, 'Free Trade and Core Labour Rights: Status Quo of a Discussion' (2001) 9(4) Tilburg Foreign Law Review; N Schrijver, 'Advancements in the Principles of International Law on Sustainable Development' in MC Cordonier Segger and HE Judge CG Weeramantry, *Sustainable Development Principles in the Decisions of International Courts and Tribunals* (London, Routledge 2017).

81 See Preparations for the 1999 Ministerial Conference—Trade and Environment, Communication from Norway (30 April 1999) WT/GC/W/176, the source for this discussion of labour issues in the Seattle Ministerial process. See also 'Ministerial Preparations On A Bumpy Ride To Seattle' *Bridges Weekly Trade News Digest* (1 November 1999) <https://ictsd.iisd.org/bridges-news/bridges/news/ministerial-preparations-on-a-bumpy-ride-to-seattle> accessed 16 December 2020.

82 A Panagariya, 'The Return of Labour Standards in the WTO?' *Economic Times* (6 November 1999) <http://www.columbia.edu/~ap2231/ET/et-06-nov99.htm> accessed 16 December 2020.

83 'Labour' *Bridges Weekly Trade News Digest* (24 November 1999) <https://ictsd.iisd.org/bridges-news/bridges/news/new-issues> accessed 16 December 2020.

84 Ibid; opposition from G-77 and others.

or trade-related investment measures. Indeed, for a large part of the WTO Rounds the CTE and CTD did not even meet. When the negotiations in Seattle failed, members were left with the *status quo*, which, as stated by the WTO AB and described by one WTO Member, appeared to be that '[a]s set out in the Preamble to the WTO Agreement ... sustainable development is an important objective for the WTO'.[85]

[85] Preparations for the 1999 Ministerial Conference—Canadian Approach to Trade and Environment in the new WTO Round—Communication from Canada (12 October 1999) WT/GC/W/358, <http://docsonline.wto.org> accessed 16 December 2020.

13

Sustainable Development in the 2001 WTO Doha Round Debates and Beyond

The 2001 World Trade Organization (WTO) Doha Declaration firmly underscored WTO members' commitment to sustainable development, and proposed negotiations in several areas which might, if realized, start to integrate social and environmental considerations into trade law and policy at the global level, including trade-related investment measures. In the 2001 Doha Ministerial Declaration which launched the Doha Round of trade negotiations, Parties distinctly refer to sustainable development as a WTO objective, and outline certain opportunities to cooperate more deeply in specific areas that have potential to address the tensions and opportunities identified earlier in this volume. In essence, in the 2001 Doha Declaration launching the new trade negotiations and in subsequent dispute settlement decisions, the WTO member States and dispute settlement mechanism (DSM) may be seen to have made small steps to integrate social and environmental considerations into the work of the WTO. In particular, certain exemptions have been expanded and clarified (more through subsequent disputes than through negotiations), States have agreed on frameworks for negotiations that could both liberalize trade in environmental goods and services and reduce subsidies that encourage over-fishing, and potentially also encourage greater cooperation on trade-related environment and social development challenges. Many advances have been made by the WTO Secretariat, led by the Members, to ensure greater transparency and accountability across the institution, and to secure higher levels of complementarity among environment, development, trade and investment discussions. However, taking into account the critiques in legal scholarship and the continuing disconnects in negotiations and in practice, the state of the discussions and the DSM also reveal certain limits to the WTO's progress in promoting more integrated international economic law and policy that can promote achievement of the world's Sustainable Development Goals (SDGs).

13.1 Sustainable Development as a WTO Objective

Sustainable development, as an objective of the WTO, is clearly noted in the Doha Declaration of 2001. While the first public Draft WTO Doha Ministerial Declaration of 26 September 2001 did not contain a special reference to sustainable development, the second draft of 27 October 2001 noted the objective in accordance with the Preamble of the WTO Agreement.[1] This affirmation was further strengthened during the conference

[1] 'We strongly reaffirm our commitment to the objective of sustainable development, as stated in the Preamble to the Marrakesh Agreement . . .': see Draft Doha WTO Ministerial Declaration (27 October 2001) <https://ictsd.iisd.org/bridges-news/bridges/issue-archive/new-ministerial-text-to-hand-ministers-a-challenge-in-doha> accessed 16 December 2020.

Crafting Trade and Investment Accords for Sustainable Development. Marie-Claire Cordonier Segger, Oxford University Press. © Marie-Claire Cordonier Segger 2021. DOI: 10.1093/oso/9780198831341.003.0013

itself. The final 2001 Doha Declaration highlights sustainable development as an objective of the WTO:

> *We strongly reaffirm our commitment to the objective of sustainable development,* as stated in the Preamble to the Marrakesh Agreement. We are convinced that the aims of upholding and safeguarding an open and non-discriminatory multilateral trading system, and acting for the protection of the environment *and the promotion of sustainable development* can and must be mutually supportive. We take note of the efforts by Members to conduct national environmental assessments of trade policies on a voluntary basis. We recognize that under WTO rules, no country should be prevented from taking measures for the protection of human, animal or plant life or health, or of the environment at the levels it considers appropriate, subject to the requirement that they are not applied in a manner which would constitute a means of arbitrary or unjustifiable discrimination between countries where the same conditions prevail, or a disguised restriction on international trade, and are otherwise in accordance with the provisions of the WTO Agreements. We welcome the WTO's continued cooperation with UNEP and other inter-governmental environmental organizations. We encourage efforts to promote cooperation between the WTO and *relevant international environmental and developmental organizations*, especially in the lead-up to the World Summit on Sustainable Development to be held in Johannesburg, South Africa, in September 2002.[2]

In the Declaration, which was reached by consensus among WTO Members, States recognized sustainable development as an objective of the WTO, and placed it into a strengthened context, referring to practical measures such as the need for cooperation with other international environment *and development* organizations in the lead-up to the 2002 World Summit on Sustainable Development (WSSD). It also provides an indication that sustainable development objectives are increasingly understood by WTO members as involving both environmental and social development actors and organizations. States appear to have been prepared to move away from the traditional 'trade only' policy, and also the 'trade and environment only' approach. The Declaration preamble follows the Appellate Body's (AB) integrated definition of the concept of sustainable development.[3] The Doha Ministerial Declaration recognizes environmental protection and social development as elements that need to be integrated into the mandate of a mainly economic organization, the WTO.

In Doha, States also agreed on two procedural mechanisms which may have potential to operationalize the sustainable development objective within the WTO itself. First, at paragraph 51, the Committee on Trade and Environment (CTE) and the Committee on Trade and Development (CTD) were asked, within their mandates, to debate the environment and development aspects of the negotiations themselves,[4] in the organization and management of the work programme section of the Declaration:

[2] Doha WTO Ministerial 2001: Ministerial Declaration, WT/MIN(01)/DEC/1 (Doha Ministerial Declaration) (emphasis added).

[3] Ibid.

[4] Ibid.

> [t]he Committee on Trade and Development and the Committee on Trade and Environment shall, within their respective mandates, each act as a forum to identify and debate *developmental and environmental aspects of the negotiations, in order to help achieve the objective of having sustainable development appropriately reflected*.[5]

An initial proposal by Canada that focused on the CTE was broadened in the negotiations to include the CTD. In effect, these Committees appear to have been given an interstitial mandate, to 'help achieve the objective of having sustainable development appropriately reflected' in the negotiations.[6] The potential contribution of impact assessments were also highlighted, with a mandate to be shared among WTO Members. Further elements of the Doha Declaration, together with subsequent negotiations and WTO disputes, suggest that the sustainable development objective of the WTO may have been important in Doha negotiations, guiding and influencing members to integrate environmental protection with trade and social development priorities, as described earlier in this volume. The Declaration does address the points of tension highlighted earlier in this volume through a few key provisions. Unfortunately, as has been noted in legal scholarship, the current lack of progress in the trade negotiations appears to have stymied these initial indications of potential, and even recent WTO cases do not appear able to contribute much that is useful in this respect.[7]

13.2 Exemptions to Prevent Trade Rules from Constraining the Regulatory Flexibility of WTO Members for Social and Environmental Purposes, in Order to Realize Sustainable Development

The negotiations launched in the Doha Ministerial Declaration do not appear intended to change or broaden the exceptions in the WTO, in order to provide greater flexibility for members seeking to regulate for environmental or social purposes.[8] Indeed, in the 2001 Doha Declaration at paragraph 31, guidance for negotiations on the relationship between trade and environment that were mandated by WTO Members specifically notes that:

> With a view to enhancing the mutual supportiveness of trade and environment, we agree to negotiations, without prejudging their outcome, on:
>
> (i) the relationship between existing WTO rules and specific trade obligations set out in multilateral environmental agreements (MEAs). *The negotiations shall be limited in scope to the applicability of such existing WTO rules as among parties to the MEA in question. The negotiations shall not prejudice the WTO rights of any Member that is not a party to the MEA in question;*[9]

[5] Ibid 51.

[6] G Sampson, *The WTO and Sustainable Development* (Tokyo, UNU 2005).

[7] UP Thomas, 'Trade and the Environment: Stuck in a Political Impasse at the WTO after the Doha and Cancun Ministerial Conferences' (2004) 4 Global Environmental Politics 9.

[8] G Dunkley, *Free Trade: Myth, Reality and Alternatives* (London, Zed Books 2004) 202–203.

[9] Doha Ministerial Declaration (n 2) (emphasis added).

There are problems with this approach, from the perspective of an integration principle that seeks to secure flexibility for States bound to deliver on sustainable development obligations in other treaties. First, the negotiations are to be limited, not addressing the difficult situations where a WTO member is not a Party to the MEA in question. Yet it is precisely those situations, as argued in Chapters 2 and 3, that cause the greatest difficulties for sustainable development policy-makers. Also, the negotiations will only focus on enhancing the mutual supportiveness of trade and environment, rather than enhancing integration of the environment and social development into trade rules. While this commitment to 'mutual supportiveness' does reflect Agenda 21, it ignores the developments since the 1992 Rio Earth Summit, especially the additional emphasis placed on social aspects of sustainable development. Paragraph 31 does, however, demonstrate an attempt at integration in the *other* direction, where it is noted in the Declaration that: 'The outcome of this work as well as the negotiations carried out under paragraph 31(i) and (ii) shall be compatible with the open and non-discriminatory nature of the multilateral trading system . . . and will take into account the needs of developing and least-developed countries.'[10]

In the Doha Implementation Decision,[11] however, WTO members do appear to have agreed to make it easier for developing country members to implement certain Uruguay Round Agreements, by clarifying the scope of existing rules and allowing developing countries more time to implement specific provisions from the WTO Agreements.[12] For instance, in the Agreement on the Application of Sanitary and Phytosanitary Measures (SPS Agreement) negotiations, developing countries were granted a longer time frame to implement new SPS standards.[13] Such flexibility in time limits could be considered a type of exemption from trade rules, especially given that many SPS measures are set in place to address environmental or health concerns, as it allows developing countries additional time to balance social development and environmental interests. Similar decisions were included for various obligations of the developing countries under the WTO Agreement on Technical Barriers to Trade (TBT Agreement).[14] This exemption was agreed due to requests from developing countries, though it is not certain that this was due to any desire on their part to use the additional time in order to address social and environmental concerns.[15] These steps remain very limited.

The most significant clarifications of the WTO exceptions have continued to be elaborated in the DSM, which has had occasion to further discuss how WTO exceptions are applied to environment and health measures in developing countries since the 'Doha Round' was launched. Two recent WTO disputes are particularly important in this regard: the *Brazil-Retreaded Tyres* dispute[16] and the *European Communities-Biotech*

[10] Ibid.

[11] Implementation-Related Issues and Concerns—Ministerial Decision (14 November 2001) WT/MIN(01)/17, <http://docsonline.wto.org>.

[12] V Jha (ed), *Environmental Regulation and Food Safety: Studies of Protection and Protectionism* (Cheltenham, Edward Elgar, 2005) 30–31.

[13] Adopted 15 April 1994, entered into force 1 January 1995, 1867 UNTS 493, art 10.

[14] Adopted 15 April 1994, entered into force 1 January 1995, 1868 UNTS 120, art 11.

[15] ICTSD, 'New Issues' *Bridges Weekly Trade News Digest* (24 November 1999) <https://ictsd.iisd.org/bridges-news/bridges/news/new-issues> accessed 16 December 2020.

[16] *Brazil—Measures affecting Imports of Re-treaded Tyres—Report of the Panel* (12 June 2007) WT/DS332/R; *Brazil—Measures affecting Imports of Re-treaded Tyres—Report of the Appellate Body* (3 December 2007) WT/DS332/AB/R.

dispute.[17]

First, the interpretation of the General Agreement on Tariffs and Trade (GATT) article XX general exception was slightly clarified in a 2005 dispute concerning a Brazilian ban on imports of re-treaded and used tyres. This was one of the first cases where a developed country (or group) challenged a developing country's environmental measure and thus poses interesting sustainable development questions. Shortly after the European Communities (as one of the main exporters of used tyres) launched formal consultations in June 2005,[18] Brazil raised the problem in the Committee on Trade and Environment, highlighting the link between their measures and sustainable development:

> Moreover, in order to achieve the cited objectives, and in harmony with the widely accepted principle of sustainable development—included in the preamble of the WTO Agreement—Brazil banned imports of used and re-treaded tyres.[19]

Brazil justified the use of health and environmental measures, based on their commitments to sustainable development, as a reason for flexibility to be sought and granted. In the *Brazil-Re-treaded Tyres* dispute, the Panel did consider whether GATT article XX applied to grant an exemption to the measures. However, the Panel focused on the way that the ban was being applied unevenly, as Brazil still allowed for re-treaded tyres from Mercosur countries, due to court orders obtained by re-treading companies in the Mercosur.[20] The Panel found that the measure generally fulfilled the requirements of article XX (b) of the GATT as being necessary to protect animal, plant and human life or health, but that it was being applied in a manner that constituted a disguised restriction on international trade and was thus not justified under the chapeau of article XX of the GATT (similar to the *US-Shrimp* dispute).

The Appellate Body (AB) upheld the Panel's decision, but provided slightly different reasoning. First, the AB emphasized the Preamble to the WTO Agreement:

> The risks at issue relate to: (i) the exposure of animals and plants to toxic emissions caused by tyre fires; and (ii) the transmission of a mosquito-borne disease (dengue) to animals.[21]

[17] *European Communities—Measures Affecting the Approval and Marketing of Biotech Products—Reports of the Panel—Annex F—Addendum* (29 September 2006) WT/DS291/R/Add.4, WT/DS292/R/Add.4, WT/DS293/R/Add.4 (*European Communities-Biotech*).

[18] On 20 June 2005, the European Communities requested consultations with Brazil under art XXII:1 of the GATT 1994 and art 4 of the Understanding on Rules and Procedures Governing the Settlement of Disputes regarding Brazil's imposition of measures that adversely affect exports of re-treaded tyres from the European Communities to the Brazilian market.

[19] Committee on Trade and Environment, *Trade in Used and Retreaded Tyres-Submission by Brazil* (12 July 2005) WT/CTE/W/241; see also Committee on Trade and Environment, *Report of the Meeting held on 6 July 2005* (2 September 2005) WT/CTE/M/40 82.

[20] KR Gray, 'Brazil: Measures Affecting Imports of Retreaded Tyres' (2008) 102 American Journal of International Law 610, 610–611.

[21] The note cites the WTO Agreement Preamble, then: 'Moreover, in the 1994 Ministerial Decision on Trade and Environment, Ministers took note, *inter alia*, of the *Rio Declaration* and *Agenda 21*. Of particular relevance is paragraph 4.19 of *Agenda 21*, which states, in part: "... society needs to develop effective ways of dealing with the problem of disposing of mounting levels of waste products and materials. Governments, together with industry, households and the public, should make a concerted effort to reduce the generation of wastes and waste products ..."' The European Communities referred to the Rio Declaration and Agenda 21 in its response to question 37 by the Panel and in para 138 of its first written submission.

Therefore, the Panel found that the objective of protection of animal and plant life and health should also be considered important.[22]

The notes refer to Agenda 21 for guidance on the waste management problem at hand, once again linking the WTO AB reasoning to international 'soft law' on sustainable development. Indeed, third parties to the dispute evinced a certain, potentially interstitial, respect for sustainable development in their arguments during the case. In Oral Statement, during the AB Hearing, Cuba:

> … emphasized the importance of the principle of sustainable development and environment preservation policies, and recalled that waste tyre management presents a challenge in particular for developing countries, given the significant environmental and economic costs it involves.[23]

Similarly, with direct reference to the WTO's sustainable development objective, China noted:

> … The preamble of Marrakech Agreement declares that one objective of WTO is to pursue 'the optimal use of the world's resources in accordance with the objective of sustainable development' and 'seeking both to protect and preserve the environment' [note omitted][24]
>
> … China hopes that the Panel will give considerations to the fact that the defending party in this case is a developing country. In fact, developing countries are facing more difficulties than developed countries in balancing their economic development and environment protection. In addition, in dealing with environmental problems, developing countries usually are less sufficient in terms of funding and less efficient in terms of technology. Therefore, the multilateral trade system should give more support and tolerance to developing countries' endeavour to improve the environment.[25]

China argued, essentially, that the WTO general exceptions should be interpreted more broadly for developing countries, linking the recognition of sustainable development as an objective explicitly to the need to balance economic development and environmental protection.

While the WTO AB upheld the Panel's conclusion on the applicability of article XX (b) GATT, the AB also recognized that certain complex public health or environmental problems may be 'tackled only with a comprehensive policy comprising a multiplicity of interacting measures'. The AB stated:

> In the short-term, it may prove difficult to isolate the contribution to public health or environmental objectives of one specific measure from those attributable to the other measures that are part of the same comprehensive policy. Moreover, the results obtained from certain actions—for instance, measures adopted in order to attenuate global warming and climate change, or certain preventive actions to reduce the incidence of diseases that may manifest

22 *Brazil—Measures affecting Imports of Re-treaded Tyres—Report of the Panel* (n 16).
23 Ibid 85.
24 Ibid 5.27.
25 Ibid 5.37.

themselves only after a certain period of time—can only be evaluated with the benefit of time. In order to justify an import ban under Article XX(b), . . . a panel might conclude that an import ban is necessary on the basis of a demonstration that the import ban at issue *is apt to* produce a material contribution to the achievement of its objective. This demonstration could consist of quantitative projections in the future, or qualitative reasoning based on a set of hypotheses that are tested and supported by sufficient evidence.[26]

This decision further lowered the burden of proof for any (developed or developing country) WTO member seeking to justify the 'necessity' of a health or environment measure, as it is likely more straightforward to demonstrate that a measure 'is apt to produce a material contribution to the achievement of its objective' than it is to demonstrate that the measure is, for instance, essential to secure the objective.[27]

The second *European Communities-Biotech* dispute[28] concerned the applicability of the exceptions in the SPS Agreement, at Article 5.7, to the European Community regulation of genetically modified organisms (GMOs) under WTO law. In particular, the dispute focused on the *de facto* European Communities' moratorium on all GMO products pending legislation aimed at their commercial regulation,[29] and their subsequent robust pre-market approval regime.[30] Aimed at protecting human health and the environment,[31] in practice, the approval process resulted in long delays for approvals.[32] In 2001 the regime was clarified with the passage of the Deliberate Release Directive,[33] with a view to removing the moratorium.[34] In 2003 the European Communities amended the regime by putting forward legislation requiring both the labelling and tracing of all GMO products commercially sold.[35] In May 2003 the conflict came to a head when the United States, Canada and Argentina challenged these measures at the WTO. They collectively claimed that the regulatory controls imposed by member States of the European Community were not in compliance with their

26 Ibid 151.

27 Gray (n 20).

28 A Negi, 'World Trade Organisation and the EC Biotech Case: Procedural and Substantive Issues' (2007) 44 International Studies 1.

29 Ibid.

30 Commission Regulation (EC) No 258/97/EC of the European Parliament and of the Council of 27 January 1997 concerning novel foods and novel food ingredients [1997] OJ L 043, <http://eur-lex.europa.eu/LexUriServ/LexUriServ.do?uri=CELEX:31997R0258:EN:HTML> accessed 10 October 2010.

31 Mary Footer, 'Post-Normal Science, in the Multilateral Trading System: Social Science Expertise and the *EC-Biotech* Panel' (2007) 6(2) World Trade Review 281, 283.

32 Lawrence A. Kogan, 'World Trade Organization Biotech Decision Clarifies Central Role of Science in Evaluating Health and Environmental Risks for Regulation Purposes' (2007) 2(3) Global Trade and Customs Journal 149, <http://www.itssd.org/Publications/GTCJ_04-offprints_Kogan%5B2%5D.pdf> accessed 16 December 2020.

33 Directive 2001/18/EC of the European Parliament and of the Council of 12 March 2001 on the deliberate release into the environment of genetically modified organisms and repealing Council Directive 90/220/EEC, [2001] OJ L 106/1, <http://www.bmwf.gv.at/fileadmin/user_upload/forschung/gentechnik/RL-2001-18-EG-_EN_.pdf> accessed 10 October 2010.

34 Ibid.

35 Commission Regulation (EC) No 1829/2003 of the European Parliament and of the Council of 22 September 2003 on genetically modified food and feed, [2003] OJ L 268/1, <https://eur-lex.europa.eu/legal-content/EN/ALL/?uri=CELEX%3A32003R1829> accessed 16 December 2020; Commission Regulation (EC) No 1830/2003 of the European Parliament and of the Council of 22 September 2003 concerning the traceability and labeling of genetically modified organisms and the traceability of food and feed products produced from genetically modified organisms and amending Directive 2001/18/EC [2003] OJ L 268/24, <http://www.food.gov.uk/multimedia/pdfs/reg18302003.pdf> accessed 10 October 2010.

obligations under the covered agreements.[36] The various versions of the final judgments speak volumes to the complexity inherent in both the legal and scientific issues underlying the dispute.[37]

It was alleged that the European Communities had, through the application of its pre-market regulatory system, imposed an 'undue delay' on the approval of GMO product applications contrary to numerous aspects of the SPS Agreement, a *de facto* moratorium.[38] It was also claimed that this 'undue delay' equated to 'less favorable treatment' in contravention of the national treatment clause of the GATT, based on the assertion that GMO and non-GMO products were sufficiently 'like' products.[39] Finally, they argued that the 'precautionary' measures imposed by the European Community and its member States were excessive in nature, lacked proper scientific evidence and were not based on an 'adequate' science-based risk assessment within the meaning of the SPS agreement.[40] The European Communities denied the moratorium, arguing in the alternative that if one existed, it was colloquial in nature and did not constitute an undue restriction on trade. They indicated that delays associated with difficult regulatory action were not trade restrictive measures as such; and the 'precautionary' safeguards imposed were temporary in nature, implemented due to the continued scientific uncertainty surrounding GMOs.[41] Underlying the European Communities' position was a reliance on the precautionary principle, and its obligations under the 2001 UN Convention on Biological Diversity (UNCBD) Cartagena Protocol on Biosafety, as discussed in Chapter 2.[42] With regard to the exceptions, in particular, the European Communities contended that the stated objective of its regulatory regime was the protection of human health and the environment,[43] which was consistent with the precautionary principle as a general principle of international law,[44] citing Agenda 21 and several treaties on sustainable development as evidence.[45] The European Communities sought to rebut the assertion that GMO and non-GMO goods could be considered 'like products'.[46] If the Panel had found, as it did in the *European Communities-Asbestos* dispute,[47] that GMO and non-GMO were not 'like products', the Party challenging the measure would have no claim of discrimination. Finally, the European Communities argued that article 5.7 of the SPS Agreement is a specific illustration of the precautionary principle,[48] which

[36] Simon Lester, 'WTO—Sanitary and Phytosanitary Measures Agreement-rules/exceptions—International Law as Interpretive Tool' (2007) 101 American Journal of International Law 453, 454.

[37] R Howse and H Horn, 'European Communities-Measures Affecting the Approval and Marketing of Biotech Products' (2009) 8(1) World Trade Review 49, 82; G Winham, 'The GMO Panel: Applications of WTO Law to Trade in Agricultural Biotech Products' (2009) 31(3) European Integration 409–441.

[38] SPS Agreement (n 13) arts 2.2, 2.3, 5.1, 5.2, 5.5, 5.6, 7 and 8, and Annexes B(1), B(2), B(5), C(1)(a), C(1)(b) and C(1)(e).

[39] Marrakesh Agreement Establishing the World Trade Organization (adopted 15 April 1994, entered into force 1 January 1995) 1867 UNTS 4 arts. I:1, III:4, X:1 and XI:1.

[40] SPS Agreement (n 13) arts 2.2, 5.1 and 5.7.

[41] *European Communities-Biotech* (n 17).

[42] Ibid.

[43] Ibid.

[44] Ibid 336. The European Communities argued that this principle could be considered by virtue of Vienna Convention on the Law of Treaties (VCLT) (signed 23 May 1969, entered into force 27 January 1980) 1155 UNTS, art 31(3)(c).

[45] Ibid; particularly the World Charter for Nature of 1982, the Rio Declaration of 1992, the 1992 United Nations Framework Convention on Climate Change and the 1992 Convention of Biological Diversity.

[46] Ibid, 71, 342.

[47] *European Community —Measures Affecting Asbestos and Asbestos-Containing Products* (12 March 2001) WT/DS135/AB/R.

[48] *European Communities-Biotech* (n 17) 97.

the European Communities relied upon to justify the implementation of their provisional safeguard measures.[49]

The Panel did not make a finding on the 'like-products' issue, but did conclude that the European Communities had implemented a *de facto* moratorium on GMO based products from June 1999 to August 2003. Subsequently, the European Communities were in violation of Annex C(1)(a) of the SPS Agreement prohibiting 'undue delay'.[50] Following the same logic, the Panel found that the 'product-specific' measures were equally in violation of Annex C(1)(a).[51] The Panel also concluded that the 'precautionary measures' of all six European Community member States violated articles 5.1 and 2.2 of the SPS Agreement,[52] as they were not based on an adequate scientific risk assessment, and that these measures were not saved by the article 5.7 exception to the SPS Agreement.[53]

To come to a final determination regarding the 'precautionary measures' of members, the Panel characterized SPS article 5.7 'as a qualified right' which shifts the burden of proof to the complaining states to prove a violation of the SPS agreement prior to the application of SPS article 5.1.[54] After considering the scientific evidence provided by the WTO member States, the Panel concluded that the 'precautionary measures' in question had not been based on scientific risk assessment.[55] Fundamentally, the Panel determined that WTO member States could not simply rely on non-governmental organization (NGO) reports or peer-reviewed journal articles as the scientific basis of a trade-restrictive measure in the face of international applicable 'risk assessment techniques', and that the scientific evidence presented did not satisfy a determination of an 'adequate risk assessment' as intended in Annex (A)(4).[56] Finding that the relevant 'precautionary measures' did not satisfy the requirements of article 5.1 of the SPS Agreement, the Panel considered exemptions under article 5.7. First, relying on *Japan-Agricultural Products II,* the Panel recognized that there were four 'cumulative' requirements in article 5.7 that must be satisfied to support the measures in question. Relevant scientific information was insufficient (article 5.7 reflected the precautionary principle in this regard[57]). The European Communities was not excused from conducting a scientific risk assessment due to the insufficiency of scientific evidence;[58] but both the European Communities' approval procedures and their scientific committees' findings were risk assessments under the SPS Agreement. As such the European Communities actually did have sufficient scientific evidence.[59] The Panel did not provide an opinion on the legal status of the precautionary principle in international law,[60] and while the Panel considered the Convention on Biological Diversity and the Cartagena Protocol, it noted that these agreements were not in force for all the WTO members in the dispute and thus did

[49] Ibid 73.
[50] Ibid 1070.
[51] Ibid 1071.
[52] Ibid 1073.
[53] Ibid.
[54] Ibid 956.
[55] Ibid 1007–1008.
[56] Ibid 150.
[57] Ibid 1008.
[58] Ibid 1023.
[59] Ibid 1023–1024.
[60] Oren Perez, 'Anomalies at the Precautionary Kingdom: Reflections on the GMO Panel's Decision' (2007) 6(2) World Trade Review 265, 267.

not need to 'be taken into account'.[61] Cumulatively, the Panel found that as the European Communities did not conduct an adequate scientific risk assessment to satisfy article 5.1, the conditions necessary to invoke article 5.7 were not present.[62]

The Decision in the 2001 Doha Declaration to extend the time periods of certain WTO obligations for developing countries may indeed prove to be helpful in terms of making compliance more straightforward for developing country WTO members, and can be recognized as one way that concerns about development effects of trade disciplines, as discussed in Chapter 2 of this volume, can be integrated into a trade agreement through the opening of 'windows' or exceptions. However, the effects of these two disputes on the scope of exceptions available to WTO members are considerably more mixed. The WTO Panel and AB in the *Brazil-Re-treaded Tyres* dispute, by finding that to demonstrate a measure is 'necessary', it is sufficient to demonstrate that there is a reasonable link between a health or environment measure and its policy objective, broadened the scope of article XX, making the exception more accessible for developing country WTO members. However, as noted by some commentators, in the *European Communities-Biotech* dispute, the scope of SPS article 5.7 as an exception was both clarified and narrowed. While some have welcomed the judicial restraint taken by the AB and Panel with regards the precautionary principle and the transfer of burden to the complainant,[63] it has also been noted that if the European Communities' scientific process was not considered a risk assessment in the scope of the SPS Agreement, it becomes hard to understand which developing country could possibly live up to the 'scientific' standard set in the WTO.[64] Furthermore, the Panel's decision disregarded references to the UNCBD and other treaties, rather than taking them into account as the Panel and AB had done in the *US-Shrimp* dispute, on the grounds that certain WTO members were not parties to those international treaties on sustainable development. As such, the decision narrowed WTO potential for integration substantially. Essentially, the Panel's view was that unless all parties to a dispute are also parties to the other international treaty on sustainable development, the WTO is not required to take the obligations of the Party that is a member of both regimes into account, or even consider the multilaterally agreed principles and definitions of that treaty. This extremely textual view has supporters in international law, in that if the principles recognized in the other treaty are not also customary law, and the other treaty is not a specialized regime (*lex specialis*), it is for the Party with the conflicting obligations to be ready to leave one for the other, incurring State responsibility if necessary.[65] The precautionary principle remains debated, especially in trade law scholarship and practice.[66] However, the decision provides an unfortunate

[61] Simon Lester, 'WTO— *Sanitary and Phytosanitary Measures* Agreement-Rules/Exceptions-International Law as Interpretive Tool' (2007) 101 American Journal of International Law 453, 457.

[62] *European Communities-Biotech* (n 17) 422.

[63] Howse and Horn (n 37).

[64] Ibid.

[65] VCLT, art 38; A Boyle and C Chinkin, *The Making of International Law* (Oxford, OUP 2007) 234–240.

[66] MC Cordonier Segger and A Khalfan, *Sustainable Development Law: Principles, Practices and Prospects* (Oxford, OUP 2004) 143–155; T O'Riordan, A Jordan and J Cameron (eds), *Reinterpreting the Precautionary Principle* (London, Cameron May 2001) 296; A Trouwborst, 'The Precautionary Principle in General International Law: Combating the Babylonian Confusion' (2007) 16 Review of European Community and International Environmental Law 185. See also M Kunz, 'Principle 11: environmental legislation' in JE Viñuales (ed), *The Rio Declaration on Environment and Development: A Commentary* (Oxford, OUP 2015); Report of the UN Secretary General, 'Gaps in International Environmental Law and Environment-Related Instruments: Towards a Global Pact for the Environment', 30 November 2018, UN Doc A/73/419.

counterpoint to the more expansive reasoning of the Panel and AB in the *US-Shrimp* dispute, limiting the opportunity for the WTO dispute settlement process to integrate social development, environmental and economic development considerations found in other treaties on sustainable development, in trade law and policy. From the view of the regulator seeking to advance sustainable development through integration, the limits of the 'purpose' approach which leaves a great deal of discretion to the trade Panel in interpreting the value of shedding light on the nature of obligations through considering relevance of object and purpose, become apparent with this decision.[67] In this instance, the WTO Panel was not willing to take into account the provisions of the other treaty in question, or to broaden its view of the article 5.7 exceptions in this light.[68] The Panel's decision has demonstrated the limits of the DSM in providing flexibility for regulators concerned with the implementation of sustainable development measures, or at the least, gives a stern warning that appeals to other international obligations are, indeed, not a 'trump card' in the WTO.[69]

13.3 Permissions and Prescriptions to Secure Additional Environmental and Social Cooperation Parallel to the Trade Agreement Itself

Given the lack of consensus between diverse WTO member States as to the utility of negotiating development and environmental issues at the WTO as opposed to other forums, it is perhaps not surprising that there was very little progress in developing parallel trade-related cooperation on social development or environmental issues in the WTO, up to the launching of the Doha Round of trade negotiations.

In the 2001 Doha Declaration at paragraph 31, certain negotiations for increased cooperation on trade and environment among WTO members were agreed, but only for:

> (ii) procedures for regular information exchange between MEA Secretariats and the relevant WTO committees, and the criteria for the granting of observer status ...[70]

With the granting of observer status to MEA Secretariats and publication of certain joint studies, there has been a certain amount of progress, but this is scarcely the type of collaborative programme that can be highlighted.[71]

The Doha Declaration, at paragraph 33, does recognize 'the importance of technical assistance and capacity-building in the field of trade and environment to developing countries, in particular the least-developed among them',[72] encouraging members to support technical assistance and to share environmental review experiences, and commits to provide a report on these activities. These initial indications of willingness to provide technical

[67] VCLT, art 31(1).

[68] R Gardiner, *Treaty Interpretation* (2nd edn, Oxford, OUP 2015).

[69] See M Footer, 'Post-Normal Science, in the Multilateral Trading System: Social Science Expertise and the *EC-Biotech* Panel' (2007) 6(2) World Trade Review 281, 283.

[70] Doha Ministerial Declaration (n 2).

[71] D Brack and K Gray, *Multilateral Environmental Agreements and the WTO* (IISD Report, September 2003) 37; D Motaal, 'The Observership of Intergovernmental Organizations in the WTO post-Doha' (2005) 5 Journal of World Intellectual property 477.

[72] Doha Ministerial Declaration (n 2).

assistance and to learn about environmental reviews, such as those discussed in Chapter 2 of this volume, may contribute to laying foundations for cooperation, over time.

In Doha, there was also narrow, limited progress in advancing cooperation on trade and social development-related issues. For instance, the Doha Decision on Technology Transfer to Least-developed Countries was welcomed by many scholars and commentators.[73] As noted throughout the 2002 Johannesburg Plan of Implementation (JPOI),[74] technology transfer is key to sustainable development, as many development, environment but also economic challenges can be improved with access to new technologies. Several environmental assessments, including Canada's 1994 Environmental Assessment of the Uruguay Round noted in Chapter 2, have signalled concerns that by fulfilling TRIPS requirements on the enforcement of licensing fees, environmental technologies became too expensive for developing countries. In this Implementation Decision, Ministers mandated the TRIPS Council to put in place a mechanism to ensure full implementation of article 66.2 of the TRIPS which asks developed countries to promote and encourage technology transfer to least developed countries. Further, in TRIPS-related negotiations, States agreed to:

> '... instruct the Council for TRIPS, in pursuing its work programme ... to examine, inter alia, the relationship between the TRIPS Agreement and the Convention on Biological Diversity, the protection of traditional knowledge and folklore, and other relevant new developments raised by Members pursuant to Article 71.1. In undertaking this work, the TRIPS Council shall be guided by the objectives and principles set out in Articles 7 and 8 of the TRIPS Agreement and shall take fully into account the development dimension.[75]

In terms of broader social development issues, however, such as labour and other human rights, there continues to be no negotiations in the WTO. Many WTO members continue to assert that the best place for such discussions is in the International Labour Organization, and in the UN Human Rights Commission.[76]

Members have made little progress on this cooperation since the 2001 Doha meeting. Negotiations under the trade and environment paragraph are stalled, as was clear from the WTO Ministerial Declarations from Hong Kong,[77] and from Geneva in 2009.[78] This point suggests that members are hesitant to even agree on the most moderate developments in this field before other aspects of the negotiations are resolved, or other demands have been met.[79] Developed countries, including the EU, are very much the *demandeurs* for a strong trade and environment agenda in the WTO.[80] There may still be potential for a 'global deal'

[73] C Bellmann, G Dutfield and R Meléndez-Ortiz, *Trading in Knowledge: Development Perspectives on TRIPS, Trade and Sustainability* (London, 2003).

[74] Johannesburg Plan of Implementation (JPOI), Report of the World Summit on Sustainable Development, 4 September 2002, UN Doc. A/CONF.199/20.

[75] Doha Ministerial Declaration (n 2).

[76] EU Petersmann, 'Taking Human Dignity, Poverty and Empowerment of Individuals More Seriously' (2002) 13 European Journal of International Law 845.

[77] Doha Ministerial Declaration (n 2).

[78] Geneva Ministerial Declaration (20 May 1998) WT/MIN(98)/DEC/1, <http://docsonline.wto.org> accessed 16 December 2020.

[79] See, e.g., S Cho, 'The Demise of Development in the Doha Round Negotiations' (2010) 45 Texas International Law Journal 573.

[80] N Schrijver and F Weiss, *International Law and Sustainable Development: Principles and Practice* (Lieden, Martinus Nijhoff 2004) 182.

in the Doha 'Development Agenda', however, at the moment, the WTO seems to lack clear direction for integrated cooperation on trade, environment and development issues.

13.4 Prescriptions for WTO Members to Liberalize Trade in Specific Economic Sectors that Contribute to Sustainable Development

As argued in Sections 2 and 3, tensions related to the potential for trade law to support expansions of unsustainable and obsolete industries, may be countered by new efforts to use trade law to liberalize trade in more sustainable goods and services. Taking advantage of this opportunity in the WTO is not without its challenges. In particular, it is difficult to determine which specific goods and services are 'more sustainable'. As noted above, members are not all parties to the same international treaties that agree to promote development of new technologies and products in order to protect the environment, respect social justice concerns and/or achieve more sustainable development.[81] A central tenet of trade law prevents WTO members from examining the process and production method (PPM) of a product in order to distinguish between 'like-products' that are entering their markets.[82] In light of this principle, it is difficult for WTO members to agree to distinguish between products that contribute to sustainable development when conferring trade advantages.[83] As mentioned earlier in this volume, it may be necessary for Parties to trade agreements to negotiate specific solutions to this tension. Indeed, the 2001 Doha Declaration did launch trade negotiations which have the possibility, for the first time, of using trade law to actually promote the expansion of more sustainable goods and services.

First, as noted above, at paragraph 31 the Doha Declaration launches specific negotiations to liberalize trade in environmental goods and services:

> (iii) the reduction or, as appropriate, elimination of tariff and non-tariff barriers to environmental goods and services.[84]

At paragraph 32, WTO Members also instruct the CTE to give particular attention to:

> (i) the effect of environmental measures on market access, especially in relation to developing countries, in particular the least-developed among them, and those situations in which the elimination or reduction of trade restrictions and distortions would benefit trade, the environment and development ...[85]

As noted by Ricardo Melendez-Ortiz and others, should these negotiations be successful, they may indeed allow the benefits of trade liberalization to support increased production and diffusion of, for instance, renewable energy technologies in support of the objectives of multilaterally agreed commitments in the field of sustainable development.[86] Further

[81] Brack and Gray (n 71).
[82] CR Conrad, *Process and Production Methods (PPMs) in WTO Law: Interfacing Trade and Social Goals* (Cambridge, CUP 2011).
[83] Ibid.
[84] Doha Ministerial Declaration (n 2).
[85] Ibid.
[86] Bellmann, Dutfield and Meléndez-Ortiz (n 73).

proposals are now being developed, alongside both the UN Framework Convention on Climate Change (UNFCCC) and WTO regimes, for a standalone or plurilateral trade agreement to promote trade in renewable energy technologies and other climate compatible goods and services.[87] At the WTO, however, negotiations have remained paralysed in the effort to define which goods and services are truly environmental. A list, which has been circulating among members for more than ten years, has yet to be finalized, with debates on whether turbines for large-scale hydrological dams should be included, for instance.[88] Given the lack of real progress in this area of the negotiations since the 2001 Doha Round was launched, the promise of this mandate remain unrealized in this area.

Trade and investment agreements might contribute to sustainable development, and the 'green economy', both by enhancing trade in more sustainable products, and by reducing perverse incentives that promote unsustainable industries.[89] Negotiations were also launched in the 2001 Doha Declaration under paragraph 28 on subsidies, in order to reduce and reform fishing subsidies, which as mentioned earlier in this volume, have been found in scientific and economic studies, including sustainability impact assessments, to be highly unsustainable as they prompt over-fishing and depletion of the world's fish stocks.[90] As noted in the Declaration: '[i]n the context of these negotiations, participants shall also aim to clarify and improve WTO disciplines on fisheries subsidies, taking into account the importance of this sector to developing countries.'[91] Unfortunately, in this area too, very little progress has been made to date.[92]

Essentially, as has been recognized by trade and investment law scholars, though the opportunity may be present, WTO negotiations have had significant difficulties to date in addressing this tension.[93] There has been little progress in agreeing to use trade rules to limit economic policies (such as subsidies) that encourage unsustainable exploitation of natural resources. And there has been even less success in encouraging increased trade in environmentally sound goods and services, or finding trade rules that incentivize 'fair trade' products which explicitly support social development. In spite of recognizing a sustainable development objective, negotiations in the WTO have been unable to realize these 'triple-win' opportunities.

[87] JA Kim, 'Facilitating Trade in Services Complementary to Climate-friendly Technologies' (2011) International Centre for Trade and Sustainable Development, Issue 15; M Wilke, 'Feed-in Tariffs for Renewable Energy and WTO Subsidy Rules: An Initial Legal Review' (2011) International Centre for Trade and Sustainable Development, Issue 4.

[88] See, e.g. Deutsche Bank Research, *Doha or Dada: The World Trade Regime at an Historic Crossroads* (28 June 2011) 13, <http://www.dbresearch.de/PROD/DBR_INTERNET_EN-PROD/PROD0000000000275048.pdf> accessed 16 December 2020.

[89] TEEB, *The Economics of Ecosystems and Biodiversity: Mainstreaming the Economics of Nature: A Synthesis of the Approach, Conclusions and Recommendations of TEEB*; UN Environmental Programme (UNEP), 'Towards a Green Economy: Pathways to Sustainable Development and Poverty Eradication', 2011, <https://www.unep.org/greeneconomy> accessed 16 December 2020; E von Weizsacker and others, *Factor Five: Transforming the Global Economy through 80% Improvements in Resource Productivity* (London, Earthscan 2009); J Monkelbaan, 'Using Trade for Achieving the SDGs: The example of the Environmental Goods Agreement' (2019) 51(4) Journal of World Trade 575.

[90] C Deere, *Net Gains: Linking Fisheries Management, International Trade and Sustainable Development* (Cambridge, IUCN Publications 2000).

[91] Doha Ministerial Declaration (n 2).

[92] Deere (n 90).

[93] D Bethlehem and others, *The Oxford Handbook of International Trade Law* (Oxford, OUP 2009); P Birnie, A Boyle and C Redgwell, *International Law & the Environment* (Oxford, OUP 2009); Schrijver and Weiss (n 80); Sampson (n 6); Report of the UN Secretary General (n 66).

14

Sustainable Development in the WTO Institutions and Trade Policy Review Mechanism (TPRM)

It is perhaps not surprising that there has been so little progress, in spite of certain promising indications during the launching of the Doha Round of negotiations, on trade and sustainable development in the World Trade Organization (WTO). The WTO has nearly 150 members, with 30 more involved in accession negotiations,[1] and these members are very diverse in their economic, social and environmental conditions, as well as their cultural and political perspectives.[2] WTO members continue to hold distinct and occasionally contradictory views on the linkages between trade and sustainable development in law and in policy, and not all are parties to other treaties or organizations on these matters.[3]

After 2001, the WTO as an institution did move to integrate environment and development issues into many aspects of its programming. As was noted by then-WTO Director General Pascal Lamy, the objective of sustainable development mandates WTO members 'to no longer compartmentalize [their] work; discussing environmental and developmental issues in isolation of the rest of what [they] do. These are issues that permeate all areas of the WTO.'[4] Indeed, WTO Director Generals have repeatedly stated that sustainable development is not just a vague concept but rather requires an integrated approach to the economic, social and environmental work of the WTO.[5] The WTO has even instituted a practice of hosting public symposia on the subject. Starting with back-to-back meetings on trade and development, and on trade environment, the events have now merged into one annual event on 'trade and sustainable development'.[6] Progress on integrating social and environmental considerations into WTO law and policy in order to realize sustainable development, however, remains poor.

[1] See <http://www.wto.org/english/thewto_e/whatis_e/tif_e/org6_e.htm> accessed 16 December 2020.

[2] See, e.g., PricewaterhouseCoopers, 'Sustainability Impact Assessment (SIA) of the negotiations of the trade agreement between the European Community and the Countries of the Cooperation Council for the Arab States of the Gulf (GCC): Final Report' (Paris, May 2004) 17–19; ECORYS, CUTS and CENTAD, "Trade Sustainability Impact Assessment for the FTA between the EU and the Republic of India: Global Analysis Report" (Rotterdam, ECORYS 2008) 43–110.

[3] The US, for instance, is not a Party to the UN Convention on Biological Diversity, or to the Kyoto Protocol to the UN Framework Convention on Climate Change. See online <http://www.cbd.int/information/parties.shtml> and <http://unfccc.int/kyoto_protocol/status_of_ratification/items/2613.php> accessed 16 December 2020.

[4] P Lamy, 'Trade Can be a Friend, and Not a Foe, of Conservation', Speech at the WTO Symposium on Trade and Sustainable Development, Geneva, 10 October 2005, <http://www.wto.org/english/news_e/sppl_e/sppl07_e.htm> accessed 16 December 2020.

[5] Ibid; P Lamy 'Lamy Highlights Environment Dimension of Trade Talks', Remarks to the Commission on Sustainable Development, 10 May 2006, <http://www.wto.org/english/news_e/sppl_e/sppl25_e.htm> accessed 16 December 2020.

[6] See, e.g., the 2005 symposium, <http://www.wto.org/english/tratop_e/envir_e/sym_oct05_e/sym_oct05_e.htm> accessed 16 December 2020.

Crafting Trade and Investment Accords for Sustainable Development. Marie-Claire Cordonier Segger, Oxford University Press. © Marie-Claire Cordonier Segger 2021. DOI: 10.1093/oso/9780198831341.003.0014

There were high initial expectations for the Doha Development Agenda, as it was widely understood as intending to place development priorities at the heart of the new negotiations. However, little progress appears to have been made, leading some commentators to announce the failure of Doha.[7] As noted above, while developing countries have made great efforts to ensure that their voices and interests are heard and taken into account, there has been little advancement on important development issues. Similarly, progress has been scant in constructively addressing overlaps between trade and human rights questions, or trade and environment questions, in a way that integrates development interests.

Few, if any, WTO members still deny the importance of sustainable development or consider its application restricted only to natural resources. There are, however, still diverse views in the WTO. Certain WTO members consider sustainable development to have first and foremost a developmental dimension and others focus mainly on the trade and environment dimensions. These divergences, as well as some signs of limited consensus, are evinced by recent discussions in the WTO TPRM.

The TPRM, which became part of the WTO in 1989, exists to facilitate the functioning of the multilateral trading system through transparency.[8] The mechanism was not intended to substitute dispute settlement procedures, but rather, provides a forum for WTO members to be reviewed on their efforts to implement trade disciplines agreed in the WTO. Initially, the mechanism was exclusively focused on economic policy decisions,[9] but it has also discussed trade and sustainable development.[10] As the European Commission (EC) and others have started to integrate social development and environmental issues into their trade and economic policy-making, this has extended to trade policy review questions. For instance, Norway introduced its trade policy by noting their commitment to 'pursuing a policy of sustainable development domestically as well as globally, endeavouring to ensure in the process that trade and environmental policies were mutually supportive'.[11] The US questioned Madagascar about environmental pollution in mining activities.[12] And China also noted its strong commitment to a collective notion of sustainable development.[13]

The EC has taken the initiative to question each WTO member undergoing a TPRM on their positions on sustainable development, trade and environment and trade and social provisions. The EC has asked, with regards to sustainable development:

> In what ways does [WTO member] think trade policy can best contribute to sustainable development? Does the issue of trade and sustainable development fit into [WTO

[7] D Kleiman, J Guinan and PC Mavroidis, 'The Doha Round: An Obituary', Global Governance Programme Policy Brief, June 2011, <https://www.aspeninstitute.org/wp-content/uploads/files/content/docs/pubs/TheDohaRound_AnObituary_June2011.pdf> accessed 16 December 2020, 6.

[8] M Gehring, 'TPRM' in M Hilf and S Oeter (eds), *WTO-Recht* (Baden-Baden, Nomos 2005); M Kende, *The Trade Policy Review Mechanism: A Critical Analysis* (Oxford, OUP 2018).

[9] VC Price, 'GATT's new Trade Policy Review Mechanism' (1991) 14 The World Economy 227.

[10] The idea to use the TPRM to shed light on WTO members' sustainable development challenges was raised by legal scholars in the WTO Trade and Sustainable Development symposia after the 2001 Doha Ministerial. See also M Gehring, *Nachhaltigkeit durch Verfahren im Welthandelsrecht* (Berlin, Duncker and Humbolt 2007) 226; and see D Esty, *Greening the GATT* (Washington, IIE 1994) 146.

[11] Trade Policy Review Norway, Trade Policy Review Body Minutes of Meeting (26 July 2000) WT/TPR/M/70, <http://docsonline.wto.org> accessed 16 December 2020.

[12] Trade Policy Review Madagascar, Trade Policy Review Body Minutes of Meeting (11 June 2001) WT/TPR/M/80, <http://docsonline.wto.org> accessed 16 December 2020.

[13] See Trade Policy Review-People's Republic of China-Minutes of Meetings (6 June 2006-12 June 2007) WT/TPR/M/161 to WT/TPR/M/181, <http://docsonline.wto.org> accessed 16 December 2020.

> member]'s overall development strategies? What steps does [WTO member] take to ensure that its trade policy does not have any negative effects on sustainable development in [WTO member] and elsewhere?

The answers to these questions, summarized in Annex 1 to this volume, are particularly revealing. The replies of WTO member States to the questions on sustainable development posed in the WTO TPRM provide evidence of continuing points of disagreement, but also of certain common understandings about the nature of a commitment to sustainable development in trade law and policy. There are essentially three main positions.

First, some WTO members remain adamant that sustainable development is purely a domestic policy issue, or argue that all social and environmental considerations, including the potential impacts of trade, should remain only in the domestic law and policy arena. Very few continue to insist that trade institutions focus only on economic issues, and do not address social and environmental impacts.[14]

Second, several WTO members such as Canada and the US recognize openly that sustainable development is an objective of the WTO Agreements, and note that as such, it is relevant to the interpretation of the treaties (as part of the object and purpose). Such members emphasize a belief that trade liberalization will nearly automatically promote sustainable development. These WTO members highlight the minimal exceptions to WTO rules as the principal manner of accommodating environment and sustainable development concerns in the WTO, and often also mention procedural innovations such as public participation, or the importance of consulting between environment, development and trade authorities at the domestic level in the making of trade law and policy.

Third, WTO members such as the European Commission also recognize that trade will not automatically deliver on a sustainable development objective, and link their commitment to the objective with the need for better integration of environmental and social considerations into trade and development policy. They recognize a need to go beyond exemptions, to negotiate tailored trade liberalization that can encourage the dissemination of 'more sustainable' goods and services, and to set up mechanisms for additional cooperation on trade-related social development and environmental challenges. These members also refer to certain procedural innovations, and some also advocate the acceptance of principles such as sustainable use of natural resources, precaution and public participation. A few of these members also refer to a 'principle of sustainable development'. Given the context in which they use it, these WTO members refer to this principle to argue that States must integrate environmental and social development considerations into their trade policies in order to achieve sustainable development, but also, *a l'envers*, that trade measures for environmental purposes must take social and economic development priorities and conditions in developing countries into account.

14 See Annex 3.

15

The Limits of Addressing Sustainable Development in the WTO Regime

In conclusion, sustainable development has been recognized as an objective of the World Trade Organization (WTO) Agreements, and of the WTO itself. The implications of this commitment remain contested, with differing approaches being advocated by different WTO member States.[1] As noted above, the WTO has a very diverse membership. However, discussions have proceeded for over twenty years on this issue. As an objective, sustainable development is now firmly embedded in the WTO legal regime. Sustainable development is clearly reflected in the 2001 Doha Ministerial Declaration, not just at paragraphs 31–33 on trade and environment, but also in reference to the liberalization of environmental goods and services to achieve environment, development and trade benefits, reductions of subsidies to prevent over-fishing and efforts to clarify traditional knowledge through intellectual property rights. Indeed, there is evidence in the WTO regime of further 'interstitial' normative influence of this objective and the related integration principle, especially in changes to the work programmes of the Committee of Trade and Environment (CTE) and the Committee on Trade and Development (CTD), in the increasing numbers of WTO members that are conducting environment and sustainability assessments of their trade policies, the replies of WTO members to Trade Policy Review Mechanism (TPRM) questions, and in the debates on sustainable development concerns in the Ministerial meetings after Doha. These small steps, while they have been interpreted to grant additional flexibility in certain dispute settlement cases, do not take the WTO nearly far enough towards integration. There is very little space for actual cooperation on trade-related aspects of environmental or development law and policy, addressing the second tension between economic liberalization agreements and sustainable development detailed earlier in this volume, and there is as yet very little progress in enhancing trade in more sustainable goods and services, though Doha negotiations continue.

A number of WTO member States have not only set sustainable development as an objective of their trade and investment policy, but are also raising arguments related to sustainable development in WTO trade negotiations, and making sustainable development claims in dispute settlement procedures, as can be seen by its definition and recognition by the Panel and Appellate Body in the 1998 *US-Shrimp* dispute, the *Brazil-Re-treaded Tyres* dispute and others. The WTO Panel and Appellate Body did not hesitate to be guided by the

[1] See M Trebilcock and R Howse, *The Regulation of International Trade* (New York, Routledge 2005); M Gehring and MC Cordonier Segger (eds), *Sustainable Development in World Trade Law* (The Hague, Kluwer Law International 2005); D Bethlehem, D McRae, R Neufeld and I van Damme, *The Oxford Handbook of International Trade Law* (Oxford, OUP 2009); J Mathis, *Regional Trade Agreements in the GATT/WTO* (The Hague, TMC Asser 2002). See also, on the WTO's growing flexibility for regulators more broadly, S Bernstein and E Hannah, 'Non-State Global Standard Setting and the WTO: Legitimacy and the Need for Regulatory Space' (2008) 11(3) Journal of International Economic Law 575.

Crafting Trade and Investment Accords for Sustainable Development. Marie-Claire Cordonier Segger, Oxford University Press. © Marie-Claire Cordonier Segger 2021. DOI: 10.1093/oso/9780198831341.003.0015

consensus commitments from the 1992 Rio United Nations Conference on Environment and Development (UNCED), the 2002 World Summit on Sustainable Development (WSSD) and the 2020 UN Conference on Sustainable Development (UNCSD), and contributed to the operationalization of a commitment to sustainable development in trade law in this case. In spite of this high-water mark, as revealed in both the *European Communities-Hormones* dispute and the *European Communities-Biotech* dispute, the WTO dispute settlement body (DSB) retains the ability to resist taking into account other treaties, and will not always be convinced by arguments based on customary principles.

Measures have been debated in the WTO with regard to all three tensions identified earlier in this volume. What progress there has been on how to prevent trade disciplines from constraining legitimate environmental and social measures through the General Agreement on Tariffs and Trade (GATT) article XX and related exemptions have advanced mainly through WTO dispute settlement decisions, and this progress is limited at best. It is not yet clear, in the WTO, what specific provisions and measures could be enacted to increase the contributions of trade and investment law to achieving the world's Sustainable Development Goals (SDGs), or what additional cooperation might be undertaken by the WTO on trade-related environmental concerns, or on trade-related social issues. The Doha 'Development Agenda' trade negotiations have become deadlocked on these points.

Among those States which recognize international linkages between trade and sustainable development, two main approaches can be traced among WTO members. The first approach characterizes sustainable development as a subset of the trade and environment debate, a policy objective that can be mainly addressed by ensuring the right exemptions in the trade agreement, then promoting stronger domestic environmental standards and international environmental cooperation (with its sustainable development component) as a separate and parallel agenda. The second approach, taken by the European Commission (EC) and also many developing countries, is overarching but more integrated, whereby sustainable development is recognized as an objective of economic cooperation (including the rules relating to trade liberalization), and mechanisms are tailored to secure the particularized integration of environment and development issues into trade and investment treaties, with efforts also being made to enhance economic progress in key areas of relevance to sustainable development.

In spite of incremental advances in the WTO, it is far from clear that the WTO members will be able to prevent or mitigate the negative impacts posited by assessments in practice, and summarized earlier in this volume, ensuring integration of social and environmental considerations in international economic law and policy as outlined above. Beyond the recognition of the interpretive value as part of the 'object and purpose' of the WTO Agreements, there has been little progress to date at the global level in finding and agreeing on specific mechanisms by which integration of environmental and social development priorities might be secured at the WTO. In the next part of this volume, therefore, the options that are being tested by States in bilateral and regional economic agreements are examined, with a careful consideration of their likely interpretation in light of an integration principle. By looking to the innovations of States in other economic treaties, the volume evaluates elements of the two principal approaches currently in general practice, to better define the meaning of the integration principle for trade and investment law, and to consider how such provisions may be interpreted in its light.

SECTION FIVE

SUSTAINABLE DEVELOPMENT-RELATED INNOVATIONS IN BILATERAL AND REGIONAL TRADE AND INVESTMENT RULES

16

Bilateral and Regional Economic Rules and Regimes

Bilateral and regional economic regimes provide opportunities for States to innovate in the elaboration and 'testing' of instruments for proposal at the global level.[1] As noted earlier in this volume, the impacts of any given trade or investment agreement depend on how it changes economic relationships between the Parties, on the prevailing social and environmental conditions in the Parties and on the depth of the liberalization commitments undertaken, among other factors. However, there are nonetheless legal measures which, if included in an economic agreement, may be interpreted to integrate environmental and social development priorities into the investment measures, addressing the key tensions and related opportunities identified above. This next part of the volume discusses the outcomes of a comparative analysis of over 110 different bilateral and regional trade and investment treaties in which member States have made commitments related to sustainable development, focusing on eight treaties that exemplify the two main approaches identified earlier in this volume among WTO members.[2] As such, this Chapter analyses whether and how, in the bilateral and regional economic treaty texts, States:

(1) provide exceptions in trade and investment treaties to prevent economic rules from constraining the regulatory flexibility of the Parties for social and environmental purposes in the field of sustainable development;
(2) establish prescriptions and permissions for cooperation to resolve environmental and social problems that could be exacerbated by the bilateral or regional economic treaty, strengthening domestic laws and supporting efforts to mitigate potential environmental and social impacts; and
(3) agree permissions and prescriptions to liberalize trade and investment in specific economic sectors that they agree will contribute to sustainable development, encouraging technologies and industries prioritized in other international treaties on sustainable development.

At the regional level, it is also possible to consider how these types of provisions are encouraged by changes in the procedures of negotiating trade and investment treaties. In essence, by examining how Parties' commitments to sustainable development are being characterized in a selection of bilateral or regional economic treaties, it is possible to analyse how related operational provisions can be interpreted in light of the principle that

[1] Roberto V Fiorentino, Luis Verdeja and Christelle Toqueboeuf, 'The Changing Landscape of Regional Trade Agreements: 2006 Update', WTO Discussion Paper No 12, 2007; Hugh Thirlway, *The Sources of International Law* (Oxford, OUP 2019).

[2] See Chapters 1–3 for details on selection of bilateral and regional economic agreements for this study, and case studies.

Crafting Trade and Investment Accords for Sustainable Development. Marie-Claire Cordonier Segger, Oxford University Press. © Marie-Claire Cordonier Segger 2021. DOI: 10.1093/oso/9780198831341.003.0016

environmental and social development considerations shall be integrated into economic decision-making concerning trade and investment.

Bilateral or regional economic treaties are discriminatory by nature, designed to grant certain trade preferences or investment protections to firms and investors from the participating countries.[3] As noted earlier in this volume, bilateral or regional economic treaties can be agreed between developed States, developing States, among both a developed and a developing State, or even across diverse groups of developed and developing States[4] such as the negotiations for a Trans-Pacific Partnership (TPP) or the Agreement on Climate Change, Trade and Sustainability. Barriers to market access diminish when States liberalize economic relations, though arrangements vary from partial trade preferences, to free trade areas, to customs unions, to common markets, to economic and monetary unions to fully integrated economic entities.[5] Only about 10 per cent of regional trade treaties are customs unions, with common rules, institutions, modes of cooperation and even judicial institutions, bringing a high level of economic, political and social collaboration.[6] The grand majority of current bilateral or regional economic treaties involve the second stage of economic integration, bilateral free trade areas, in which Parties agree to remove substantially all border tariffs, quotas and preferences amongst Parties, while maintaining their own tariff policies with respect to non-Parties.[7] As at April 2021, some 481 regional trade agreements (RTAs) had been notified to the General Agreement on Tariffs and Trade (GATT)/ World Trade Organization (WTO), and 302 of these bilateral or regional economic treaties were in force.[8] Concerns have been raised, particularly by WTO analysts, about this proliferation.[9] However, as proponents argue, small-scale trade and investment agreements can provide a convenient testing ground for legal innovations.[10] Indeed, regional and bilateral trade and investment agreements:

> can also be used by some countries as a vehicle for promoting deeper integration of their economies than is presently available through the WTO, particularly for issues which are not fully dealt with multilaterally, such as investment ... environment and labour standards.[11]

[3] M Trebilcock and R Howse, *The Regulation of International Trade* (New York, Routledge 2005) 14–24; CA Cooper and BF Massell, 'Toward a General Theory of Customs Unions for Developing Countries' (1965) Journal of Political Economy 461; JN Bhagwati, P Krishna and A Panagariya (eds), *Trading Blocs: Alternative Approaches to Analyzing Preferential Trade Agreements* (Boston, MIT Press 1999). A Krueger, 'Free Trade Agreements versus Customs Unions', NBER Working Paper No 5084, 1995; BA Balassa, *The Theory of Economic Integration* (London, Allen and Unwin 1961).

[4] Trebilcock and Howse (n 3) 14–24.

[5] Bhagwati, Krishna and Panagariya (n 3).

[6] Krueger (n 3). See also WTO Regional Trade Agreements Gateway 2011 <http://www.wto.org/english/tratop_e/region_e/region_e.htm> accessed 16 December 2020.

[7] E Ornelas, 'Trade Creating Free Trade Areas and the Undermining of Mulitlateralism' (2004) 49 European Economic Review 1717.

[8] WTO, 'Figures on Regional Trade Agreements notified to the GATT/WTO and in force', <http://rtais.wto.org/UI/publicsummarytable.aspx> accessed 16 December 2020.

[9] WTO, 'Regional Trade Agreements: Scope of RTAs', http://www.wto.org/english/tratop_e/region_e/scope_rta_e.htm accessed 16 December 2020.

[10] L Bartels and F Ortino (eds), *Regional Trade Agreements and the WTO Legal System* (Oxford, OUP 2006).

[11] WTO Secretariat, 'The Changing Landscape of RTAs' Seminar on Regional Trade Agreements and the WTO (2003) <http://www.wto.org/english/tratop_e/region_e/sem_nov03_e/boonekamp_paper_e.doc> accessed 16 December 2020, 23.

These final sections of the present volume compare how sustainable development is addressed in bilateral or regional economic treaties including those engaging the UK, Europe and the Americas.[12] In these treaties, States are 'testing' various innovations which can address the three key integration tensions identified earlier in this volume, offering different options to realize sustainable development through a trade and investment agreement. As discussed, if a customary norm of integration is emerging that can inform the interpretation of trade and investment treaties, or the further development of interactional economic regimes, the provisions of these recent bilateral or regional economic treaties offer useful comparisons.

In the Americas, two principal models of economic treaty address sustainable development explicitly, responding to the distinct viewpoints on the relationship that were identified in the Trade Policy Review Mechanism (TPRM) replies analysed earlier.[13] The Chile-US Free Trade Agreement (FTA),[14] together with the US-Peru Trade Promotion Agreement (TPA), the Chile-Colombia FTA and the Canada-Colombia-Peru FTA,[15] exemplify the first approach. The Chile-US FTA has a structure very similar to the venerable 1994 North American Free Trade Agreement (NAFTA)[16] between the US, Canada and Mexico, which has provided a prototype for many FTAs.[17] This is similar to the free trade agreements negotiated by the US with Peru, Colombia and Panama;[18] the FTAs of Canada with Costa Rica, Chile, Colombia and Peru;[19] and the FTAs of Mexico with Uruguay, Chile, Bolivia, Nicaragua, and with El Salvador, Honduras and Guatemala,[20] among others.

Chile and the United States announced their negotiations of a trade and investment treaty on 29 November 2000.[21] After fourteen rounds, the negotiations concluded on 11 December 2002, and the accord was signed in Miami on 6 June 2003. In the United States, the treaty was approved through the US-Chile FTA Act.[22] In Chile, the Agreement was approved by the Congress on 23 October 2003.[23] The US-Chile FTA entered into force on

12 There are few systemic legal comparisons of this nature, to date. See OECD, *Environment and Regional Trade Agreements* (Paris, 2007); L Bartels, 'Social Issues: Labour, Environment and Human Rights' in S Lester and B Mercurio (eds), *Bilateral and Regional Trade Agreements: Commentary, Analysis and Case Studies* (Cambridge, CUP 2008) which builds on the typology that, based on the research done for this volume, was proposed in MC Cordonier Segger, 'Sustainable Development in Regional Trade Agreements' in M Gehring and MC Cordonier Segger (eds), *Sustainable Development in World Trade Law* (The Hague, Kluwer Law International 2005).

13 A third type of trade treaty, 'Partial Preference Agreement', was facilitated by the Latin American Integration Association (ALADI) in the 1990s. This study did not review existing Partial Preference Agreements in any depth, few of which contain any references to sustainable development. See K Steinfatt, 'Preferential and Partial Scope Trade Agreements' in S Xirinachs and M Roberts (eds), *Towards Free Trade in the Americas* (Hagerstown, Maryland, Phoenix Colour 2001) 108.

14 Adopted 2003, entered into force 1 January 2004, <https://ustr.gov/trade-agreements/free-trade-agreements/chile-fta/final-text> accessed 16 December 2020. See also Factual Reports, <http://www.sice.oas.org/TPD/CHL_USA/CHL_USA_e.asp#articles> accessed 16 December 2020

15 US-Peru TPA (adopted 12 April 2006); Canada-Colombia FTA (entered into force 15 August 2011); Chile-Colombia FTA (adopted 27 November 2006).

16 Entered into force 1 January 1994.

17 L Crump, 'Negotiation Process and Negotiation Context' (2011) 16 International Negotiation 197, 213.

18 US-Peru TPA (n 15); US-Colombia TPA (signed 22 November 2006); US-Panama TPA (signed 28 June 2007).

19 Canada-Costa Rica FTA (entered into force 1 November 2002); Canada-Chile FTA (entered into force 5 July 1997); Canada-Colombia FTA (n 14); Canada-Peru FTA (signed 29 May 2008, entered into force 1 August 2009).

20 Mexico-Uruguay FTA (entered into force 15 July 2004); Mexico-Chile FTA (entered into force 1 August 1999); Mexico-Bolivia FTA (entered into force 7 June 2010); Mexico-Nicaragua FTA (entered into force 1 July 1998); Mexico-Northern Triangle FTA (entered into force 15 March 2001).

21 H Corbin, 'The Proposed United States–Chile Free Trade Agreement: Reconciling Free Trade and Environmental Protection' (2003) 14 Colorado Journal of International Environmental Law and Policy 119.

22 US HR 2738 (24 July 2003) US Public Law 108-77 (3 September 2003), Proclamation 7746 of 30 December 2003, Federal Register Vol 68, No 250, 75789.

23 Chile Decree 312, Chile Presidential Proclamation 7746 (1 December 2003).

1 November 2004. The treaty takes on substantive liberalization obligations in many important areas of trade and investment law and policy, extending beyond the Parties' WTO commitments. Its institutions are straightforward. In article 21.1, the Parties establish a cabinet-level Free Trade Commission responsible for supervision, dispute resolution, establishing committees and working groups, and approving modifications of the tariff elimination schedules and other commitments. Parallel to the economic accord, an Environmental Side Agreement and a Labour Side Agreement were agreed. Building on the trade and investment agreement, they established both an Environmental Affairs Council and Joint Commission for Environmental Cooperation with sustainable development mandates, as well as a separate Labour Affairs Council and Labour Cooperation Mechanism, in which sustainable development elements are not highlighted.

The second model places greater emphasis on dialogue and cooperation, and has been adopted by the European Union (EU) for economic cooperation negotiations with countries in the Americas. The EU-Chile Association Agreement[24] (EU-Chile AA) provides a second case study in this volume, supplemented by examples from similar recent treaties such as the EU-Central America AA,[25] the EU-Colombia-Peru FTA[26] and the EU-CARIFORUM Economic Partnership Agreement (EPA).[27] Negotiations on the EU-Chile AA began when Chile and the EU signed a Framework Cooperation Agreement on 21 June 1996, in Florence to lay foundations for progressive and reciprocal liberalization of their economies, and to develop a new 'political and economic association' between the European Community and its member States and Chile. From inception, negotiations went further than a simple free trade agreement. After ten intensive rounds, an accord was signed on 18 November 2002. At the time, the treaty was promoted as 'the most significant EU Agreement with a third country', outlining new commitments to political dialogue, cooperation, trade and certain minimal establishment provisions for investors. In the EU-Chile AA, Parties established a more complex institutional framework than is found in the US-Chile FTA. At Part I, the Parties establish an Association Council of the Association Committees and a series of Special Committees for development and implementation of the Agreement, together with a Political Dialogue supported by an Association Parliamentary Committee, and a Joint Consultative Committee which provides a mechanism for the engagement of civil society.[28] The Political Dialogue, covered in Part II of the Agreement, focuses on promotion, dissemination, further development and common defence of democratic values, and is carried out through periodic meetings of Heads of State, Ministers and senior officials. Priorities for cooperation are outlined in Part III, which includes sustainable development, and Trade liberalization is covered in Part IV, where the EU reduces or eliminates customs duties and liberalizes trade beyond WTO disciplines in, *inter alia*, services, government procurement

[24] Agreement establishing an association between the European Community and its member States, of the one part, and the Republic of Chile, of the other part, signed 18 November 2002, entered into force 1 February 2003 [2002] OJ L 352 [EU-Chile AA].

[25] Signed 29 June 2012, entered into force 1 August 2013. On 31 July 2013, the European Commission announced the provisional application of the EU Free Trade Agreement with Honduras, Nicaragua and Panama starting on 1 August 2013. The agreement entered into force on 1 October 2013 for Costa Rica and El Salvador, and on 1 December 2013, the agreement entered into force for Guatemala.

[26] Signed 30 March 2010.

[27] Signed 15 October 2008, entered into force 29 December 2008.

[28] EU-Chile Association Council, 'First Meeting of the EU-Chile Association Council: Joint Communiqué' (27 March 2003) UE-CL 3903/03 (Presse 97).

and investment, as well as making special provisions for sanitary and phytosanitary (SPS) and other measures.

Several brief observations can be made on the extent of the liberalization contemplated in these two treaties.

First, both types of bilateral or regional economic treaties significantly reduce tariffs between the Parties. As noted earlier in this volume, the EU previously maintained high tariffs on a number of goods in industrial sectors such as chemicals and textiles, as well as for agriculture, forest products and fisheries, processed foods and wines.[29] The EU-Chile AA commits the EU to full liberalization of industrial sectors, and to deep liberalization of fishing and agriculture, excluding only certain sensitive sectors. For the EU's imports, 99.7 per cent of imports by value are covered immediately. For Chile's imports, the EU-Chile AA covers 97 per cent of imports by value over seven years, with 94 per cent of imports by value immediately.[30] Up to ten years were provided as a transition period for certain products, and tariff quotas are applied for a limited number of products such as fisheries, mainly as a transitional measure. Similarly, in the US-Chile FTA, the US significantly reduced tariffs in key sectors. Upon entry into force, zero tariffs were set for more than 85 per cent of consumer and industrial goods. Other duties were also reduced, subject to a phase-in period of twelve years.[31]

Second, both bilateral or regional economic treaties liberalize important sectors of the Chilean economy for sustainable development. For instance, mining exploration and exploitation is opened to investment by firms from the Parties to the treaties,[32] And with regard to Chile's many fruit products, including wine and spirits, the accords include obligations not to use geographical or local product names.[33] But neither the US-Chile FTA nor the EU-Chile AA provide open access to fish in Chilean waters by foreign-flagged vessels, or port access for foreign fishing vessels, or change Chilean fishing quotas, and both guarantee respect for Chile's 200 miles exclusive economic zone.[34]

Third, both treaties extend further than the GATT/WTO regime in areas of national and international economic policy that can have important social and environmental impacts. For instance, in both treaties, Parties take on additional obligations in government procurement and investment/establishment, as well as services, though the US-Chile FTA commits to severe disciplines on investment measures and binding investor-state dispute settlement, while the EU-Chile AA simply provides for additional rules for the establishment of EU firms.[35] In both treaties, Parties also establish cooperative mechanisms to promote greater reductions in SPS and technical trade (TBT) barriers.[36] Such mechanisms are engaged, in further bilateral or regional economic treaties, to promote liberalization of other sectors of importance to sustainable development, as is discussed below.

[29] Government of Chile/European Union, 'Subsecretario Participó en V Comité De Asociación Chile-Unión Europea' (7 December 2007) <http://www.sice.oas.org/TPD/CHL_EU/CHL_EU_s.ASP> accessed 16 December 2020.

[30] Planistat, *Sustainable Impact Assessment (SIA) of the Trade Aspects of Negotiations for an Association Agreement between the European Communities and Chile* (Santiago 2002) [EU-Chile SIA].

[31] US-Chile FTA (n 13).

[32] US-Chile FTA (n 13) Annex 19.3; EU-Chile AA (n 23) art 35.

[33] US-Chile FTA (n 13) chapter 9, art 9.2; EU-Chile AA (n 23) art 139.

[34] US-Chile FTA (n 13); EU-Chile AA (n 23).

[35] US-Chile FTA (n 13) chapter 9; EU-Chile AA (n 23) title IV.

[36] US-Chile FTA (n 13) chapter 7; EU-Chile AA (n 23) art 83.

As noted in an initial review, from the entry into force of the EU-Chile AA, Chilean exports to the EU increased from US$ 4.3 billion to US$ 15.9 billion, a jump from 24.5 per cent to 27.5 per cent, and bilateral trade between the EU and Chile nearly tripled, from US$ 7.4 billion in 2002 to US$ 21.1 billion in 2006.[37] Chile moved up to 23rd in the world, in terms of providing goods and services to the EU, from 34th place previously. In other words, the EU-Chile AA appears to have increased Chile's exports to the EU significantly, especially in the Netherlands, Spain, Germany and Italy.[38] Trade between Chile and the United States also increased steeply after entry into force of the US-Chile FTA, from US$ 6 billion in 2003 to over US$ 11 billion by 2007. In this time frame, Chile exported more to the US than was imported, mainly in metals. Further, 7,675 types of products or 97.1 per cent of real exports benefitted from zero tariffs; this is to reach 100 per cent after twelve years, by 2015. The tariff-free exports grew from US$ 3,310,2 million in 2003 before the FTA entered into force to US$ 5,405,0 million in 2007.[39] In essence, both bilateral or regional economic treaties appear to have been successful economic deals for both Parties. The question remains as to how the social and environmental sustainability considerations identified in impact assessments reviewed earlier in this volume were integrated, if at all.

In this research, the comparative review of over 110 bilateral or regional economic treaties, many from the Americas, permitted analysis of how innovative mechanisms to address sustainable development issues can be interpreted in the context of trade and investment agreement. Responding to the three principal tensions identified earlier in this volume, and the opportunities highlighted with relation to the integration principle, an analytical framework (typology) can be proposed which identifies a series of legal options for States seeking to deliver on a commitment to sustainable development in a bilateral or regional economic treaty.[40] The framework assists in understanding the measures that are linked to sustainable development in their trade and investment agreements, in the context of a customary principle that requires environmental and social development concerns to be integrated into economic decision-making.

Initially, Parties may, in accordance with the intentions reflected in the 1992 Agenda 21, the 2002 Johannesburg Plan of Implementation (JPOI), the 2012 UN Conference on Sustainable Development (UNCSD), the 2015 Sustainable Development Goals (SDGs) and other key 'soft law' consensus instruments discussed earlier in this volume, be using introductory provisions to signal a joint commitment to a sustainable development purpose. These include a 'joint resolution' to 'promote sustainable development' by Parties in the Preambles of trade and investment accords; affirmations that sustainable development

[37] Chile/European Union, 'Subsecretario Participó en V Comité De Asociación Chile-Unión Europea' (7 December 2007) <http://www.sice.oas.org/TPD/CHL_EU/Implementation/Joint_Council/VCouncil_s.pdf> accessed 16 December 2020; Dirección General de Relaciones Económicas Internacionales del Ministerio de Relaciones Exteriores de Chile, 'Evaluación De Las Relaciones Económicas Y De Cooperación Entre Chile Y Los Países De La Unión Europea: A Cuatro Años de Vigencia del Acuerdo De Asociación' (October 2007) (EU-Chile DIRECON Study) <http://www.sice.oas.org/TPD/CHL_EU/Studies/Evaluacion2007_s.pdf> accessed 16 December 2020, 7.

[38] EU-Chile SIA (n 29) 10.

[39] Dirección General de Relaciones Económicas Internacionales del Ministerio de Relaciones Exteriores de Chile, 'Evaluación De Las Relaciones Económicas Y De Cooperación Entre Chile y los Estados Unidos: A Tres Años de Vigencia del Acuerdo del Libre Comercio' (January 2007) (Chile-US DIRECON Study) <http://www.sice.oas.org/TPD/CHL_USA/Studies/EvaChUS0107.pdf> accessed 16 December 2020.

[40] The original decision to focus on designing this typology was an outcome of discussions with Professors Dan Sarooshi and Chris McCrudden at Oxford University, and exchanges concerning inter-actional theories with Professor Stephen Toope at McGill University and the University of Cambridge. Their insights have been invaluable for this volume.

is an objective of the treaty; other initial statements of Parties' intentions to implement the accord in accordance with a 'principle of sustainable development' and even, most recently, full Articles characterizing their treaty as a new 'Partnership for Trade and Sustainable Development'. As discussed below, a regulator will find many such commitments in recent trade and investment agreements of the Americas.

Then, as a second step, there are operational provisions that may be interpreted in light of this sustainable development purpose, particularly given the emerging customary principle to integrate environmental protection and social development with economic development.

In a first category, addressing the first tension identified in this volume, the regulator finds exemptions from trade and investment rules, where liberalization obligations or disciplines might otherwise constrain regulators and policy-makers, mitigating their effects. These include:

(1) general exceptions related to the conservation of natural resources, and to the use of measures, including environmental measures, necessary to protect human, animal, or plant life or health;
(2) specific exceptions in sections of the Agreement where economic rules on *inter alia* sanitary and phytosanitary standards, technical barriers to trade, intellectual property rights, government procurement, services, or investment, might constrain the use of environmental and social measures;
(3) explicit 'non-application notes' by the Parties to prevent socially or environmentally sensitive sectors from being disciplined by new trade and investment liberalization commitments, such as keeping parks and natural resources from being subject to investment provisions, or health and education sectors from being subject to services disciplines;
(4) general interpretive statements to guide potential areas where trade and investment rules could otherwise constrain the use of measures agreed in other international (or regional) agreements.

In a second category, which has become more prevalent than one might expect from WTO experiences, the regulator finds provisions that can permit or prescribe 'mitigation-oriented' social and environmental cooperation activities among the Parties, to strengthen domestic environmental or social laws, such as:

(1) parallel agreements (or chapters, or both) for cooperation on environmental and social matters,
(2) joint coordination of new institutions for social and environmental cooperation,
(3) common work programmes on specific environmental or social projects, often accompanied by capacity-building, technology transfer and financing commitments,
(4) factual report/complaints mechanisms to provide recourse when environmental or social rules appear to be violated to attract trade or investment.

In a third category, addressing the third tension identified in this volume, the regulator will find new commitments to liberalize or enhance trade or investment in sectors that contribute to sustainable development. These opportunities appear specific to each economic relationship, but can include:

(1) sanitary and phytosanitary provisions which promote scientific cooperation and risk assessment to improve levels of health or environment protection;
(2) government procurement provisions which make public purchasing of sustainable development goods or services more affordable;
(3) technical barriers to trade provisions which improve certification processes, promoting mutual recognition of environmental or social standards;
(4) intellectual property rights provisions which support biodiversity protection and the recognition of traditional knowledge;
(5) measures to enhance liberalization of environmental goods and services;
(6) investment provisions which privilege socially responsible corporations;
(7) measures to reduce illegal trade in forestry products; and promote trade in certified sustainable wood;
(8) measures to secure reductions in unsustainable fishery and other subsidies; and
(9) measures to promote trade or investment in renewable energy and eco-innovation.

Such measures have been proposed in trade and environment, or trade- and labour- related literature over the decades of WTO debates; they are also being increasingly debated in the context of bilateral investment treaties (BITs), and considered by international investment arbitration institutions and tribunals. This research finds they are starting to be included in recent bilateral or regional economic treaties. This volume brings them together within an analytical framework based on their normative effects, in order to examine how such provisions might be interpreted to better integrate environmental and social concerns into trade and investment agreements for the realization of sustainable development.

The comparative review of negotiations in the surveyed treaties also reveals certain procedural innovations undertaken by the Parties that are assisting in identifying useful innovations that might be included in a bilateral or regional economic treaty. In particular, sustainable development proposals are being made during the following procedures:

(1) *ex-ante* (or ongoing) environment, development, human rights or sustainability impact assessments and reviews of trade and investment liberalization policies and draft treaties;
(2) consultations between economic, environment and development authorities,
(3) mechanisms to ensure transparency and public participation in trade and investment negotiations,
(4) mechanisms to inform tribunals about sustainable development issues, including expert consultation and public participation measures.

In the following chapters, drawing on examples from the eight focus treaties and over one hundred other bilateral or regional economic treaties comparatively reviewed in this research, examples of these types of provisions are analysed, from the perspective of how they address the key tensions identified in the review of assessments provided in Section 2 of this volume, by integrating environmental and social concerns into the bilateral or regional economic treaties as discussed in Section 3, overcoming the limits of addressing these issues effectively in the WTO, as discussed in Section 4.

Up until recently, many such opportunities were only theoretically canvassed in academic literature, but not yet adopted in actual economic agreements. However, the research for this book found that among the bilateral or regional economic treaties negotiated in the span of years between the 1992 UN Conference on Environment and Development (UNCED), the 2002 World Summit on Sustainable Development (WSSD), the 2012 UNCSD and beyond the 2015 SDGs, new types of provisions are being adopted by States. Rather than simply promoting *any* kind of economic growth, it can be argued that these recent bilateral or regional economic treaties are seeking ways to integrate social and environmental considerations to contribute to a more sustainable type of growth. The question of how is the focus of the next chapter.

17

Provisions to Integrate Environmental and Social Considerations into a Bilateral and Regional Trade and Investment Agreements for Sustainable Development

17.1 Sustainable Development Purpose of Bilateral or Regional Economic Treaties

In bilateral and regional trade and investment agreements, just as in the World Trade Organization (WTO), States are signalling a commitment to sustainable development in carefully worded introductory provisions. In most of the bilateral or regional economic treaties analysed in this research, the Parties explicitly commit to increases in trade and investment that support sustainable development.[1] In the treaties that follow a model similar to the 1994 North American Free Trade Agreement (NAFTA), this is simply framed as a 'joint resolution' of the Parties 'to promote sustainable development' in the Preamble. For instance, in the Preamble of the 2003 US-Chile Free Trade Agreement (FTA), Parties stated that:

> The Government of the Republic of Chile and the Government of the United States of America, resolved to: . . . promote sustainable development . . . have agreed as follows . . .[2]

This commitment appears in a list alongside over a dozen other preambular assurances such as to 'create an expanded and secure market for the goods and services produced in their territories' and to 'establish clear and mutually advantageous rules governing their trade'. In the treaty objectives, Parties narrow their focus to trade and investment liberalization:

> The objectives of this Agreement ... including national treatment, most-favored-nation treatment, and transparency, are to: ... (a) encourage expansion and diversification of trade between the Parties; ... (d) substantially increase investment opportunities in the territories of the Parties . . .[3]

[1] See Table of RTAs, whereby 57 of 116 treaties commit to sustainable development in preambular or other introductory provisions.

[2] US-Chile FTA (adopted 2003, entered into force 1 January 2004) <https://ustr.gov/trade-agreements/free-trade-agreements/chile-fta/final-text> accessed 16 December 2020, Preamble.

[3] Ibid, chapter 1, art 1.2 on objectives.

Crafting Trade and Investment Accords for Sustainable Development. Marie-Claire Cordonier Segger, Oxford University Press. © Marie-Claire Cordonier Segger 2021. DOI: 10.1093/oso/9780198831341.003.0017

However, in other recent treaties, especially those involving the European Union, more diverse formulations are adopted. For instance, in the EU-Chile Association Agreement (AA), the Preamble states:

> Considering the traditional links between the Parties and with particular reference to . . . the need to promote economic and social progress for their peoples, taking into account *the principle of sustainable development* and environmental protection requirements . . . the Parties have decided to conclude this Agreement . . . (emphasis added).

It is then further emphasized, at Part I, Title 1 on Nature and Scope of the AA in article 1 on Principles, that:

> 2. The *promotion of sustainable economic and social development* and the equitable distribution of the benefits of the Association are *guiding principles* for the implementation of this Agreement . . .[4]

Only at Part IV on Trade and Trade-related Matters, do the objectives of the treaty focus specifically on trade and investment liberalization, emphasizing objectives such as '(a) the progressive and reciprocal liberalisation of trade in goods' and 'the improvement of the investment environment . . .',[5] among others.

These approaches can be compared. In the first case, the Parties simply note that they are resolved to 'promote sustainable development' and hence are concluding a free trade agreement. This is the approach found in the NAFTA and the United States of America, the United Mexican States, and Canada Agreement (USMCA),[6] and in many trade and investment agreements involving NAFTA Parties such as the Canada-Chile FTA,[7] the Canada-Costa Rica FTA,[8] and the Peru-United States TPA.[9] It is also found, in Spanish, in the Andean-MERCOSUR FTA, in the Bolivia-MERCOSUR FTA and in the Bolivia-Mexico FTA,[10] which state:

> El Gobierno de los Estados Unidos Mexicanos y el Gobierno de la República de Bolivia, decididos a . . . promover el desarrollo sostenible . . . celebran este tratado de libre comercio.

The Preamble of the Chile-New Zealand-Singapore-Brunei-Darussalam Trans-Pacific Strategic EPA states that Parties will:

> be mindful that economic development, social development and environmental protection are interdependent and mutually reinforcing components of sustainable development

[4] Agreement establishing an association between the European Community and its Member States, of the one part, and the Republic of Chile, of the other part, signed 18 November 2002, entered into force 1 February 2003 [2002] OJ L 352 [EU-Chile AA].

[5] Ibid, Part IV on Trade and Trade-related Matters in Title 1, art 55 on objectives.

[6] See NAFTA (entered into force 1 January 1994) Preamble. See also US-Mexico-Canada Agreement (entered into force 1 July 2020), as it contains similar provisions.

[7] See Canada-Chile FTA (entered into force 5 July 1997) Preamble.

[8] Canada-Costa Rica FTA (entered into force 1 November 2002).

[9] US-Peru TPA (adopted 12 April 2006).

[10] Mexico-Bolivia FTA (entered into force 7 June 2010).

> and that closer economic partnership can play an important role in promoting sustainable development.[11]

In this version, Parties seem to accept the assumption challenged in the review of impact assessments earlier in this volume, that trade and investment liberalization will automatically deliver sustainable development.

As part of the Preamble, according to the Vienna Convention on the Law of Treaties (VCLT) at article 31 (2), as discussed in earlier in this volume, these provisions are relevant to interpretation as part the context of the treaty, in light of its object and purpose.[12] As noted in previous sections of this book, the US carried out an Environmental Review (ER) of the proposed US-Chile FTA.[13] In the final ER Report, the United States Trade Representative (USTR) stated that the:

> ... preamble to the Agreement expresses the Parties' *common goals* regarding trade and the implementation of the Agreement. The US-Chile Agreement preamble recognizes environmental issues, stating that the Parties are, 'resolved to: ... Promote sustainable development.[14]

The USTR argues that the Parties commitment to promote sustainable development is a *common goal* of the trade and investment agreement. In this light, a 'joint resolution to promote sustainable development' can be interpreted in the same way as the WTO Agreement Preamble reference to sustainable development, which was analysed by the WTO Panel and Appellate Body (AB) in the WTO *US-Shrimp Case,* and in the WTO 1994 Decision on Trade and Environment, as discussed earlier in this volume. In particular, it suggests that sustainable development is part of the 'object and purpose' of the trade and investment agreement. As the treaty in question contains a specific section titled 'Objectives' which focuses only on the economic objectives of the treaty, and taking into account the distinction between an 'objet' and a 'but' discussed in this book, this preambular 'common goal' to promote sustainable development may best be characterized as part of the *purpose* of the trade and investment treaty.[15] The object (*objet*) of the treaty may well focus mainly on economic matters, but the overarching purpose (*but*) includes sustainable development. In the US-Chile ER, however, USTR also characterizes sustainable development as a subset, one of several 'environmental issues'—the one which involves linking environment to development priorities. With this formulation, the provisions of the trade and investment liberalization treaty may indeed be interpreted in light of a sustainable development purpose. However, a future tribunal (or, more likely, regulator) could take the commitment to sustainable development into account in a quite narrow sense, focusing on environmental issues only. Furthermore,

[11] Chile-New Zealand-Singapore-Brunei Darussalam Trans-Pacific Strategic EPA (adopted 3 June 2005, entered into force 1 January 2006) Preamble.

[12] See earlier discussions of customary rule of *ut magis valeat quam pereat*, as reflected in the VCLT (signed 23 May 1969, entered into force 27 January 1980) 1155 UNTS 331, art 31(1) in Chapter 3, and for the WTO Chapter 4. See also VCLT, art 31(2) which notes that treaty text can include Preamble and annexes.

[13] USTR, *Final Environmental Review of the US-Chile FTA* (Washington, 2003) <https://ustr.gov/sites/default/files/chilefinal.pdf> [US-Chile Final ER] accessed 16 December 2020.

[14] Ibid 9 (emphasis added).

[15] DS Jonas and TN Saunders, 'The Object and Purpose of a Treaty: Three Interpretive Methods' (2010) 43(3) Vanderbilt Journal of Transnational Law 565–610; R Gardiner, *Treaty Interpretation* (2nd edn, Oxford, OUP 2015).

as noted in the *Case Concerning the Arbitral Award of 31 July 1989*, an argument based on an 'object and purpose' to promote sustainable development will not prevail against any clear obligations in the treaty itself to do otherwise.[16] To integrate environment and social development considerations into the economic project of the trade and investment liberalization agreement in the deeper sense discussed earlier in this volume, the use of such preambular language alone in the US and Canadian free trade accords, seems a weak and incomplete manner to proceed.

In contrast, the initial provisions on sustainable development in the EU-Chile AA highlight economic and social considerations in a more integrated way. At article 1 on Principles, the Parties agree that '[t]he promotion of sustainable economic and social development'[17] is a *guiding principle* for the implementation of the Agreement. This statement can be read with article 16.2 of the EU-Chile AA, which firmly states that one of the treaty objectives is '(b) promoting social development, which should go hand in hand with economic development and the protection of the environment'.[18] Slightly weaker, the EU-Mexico EPA,[19] in its Preamble, is 'MINDFUL of the importance that both Parties attach to the proper implementation of the principle of sustainable development, as agreed and set out in Agenda 21 of the 1992 Rio Declaration on Environment and Development'.[20] Similar provisions are found in the EU-Colombia-Peru FTA.[21] In essence, these bilateral or regional economic treaties recognize both a principle that the economic agreement will promote social development together with economic development and the protection of the environment, and a *purpose* that cooperation will support sustainable development in a manner that is stronger and more integrated than the first approach.

These two sets of commitments may be simply structurally different, but given current controversy in the WTO and other debates, a more likely possibility is that a clear signal is being sent by Parties. In the NAFTA-style treaties, sustainable development is part of the context, and may be used to indicate the *object and purpose* of the treaty,[22] similar to the point reached in the WTO and discussed above. However, the text then focuses on economic principles and objectives, while sustainable development commitments are relegated to a subset of environmental cooperation. In the EPA-style treaties, the commitment to sustainable development is stronger. Parties are noting an intention to take account of environmental and social development objectives, as 'the promotion of sustainable social and economic development' is recognized as a guiding principle for the implementation of the free trade agreement in question, as well as an overarching 'object and purpose' of the treaty.

Trade and investment law did not stop evolving, however. The 2011 European Union-Central America AA is considerably more assertive. In the Preamble, the Parties affirm a:

16 *Case Concerning the Arbitral Award of 31 July 1989* (*Guinea-Bissau v. Senegal*) [1991] ICJ Rep 53, 53–76, 72, paras 55 and 56. See also P Sands, 'Treaty, Custom and Cross-Fertilization of International Law' (1998) 10 Yale Human Rights and Development Law Journal 3, 11–12.

17 EU-Chile AA (n 4) art 1.2.

18 Ibid, art 16.2(b).

19 EU-Mexico Economic Partnership, Political Coordination and Cooperation Agreement, signed 8 December 1997, entered into force 1 October 2000, [2000] OJ L 276, 1.

20 Ibid, Preamble.

21 EU-Colombia-Peru FTA (signed 30 March 2010) Preamble, arts 4 and 107.

22 I Buffard and K Zemanek, 'The Object and Purpose of a Treaty: An Enigma?' (1998) 3 Austrian Review of International and European Law 311.

> commitment to working together in pursuit of the objectives of poverty eradication, job creation, equitable and sustainable development, including aspects of vulnerability to natural disasters, environmental conservation and protection and biodiversity, and the progressive integration of the Republics of the CA Party into the world economy;[23]

The Preamble also emphasizes their conviction that:

> this Agreement will create a climate conducive to growth in sustainable economic relations between them, more particularly in the trade and investment sectors;[24]

Parties further identify:

> the need to promote sustainable development in both regions through a development partnership involving all relevant stakeholders, including civil society and the private sector, in line with the principles set out in the Monterrey Consensus and the Johannesburg Declaration, and its Plan for Implementation;[25]

The Parties also 'reaffirm' that 'the States in their exercise of sovereign power to exploit their natural resources, according to their own environmental and developmental policies, should promote sustainable development.'[26] These preambular intentions are further reflected in objectives, and also, as in further sections, in certain operational provisions. First, in the objectives of the EU-Central America AA at article 1.2, the Parties:

> confirm their commitment to the promotion of sustainable development, which is a guiding principle for the implementation of this Agreement, taking notably into account the Millennium Development Goals. The Parties shall ensure that an appropriate balance is struck between the economic, social and environmental components of sustainable development.[27]

They further determine, in article 2(b), to:

> develop a privileged political partnership based on values, principles and common objectives, in particular the respect for and the promotion of democracy and human rights, sustainable development, good governance and the rule of law... [and to]
>
> enhance bi-regional co-operation in all areas of common interest with the aim of achieving more sustainable and equitable social and economic development in both regions;

It is further reaffirmed, at article 78(j) in the objectives section of the chapter on trade, that one of the objectives of this section is 'the promotion of international trade and investment between the Parties in a way that contributes to the objective of sustainable development

23 EU-Central America AA (signed 29 June 2012, entered into force 1 August 2013) Preamble.
24 Ibid.
25 Ibid.
26 Ibid.
27 Ibid, art 1.2.

through joint collaborative work'. A similar approach is taken in the EU-Colombia-Peru FTA and the EU-South Africa Trade Development Cooperation Agreement.[28] For the regulator, this approach denotes a serious consideration of sustainable development, as both purpose and principle, clearly affirming the Parties' commitment in more than a preambular manner.

Parties took an even more comprehensive approach a few years previously, in the 2008 EU-CARIFORUM EPA.[29] In the Preamble, they affirm their commitment to sustainable development in three provisions. First, they note:

> ... the need to promote economic and social progress for their people in a manner consistent with sustainable development by respecting basic labour rights in line with the commitments they have undertaken within the International Labour Organisation and by protecting the environment in line with the 2002 Johannesburg Declaration;[30]

This statement clearly engages both social development and environmental protection as part of sustainable development, tying both to multilateral collaboration. Further, they 're-affirm' a '... commitment to work together towards the achievement of the objectives of the Cotonou Agreement, including poverty eradication, sustainable development and the gradual integration of the African, Caribbean and Pacific (ACP) States into the world economy'[31] and a commitment to 'help them to face the challenges of globalisation and achieve the economic growth and social progress compatible with sustainable development to which they aim'.[32]

These preambular provisions alone suggest that sustainable development is intended as part of the 'purpose' of the economic accord. But the Parties assert the commitment further in Part 1, named appropriately 'Trade Partnership for Sustainable Development', at article 1 of the objectives, which include '(a) Contributing to the reduction and eventual eradication of poverty through the establishment of a trade partnership consistent with the objective of sustainable development, the Millennium Development Goals and the Cotonou Agreement'.[33] In article 3, the Parties also provide a definition of what is intended by this commitment to a trade agreement for sustainable development. It is worth reproducing these provisions:

> 1. The Parties reaffirm that the objective of sustainable development is to be applied and integrated at every level of their economic partnership ... especially the general commitment to reducing and eventually eradicating poverty in a way that is consistent with the objectives of sustainable development.
> 2. The Parties understand this objective to apply in the case of the present Economic Partnership Agreement as a commitment that: (a) the application of this Agreement shall fully take into account the human, cultural, economic, social, health and environmental best interests of their respective population and of future generations;

[28] See, e.g., EU-Colombia-Peru FTA (n 21) art 4; EU-South Africa Trade Development and Cooperation Agreement (signed 11 October 1999) art 1.
[29] EU-CARIFORUM EPA (signed 15 October 2008, entered into force 29 December 2008).
[30] Ibid, Preamble.
[31] Ibid.
[32] Ibid.
[33] Ibid, art 1.

(b) decision-taking methods shall embrace the fundamental principles of ownership, participation and dialogue.

3. As a result the Parties agree to work cooperatively towards the realisation of a sustainable development centred on the human person, who is the main beneficiary of development.[34]

This comprehensive Part 1 develops and builds on the approach first used in the EU-Chile AA, but extends it considerably further. Not only is it made clear that sustainable development is a *principal* object and purpose of the trade agreement, but this commitment is actually defined. In article 3, both substantive and procedural aspects of sustainable development are highlighted. In substance, the Parties agree to fully take into account both the health and environmental, and also human, cultural and social best interests of their populations and of future generations more broadly, alongside and equal to their economic interests. The human development dimension is strongly emphasized.[35] This can be understood as a fulsome expression of the social development and environmental integration principle discussed above. In procedural terms, the Parties also agree that inclusive, participatory decision-making methods are required. They require ('shall') dialogue, partnership and ownership. As discussed below, they also provide for continuing impact assessment.[36] Article 3 provides a first attempt to explain clearly what sustainable development may mean in a trade treaty, in a way similar to article 6 of the FAO Seed Treaty discussed earlier in this volume.[37] Agreed between Parties from the European Union (27 countries) and the CARIFORUM (another 15 States and dependencies), and as analysed in the context of this volume, this treaty is clearer in firmly supporting sustainable development, particularly with respect for the integration principle.

In the decade since countries agreed, at Part V paragraph 51 of the 2002 World Summit on Sustainable Development (WSSD), to 'Strengthen regional trade and cooperation agreements ... with a view to achieving the objectives of sustainable development',[38] these examples suggest certain 'pilot' advances are occurring in regional trade law. These preambular and other preliminary statements demonstrate a certain acceptance of sustainable development as a 'purpose', and among the set of treaties negotiated by the EU, a growing respect for the integration principle. In the two most recent treaties, the principle can be interpreted as expressing an intention to integrate—or at least take into account—both social development and the protection of the environment in the trade agreement, in order to create a trade partnership for sustainable development.

In light of the discussions earlier in this volume on the global policy reasons and European legal reasons for integration, and on the limits of WTO law, this research demonstrates that in certain bilateral or regional economic treaties, Parties are exploring new ways to express a more firm commitment to sustainable development. At the very least, the most recent trade and investment accords demonstrate what is possible between like-minded

[34] Ibid, art 3.

[35] EU-Central America EPA (n 23) arts 21, 46.

[36] Ibid, art 26.

[37] International Treaty on Plant Genetic Resources for Food and Agriculture of the Food and Agriculture Organization (adopted 3 November 2001, entered into force 31 March 2004) (FAO Seed Treaty) art 6.

[38] Johannesburg Declaration and Johannesburg Plan of Implementation (JPOI), Report of the World Summit on Sustainable Development, 4 September 2002, UN Doc. A/CONF.199/20, part V para 3.

Parties concerned about sustainable development. It is clear that in certain treaties, particularly the EU-CARIFORUM EPA and the EU-Central America AA, a strengthened commitment to sustainable development through trade has been adopted. For the purposes of interpretation, these last two region-to-region economic treaties go further than outlining sustainable development as part of the object and purpose,[39] to assist in determining the ordinary meaning of the terms of treaty exceptions, as in the WTO's 'high-water mark' *US-Shrimp* dispute.[40] Instead, a strong intention is expressed by the Parties to ensure integration of social and environmental commitments throughout the application of the accord, as a principle, in order to ensure that their bilateral or regional economic treaties fully support sustainable development.[41] These are, however, simply expressions of intention (object and purpose) and principle in the trade and investment agreements. How are such intentions operationalized in the terms of the bilateral or regional economic treaties themselves?

17.2 Provisions to Integrate Social and Environmental Considerations into Free Trade Agreements

This section examines innovative operational provisions from bilateral or regional economic treaties discussed in this volume which explicitly mention sustainable development. The provisions are examined in light of their potential to respond to the three tensions identified earlier in this volume, and the corresponding rationale and opportunities for integration identified, including the potential interpretations of the mechanisms in light of the integration principle. In the first category, responding to the first type of tension identified in Section 2 and the integration opportunity identified in Section 3 and the limits of the WTO in this respect, provisions are identified which can be interpreted as preventing trade rules from constraining the regulatory flexibility of the Parties for social and environmental purposes in the field of sustainable development. In the second category, responding to the second type of tensions and opportunities identified above, provisions are identified which can be interpreted as securing additional environmental and social cooperation to strengthen domestic laws, parallel to the trade agreement itself. In the third category, responding to the third type of tensions and integration opportunities identified above, provisions are identified that can be interpreted as enhancing trade liberalization in specific economic sectors that deliver sustainable development benefits. In a further section, procedural innovations are highlighted, as this research found that changes in the way that trade and investment agreements are negotiated, as well as sustainable development-related innovations contained in the procedural rules of the bilateral or regional economic treaties, from an interactional view, have implications for the way the treaty texts integrate for sustainable development. Finally, as illustrative examples of the contributions that are possible, trade and investment treaty provisions from bilateral, regional or region-to-region economic treaties which specifically contribute to targets adopted under the seventeen Sustainable Development Goals (SDGs) are highlighted.

[39] VCLT, art 31(1).
[40] Ibid; Gardiner (n 15); see also discussions in Chapters 3 and 4.
[41] Gardiner (n 15). Brunnee J and Toope SJ, *Legality and Legitimacy in International Law* (Cambridge, CUP 2010) 15–19, 56–76.

17.2.1 Social/Environmental 'Mitigation Provisions' in Trade and Investment Rules

In both the EU-Chile AA and the US-Chile FTA, the joint commitment to promote sustainable development, considered in light of the integration principle, suggests that the Parties do not desire the rules of the trade and investment agreement to inadvertently *frustrate* their efforts to achieve more sustainable development. However, as discussed earlier in this volume with regards the potential regulatory impacts of trade agreements, in certain instances legitimate environmental and social regulations may be constrained by the application of new trade or investment disciplines. Many of these instances are identified in the EU-Chile Sustainable Impact Assessment (SIA)[42] and in the US-Chile Environmental Review,[43] among the other assessment experiences. The most prevalent types of trade and investment agreement sustainable development provisions to address this tension are the 'preventive' exceptions for such measures from the economic rules themselves.

The integration principle, as explained in Section 3 above, is not a 'trump card' but rather a call for balance, and furthermore as a customary principle, simply assists in treaty interpretation, in the sense of VCLT, article 31(3)(c) as a relevant rule of international law applicable in the relations between the Parties as shaped by inter-actional shared understandings.[44] But as discussed below, by explicitly incorporating these 'prevention' provisions, the Parties shed certain light on the nature of the sustainable development balance they seek to strike between trade, environment and social development interests. Such provisions can guide domestic authorities and trade tribunals, as well as firms, non-governmental organizations (NGOs) and others whose work is carried out 'in the shadow of the trade law' by indicating where new trade and investment rules are not meant to prevent Parties from adopting or implementing legitimate measures to promote more sustainable development. As demonstrated in this research, Parties have not limited themselves to GATT, article XX-style general exceptions (see Bilateral and Regional Economic Treaties Table, Annex 3).

17.2.2 Exceptions for Social Development and Environmental Measures

Many free trade and investment agreements contain exceptions for important sustainable development-related public policy priorities such as health, the environment and the conservation of natural resources. First, these include general exceptions similar to or directly referencing GATT article XX or the General Agreement on Trade in Services (GATS) article XIV.[45] In the bilateral or regional economic treaties analysed for this volume, the

42 Planistat, *Sustainable Impact Assessment (SIA) of the Trade Aspects of Negotiations for an Association Agreement between the European Communities and Chile* (Santiago, 2002) [EU-Chile SIA].

43 US-Chile Final ER (n 13).

44 Gardiner (n 15); see Chapter 3; See Brunnee and Toope (n 41).

45 See, e.g., art 12 of the Australia-Singapore FTA (signed 17 February 2003, entered into force on 28 July 2003) art 1601 of the *Australia-Thailand FTA* (entered into force 1 January 2005) art 703(1), art 22.1 of the Australia-US Free Trade Agreement (signed 18 May 2004); art 11.22(2) of the Chile-New Zealand-Singapore-Brunei Darussalam Trans-Pacific Strategic EPA (n 11) as noted in L Bartels, 'Social Issues: Labour, Environment and Human Rights' in S Lester and B Mercurio (eds), *Bilateral and Regional Trade Agreements: Commentary, Analysis and Case Studies* (Cambridge, CUP 2008) 29. See MC Cordonier Segger, 'Sustainable Development in Regional Trade Agreements' in L Bartels and F Ortino (eds), *Regional Trade Agreements and the WTO Legal System* (Oxford, OUP 2006).

Parties reiterate and strengthen WTO commitments on market access for goods, taking on binding obligations to lower tariffs, to accord each other national treatment (non-discrimination), to provide 'most-favoured-nation' status and to ensure transparency. They affirm and strengthen commitments to jointly reduce technical barriers to trade (TBTs) which may include environmental labels and other requirements, and they agree to further limit the use of SPS. They further agree to deeper liberalization commitments than in the WTO Agreements, in areas such as government procurement and investment, as well as services, trade disciplines, subsidies disciplines and intellectual property rights. Many of these 'WTO and beyond' obligations are subject to exceptions for environmental and social measures, both with regard to trade in goods (including related TBT and SPS standards), and with regard to important new areas such as positive-listed trade in services, government procurement and investment. In this way, the Parties signal an intention to avoid or mitigate otherwise constraining consequences of the trade rules for health, environment and natural resources measures. As demonstrated earlier in this volume, from WTO experience, provisions permit the Parties certain flexibility to use measures that would be disallowed should the exemptions not be included in the treaty.

General exceptions

The principal general exception in the Chile-US FTA is found at article 23.1, which provides exceptions to obligations covering national treatment and market access for goods, rules of origin and origin procedures, customs administration, sanitary and phytosanitary measures and technical barriers to trade. It states that:

> Article XX of GATT 1994 and its interpretive notes are incorporated into and made part of this Agreement, *mutatis mutandis*. The Parties understand that the measures referred to in Article XX(b) of GATT 1994 include environmental measures necessary to protect human, animal, or plant life or health, and that Article XX(g) of GATT 1994 applies to measures relating to the conservation of living and non-living exhaustible natural resources.[46]

The Chile-US FTA approach is based on the NAFTA,[47] an approach still echoed in the USMCA, and provides for exceptions by incorporating references to exceptions in the General Agreement on Tariffs and Trade (GATT) article XX.[48] This approach is taken by other similar regional trade and investment treaties.[49] Such provisions, as discussed earlier in this volume, expressly grant exceptions for measures that are necessary to protect human, animal or plant life or health (article XX(b) of the GATT 1994) and for measures related to the conservation of natural resources in certain conditions (article XX(g) of the GATT 1994). This exception also incorporates article XX(d) of the GATT 1994, which exempts measures necessary to secure compliance with laws or regulations that are not inconsistent with the trade and investment agreements.

46 US-Chile FTA (n 2) art 23.1: general exceptions.

47 See, e.g., Australia-US FTA (signed 18 May 2004) art 22.1; art O-01 Canada-Chile FTA (n 7); as noted in Bartels (n 45) 31.

48 Adopted 30 October 1947, provisionally entered into force 1 January 1948, 55 UNTS 194, CTS No 31 (1948).

49 See, e.g., Canada-Costa Rica FTA (n 8); or Central America-Dominican Republic FTA (signed 16 April 1998).

The EU-Chile AA also provides a general exception for health, environment and natural resources measures. In particular, at article 91, the Parties agree that for the provisions in their Title II on Free Movement of Goods:

> Subject to the requirement that such measures are not applied in a manner which would constitute a means of arbitrary or unjustifiable discrimination between the Parties where the same conditions prevail, or a disguised restriction on trade between the Parties, nothing in this Title shall be construed to prevent the adoption or enforcement by either Party of measures which: ...
>
> (b) are necessary to protect human, animal or plant life or health;
> (c) are necessary to secure compliance with laws or regulations which are not inconsistent with this Agreement ...
> (f) relate to the conservation of exhaustible natural resources if such measures are made effective in conjunction with restrictions on domestic production or consumption ...[50]

This general exception provides for many of the same exemptions as the Chile-US FTA, though it simply draws upon elements of the text of article XX of the GATT rather than expressly incorporating WTO law. It allows the Parties greater flexibility in the interpretation of their terms, as they are less tied to the WTO approach which, as discussed above, is still being refined through Panel and AB decisions.

The Chile-EU AA also includes a second exception for trade in services, financial services and establishment (investment), and other matters. After a similar 'chapeau', Article 135 exempts measures:

> ... (b) necessary to protect human, animal or plant life or health;
> (c) relating to the conservation of exhaustible natural resources if such measures are applied in conjunction with restrictions on the domestic supply or consumption of services or on domestic investments ...;
> (e) necessary to secure compliance with laws or regulations which are not inconsistent with the provisions of this Title including those relating to ... (iii) safety.[51]

These exceptions were the outcomes of negotiations with Chile. Both are distinct from the exceptions used by the EU in most other regional economic agreements, which are based on article 30 of the EU Treaty and do not include an exception for natural resources.[52] The European Court of Justice (ECJ) has interpreted this clause in several cases, taking a 'proportionality approach' that balances the trade restrictiveness of the measure with its public policy goals.[53] The approach in the treaty, in contrast, broadens the flexibility for

[50] EU-Chile AA (n 4) chapter III, art 91: general exception. The treaty also, in art 194, offers exceptions for national security, which is as broad as the provisions in the WTO discussed in Chapter 2. Exception 1 (iv) for measures 'taken in time of war or other emergency in international relations'; might also serve to exempt certain actions taken to address health or environmental emergencies.

[51] Ibid, art 135.

[52] Treaty establishing the European Community (Nice Consolidated Version) [2002] OJ C 325, P. 0047-0047, art 30.

[53] See Case C-340/97 *Nazli* [2000] ECR I-957, paras 55–56, and J Neumann and E Türk, 'Necessity Revisited: Proportionality in World Trade Organization Law After *Korea-Beef*, *EC-Asbestos* and *EC-Sardines*' (2003) 37 Journal of World Trade 199, as cited in Bartels (n 45).

natural resources conservation, and may provide useful flexibility for sustainable development regulators.

As such, in both treaties a general exception exists for measures that would otherwise violate market access obligations on goods and services, through the incorporation of WTO-style general exceptions, with certain specific refinements. If an otherwise inconsistent measure can be shown to fall under certain limited exceptions, and also to comply with the 'chapeau' which requires that it does not result in arbitrary or unjustifiable discrimination and does not constitute disguised protectionism, it can be permitted by the exception. Once a trade or investment discipline is restricted, the burden of proof is, however, on the Party claiming the exception.

With regard to the integration of environmental protection and social development with economic development, these general exceptions do respond to the commitments of Parties to promote sustainable development. Against a background of continuing WTO debates, in the case of the US-Chile FTA, the Parties set out certain understandings to explicitly broaden the interpretation of the GATT exceptions in relation to environmental measures, and article 135(e) is particularly relevant. In the *Korea-Various Measures on Beef* dispute, the WTO AB noted that to qualify for such an exception: 'First, the measure must be one designed to "secure compliance" with laws or regulations that are not themselves inconsistent with some provision of the GATT 1994. Second, the measure must be "necessary" to secure such compliance.'[54] While the measure itself would require an exception, the broader law or regulation which it implements must already be consistent with the trade disciplines. In the US-Chile ER, the USTR has specifically noted that these exceptions could, indeed, cover measures to ensure compliance with environmental laws, as the obligation '... specifically reflects the Parties' understanding that environmental measures may fall within the above exceptions'.[55] Presumably, this is an explicit reference to insights gained in the WTO *US-Shrimp* dispute and the other earlier cases. In particular, in the WTO *US-Gasoline* dispute, as the term 'environment' was not included in the WTO Agreements, the Parties agreed that pollution, in particular ground-level ozone and toxic substances, presented health risks to humans, animals and plants. In this case, the AB also stated that:

> the ability of any WTO Member to take measures to ... protect the environment, is [not] at issue ... WTO Members have a large measure of autonomy to determine their own policies on the environment ... and the environmental legislation they enact and implement.[56]

However, as the AB cautioned:

> 'that autonomy is circumscribed ... by the need to respect the requirements of the General Agreement and the other covered agreements.[57]

[54] *Korea-Various Measures Affecting Imports of Fresh, Chilled and Frozen Beef - Report of the Appellate Body* WT/DS161/AB/R, adopted 10 January 2001, DSR 2001:I, 5, para 157.

[55] US-Chile Final ER (n 13) 12.

[56] *United States—Standards for Reformulated and Conventional Gasoline—Report of the Appellate Body* (29 April 1996) WT/DS2/AB/R, 30–31.

[57] Ibid.

Later, as discussed earlier in this volume, GATT article XX was interpreted in light of the WTO commitment to sustainable development by the WTO Panel and AB in the *US-Shrimp* dispute, where several WTO members maintained that article XX(g) referred only to the conservation of non-living natural resources (in this instance, arguing that sea turtles should not be covered), while the US maintained that its scope was broader, and the AB found that living natural resources were indeed covered by the article XX(g) exception. Both the EU-Chile SIA, and the US-Chile ER[58] raised concerns about exhaustible living natural resources, including impacts of international trade-led increases of exploitation of marine mammals, fisheries and forests.[59] The explicit clarification by the Parties in the Chile-US FTA with regard to article XX of the GATT and its applicability indicates that the Parties intend to give more policy space to their regulators, to explicitly permit the use of environmental measures, and measures for the conservation of living as well as non-living natural resources, even where such measures might violate other obligations of the trade treaty. Such an exemption, conditioned though it is by the chapeau of the exception, is likely helpful to ensure a more balanced integration or at least to prevent one priority (trade) from almost always overriding the others (environment, natural resources conservation, health). However, this exception is no *carte blanche*. Particularly with regards to GATT article XX(b), it has proven a heavy burden for a Party to demonstrate, in trade law, as required by the Panel at 6.22 in the *US-Gasoline* dispute, 'whether these inconsistent measures were necessary to achieve the policy goal . . .', when 'necessary' is found somewhere between 'indispensable' and 'making a contribution' to the goal. Even under the new standard suggested in the *Brazil-Re-treaded Tyres* dispute,[60] many legitimate measures can fail the article XX test.

In the EU-Chile AA, and other similar regional trade treaties, the exemptions chosen by the Parties take a slightly different approach.[61] In particular, the provisions appear to be based on the text of the WTO article XX but do not actually refer to either the GATT or the GATS. The lack of an explicit reference suggests that Parties would not necessarily interpret the exception in a way that is guided by the decisions of the WTO AB. This may permit health, environment and natural resources regulators greater flexibility to lessen the burden on the Party claiming the exemption, particularly with regard to the interpretation of the chapeau which has considerably restricted access to the WTO general exceptions. It also does not tie the Parties, particularly the EU, to the notion that a commitment to sustainable development is simply an objective of the treaty, without carrying additional normative weight.

Specific exceptions

Many of over 60 free trade agreements studied also include various specific exceptions for areas of trade liberalization which go beyond existing commitments in the WTO.[62] Two initial examples include the specific exceptions for trade in services and investment (or

[58] US-Chile Final ER (n 13).

[59] EU-Chile SIA (n 42).

[60] *Brazil—Measures affecting Imports of Re-treaded Tyres—Report of the Panel* (12 June 2007) WT/DS332/R; *Brazil—Measures affecting Imports of Re-treaded Tyres—Report of the Appellate Body* (3 December 2007) WT/DS332/AB/R.

[61] See, e.g., EU-Colombia-Peru FTA (n 21); EU-South Africa Trade Development and Cooperation Agreement (n 28).

[62] Ibid.

'establishment' only, in the case of the EU-Chile AA), and the specific exceptions for government procurement disciplines. These specific exceptions may provide further flexibility for sustainable development regulators, addressing concerns raised in the EU-Chile SIA[63] and the US-Chile ER, as noted in Chapter 2.[64]

With regard to services and investment/establishment, debates persist about which types of measures might require general exceptions. In 1995 the WTO Committee on Trade in Services sought guidance from the WTO Committee on Trade and Environment on sustainable development issues related to services,[65] but negotiations to date have been inconclusive. Perhaps reflecting this uncertainty, both treaties establish specific exceptions related to the services and investment/establishment disciplines in the trade agreement.

In the US-Chile FTA, Parties agreed on fairly stringent services and investment obligations, going beyond WTO commitments. Services obligations apply to cross-border supply of services, including those delivered electronically, or through the travel of services professionals across borders. In the US-Chile FTA Services chapter, Parties agreed to extend national treatment and most-favoured-nation treatment for services suppliers in 'like circumstances', and to avoid application of certain non-discriminatory measures.[66] Furthermore, measures to ensure that qualification requirements and procedures, technical standards and licensing requirements are disciplined to avoid burdensome or unnecessary barriers to trade in services.[67]

With regard to the integration of environmental and social concerns into the trade and investment liberalization agreement, and in particular, the need to secure certain flexibility for regulators in order to ensure the bilateral or regional economic treaty does not constrain sustainable development measures, this could become problematic. Such requirements to demonstrate that any measures should not be 'more burdensome than necessary to ensure the quality of the service' and 'not . . . a restriction on supply' could place a heavy obligation on health, environment and natural resources regulators. For example, in the impact assessments concerns were expressed that too many tourism suppliers could degrade fragile ecosystems, and such restrictions may not permit regulators to cap distribution of operating licences unless both necessity and lack of restriction are proven.[68] A clear exception can send important signals to legislators and industry decision-makers to ensure correct interpretation of such a stipulation. Indeed, in the Chile-US FTA chapters on cross-border trade in services, telecommunications and electronic commerce, Parties agreed:

> Article XIV of GATS (including its footnotes) is incorporated into and made part of this Agreement. . . . The Parties understand that the measures referred to in Article XIV(b) of GATS include environmental measures necessary to protect human, animal, or plant life or health.[69]

[63] EU-Chile SIA (n 42).
[64] US-Chile Final ER (n 13).
[65] WTO Council for Trade in Services, *Ministerial Decision on Trade in Services and the Environment*/C/M/1, adopted 1 March 1995, S/L/4.
[66] US-Chile FTA (n 2) arts 11.2 and 11.3.
[67] Art 11.8 on domestic regulation, 2.
[68] EU-Chile SIA (n 42); US-Chile Final ER (n 13).
[69] US-Chile FTA (n 2) art 23.1.

This exception could accommodate the example of tourism operators in fragile ecosystems, in reasonable circumstances.[70] By choosing a GATS-style exception to apply in case of obligations related to services, the Parties appear to be simply following the model laid out by WTO GATS[71] article XIV(b). And by emphasizing their understanding that the measures referred to in the GATS include environmental measures, the Parties are both highlighting their intention to provide exceptions for environmental standards, and also, perhaps, seeking to influence eventual WTO negotiations.

However, the US-Chile FTA exceptions for services are actually narrower than the WTO exceptions in an important way. The GATS used a positive-list approach to specify the scope of its obligations (i.e. any service not listed is not covered).[72] In contrast, the US-Chile FTA uses a negative-list approach. As such, any service not specifically reserved is covered, just as it is in the NAFTA model for services, or the GATT model for goods.[73] And in addition to the negative-list approach, by choosing a GATS rather than GATT-style exception, the Parties exclude exceptions for measures related to the conservation of natural resources. While Parties do exclude services supplied in the exercise of governmental authority (i.e. neither on a commercial basis, nor in competition with one or more services suppliers), unless other types of 'exemptions' (such as specific reservations) are not also set in place, this omission could cause problems in sensitive sectors identified in the impact assessments described earlier in this volume. From the viewpoint of integration, it is hard to see how, if new disciplines in the US-Chile FTA are applied strictly, to prevent the agreement from frustrating sustainable development, and limiting rather than supporting social and environmental policy. For instance, new or existing environment and development measures related to services in natural resources sectors, including controversial issues related to oil and gas pipelines, electricity transmission lines, tourism, marine shipping, even water and sanitation[74] —sectors that are not necessarily covered by the GATS for many countries—are soon open to challenge under the trade agreement. Further, in the US-Chile FTA, the two Parties commit to strong and detailed disciplines on regulatory transparency. However, as noted in the US-Chile ER process, if substantial access were granted to foreign service providers in sectors of importance to sustainable development, such as health, safety, consumer protection or environmental measures related to energy distribution services, tourism or maritime shipping, and these providers were either unaware of local social and environmental conditions or unwilling to comply with currently voluntary (and in some cases, non-existent) standards,[75] the trade agreement could make the adoption of new sustainability-oriented standards more difficult and burdensome. As such, while the US-Chile FTA does include specific exceptions for certain environmental measures, it also presents certain risks for other non-covered measures related primarily to the sustainable development of natural resources. This does not appear consistent with the integration principle.

70 USTR, *Interim Environmental Review of the US-Chile FTA* (Washington, 2001) (US-Chile Interim ER).

71 General Agreement on Trade in Services (adopted 15 April 1994, entered into force 1 January 1995) 1869 UNTS 183 art XIV.

72 GC Hufbauer and C Cimino-Isaacs, 'How Will TPP and TTIP Change the WTO System?' (2015) 18(3) Journal of International Economic Law 679–696.

73 See for negative-list case studies, IN Mukherji, 'The Bangkok Agreement: A Negative List Approach to Trade Liberalization in Asia and the Pacific' (2005) 1 Asia-Pacific Trade and Investment Review 27.

74 US-Chile Interim ER (n 70) 23–25.

75 Ibid 9–44.

The EU-Chile AA also lays down fairly strict requirements in regard to services liberalization. However, the EU-Chile AA exceptions are slightly broader. In particular, the general exceptions for trade in services include (unlike the GATS) a GATT-style specific exception for measures related to the conservation of natural resources. Article 135 explicitly exempts measures:

> c) relating to the conservation of exhaustible natural resources if such measures are applied in conjunction with restrictions on the domestic supply or consumption of services or on domestic investments.

As such, it appears that the EU-Chile AA, with its explicit recognition of a principle of sustainable development, goes slightly further in ensuring that natural resources-related measures will be given flexibility under the economic agreement in the area of services. In this instance, the agreed 'sustainable development principle' may act as an interstitial norm, influencing Parties to respect other more specific principles such as integration of environment and social considerations into trade and investment treaty provisions, and sustainable use of natural resources.

With regard to the integration of social and environmental considerations into economic treaties, a further point can be underlined relating to health exceptions. The 'broadening clarifications' in the US-Chile FTA refer to environmental measures necessary to protect human health, hence opening policy space for regulators in relation to health matters. In medical and environmental science, environmental conditions are often considered a determinant of population health.[76] Indeed, in the WTO *European Communities-Asbestos* dispute,[77] a partial ban on white chrysotile asbestos, for example, to prevent the carcinogen from being inhaled by 22,000 do-it-yourself enthusiasts in France, was so characterized.[78] As noted above in this book, with regards the EU-Chile SIA, one of the concerns regarding the health impacts of trade and investment agreements involved damage to the health of workers in Chile's fruit and flowers industries—if liberalization led to much higher use of pesticides and fungicides and health laws and standards were not able to keep pace with increased production.[79] The health provisions in this exception could, in such an instance, secure useful policy space for regulators seeking to improve health standards in these industries, without exposing them to accusations of imposing unnecessary technical barriers to trade. Such a measure would likely be covered by both the EU-Chile AA human health exception, and the broadened environment and health measures exceptions in the US-Chile FTA.

Both the EU-Chile SIA and the US-Chile ERs raised other important social issues related to sustainable development. Yet it seems the exception for 'measures necessary to protect human ... health' is the only type of measure from the 'social pillar' of

[76] World Health Organization (WHO), *Summary Measures of Population Health: Concepts, Measures, Ethics and Applications* (Geneva, 2010) 4–5. See also WTO and WHO, *WTO Agreements and Public Health: A Joint Study between the WHO and the WTO Secretariat* (Geneva, 2002) <http://www.wto.org/english/res_e/booksp_e/who_wto_e.pdf>.

[77] See *European Communities—Measures Affecting Asbestos and Asbestos-Containing Products* (12 March 2001) WT/DS135/AB/R.

[78] ML Busch and KJ Pelc, 'Words Matter: How WTO Rulings Handle Controversy' (2019) 63(3) International Studies Quarterly 464–476.

[79] EU-Chile SIA (n 42).

sustainable development that is explicitly included in the exceptions. Other social issues are notably absent. For the purpose of comparison, the Parties to the Canada-Chile FTA do include further specific exceptions to services obligations, for 'measures necessary to secure compliance with laws or regulations that are not inconsistent with the provisions of this Agreement, *including those relating to health and safety and consumer protection*'.[80] Essentially, in the US-Chile FTA, the Parties did not take the opportunity to explicitly extend the specific exemptions to measures related to consumer protection, nor to directly address other issues raised in the Agenda 21, the Johannesburg Plan of Implementation (JPOI), the UN Conference on Sustainable Development (UNCSD) and the SDGs themselves such as gender equality, access to clean water and sanitation, access to quality education, or collective rights of indigenous peoples, unless these could be characterized as life or health measures.

The specific reference in the US-Chile FTA to consumer protection, as well as to health and safety laws, highlights that an exception to services disciplines can provide more explicitly for the social dimension of sustainable development.[81] Of course, such a specific exception still does not hand the Parties a *carte blanche*, but rather, a mechanism for seeking balance. The legal bar is high—a Party seeking to benefit from the exception to save a health measure would need to demonstrate that a measure is necessary to secure compliance, that it is aimed at compliance with a law or regulation not inconsistent with the trade rules and that it is not applied in the manner noted above. However, as the customary integration principle becomes more accepted, there exists the possibility that it may also be extended to cover other social measures, as the list is non-exhaustive. Such a trade-off appears in an accord that commits 'to promote sustainable development' as a purpose, and demonstrates that balanced integration can be achieved through specific exceptions, as well as general ones.

As a second example, the US-Chile FTA, as discussed earlier in this volume, makes important NAFTA Chapter 11-style commitments in the area of investment promotion and protection. Several concerns were raised in the US-Chile ER process with regard to the scope of potential restrictions on regulators that would arise due to new provisions disciplining investment rules.[82] And in the US-Chile FTA Parties agreed specific exceptions in the area of investment rules, particularly with regard to performance requirements, to allay these concerns and provide greater clarity. In particular, at article 10.5 (3), States agreed similar GATT-style exceptions for investment.[83]

Further, with respect to the concerns of an over-broad protection for investors that were raised in the ER process, the treaty also states at Annex 10-D that 'Article 10.9(1) on expropriation is intended to reflect customary international law . . .' A further specific exception at Annex 10-D clarifies directly that:

> (b) Except in rare circumstances, nondiscriminatory regulatory actions by a Party that are designed and applied to protect legitimate public welfare objectives, such as public health, safety, and the environment, do not constitute indirect expropriations.

80 Canada-Chile FTA (n 7) art G-01.
81 See, e.g., US-Chile FTA (n 2) Annex 11.9 Section A, 2(h) for consumer protection and professional services.
82 US-Chile Interim ER (n 70) 62–68.
83 US-Chile FTA (n 2).

By explicitly exempting the application of disciplines to regulatory expropriation relating to health, safety and the environment, Parties appear to be integrating concerns raised in the impact assessment, and documented in secondary literature, regarding prejudice to environmental, health and safety objectives with the new rights for investors.[84]

In contrast, the EU-Chile SIA also raised concerns as to the impacts of these rights, and the EU-Chile AA avoids providing broad new rights for investors. Only certain narrow investment-related obligations, such as general commitments to national treatment and most-favoured-nation treatment with regard to the establishment of investors, a simple affirmation of a shared 'objective of progressive liberalisation of investment conditions' and a 'commitment to review the investment legal framework, the investment environment and the flow of investment between them consistent with their commitments in international investment agreements' at a later date. This narrow scope of obligations is not, however, necessarily due to any sensitivity about the sustainability issues related to investment disciplines, though many concerns were raised in the EU-Chile SIA process.[85] Rather, jurisdiction over investment negotiations was national rather than at community level in the EU, in the time of the Chile-EU AA negotiations.[86] Indeed, separate provisions on cooperation in the AA note the Parties intentions to develop 'a legal framework for the Parties that favours investment, by conclusion, where appropriate, of bilateral agreements between the Member States and Chile to promote and protect investment and avoid dual taxation'.[87] In other more recent European treaties that do adopt certain limited provisions on investment, similar specific exceptions can be identified.[88]

As a third example, both treaties provide similar but nuanced specific exceptions in the area of government procurement. The procurement chapter of the US-Chile FTA is modelled on commitments of the Parties in the WTO's presently plurilateral Government Procurement Agreement, which prescribes non-discrimination, transparency, predictability and accountability in the government procurement process.[89] Parties commit to provide reciprocal, competitive government procurement opportunities to suppliers in each Party's government procurement market; an extensive set of new obligations. However, the treaty also provides specific exceptions to its disciplines in several ways. First, in the procurement chapter, Parties place restrictions on the type of requirements and evaluation criteria that will be taken into account for government procurement contracts over a certain low threshold. Article 9.10 of the US-Chile FTA specifies that—unless an entity determines that it is not in the public interest to award a contract—contracts shall be awarded to suppliers that are fully capable of undertaking the contract and whose tender is determined to

[84] Ibid; A Newcombe, 'Sustainable Development and Investment Treaty Law' (2007) 8 Journal of World Investment & Trade 357, 65–69.

[85] EU-Chile SIA (n 42) 141–154.

[86] J Ceyssens, 'Towards a Common Foreign Investment Policy? Foreign Investment in the European Constitution' (2005) 32 Legal Issues of Economic Integration 259–291; M Krajewski, 'External Trade Law and the Constitution Treaty: Towards a Federal and More Democratic Common Commercial Policy?' (2005) 42 Common Market Law Review 91–127.

[87] Art 21, 2 (b).

[88] See, e.g., EU-CARIFORUM EPA (n 29); EU-Colombia-Peru FTA (n 21).

[89] Agreement on Government Procurement (adopted 15 April 1994, entered into force 1 January 1995) 1867 UNTS 194; C McCrudden, 'International Economic Law and Human Rights: A Framework for Discussion of the Legality of "Selective Purchasing" Laws under the WTO Government Procurement Agreement' (1999) 2 Journal of International Economic Law 3.

be the most advantageous in terms of the requirements and evaluation criteria set out in the tender documentation.[90] This does not limit considerations to price only, as some treaties have sought to do,[91] but simply narrows the policy-makers' discretion to choose a supplier. Procurement programmes designed, for instance, to ensure employment for forcibly relocated indigenous peoples, or otherwise deliver on important social or environmental policy objectives, might still be restricted by the trade and investment agreement, absent other exemptions. And indeed, the specific exceptions address these concerns in large part. In article 9.16, Parties echo the GATT article XX, adding that: 'The Parties understand that subparagraph (b) includes environmental measures necessary to protect human, animal, or plant life or health.'[92] Further, in the Scope at article 9.1, Parties clarify that these disciplines do not apply to 'subsidies, guarantees, cooperative agreements, government provision of goods and services to persons or to a regional or local level of government'.[93]

In the US-Chile FTA, the Parties commit, at article 9.7, that technical specifications will be made in terms of performance requirements rather than design or descriptive characteristics; and based on international standards where applicable, or otherwise on national rules. They specifically forbid references to trademarks or trade names, patents, designs or types, specific origins, producers or suppliers. Related concerns were raised in the impact assessments.[94] But these provisions would appear to block the potential for government procurement competitions to address issues raised in the impact assessments by privileging, for instance, wood products with sustainability certifications such as the Forest Stewardship Council,[95] or more sustainable building codes and certification schemes,[96] or textiles that comply with specific human rights codes.[97] To address such concerns, however, at article 9.7 (5) the Parties include a further specific exception to emphasize that '... this Article is not intended to preclude a Party from preparing, adopting, or applying technical specifications to promote the conservation of natural resources'.[98] This exception, by preventing the treaty from being applied to frustrate regulations to secure more sustainable use of natural resources, could help to integrate environmental protection and social development in the trade treaty, contributing to the sustainable development objective.

The EU-Chile AA also makes significant commitments to liberalize government procurement. Overall, the disciplines are less stringent, though the trade agreement does provide at article 149 (3) that technical specifications prescribed by entities shall:

> (a) be in terms of performance and functional requirements rather than design or descriptive characteristics; and (b) be based on international standards, where these exist

[90] US-Chile FTA (n 2) art 9.10.
[91] C McCrudden, 'Using Public Procurement to Achieve Social Outcomes' (2004) 28(4) Natural Resources Forum 257.
[92] US-Chile FTA (n 2) art 9.16.
[93] Ibid, art 9.1.
[94] US-Chile Interim ER (n 70) 61.
[95] P Newell, 'Managing Multinationals: The Governance of Investment for the Environment' (2001) 13 Journal of International Development 907.
[96] SM Wheeler and T Beatley, *The Sustainable Urban Development Reader* (London, Routledge 2004); CJ Kilbert, *Sustainable Construction: Green Building Design and Delivery* (New Jersey, John Wiley and Sons 2008).
[97] S Charnovitz, 'The Labor Dimension of the Emerging Free Trade Area of the America' in P Alston (ed), *Labour Rights as Human Rights* (Oxford OUP 2005).
[98] US-Chile FTA (n 2) art 9.7(5).

or, in their absence, on national technical regulations, recognised national standards, or building codes.

However, these provisions 'do not apply when the entity can objectively demonstrate that the use of technical specifications referred to in that paragraph would be ineffective or inappropriate for the fulfilment of the legitimate objectives pursued'. Further, article 153 on the awarding of contracts notes at (1) that to be considered for award a tender must, at the time of opening, 'conform to the essential requirements of the notices or tender documentation and be submitted by a supplier which complies with the conditions for participation'. And at (2), the rules specify that entities shall 'make the award to the tenderer whose tender is either the lowest tender or the tender which, in terms of the specific objective evaluation criteria previously set forth in the notices or tender documentation, is determined to be the most advantageous'. Concerns were raised in the SIA, which specifically noted for example that:

> Chemical and Non-Ferrous metals industries are heavily involved in the pressure operated on the environment ... despite voluntary engagements and new regulations, the environmental scale effect resulting from the EU-Chile agreement is likely to overweigh the expected technique effect.[99]

The chapeau to article 161 of the EU-Chile AA is similar to the one in the US-Chile FTA, but the Parties separate the specific exceptions slightly to read: '(b) necessary to protect human life, health or security; and (c) necessary to protect animal or plant life or health.'[100] Essentially, the Parties emphasize, in their procurement disciplines, the need to ensure that Parties can maintain measures for animals and plants, and also that measures may specifically address 'human security' objectives.

Further, Chile and the EU also provide a series of specific exceptions for certain types of international contracts, cooperation programmes, natural resources, arbitration, employment and research or development services,[101] addressing other key concerns raised in impact assessments discussed earlier in this volume.[102]

These specific exceptions are by no means unique. In many of the bilateral, regional and region-to-region economic treaties discussed in this volume, similar exceptions had been inserted at key points where new disciplines were being agreed,[103] providing flexibility for regulators on health, environment, safety and natural resources or other issues raised in the assessments.[104]

99 EU-Chile SIA (n 42) 218.

100 US-Chile FTA (n 2) art 161.

101 EU-Chile AA (n 4) arts 91, 133, 135.

102 EU-Chile SIA (n 42) 217–218.

103 See Annex 2 of this volume, particularly with regard to references to EU-CARIFORUM EPA (n 29); EU-Colombia-Peru FTA (n 21).

104 MC Cordonier Segger, 'Inspiration for Integration: Interpreting International Trade and Investment Accords for Sustainable Development' (2017) 3(1) Canadian Journal of Comparative and Contemporary Law 159; Eric Neumayer, *Greening Trade and Investment: Environmental Protection without Protectionism* (London, Routledge 2017); MC Cordonier Segger, Peter Holmgren and D Andrew Wardell, 'Financing Sustainable Landscapes through Innovative International Economic Law and Governance Instruments' (2018) 7(1) Global Journal of Comparative Law 169, 169–205.

These exceptions do not provide a *carte blanche* for the Parties to ignore non-discrimination or other disciplines in favour of health, environment or other legislation. Indeed, the burden on the regulator to defend new measures with scientific evidence and other arguments, in many instances, may be heavy. However, for the regulators and others developing new domestic laws and instruments in the area of sustainable development, the provisions can be interpreted to demonstrate that States did not intend to stifle or constrain legitimate measures for sustainable development.[105] The customary principle of integration highlights a need for balance between economic and environmental objectives. With these specific exceptions focused on issues raised in the impact assessments surveyed earlier in this volume,[106] under the VCLT, the provisions could interpreted,[107] especially taking the customary principle of integration into account,[108] so as to prevent new measures needed for sustainable development from being disallowed. For a regulator, being questioned on the trade or investment liberalization acceptability of a proposed measure in one of these specific areas, this interpretation would make all the difference. Such exceptions may provide a useful integration tool to prevent harm for sustainable development, as a precondition for integration.

'Non-application notes' for laws and policies on sustainable development

General and specific exceptions can secure exemptions to prevent a trade agreement from constraining environmental and social regulators. A further tool involves the insertion of specific agreed footnotes or annexed tables, focusing on particular regulatory measures identified in an impact assessment, to ensure these measures are not disciplined or prevented by the new trade rules. While general exceptions may provide guidance for future situations, by exempting future regulatory measures, and specific exceptions make it clear that disciplines are not meant to restrict social or environmental regulations in certain special contexts, such footnotes or annexes are being used in regional trade agreements to clarify that the trade rules will not apply to their existing laws and policies.[109] In both treaties, entire categories of social and environmental regulations are directly designated by each of the Parties separately.[110] These provisions are often called 'reservations' in the trade treaties, though they are mutually accepted by the Parties during negotiations.[111] Information on the legal measures that the Party has designated as non-applicable, and the relevant legislation, is provided in annexes to the treaties. In this way, each of the Parties

[105] VCLT, art 31(3)(c) permits other relevant rules of international law, see J Pauwelyn, *Conflict of Norms in Public International Law: How WTO Law Relates to Other Rules of International Law* (Cambridge, CUP 2003) 253–254 where it is explained that this rule permits customary norms to assist in giving meaning to the terms of the treaty, such as these exceptions.

[106] VCLT, art 32, which permits reference to *travaux préparatoires* to confirm meanings; Gardiner (n 15).

[107] An interpretation of these exceptions, in good faith in accordance with their ordinary meaning, in light of a 'purpose' of sustainable development, suggests that disciplines are not meant to block regulations in this area, VCLT, art 31.

[108] See n 106, and see T Cottier and M Foltea, 'Constitutional Functions of the WTO and RTAs' in Bartels and Ortino (n 45) 51–52.

[109] See C Redgwell 'Universality or Integrity? Some reflections on Reservations to General Multilateral Treaties' 64 (1993) British Yearbook of International Law 245; I Ziemele (ed), *Reservations to Human Rights Treaties and the Vienna Convention Regime, Conflict, Harmony or Reconciliation* (The Hague, Martinus Nijhoff 2004); Gardiner (n 15).

[110] The Canada-Chile FTA (n 7) contains reservations for services at art H-06; the Canada-Costa Rica FTA (n 8) contains reservations to services at art VIII.3

[111] Gardiner (n 15).

seeks to preserve regulatory flexibility, while also securing transparency for firms and others that rely on the trade or investment liberalization rules. These non-application notes specifically address issues raised in the *ex-ante* environmental and sustainability assessment processes on several occasions.

The US-Chile FTA contains several broad non-application notes of relevance to sustainable development, directly addressing issues highlighted in the Chile-US ER, and raised in the 2002 JPOI. First, while general exceptions mainly emphasize health and environment concerns as noted above, more specific notes are being used to ensure that trade disciplines do not threaten important social development laws and policies. Returning to the examples of trade in services and investment, in the US-Chile FTA chapter on cross-border services and investment, the Parties make extensive commitments to national treatment, most-favoured nation and transparency and also, for investment, to discipline their use of performance requirements, expropriation and other regulatory tools. These commitments raised environmental concerns in the Chile-US ER.[112] In the Chile-EU SIA, further social concerns were raised about the same provisions.[113]

One of the concerns was that economic measures to benefit displaced or marginalized peoples, including past measures to compensate indigenous peoples who were removed from their lands to permit hydroelectric, mining or other development, could be questioned under the trade and investment agreement.[114] These issues are directly addressed in the US-Chile FTA through specific 'non-application notes' included by each Party. In Annex II-CH-6, Chile notes its decision, agreed by the other Party, to set aside:

> the right to adopt or maintain any measure according rights or preferences to socially or economically disadvantaged minorities.[115]

In Annex II-CH-7, to be precise, Chile specifically notes that the economic agreement does not cover 'any rights or preferences provided to indigenous peoples'.[116] In the EU-Chile SIA, concerns were raised about increased privatization of health or education services and other social services.[117] In Annex II-CH-8 of the US-Chile FTA, Chile sets aside the right to 'adopt or maintain any measure relating to natural persons who render educational services ...'[118] And at Annex II-CH-12 Chile also makes it clear that disciplines will not apply to their regulations concerning:

> the right to adopt or maintain any measure with respect to ... income security or insurance, social security or insurance, social welfare, public education, public training, health care, and child care.[119]

112 US-Chile Interim ER (n 70) 66–68.
113 EU-Chile SIA (n 42) 217–218.
114 Ibid 20; US-Chile Interim ER (n 70) 9–44 for general concerns.
115 US-Chile FTA (n 2) Annex II, CH-6.
116 Ibid, Annex II, CH-7.
117 EU-Chile SIA (n 42) 191–192.
118 US-Chile FTA (n 2) Annex II, CH-8.
119 Ibid, Annex II CH-12.

The social 'non-application' notes by the US are found in Annex II-US-2, and they are also fairly broad. With respect to obligations related to national treatment, most-favoured-nation treatment, local presence and performance requirements, the US:

> reserves the right to adopt or maintain any measure with respect to ... income security or insurance, social security or insurance, social welfare, public education, public training, health, and child care.[120]

And at Annex II-US-3, the US further sets aside:

> the right to adopt or maintain any measure according rights or preferences to socially or economically disadvantaged minorities, including corporations organized under the laws of the State of Alaska in accordance with the *Alaska Native Claims Settlement Act*.[121]

As such, in terms of the first type of integration—the inclusion of provisions to ensure that the trade and investment liberalization agreement does not inadvertently constrain or frustrate social development or environmental law, such non-application notes (called 'reservations') are a third tool being used by Parties to bilateral, regional or region-to-country economic treaties. In the accords surveyed, the Parties may ensure the social issues highlighted in Agenda 21 and in the JPOI, such as agreements on education, training or economic preferences for indigenous peoples, or public health measures, while not necessarily covered by plurilateral general exceptions, are being protected through these specific notes.[122]

Second, non-application notes are also included by each Party to secure exemptions for measures aimed at ensuring sustainable management of natural resources, in both the developed and the developing countries concerned. Both the EU-Chile SIA and the US-Chile ER processes identified fisheries as a major area of potential concern, with regard to potential material and normative impacts.[123] In the US-Chile FTA, with regard to fisheries, non-application notes are particularly extensive. At Annex II-CH-10, Chile retains the right to control the activities of foreign fishing, including fish landing, first landing of fish processed at sea, and access to Chilean ports (port privileges), as well as to control the use of beaches, land adjacent to beaches (*terrenos de playas*), water-columns (*porciones de agua*) and sea-bed lots (*fondos marinos*) for the issuance of maritime concessions.[124] Also, at Annex I-CH-8, Chile declares that market access and investment liberalization will not apply to aquaculture and artisanal (small-scale) fishing licences and concessions.[125]

120 Ibid, Annex II US-2.

121 Alaska Native Claims Settlement Act 43 USC §§ 1601 et seq.

122 See Annex 2 of this volume. See, as examples, EU-CARIFORUM EPA (n 29); EU-Colombia-Peru FTA (n 21).

123 EU-Chile SIA (n 42) 113–127; US-Chile Interim ER (n 70) 13–15.

124 *Decreto Ley 2.222*, Diario Oficial, mayo 31, 1978, *Ley de Navegación Decreto con Fuerza de Ley 340*, Diario Oficial, abril 6, 1960, sobre *Concesiones Marítimas Decreto Supremo 660*, Diario Oficial, noviembre 28, 1988, *Reglamento de Concesiones Marítimas*. Similarly, according to Annex I-CH-28: 'Anyone unloading, transshipping, and, generally, using continental or insular Chilean ports, particularly for landing fish catches or processing fish catches on board, shall also be required to be a Chilean natural or juridical person.'

125 Measures: *Ley 18892*, Diario Oficial enero 21, 1992, *Ley General de Pesca y Acuicultura*, Títulos I y VI.

In another example related to energy, which was also identified as a concern in the impact assessment processes, Chile clarifies at Annex I-CH-5 that the:

> exploration, exploitation, and treatment (*beneficio*) of liquid or gaseous hydrocarbons . . . can be the object of administrative concessions or special operating contracts . . . [126]

Moreover, Chile confirms that the 'production of nuclear energy for peaceful purposes may only be carried out by the *Comisión Chilena de Energía Nuclear* or, with its authorization . . .'[127] In a third example related to lithium mining, at Annex I-CH-6 and Annex I-CH-7, Chilean investment obligations related to national treatment and performance requirements are subject to careful control,[128] and rights of first refusal for thorium or uranium supplies.[129] And with regard to the development concerns raised during the impact assessments about water privatization,[130] at Annex II-CH-13, Chile

> '. . . reserves the right to adopt or maintain any measure imposing the requirement that the production and distribution of drinking water, the collection and disposal of waste water, and sanitation services, such as sewage systems, waste disposal, and waste water treatment . . .'[131]

This non-application note appears to directly addresses the concern raised in the sustainability impact assessment carried out during the negotiations. It integrates in reverse, by providing a further tool to prevent the treaty from directly frustrating these social and environmental concerns.

The US-Chile ER also raised potential impacts surrounding increased trade in used goods.[132] Concerns were expressed, as explained above, that measures to facilitate the import of used goods would result in older models of polluting or unsafe products being exported to Chile where regulations might be more lax and disposal less careful.[133] And in the Chile-US FTA, Parties agree that the disciplines of the trade agreement will not apply to 'measures of Chile relating to imports of used vehicles'.[134]

The non-application notes related to natural resource management are not confined only to the developing country Party. For instance, as mentioned earlier, both the EU-Chile SIA and US-Chile ER identified impacts that might occur should the trade rules interfere with regulations to ensure more sustainable forest management or to secure value-added processing of wood in either the United States or Chile.[135] In the Chile-US FTA, national treatment obligations covering trade in goods do not apply to controls by the United States 'on

126 US-Chile FTA (n 2) Annex I, CH-5.

127 Measures: *Constitución Política de la República de Chile*, Capítulo III; *Ley 18097*, Diario Oficial, enero 21, 1982, *Ley Orgánica, Constitucional sobre Concesiones Mineras*, Títulos I, II, y III; *Ley 18248*, Diario Oficial, octubre 14, 1983, *Código de Minería*, Títulos I y II; *Ley 16319*, Diario Oficial, octubre 23, 1965, crea la Comisión Chilena de Energía Nuclear, Títulos I, II, y III.

128 Ibid.

129 Ibid.

130 US-Chile Interim ER (n 70) 20–21.

131 US-Chile FTA (n 2) Annex I-CH-13.

132 US-Chile Interim ER (n 70) 69–70.

133 Ibid.

134 US-Chile FTA (n 2) Section B—Measures of Chile, art 3.11.

135 US-Chile Interim ER (n 70) 16–19; EU-Chile SIA (n 42) 91–100.

the export of logs of all species'.[136] With respect to investment obligations in the area of coal, and oil and gas, Annex I-US-4 of the US-Chile FTA, also notes that according to the US Mineral Lands Leasing Act of 1920:

> aliens and foreign corporations may not acquire rights-of-way for oil or gas pipelines, or pipelines carrying products refined from oil and gas, across onshore federal lands or acquire leases or interests in certain minerals on on-shore federal lands, such as coal or oil . . .'[137]

With respect to the (positive-list) government procurement obligations, US state-level non-application notes affect procurement in a range of goods and services. Washington State, as one example, excludes 'procurements of fuel, paper products, boats, ships and vessels'. Further, non-application notes state, specifically, that nothing in the procurement disciplines shall 'prevent any state entity from applying restrictions that promote the general environmental quality in that state, as long as such restrictions are not disguised barriers to international trade'.[138] The treaty also notes that the procurement rules 'shall not apply to preferences or restrictions associated with programs administered by entities that promote the development of distressed areas and businesses owned by minorities, disabled veterans, and women'.[139] Section H, in the Schedule of the US Act, also states at 1 that the disciplines do 'not apply to set-asides on behalf of small and minority businesses'.[140]

Interestingly, the Chilean authorities, so cautious with regard to social programmes for services or investment, do not opt out from the accord's procurement schedules and chapters, listing all municipalities and a great number of government agencies. The Chilean policy, it appears, has been to explicitly open procurement contracts above the threshold to all contenders, aiming for the best possible quality and price. In the EU-Chile AA, similarly, Chile provides an extensive list of central government entities and sub-national bodies, including municipalities, opting out of nothing, while the Europeans provide detailed schedules of measures to which disciplines are non-applicable if not in conformity, country by country. The Chilean approach exposes the regulators to certain risks and burdens from the perspective of integration. If a new Chilean green or social procurement programme were questioned,[141] Chilean authorities would only be able to rely on the general exceptions in the procurement chapter to make their case (and it is likely that the legal fees alone, for a municipality, would create their own barriers).

In more recent bilateral, region-to-region, or region-to-country economic treaties, further non-application notes and annexes opened space for laws regarding the marking and labelling of products in view of concerns to human and animal health or environmental issues.[142] These appear to directly address particular concerns raised in the SIAs to these treaties.[143]

[136] Annex 3.2 on national treatment and import and export restrictions at Section A—Measures of the United States, art 3.2 and art 3.11 of the US-Chile FTA (n 2).

[137] 'Non-US citizens may own a 100 percent interest in a domestic corporation that acquires a right-of-way for oil or gas pipelines across on-shore federal lands . . .': Mineral Lands Leasing Act of 1920, 30 USC §§ 181, 185(a), chapter 3A 10 USC § 7435.

[138] US-Chile FTA (n 2) note 2 of Annex 9.1.

[139] Annex 9.1, Section B on sub-central level government entities, US note 6.

[140] For a broader discussion of the labour debates, see C McCrudden and A Davies, 'A Perspective on Trade and Labour Rights' in M Gehring and MC Cordonier Segger (eds), *Sustainable Development in World Trade Law* (The Hague, Kluwer Law International 2005).

[141] C Weller, E Claro and H Blanco, *Sustainable Public Procurement: Where do we stand in Chile?* (Winnipeg, IISD 2008).

[142] EU-Colombia-Peru FTA (n 21). CH 4 TBT, art 81(d).

[143] Development Solutions, *EU-Andean Trade Sustainability Impact Assessment: Draft Final Report* (Brussels, Development Solutions July 2009) [EU-Andean SIA] 133; US-Oman interim Environmental Review (April 2005) 2.

Specific non-application notes, then, are one mechanism used extensively by Parties to ensure integration, by preventing their trade and investment liberalization commitments from unduly constraining their ability to regulate in important areas related to sustainable development. There appears to be tangible links between the concerns signalled in the assessments, and the decisions of States to include specific footnotes, annexes and other exemptions. Parties, ideally, would be taking the risks and data garnered by the assessment to identify sensitive sectors where more caution is needed.[144] The customary principle of integration highlights a need for balance between economic and environmental objectives.[145] With non-application notes and annexes that can be considered part of the treaty in accordance with the VCLT,[146] these provisions might be interpreted to detain application of the trade disciplines where regulations are still under development, or otherwise sensitive to sustainable development interests.[147] By integrating non-application notes for environmental and social development measures as appropriate, the Parties are 'reverse integrating'—they are able to change the scope of the trade and investment liberalization treaty, providing space for sustainable development regulations.

Rules on relationships between environmental, social and economic liberalization treaties

When trade, environment and social development regimes overlap, there is seldom a direct conflict of legal obligations, as discussed earlier in this volume.[148] However, trade and investment treaty provisions can appear to specifically forbid or condition the use of market measures which may be essential for the other treaty on sustainable development. The challenges discussed above, including the problems related to the phasing out of persistent organic pollutants (POPs), and difficulties for Chile with regard to their commitments under the UN Convention on Biological Diversity (UNCBD) and its Cartagena Protocol, provided examples situations where regimes overlap, raising tensions.[149]

Of value to interpretation, many bilateral or regional economic agreements provide for 'relations with other agreements' clauses which clarify which treaty is meant to govern. Article VCLT article 30(2) provides that when a treaty specifies that it is subject to, or that it is not to be considered as incompatible with, an earlier or later treaty, the provisions of that other treaty prevail. Several of these sorts of clauses are found in trade and investment liberalization accords. Article 1.3 of the Chile-United States FTA on relation to other agreements states that: 'The Parties affirm their existing rights and obligations with respect to each other under ... other agreements to which both Parties are party.'[150] While this provision may have been focused on trade agreements and other arrangements in which the Parties are involved, including the NAFTA and the Mercosur in which Chile is an associate member, it

144 VCLT, art 31(3)(c) permits other relevant rules of international law, see Pauwelyn (n 105) 253–254 where it is explained that this rule permits customary norms to assist in giving meaning to the terms of the treaty, such as these exceptions.

145 An interpretation of these exceptions, in good faith in accordance with their ordinary meaning, in light of a 'purpose' of sustainable development, suggests that disciplines are not meant to block regulations in this area, VCLT, art 31.

146 VCLT, art 31 which permits recourse to annexes as part of the 'context' of the treaty: Gardiner (n 15).

147 C Thomas and J Trachtman (eds), *Developing Countries in the WTO Legal System* (Oxford, OUP 2009) 51–52.

148 See O Holliday Charles Jr, Stephan Schmidheiny and Philip Watts, *Walking the Talk: The Business Case for Sustainable Development* (London, Routledge 2017); Soo-Hyun Lee, 'The Role of WTO in Sustainable Development Governance Revisited' (2018) 10 135, 135; Gregory C Shaffer and Mark A Pollack, 'Hard vs. Soft Law: Alternatives, Complements, and Antagonists in International Governance' (2009) 94 Minnesota Law Review 706, 706.

149 See Chapter 2.

150 US-Chile FTA (n 2) art 1.3.

could be interpreted in light of the customary integration principle to safeguard the rights and obligations of the Parties in other treaties—if these were signed before 2003.[151] Similar provisions are found in other accords, such as article 4 of the EFTA-Singapore FTA which states that the provisions of the Agreement '... shall be without prejudice to the rights and obligations of the Parties under the [WTO Agreement] and any other international agreement to which they are a party'.[152]

In the bilateral or regional economic treaties examined for this research, further guidance is provided to exempt or at least limit such constraints, guiding overlaps of trade and environment regimes where one might otherwise prevent another. In particular, the Chile-US FTA at article 19.9, notes:

> The Parties recognize the importance of multilateral environmental agreements, including the appropriate use of trade measures in such agreements to achieve specific environmental goals.

This formulation does not specify whether the Parties are referring to agreements to which they are both Parties (for instance, the Montreal Protocol), or agreements where only one is a Party (such as the UN CBD to which only Chile is a Party, and its Cartagena Protocol, which Chile is considering ratifying). Such a provision, while perhaps not offering a clear solution to the problem of overlaps or conflicts, might indeed guide a tribunal or regulator faced with a claim that the actions of one Party to the trade treaty, taken in order to comply with the trade measures in an agreement on sustainable development are somehow illegitimate or inappropriate. Further, the US-Chile FTA defers discussions on multilateral environment agreements (MEAs) to the WTO Doha Round, recognizing the 'negotiations on the relationship between existing WTO rules and specific trade obligations set out in multilateral environmental agreements' while leaving space for flexibility in that 'the Parties shall consult on the extent to which the outcome of the negotiations applies to this Agreement'.[153]

The EU-Chile AA, on the other hand, does not contain similar rules on overlaps or conflicts between agreements. The AA does state at article 14 on cooperation in the field of foreign and security policy that: 'the Parties shall, as far as possible, coordinate their positions and undertake joint initiatives in the appropriate international fora, and cooperate in the field of foreign and security policy'.[154] This is scarcely guidance in the event of a conflict or overlap of obligations. However, at article 44 on social cooperation, the EU-Chile AA commits that the Parties 'will give priority to ... respect for fundamental social rights, notably by promoting the relevant conventions of the International Labour Organisation' and that '[m]easures may be coordinated with those of the Member States and the relevant international organisations'.[155] And at article 49, the Parties agree to 'use all existing cooperation instruments to promote' regional cooperation and regional integration, giving priority to

[151] Pauwelyn (n 105) 362–365.

[152] EFTA-Singapore Free Trade Agreement (signed 26 June 2002, entered into force 1 January 2003) <http://www.efta.int/content/legal-texts/third-country-relations/singapore/Overview.doc> accessed 16 December 2020. See also art 18.2 of the Chile-New Zealand-Singapore-Brunei Darussalam Trans-Pacific Strategic EPA (n 11) as cited by Bartels (n 45).

[153] US-Chile FTA (n 2) art 19.9.

[154] EU-Chile AA (n 4) art 14.

[155] Ibid, art 44.

'(a) promoting trade and investment in the region; and (b) developing regional cooperation on the environment'.[156] Article 50 on triangular and bi-regional cooperation further states that: 'The Parties recognise the value of international cooperation for the *promotion of equitable and sustainable development* processes . . .'[157]

Unlike the explicit provisions in the US-Chile FTA, these provisions do not appear to be able to directly guide Parties in the event of a conflict between the trade rules enshrined in Part IV of the EU-Chile AA, and an existing (or new) international treaty on environmental or social development goals, beyond the commitment to cooperate. They do not grant precedence to such measures. However, it is possible that the integration principle, as recognized in the treaty, can serve to guide treaty interpretation in such instances, whereby the commitments of Parties in other treaties on sustainable development are expected to be taken into account should overlaps appear.

Several general observations can be made with respect to preventing these 'potential regime overlaps'. First, where constraints are not intended by the Parties, the bilateral or regional economic treaties can include a specific statement which clarifies that the trade and investment liberalization rules are subject to, or are not to be considered as incompatible with, other agreements.[158] If such a statement is included, and it often is, then according to rules of treaty law in the VCLT, the provisions of the other treaties would prevail in the event of actual conflicts.[159] Such a 'conflicts clause' would preclude agreed market measures under MEAs and other sustainable development treaties from the purview of the regional or bilateral trade and investment disciplines, providing greater stability to interpretation for all treaty regimes. Such provisions were included in the NAFTA,[160] and also appear in the Canada-Chile FTA at articles A-03 and A-04,[161] and the Canada-Costa Rica FTA at articles I.3 and I.4,[162] among others. Chapter 1 of the NAFTA sets forth the NAFTA's basic objectives and rules of interpretation. Article 102 states its objectives, and agrees that it will be interpreted in accordance with the applicable rules of international law. Article 103 affirms existing rights and obligations under both bilateral and multilateral agreements, including the WTO Agreements, providing that the NAFTA prevails in the event of any inconsistency between it and such other international agreements, except as otherwise noted.[163] Article 104 then reverses the general rule of article 103 in regard to certain international environmental agreements, stating:

1. In the event of any inconsistency between this Agreement and the specific trade obligations set out in [various accords where Parties use specific trade obligations including the Basel Convention] such obligations shall prevail to the extent of the inconsistency, provided that where a Party has a choice among equally effective and reasonably

[156] Ibid, art 49.
[157] Ibid, art 50.
[158] VCLT, art 30(2), which provides that when a treaty specifies that it is subject to, or that it is not to be considered as incompatible with, an earlier treaty or later treaty, the provisions of that other treaty prevail.
[159] Pauwelyn (n 105) 268–274, 361, but see 385 with reference to *lex specialis*.
[160] NAFTA (n 6) art 104; JJ Kirton and VW Maclaren (eds), *Linking Trade, Environment, and Social Cohesion* (Aldershot, Ashgate 2002).
[161] Canada-Chile FTA (n 7) arts A-03, A-04.
[162] Canada-Costa Rica FTA (n 8) arts 1.3 and 1.4.
[163] NAFTA (n 6) art 103.

available means of complying with such obligations, the Party chooses the alternative that is the least inconsistent with the other provisions of this Agreement.

2. The Parties may agree in writing to modify Annex 104.1 to include any amendment to an agreement referred to in paragraph 1, and any other environmental or conservation agreement.[164]

As such, this provision specifies three pre-existing MEAs and provides for others in an 'open-ended' Annex. Upon 'inconsistencies' between the NAFTA and the MEA obligations, the latter shall prevail to the extent of the inconsistency, with a caveat for instrument choice. The 'listed MEAs' were already in force during the negotiation of the NAFTA in 1994, and each authorizes the use of market-based instruments. These measures include, as discussed earlier in this book, trade bans against products made with chlorofluorocarbons in non-parties to discourage 'free-riders',[165] bans on trade and investment in endangered species products to discourage their exploitation[166] and bans on investment in or the import/export of hazardous wastes, as well as other restrictions.[167] If not for article 104, these measures would be disallowed by the disciplines of the trade and investment accord, the opposite of a balanced integration of the environment into economic development law and policy. Further, to prevent Parties from bringing trade cases related to these MEAs to other bodies, a choice of forum provision was added at article 2005 so that the Party which relied on the MEA in their defence could have the dispute adjudicated under a NAFTA Panel or another mechanism of their choice. Under the NAFTA, however, article 2005(3) states that if NAFTA article 104 is being used as a defence, recourse exists only under the NAFTA. Without such a provision, the Complaining Party could simply pursue any claims at the WTO, which might not apply a NAFTA 'precedence' provision.[168] The choice of forum provisions in the NAFTA do not appear to extend to Parties being able to access the non-compliance procedures increasingly used to augment traditional dispute settlement

164 Ibid.

165 D Brack, *International Trade and the Montreal Protocol* (London, Earthscan 1996); Montreal Protocol on Substances that Deplete the Ozone Layer (adopted 16 September 1987, entered into force 1 January 1989) 1522 UNTS 3 arts 2 and 4; Basel Convention on the Control of Transboundary Movements of Hazardous Wastes and their Disposal (adopted 22 March 1989, entered into force 5 May 1992) 1673 UNTS 57, arts 3–6, 8–9.

166 Convention on International Trade in Endangered Species of Wild Fauna and Flora (CITES) (adopted 3 March 1973, entered into force 1 July 1975) 993 UNTS 243; Brack (n 165); UNEP and IISD, *Environment and Trade: A Handbook* (2nd edn, Winnipeg, UNEP and IISD 2005); 'Process of preparation of the Environmental Perspective to the Year 2000 and Beyond, Meeting no. 102' UNGA Res 38/161, 19 December 1983, UN Doc A/RES/38/161.

167 Basel Convention (n 165).

168 NAFTA (n 6) art 2005(3). This provision is being tested at present. On 9 March 2009 Mexico requested that a WTO Panel be established to review Mexico's claims that US law limiting the use of the 'dolphin safe' label on tuna and tuna products is inconsistent with US obligations under the WTO Agreement. In response, the United States invoked the NAFTA choice of forum provision (art 2005(4) of the NAFTA) on 24 March 2009. The more appropriate forum may be NAFTA chapter 20 rather than the WTO's Dispute Settlement Body. While in general NAFTA Parties have the option of selecting either the WTO or the NAFTA forum (NAFTA, art 2005(1), measures to protect human, animal or plant life or health or relating to the environment are clearly supposed to be submitted to dispute settlement under NAFTA, art 20. However, the WTO AB in the *Mexico-Taxes on Soft Drinks* dispute, shows that WTO Panels do not often defer to RTAs, also NAFTA Parties have never agreed on a chapter 20 roster, delaying the functioning of art 2011. See D Gantz, 'Dispute Settlement Under the NAFTA and the WTO: Choice of Forum Opportunities and Risks for the NAFTA Parties' (1998) 14 American University International Law Review 1025.

provisions in MEAs.[169] However, other provisions for cooperation to implement MEAs may permit, or even encourage precisely this choice, as discussed below.[170]

Mutual supportiveness and integration imply an element of balance between overlapping provisions. A straightforward declaration that all other treaties will have *precedence* in the event of conflicts may not actually provide for an integrated or balanced relationship between trade, environment and social obligations. However, in this instance, the granting of precedence *is* actually balanced by certain conditions. First, the MEA prevails only to the extent of the inconsistency. Second, the Party to the MEA must still choose the alternative least inconsistent with NAFTA, and third, the measure must be a specific trade obligation.[171] The Party introducing the measure has the burden of demonstrating that their measure meets the conditions. This introduces an element of balance. It is also important to take into account that the non-application of NAFTA disciplines to these limited instances would not necessarily have a great impact on the NAFTA's effectiveness or other trade liberalization objectives, but non-application of the MEA trade measures could act as a significant and disproportionate constraint on the ability of Parties to the MEAs to implement these legitimate treaty regimes.[172]

Two further observations can also be made with respect to these provisions. First, though they do provide for further accords to be 'placed under the protection' of this limited exemption from NAFTA rules disallowing trade measures of this sort, no such further accords have as yet been designated, and one of the signatories (the US) is not a Party to many other MEAs, which are not mentioned in article 104.[173] As other sustainable development-related treaties signed later than the original select MEAs are listed and Parties avail themselves of NAFTA article 103 provisions in the event of 'inconsistencies', the mechanism's effectiveness will become clearer.[174] Second, these provisions contemplate only environmental agreements. However, if the social pillar of sustainable development is to be taken seriously, it might be equally important that the relationship between the trade agreement and social development accords, including human rights covenants and other instruments, be made clear.

The original NAFTA, and now the USMCA approach is by no means the most current state of the trade and investment law in relation to such overlaps of regimes. For further comparison, the Peru-US TPA at article 18.10 states:

> 1. The Parties recognize that multilateral agreements to which they are all party, play an important role globally and domestically in protecting the environment and that their

[169] NAFTA (n 6) arts 103, 104 and 2005. JH Knox, 'The Judicial Resolution of Conflicts between Trade and the Environment' (2004) 28 Harvard Environmental Law Review 1; SR Miller, 'NAFTA: A Model for Reconciling the Conflict between Free Trade and International Environmental Protection' (1994–1995) 56 University of Pittsburgh Law Review 483.

[170] See Section 17.3.

[171] J-F Morin and C Bialais, 'Strengthening Multilateral Environmental Governance through Bilateral Trade Deals' Policy Brief No. 123, Centre for International Global Innovation.

[172] Kirton and Maclaren (n 160); A Cosbey, 'NAFTA's Chapter 11 and the Environment' (2003) Discussion Paper for the CEC's Public Workshop on NAFTA's Chapter 11, <http://www.iisd.org/pdf/2003/investment_jpac.pdf>; C Deere and D Esty (eds), *Greening the Americas: NAFTA's Lessons for Hemispheric Trade* (Boston, MIT Press 2002).

[173] Deere and Esty (n 172).

[174] See K Gray 'Accommodating MEAs in Trade Agreements' (Presentation given at the International Environmental Governance Conference in Paris, March 2004).

respective implementation of these agreements is critical to achieving the environmental objectives thereof. The Parties further recognize that this Chapter and the ECA can contribute to realizing the goals of those agreements. Accordingly, the Parties shall continue to seek means to enhance the mutual supportiveness of multilateral environmental agreements to which they are all party and trade agreements to which they are all party.

2. To this end, the Parties shall consult, as appropriate, with respect to negotiations on environmental issues of mutual interest.
3. Each Party recognizes the importance to it of the multilateral environmental agreements to which it is a party.[175]

The context is different to articles 103 and 104 of the NAFTA, or the comparable Canada-Chile FTA,[176] Canada-Costa Rica FTA,[177] and Chile-US FTA provisions.[178] In the Peru-US TPA, the provisions appear in the environmental chapter of the trade and investment treaty, not as clearly operational economic law obligations themselves, but rather, part of the treaty context.[179] Also, the Peru-US TPA does not commit to *precedence* in the event of conflict. Rather, it simply commits to seek means to enhance 'mutual supportiveness', and that Parties will consult, as appropriate, on 'issues of mutual interest'. Finally, while the set of MEAs to which it applies are broader than the NAFTA approach, the current proposal still limits the commitment to MEAs of which the Parties of the Peru-US TPA are 'all Parties,' and to trade agreements to which they are all Parties. The commitment to mutual supportiveness would not apply to measures taken under environmental agreements to which some of the economic agreement Parties are Parties, but others are not. This problem is clearly acknowledged in the final provision that '[e]ach Party recognizes the importance to it' of the MEAs to which it is a Party. These provisions, in short, do not resolve the problem. A similar problem arises from the streamlined approach taken in the Australia-Thailand FTA, where the Parties 'affirm with respect to each other their existing rights and obligations relating to technical regulations' not only under the TBT Agreement but also under 'all other all other international agreements, including environmental and conservation agreements, to which the Parties are party'.[180]

In the most recent treaties, 'relations with other agreement' clauses provided are more general, for example, the EU-Central America AA, which states that:

> The Parties recognise that international environmental governance and agreements are important elements to address global or regional environmental problems and stress the need to enhance the mutual supportiveness between trade and environment. The Parties commit to consult and co-operate as appropriate on trade-related environmental issues of mutual interest.[181]

175 US-Peru TPA (n 9).
176 Canada-Chile FTA (n 7).
177 Canada-Costa Rica FTA (n 8).
178 US-Chile FTA (n 2).
179 US-Peru TPA (n 9) chapter 18.
180 Australia-Thailand FTA (n 45), as cited by Bartels (n 45).
181 EU-Central America AA (n 23) art 287.1.

The treaty also specifically notes seven major MEAs, reaffirming the commitment of the parties to these treaties.[182] Such provisions are more directly respectful of the integration principle discussed in Chapter 3, and can directly address particular concerns raised in the SIA to this treaty. For instance, the EU-Central America SIA expressed concerns about environmental impacts linked to expected changes in land use for the fruits, vegetables and nuts sector, such as the doubling of banana and other large-scale fruit plantations, that could lead to increased deforestation and resulting biodiversity loss.[183] This would have a contrary effect to State commitments under the UNCBD. The EU-Central America SIA also notes that greenhouse gas emissions would likely increase due to the treaty, which would affect commitments under the UN Framework Convention on Climate Change (UN FCCC).[184] Further, this impact assessment directly mentions challenges in implementing MEAs in Central America, and recommends a 'commitment to signing and enforcing MEAs, in order to combat climate change, preserve biodiversity and ecosystems ...'[185] While such provisions may be able to guide interpretation in situations where both Parties to the economic agreement are also Parties to overlapping MEAs, problems remain unresolved for other accords related to sustainable development to which all are not both Parties.

With regard to social development, the 2003 US-Chile FTA[186] and the later Peru-US TPA both provide an example of an innovative provision in the body of the text which indicates the relationship of the trade and investment agreement to international social development (labour) treaties and bodies. In particular, in the US-Peru TPA at article 17.1: Statement of Shared Commitments:

> 1. The Parties reaffirm their obligations as members of the International Labor Organization (ILO) and their commitments under the ILO Declaration on Fundamental Principles and Rights at Work and its Follow-Up (1998) (ILO Declaration) 1. Each Party shall strive to ensure that such labor principles and the internationally recognized labor rights set forth in Article 17.7 are recognized and protected by its law. 2. The Parties reaffirm their full respect for their Constitutions and recognize the right of each Party to adopt or modify its labor laws and standards. Each Party shall strive to ensure that it provides for labor standards consistent with the internationally recognized labor rights set forth in Article 17.7 and shall strive to improve those standards in that light.[187]

This commitment is made operational at article 17.5 (and following) which establishes a Labour Cooperation and Capacity-Building Mechanism. These provisions reaffirm the obligations of the Parties as ILO members, and commit to 'strive' to ensure that such principles and the rights set forth in article 17.7 are realized. These include: (a) the right of association; (b) the right to organize and bargain collectively; (c) a prohibition on the use of any form of forced or compulsory labour; (d) labour protections for children and minors, including a minimum age for the employment of children and the prohibition and elimination of the

[182] Ibid, art 287.2.

[183] ECORYS, *Trade Sustainability Impact Assessment of the Association Agreement to be negotiated between the EU and Central America: Draft Final Report* (Rotterdam, July 2009) [EU-Central America SIA] 17.

[184] Ibid 42.

[185] Ibid 95.

[186] US-Chile FTA (n 2) art 19.3.

[187] US-Peru TPA (n 9) art 17.1.

worst forms of child labour; and (e) acceptable conditions of work with respect to minimum wages, hours of work and occupational safety and health, but not a common minimum wage.[188] Furthermore, the provision does not commit to precedence for all labour agreements, as such. The ILO enshrines over 190 Conventions, but the TPA only mentions ILA Convention No 182 Concerning the Prohibition and Immediate Action for the Elimination of the Worst Forms of Child Labour.[189] Nor does it address other human rights, such as the right to health. However, even just the specific mention of this Declaration and ILO Convention No 182, coupled with the 'open-ended' nature of the final provision ('to further advance common commitments regarding labor matters') offers broader flexibility to the Parties than earlier examples. In other ways, the provisions are still quite limited. They only extend to social agreements to which all Parties are already Parties, suggesting that in other cases, trade rules will 'trump' labour standards. Essentially, this approach provides a commitment to a labour cooperation and capacity-building mechanism on fundamental principles and rights at work, and compliance with prohibitions on child labour, with more later, perhaps. Such provisions might become tools for reconciliation, if not yet integration, if they built cooperative agendas on social development issues over time.

As such, with regard to the integration of social and environmental norms with international economic law, it appears Parties to trade and investment liberalization agreements are still experimenting on how to address the potential for bilateral or regional economic treaties to constrain the use of social or environmental measures, affecting Parties' ability to implement other important social or environmental commitments and frustrating the integration principle. As seen above, several of the bilateral or regional economic treaties that commit to sustainable development do include specific provisions to clarify such overlaps, but even in these treaties, Parties hesitate to designate rules of precedence for other international treaties on sustainable development that contain specific trade obligations, including MEAs, where the Parties to the trade and investment negotiation are not all Parties to the other treaty.[190] Conflicts clauses, according to VCLT article 30, will govern the relationship where provided.[191] If conflicts provisions are included, the interpreter shall see them as a clear signal (either way) to relevant actors to either limit new regulations appropriately,[192] or to prevent the treaty rules from being used to 'chill' new regulations. If there is no clear conflicts clause at all, the relevant obligations might be interpreted to ensure that the environmental and other rules have precedence in cases of actual conflict, depending which one was agreed earlier in time, and also whether one could be said to be 'a special rule' between the Parties. The customary principle of integration highlights a need for balance between economic and environmental objectives, and to find a solution through interpretation may be important.[193] But as discussed earlier in this volume, it cannot be used to override clear directions in the treaty itself. In a trade or investment liberalization agreement

[188] Ibid; Charnovitz (n 97); A Panagariya, 'The Return of Labour Standards in the WTO?' *Economic Times* (6 November 1999) <http://www.columbia.edu/~ap2231/ET/et-06-nov99.htm> accessed 16 December 2020.

[189] Adopted 17 June 1999, entered into force 10 November 2000, 38 ILM 1207 7.1 and 8.

[190] An interpretation of these exceptions, in good faith in accordance with their ordinary meaning, in light of a 'purpose' of sustainable development, suggests that disciplines are not meant to block regulations in this area, VCLT, art 31.

[191] VCLT, art 30; Pauwelyn (n 105). See also Gardiner (n 15).

[192] Thomas and Trachtman (n 147) 51–52.

[193] VCLT, art 31(3)(c) permits other relevant rules of international law, see Pauwelyn (n 105) 253–254 where it is explained that this rule permits customary norms to assist in giving meaning to the terms of the treaty, such as these exceptions.

where sustainable development is treated as both an objective and a binding 'integration' principle, in contrast, it is possible that rather than detailed rules, this is precisely an area where the integration principle is expected to operate, requiring Parties to seek mutually supportive solutions to any overlaps, to integrate environmental and social development priorities into the trade, investment and other economic plans and policies and to mitigate unintended consequences in favour of a balanced outcome.

17.2.3 Not Lowering Standards to Attract Investment

One further type of provision to mitigate or avoid sustainable development impacts from bilateral or regional economic treaties involves the inclusion of specific commitments not to use lower environmental standards as a way of securing competitive advantages, in order to avoid a so-called 'race to the bottom' phenomena.[194] Similar obligations in relation to the social pillar of sustainable development are not often included, though commitments to respect certain minimum international labour standards are becoming more common, as discussed above. Such provisions may offer guidance to regulators seeking to integrate or at least balance environmental, social and economic aspects of a trade treaty.

As noted in a 2007 Organisation for Economic Co-operation and Development (OECD) Study on Environment and Trade, differences among countries' environmental standards can result in competitive advantages. To promote a level playing field for environmental regulation,[195] as mentioned in both the Chile-US ER, and the Chile-EU SIA, it is important to prevent regulators from being tempted to weaken environmental standards to secure investment, and industries from playing different host States against each other.[196] Many trade and investment agreements now adopt clauses stating that it is inappropriate to reduce the protections of domestic environmental laws:

> Parties do not waive or otherwise derogate from, or offer to waive or otherwise derogate from, such laws in a manner that weakens or reduces the protections afforded in those laws as an encouragement for trade with the other Party, or as an encouragement for the establishment, acquisition, expansion, or retention of an investment in its territory.[197]

Other trade accords include similar provisions.[198] For instance, in the Trans-Pacific Strategic Economic Partnership negotiations, Parties agreed that 'it is inappropriate to relax, or fail to enforce or administer, their environment laws and regulations to encourage trade and investment'.[199] These provisions aimed to prevent strategic distortions of trade

194 I Bastiaens and E Postnikov, 'Greening up: The Effects of Environmental Standards in EU and US Trade Agreements' (2017) 26(5) Environmental Politics 847–869.

195 OECD, *Environment and Regional Trade Agreements* (Paris, 2007) executive summary, 2.

196 EU-Chile SIA (n 42) 282–283; US-Chile Interim ER (n 70) 45–82.

197 Article 19.2.2 of the US-Australia Free Trade Agreement (signed 18 May 2004, entered into force 1 January 2005) US-Chile FTA (art 19.2.2); the similar clause in the US-Jordan Agreement (art 5.1) applies only to trade, as cited in OECD (n 195) 108.

198 See CARIFORUM-EU EPA, Canada-Peru FTA, Chile-Colombia FTA and Canada-Colombia FTA for more examples of agreements with 'not lower enviro standards' language.

199 Environmental Cooperation Agreement among the Parties to the Trans-Pacific Strategic Economic Partnership (n 1006) art 2.5.

and investment flows from 'pollution havens'. However, even though empirical studies have found either a lowering of standards or lack of enforcement, the phenomenon may be related more to lack of capacity than strategic intent.[200] In this case, such agreements 'not to lower standards', if construed narrowly, may not contribute a great deal to the improvement of social and environmental standards.[201]

Of the types of bilateral or regional economic treaties studied, as mentioned above, only those designed like the NAFTA and its USMCA successor (for relations between Canada and the US with Mexico, but not between Canada and the US), and the US-Chile FTA contain a chapter setting out specific investment-related disciplines. Article 10.12 notes that nothing in the investment chapter 'shall be construed to prevent a Party from adopting, maintaining, or enforcing any measure otherwise consistent with this Chapter that it considers appropriate to ensure that investment activity in its territory is undertaken in a manner sensitive to environmental concerns'.[202] Furthermore, at Article 19.2(2) on environmental cooperation, the Parties:

> recognize that it is inappropriate to encourage trade or investment by weakening or reducing the protections afforded in domestic environmental laws. Accordingly, each Party shall strive to ensure that it does not waive or otherwise derogate from, or offer to waive or otherwise derogate from, such laws in a manner that weakens or reduces the protections afforded in those laws as an encouragement for trade with the other Party, or as an encouragement for the establishment, acquisition, expansion, or retention of an investment in its territory.[203]

As noted in the OECD Study, however, civil, administrative and criminal enforcement of environmental laws also requires strong institutions, trained judiciary, dedicated financial resources and qualified personnel:

> Developing countries face the formidable challenge of improving their environmental frameworks, even where more stringent regulations may withdraw some of the advantages associated with existing lower standards. Moreover, access to technology required for meeting more stringent standards may require significant investments that emerging local industry finds hard to finance in a highly competitive marketplace for capital.[204]

[200] Cosbey (n 172); A Jaffe, SR Peterson and PR Portney, 'Environmental Regulation and the Competitiveness of US Manufacturing: What Does the Evidence Tell Us?' (1995) 33 Journal of Economic Literature 132–163; P Low and A Yeats, 'Do Dirty Industries Migrate?' in P Low (ed), *International Trade and Environment* (World Bank Discussion Paper No 159, 1992); JA Tobey, 'The Effects of Domestic Environmental Policies on Patterns of World Trade: An Empirical Test' (1990) 43(2) Kyklos 191–209; VD McConnell, and RM Schwab, 'The Impact of Environmental Regulation on Industry Location Decisions: The Motor Vehicle Industry' (1990) 66(1) Land Economics 67–81; REB Lucas, D Wheeler, and H Hettige, 'Economic Development, Environmental Regulation, and International Migration of Toxic Industrial Pollution: 1960-1988,' in Low (n 200) 67–86; N Birdsall and D Wheeler, 'Trade Policy and Industrial Pollution in Latin America: Where are the Pollution Havens?' (1993) 2(1) Journal of Environment and Development 137–149; SG Eskeland and AE Harrison, 'Moving to Greener Pastures? Multinationals and the Pollution Haven Hypothesis', World Bank Policy Research Working Paper No 1744, Washington, 1997.

[201] Jaffe, Peterson and Portney (n 200) 133.

[202] US-Chile FTA (n 2) art 10.12.

[203] Ibid, art 19.2(2).

[204] OECD (n 195) 108.

Indeed, cooperation and capacity-building mechanisms may be needed to complement this type of commitment. As is discussed below, trade agreements that include commitments not to lower environmental standards, such as the US-Chile FTA and the EU-Chile AA, can also provide for environmental cooperation and capacity-building, which ultimately aims at achieving a more level playing field, as regards appropriate environmental standards, among the Parties.[205] With regards to the potential of such provisions to integrate environment and social development into trade and investment agreements, it may indeed be useful to ensure that standards are not lowered, in order to attract trade or investment, as part of an effort to ensure that the trade agreement does not frustrate or prevent sustainable development events. Cooperation, however, is possibly even more important.

17.3 Sustainable Development-Related 'Cooperation Measures' for Trade and Investment Agreements

In many bilateral or regional economic treaties, beyond reactive 'mitigation' mechanisms which prevent the trade and investment treaty from actually *frustrating* sustainable development measures, States also commit to undertake new trade- or investment-related cooperation programmes in order to strengthen their laws to address existing environmental and social problems.

Among OECD members, Canada, the EU, New Zealand and the US include the most comprehensive environmental cooperation provisions, with Parties to the US Agreements attempting to put trade and environmental commitments on an equal footing and Parties to the EU Agreements including entire cooperation arrangements and partnership chapters on sustainable development. There are also further non-OECD efforts: the MERCOSUR has a Framework Agreement on the Environment, while Chile includes environmental cooperation side agreements or chapters in its new bilateral economic treaties.[206]

Such initiatives can contribute directly to the realization of sustainable development—they provide space for a proactive cooperation agenda. While labour cooperation tends to focus narrowly on the realization of human rights, cooperation related to strengthening laws on environment, natural resources, and corporate responsibility is often linked to sustainable development in bilateral or regional economic treaties.[207]

Trade and investment liberalization agreements can include parallel accords or chapters which commit to new cooperation on sustainable social and economic development, environmental protection and related matters.

The approach found in treaties involving North America differs from the one in treaties involving the EU. The North American approach tends to include quite specific and separated commitments, one on trade-related environmental issues and one on labour rights. There is little attempt to integrate, except inasmuch as sustainable development links to some environmentally related development concerns. The EU approach focuses on the Parties' general development priorities, establishing a framework for cooperation and an

[205] Ibid 105–110.
[206] Ibid 156–161.
[207] Ibid 157.

ongoing process of dialogue on all issues related to the treaty including economic and social development and environmental protection, while leaving details of cooperation to the future joint policy-making processes. The bilateral economic treaties provide examples of each distinct approach.

17.3.1 Parallel Agreements/Chapters for Cooperation on Environmental and Social Matters

In the Chile-US FTA labour chapter 18, Parties lay out a cooperative agenda to promote worker rights, establishing a Labour Cooperation Mechanism in Annex 18.5. Neither mentions sustainable development, focusing instead specifically and only on worker's rights.

The environmental chapter 19, identifies sustainable development as part of the purpose of the chapter at article 1, where Parties agree 'to collaboratively promote the optimal use of resources in accordance with the objective of sustainable development,' as well as to strengthen enforcement of domestic environmental laws, and to provide a framework for environmental collaboration.[208] Annex 19.3 on environmental cooperation identifies a series of initial joint cooperation projects. There is also a further and parallel 2003 Chile-US Environmental Cooperation Agreement which begins by 'reaffirming that economic development, social development and environmental protection are interdependent and mutually reinforcing components of sustainable development' and 'considering the necessity of augmenting institutional, professional and scientific capacity to achieve this objective for the well-being of present and future generations', then details further mechanisms to implement cooperation between the Parties, including creation of an Environmental Affairs Council that sets priorities for joint cooperation in biennial work programmes.[209] Essentially, the Parties negotiated labour and environmental provisions within the trade treaty, and also concluded separate parallel 'side agreements' with specific cooperative institutions and work programmes to address common priorities.[210] Sustainable development is highlighted as a purpose of the environmental chapters and the parallel environmental accords, and is clearly identified with economic, environmental *and* social development elements within these chapters. It is also reflected in provisions that address the private sector, such as for Parties to encourage standards of corporate responsibility. Such cooperation arrangements are also used in the US-Peru TPA,[211] the US-Colombia TPA,[212] the Canada-Peru FTA[213] and the Canada-Colombia FTA,[214] among other treaties discussed in this volume.

[208] US-Chile FTA (n 2) environmental chapter, art 1.

[209] Agreement on Environmental Cooperation between the Governments of Canada and the Republic of Chile (CCAEC) (adopted 6 February 1997, entered into force 5 July 1997) 36 ILM 1196.

[210] A Sloan, 'An Empirical Study on the Impact of the United States Chile Free Trade Agreement on Chilean Employment and Value Added' (Major Paper Presented to the Department of Economics of the University of Ottawa, 2019).

[211] US-Peru TPA (n 9) see chapter 18: objective.

[212] US-Colombia TPA (signed 22 November 2006) see chapter 18: objective.

[213] Canada-Peru FTA (signed 29 May 2008, entered into force 1 August 2009) art 1701, <http://www.sice.oas.org/TPD/AND_CAN/Final_Texts_CAN_PER_s/Index_s.asp> accessed 16 December 2020.

[214] Agreement on the Environment between Canada and the Republic of Colombia (signed 21 November 2008) as a side agreement to the Canada-Colombia FTA (entered into force 15 August 2011) Preamble, <http://www.international.gc.ca/trade-agreements-accords-commerciaux/agr-acc/colombia-colombie/can-colombia-toc-tdm-can-colombie.aspx> accessed 16 December 2020.

An earlier variation involves a format of separate side agreements that establish new institutions and non-enforcement claims procedures for other Parties and civil society. These mechanisms were originally pioneered by Canada, the US and Mexico in NAFTA and its related North American Agreement on Environmental Cooperation (NAAEC) and North American Labour Cooperation Agreement (NALCA). Most free trade agreements involving Canada since the NAFTA, including the Canada-Costa Rica FTA[215] and the Canada-Chile FTA,[216] are accompanied by parallel 'environmental side agreements' and 'labour side agreements'. This includes the 2018 US-Mexico-Canada treaty that superseded the NAFTA when it entered into force in 2020. Chile's other trade agreements also contain minimalist agreements on environmental cooperation, including, for instance, the Environmental Side Agreement of the Chile, New Zealand, Singapore and Brunei Darussalam Trans-Pacific Strategic EPA which acknowledges that all Parties 'share a similar commitment to a high level of environmental protection and standards, and to upholding these in the context of sustainable development' and recognize 'that environment and trade policies should be mutually supportive, with a view to achieving sustainable development' committing at Article 2 to 'fulfil their respective multilateral environment commitments and international plans of action designed to achieve sustainable development'.[217]

This NAFTA-style approach suggests that Parties view a commitment to sustainable development as a goal, a reason for including separate environmental collaboration agreements within (or parallel to) their trade agreements. In certain contexts, further provisions on sustainable development are also described as sub-components of the environmental cooperation agenda, a 'softer way' of referring to environmentally sound development that is to be carried out mainly in the developing country trading partner. This approach also reveals the somewhat impoverished concept of sustainable development discussed earlier in this volume, in that the parallel labour provisions do not even mention the role of labour protections in securing the 'social pillar' of sustainable development.[218] Labour cooperation can be seen as a completely separate agenda, rather than an integrated aspect of the sustainable development objective and provisions. Further, found in separated side agreements, resulting sustainable development obligations may be used as an aid to interpretation for the trade or investment liberalization agreement itself but rather, part of a more specific commitment to environmental cooperation. This may have implications should the provisions be raised in a dispute settlement. Under the VCLT, the explicit commitments to sustainable development could be interpreted to assist in integration.[219] However, a tribunal may find that such a clause, if only included in a separate environmental agreement or chapter, is simply an 'agreement relating to the treaty which was made between all the Parties in connection with the conclusion of the treaty', part of the context of the terms of the treaty, for the purpose of interpretation, rather than as a specific 'term' of the treaty, providing explicit guidance for the overlap.[220] The customary principle of integration highlights a need

215 Agreement on Environmental Cooperation between the Government of Canada and the Government of the Republic of Costa Rica (signed 23 April 2001, entered into force 1 November 2002) <http://www.ec.gc.ca/international/costarica/index_e.htm>.

216 CCAEC (n 209).

217 Environmental Side Agreement of the Trans-Pacific Strategic Economic Partnership Agreement (n 1006).

218 Charnovitz (n 97).

219 An interpretation of these provisions, in good faith in accordance with their ordinary meaning, in light of a 'purpose' of sustainable development, would demonstrate that the RTA is not meant to frustrate the Environmental Side Agreement, see VCLT, art 31(2)(a).

220 VCLT, art 31(3)(c) permits other relevant rules of international law; see Pauwelyn (n 105) 253–254 where it is explained that this rule permits customary norms to assist in giving meaning to the terms of the treaty.

for balance between economic and environmental objectives. This outcome would scarcely provide such balance.

A second and quite distinct approach is found in the EU-Chile EPA, and is commonly taken in other association agreements negotiated by the EU. In these treaties, the Parties have incorporated broad provisions for high-level political dialogue in the Association Council and its Committees, and for international cooperation on joint priorities related to social development, the environment and other issues.[221] These provisions provide forums for the Parties to develop cooperation programmes at different levels.[222] In contrast to the detailed chapters and side agreements of the US-Chile FTA, in the EU-Chile AA, the Parties focus on general topics for their cooperation programmes. In these articles, they refer directly to social and economic development priorities similar to those highlighted in the JPOI and the SDGs, and underscore the importance of integrated decision-making for environmental, economic and social policy. All cooperation is intended to take into account the principle of sustainable development, not just the environmental agreement. In addition, though, the EU-Chile AA's article 28 on cooperation on the environment recognizes the rational use of natural resources and ecosystems 'in the interests of sustainable development' as an objective, and article 44 on social development prioritizes the promotion of 'human development, the reduction of poverty and the fight against social exclusion'. Rather than separate and detailed mechanisms for only labour or environment priorities, the treaty provides for an integrated structure of dialogues, cooperation and financing. This approach is also taken in the EU-Israel AA,[223] the EU-Egypt AA,[224] the EU-Mexico EPA,[225] and the other EU association agreements.

As such, the US-Chile FTA contains detailed parallel provisions on the environment and labour. This is a change from the NAFTA model of completely separate side agreements, and a welcome one, as it makes these provisions part of the treaty's context for interpretive purposes under article 31 of the VCLT, both as annexes, and also as agreements done by Parties and related to the treaty, under article 31 2(a) and 2(b) of the VCLT.[226] Further, the principle of integration requires that States ensure environmental aspects of economic development policies, at the least, are integrated into these policies. While they are part of the treaty, as a separate chapter with certain provisions that only apply to the treaty itself, it is not clear that this type of approach, in all of these accords, can actually secure such integration. It will be for the tribunal or the regulator to decide, depending on the specific provisions agreed in each bilateral or regional economic treaty. However, the integrated provisions and institutions used by the Parties in the EU-Chile AA also have their weaknesses. In particular, the lack of detailed mechanisms for monitoring and implementation suggests that, while the Association Council may make integrated decisions, it may not be able to ensure that sustainable development priorities are actually implemented in practice, among other issues.

Certain common elements can also be identified between the two approaches. In particular, in both types of accords, Parties often include provisions to establish new senior-level

[221] Title I; see Chapter 3 of this volume.

[222] M Maresceau, 'Bilateral Agreements concluded by the European Community' (2004) 309 Recueil des Cours de l'Académie de Droit International 125, 311; Ignacio Garcia Bercero, 'Dispute Settlement in European Union Free Trade Agreements: Lessons Learned?' in Bartels and Ortino (n 45) 383.

[223] EU-Israel AA (signed November 1995, entered into force June 2000) [2000] OJ L 147, art 50.

[224] EU-Egypt AA (signed June 2001, entered into force June 2004) COM(2001) 184 final, art 44.

[225] EU-Mexico EPA (signed 8 December 1997, entered into force 1 October 2000) [2000] OJ L 276, art 34.

[226] VCLT, art 31(1) and (2), and see Gardiner (n 15). See also discussion in Chapter 3.

councils or other similar institutions, with regular meetings. In these treaties, the Parties also agree to undertake common work programmes on specific *trade-related* environmental or social initiatives, accompanied by commitments to provide capacity-building, technology transfer and financing. Collaboration projects as part of these initiatives can address issues identified in the environmental and labour reviews, and in the sustainability impact assessments of the trade and investment liberalization agreements themselves.

Certain accords also provide recourse through State-to-State dispute settlement, factual report processes or other complaints mechanisms when environmental or social rules are violated. These further cooperative social and environmental mechanisms are comparatively analysed in turn below.

17.3.2 Institutions for social and environmental cooperation

In many trade agreements or related side agreements, the Parties have set up specific institutions to implement cooperation related to sustainable development. These institutions manage the cooperation arrangements between the Parties. Their mandates and levels of responsibility vary, depending on the types of commitments undertaken by the Parties in corresponding free trade and parallel social or environmental treaties.

In the US-Chile FTA environment chapter 19, at article 19.3, Parties establish an Environment Affairs Council comprising cabinet level or equivalent representatives of the Parties, or their designees, who meet at least once a year to discuss implementation. It is mandated to hold public sessions, and to ensure a process for promoting public participation in its work, to develop and implement cooperative environmental activities. According to Article 19.3, all decisions of the Council shall be taken by mutual agreement and shall be made public unless otherwise decided. Each Party may convene a national consultative or advisory committee to advise it on implementation issues. In article 19.5, the Parties 'recognize the importance of strengthening capacity to protect the environment and *promote sustainable development* in concert with strengthening trade and investment relations between them', and agree to undertake specific cooperative projects in Annex 19.3; as well as to promptly negotiate a US-Chile Environmental Cooperation Agreement to establish priorities for further cooperative environmental activities. Each Party commits to take into account public comments and recommendations and to share information on their experiences in assessing and taking into account positive or negative environmental effects of trade agreements and policies. Due to this exchange, such IAs may well be considered part of the *travaux préparatoires* and subsequent practices of the treaty regime under the rules of the VCLT article 32, as supplementary means of interpretation that can assist in confirming the ordinary meaning of terms, since these can include all materials available to negotiators of all the Parties.[227]

On 17 June 2003, as agreed in chapter 19 and Annex 19.3, Chile and the United States signed an Agreement on Environmental Cooperation as part of the US-Chile FTA.[228] In the Preamble, the Parties reaffirm that 'economic development, social development and

[227] Gardiner (n 15) 99–106, but see *Chile-Price Band* dispute (n 27 of Chapter 10) 230.

[228] Chile-US Agreement on Environmental Cooperation (signed 17 June 2003, entered into force 1 November 2004) <http://www.sice.oas.org/TPD/CHL_USA/ECA/ECA_e.pdf> accessed 16 December 2020.

environmental protection are interdependent and mutually reinforcing components of sustainable development'. Article 1 states that the 'objective of this Agreement is to establish a framework for cooperation between the Parties to promote the conservation and protection of the environment, the prevention of pollution and degradation of natural resources and ecosystems, and the rational use of natural resources, *in support of sustainable development*' (emphasis added). According to article II, the Parties establish a Joint Commission for Environmental Cooperation that is co-chaired by designated high level officials of the Department of State of the United States and the Ministry of Foreign Affairs of Chile. Each Party's Chair designates up to five representatives from its government agencies to serve on the Commission, and identifies a point of contact. The Commission is responsible for establishing and developing programmes of work; examining and evaluating cooperative activities; making recommendations and undertaking other activities. It meets at least every two years and each Party assumes the costs of its own participation. In article IV, the Parties also agree that the Commission should promote the development of opportunities for public participation in cooperative projects and that each Party should engage its public in accordance with its own domestic procedures.

These provisions are highly streamlined versions of the institutions established in the NAAEC between Canada, Mexico and the United States, which is the prototype for the 'separate, parallel' institutional approach.[229] Under this agreement, Canada, the US and Mexico established a Commission for Environmental Cooperation (CEC) with a Council of Ministers, a Joint Public Advisory Committee and a professional Secretariat. The Council is the CEC governing body which, composed of Environment Ministers and equivalents, meets at least once a year to discuss CEC programmes and activities.[230] The Joint Public Advisory Committee (JPAC) is composed of fifteen members, five from each of the three countries (Canada, Mexico and the United States).[231] Its members act independently and their responsibility is to provide the Council with their advice on all matters within the scope of the NAAEC. A few years of experience with the distinct models reveals that for sustainable development, the existence of an active secretariat can be a key factor for success.[232] The NAAEC Secretariat is located in Montreal with a liaison office in Mexico City. It provides technical and operational support to the Council, as well as to committees and groups set up by the Council, and implements initiatives and conducts research in core programme areas on North American environment, environmental law and standards and other environment and trade issues, in addition to processing citizen submissions on enforcement

[229] See MC Cordonier Segger, 'Enhancing Social and Environmental Cooperation in the Americas,' in MC Cordonier Segger and M Leichner Reynal (eds), *Beyond the Barricades: The Americas Trade and Sustainable Development Agenda* (Aldershot, Ashgate 2005) 183–222; Deere and Esty (n 172). See also A de Mestral, 'The NAFTA Commission on Environmental Cooperation-Voice for the North American Environment?' in A Kiss, D Shelton and K Ishibashi (eds), *Economic Globalization and Compliance with International Environmental Agreements* (The Hague, International Environmental Law and Policy Series 63, Kluwer Law International 2003); HL Kong and LK Wroth, *NAFTA and Sustainable Development* (Cambridge, CUP 2015).

[230] Specifically, the Council has a cooperative work plan based on priority areas, including: establishing limits for specific air and marine pollutants; environmental assessments of projects with transboundary implications; and reciprocal court access for damage or injury resulting from transboundary pollution.

[231] A de Mestral, 'The North American Free Trade Agreement: a comparative analysis' (1998) 275 Recueil des Cours de l'Académie de Droit International 219, 375; see also CEC, <http://www.cec.org/who_we_are/jpac/index.cfm> accessed 16 December 2020.

[232] Interview with Andy Bowcott, Manager, International Relations, Environment Canada, and Canada's Chief Negotiator for the Canada-Chile, Canada-Costa Rica, Canada-Central America Environmental Side Agreements (Ottawa, January–April 2003).

matters. A more recent model is found in the Canada-Chile Agreement on Environmental Cooperation (CCAEC),[233] which also provides a framework for bilateral cooperation on environmental issues.[234] The CCAEC establishes a commission for environmental cooperation, mechanisms for access to environmental information and a joint public advisory council process.[235] The annexes, which phase the agreement into Chilean environmental law, led to a comprehensive and valuable revision of environmental law enforcement in Chile.[236] Rather than one common Secretariat, the Parties established national secretariats to implement the CCAEC, recognizing prior commitments under other environmental agreements. These institutional arrangements are not, of course, the only option available to the Parties. For example, under the US-CAFTA-DR FTA, an existing institution, the Secretariat for Central American Economic Integration (SIECA) provides a Secretariat to deal with public submissions by citizens from all Parties, except US citizens, who may bring submissions before the CEC established under the NAAEC.

With regard to social development and labour rights, the US-Chile FTA labour chapter 18 lays out a cooperative agenda to promote workers' rights. In this accord, Parties agree that it is inappropriate to weaken or reduce domestic labour protections to encourage trade or investment, and requires that Parties shall effectively enforce their own domestic labour laws. A cooperative mechanism is provided specifically to promote respect for the principles embodied in the 1998 ILO Declaration on Fundamental Principles and Rights at Work,[237] and to promote compliance with ILO Convention 182 on the Worst Forms of Child Labour.[238] In article 18.4 the Parties establish a Labour Affairs Council of cabinet-level representatives, to pursue agreed labour objectives and to oversee chapter implementation and the activities of a Labour Cooperation Mechanism established under article 18.5, with a public session. It establishes a system of contact points within labour ministries, and agrees that the Council shall establish its own work programme and procedures, such as expert groups, or consultations with NGOs. All decisions of the Council are taken by mutual agreement of the Parties and made public, unless otherwise decided, and each Party has the option to convene a public national consultative or advisory committee. A Labour Cooperation Mechanism is also set out in Annex 18.5. Although the 2002 WSSD outcomes, including the JPOI, place high emphasis on the social pillar of sustainable development and the contribution of social and labour rights institutions, none of these provisions mentions sustainable development. Essentially, the US-Chile FTA labour chapter 18 builds on earlier institutional models pioneered in the 1994 NAALC, which commits the Parties to 'improve working conditions and living standards' in all parties, to 'protect, enhance and enforce basic workers' rights', through eleven core labour principles.[239] The NAALC establishes a

233 CCAEC (n 209) arts 2 and 10, Sections 1 and 2.

234 Notes of interviews with A Bowcott, Manager, Environment Canada, International Relations Canada, and Canada's Chief Negotiator for the Canada-Chile, Canada-Costa Rica, Canada-Central America Environmental Side Agreements, January-April 2003, on file with the author.

235 W Durbin, *A Comparison of the Environmental Provisions of the NAFTA, the Canada-Chile Trade Agreement and the Mexican-European Community Trade Agreement* (New Haven, Yale Centre for Environmental Law and Policy 2000).

236 Ibid. See also MC Cordonier Segger, 'Enhancing Social and Environmental Cooperation in the Americas' in Cordonier Segger and Leichner Reynal (n 229) 181, 204–205.

237 ILO, Declaration on Fundamental Principles and Rights at Work (19 June 1998) 37 ILM 1237.

238 ILO Convention No 182 Concerning the Prohibition and Immediate Action for the Elimination of the Worst Forms of Child Labour (adopted 17 June 1999, entered into force 10 November 2000) 38 ILM 1207.

239 NAFTA (n 6) art 1.

Commission for Labour Co-operation, with a Ministerial Council and Secretariat, assisted by national administrative offices (NAOs) in each country.[240]

In contrast, the EU-Chile AA does not charge particular institutions with environmental, social development or labour-related cooperation as such. However, the agreement establishes an Association Council and an Association Committee, special committees for specific issues, a political dialogue supported by an Association Parliamentary Committee and a Joint Consultative Committee as a mechanism for the engagement of civil society. These institutions are established in recognition by the Parties of a 'need to promote economic and social progress for their peoples, taking into account the principle of sustainable development' and are guided by principles of 'promotion of sustainable economic and social development and equitable distribution of the benefits of the Association'.[241]

The Association Council is composed of high-level representatives such as the EU President of the Council of the European Union and the Minister of Foreign Affairs of Chile. It meets and examines major issues of common interest and is entitled to take decisions that are binding on both Parties. It is governed by specific procedures agreed in Athens on 27 March 2003.[242] The Association Committee is in charge of the implementation of the Association Agreement, and composed of EU and Chilean senior officials. Both Council and Committee are chaired alternately by the EU or Chile, and the Council can create Special Committees to address any specific issues of interest. The Parliamentary Committee integrates members of the European Parliament and of the Chilean National Congress. In the Political Dialogue, the Parties 'commit to discuss and exchange information on joint initiatives concerning any issue of mutual interest and any other international issue with a view to pursuing common goals, in particular, security, stability, democracy and *regional development*',[243] through periodic meetings of heads of State, foreign affairs Ministers and senior officials. The Joint Consultative Committee assists the Association Council to promote dialogue and cooperation between European and Chilean civil society on all economic and social aspects of the relations between the Community and Chile, either upon request by the Association Council or on its own initiative. As such, a special committee, parliamentary exchange or political dialogue session could, conceivably be struck on any issue related to the environment, social or economic development issues covered in the agreement, and these processes would be carried out in accordance with the principle of sustainable development.

Similar provisions are found in the most recent EU-Central America EPA, EU-CARIFORUM EPA, and EU-Colombia and Peru FTA, where Parties commit to cooperation on environmental or social agendas. For example, the EU-CARIFORUM EPA established a Trade and Development Committee responsible, among other things, for overseeing the implementation of the trade and development provisions of the treaty, which would include provisions linked to sustainable development.[244] For instance, the committee would

[240] Ibid, arts 8–9, 12, 15 and 21. See NAALC Secretariat, <http://www.naalc.org> accessed 16 December 2020. See also, in particular, Commission for Labour Cooperation, *Comparative Guide to Labour and Employment Laws in North America. Labour Relations Law in North America* (Washington, NAALC 2000).

[241] EU-Chile AA (n 4) Preamble.

[242] EU-Chile Association Council, 'First Meeting of the EU-Chile Association Council: Joint Communiqué' (27 March 2003) UE-CL 3903/03 (Presse 97) <http://www.sice.oas.org/TPD/CHL_EU/Implementation/Joint_Council/ICouncil_e.pdf> accessed 16 December 2020.

[243] Ibid (emphasis added).

[244] EU-CARIFORUM EPA (n 29) art 230.

be involved in overseeing collaboration in areas such as quality standards for food production and marketing,[245] or promotion of private investment and public–private partnerships in viable production.[246] As another illustration, the EU-Central America EPA leaves the authority for sustainable development-related measures directly under the purview of the Association Council itself, assisted by the Association Committee.[247]

These provisions could directly address particular opportunities raised in the SIAs to these treaties. For instance, the EU-ACP SIA noted a strong need for coordination in a variety of areas regarding trade and over-exploitation of fisheries.[248]

For a customary principle that environmental and social concerns must be integrated into economic development plans, with the costs of such integration to be borne by the proponents, these new types of institutions for sustainable development cooperation may be important. For instance, periodic SIAs could identify appropriate mitigation measures, leading to exchanges among the Parties at several levels and even binding decisions on actions to address the concerns raised. This iterative process, while slow, would allow environmental and social to be slowly integrated into the economic and broader political cooperation agenda of the Parties as their economies and markets also became more open to each other.

17.3.3 Common Work Programmes on Specific Environmental or Social projects

Many of the bilateral or regional economic treaties studied provide for common work programmes that include plans to strengthen laws, regulations and standards on environmental quality, on social development and on other matters related to sustainable development. By cooperating to strengthen these laws and regulations, in parallel to the trade treaty, Parties can send a strong signal that they do not mean to weaken existing domestic laws, while also directly addressing concerns associated with the second key tension identified earlier in this volume.

For instance, in the environment chapter 19 of the US-Chile FTA at article 19.5 on environmental cooperation, the Parties recognize 'the importance of strengthening capacity to protect the environment and *promote sustainable development in concert with strengthening trade and investment relations*',[249] and establish an Annex 19.3 on environmental cooperation, noting that 'cooperation on environmental matters provides enhanced opportunities to improve the environment and to advance common commitments on sustainable development'.[250] Several initiatives are prioritized in Annex 19.3, most of which require strengthened laws and regulations:

- developing a pollutant release and transfer register (PRTR) in Chile;
- reducing mining pollution;

245 Ibid, art 43.2(c).
246 Ibid, art 43.2(d).
247 EU-Colombia-Peru FTA (n 21) art 154.2.
248 PricewaterhouseCoopers, *Sustainability Impact Assessment of the EU-ACP Economic Partnership Agreements: Key Findings, Recommendations and Lessons Learned* (Paris, 2007) [EU-ACP SIA] arts 6 and 7.
249 US-Chile FTA (n 2) art 19.5 on environmental cooperation (emphasis added).
250 Ibid, Annex 19.3 on environmental cooperation.

- increasing the use of cleaner fuels;
- sharing private sector expertise;
- reducing methyl bromide emissions;
- improving agricultural practices;
- improving wildlife protection and management; and
- improving environmental enforcement and compliance assurance;

These relate to concerns highlighted in the US-Chile ER process, which as discussed above emphasized potential impacts of pollution due to increases in mining and transport activities,[251] impacts of increases in methyl bromide emissions and other expanding agricultural trade[252] and potential loss of species and habitat due to deforestation for forestry exports.[253] These initiatives attempt to mitigate those concerns in practical ways, through cooperation.[254] According to the United States, these initiatives are being pursued 'for the advancement of our common commitment to achieve sustainable development'.[255]

Commitments to strengthen laws through cooperation are further operationalized in the 2003 US-Chile Environmental Cooperation Agreement and its subsequent work programmes,[256] with the objective at article 1 being carried out *in support of sustainable development*.[257]

In article III, the Parties commit to establish work programmes based on national priorities. Activities include the exchange of information on environmental policies, laws and practices in both countries; the exchange of information on the implementation of multilateral environmental agreements to which the United States and Chile are both Parties and the promotion of 'good domestic practices leading to sustainable management of the environment.'

In spite of the commitment made in the US Trade Promotion Act that equivalent provisions will be set up for trade, environment and labour in any US Trade Agreement,[258] the US–Chile Environmental Cooperation Agreement establishes a framework for cooperation that seems significantly less detailed and binding than the economic disciplines found in the trade agreement.[259] A great deal is left to future elaboration in a series of annual joint US-Chile work programmes, which fortunately have not been inconsequential.[260] For

[251] Ibid 33–37.
[252] US-Chile Interim ER (n 70) 31–32.
[253] Ibid, 16–19.
[254] US-Chile Final ER (n 13) 19–26.
[255] Department of State, 'U.S.-Chile Sign Agreement on Environmental Cooperation' Remarks at the Signing of an Agreement Between the United States and the Republic of Chile on Environmental Cooperation by Paula J Dobriansky, Santiago, Chile, 17 June 2003, <http://www.state.gov/g/rls/rm/2003/21772.htm> accessed 16 December 2020.
[256] Agreement between the Government of the United States of America and the Government of the Republic of Chile on Environmental Cooperation (signed 17 June 2003, entry into force 1 November 2004) <http://www.sice.oas.org/TPD/CHL_USA/ECA/ECA_e.pdf> accessed 16 December 2020, Preamble.
[257] Ibid, art 1.
[258] Trade Act of 2002, 107 PL 210; 116 Stat 933; 2002 Enacted HR 3009; 107 Enacted HR 3009 <http://www.sice.oas.org/ctyindex/USA/tradeact/act1.asp> accessed 16 December 2020.
[259] OECD (n 195) 93. Gratitude is due to R Tarasofsky and D van Hoogstraten for their advice on these points.
[260] E Gitli and C Murillo, 'A Latin American Agenda for a Trade and Environment Link in the FTAA', in Deere and Esty (n 172) 273.

2005–2006, for instance, area 3 of this work programme lays out detailed priorities, activating means also highlighted in the 2002 JPOI such as:

> capacity building ... to improve the effectiveness of enforcement and compliance with environmental laws, norms and regulations; encouraging ... sound environmental practices and technologies, particularly in business enterprises; promoting sustainable development and management of environmental resources, including wild fauna and flora, and protected wild areas; civil society participation in the environmental decision-making process; and environmental education ...

These five areas do respond directly to concerns identified during the US-Chile ER process, committing to strengthen enforcement and compliance with environmental laws, norms and regulations.[261]

For such joint work programmes to succeed in strengthening laws and standards, they must be implemented effectively. Information exchange and capacity-building, technical assistance, financing and constant monitoring are needed to ensure that compliance actually improves.[262]

In the US-Chile Environmental Cooperation Agreement, there are provisions for these elements. At article III(2)(b), the Agreement commits the Parties to 'the exchange of information on environmental policies, laws and practices in both countries'.[263] Provisions on environmental information exchange and capacity-building provisions address both levels of concerns: building domestic environmental management and sustainable development capacity, and improving capacity to implement MEAs. At article 19.9 and in Annex 19.3 on environmental cooperation at article 2b(vi) of the US-Chile FTA, Parties declare that the US-Chile Environmental Cooperation Agreement will 'promote the understanding and effective implementation of [MEAs] to which both Parties are Party'. In the Environmental Cooperation Agreement itself at article III(c,d) this becomes a commitment for 'the exchange of information on the implementation of [MEAs] to which the United States and Chile are both Parties; and the promotion of good domestic practices leading to sustainable management of the environment'. The Canada-Chile Environmental Cooperation Agreement[264] and the Canada-Costa Rica Environmental Cooperation Agreement,[265] respectively, also commit to support and build on MEAs through cooperative ventures. Similarly, in the US-Peru TPA[266] and the United States-Colombia TPA,[267] Parties agree to build capacity to implement their MEAs, developing joint projects to improve compliance. It has been noted that:

> the most impressive results of capacity building associated with [an RTA] have come out of the North American Commission for Environmental Co-operation (NACEC)—the

261 US-Chile Interim ER (n 70).

262 OECD (n 195) 99–101.

263 Agreement between the Government of the United States of America and the Government of the Republic of Chile on Environmental Cooperation (n 256) art III(2)(b).

264 Canada-Chile Environmental Cooperation Agreement (adopted 6 February 1997) 36 ILM 1196.

265 Canada-Costa Rica Environmental Cooperation Agreement (adopted 23 April 2001, entered into force 1 November 2002).

266 US-Peru TPA (n 9) art 18.13.

267 US-Colombia TPA (n 212) art 18.13.

institution set up to administer the NAAEC. Capacity building is only one part of the activities of the CEC, which has two other priority areas for trilateral co-operation: information for decision-making, and trade and environment. But to some extent, all CEC activities result in increased capacity for environmental management.[268]

Technical assistance is also required to implement joint work programmes, and the US-Chile Environmental Cooperation Agreement at article V highlights several practical co-operative mechanisms, including the exchange of professionals, technicians and specialists; the organization of joint seminars, training sessions and outreach programmes; support for environmental research and technology; facilitation of academic, industry and government links and consultation on national environmental programmes. According to article VI, the CEC can facilitate direct cooperation between firms, universities and others on these matters, even concluding arrangements under the Agreement, engaging other stakeholders. Article 19.4 (2, 3) of the environmental cooperation chapter also commits to promote public participation in implementation, and in Article 2(a) of the US-Chile FTA at Annex 19.3 on environmental cooperation, the Parties note that they 'have agreed to take into account public input regarding priority areas for bilateral cooperation' in the future.

Furthermore, financing is key to success for such work programmes. As noted in an OECD review:

> Adequate financing is a crucial element in the implementation of the environmental co-operation activities foreseen in the context of bilateral or regional economic treaties. Nevertheless, few trade and investment agreements or side agreements on the environment specifically address financial issues. When they do, it is generally in an open-ended way.[269]

This challenge is manifest in the US-Chile Environmental Cooperation Agreement. At article VII, Parties simply recognize that all 'cooperative activities under this Agreement shall be subject to the availability of funds and human resources and to the applicable laws and regulations in each Party'. Such arrangements may include:

a) cooperative activities jointly financed as agreed by the Parties;
b) cooperative activities in which each institution, organization, or agency will assume the costs of its own participation; and
c) cooperative activities financed, as appropriate, by private institutions, foundations, or public international organizations.[270]

The Canada-Costa Rica FTA provides that funding for the cooperative activities agreed by the Parties will be determined on a case-by-case basis.

[268] OECD (n 195) 81.
[269] Ibid 86.
[270] Agreement between the Government of the United States of America and the Government of the Republic of Chile on Environmental Cooperation (n 256) art VII.

> Behind those general statements in the body of the Agreement, however, are often detailed programmes and the corresponding budgets, which reflect the willingness of the [P]arties to effectively implement their environmental co-operation programmes. These budgets include funding to support the institutions established under the RTA on institutional arrangements, as well as the various programmes of co-operation.[271]

While only general provisions are found in the treaty, this does not mean no resources have been made available. Indeed, both Chilean and US sources have been funding programmes under the treaty, consistently, though there is ample space for further investments.[272]

Monitoring and evaluation is also key to ensure these accords are implemented effectively. The US-CAFTA-DR Environmental Cooperation Agreement provides a cooperative framework of priorities and periodically agreed work programmes, like the others. However, among its innovative features, the US-CAFTA-DR Environmental Cooperation Agreement also establishes benchmarks to identify short, medium and long-term goals for improving environmental protection, and provides for independent, outside monitoring of progress in meeting the benchmarks. According to a recent study by the Organization of American Studies (OAS), such provisions can also advance the agenda for environmental cooperation significantly.[273]

With regard to the 'social pillar' of sustainable development, the Chile-US labour chapter 18 and its related Labour Cooperation Mechanism are much less explicitly linked to sustainable development. Essentially, the Parties agree that:

> cooperation provides enhanced opportunities for the Parties to promote respect for the principles embodied in the *ILO Declaration on Fundamental Principles and Rights at Work and its Follow-up (1998)*, compliance with *ILO Convention 182 Concerning the Prohibition and Immediate Action for the Elimination of the Worst Forms of Child Labor (1999)*.[274]

They establish a Labour Cooperation Mechanism, which is set out in an Annex 18.5. In this Annex, they commit to cooperate on:

> issues such as (a) *fundamental rights and their effective application*; ... (b) *labor relations*, [... including] the resolution of labor disputes; (c) *working conditions* [... including] occupational safety and health; (d) *issues related to small and medium enterprises* [... including] improvement of working conditions; (e) *social protections* [... including] social programs for workers and their families; [...] and (g) implications of economic integration between the Parties for advancing each Party's labor objectives.[275]

With regard to implementation, at 5 the Parties agree to carry out cooperative activities under this Annex, including, *inter alia*, through exchanges of government delegations,

[271] OECD (n 195) 86.

[272] Follow-up interviews with Dr Edda Rossi, International Affairs Ministry, Government of Chile, and David van Hoogstraten, former Senior Official, USTR.

[273] OAS, ECLAC and IDB, *A Comparative Guide to the Chile-United States Free Trade Agreement and the Dominican Republic-Central America-United States Free Trade Agreement* (Washington, OAS 2005).

[274] Labour Cooperation Mechanism, chapter 18 on labour cooperation, art 18.5.

[275] Ibid.

academics, information sharing and by drawing on the expertise of academic and other institutions. At 6 they also commit to consider views of their respective worker and employer representatives, as well as other members of civil society in identifying areas for co-operation and carrying out cooperative activities.[276] Similar 'labour rights' chapters and side-agreements have been included in other regional trade agreements.[277] However, as mentioned above, these commitments, while consistent with the 'social pillar' of sustainable development, do not explicitly incorporate any reference to sustainable development. The Parties appear to consider labour rights as a separate agenda unrelated to sustainability.

A distinct and integrated approach governs cooperative activities under the EU-Chile AA and other similar accords. In these treaties, there is clearer integration between social, environmental and economic priorities. Detailed programmes are not included in the treaty, but instead, Parties agree to use economic, financial and technical cooperation to implement the AA's objectives and principles in a range of key areas that are similar to those highlighted in the 2002 JPOI and in the 2015 SDGs.

For instance, in the EU-Chile AA, Part III of the Association Agreement focuses on an integrated cooperation agenda. At article 16.1, Parties commit to establish close cooperation to promote '*social development, which should go hand in hand with economic development and the protection of the environment*'.[278] At article 28, covering cooperation on the environment, the Parties agree to encourage conservation and improvement of the environment, prevention of contamination and degradation of natural resources and ecosystems and rational use of the latter in the interests of sustainable development. They recognize as priorities:

- the relationship between poverty and the environment;
- the environmental impact of economic activities;
- environmental problems and land-use management;
- projects to reinforce Chile's environmental structures and policies;
- exchanges on environmental standards and models, training and education; and
- environmental education and training to involve citizens more.

These last three, especially, are important for strengthening laws and law enforcement, within a broader agenda of reinforcement, capacity-building and exchange.

These priorities respond to concerns raised in the SIA,[279] but do not focus only on these concerns. Rather, broad topics are being identified, including for instance 'exchanges on environmental standards and models, training and education', as markers for governments, civil society, academics, the private sector and others to propose collaborative ventures. Further topics for cooperation hold new potential to deliver on sustainable development-related agendas as well. In article 29 on consumer protection, for instance, the Parties

[276] MJ Bolle, 'Overview of Labor Enforcement Issues in Free Trade Agreements' (CRS Report prepared for Members and Committees of Congress. Order Code RS22823, 2016). (2016); S Polaski, 'Protecting Labor Rights through Trade Agreements' (2004) 10 University of California Davis Journal of International Law and Policy 13.

[277] Bolle (n 276).

[278] EU-Chile AA (n 4) art 16.1; see also EU-CARIFORUM EPA (n 29) art 3.2(a). 'The application of this Agreement shall fully take into account the human, cultural, economic, social, health and environmental best interests of their respective population and of future generations.'

[279] EU-Chile SIA (n 42) 193–200 for summary of environmental impacts.

prioritize the need to establish mutual interconnected warning systems for dangerous goods. This programme has been set up in recent years, and linked to others.[280]

The EU-Colombia-Peru FTA:

> recognises the sovereign right of each Party to establish its domestic policies and priorities on sustainable development, and its own levels of environmental and labour protection, consistent with internationally recognized standards and agreements referred to in Articles 269 and 270, and to adopt or modify accordingly its relevant laws, regulations and policies; each Party shall strive to ensure that its relevant laws and policies provide for and encourage high levels of environmental and labour protection.[281]

The EU-CARIFORUM EPA contains similar commitments at article 184, though it focuses on health rather than labour, whereby each CARIFORUM State shall 'seek to ensure that its own environmental and public health laws and policies provide for and encourage high levels of environmental and public health protection, and shall strive to continue to improve those laws and policies'. These promises to 'strive' are not particularly promising, but respond to the priorities highlighted in the SIAs. Opportunities for collaboration to strengthen environmental and other laws were identified in the EU-Andean SIA,[282] and also in the EU-ACP SIA.[283]

These commitments can be compared to the MERCOSUR Framework Agreement on Environment[284] in which Parties agree on a sustainable development objective, and commit to work together to secure and to coordinate their compliance with MEAs and national policies and to harmonize their legislation on environment and natural resources. Specific thematic areas identified for this cooperation include 'sustainable management of natural resources' and 'environmentally sustainable productive activities'. Parties develop Work Plans and the MERCOSUR bodies follow up. The 2005 Declaration on a MERCOSUR Biodiversity Strategy also includes detailed action for cooperation among Parties.[285] While these mechanisms are still weak, they have survived successive rounds of budget cuts, and even now, attract certain levels of financing for implementation.[286]

In the EU EPAs, there are also provisions for information exchange, capacity-building and technical assistance to strengthen laws, though where there are less marked differences in levels of development, it is mainly aimed at sharing and exchanging information. As noted by the OECD: '[i]nformation is a critical part of establishing comparable methodologies and common indicators for the effective monitoring and response to environmental problems.' The EU-Chile AA emphasizes the need to build and strengthen scientific, technical, human and institutional capacity for environmental management. However, according to the OECD:

> ... the failure of the agreements to identify more concrete projects and to create specific institutions to advance co-operation activities could prevent such comprehensive

280 Ibid.
281 EU-Colombia-Peru FTA (n 21) art 268.
282 EU-Andean SIA (n 143) 42–56.
283 EU-ACP SIA (n 248) 28–51, 155–186.
284 Acuerdo Marco sobre Medio Ambiente del Mercosur (signed 22 June 2001) reprinted in Ley Nacional 25.841 Argentinean Official Bulletin (15 January 2004) (Mercosur Framework Agreement on the Environment).
285 Lineamientos para una Estrategia Mercosur sobre Conservación y Manejo Sostenible de la Biodiversidad (adopted 18 November 2005) Mercosur decision MERCOSUR/IV RMMAM/ACUERDO Nº 03/05.
286 Interview with D van Hoostraten, former senior negotiator, USTR.

provisions from being implemented. The provisions incorporated in these agreements establishing the approximation of laws, including legislation on the environment and on natural resources, as a condition of strengthening the economic links between the parties, may already be defining the priorities for future co-operation.[287]

The Memorandum of Understanding (MoU) on EU-Chile Cooperation, which defines cooperation programme guidelines for 2000–2006, includes an Integrated Natural Resources Management Programme, noting that the 'economic growth model of the country based on raw material export produced pressure on the natural resources, especially at the level of the non-renewable, which can endanger the viability of the various eco-systems in the future'.[288] To address this problem, the MoU sets out various strategies and provides specific technical and financial assistance. Some is specifically trade related, but it also aims to improve laws and policies for sustainable resources development, including for regional development and land-use planning. At article 50 on triangular and bi-regional co-operation, the 'Parties recognise the *value of international cooperation for the promotion of equitable and sustainable development processes*'.

Turning to the social agenda, the EU-Chile AA also makes commitments for social co-operation at Title V. In article 43, the Parties establish a social dialogue, to improve living conditions and integration into society for 'social partners' (minorities, etc). In article 44 on social cooperation, the Parties recognize 'the importance of social development, which must go hand in hand with economic development'. They agree to:

> give priority to the creation of employment and respect for fundamental social rights, notably by promoting the relevant conventions of the International Labour Organisation.[289]

This social cooperation work programme includes, *inter alia*, 'promoting human development, the reduction of poverty and the fight against social exclusion, by generating innovative and reproducible projects involving vulnerable and marginalized social sectors; promoting the role of women in the economic and social development process and promoting specific programmes for youth; . . . developing an efficient and equitable health system, based on solidarity principles; promoting projects and programmes which generate opportunities for the creation of employment within micro-, small and medium-sized enterprises; and promoting programmes of land management with special attention to areas with higher social and environmental vulnerability'.[290] Indeed, in article 45 on cooperation related to gender, the Parties prioritize cooperation that will 'contribute to easing women's access to all necessary resources for the full exercise of their fundamental rights'.

These are substantive commitments in international economic, environmental and social areas, and the Parties have agreed to implement them in accordance with a principle of sustainable development. The Parties are given space to implement through voluntary

[287] OECD (n 195) 95.
[288] As cited in ibid 86.
[289] Article 44, social cooperation.
[290] EU-Chile AA (n 4) art 44.

initiatives and through the Association Council and Committees, which can, if necessary, balance priorities. The specific implementation structures and budget provisions are considerably less detailed than those included in the US-Chile FTA and related side agreements or cooperation mechanisms. However, certain steps have still been taken to secure implementation, and activate the cooperation envisioned. The problem here, of courses, is to ensure that sustainable development has space on a crowded cooperation agenda. It is certainly not the only priority. As noted in the 2005 Joint Declaration of the EU-Chile Association Council:

> 8. Ministers acknowledged that the EU-Chile policy dialogues on sectoral issues within the framework of Article 52 of the Association Agreement ... represent a new approach that leads to a strengthening and deepening of our bilateral relationship. Ministers took note of the Parties intention to extend this policy dialogue to other areas such as employment and social policies, youth, culture, the information society, environment and others.[291]

Implementation is being reported and further encouraged through regular meetings of the Parties at all levels, with policy priorities being set jointly by the Parties in their Association Councils. According to the third Association Council Meeting of May 2008, which adopted the 2008 Joint Declaration of the EU-Chile Association Council, the focus of 2007–2010 work programme cooperation activities by the Association was on innovation and competitiveness, post-secondary education cooperation and social cohesion. These issues are specifically highlighted in Agenda 21 and as part of the 'social pillar' of the JPOI. In the Association Agreement, they are addressed in an integrated way that is consistent with the JPOI. Financing is a challenge for this treaty. In article 53 on resources, Parties commit to 'providing, within the limits of their capacities and through their own channels, the appropriate resources, including financial resources'. However, these financing commitments do, actually, appear to have channelled certain resources towards implementation of the treaty.[292] The EC, the government of Chile and related partners support these priorities with new financing commitments totalling more than EUR 45 million.[293] Both work programmes under the two agreements concluded with Chile, are to some extent under implementation.[294]

[291] European Commission 'Joint Declaration of the II. EU-Chile Association Council' (EU Doc 9352/05) Luxembourg, 26 May 2005 (Press Release 125).

[292] Parties agreed to concentrate bilateral development cooperation for the 2007–2010 period on the following priority sectors: (1) Innovation and competitiveness, which will have a total budget of EUR 20.5 million over four years, of which EUR 10.25 million are EC funds; (2) Social cohesion, with an emphasis on cooperation programmes focused on supporting education, social protection and employment. To this end, a total of EUR 20.5 million will be allocated, of which 10.25 million euros will be EC funds for the same period; (3) Higher education, through the launching of an Erasmus Mundus External Cooperation Window-Chile, for which the EC contribution amounts to EUR 4.92 million (100 per cent) to finance 140 masters, doctoral and post-doctoral scholarships for Chilean students in Europe.

[293] Council of the European Union 'Joint Communiqué 9540/08 of the third Chile-EU Troika Summit' (EC Doc C/08/131), Lima, Peru, 17 May 2008 (Press Release 131).

[294] Notes from interviews with P Rosas, Chilean Representative, DIRECON and V Duran, Professor of Environmental Law, University of Chile, on file with author.

17.3.4 Factual Report/Complaint Mechanisms to Provide Recourse When Environmental or Social Rules are Violated

The 'need to maintain and improve laws providing for high levels of health, safety, and environmental protection is matched by an equally important consideration: the need to enforce laws that are enacted'.[295] In the NAFTA and its related USMCA, the Canada-Chile FTA, the US-Chile FTA and other similar accords, Parties established mechanisms to challenge governments in cases where non-enforcement is believed to be occurring.[296]

Even in the NAFTA and its NAAEC, as carried through and strengthened in the USMCA that entered into force on 1 July 2020, the Parties retain the right to exercise sovereign discretion with respect to investigatory, prosecutorial, regulatory and compliance matters, and to make decisions regarding the allocation of resources to enforcement.[297] These discretions permit each Party with a great deal of flexibility; a government might excuse itself from enforcement due to 'other priorities' or limited resources.[298] In some treaties, such discretion is conditioned: a Party is in compliance with the obligation to effectively enforce laws where a course of action or inaction reflects a *reasonable exercise* of such discretion, or results from a *bona fide* decision regarding resources allocation.[299] This obligation to effectively enforce environmental laws is often linked with commitments that Parties will provide adequate procedural guarantees for those affected.[300]

Further, to reinforce accountability, public submission mechanisms can be used.[301] The strongest mechanisms were agreed by Parties to the NAAEC,[302] the Canada-Chile Agreement for Environmental Cooperation,[303] and US-CAFTA-DR Environmental Cooperation Agreement.[304] These have been called 'pioneering from the international legal perspective, in that they focus not on the State's compliance with international legal obligations, but rather on its enforcement of purely domestic law'.[305] The process seeks to strengthen the regulatory regime of the Parties, by allowing citizens to make submissions if they find that environmental laws are not being effectively enforced.[306] Where it is judged that the submission is valid, a factual record is produced, documenting the facts of the case,

[295] OECD (n 195).

[296] de Mestral (n 229) 364 and De Mestral 'NAFTA Dispute Settlement: Creative Experience or Confusion?' in Bartels and Ortino (n 45) 359, 377.

[297] MC Cordonier Segger, *Beyond the Barricades: The Americas Trade and Sustainable Development Agenda* (London, Routledge 2017); Hoi L Kong and L Kinvin Wroth, *NAFTA and Sustainable Development* (Cambridge University Press, CUP 2015).

[298] Cordonier Segger (n 297).

[299] OECD (n 195) 109.

[300] Ibid.

[301] For general commentary in the NAFTA context, see DA Gantz, 'Government to Government Dispute Resolution under NAFTA's Chapter 20: A Commentary on the Process' (2000) 11 American Review of International Arbitration 481.

[302] North America Agreement on Environmental Cooperation (adopted 14 September 1993, entered into force 1 January 1994) 32 ILM 1480.

[303] CCAEC (n 209).

[304] Agreement among the Governments of Costa Rica, the Dominican Republic, El Salvador, Guatemala, Honduras, and the United States of America on Environmental Cooperation (signed 18 February 2005, entered into force 1 January 2009) [for the last Party Costa Rica] <http://www.sice.oas.org/Trade/CAFTA/CAFTADR_e/environment/envcoop_e.asp>.

[305] OECD (n 195) 119.

[306] de Mestral (n 229). See GA Ortega, 'Public Participation within NAFTA's Environmental Agreement', and S Wilson, 'Article 14-15 of the North American Agreement on Environmental Cooperation: Intent of the Founders,' in Kirton and Maclaren (n 160).

and released publicly. This can bring problems to light, encouraging States to resolve them quickly to avoid public scrutiny and the pressure of other Parties.[307] In the NAAEC, article 14 allows for public submissions on alleged non-enforcement of environmental laws by either Party, and article 15 instructs that a Factual Record be prepared upon recommendation of the Petition Review Committee and accepted by either Party in the Council.[308]

The mechanism has garnered cautious approval, mainly because it is activated for enforcement. Under the NAAEC, as of September 2011, there had been seventy-nine citizen submissions. Of these, forty-one originated from Mexico, twenty-eight from Canada and only ten from the United States.[309] Evidence is building that the process does improve environmental protection, and that it: '... may help promote citizen involvement in environmental issues in countries where traditionally no such opportunities existed.'[310] The Chile-Canada citizen submission had also been used five times by 2012. As the OECD notes: 'the mechanism may be the most effective of the various tools available for fostering compliance with domestic environmental laws, and may have the side benefit of empowering civil society to help protect environmental integrity.'[311]

Observers have expressed concern about the overall inadequacy of the submission process[312] and possible decline of the citizen submission procedures over recent years.[313] In the US-CAFTA-DR FTA[314] and Environmental Cooperation Agreement, innovations are introduced to the NAAEC model, perhaps strengthening it. First, US citizens and non-governmental organizations are not entitled to file complaints under article 17 concerning alleged non-enforcement by the United States, but can directly access the NAAEC process.[315] Other citizens or NGOs of any other Party may file complaints of non-enforcement against the United States, under specific criteria. In addition, a Factual Record is undertaken, and must be made public, by the vote of any Council Member.[316] There is also a follow-up procedure: upon Factual Record completion, the Environmental Affairs Council may provide recommendations on matters addressed in the Factual Record, including on further development of a Party's mechanisms for monitoring its own enforcement. With regards these innovations, the OECD notes that it is 'difficult, and too early, to assess the efficiency of this type of commitment and mechanism ... For developing country Parties, entering this commitment may constitute a challenge—but also an opportunity to have a closer look at their own environmental regulation and enforcement systems, and enhance their effectiveness.'[317]

[307] Ibid.
[308] Ibid.
[309] According to data gathered by the CEC, <http://www.cec.org/Page.asp?PageID=751&SiteNodeID=250&BL_ExpandID=99>.
[310] OECD (n 195) 118–131.
[311] Ibid.
[312] J Todd, 'Trade Treaties, Citizen Submissions, and Environmental Justice' (2017) 44 Ecology Law Quarterly 89.
[313] J Ayres, 'Power Relations under NAFTA: Reassessing the Efficacy of Contentious Transnationalism' (2004) 74 Studies in Political Economy 101, 113.
[314] Dominican Republic-Central America FTA (signed 5 August 2004) 19 USC, <http://www.ustr.gov/trade-agreements/free-trade-agreements/cafta-dr-dominican-republic-central-america-fta/final-text> (US-CAFTA-DR FTA).
[315] PL Stenzel, 'Free Trade and Sustainability through the Lens of Nicaragua: How CAFTA-DR should be amended to promote the Triple Bottom Line' (2010) 34 William and Mary Environmental Law and Policy Review 653, 664.
[316] Ibid 687; US-CAFTA-DR FTA (n 314) arts 17.7–17.11.
[317] OECD (n 195) 109.

In another innovation, a less formal process and perhaps weaker process was incorporated into the Canada-Costa Rica Agreement on Environmental Cooperation.[318] Any member of the public may submit questions to either Party relating to its obligations to effectively enforce its environmental laws.[319] Upon receipt of a question, the Parties agree to acknowledge the question in writing, provide a timely response and make summaries of questions and answers publicly available on a website.[320] Similar informal public submission processes were included in the US-Chile FTA at chapter 19. This builds environmental information exchange and capacity for domestic environmental enforcement and monitoring, but does not have the same weight (or cost) as factual reports or claims processes.[321] Citizens' rights to request information from any Party on the effective implementation of environmental law in its territory are simply recognized, along with a duty to respond publicly to this request.

The EU-Chile AA and other similar treaties do not activate such mechanisms to secure enforcement in the same way. They focus instead on a broad spectrum of topic areas in which Chile and the EU commit to encourage dialogue and cooperation.[322] However, such measures may not be necessary, as the EU-Chile AA provides other formal institutional mechanisms for public participation in the overall treaty, including through a Civil Society Consultative Committee, and this committee can act on its own initiative to investigate issues and raise them directly with the Association Council.[323] Similarly, the EU-CARIFORUM EPA also establishes a Consultative Committee, which is broadly representative of civil society organizations, including the academic community and social and economic partners, and which is able to carry out activities on its own initiative, and can make formal recommendations to the Joint CARIFOUM-EC Council and its Trade and Development Committee.[324]

In the EU-Colombia-Peru EPA and the EU-CARIFORUM EPA, innovative provisions are agreed to permit further accountability. For example, the EU-Colombia-Peru FTA provides that:

> Each Party shall consult domestic labour and environment or sustainable development committees or groups, or create such committees or groups when they do not exist. Such committees or groups may submit opinions and make recommendation or this Title, including on their own initiative, through the respective internal channels of the Parties.[325]

Financing mechanisms are also provided in the new EU EPAs, however. Indeed, rather than simply making bilateral aid or cooperation funds available, in the EU-CARIFORUM EPA at article 8(3) the Parties 'agree on the benefits of a regional development fund representative of the interests of all CARIFORUM States to mobilise and channel EPA-related development resources from the EDF and other potential donors'. The treaty committed

[318] Canada-Costa Rica Environmental Cooperation Agreement (n 265) art 9.
[319] Ibid.
[320] Ibid.
[321] Ibid.
[322] Durbin (n 235).
[323] Ibid.
[324] EU-CARIFORUM EPA (n 29) art 232(1)–(5).
[325] EU-Colombia-Peru FTA (n 21) art 281.

CARIFORUM countries to establish this fund within two years. There are signs that it is already starting to access European Development Fund (EDF) resources.[326]

Overall, three points can be underlined from this comparison of the parallel and integrated environmental, social and development cooperation provisions in different Americas bilateral or regional economic treaties.

First, this survey revealed many innovations which could be used to address the second key tension raised in the impact assessments; the concern that the effect of new trade rules will be to weaken existing domestic environmental laws and standards, or limit their enforcement. By assistance to strengthen laws instead, in accordance with jointly agreed priorities and work programmes, and by engaging citizens in monitoring to support enforcement, the 'integration tension' is converted to an opportunity. Indeed, many of the specific innovations in work programmes appear to respond directly to concerns raised in impact assessments.

Second, two distinct approaches to strengthening laws are revealed, each with strengths and weaknesses. Environment and labour matters are addressed in the US-Chile FTA and similar treaties, but the provisions, even if addressing trade-related issues, are kept separate through environmental and labour chapters, annexes and side agreements. A link between labour agreements and chapters and sustainable development is not obvious. The environmental measures, only, explicitly seek to operationalize the trade treaty objective to promote sustainable development. Indeed, a second sustainable development commitment is agreed in the Preamble and provisions of the separate environment chapters, annexes/environmental side agreements and work programmes. It is possible that in the US-Chile FTA and related accords, the Parties subscribe to a limited definition of sustainable development where—contrary to the 2002 WSSD JPOI outcomes—the concept is still seen only as a sub-goal of environmental policy. This is different from the EU-Chile AA approach, which is broader and more integrated, along the lines recommended by the 1992 Agenda 21, the 2002 JPOI and the 2012 UNCSD, and noted in the 2015 SDGs. This latter approach responds more clearly to the principle that environmental and social considerations should be integrated into economic decision-making, and the EU's acceptance of an 'integration principle' in its law and policy may be informing the differences.

Third, the separated environmental and labour side agreements in the US-Chile FTA and similar treaties, including the US-CAFTA-DR FTA, which take the 'sustainable development treaty purpose only' approach, tend to use detailed, specific and limited measures. Innovative mechanisms are provided to ensure that the treaty strengthens environmental and labour laws and their enforcement environmental cooperation and social development through obligations, backed by committees or councils, leading ongoing cooperation agendas or work programmes that have access to information exchange, capacity-building, technical assistance, monitoring and financing. These accords also provide for enforcement-strengthening mechanisms to investigate claims and otherwise encourage public and civil society engagement in the process. In contrast, in the EU-Chile AA and other similar treaties which take the 'treaty purpose, object and integration principle' approach tend not

[326] The eleventh EDF 2014 to 2020 has been allocated EUR 30.5 billion, an increase of about 34 per cent as the tenth EDF was initially allocated EUR 22.7 billion for 2008–2013. See A D'Alfonso, 'European Development Fund, Joint Development Cooperation and the EU Budget: Out or In?' (European Parliamentary Research Service. Members' Research Service. PE 542.140, 2014).

to provide such specific implementation measures in treaty texts themselves, leaving actual cooperation programmes and activities open to be shaped by dialogue among partners, new developments and other factors.

17.4 Sustainable Development-Oriented Trade and Investment Rule Enhancement Initiatives

Beyond the inclusion of different types of exemptions to prevent bilateral or regional economic treaties from constraining the adoption of new laws on sustainable development, and the activation of parallel cooperative measures to strengthen the application and enforcement of existing laws which can prevent sustainable development problems from being exacerbated by a trade or investment treaty, the analysis of impact assessments earlier in this volume revealed a third tension. In particular, there is a concern that rather than contributing to sustainable development, trade and investment liberalization will stimulate growth in obsolete, unsustainable industries, especially in developing countries. The integration opportunity that responds to this tension involves the potential to develop an *integrated* agenda that promotes *more trade, but in sustainable goods and services*. Here, the focus is on new 'green economy' goods and services that States, in other international treaties, have agreed are more sustainable.[327] The opportunity is not simply to use trade and investment liberalization rules, alongside much more direct economic stimulus measures set in place to 'build back better' from the global COVID-19 pandemic, to enhance more sustainable industries and sectors,[328] but also to use trade and investment disciplines to remove incentives for unsustainable development, such as subsidies that encourage over-fishing.[329] Through trade agreements, subsidies (e.g. fossil fuel subsidies) can also be tackled for their sustainability impacts, and not just their negative trade or protectionism effects. In the new Agreement on Climate Change, Trade and Sustainability (ACCTS), States are currently negotiating specific rules for eliminating fossil fuel subsidies.[330] In this book, the emergence of this new 'sustainable trade agenda' was traced in new global and regional trade and investment treaty negotiations.

[327] For discussions of how liberalization can promote trade in environmental goods and services, see Gehring and Cordonier Segger (n 140); G Sampson, *The WTO and Sustainable Development* (Tokyo, United Nations University Press 2005); P Birnie, A Boyle and C Redgwell, *International Law & the Environment* (Oxford, OUP 2009); TEEB, *The Economics of Ecosystems and Biodiversity: Mainstreaming the Economics of Nature: A Synthesis of the Approach, Conclusions and Recommendations of TEEB* (TEEB, 2010); UNEP, 'Towards a Green Economy: Pathways to Sustainable Development and Poverty Eradication' (2011) <https://ww.unep.org/greeneconomy> accessed 16 December 2020; E von Weizsacker and others, *Factor Five: Transforming the Global Economy through 80% Improvements in Resource Productivity* (London, Earthscan 2009).

[328] For a discussion of the need to promote trade in clean energy and climate-friendly technologies and other carbon markets, and how this is prioritized in the UN Framework Convention on Climate Change, see C Streck and D Freestone, *Legal Aspects of Carbon Trading: Kyoto, Copenhagen and Beyond* (Oxford, OUP 2009). For a discussion of a need to carefully encourage trade in more sustainable agricultural and biodiversity products, and how this is prioritized in the UN Convention on Biological Diversity, see J Cabrera, *Propriedad Intelectual, Biodiversidad y Comercio. Opciones para establecer sinergias entre los Acuerdos Ambientales y los Tratados de Comercio* (San Jose, Universidad Nacional Estatal a Distancia 2009).

[329] On trade in certified sustainable fisheries, see CA Roheim and others, 'Evolution and Future of the Sustainable Seafood Market' (2018) 1(8) Nature Sustainability 392–398; Gabriel S Sampson and others, 'Secure Sustainable Seafood from Developing Countries' (2015) 348(6234) Science 504, 504–506.

[330] ILA, *Sustainable Development and The Green Economy in International Trade Law* (ILA, 2020).

As explained earlier, in the deadlocked negotiating agenda of the WTO Doha 'Development Round', three such innovations include commitments to negotiate reductions in fisheries subsidies that encouraged over-fishing, negotiations on how intellectual property rights might protect indigenous traditional knowledge and negotiations to facilitate trade in environmental goods and services. Further sustainable development-oriented trade enhancement initiatives are being adopted in regional trade agreements. The Chile-US FTA and other more recent treaties, and especially the EU- Chile AA and other related inter-regional accords, provide examples of such innovations. This section discusses several instructive examples. It starts with a consideration of the examples highlighted from the survey of trade and investment liberalization impact assessments discussed earlier in this volume: SPS measures, government procurement and investment liberalization. Then it turns to more advanced and innovative new measures.

17.4.1 Sanitary and Phytosanitary Scientific Cooperation and Risk Assessment

Across three decades of impact assessments, concerns have been raised that trade agreements can be used as forums to challenge the efforts of Parties to secure high SPS standards, weakening protections for health, the environment and animal welfare.[331] Regional SPS provisions could also be used to promote scientific cooperation and risk assessment in order to improve levels of health, environment and animal protection in the territories of both developed and developing country trading partners.[332] Such mechanisms, in a trade agreement, would be an opportunity to secure well-designed and more effective standards in all Parties to a trade or investment agreement.

Many of the bilateral or regional economic treaties analysed in this volume commit to implement and go beyond the WTO SPS Agreement. They also establish SPS cooperation mechanisms (such as committees) which are mandated to undertake cooperative development of standards, as well as efforts to reduce trade and investment barriers.

For instance, in the US-Chile FTA at article 6.3, Parties agree to establish a committee on SPS matters to enhance the implementation by each Party of the WTO SPS Agreement, specifically noting that its objective is also to protect human, animal and plant life and health, and enhance consultation and cooperation on SPS matters, as well as to facilitate trade between the Parties.[333] They agree that the committee will coordinate positions in international and regional fora on food safety and human, animal and plant health; and also that it will coordinate technical cooperation programmes on SPS matters.[334] Such a committee has the potential to facilitate cooperation to improve standards. However, it could also become

331 EU-Chile SIA (n 42) 219. See T O'Riordan, A Jordan and J Cameron (eds), *Reinterpreting the Precautionary Principle* (London, Cameron May 2001) 296; A Trouwborst, 'The Precautionary Principle in General International Law: Combating the Babylonian Confusion' (2007) 16 Review of European Community and International Environmental Law 185. See also *European Communities—Measures Affecting the Approval and Marketing of Biotech Products—Reports of the Panel* (29 September 2006) WT/DS291/R/Add.4, WT/DS292/R/Add.4, WT/DS293/R/Add.4 and *European Communities—Measures Concerning Meat and Meat Products (Hormones)* (13 February 1998) WT/DS26/AB/R and WT/DS48/AB/R.

332 See Sampson (n 327) 161; Gehring and Cordonier Segger (n 140) 399; Cordonier Segger and Leichner Reynal (n 229) 25.

333 US-Chile FTA (n 2) art 6.3.

334 Ibid.

a forum for Parties to challenge other Parties' SPS measures on trade grounds alone before they even reach completion, weakening standards. The mechanism is, essentially, double-edged rather than balanced between environment, social and economic objectives, with a creative ambiguity that has yet to be proven in practice.

In the EU-Chile AA, the Parties also commit at article 89 to work together to enhance their implementation of the WTO SPS Agreement. However, they go further, including two sets of innovative cooperative measures on issues highlighted in the SIAs, the Agenda 21,[335] the JPOI,[336] and the SDGs themselves. For instance, in article 24 on cooperation on agriculture and rural sectors and sanitary and phytosanitary measures, the Parties establish their intention 'to support and stimulate agricultural policy measures in order to promote and consolidate the Parties' efforts towards sustainable agriculture and agricultural and rural development'.[337] The cooperation envisioned focuses on capacity-building, infrastructure and technology transfer. But the Parties also commit to undertake 'specific projects aimed at supporting sanitary, phytosanitary, environmental and food quality measures', as well as 'technical assistance for the improvement of productivity and the exchange of alternative crop technologies' and 'technical assistance for the strengthening of sanitary and phytosanitary control systems, with a view to supporting as far as possible the promotion of equivalence and mutual recognition agreements'.[338]

In further bilateral or regional economic treaties that were surveyed in this volume, both the EU and Chile are also innovating to strengthen SPS control systems in order to encourage trade in products that can support sustainable agricultural development. For instance, in the EU-Central America AA at article 61, the EU and Central America commit to enhance Central American adherence to European SPS standards by:

> capacity building of the Central American entities responsible for export promotion, in particular supporting [medium and small enterprises] from urban and rural sectors, necessary for the production and export of organic goods, including on customs procedures, technical regulations and quality standards required in the European Union market.[339]

At present, according to the SIA, Central American organic fruits, vegetables and other producers are facing increasing demand in produce due to the popularity of these organic goods in Europe.[340] A collaborative effort to improve social and environmental standards in Central American agricultural practices, while also tailoring European SPS measures to facilitate rather than frustrate organic products from Central America, could achieve a great deal. If applied carefully, this treaty may offer one instance where through integration, trade and investment flows might enhance sustainable development.

In another example, in the Chile, New Zealand, Singapore and Brunei Darussalam Trans-Pacific Strategic EPA, the Parties agreed on Implementing Arrangements.[341] Chapter 16 on

[335] Agenda 21, Annex 2 Report of the UN Conference on Environment and Development, 13 June 1992, UN Doc A/CONF.151/26 (Vol I).
[336] JPOI (n 38) 54.
[337] EU-Chile AA (n 4) art 24.
[338] Ibid.
[339] EU-Central America AA (n 23) art 61.
[340] EU-Central America SIA (n 183) 60.
[341] Chile, New Zealand, Singapore and Brunei Darussalam Trans-Pacific Strategic EPA, Implementing Agreements (n 11).

strategic partnership commits in the area of primary industry to share experience and identify possible joint research for sustainable agricultural practices.[342] Such techniques are, as mentioned earlier in this volume, also prioritized in the FAO Seed Treaty article 6 to support sustainable use of agricultural resources.[343] It is possible, indeed, that by fully implementing the economic treaties, the Parties will be strengthening their ability to implement the FAO Seed Treaty on matters of sustainable agricultural development. These 'sustainable development' cooperation arrangements, included within the text of a treaty seeking to liberalize trade in agriculture, appear to provide part of the balance that a principle of integration would expect. Rather than simply agreeing to dismantle or streamline SPS standards in the area of agriculture, the Parties are agreeing to jointly research ways to promote more sustainable agricultural practices. If the proposed cooperation is successful, and the sustainable agricultural products are able to gain access to wider markets, there is the possibility that environmental, economic and social development interests will benefit together.

These last two innovations appear to respond to the Parties' commitment to promote sustainable development, by activating trade and investment rules to support economic growth in more sustainable products which do not use pesticides, fertilizers or other pollutants, and are healthier for agricultural labourers.[344] Essentially, States appear to have agreed, in their economic accord, to use trade and investment law to jointly strengthen SPS control systems and seek mutual recognition, in order to encourage trade and investment in products that can support sustainable agricultural development.

17.4.2 More Sustainable and Accountable Public Purchases

Impact assessments and other studies canvassed earlier in this volume raised concerns that public procurement disciplines in trade agreements could impose strict standards on governments, constraining an important tool for sustainable development.[345] Government procurement provisions are currently used to secure more affordable and sustainable goods or services, for instance by promoting the use of environmentally sound design and construction techniques in infrastructure development cooperation,[346] supporting adoption of social or environmental certification systems for forest products or textiles used by governments[347] or respecting set-asides for economic empowerment of vulnerable or marginalized groups.[348] As noted by Weller, Claro and Blanco, in Chile at the time of the negotiations, public authorities were the largest consumers in the economy:

> on average spending 45 to 65 per cent of their budgets on public procurement, amounting to 13 per cent to 17 per cent of the GDP. If governments make a concerted effort to purchase environmentally- and socially-preferable products and services, their substantial

[342] Ibid, chapter 16.

[343] FAO Seed Treaty (n 37) art 6.

[344] C Badgley and others, 'Organic Agriculture and the Global Food Supply' (2007) 22(2) Renewable Agriculture and Food Supply 86.

[345] EU-Chile SIA (n 42) 140.

[346] Weller, Claro and Blanco (n 141); Gehring and Cordonier Segger (n 140) 154; UNEP (n 327) 329–372.

[347] UNEP (n 327) 153–196.

[348] L Kaye Nijaki and G Worrel, 'Procurement for Sustainable Local Economic Development' (2012) 25 International Journal of Public Sector Management 133.

buying power will drive the delivery of sustainable development policies and stimulate markets for sustainable products and services.[349]

At present such procurement tools, as mentioned earlier in this chapter, simply benefit from specific exceptions in the trade agreement. However, further innovations can also be highlighted in two areas.

First, in the EU-Chile AA, at article 33 on public procurement, the Parties agree to co-operate to provide technical assistance, 'paying special attention to the municipal level'. Further technical assistance might, if focused appropriately, contribute to sustainable development-related public procurement in Chile. While Parties stop short of promising procurement benefits, they do address the needs of small and medium-sized enterprises, a sector highlighted as important for sustainable development at many points of the JPOI[350] and highlighted in the SDGs. As noted in the EU-Chile SIA, among others surveyed for this volume, this sector faces particular risks from trade-induced structural economic changes.[351] In the EU-Chile AA, Parties agree at article 19 to undertake cooperation on small and medium-sized enterprises, in particular to:

> promote a favourable environment for the development of small and medium-sized enterprises (SMEs) through technical assistance; conferences, seminars, prospecting for industrial and technical opportunities ... promoting contacts between economic operators, encouraging joint investment and establishing joint ventures ... ; ... facilitating access to finance, providing information and stimulating innovation.

Similarly, the EU-CARIFORUM EPA agrees that Parties will collaborate to provide: 'support measures aimed at promoting private sector and enterprise development, in particular small economic operators, and enhancing the international competitiveness of CARIFORUM firms and diversification of the CARIFORUM economies'.[352] The EU-Colombia-Peru FTA also encourages the Parties to collaborate, including in public procurement, in order to promote 'the development of Micro and SMEs, using trade as a tool for reducing poverty'.[353] Negative impacts of trade liberalization on SMEs, which employ many of the poorest people in Central America and the Caribbean, were raised in the SIAs as a way of addressing the social and economic pillars of sustainable development.[354] These concerns appear to have been taken into account. In the latter example, the cooperation measures aimed at socially and economically marginalized sectors, could encourage Parties to find innovative ways to enhance SME participation in procurement, while maintaining accountable and transparent processes.

Further, specific provisions are being used to clarify that procurement liberalization commitments are not intended to block Parties from integrating environment or social

[349] Weller, Claro and Blanco (n 141) 2. See also A Madariaga, *El Estado y la Responsabilidad Social: Estrategia de Incorporación de Criterios de Responsabilidad Social y Ambiental en las Compras Públicas* (Santiago, CENDA 2008) <http://cendachile.cl/files/doc.%20estado%20final.pdf> accessed 16 December 2020.

[350] JPOI (n 38) 19 c).

[351] EU-Chile SIA (n 42) 51. Indeed, in Chile, new web-based procurement systems have been established, facilitating access to government procurement for small and medium-sized enterprises (Chile Compra, Santiago 2012).

[352] EU-CARIFORUM EPA (n 29) art 8.1(iii).

[353] EU-Colombia-Peru FTA (n 21) art 324.2(b).

[354] EU-ACP SIA (n 248) 23, 26 (includes CARFORUM); EU-Andean SIA (n 143) 20–21.

development considerations into their procurement contracts. For instance, in the Peru-US FTA, Parties agreed that government agencies may include provisions in their procurement bids for tender to promote environmental protection, and requirements that suppliers must comply with core labour laws in the country where they make a product or perform a service. At article 9.6(7), it is agreed that:

> 7. For greater certainty, this Article is not intended to preclude a procuring entity from preparing, adopting, or applying technical specifications: (a) to promote the conservation of natural resources and the environment; or (b) to require a supplier to comply with generally applicable laws regarding (i) fundamental principles and rights at work; and (ii) acceptable conditions of work with respect to minimum wages, hours of work, and occupational safety and health, in the territory in which the good is produced or the service is performed.[355]

In SIAs, concerns were raised about how to promote socially and environmentally sound practices through technical specifications in bids for tender, if companies that are distant from the government entity are permitted to bid on contracts, and their performance records are hard to confirm.[356] Through a specific mechanism to address related good governance concerns, Parties address this concern as well. At article 9.10 on ensuring integrity in procurement practices further to article 19.9 (anti-corruption measures), the Parties to the Peru-US FTA commit to 'establish or maintain procedures to declare ineligible for participation in the Party's procurements, either indefinitely or for a stated period of time, suppliers that the Party has determined to have engaged in fraudulent or other illegal actions in relation to procurement'.[357] Essentially, through the trade and investment liberalization treaty, a mechanism is established to block firms with records of fraud and illegality. On 'the request of a Party, the Party receiving the request shall identify the suppliers determined to be ineligible under these procedures, and, where appropriate, exchange information regarding those suppliers or the fraudulent or illegal action'.[358] This mechanism could assist in integrating environmental and social priorities into economic development. If a supplier fraudulently represents themselves as holding an environmental certification, incorrectly claimed experience in addressing fundamental rights at work or had carried out procurement contracts while breaking environmental or social laws, an inquiry could be carried out, and consequent cautions would result. Social and environmental specifications of a procurement bidding process would be less likely to be bypassed by a company whose record is not known in the other country. While again, the treaty provision does not require all procurement tendering processes to take environmental or social considerations into account, it can ensure that firms that have not kept environmental and social commitments to governments in the past can be identified and sanctioned. Such innovations, if adopted in other bilateral or regional economic treaties and consistently implemented, may therefore assist in the promotion of sustainable development.

[355] US-Peru TPA (n 9) art 9.6(7).

[356] See, e.g., EU-Andean SIA (n 143) 114–118; F Trionfetti, 'Discriminatory Public Procurement and International Trade' (2002) 23 World Economy 57.

[357] US-Peru TPA (n 9) art 9.10.

[358] Ibid.

17.4.3 Investment Incentives for Corporate Social Responsibility

Concerns were expressed in the impact assessments discussed above that investment liberalization provisions might protect investors at the expense of host country government attempts to regulate in the interests of social and environmental protection. Commitments not to lower environmental standards to attract investment are one means of avoidance. Recent academic work on trade, investment and corporate social responsibility has also suggested that investment treaties could find ways to privilege firms which adopt corporate social responsibility (CSR) commitments.[359] This responds to the 2002 JPOI mandate on corporate social responsibility, in which States commit, at 49, to:

> [a]ctively promote corporate responsibility and accountability, based on the Rio principles, including through the full development and effective implementation of intergovernmental agreements and measures, international initiatives and public-private partnerships and appropriate national regulations, and support continuous improvement in corporate practices in all countries.[360]

It also responds to the calls for corporate social responsibility in the 2015 SDGs and in the UN Global Compact.

Parties to the US-Chile FTA, at article 19.10, commit to principles of corporate stewardship. They recognize 'the substantial benefits brought by international trade and investment as well as the opportunity for enterprises to implement policies for sustainable development that seek to ensure coherence between social, economic and environmental objectives', and agree that 'each Party should encourage enterprises operating within its territory or jurisdiction to voluntarily incorporate sound principles of corporate stewardship in their internal policies, such as those principles or agreements that have been endorsed by both Parties'.[361] This is followed by Annex 19.3 1 (d) on Sharing Private Sector Expertise, where the Parties agree to 'seek to increase environmental stewardship by inviting enterprises of each Party to share their experiences in developing and implementing programmes that have reduced pollution, including, where appropriate, demonstrating the financial benefits of these measures'. Further, in the US-Chile Environmental Cooperation Agreement at article III 2.d), Parties prioritize 'the promotion of good domestic practices leading to sustainable management of the environment' and at Article V d), agree to facilitate 'linkages among representatives from academia, industry, and government to promote the exchange of best practices and environmental information and data of interest to the Parties'. If these commitments are consistently implemented, rather than simply 'not lowering' environmental standards, the treaty could promote more sustainable investments. Indeed, in the 2005-2006 Work Programme of the Chile-US Environmental Cooperation, which can be considered subsequent treaty practice as it is formally agreed by both Parties, priority area 2 has been formed to undertake efforts to '[e]ncourage development and adoption of sound

[359] J Hepburn and V Kuuya, 'Corporate Social Responsibility in Investment Treaties' in M Gehring, MC Cordonier Segger and A Newcombe (eds), *Sustainable Development in World Investment Law* (Alphen aan de Rijn, Kluwer Law International 2010), IISD, *Model Investment Agreement* (Winnipeg, 2006); M Kerr, R Janda and C Pitts, *Corporate Social Responsibility-A Legal Analysis* (Toronto, Lexis-Nexis Canada 2009).

[360] JPOI (n 38) 49.

[361] Article 19.10.

environmental practices and technologies, particularly in business enterprises',[362] in order to 'encourage enterprises to develop and adopt sound environmental practices and technologies, and to show that doing so not only benefits the environment, but can be done in a manner consistent with maintaining international competitiveness'.[363]

Such commitments can be contrasted with other similar provisions agreed by the Parties to the Canada-Peru FTA. The Preamble notes both Parties' intention to 'promote sustainable development' and also to 'encourage enterprises operating within their territory or subject to their jurisdiction, to respect internationally recognized corporate social responsibility standards and principles and pursue best practices'.[364] Moreover, the Parties include further provisions on corporate social responsibility at article 810 in the investment chapter of the trade agreement, stating that:

> Each Party should encourage enterprises operating within its territory or subject to its jurisdiction to voluntarily incorporate internationally recognized standards of corporate social responsibility in their internal policies, such as statements of principle that have been endorsed or are supported by the Parties. These principles address issues such as labour, the environment, human rights, community relations and anti-corruption. The Parties therefore remind those enterprises of the importance of incorporating such corporate social responsibility standards in their internal policies'.[365]

These provisions were included in the Canada-Peru FTA after considerable negotiation. The commitment to a sustainable development objective, and the specific 'soft law' provisions in the JPOI were used by officials within the Canadian government to guide their decision to accept negotiating proposals of Peru.[366] Progress achieved in such a manner suggests that a sustainable development objective does carry a form of interstitial influence. Further, industries with strong CSR records, given this commitment, may find governments able take CSR into account in facilitating investments or granting licenses.

In the EU-CARIFORUM EPA, Parties similarly agree to promote 'corporate social responsibility through public information and reporting'.[367] In the EU-South Korea FTA, in a more detailed elaboration, the Parties agree to collaborate in order to promote the:

> exchange of information and co-operation on corporate social responsibility and accountability, including on the effective implementation and follow-up of internationally agreed guidelines, fair and ethical trade, private and public certification and labelling schemes including eco-labelling and green public procurement;[368]

These provisions respond directly to impacts and opportunities identified in the SIAs. For instance, the EU-ACP SIA noted that 'commercial presence in the tourism sector presents opportunities and challenges and can raise industry standards where CSR and codes of

362 2005–2006 Work Programme of the Chile-US Environmental Cooperation, priority 2.
363 Ibid.
364 US-Peru TPA (n 9) Preamble.
365 Canada-Peru FTA (n 213) art 810.
366 Interview with David Henry, Senior Policy Advisor Americas, Environment Canada (Ottawa, May 2007).
367 EU-CARIFORUM EPA (n 29) art 196.2(d).
368 EU-South Korea FTA (signed 6 October 2010) Annex 13, art 1(d).

conduct are adopted'.[369] The EU-South Korea SIA also noted that 'cooperative approaches should be developed for the development of standards in areas such as animal welfare and environmental eco-labels as well as Corporate Social Responsibility'.[370] Here, the SIA recommendations would appear to have been taken into account.

These provisions, while mainly hortatory in stating that Parties 'should encourage enterprises ... to voluntarily' and then 'remind those enterprises', contribute to setting up expectations among companies that the Parties welcome CSR efforts. While not going so far as to impose obligations on the Party that regulates the investors, it sends a signal to investors that CSR efforts are encouraged, and may even be taken into account in investment decision-making processes.[371] If such CSR standards bring higher costs for investors, such encouragement in the other direction could be helpful for a more integrated bilateral or regional economic treaty.

17.4.4 Further Regional Trade and Investment Enhancement Innovations Related to Sustainable Development

Trade and investment enhancement can, if tailored, contribute to sustainable development.[372] Depending on economic, social and environmental conditions prevailing among the Parties, and concerns raised in the impact assessment, different opportunities exist. Further innovations may include cooperation: to reduce technical barriers to trade by mutually recognizing sustainability certification schemes; to secure respect for intellectual property rights over traditional knowledge on biodiversity; to liberalize, transfer and encourage investment in innovative technologies and renewable energy resources; and to reduce trade in the products of illegal logging.

Reducing technical barriers to trade by mutually recognizing sustainability *certification schemes*

Concerns have been raised that trade measures cannot be based on production and processing methods, especially in the WTO.[373] However, the idea of using trade and investment disciplines to support efforts to promote higher social and environmental standards (including sustainability certification schemes) has also gained currency, especially in the EU,[374] and been reflected in bilateral or regional economic treaties. In the EU-Chile AA at

369 EU-ACP SIA (n 248) 68.

370 IBM Belgium, *Trade Sustainability Impact Assessment of the EU-Korea FTA: Final Report* (Brussels, June 2008) [EU-South Korea SIA] 25.

371 Hepburn and Kuuya (n 359) 585.

372 MC Cordonier Segger and others, *Trade Rules and Sustainability in the Americas* (Winnipeg, IISD 1999) 17; Gehring and Cordonier Segger (n 140) 191, Cordonier Segger and Leichner Reynal (n 229) 253, H Blanco, L Togeiro de Almeida and K Gallagher (eds), *Globalizacion y Medio Ambiente: Lecciones desde las Americas* (Santiago, RIDES-GDAE 2005); H Blanco, M Araya and C Murillo, *ALCA y medio ambiente: Ideas desde Latinoamerica* (Santiago, CIPMA-GETS-CINPE 2003); D Esty, *Greening the GATT* (Washington, IIE 1994) 208; M Gehring, *Nachhaltigkeit durch Verfahren im Welthandelsrecht* (Duncker and Humbolt Berlin 2007) 18.

373 Sampson (n 148) 80; Gehring and Cordonier Segger (n 140) 44; R Tarasofsky, 'Ensuring Compatibility between Multilateral Environmental Agreements and GATT/WTO' (1996) 7 Yearbook of International Environmental Law 52; S Shaw, 'Business and the Environment: Is there More to the Story?' (2005) 40 Business Economics 40.

374 L Van den Putte and J Orbie, 'EU Bilateral Trade Agreements and the Surprising Rise of Labour Provisions' (2015) 31 International Journal of Comparative Labour Law and Industrial Relations 263.

article 18 on cooperation on standards, technical regulations and conformity assessment procedures, Parties state their intention to promote 'compatibility of technical regulations on the basis of international and European standards; and technical assistance to create a network of conformity assessment bodies on a non discriminatory basis', and agree to 'encourage any measure aiming at improving convergence and compatibility between the respective system of the Parties'.[375] Similarly, the US-Chile FTA states at article 7.4 on trade facilitation that the Parties 'shall intensify their joint work in the field of standards, technical regulations, and conformity assessment procedures with a view to facilitating access to each other's markets'.[376] In particular, the Parties shall seek to identify 'bilateral initiatives that are appropriate for particular issues' to encourage 'convergence or equivalence of technical regulations and standards, alignment with international standards ... and use of accreditation to qualify conformity assessment bodies, as well as cooperation through mutual recognition'.[377] At article 7.8, the Parties create a committee on technical barriers to trade (TBTs) to, *inter alia*, facilitate 'sectoral cooperation among governmental and non-governmental conformity assessment bodies in the Parties' territories'.[378] Such a committee has the potential to facilitate cooperation to improve standards. However, it could also become a forum for a Party to challenge the TBT measures of the other on trade grounds alone, weakening environmental and social standards. In this case, the trade treaty provides a *potential* forum for constructive collaboration, but the potential of this mechanism to serve as an instrument for integration still depends a great deal on how it is used by the Parties over time.

More recent bilateral or regional economic treaties demonstrate certain progress. In particular, the EU-CARIFORUM EPA at article 51 encourages collaboration in overcoming technical barriers to trade, and mandates the:

> Establishment of the appropriate arrangements for the sharing of expertise, including appropriate training intended to ensure adequate and enduring technical competence of the relevant standard setting, metrology, accreditation, market surveillance and conformity assessment bodies, in particular those in the CARIFORUM region.[379]

This responds to the SIA which called for the establishment of 'a permanent EU-ACP Cooperative Dialogue for Public Participation and Capacity Building for Sustainability' in particular to 'Coordinate technical assistance in support of sustainability'.[380] Similarly, co-operation on eco-certification is agreed in the EU-Central American AA at article 54(b), for example, where the Parties agreed to provide 'expertise and capacity building on customs issues (certification and verification of origin to the competent authorities, among others) and technical matters to enforce regional customs procedures'.[381] This appears to respond to recommendations highlighted with regard to 'making sector-specific regulations (certification systems), e.g. in relation to endangered wood species and the (eco-) tourism sector which can have a profound effect on the environment' in the SIA.[382]

375 EU-Chile AA (n 4) art 18.
376 US-Chile FTA (n 2) art 7.4.
377 Ibid.
378 Ibid art 7.8.
379 EU-CARIFORUM EPA (n 29) art 51(2)(a).
380 EU-ACP SIA (n 248) 6–7 (includes CARIFORUM).
381 EU-Central America AA (n 23) art 54(b).
382 EU-Central America SIA (n 183) 95.

Securing respect for intellectual property rights over traditional knowledge *on* biodiversity

Intellectual property (IP) rights protections, as noted in the literature and SIAs, could support sustainable development of bio-prospecting industries, securing better enforcement of access and benefit sharing for biological inventions based on sovereign biological resources and the traditional knowledge of indigenous peoples.[383] In the US-Chile FTA, very little is agreed for biodiversity IP concerns, though in the environmental cooperation Annex 19.3 the Parties do prioritize, at article 1 on improving wildlife protection and management, new cooperation to protect wildlife in Chile and the Latin American region, and to build capacity to promote the management and protection of biological resources in the region.[384]

In the US-Peru TPA, Parties agree several innovations. At article 18.11 on biological diversity, the Parties 'recognize the importance of the conservation and sustainable use of biological diversity and their role in achieving sustainable development', emphasize their commitment to 'promoting and encouraging the conservation and sustainable use of biological diversity and all its components and levels, including plants, animals, and habitat', and 'recognize the importance of respecting and preserving traditional knowledge and practices of indigenous and other communities that contribute to the conservation and sustainable use of biological diversity'.[385] Both commit to 'enhance their cooperative efforts on these matters', underpinned by public participation and consultations in accordance with domestic law, and the possibility to 'make information publicly available about programs and activities, including cooperative programs, [undertaken for] the conservation and sustainable use of biological diversity'.[386] This may send signals of good intentions, but the question of how a trade agreement can actually contribute to achieve them is important. In this case, an April 12 2006 MoU regarding biodiversity and traditional knowledge appears to provide further detail. In this MoU, the Parties recognize a potential contribution of traditional knowledge and biodiversity to cultural, economic and social development, as well as the importance of obtaining informed consent from the appropriate authority prior to accessing genetic resources under the control of such authority; equitably sharing the benefits arising from the use of traditional knowledge and genetic resources; and promoting quality patent examination to ensure the conditions of patentability are satisfied.[387] They refer to access and benefit sharing (ABS) contracts that reflect mutually agreed terms between users and providers.[388] They commit to seek ways to share information that may have a bearing on the patentability of inventions based on traditional knowledge or genetic resources through publicly accessible databases and an opportunity to cite, in writing, to the appropriate examining authority that may have a bearing on patentability.[389] Together, these recognitions and commitments open a door alongside the trade agreement to deeper cooperation on IP rights from traditional knowledge and biological resources, as agreed in

383 C Bellmann and R Melendez-Ortiz, *International Legal Protection for Genetic Resources, Traditional Knowledge and Folklore: Challenges for the Intellectual Property System–Weerawit Weeraworawit* (London, Routledge 2013) 174; Blanco, Togeiro de Almeida and Gallagher (n 372); Blanco, Araya and Murillo (n 372); Sampson (n 327) 154; Gehring and Cordonier Segger (n 140) 309; MJ Krieger, 'Intellectual Property Rights and Traditional Knowledge: Biopiracy or Bioprospecting?' (2008) ETH Research Reports Working Paper 15.

384 US-Chile FTA (n 2) art 2 (b)(vi).

385 US-Peru TPA (n 9) art 18.11.

386 Ibid.

387 Bilateral Understanding between the US and Peru on Biodiversity and Traditional Knowledge.

388 Ibid.

389 Ibid.

Article 8j of the UN Convention on Biological Diversity, and in the Nagoya Protocol.[390] By integrating the concerns about genetic resources into the trade agreement, and providing for deeper collaboration on ways that IP rights could be made to contribute to biodiversity conservation, the Parties make constructive collaboration possible, on a matter of both social and environmental concern. This appears extraordinary, given that the US is not actually a Party to the UN Convention on Biological Diversity, and has not taken on the same commitments at the multilateral level.[391] However, it is important to note, as discussed in Chapter 3, that such agreements, if not clearly 'related to the trade treaty' and accepted as such by the Parties, will be less useful to the treaty interpreter under VCLT article 30(1) and 30(2). If the MoUs are not seen as sufficiently 'related' to the treaty, their good intentions will not be taken into account in interpreting clauses which might weaken laws to implement the UN CBD in other circumstances. This may have implications should the matter be raised in a dispute settlement. Under the VCLT, these provisions may be helpful in the interpretation of any overlapping obligations to respect IPRs in the RTA.[392] However, a tribunal may find that such a clause, rather than specific 'term' of the treaty providing explicit guidance, is an 'agreement relating to the treaty which was made between all the Parties in connection with the conclusion of the treaty', part of the context of the terms of the treaty, for the purpose of interpretation, or even an unrelated agreement.[393] The customary principle of integration highlights a need for balance between economic and environmental objectives. This outcome would scarcely provide such balance.

There are few comparable provisions in the EU-Chile AA. However, in the EU-CARIFORUM EPA, Parties directly 'agree that the patent provisions of this subsection and the Convention on Biological Diversity shall be implemented in a mutually supportive way'.[394] Further, the EU-Peru-Colombia AA at article 272 indicates, with regard to intellectual property rights and biodiversity protection, that:

> The Parties recognise their obligation in accordance with the CBD to, subject to their domestic legislation, respect, preserve and maintain knowledge, innovations and practices of indigenous and local communities embodying traditional lifestyles relevant for the conservation and sustainable use of biodiversity and promote their wider application conditioned to the prior and informed consent of the holders of such knowledge, innovations

[390] United Nations Convention on Biological Diversity (UNCBD) (opened for signature 5 June 1992, entered into force 29 December 1993) 1760 UNTS 79, 143, art 8j; CBD Secretariat, *Bonn Guidelines on Access to Genetic Resources and Fair and Equitable Sharing of the Benefits Arising out of their Utilization* (Montreal, 2002); JPOI (n 38) 44 j); K Bottriel and D French, 'The Duty of States to Ensure Sustainable Use of Natural Resources' (Montreal, CISDL 2005) CISDL Legal Working Papers on Recent Developments in International Law Related to Sustainable Development, <http://www.cisdl.org/pdf/sdl/SDL_Sustainable_Use.pdf> accessed 16 December 2020; J Hepburn and A Khalfan, 'The Principle of Equity and the Eradication of Poverty' (Montreal, CISDL 2005) CISDL Legal Working Papers on Recent Developments in International Law Related to Sustainable Development, <http://www.worldfuturecouncil.org/fileadmin/user_upload/papers/CISDL_P2_Equityetc.pdf> accessed 16 December 2020; Cabrera (n 328).

[391] See PG LePrestre (ed), *Governing Global Biodiversity: The Evolution and Implementation of the Convention on Biological Diversity* (Aldershot, Ashgate 2002).

[392] An interpretation of these provisions, in good faith in accordance with their ordinary meaning, in light of a 'purpose' of sustainable development, suggests that while scarcely giving precedence to biodiversity, neither are IP provisions meant to dominate, see VCLT, art 31(2)(a).

[393] VCLT, art 31(3)(c) permits other relevant rules of international law, see Pauwelyn (n 105) 253–254 where it is explained that this rule permits customary norms to assist in giving meaning to the terms of the treaty.

[394] EU-CARIFORUM EPA (n 29) art 150.3.

> and practices, and encourage the fair and equitable sharing of benefits arising from the utilisation of such knowledge, innovation and practices.[395]

This responds directly and clearly to the SIA which noted, for example, that: 'Further intellectual property protection schemes for plant varieties are required to balance traditional knowledge and rights of indigenous communities, biodiversity considerations, seed harvesting by local farmers and food security.[396]

Liberalizing, incentivizing investment and transferring eco-innovations, green *technologies* and renewable energy

It has been suggested that by liberalizing environmental goods and services, and incentivizing investment in renewable energy and other eco-innovation technologies, States can deliver simultaneous improvements for trade and the environment.[397] While the Doha Round remains frozen on these issues, regional and bilateral treaties have made progress. In the Agreement on Environmental Cooperation of the US-Chile Free Trade Agreement and the US-CAFTA-DR Free Trade Agreement, 'developing and promoting environmentally beneficial goods and services' is included among commitments for cooperation.[398] The interest is commercial as well as environmental. A trade negotiating objective in the US Trade Act of 2002 is defined 'to seek market access … for United States environmental technologies, goods, and services', and the US systematically seeks to encourage trade liberalization in this area.[399] Such liberalization may deliver environmental benefits in Chile, as access to environmental services improves for industry and for consumers, and as the most recent technologies can be imported.[400]

In the EU-CARIFORUM EPA, Parties agree broadly to collaborate in order to promote 'public awareness and education programmes in respect of environmental goods and services in order to foster trade in such products between the Parties'.[401] The EU-South Korea FTA is more precise:

> The Parties shall strive to facilitate and promote trade and foreign direct investment in environmental goods and services, including environmental technologies, sustainable renewable energy, energy efficient products and services and eco-labelled goods, including through addressing related non-tariff barriers. The Parties shall strive to facilitate and promote trade in goods that contribute to sustainable development, including goods that are the subject of schemes such as fair and ethical trade and those involving corporate social responsibility and accountability.[402]

395 EU-Colombia Peru AA (n 28) art 272.4.

396 EU-Andean SIA (n 143) 121.

397 Sampson (n 327) 44.

398 Agreement on Environmental Cooperation of the US-Chile Free Trade Agreement and the US-CAFTA-DR Free Trade Agreement.

399 OECD (n 195) 97–99; US Trade Act of 2002 s 2102(b)(11)(F).

400 A Dufey, E Claro and N Borregaard, 'Liberalising Trade in Environmental Goods and Services in the Czech Republic' (2005) OECD Trade and Environment Working Paper, OECD, Paris; S Giljum and N Eisenmenger, 'North-South Trade and the Distribution of Environmental Goods and Burdens: A Biophysical Perspective' (2004) 13 Journal of Environment Development 73.

401 EU-CARIFORUM EPA (n 29) art 190.2(f).

402 EU-South Korea FTA (n 368) art 13.6.2.

These provisions could directly address particular opportunities raised in the EU-South Korea SIA which notes the interest of both Parties to encourage the development of a 'global green economy'.[403]

Similarly, cooperation and enhanced trade and investment in renewable energy and carbon markets is agreed in article 275 of the EU-Colombia-Peru FTA, and in EU-Central American AA at article 50(3)(d), for example, where the Parties agreed that 'co-operation shall seek to facilitate joint initiatives in the area of climate change mitigation and adaptation to its adverse effects, including the strengthening of carbon market mechanisms'.[404] This appears to respond to opportunities highlighted with regard to climate change in the SIA, which noted that an AA constituted an opportunity to include specific provisions to 'stimulate the commitment to and implementation of international and MEAs, thereby encouraging further progress on issues of international concern such as climate change, biodiversity and natural resources'.[405]

There is scope for integration of social and environmental considerations by enhancing trade and investment in goods and services that, according to other accords, are important to encourage for more sustainable development. Advancement achieved in the identification and liberalization of trade in environmental goods and services in the framework of RTAs may eventually translate into progress at the WTO. As discussed above, the Doha Development Agenda establishes negotiations on this issue, and the WTO Committee on Trade and Environment has sought to define a list of environmental goods and services for tariff reductions.[406] Very little progress has been made to date. Depending on the experience in these treaties, it may eventually be possible, as the US and EU have jointly proposed, to negotiate measures within the WTO to facilitate trade in climate-friendly goods and services.[407] The bilateral or regional economic treaties analysed above provide initial signs of openness among States to this proposal.

Reducing trade in the products of illegal logging

A final and telling example involves the potential for trade and investment liberalization to actually support the enforcement of forestry laws to limit illegal logging and trade in wildlife.[408] The Chile-US ER highlights illegal logging and unsustainable exploitation of native forests as a major area of concern.[409] Similar challenges were raised in the US-Peru ER, which noted that if trade in forestry products were liberalized without adequate legal protections to prevent illegally extracted wood and wildlife products from being sold as legitimate, firms from countries where laws are effectively enforced would find it difficult to compete with lower priced products.[410] Stakeholders proposed the use of trade and

403 EU-South Korea SIA (n 370) 204.

404 EU-Central America AA (n 23) art 50(3)(d).

405 EU-Central America SIA (n 183) 17.

406 Doha WTO Ministerial 2001: Ministerial Declaration, WT/MIN(01)/DEC/1 (Doha Ministerial Declaration) 31, also noted in the JPOI (n 38) 99 b).

407 ICTSD, 'EU, US Call for Eliminating Trade Barriers to Climate-Friendly Goods and Services', <http://ictsd.org/i/news/bridgesweekly/7778/> accessed 16 December 2020.

408 R Glastra, *Cut and Run: Illegal Logging and Timber Trade in the Tropics* (Ottawa, International Development Research Centre 1999); A Contreras-Hermosilla., R Doornbosch., & M Lodge, M. (2008). *The Economics of Illegal Logging and Associated Trade* (Paris, OECD 2007); G Hayman and D Brack, *International Environmental Crime: The Nature and Control of Environmental Black Markets* (London, RIIA 2002).

409 US-Chile Final ER (n 13).

410 USTR 'Interim Environmental Review United States-Andean Free Trade Agreement' (2005) <http://www.ustr.gov/sites/default/files/perinter.pdf> accessed 16 December 2020, 12.

investment measures to actually prevent illegally extracted forest materials and species from being traded internationally.[411] The US-Peru TPA responded by incorporating Annex 18.3.4 on forest sector governance, with detailed and mandatory provisions to address illegal logging and trade in wildlife. These provisions appear tailored to a specific and particular concerns raised in the impact assessment. Peru is the world's top exporter of mahogany and other endangered species of trees listed under CITES, and the US is the main importer. Recognizing the environmental and economic consequences of trade and investment associated with illegal logging, and illegal trade in wildlife, in this Annex the Parties provide a new trade-related certification and verification mechanism to 'enhance forest sector governance and promote legal trade in timber products'. Parties recognize that:

> trade associated with illegal logging, and illegal trade in wildlife, including wildlife trafficking, undermine trade in products from legally harvested sources, reduce the economic value of natural resources, and weaken efforts to promote conservation and sustainable management of resources.[412]

Accordingly, each Party commits to combat trade associated with illegal logging and illegal trade in wildlife. They also note that 'good forest sector governance is critical to promoting the economic value and sustainable management of forest resources', and establish a new mechanism, a Sub-Committee on Forest Sector Governance, under both the Committee on Trade in Goods and the Environmental Affairs Council, to facilitate consultation and information exchange, and secure implementation. Among the agreed measures, Peru will develop systems to track harvest, transport, processing and exports of tree species protected under CITES.[413] The Parties will undertake verification and action against traders in case of non-compliance under set time periods, and Peru will identify a focal point with sufficient authority and staff to investigate violations. The US can detain questionable shipments pending verification that the timber was legally harvested, and send inspectors to accompany Peruvian authorities. According to the Annex, Peru will also craft and adopt a strategic plan of action on broad-leaf mahogany in order to comply with CITES Annex II 'severely restricted' species obligations, including an annual export quota, and secure financial resources for implementation.[414] The mechanism was greeted with cautious approval from experts and other institutions working on illegal logging.[415] It may provide a model for discussions, currently in preliminary stages, for a legally binding instrument on forests.[416] This particular mechanism provides for trade liberalization, public sector investments and market access with appropriately integrated balancing measures, in order to ensure that there is less chance of unintended and detrimental consequences to the forests, and to the forestry competitors in the trading partner where illegal logging is less common. Such a

[411] Dudley and others, *Bad Harvest?* (Gland, WWF 1995); D Brack, K Gray and G Hayman, *Controlling the International Trade in Illegally Logged Timber and Wood Products* (London, RIIA 2002).

[412] Annex 18.3.4 on forest sector governance.

[413] CITES (n 166) Annex II.

[414] ICTSD, 'US-Peru Bilateral to Address Illegal Logging, Boost MEA Implementation' Bridges Trade BioRes, 22 June 2007, <http://ictsd.net/i/news/biores/9122 > accessed 16 December 2020.

[415] RIIA, 'US-Peru Bilateral to Address Illegal Logging' (2007) <http://www.illegal-logging.info> accessed 16 December 2020.

[416] See 'Non-legally binding instrument on all types of forests' UNGA Res A/C.2/62/L.5 (2007) Sixty-second Session, 2nd Cte, 22 October 2007.

trade and investment measure has the potential to deliver both environment and development benefits, by seeking to secure better governance,[417] and more sustainable use of natural resources.[418] The EU-Central America AA also directly agrees that:

> In order to promote the sustainable management of forest resources, the Parties commit to work together to improve forest law enforcement and governance and to promote trade in legal and sustainable forest products through instruments that may include, inter alia: effective use of CITES with regard to endangered timber species; certification schemes for sustainably harvested forest products; regional or bilateral Forest Law Enforcement Governance and Trade ('FLEGT') Voluntary Partnership Agreements.[419]

This provision could directly address particular concerns raised in the SIA, which signalled:

> In Central America, increased investment in the forestry and agriculture sectors might stimulate illegal logging for timber production or agricultural frontier expansion if policies are not established to control these. Flanking measures will be needed to mitigate the harmful secondary effects of deforestation including reduced land and water quality. In the EU, purchases of illegally logged timber or products made thereof, needs to be clearly discouraged and limited.[420]

Overall, this analysis revealed many innovations which could address the third key tension raised in impact assessments; the concern that trade and investment liberalization treaties will simply encourage the growth of obsolete industries that in other treaties, States are attempting to phase out. Many of the specific trade and investment enhancement endeavours appear to respond directly to concerns raised in assessments. The integration of social and environmental opportunities into the economic decision-making permits States to identify opportunities to enhance market access for more sustainable goods and services, while agreeing trade disciplines which reduce existing subsidies for unsustainable (and in the case of forests, illegal) industries, even to the extent of agreeing new monitoring and enforcement systems. This integration converts a tension into an opportunity, and though relatively new, offers perhaps an interesting way forward for bilateral or regional economic treaties to contribute to sustainable development.

417 N Chowdry and CE Skarstedt, 'The Principle of Good Governance' (Montreal, CISDL 2005) CISDL Legal Working Papers on Recent Developments in International Law Related to Sustainable Development, <http://www.cisdl.org/pdf/sdl/SDL_Good_Governance.pdf> accessed 16 December 2020.
418 Bottriel and French (n 390).
419 EU-Central America AA (n 23) art 289.
420 EU-Central America SIA (n 183) 84.

18

Procedural Innovations Related to Sustainable Development

Various procedural innovations have been undertaken by the Parties during trade and investment negotiations, as has been noted above. New procedures are being used by Parties to identify potential environmental and sustainability impacts, and to consider innovative measures for inclusion in their economic agreements. Discussions on how trade and investment could promote more sustainable development are taking place through four main procedural innovations: impact assessments and reviews of trade and investment liberalization policies and draft treaties; consultations between domestic-level economic, environment and development authorities; transparency and public participation mechanisms; and new dispute settlement provisions. Each is briefly discussed in turn below, examining how these processes help environment and social development aspects to be integrated into economic planning, including trade treaty-making, in order to achieve sustainable development.

18.1 Impact Assessments of Trade and Investment Liberalization Policies and Draft Treaties

Social and environmental concerns raised in the impact assessments of trade and investment liberalization agreements were discussed earlier. Here, the focus is on the origins and scope of impact assessment processes, their mandates and methodologies, their role in integrating social and environmental issues into economic trade policy and how they could be improved.

Impact assessments were recommended for trade and investment agreements in scholarly and scientific literature prior to the 1992 UN Conference on Environment and Development (UNCED).[1] The environmental cooperation body of the venerable North American Free Trade Agreement (NAFTA), the North American Commission for Environmental Cooperation (NACEC), proposed an initial methodology,[2] leading to a series of studies for review in an ongoing North American Symposium for the Assessment of Trade and Environment.[3] The United Nations Environment Programme (UNEP) also

[1] See for historical overview, J Salzman, 'Executive Order 13.141 and the Environmental Review of Trade Agreements' (2001) 95 American Journal of International Law 368, 368.

[2] NACEC, 'Assessing the Environmental Effects of Trade' (NACEC, 1999).

[3] CEC, Fourth North American Symposium on Assessing the Environmental Effects of Trade: Services and the Environment, 23 April 2008, <http://www.cec.org/calendar/details/index.cfm?varlan=english&ID=2088>.

Crafting Trade and Investment Accords for Sustainable Development. Marie-Claire Cordonier Segger, Oxford University Press. © Marie-Claire Cordonier Segger 2021. DOI: 10.1093/oso/9780198831341.003.0018

carried out national-level sector-specific environmental impact evaluations,[4] and experts from the UN Human Rights Council (UNHRC) theorized human rights impact assessments.[5] These efforts gradually led to more sophisticated analysis,[6] generating methods that can assess social, environmental and economic impacts based on probable scenarios of trade and investment negotiation outcomes.

A general description of the two main models of review of assessment was explained earlier in this volume. The first model of assessment involves undertaking separate national or regional environmental and labour assessments or reviews of new trade and investment treaties, to identify the most significant material and regulatory *environmental* or *labour* impacts of the economic activity stimulated by a particular trade or investment agreement. The US and Canada both conduct *ex-ante* environmental assessments of economic negotiations which highlight sustainable development as part of their *raison d'être*.[7] Methods used for these assessments are similar in Canada and the US.[8] Government officials prepare scenarios predicting the economic changes that could be directly attributed to a new trade treaty, and then consider potential material environmental impacts of those economic effects in that country. They also consider potential impacts on environmental regulations. An initial screening is done, and through public consultation processes, industry associations, academics and civil society organizations raise relevant concerns. If significant concerns are found, a second more in-depth assessment is done to address those issues. Then, an inter-departmental committee and advisors screen the final outcomes, and these are published as a final report.[9] Environmental Reviews (ERs) do not consider social or development impacts, nor are they permitted to take cumulative impacts into account.[10] The Canadian assessments do not consider impacts that could occur in the territories of their trading partners, while the US reviews may consider such impacts to identify areas for future environmental cooperation. In Canada, EAs are mandated by Cabinet Directive.[11] In the United States, ERs are required by Executive Order 13141 on Environmental Review

[4] See Centro de Investigación y Planificación del Medio Ambiente (CIPMA), *Environmental Impacts of Trade Liberalization and Policies for the Sustainable Management of Natural Resources: A Case Study of Chile's Mining Sector* (Geneva, UNEP 1999).

[5] See S Walker, 'Human Rights Impact Assessments of Trade-Related Policies' in M Gehring and MC Cordonier Segger (eds), *Sustainable Development in World Trade Law* (The Hague, Kluwer Law International 2005) 217–256.

[6] Patrick Reynaud, 'Sustainable Development and Regional Trade Agreements: Toward Better Practices in Impact Assessments' (2012) 8 McGill International Journal of Sustainable Development Law and Policy 205, 205; Sikina Jinnah and Elisa Morgera, 'Environmental Provisions in American and EU Free Trade Agreements: A Preliminary Comparison and Research Agenda' (2013) 22(3) Review of European, Comparative & International Environmental Law 324–339.

[7] General Council—Preparations for the 1999 Ministerial Conference—Trade and Sustainable Development-Communication from the United States (6 August 1999) WT/GC/W/304 99-3364; General Council-Preparations for the 1999 Ministerial Conference—Canadian Approach to Trade and Environment in the New WTO Round—Communication from Canada (12 October 1999) WT/GC/W/358 99-4298, <http://docsonline.wto.org>.

[8] J Salzman, 'Executive Order 13.141 and the Environmental Review of Trade Agreements' (n 1); see also J Salzman, 'Seattle's Legal Legacy and Environmental Reviews of Trade Agreements' (2001) 31 Environmental Law 501, 513–514.

[9] See Annex 1 of this volume.

[10] C George, 'Developments in Regional Trade Agreements and the Environment: 2012 Update', OECD Trade and Environment Working Papers, No. 2013/04 (Paris, OECD 2013) <https://doi.org/10.1787/5k43m4nxwm25-en>.

[11] Government of Canada, *The Cabinet Directive on the Environmental Assessment of Policy, Plan and Program Proposals* (Ottawa, Privy Council Office and Canadian Environmental Assessment Agency 2004) <http://www.ceaa-acee.gc.ca/016/CEAA-StrategicFinal_e.pdf>.

of Trade Agreements[12] and the implementing Guidelines.[13] Order 13141 responds to US Trade Act negotiation objectives that include:

> to strengthen the capacity of US trading partners to protect the environment through the promotion of sustainable development;
>
> to reduce or eliminate government practices or policies that unduly threaten sustainable development.[14]

This implies that the US sees the promotion of sustainable development as a method to achieve environmental protection, but also recognizes that certain government practices and policies, including trade policies, can jeopardize sustainable development.[15] Presumably, the task is to uncover which ones do so 'unduly'. To evaluate regulatory effects, the US Trade Policy Staff Committee subcommittees are subdivided into smaller groups to analyse the text in each chapter of the Agreement.[16] Though the ERs focus on identifying trade and investment agreement commitments that may affect, positively or negatively, the ability of US governments to enact, enforce or maintain environmental laws and regulations, provisions affecting the ability to fulfil international obligations or participate in international cooperative fora are also considered.

The US Trade Act provides that ERs shall be conducted and reported to the Committee on Ways and Means of the House of Representatives and the Committee on Finance of the Senate.[17] These reviews seek to ensure that policy-makers are informed about reasonably foreseeable environmental impacts of trade agreements (both positive and negative), to identify complementarities between trade and environmental objectives, and to help shape appropriate responses if environmental impacts are identified.[18] Indeed, the final reports are often prepared once negotiations are nearly concluded, and have a tendency to explain measures that address concerns, to the point that they obscure the actual concerns themselves.

The second model involves assessing the broader impacts of an economic treaty on its Parties' potential for *sustainable development*. The EU, with particularly key contributions from UK experts, has developed technical guidelines and handbooks to explain how to carry out sustainable impact assessments (SIA).[19] The method analyses specific development scenarios likely to result from liberalization obligations agreed in an economic integration treaty, sector by sector, then examines their effects on certain social, economic and environmental indicators (see Table 18.1 below).[20] Most SIAs now include a strong social dimension.[21]

[12] 64 FR 63169, 18 November 1999.

[13] 65 FR 79442, 19 December 2000.

[14] US Trade Act of 2002, s 2102(b)(11)(D-E), s 2102(c)(4), Executive Orders 13277 (2002) and 13141 (1999); Salzman (n 1).

[15] J Creason and others, 'The Environmental Impacts of Trade Liberalisation: A Quantitative Analysis for the United States using TEAM' (2005) 34 Agricultural and Resource Economics Review 90, 90.

[16] USTR, *Interim Environmental Review of the US-Chile FTA* (Washington 2001) 7.

[17] Salzman (n 1).

[18] Ibid.

[19] EC, *Handbook for Trade Sustainability Impact Assessment* (Brussels, 2006).

[20] See, e.g., C Kirkpatrick and N Lee, *Sustainable Development in a Developing World: Integrating Socio-Economic Appraisal and Environmental Assessment* (Cheltenham, Edward Elgar 1997).

[21] H Blanco, 'Evaluacion de la sustentabilidad de los acuerdos comerciales y su aplicacion en el contexto latinoamericano y del ALCA' in H Blanco, M Araya and C Murillo, *ALCA y medio ambiente: Ideas desde Latinoamerica* (CIPMA-GETS-CINPE, Santiago 2003).

Table 18.1 SIA Indicators

I. Economic
1. Real income (Net value added)
2. Net fixed capital formation (Private, public capital formation)
3. Employment (Self-employment, informal employment)
4. Consumer effects (Prices, variety of goods and services)
II. Social
5. Poverty (income and other social dimensions of poverty)
6. Health and education (life expectancy; mortality rates; nutritional levels, literacy rates; primary, secondary and tertiary enrolment rates)
III. Environmental
7. Environmental quality (air, water, and land quality indicators)
8. Biological diversity (designated eco-systems, endangered species)
9. Other natural resource stocks (energy resources; other non-renewable and renewable resources)

Source: SIA handbook, studies and literature[22]

Such SIA methods are more sophisticated than an ER alone.[23] An SIA involves prioritization and identification of key issues (screening and scoping); development of negotiation scenarios; elaboration of country groupings and case studies (broad country groupings are subdivided as appropriate for each of the main sectors, making use of available data); consideration of indicators; identification of cross-sectoral linkages and cumulative impacts (related to scale effects, technology effects, structural effects, location effects and sometimes regulatory effects); evaluation of alternative prevention, mitigation and enhancement (M&E) measures; monitoring and *ex post* evaluation; consultation and stakeholder participation; and technical analysis of potential impacts (using both quantitative and qualitative data).[24] Technical analysis includes consideration of submissions from stakeholders, experts and other interested parties and analysis of results of economic modelling studies, but it also includes reviews of empirical evidence of potential economic, social and environmental impacts and causal chain analysis.[25]

SIAs can consider cumulative effects of a trade agreement, and are expected to focus on potential impacts in the developing country partner's economy, environment and society.[26] The European Community (EC) commissions an independent SIA of each new trade

[22] See also C George, 'Sustainable Development and Global Governance' (2007) 16 Journal of Environment and Development 102; C George and C Kirkpatrick, 'Trade and Development: Assessing the Impact of Trade Liberalization on Sustainable Development' (2004) 38 Journal of World Trade 441; C George and C Kirkpatrick, 'The Influence of the European Union's Sustainability Impact Assessment of Multilateral and Regional Trade Negotiations' (2006) Institute for Development Policy & Management Working Paper No. 14/2006, <http://citeseerx.ist.psu.edu/viewdoc/download?doi=10.1.1.530.5253&rep=rep1&type=pdf> accessed 16 December 2020; Kilpatrick and Lee (n 20).

[23] Gehring and Cordonier Segger (n 5) 204–205; M Perrin, 'Sustainability Assessments of Trade Liberalisation Agreements', Paper presented at Workshop on Methodologies for Environmental Assessment of Trade Liberalisation Agreements, Paris, OECD October 1999.

[24] EC (n 19).

[25] For a review of methodological issues in SIAs, see Hugo Rojas-Romagosa, 'Overview of the Evolution of the Methodology and Coverage of EU Ex-Ante Trade Sustainability Impact Assessments over Time' (RESPECT mimeo 2018); Reynaud (n 6).

[26] Gehring and Cordonier Segger (n 5) 209–212; EC (n 19); Kirkpatrick and George (n 22).

agreement that it negotiates, and publishes a response. The purpose of the EU SIAs is to integrate sustainability into trade policy by informing negotiators of the possible social, environmental and economic consequences of a trade agreement. SIAs suggest new domestic policies and international initiatives that could yield better outcomes, not just in terms of liberalization and economic growth, but also for other social and environmental components of sustainable development.[27] An SIA offers possible accompanying policy measures, to maximize the positive impacts of the trade negotiations in question, and reduce any negative impacts.[28]

Like the US and Canadian assessments, the EU SIAs have generated a significant body of scientific and technical analysis.[29] However, while the US ERs and Canadian Environmental Assessments (EAs) are seen as public education on the importance of trade liberalization, the EU SIAs attempt to provide systematic analysis of potential effects for identification of mitigation and flanking measures. All assessment reports to date highlight that the process is meant to support sustainable development through integration.[30]

Assessments can be continual. In certain treaties of the EU, such as the EU-Colombia-Peru AA, Parties agree to: 'review, monitor and assess the impact of the implementation of this Agreement on labour and the environment, as it deems appropriate, through its respective domestic and participative processes'.[31] In the EU-South Korea Free Trade Agreement, Parties agree on:

> ... reviewing, monitoring and assessing the impact of the implementation of this Agreement on sustainable development, including the promotion of decent work, through their respective participative processes and institutions, as well as those set up under this Agreement, for instance through trade-related sustainability impact assessments.[32]

SIA monitoring is now meant to occur after the trade treaty negotiation process, as part of the ongoing cooperative process to implement the treaties.

One of the implications of this volume is that SIAs could benefit from a serious component of regulatory impact assessment. In few SIAs are potential regulatory impacts considered seriously. A pioneer examines potential impacts on a Party's ability to implement Rio Declaration principles,[33] and on national sustainable development strategies.[34] But efforts are rudimentary and could benefit from considerable improvement.[35] By focusing on the three key regulatory tensions identified in this research, SIAs could uncover: (1) which new laws and regulations, including international market based instruments, trade or investment measures, might be unduly constrained by the new trade and investment

[27] EC (n 19) 11–12.
[28] The Commission has produced revised Guidelines on how to conduct the required analysis: see EC (n 19).
[29] Kirkpatrick and George (n 22); Gehring and Cordonier Segger (n 5) 204–205, 209–212.
[30] See Annex 1 of this volume.
[31] EU-Colombia-Peru FTA (signed 30 March 2010) art 279.
[32] EU-South Korea FTA (signed 6 October 2010) art 13.10.
[33] IARC, *Trade Sustainability Impact Assessment (SIA) of the Association Agreement under Negotiation between the European Community and Mercosur: Final Overview Report Trade SIA EU-Mercosur* (Manchester, March 2009) [EU-Mercosur SIA].
[34] OECD, 'National Strategies for Sustainable Development: Good Practices in OECD Countries' (8 September 2005) SG/SD(2005)6.
[35] For a review of methodological issues in SIAs, see Kirkpatrick and George (n 22).

liberalization agreements, and how these laws or treaties could be accommodated by a form of exception; (2) which existing laws and regulations on sustainable development, including multilateral environmental assessments (MEAs), could be weakened by the new economic agreements, and how they might be strengthened by trade- or investment-related cooperation, including citizen submissions and other mechanisms to improve enforcement; and (3) which future laws and regulations might promote development, incentivize investment and encourage trade in sustainable goods and services, and could benefit from trade and investment enhancement measures. The outcomes of this legal element of the assessment could assist States in their economic negotiations.

As this volume has shown, impact assessment findings are making their way into bilateral, regional and international economic treaty regimes themselves. The tool itself is also gaining currency, as other major trading States also increasingly begin to undertake such assessments.[36] The WTO notes that the importance of impact assessments was confirmed in the 2001 Doha Ministerial Declaration, which encourages governments to share their expertise and experience with other members who wish to perform the reviews.[37]

Impact assessments are conducted prior to consensus on trade and investment treaty objectives. The treaty itself has not yet been agreed, nor has its object and purpose been set. As such, the investments of resources entailed, including inter-agency and public engagement, also good faith attempts to address findings in trade and investment treaty negotiations, are unlikely to have been affected by a commitment to the treaty purpose of sustainable development. Rather, as discussed above, such procedural innovations may provide certain evidence of an interstitial influence of State commitments to promote sustainable development. This influence may also be encouraging States to respect the requirement that environmental and social considerations be integrated into trade, investment and other economic decisions.

18.2 Consultations between Economic, Environment and Development Authorities

According to the World Trade Organization (WTO) and others, inadequate coordination among decision-makers at the national level can be one reason for tensions.[38] Consultations between economic, environmental and social development authorities can secure more integrated and coherent trade and investment policy-making.[39] For instance, effectively addressing environmental issues in bilateral or regional economic treaties requires:

[36] Kirkpatrick and George (n 22); Gehring and Cordonier Segger (n 5) 204–205, 209–212.

[37] Kilpatrick and George (n 22). See also WTO Report to the Fifth Session of the WTO Ministerial Conference in Cancún; paras 32 and 33 of the Doha Ministerial Declaration WT/CTE/8 (11 July 2003); European Communities, Documentation pertaining to an EC Seminar on Sustainability Impact Assessment of Trade Agreements WT/CTE/W/224; (21 February 2003); Canada, Initial Environmental Assessment: Trade Negotiations in the World Trade Organization, Submission by Canada. WT/CTE/W/221, (24 January 2003); European Communities; Sustainability Impact Assessment; WT/CTE/W/208, also WT/COMTD/W/99 and TN/TE/W/3), (3 June 2002). See <http://www.wto.org/english/tratop_e/envir_e/reviews_exper_e.htm>.

[38] H Nordström and S Vaughan, *Trade and Environment* (Special Studies 4, Geneva, WTO 1999) 73; Singapore Ministerial Declaration (adopted on 13 December 1996), WT/MIN(96)/DEC (18 December 1996) para 16.

[39] Gehring and Cordonier Segger (n 5) 191–192; Perrin (n 23).

preparation, coordination among trade and environment officials (who, often, have often never previously worked together), setting of priorities, and reconciling conflicting views. Moreover, once a text is agreed on, continuous efforts are needed to ensure effective integration of trade and environmental issues throughout the life of the agreement.[40]

In the negotiation processes for the trade and investment liberalization treaties studied in this research, such procedural innovations were adopted by Chile and other countries, as well as the US and the EU. In particular, Chilean negotiations with the US and the EU led to great public debates in the Chilean Congress, business associations, labour unions, non-governmental organizations (NGOs) and others. During the negotiation of both the US-Chile FTA and the EU-Chile AA, the Chilean Office of International Economic Relations (DIRECON) sought to facilitate public participation. The Chilean experience is documented in a DIRECON Study of Lessons Learned, and as a developing country experience, provides a useful example.[41] As noted in a Chilean DIRECON Study, there was a need to develop coherent national positions on the main issues of the negotiations:

> The definition of unified positions starts with the work within the government itself. This task is complex, given the big number and diversity of agencies involved in the negotiations [including 90 public officers from 10 different ministries and 8 specialized agencies]. During the two years negotiation, these public officials could not abandon the agenda of their own ministry, which meant an additional tension in the process of building cohesive governmental positions.[42]

Further, 'behind each ministry or agency, there are institutional attributions or administrative practices that very often are not easy to modify'.[43] For an outward looking economy such as Chile, the trade agenda 'is a vital aspect of its economic policy and covers decisions that involve several ministries'.[44] The Chilean solution was to create an Inter-ministerial Committee for Foreign Economic Affairs led by the Minister of Foreign Affairs, with participation from the Ministers of Finance, Economy, Agriculture and the General Secretariat of the Government.[45] The Director General of International Economic Relations served as technical secretary. As the DIRECON Study notes, this 'inter-ministerial committee was very useful in the negotiations with the EU ... and with the US, since it assessed the course of the negotiations and made the main decisions'.[46] At certain moments during Chile-US negotiations, the Committee met with the President to define the strategy and take final decisions. It was supported by a group of advisors that prepared the documents for the ministerial meetings. During US-Chile FTA negotiations, from March 2000, it met more than 25 times.[47]

[40] OECD, *Environment and Regional Trade Agreements* (Paris, 2007) 156.

[41] O Rosales, 'Chile-U.S. Free Trade Agreement: Lessons and Best Practices', Paper presented at the American Chamber of Commerce, Washington, 28 April 2003.

[42] Dirección General de Relaciones Económicas Internacionales del Ministerio de Relaciones Exteriores de Chile, 'Evaluación De Las Relaciones Económicas Y De Cooperación Entre Chile Y Los Países De La Unión Europea: A Cuatro Años de Vigencia del Acuerdo De Asociación' (October 2007) (EU-Chile DIRECON Study) <http://www.sice.oas.org/TPD/CHL_EU/Studies/Evaluacion2007_s.pdf> (translation by author).

[43] Ibid.

[44] Ibid.

[45] Ibid.

[46] Ibid.

[47] Ibid.

The US and the EU also have extensive inter-departmental and inter-directorate consultation mechanisms in place which, while they might not serve as realistic models for developing countries due to their complexity and expense, secured several avenues for the integration of economic, social and environmental policy in the negotiations of the US-Chile FTA,[48] and the EU-Chile AA.[49] Similarly, in Canada major trade and investment policy decisions are made with full involvement of thirty federal departments, and even impact assessments are chaired by a Steering Committee of officials from many departments.[50] Such inter-departmental collaboration processes are one mechanism to secure more integrated economic policy-making. They also provide a further forum where interstitial effects of State commitments to sustainable development may be observed.

18.3 Transparency and Public Participation in Trade and Investment Negotiations

Public participation mechanisms are seen as a way to promote sustainable development, including in Agenda 21, the Johannesburg Plan of Implementation (JPOI), the Sustainable Development Goals (SDGs) and also the Aarhus and Escazu Conventions.[51] The innovations in the trade and investment agreements analysed in this book reveal two facets. First, during the negotiations of each economic agreement, public participation was facilitated by the Parties, especially on issues related to sustainability. Second, the treaties themselves contain substantive mechanisms to secure access to information, public participation and even a certain limited access to dispute settlement.

18.3.1 Transparency and Public Participation Practices in Trade and Investment Agreement Negotiations

Chilean experience provides a good example of how facilitating transparency and public participation can promote integration of social and environmental considerations into trade and investment policy. In the 1999 Joint Declaration at the initiation of negotiations for the EU-Chile AA, Parties affirmed that negotiations 'shall be conducted in an open and transparent manner. To this end contacts will be maintained in the EU and Chile with representatives of civil society.'[52] In the negotiations with the EU and others, the Chilean government had worked closely with the private sector to define sensitive areas, modalities of negotiations and build convergences. However, as the DIRECON Study notes, 'historically there has not been a similar dialogue with other sectors of society.'[53] In the context of 2002

[48] J Richardson (ed), *European Union-Power and Policy-Making* (London, Routledge 2005); see also art 6 of the EC Treaty.
[49] Executive Order 13.141 of 16 November 1999, Federal Register 64 No 222, 63.169.
[50] F Bouder, *Governance for Sustainable Development in Canada* (Paris, OECD 2001) 13.
[51] Convention on Access to Information, Public Participation in Decision-Making and Access to Justice in Environmental Matters (adopted 25 June 1998, entered into force 30 October 2001) 2161 UNTS 447.
[52] Council of the European Union, 'First Meeting of the European Union-Chile Joint Council' (EC Doc. 13291/99), 24 November 1999 (Press Release 372).
[53] Ibid.

World Summit on Sustainable Development (WSSD) preparations, a more inclusive dialogue was opened.

First, a Civil Society Consultative Committee was established to advise the Inter-Ministerial Committee. With 20 Members of Parliament, academics, former ambassadors to the US and former ministers with experience in US trade and economic relations, the Committee were briefed as negotiations proceeded, gave advice on particular points, and met directly with the Inter-Ministerial Committee eight times. Several Council members participated in missions to Washington to meet counterpart Members of Congress, authorities, NGOs, entrepreneurial and labour organizations. The Committee played a constructive role in engaging broader elements of Chilean civil society. 'To the extent that the members of the Council are influential in the public opinion, they transform themselves into valuable allies to transmit messages ... ', the DIRECON Study notes. Furthermore, three 'rooms next door' were established (for business owners, labour unions, and small and medium-sized enterprises (SMEs)) to inform and consult during the successive rounds of negotiations. From the tenth round of US-Chile FTA negotiations (Miami, December 2001) onwards, the 'rooms next door' were kept open during bilateral negotiating rounds themselves. As DIRECON noted: 'This experience helped to build trust between negotiators and private and labor organizations, very useful in the last parts of the negotiation that requires fast and urgent decisions.'[54] The 'rooms next door' process has continued through implementation of the treaty, with high political visibility, through open invitations which received 'a good response'.[55]

Second, in the mid-1990s, Chile built foundations for dialogue with a broader spectrum of civil society organizations (environmental NGOs, social justice organizations and academics) in international economic negotiations. In 2000, a Presidential Decree called for dialogue with civil society in all levels 'to obtain increased awareness, education and participation about trade negotiation process ... to access inputs regarding trade issues by informed civil society participants' and 'to generate a greater analysis and evaluation of results and impact of trade negotiations, increasing the legitimacy and consensus about trade policy issues, deepening the democratic feature of trade negotiation process, with greater civil society participation'.[56] An open invitation was issued, backed by newspaper inserts, official public activities, trade negotiations information dissemination and joint initiatives with interested sectors of civil society. In 2001–2002, during EU and US trade negotiations, seminars were held across Chile to receive public comments.[57] Outreach sessions were hosted with rural women, indigenous groups, environmental organizations, fair trade groups, workers' unions and cooperatives, and SME associations.[58] These sessions led the

[54] Rosales (n 41).

[55] Interview with Dr Eda Rossi, Director General, International Affairs Ministry, Government of Chile, March 2007.

[56] Ibid.

[57] Examples include Seminars in Santiago on 'Economic and Labor Perspectives on a Chile-United States Agreement' with the Chilean Central Workers' Union (CUT); meetings with CAMPOCOOP (National Confederation of Farming Cooperatives representing small farmers), seminars with the Center for Environmental Investigation and Planning (CIPMA) on the environmental impact of an Agreement between Chile and the United States from a sustainable development perspective; a meeting with Aymaras (indigenous communities from the First Region of Chile) in Arica; and a sessions with Mesa Mujer Rural (a rural women's organization) at the headquarters of SERNAM (National Women's Service).

[58] Ibid.

civil society groups to engage with trade negotiations, and also provided an outlet for information exchanges, which later influenced parallel cooperative work programmes.

Third, with regard to basic access to information (transparency), during and after each round of negotiation, the Chilean government and the governments of trading partners also provided public progress reports on a website.[59] Chilean positions and negotiations briefings were posted on this website, which provided a forum for public comments and feedback, identifying specific issues and potential impacts.[60]

The US and the EU also hold extensive public participations and use diverse engagement mechanisms, although these may not serve as realistic models for developing countries due to their complexity and cost.[61] These mechanisms secured avenues for transparency and public involvement in the negotiations of the Chile-US FTA, and the EU-Chile AA.[62] Transparency and participation measures used by the US and EU in the negotiations of the accords with Chile illustrate several challenging innovations. First, the US trade negotiations mandate was, of course, publicly debated in the US Congress as part of the 2002 US Trade Act.[63] However, the United States Trade Representative (USTR) also established formal mechanisms for US civil society representatives to give advice during the ER, to participate in advisory councils for the trade treaty and respective environment and labour co-operation agreements and to attend briefings during trade negotiations themselves.[64] While participation was, perhaps, dominated by large and effectively organized actors, the debates themselves were held openly. In both Canada and the United States, in several economic negotiations studied during this book, reasoned civil society input directly influenced the outcomes of the trade and investment negotiations, particularly leading to the inclusion of key topics in the new cooperative environmental work programmes, or reservations to the treaty to accommodate social priorities.[65]

Similarly, the EU hosted forums and events to inform and engage European civil society on trade issues during the negotiations. For instance, on 12 October 2000, the European Commission (EC) hosted a conference in Brussels with representatives from the European civil society to exchange views on both the EU-Mercosur and the EU-Chile AA negotiations, focusing on how to improve consultation processes.[66] The conference brought together different sectors of civil society including environmental organizations who planned to participate in the SIA, business and industry groups who planned a series of consultations

59 Interview with Dr Pablo Lasso, Head of Civil Society Consultative Forum, Government of Chile, March 2007; P Newell and D Tussie, 'Public Participation in Trade Policy-Making in Latin America: Reflections and Lessons' (May 2006) IDS Working Paper No. 267, <https://assets.publishing.service.gov.uk/media/57a08c46e-5274a27b20010c7/1052734521-newell_etal.2006-civil.pdf> accessed 16 December 2020.

60 Ibid.

61 Gehring and Cordonier Segger (n 3) 205–212.

62 US-Chile FTA (adopted 2003, entered into force 1 January 2004) <https://ustr.gov/trade-agreements/free-trade-agreements/chile-fta/final-text> accessed 16 December 2020, and Agreement establishing an association between the European Community and its Member States, of the one part, and the Republic of Chile, of the other part, signed 18 November 2002, entered into force 1 February 2003 [2002] OJ L 352 [EU-Chile AA]; MC Cordonier Segger and M Leichner Reynal (eds), *Beyond the Barricades: The Americas Trade and Sustainable Development Agenda* (Aldershot, Ashgate 2005) 227.

63 Salzman (n 1); Salzman (n 8).

64 Ibid.

65 Interview with David van Hoogstraten, USTR, May 2007; Interview with Richard Tarasofsky, DFAIT, May 2009. See also JT Mathews, 'Power Shift' (1997) 76 Foreign Affairs 50.

66 EC External Relations, 'Conference on EU-Mercosur and the EU-Chile Association Negotiations with Representatives from the European Civil Society, Business Community and Academic Community: Summary Report' (Brussels, 12 October 2000).

through the Mercosur-EU Business Forum (MEBF), workers' rights groups engaged through the European Confederation of Trade Unions (CES), and scientific institutes that had formed an academic 'Groupe de Suivi' network for the negotiations.[67] Further, the Global Affairs Canada (formerly Department of Foreign Affairs and International Trade),[68] the USTR[69] and the EC Trade Directorate General[70] established websites with extensive information about the trade and investment negotiations. And the Organization of American States' (OAS) Foreign Trade Information System (SICE)[71] also maintains a comprehensive website which provides sources of detailed information, copies of studies and reports produced by Parties to the treaties and economic authorities.

In summary, it is clear that in addition to the public engagement component of the impact assessments and reviews surveyed above, public participation and transparency were facilitated during the negotiations for the trade agreements (and their cooperation provisions) through three principal mechanisms that included (1) formal advisory councils and engagement in negotiations; (2) consultations, public meetings and outreach processes; and (3) releases of information (including draft treaty texts) by print and on websites providing avenues for civil society commentary.

It is worth noting that in all three types of mechanisms, States appeal to the objective of sustainable development. Consultations funded by States and held parallel to trade negotiations and leaders' summits are titled 'WTO Symposium on Trade and Sustainable Development'[72] and 'Hemispheric Trade and Sustainability Symposium',[73] international trade briefings are held under a banner of 'Sustainable Development and Regional Trade Agreements',[74] civil society input is delivered as 'The WTO and Sustainable Development: An Independent Assessment',[75] and websites feature sections on 'Trade and Sustainable Development'.[76] Furthermore, States approve work plans of international institutions for training and research on trade, the environment and sustainable development.[77] The concept is not yet agreed as an objective of the economic treaty itself, as negotiations were only just launched, but still influences the entire context of the negotiations. These trends offer evidence of the interstitial normativity described earlier in this book. In bilateral or regional economic treaties, it is nearly general practice for States to provide mechanisms for transparency, and for public participation, and this obligation is linked in the discourse to their commitment to integration to achieve sustainable development.

[67] Ibid.

[68] Global Affairs Canada (GAC), <https://www.international.gc.ca/global-affairs-affaires-mondiales/home-accueil.aspx?lang=eng> accessed 16 December 2020.

[69] USTR, <https://www.ustr.gov> accessed 16 December 2020.

[70] EC DG Trade, Civil Society Dialogue, <http://trade.ec.europa.eu/civilsoc/index.cfm> accessed 16 December 2020.

[71] OAS SICE, <http://www.sice.oas.org/tpd_e.asp> accessed 16 December 2020.

[72] <https://www.wto.org/english/tratop_e/envir_e/sym_oct05_e/sym_oct05_e.htm> accessed 16 December 2020.

[73] <https://www.iisd.org/articles/chairs-hemispheric-trade-and-sustainability-symposium-release-policy-statement-ftaa-and> accessed 16 December 2020.

[74] <http://www.eclac.org/dmaah/noticias/paginas/5/27685/agenda_costarica_in.pdf> accessed 16 December 2020.

[75] <http://www.iisd.org/publications/pub.aspx?pno=285> accessed 16 December 2020.

[76] <http://www.oas.org/dsd/EnvironmentLaw/DEFAULTTRADEANDSUSTDEV.htm> accessed 16 December 2020.

[77] <http://www.eclac.org/dmaah/> accessed 16 December 2020.

18.3.2 Transparency and Public Participation Provisions in Trade and Investment Agreements

In both the US-Chile FTA and the EU-Chile AA Parties agreed to certain provisions to ensure that opportunities continue to be made available for civil society to participate in decision-making related to the cooperation and trade aspects of the treaty. These guarantees can be analysed in terms of four principal sets of commitments.

First, Parties agree in the economic treaties to transparency provisions including notification, the right to be consulted when changes are planned to domestic laws or policies and other measures to facilitate access to information for industry groups, importers and exporters.[78] These include provisions for access to information or more in relation to intellectual property rights, competition policy, government procurement, sanitary and phytosanitary measures or technical barriers to trade.[79] For example, in the US-Chile FTA at chapter 20 on transparency, at article 20.2 on publication, each Party commits to ensure that its laws, regulations, procedures and administrative rulings of general application are promptly made available to enable interested persons and the other Party to become acquainted with them. Furthermore, it commits that, to the extent possible, each Party shall both publish in advance any such measure that it proposes to adopt; and provide interested persons and the other Party a reasonable opportunity to comment on such proposed measures.[80] While geared mainly to exporters and importers, the additional transparency benefits all.

Second, as mentioned above, in both trade and investment liberalization agreements the Parties make several significant guarantees to secure access to information for the public, in treaty chapters and side agreements on the environment and labour, or on broader cooperation agendas.[81] For instance, in the EU-Chile AA at article 11 on civil society, the Parties commit to promote regular meetings of representatives of the Chilean and the EUs civil societies, including the academic community, social and economic partners and NGOs to discuss implementation and gather suggestions for improvement.

Third, as also mentioned above, there are provisions for formal participation and advice by civil society in the councils, committees and other institutions established by the two treaties.[82] For instance, in the institutional provisions of the EU-Chile AA at article 10 the Parties create a Joint Consultative Committee, which assists the Association Council to promote dialogue and cooperation between the various economic and social organizations of civil society in the EU and those in Chile. According to article 10.1, such dialogue and cooperation shall encompass all economic and social relations for implementation of the Agreement. The Committee members are drawn from the European Economic and Social Committee and corresponding Chilean institutions. It can be consulted by the Association

78 See RA Chumacero, R Fuentes and K Schmidt-Hebbel, 'Chile's Free Trade Agreements: How Big is the Deal?' (June 2004) Central Bank of Chile Working Paper No 264, 26–33. See also H Corbin, 'The Proposed United States—Chile Free Trade Agreement: Reconciling Free Trade and Environmental Protection' (2003) 14 Colorado Journal of International Environmental Law and Policy 119; W Durbin, *A Comparison of the Environmental Provisions of the NAFTA, the Canada-Chile Trade Agreement and the Mexican-European Community Trade Agreement* (Yale Centre for Environmental Law and Policy, New Haven 2000); Rosales (n 41).

79 Durbin (n 78).

80 Ibid.

81 Ibid.

82 Ibid.

Council or act on its own initiative, to promote dialogue between various economic and social representatives. Similarly, in the US-Chile FTA, the Trade Commission established under article 21 has the discretion to seek the advice of non-governmental persons or groups (normally trade experts and economists).

At the labour chapter 18.3 (2), each Party also commits to ensure that its proceedings for the enforcement of its labour laws are fair, equitable and transparent; and at (5) to promote public awareness of its labour laws. At article 18.4, which establishes a Labour Affairs Council, the Parties agree that each meeting of the Council shall include a public session; that each Party shall designate a point of contact with the public; that the Council may consult with or seek advice of NGOs or persons; and that decisions shall be made public. Each Party also may convene a national consultative or advisory committee, as appropriate, comprising members of its public, including representatives of its labour and business organizations.[83] The other bilateral or regional economic treaties studied above are replete with similar structures.

Fourth, as mentioned above in the analysis of the citizen factual reports and other processes, trade and investment treaties provide certain guarantees to ensure opportunities for public participation, including to ensure Parties take public participation and input into account once it is provided. For instance, the US-Chile FTA labour chapter 18 at 7 states that each Party's point of contact shall provide for the submission, receipt and consideration of public communications on matters related to this chapter, shall make such communications available to the other Party and the public and shall review such communications, as appropriate, in accordance with its domestic procedures.[84] Similarly, in chapter 19 on environmental cooperation at article 19.4 on opportunities for public participation, each Party commits to provide for the receipt and consideration of public communications, promptly make available to the other Party and to its public all communications it receives and review and respond to them in accordance with its domestic procedures. Each Party also commits to make best efforts to respond favourably to requests for consultations by persons or organizations in its territory regarding the Party's implementation of these provisions.

In contrast, the EU-Chile AA uses a more integrated approach. At article 48 on participation of civil society in cooperation, the Parties recognize the complementary role and potential contribution of civil society in the cooperation process.[85] They agree that civil society may participate in consultations on cooperation policies and strategies, including strategic priorities; may receive financial resources; and may participate in the implementation of cooperation projects and programmes in the areas that concern them.[86] It appears that both in negotiations, and in the actual text of bilateral or regional economic treaties, certain progress is being made to secure greater transparency and public participation,[87] and this can contribute to the integration of social and environmental considerations.

[83] Ibid.
[84] Ibid.
[85] EU-Chile AA (n 62).
[86] Ibid.
[87] Emily Barritt, 'Global Values, Transnational Expression: From Aarhus to Escazú' Research Handbook on Transnational Environmental Law (Cheltenham, Edward Elgar 2020); Sidney Guerra and Giulia Parola, 'Implementing Principle 10 of the 1992 Rio Declaration: A comparative study of the Aarhus Convention 1998 and the Escazú Agreement 2018' (2019) 2 1, 1–33 Revista Juridica.)

18.4 Rules on Trade and Investment Dispute Settlement and Sustainable Development

Specific provisions in State-to-State dispute settlement rules can ensure independent arbitrators, permit arbitrators to seek outside advice on social or environmental matters beyond trade, permit arbitrators to accept *amicus curia* briefs from environmental or human rights NGOs or permit open hearings in cases where sustainable development questions are being disputed.[88] Such measures can facilitate consideration of social and environmental implications of trade and investment disputes where these issues arise, contributing to more sustainable trade dispute settlement.[89]

Both types of bilateral or regional economic treaties establish State-to-State dispute settlement mechanisms for trade disputes,[90] and the US-Chile FTA also provides for State-to-State environmental and labour disputes to use the same mechanism. The first step, as noted in the US-Chile FTA at article 22.5, is determined by the Trade Commission, and this body:

> ... may: (a) call on such technical advisers or create such working groups or expert groups as it deems necessary; (b) have recourse to good offices, conciliation, mediation, or such other dispute resolution procedures; or (c) make recommendations, as may assist the Parties to reach a mutually satisfactory resolution of the dispute.

However, in article 22.10 (4), the Parties establish a formal trade dispute settlement process, with a trade roster of fifteen individuals from which a three-member tribunal is drawn to make findings, determinations and recommendations and deliver the written reports. The same mechanism is established by the Parties to the EU-Chile AA, with minor nuances, according to annex XV at article 189.

According to USTR, the dispute settlement provisions in the US-Chile FTA set high standards for openness and transparency, including provisions for open public hearings, public release of submissions and rights for interested third parties to submit views.[91]

First, in the EU-Chile AA and in the US-Chile FTA, the Panelists and others engaged in the dispute settlement process are bound by a strict code of conduct which requires their independence and impartiality.

Second, in the EU-Chile AA and in the US-Chile FTA, as long as Parties do not object, the Panel may on its own initiative seek expert advice on environmental, social and other issues.[92] As noted in the US-Chile FTA at article 22.11, 'unless the Parties disapprove, on its own initiative, the panel may seek information and technical advice ... concerning environmental, labor, health, safety ... from any person or body that it deems appropriate ...'. Before seeking such advice the Panel must consult the Parties, and once advice is received, it must give them an opportunity to respond. A less involved procedure is contemplated in

[88] Gehring and Cordonier Segger (n 5) 153–168; H Horn, 'The Burden of Proof in Trade Disputes and the Environment' (2011) 62 Journal of Environmental Economics and Management 15; D Sarooshi, 'The Future of the WTO and its Dispute Settlement System' (2005) 2(1) International Organizations Law Review 129.

[89] Horn (n 88).

[90] The US-Chile FTA (n 62) also establishes a controversial investor-state mechanism to cover the obligations contained in the investment chapter, as will be discussed later.

[91] USTR, 'Free Trade with Chile: Summary of the U.S.-Chile Free Trade Agreement' (12 November 2002) <https://ustr.gov/trade-agreements/free-trade-agreements/chile-fta> accessed 16 December 2020, 5.

[92] Durbin (n 78); Rosales (n 41).

the EU-Chile AA at annex XV, at article 189(2), which states that 'on its own initiative, the arbitration panel may obtain information and technical advice from any person or body that it deems appropriate. Any information so obtained shall be submitted to the Parties for comments'. This independence to seek, and accept, counsel from non-trade experts has long been considered key to more balanced decision-making by trade tribunals, particularly when disputes concern public policy priorities such as health, the environment or other issues.[93]

Third, the US-Chile FTA provides that panel hearings may be open to the public if both Parties agree (except for confidential business information). This can be contrasted with the EU-Chile AA, which only permits this in the instance that both Parties agree, as an exception to the rule of closed hearings. In particular, in annex XV, article 189(2) at 23, the EU-Chile AA states that the 'hearings of the arbitration panels shall be closed to the public, unless the Parties decide otherwise'. If the Parties decide that the hearing is open to the public, part of the hearing may still be closed because of confidential information.

Fourth, openness to *amicus curiae* briefs by tribunals is a key procedural factor that has been sought by NGOs engaged in sustainable development debates for a long time.[94] In the context of the WTO, the right of the Panel to solicit or independently accept such advice has been extremely contentious.[95] However, the tribunals in both dispute settlement mechanisms have the right to accept third party submissions, including *amicus curia* briefs from NGOs.[96] The *US-Chile FTA* specifies that the Panel may receive *amicus curiae* submissions, unless the Parties agree otherwise. In the EU-Chile AA Parties agree to develop model rules of procedure so that the Panel shall consider requests from external stakeholders to provide written views and give the Parties an opportunity to respond.[97]

There are two further innovations in the US-Chile FTA which bear examination. First, as noted earlier, at chapter 10 the Parties agreed to permit investor-State dispute settlement.[98] While the Parties have ensured transparency in certain aspects of the process such as publication of arbitral documents, acceptance of *amicus curia* briefs and hearings open to the public, the decision to grant rights to investors without corresponding responsibilities has raised concerns about accountability and regulatory chill.[99] As noted above, at 10-D the Parties agree that 'except in rare circumstances, non-discriminatory regulatory actions by a Party that are designed and applied to protect legitimate public welfare objectives, such as public health, safety, and the environment, do not constitute indirect expropriations'. However, this raises concern for sustainable development.

[93] S Charnovitz, 'Regional Trade Agreements and the Environment' (1995) 37(6) Environment: Science and Policy for Sustainable Development 16–45.

[94] D Esty, 'Non-Governmental Organizations at the World Trade Organization: Cooperation, Competition, or Exclusion' (1998) 1 Journal of International Economic Law 123.

[95] G Marceau and M Stilwell, 'Practical Suggestions for Amicus Curiae Briefs before WTO Adjudicating Bodies' (2001) 4 Journal of International Economic Law 155.

[96] EU-Chile AA (n 62) annex XV, art 189(2) 35–37; R Polanco, 'Third-Party Rights and Transparency in Foreign Investment International Arbitration' (2010) Revista de Derecho Económico, año XLVII, No 75, Chile.

[97] EU-Chile AA (n 62) art 186.

[98] Roberto Echandi, Investor-State Dispute Settlement and Impact on Investment Rulemaking (New York; Geneva, United Nations Publications 2007); Dimitrij Euler and others, *Transparency in International Investment Arbitration: A Guide to the UNCITRAL Rules on Transparency in Treaty-Based Investor-State Arbitration* (Cambridge, CUP 2015).

[99] E Neumayer, *Greening Trade and Investment-Environmental Protection without Protectionism* (London, Earthscan 2001) 78; K Gray, 'Foreign Direct Investment and Environmental Impacts—Is the Debate Over?' (2002) 11 Review of European Community and International Environmental Law 306, 306, 312.

Second, the obligation to effectively enforce environmental laws is subject to the dispute settlement provisions.[100] The State-to-State mechanism provides for a consultation process under which 'a Party may request consultations with the other Party regarding any matter under the environment chapter'. Formal dispute settlement proceedings with an environmental roster are only available in the case of alleged failure by a Party to effectively enforce its environmental laws, requested by another Party, and there has been a notable lack of candidates willing to 'cast the first stone'. If a 'non-implementation of environmental law dispute' were to be won, the US-Chile FTA provides for monetary assessments up to US$ 15 million for an environmental fund to be spent in the territory of the Party in breach.[101] Should the assessment go unpaid, the complaining Party is permitted to impose retaliatory tariffs. As noted by the Organisation for Economic Co-operation and Development (OECD), there are questions about how effective the State-to-State mechanisms have been in achieving their dual objectives of improved environmental enforcement capacity and reduced trade friction from uneven regulatory playing fields:

> There are few concrete criteria by which to evaluate them, but one must surely be the frequency to which they have been put to use. To date, none has ever been exercised, even to the extent of recourse to the pre-dispute facilities for consultation and good offices ... [though] there are few States in which enforcement of such laws is flawlessly executed ... Countries may simply hesitate to incur the costs-financial, political, and other-of initiating a dispute leading to imposing penalties on another country, even if the letter of the agreement would entitle them to do so.[102]

However, such dispute settlement mechanisms may still be effective as deterrents to strategic under-enforcement of environmental standards. And there is further evidence of an interstitial norm at work. Through innovations in trade and investment dispute settlement rules, the Parties appear to be moving towards more transparent and inclusive decision-making as part of their efforts to contribute towards sustainable development.

100 Durbin (n 78).

101 JV Sagar, 'The Labor and Environment Chapters of the United States-Chile Free Trade Agreement: An Improvement over the Weak Enforcement Provisions of the NAFTA Side Agreements on Labor and the Environment?' (2004) 21 Arizona Journal of International & Comparative Law 913, 928–929.

102 OECD (n 40) 124.

SECTION SIX

TRADE AND INVESTMENT LAW CONTRIBUTIONS TO THE SUSTAINABLE DEVELOPMENT GOALS

19

Trade and Investment Accords for Sustainable Development Goals 1–5

Introduction

In New York in 2015, after nearly three decades of international policy debates on sustainable development and years of consultations with stakeholders through an Open Working Group, governments adopted 'Transforming our World: The 2030 Agenda for Sustainable Development' which as discussed earlier in this volume, provides for seventeen Sustainable Development Goals (SDGs) encompassing 169 specific targets. Under each SDG, the ambitious, time-bound targets set aspirational objectives for governments, international organizations and other stakeholders seeking to support sustainable development to achieve by 2030 or before, as well as indicators to facilitate measurement of attainment levels.[1] In setting out the SDG targets, governments focused both on sustainable development outcomes, and also process targets that lay out means of implementation for achieving those outcomes.[2] These means of implementation targets are commonly directed towards international cooperation and partnerships, but also specifically reference, in SDG 17 which covers trade, investment and financial collaborations among other forms of partnership, the need for economic cooperation arrangements to support sustainable development.

The penultimate three chapters of this volume, building on several research collaborations,[3] explore provisions from over 110 innovative bilateral and regional economic treaties that could facilitate achievement of certain SDGs and their associated targets. Ideally, this analysis will be of interest to trade and investment agreement negotiators, as well as scholars and stakeholders involved in implementation of these treaties, so that countries can maximize opportunities for their economic accords to assist in effectively contributing towards achievement of the SDG targets, particularly in a time of post-pandemic economic recovery. This chapter addresses trade and investment agreements provisions relevant to a first set of SDGs which target 'basic needs' challenges: eradicating poverty (SDG 1); ending hunger (SDG 2); promoting health and wellbeing (SDG 3); ensuring quality education (SDG 4) and achieving gender equality (SDG 5). The following chapter addresses trade and investment provisions which could help meet targets under the SDGs which seek to secure access to clean water and sanitation (SDG 6) and affordable, clean energy (SDG

1 The indicators were developed by the Inter-Agency and Expert Group on SDG Indicators (IAEG-SDGs) and agreed to at the Forty-Seventh Session of the UN Statistical Commission in 2016.

2 These targets are identified with letters instead of numerals: e.g. 1.A (for convenience 'means of implementation' targets).

3 Acknowledgements and warmest thanks are due to Oliver Taherzadeh and Emily Morrison, University of Cambridge graduate students without whose excellent research skills and substantive insights, these chapters would have been much more difficult. See O Taherzadeh, 'Provisions for the UN Sustainable Development Goals in Bilateral and Multilateral Trade Agreements' (2019) <https://doi.org/10.7910/DVN/ZDODUM>, Harvard Dataverse, V1.

Crafting Trade and Investment Accords for Sustainable Development. Marie-Claire Cordonier Segger, Oxford University Press. © Marie-Claire Cordonier Segger 2021. DOI: 10.1093/oso/9780198831341.003.0019

7), decent work and economic growth (SDG 8), innovation and infrastructure (SDG 9), reduced inequality (SDG 10) and sustainable cities and communities (SDG 11). The next chapter then explores trade and investment provisions which can assist in achieving further SDGs which focus on responsible consumption and production (SDG 12), climate change (SDG 13), protecting life below water (SDG 14) and life on land (SDG 15), also the need for peace, justice and good governance (SDG 16). Concluding remarks also address SDG 17, which underpins all other SDGs, calls for a global partnership for the SDGs, and directly addresses trade, investment and development cooperation priorities for sustainable development.

Goal 1. End Poverty in all its Forms Everywhere

In the first of the SDGs—to end poverty in all forms everywhere—governments agreed that by 2030, countries are to eradicate extreme poverty for all people everywhere; reduce at least by half the proportion of men, women and children living in poverty; implement social protection systems; ensure all men and woman have equal rights to economic resources and basic services; build the resilience of the poor and vulnerable and reduce their exposure to climate-related extremes; ensure significant mobilization of resources to help developing countries and least developed countries to end poverty; and create policy frameworks that support accelerating investment in poverty eradication actions.

According to the 2019 Report of the Secretary General,[4] the decline of global extreme poverty has slowed, indicating that at present, the world is not on track to achieve the target of less than 3 per cent of the world living in extreme poverty by 2030. Trade and investment agreements may contribute to efforts to increase ambition towards eradicating poverty. A number of bilateral and regional economic treaties address the need to raise living standards in their preambular statements, investment standards and economic integration provisions. By way of example, in the Preamble of the China-Peru FTA, the Parties recognize that the agreement, 'should be implemented with a view toward raising the standard of living, creating new employment opportunities, reducing poverty and promoting sustainable development in a manner consistent with environmental protection and conservation'.[5]

In the first of the objectives of the EU-ESA Interim EPA, which has provisionally applied since 14 May 2012, the Parties seek to contribute 'to the reduction and eventual eradication of poverty through the establishment of a strengthened and strategic trade and development partnership consistent with the objective of sustainable development, the Millennium Development Goals and the Cotonou Agreement',[6] thereby making specific reference to the predecessors of the SDGs. In the CARIFORUM-EU EPA, Parties are more explicit: in addition to establishing 'contributing to the reduction and eventual eradication of poverty through the establishment of a trade partnership consistent with the objective of sustainable development, the Millennium Development Goals and the Cotonou Agreement' as one of its objectives,[7] it also provides that the agreement's 'fundamental objective' is 'the sustainable

4 Report of the Secretary-General, Special edition: progress towards the Sustainable Development Goals (2019).
5 China-Peru FTA (entered into force 1 March 2010) Preamble.
6 EU-ESA Interim EPA (provisionally entered into force 14 May 2012), art 2(a) 'Objectives of the EPA'.
7 CARIFORUM-EU EPA, art 1(a).

development and the eradication of poverty in CARIFORUM States, and the smooth and gradual integration of these economies into the global economy'.[8] Such provisions in trade and development partnerships, such as the EU-ESA Interim EPA and CARIFORUM-EU EPA, may facilitate implementation of target 1.A, which requires countries to 'ensure significant mobilization of resources from a variety of sources, including through enhanced development cooperation, in order to provide adequate and predictable means for developing countries, in particular least developed countries, to implement programmes and policies to end poverty'. Provisions requiring developed country governments to allocate resources to essential services and poverty reduction programmes in partnered developing and least developed countries will further aid achievement of target 1.A. Additionally, economic integration provisions can facilitate achievement of target 1.4, which asks countries to ensure equal rights of all men and women to economic resources.

With respect to compensation for loss of investment, the Comprehensive Economic and Trade Agreement's (CETA's) investment chapter requires that each Party accord to investors of the other Party 'whose covered investments suffer losses owing to armed conflict, civil strife, a state of emergency or natural disaster in its territory, treatment no less favourable than that it accords to its own investors or to the investors of a third country, whichever is more favourable to the investor concerned'.[9] Agreements that provide for protections in case of investment losses due to social, economic and environmental disasters facilitate achievement of target 1.5, which seeks to reduce the exposure and vulnerability of the poor and those in vulnerable situations to climate-related extreme events and other economic, social and environmental shocks and disasters by 2030. Achievement of this target would be further aided by cooperative provisions encouraging countries to work together to formulate national disaster risk reduction plans.

Another mechanism through which trade and investment agreements seek to reduce poverty is through promotion of small and medium enterprises. The objectives of the Canada-Colombia FTA's chapter on trade-related cooperation include 'to promote sustainable economic development, with an emphasis on small and medium sized enterprises, in order to contribute to the reduction of poverty through trade'.[10] Similarly, areas of cooperation in EU-ESA's title on inland fisheries and aquaculture development include investment and finance to contribute to 'providing access to credit facilities for the development of small to medium scale enterprises as well as industrial scale inland fisheries',[11] and also 'socio-economic and poverty alleviation measures'. These measures encompass 'contributing to the promotion of small and medium scale fisheries, processors, and fish traders by building the capacity of ESA States to participate in trade with the EC Party' and 'encouraging participation of marginal groups in the fishing industry, for example, through the promotion of gender equality in fisheries by developing the capacity of women engaged in fisheries, as well as other disadvantaged groups with the potential to engage in fisheries for sustainable social economic development'.[12] Supporting gender equality in particular industries is one way that countries can use trade and investment agreements to facilitate achievement of target 1.B, which asks for creation of 'sound policy frameworks at the national, regional

[8] Ibid, art 37(1).
[9] CETA, art 8.15.5(b).
[10] Canada-Colombia FTA, art 1801(d).
[11] EU-ESA Interim EPA, art 35(1)(e)(ii).
[12] Ibid, art 35(1)(f).

and international levels, based on pro-poor and gender-sensitive development strategies, to support accelerated investment in poverty eradication actions', as well as target 1.4, which requires equal rights of men and women to economic resources and financial services, including microfinance, and appropriate new technology, among other things.

Goal 2. End Hunger, Achieve Food Security and Improved Nutrition and Promote Sustainable Agriculture

Goal 2 seeks to end world hunger, achieve food security and improve nutrition and sustainable agriculture. Achieving SDG 2 is a mounting challenge, with hunger on the rise globally and public investment in agriculture declining. The 2019 Report of the Secretary General notes a continuous downward trend in export subsidy outlays reported to the WTO and falls in aid to agriculture in developing countries.[13] Increased investment in infrastructure and technology for sustainable agriculture, and greater support for small-scale food producers and farmers is urgently required.[14] Trade and investment agreements have the potential to facilitate closures of these gaps, with current Economic agreements demonstrating a range of procedural and substantive mechanisms for achieving food security and agricultural cooperation, but more ambitious provisions are clearly required.

Countries' targets towards advancing SDG 2 include, by 2030, to ensure access by all people to safe, nutritious and sufficient food at all times; end all forms of malnutrition; double agricultural productivity and incomes of small-scale food producers; ensure sustainable food production systems and implement resilient agricultural practices. With respect to genetic resources, States are asked to, by 2020, take measures to maintain genetic diversity of seeds, plants and animals, and promote access to fair and equitable benefit-sharing. Current economic agreements address a number of these targets.

With respect to food safety, CETA requires Parties to notify one another of significant food safety issues relating to products traded between the Parties,[15] which is conducive to achieving target 2.1: ensuring 'access by all people, in particular the poor and people in vulnerable situations, including infants, to safe, nutritious and sufficient food all year round'.[16]

With respect to ensuring sustainable food production systems and implementing resilient agricultural practices, the Peru-Korea FTA requires Parties, subject to their capacities, to adopt policies and measures on issues such as energy efficiency improvement and research, promotion, development and use of renewable and environmental technologies 'that do not affect food security or the conservation of biological diversity'.[17] Provisions such as this, which promote innovation whilst having regard to the need to maintain food security, can help trading countries to ensure sustainable food production systems and implement resilient agricultural practices that increase productivity and production, help maintain ecosystems, strengthen capacity for adaptation to climate change and other weather extremes and progressively improve land and soil quality.[18]

[13] Report of the Secretary General (n 4).
[14] Ibid.
[15] CETA, art 5(11).
[16] SDG 2, target 2.1.
[17] Peru-Korea FTA, art 19.8.
[18] See target 2.4.

With respect to preserving genetic resources and benefit-sharing, the EU-South Korea FTA requires Parties to, subject to their legislation, 'respect, preserve and maintain knowledge, innovations and practices of indigenous and local communities embodying traditional lifestyles relevant for the conservation and sustainable use of biological diversity and promote their wider application with the involvement and approval of the holders of such knowledge, innovations and practices and encourage the equitable sharing of the benefits arising from the utilization of such knowledge, innovations and practices'.[19] This comprehensive provision correlates directly with target 2.5, which asks countries to promote access to and fair and equitable sharing of benefits arising from the utilization of genetic resources and associated traditional knowledge.

Trade and investment agreements also include provisions that facilitate market access. In the CARIFORUM-EU EPA, Parties commit to 'undertake prior consultations on trade policy developments that may impact on the competitive positions of traditional agricultural products . . . in the market of the EC Party', and the EC Party 'shall endeavour to maintain significant preferential access within the multilateral trading system for these products originating in the CARIFORUM States for as long as is feasible and to ensure that any unavoidable reduction in preference is phased in over as long a period as possible'.[20] These provisions may assist countries to double agricultural productivity and incomes of small-scale food producers, in particular women, indigenous peoples, family farmers, pastoralists and fishers, including through secure and equal access to markets.[21]

The means of implementation targets under SDG 2 relate directly to trade and investment, asking States first, to 'increase investment, including through enhanced international cooperation, in rural infrastructure, agricultural research and extension services, technology development and plant and livestock gene banks in order to enhance agricultural productive capacity in developing countries, in particular least developed countries' (target 2.A); second, to 'correct and prevent trade restrictions and distortions in world agricultural markets, including through the parallel elimination of all forms of agricultural export subsidies and all export measures with equivalent effect, in accordance with the mandate of the Doha Development Round' (target 2.B); and third, to 'adopt measures to ensure the proper functioning of food commodity markets and their derivatives and facilitate timely access to market information, including on food reserves, in order to help limit extreme food price volatility' (target 2.C).

The China-Peru FTA's provisions on agricultural cooperation are synonymous with advancing target 2.A. The aim of agricultural cooperation under the FTA, is 'to promote sustainable rural development through the exchange of experience, generation of partnership and execution of projects in areas of mutual interest such as: agricultural innovation and technology transfer for the development of small farming, the conservation and management of the water resource for agricultural use, the application of good agricultural and agro industrial practices, including gender approach in development policies and strategies, among others'; to 'promote the exchange of relevant information for agricultural exports between the 2 markets'; and to 'develop a training program addressed to leader producers, technicians and professionals for the application of new technologies in order to increase

[19] EU-South Korea FTA, art 10.40(1).
[20] CARIFORUM-EU EPA, art 40.
[21] See target 2.3.

and improve agriculture and animal husbandry productivity and competitiveness, in particular of value added products'.[22] The CARIFORUM-EU EPA also includes an article on cooperation wherein Parties agree to cooperate with respect to 'improvement in the competitiveness of potentially viable production, including downstream processing, through innovation, training, promotion of linkages and other support activities, in agricultural and fisheries products, including both traditional and non-traditional export sectors'.[23]

The China-Peru FTA directly addresses target 2.B, stating that, with respect to agricultural subsidies, the Parties 'share the objective of the multilateral elimination of export subsidies for agricultural goods, and shall work together toward an agreement in the WTO to eliminate those subsidies, and avoid its reintroduction in any form', and adding that 'no Party may maintain, introduce or reintroduce any export subsidy on any agricultural good destined for the territory of the other Party'.[24] Further, 'in order to establish a fair and market-oriented agriculture trading system, the Parties agree to cooperate in the WTO agricultural negotiations on domestic support measures to provide for substantial progressive reduction in agriculture support and protection, resulting in correcting and preventing restrictions and distortions in world agricultural markets'.[25] The agreement also provides an institutional mechanism for combatting obstacles to trade of agricultural and fishery goods between the Parties, by requiring the Committee on Trade in Goods to establish an Ad-Hoc Working Group on Trade in Agricultural and Fishery Goods.[26] These mechanisms also facilitate achievement of target 2.C, by helping to ensure proper functioning of food commodity markets.

Similarly, the CARIFORUM-EU EPA chapter on agriculture and fisheries explicitly recognizes that food security is critical to the pursuit of sustainable development and that there is a need to avoid major disruption of markets for agricultural, food and fish products in CARIFORUM States.[27] The Parties also 'acknowledge that the removal of barriers to trade between the Parties' envisaged by the EPA 'may pose significant challenges to CARIFORUM producers in the agricultural, food and fisheries sectors and to consumers and agree to consult with each other on these issues'.[28] Importantly, the EPA has procedural mechanisms for ensuring food security that move beyond a requirement for consultation, allowing signatory CARIFORUM States to take particular safeguard measures in cases where compliance with the provisions of the agreement 'leads to problems with the availability of, or access to, foodstuffs or other products essential to ensure food security of a Signatory CARIFORUM State and where this situation gives rise or is likely to give rise to major difficulties for such a State'.[29] The EU-ESA Interim EPA contains a similar allowance for safeguard measures to be taken where a product originating in one Party is being imported into the territory of the other Party in such increased quantities and under such conditions as to cause or threaten to cause disturbances in a sector of the economy of the importing Party or in the markets of agricultural like or directly competitive products (among other things).[30] These safeguard

22 China-Peru FTA, art 164.
23 CARIFORUM-EU EPA, art 43(2)(a).
24 China-Peru FTA, art 16.
25 Ibid, art 18.
26 Ibid, art 20.
27 CARIFORUM-EU EPA, art 37.
28 Ibid, art 40(1).
29 Ibid, art 40(2). For safeguard measures, see art 25 paras 7(b)–(d), 8 and 9.
30 EU-ESA Interim EPA, art 21(2).

mechanisms can provide an important means for ensuring more equitable market access and protecting agricultural industries in developing countries.

Goal 3. Ensure Healthy Lives and Promote Wellbeing for all at all Ages

Ensuring health and promoting wellbeing requires countries requires countries to, by 2030, reduce the global maternal mortality ratio to less than 70 per 100,000 live births; end preventable deaths of new-borns and young children; end the epidemics of AIS, malaria and other tropical communicable diseases; reduce by one third premature mortality from non-communicable diseases; and ensure universal access to sexual and reproductive health-care services; and substantially reduce the number of deaths and illnesses from hazardous chemicals and air, water and soil pollution and contamination. By 2020, the world aims to halve the number of global deaths and injuries from road traffic accidents.

The means of implementation targets towards advancing SDG 3 require countries to strengthen implementation of the World Health Organization Framework Convention on Tobacco Control, support research and development of vaccines and medicines for the communicable and non-communicable diseases that primarily affect developing countries, provide access to affordable essential medicines and vaccines (in accordance with the Doha Declaration on the Trade-Related Aspects of Intellectual Property Rights (TRIPS) Agreement and Public Health) and provide access to medicines for all. Countries are also to increase health financing and recruitment and training of the health workforce in developing countries, and build capacity for managing health risks.

Goal 4. Ensure Inclusive and Equitable Quality Education and Promote Lifelong Learning Opportunities for all

Achieving SDG 4 requires that by 2030, countries ensure that all girls and boys complete free, equitable and quality primary and secondary education leading to effective learning outcomes;[31] ensure access to quality early childhood development, care and pre-primary education;[32] provide equal access for all women and men to affordable, quality technical, vocational and tertiary education;[33] substantially increase the number of youths and adults with relevant skills; eliminate education gender disparities; ensure that all youths and a substantial proportion of adults achieve literacy and numeracy; and ensure that all learners acquire the skills and knowledge needed for promoting sustainable development. With respect to means of implementation, countries are to build and upgrade child, disability and gender sensitive education facilities and provide all with safe, inclusive, non-violent and effective learning environments; substantially increase the supply of qualified teachers by

[31] Target 4.1.
[32] Target 4.2.
[33] Target 4.3.

2030; and have substantially expanded globally numbers of scholarships available to developing countries by 2020.

As the Report of the Secretary General notes, rapid technological changes present opportunities for improving education access, and countries must invest effort in improving full life-cycle learning outcomes, particularly for women, girls and people who are marginalized and vulnerable. Cooperative provisions in a number of trade and investment agreements are strongly conducive to facilitating improved education, but tend to focus on higher education, and need to be broadened to address full life-cycle learning.

The Canada-Peru and Peru-Korea FTAs each contain provisions that may assist countries to advance their targets of substantially increasing numbers of youths and adults with relevant skills for employment, decent jobs and entrepreneurship.[34] The Canada-Peru FTA provides for cooperative labour activities, which include cooperation with respect to organizing joint conferences, workshops, training and education programmes.[35] The Peru-Korea FTA specifically targets intellectual property skills, requiring Parties to encourage and facilitate educational projects on the use of intellectual property, training courses on intellectual property rights, patent technology and market intelligence and exchange of technical expertise.[36]

In the China-Peru FTA, comprehensive provisions on education cooperation go further, spanning pre-school to higher and technical education—thus facilitating full life cycle learning—and encouraging joint planning of programmes, information exchange, professional development and collaboration between education institutions and enterprises. This article directly addresses several of the SDG 4 targets, including:[37]

1. The aims of education cooperation will be:
   (a) to build on existing agreements or arrangements already in place for cooperation in education; and
   (b) to promote networking, mutual understanding and close working relationships in the area of education between the Parties.
2. In pursuit of the objectives in Article 149 (Objectives), the Parties shall encourage and facilitate, as appropriate, exchanges between and among their respective education-related agencies, institutions, organizations, in fields such as:
   (a) education quality assurance processes;
   (b) pre-school, primary and secondary education systems;
   (c) higher education;
   (d) technical education; and
   (e) enterprise and industry collaboration for technical training.
3. The Parties shall encourage cooperation in education focusing on:
   (a) exchange of information, teaching aids, and demonstration materials;
   (b) joint planning and implementation of programs and projects, and joint coordination of targeted activities in agreed fields;

[34] Target 4.4.
[35] Canada-Peru FTA, Annex 18-A.
[36] Peru-Korea FTA, art 17.1.
[37] China-Peru FTA, art 154.

(c) development of collaborative training, exchange of experiences, joint research and development, across graduate and postgraduate studies;
(d) cooperation between the institutions of higher education of the Parties through the exchange of teaching staff, researchers and students in relation to academic programs;
(e) developing a better understanding of each Party education systems and policies including information on evaluation of qualifications;
(f) development of innovative quality assurance resources;
(g) means and methods to support learning and assessment, as well as the professional development of teachers and trainers;
(h) collaboration between higher education institutions and enterprises, to develop the level of specialized knowledge and skills to the labor market; and
(i) development of an information system on educational statistics.

Goal 5. Achieve Gender Equality and Empower all Women and Girls

The goal of achieving gender equality requires countries to end all forms of discrimination against women and girls; eliminate all forms of violence against all women and girls and all harmful practices; recognize and value unpaid care and domestic work through provision of public services, infrastructure and social protection policies; ensure full and effective participation of women and equal leadership opportunities; and ensure universal access to sexual and reproductive health and reproductive rights.[38] Countries are further required to undertake reforms to give women equal rights to economic and natural resources and financial services (among other things); enhance use of enabling technologies to promote empowerment of women; and adopt and strengthen sound policies and enforceable legislation that promotes gender equality and female empowerment.

The Chinese Taipei-Nicaragua FTA's provisions on cooperative activities on labour issues explicitly address the need to end all forms of discrimination against women and girls everywhere,[39] providing that such cooperative activities include 'gender issues, including the elimination of discrimination in respect of employment and occupation'. Including non-discrimination clauses in economic agreements can also facilitate countries' achievement of target 5.5, ensuring women's full and effective participation and equal opportunities for leadership at levels of decision-making in political, economic and public life.

A number of economic agreements feature provisions that assist countries to 'undertake reforms to give women equal rights to economic resources, as well as access to ownership and control over land and other forms of property, financial services, inheritance and natural resources, in accordance with national laws' (target 5.A), through, firstly, provisions encouraging gender equality in agriculture and fisheries industries, and second, provisions facilitating regional cooperation.

[38] In accordance with the Programme of Action of the International Conference on Population and Development and the Beijing Platform for Action and the outcome documents of their review conferences

[39] Target 5.1.

First, the China-Peru FTA asks for a 'gender approach in development policies and strategies' as part of the application of good agricultural and agro industrial practices to promote sustainable rural development.[40] The EU-ESA Interim EPA's provisions on inland fisheries and aquaculture cooperation require socio-economic and poverty alleviation measures to encourage 'participation of marginal groups in the fishing industry, for example, through the promotion of gender equality in fisheries by developing the capacity of women engaged in fisheries'.[41]

Second, with respect to regional integration, article 38 of the EU-ESA Interim EPA provides for cooperation on 'gender mainstreaming'.[42] The agreement's annexed Development Matrix,[43] which forms part of the basis for the Parties' cooperation (i.e. financial and non-financial support to the Eastern and South Africa (ESA) region) on regional integration and development strategies,[44] includes gender as a 'key area': cooperation in this area includes promotion of female entrepreneurship through targeted interventions, which may involve 'support programmes to help women improve access to all resources in particular those for trade and development' and promoting 'female entrepreneurship to facilitate participation in regional and global markets'.[45]

[40] China-Peru FTA, art 164.
[41] EU-ESA Interim EPA, art 35.
[42] Ibid, art 38.
[43] Ibid, Annex 2.
[44] Ibid, art 36.
[45] Ibid, Annex 2 art 2(g).

20

Trade and Investment Accords for Sustainable Development Goals 6–11

Introduction

In this chapter, SDGs 6 to 11 are canvassed, which focus primarily on employment, equality, water, energy, innovation and infrastructure development, and how trade and investment agreements may serve as mechanisms for enabling countries to advance the achievement of their targets under these further SDGs.

Goal 6. Ensure Availability and Sustainable Management of Water and Sanitation for all

In SDG 6, governments agreed to try, by 2030, to achieve universal and equitable access to safe and affordable drinking water for all, as well as universal access to sanitation and hygiene (paying special attention in this regard to the needs of women, girls and people in vulnerable situations); improve drinking water quality through reducing pollution and dumping; increase water-use efficiency across all sectors; and implement integrated water resources management at all levels. By 2020, countries are to protect and restore water-related ecosystems. In order to achieve these outcomes, countries are called on to support and strengthen the participation of local communities in improving water and sanitation management, and, by 2030, expand international cooperation and capacity-building support to developing countries in activities and programmes relating to water and sanitation.

Upscaling ambition with respect to SDG 6 is urgently needed, as on current data achieving universal access to basic sanitation services by 2030 will require that the current annual rate of progress doubles. The Report of the Secretary General indicates that on current information, most countries are unlikely to fully implement integrated water resources management by 2030. Trade and investment agreements could play a crucial role in enhancing States' efforts, particularly in the international cooperation space.

Trade and investment agreements that address SDG 6 focus on water and sanitation in a variety of ways, from encouraging trade in environmental products and services that facilitate the SDGs, such as improved sanitation, to providing infrastructural support to developing countries for water storage and irrigation activities, and cooperating on sustainable water resource management. The Comprehensive Economic and Trade Agreement's (CETA's) market access schedule includes annexes detailing the thresholds that apply to procurement by listed entities and for listed activities. It provides for an exception for the supply of drinking water to the public, subject to conditions.[1] One of those conditions is

[1] CETA, Annex 19-3, notes to the European Union's Annex 19-3, note 3.

Crafting Trade and Investment Accords for Sustainable Development. Marie-Claire Cordonier Segger, Oxford University Press. © Marie-Claire Cordonier Segger 2021. DOI: 10.1093/oso/9780198831341.003.0020

that supply to the public network depends only on the entity's own consumption and has not exceeded 30 per cent of the entity's total production of drinking water. Providing for such exceptions is one mechanism by which countries can promote universal and equitable access to affordable drinking water.[2]

The Japan-Switzerland Free Trade Agreement (FTA) offers a different approach, in its provisions promoting trade in environmental products and services. It specifies that:

> Parties shall encourage trade and dissemination of environmental products and environment-related services in order to facilitate access to technologies and products that support the environmental protection and development goals, such as improved sanitation, pollution prevention, sustainable promotion of renewable energy and climate-change-related goals.[3]

Promoting trade in environmental goods and services is a common feature of recent economic agreements, and explicitly incorporating references to sanitation and pollution reduction may offer a simple but effective avenue for countries to facilitate access to adequate and equitable sanitation and hygiene for all and end open defecation, as target 6.2 requires,[4] and to improve water quality by reducing pollution, as required by target 6.3.[5]

It should also be noted that this provision in the Japan-Switzerland FTA, which entered into force in 2009, makes explicit reference to development goals (albeit the Millennium Development Goals, which preceded the introduction in 2015 of the SDGs). This explicit promotion of access to technologies and products that support environmental protection and the development goals opens doors for promoting trade in all goods that facilitate sustainable development.

Cooperative provisions are a further important mechanism for facilitating SDG 6. The CARIFORUM-EU Economic Partnership Agreement (EPA) features a provision on 'cooperation on eco-innovation and renewable energy', and includes 'projects related to environmentally-friendly products, technologies, production processes, services, management and business methods, including those related to appropriate water-saving and Clean Development Mechanism applications' in its list of areas in which the Parties agree to cooperate, including by facilitating support.[6] Support provisions such as this directly engage target 6.A, which asks for expanded 'international cooperation and capacity-building support to developing countries in water- and sanitation-related activities and programmes, including water harvesting, desalination, water efficiency, wastewater treatment, recycling and reuse technologies' by 2030. It may also serve to aid achievement of the water-use efficiency component of target 6.4, which calls for substantially increased 'water-use efficiency across all sectors and ensure sustainable withdrawals and supply of freshwater to address water scarcity and substantially reduce the number of people suffering from water scarcity' by 2030. The Chinese Taipei-Nicaragua FTA engages more directly with the latter part of target 6.4, by providing that its programme of work (a programme to be developed to reflect the Parties' priorities for cooperative activities), may include long- medium- and

[2] Target 6.1.
[3] Japan-Switzerland FTA, art 9.
[4] Target 6.2.
[5] Target 6.3.
[6] CARIFORUM-EU EPA, art 138(2)(a). See further discussion at SDG 7.

short-term activities relating to 'facilitating technology development, transfer and training on protection, conservation and preservation of basins and water bodies'.[7]

The EU-ESA Interim EPA's articles on water resources and cooperation with respect to natural resources provide particularly comprehensive examples of advancing SDG 6 through trade provisions. They are encompassed within its title on natural resources and the environment, the first article of which states that the Parties 'recognise the importance of cooperation in the sustainable management of natural resources and environment. Cooperation in this area shall take account of differentiated and trans-boundary needs of ESA States.'[8] Article 50 then deals specifically with water resources. First, in the article Parties 'recognise the importance of cooperation in the development of water resources (including irrigation, hydropower and water supply) for the improvement of the livelihoods of the populations'.[9] The objectives of such cooperation are 'the sustainable development and management of water resources in the region' and 'regional cooperation for the sustainable utilisation of transboundary water resources'.[10] Second, in article 50 a range of activities is listed on which the Parties agree to cooperate, namely, development of infrastructure of water resources in the region; development of the legal and regulatory frameworks; promotion of integrated water management; capacity building in human resources, improvement in service standards, water management and institutional structures; encouragement and facilitation of EU-ESA partnerships, linkages, regional water partnerships and joint ventures between economic operators; technology development, transfer and applications, research and development, innovation, information exchange and networks; water pollution control, purification and conservation, wastewater treatment and sanitation; and promotion of sustainable irrigation schemes.

In addition, the EU-ESA Development Matrix addresses water supply for production as a key area for infrastructure development. Cooperation in this area relates to developing water supply infrastructure for 'water harnessing, treatment and disposal management systems and sustainable utilisation of transboundary water resources for productive purposes'. This may include such activities as constructing water dams, irrigation and hydro-electric infrastructure and promotion of sustainable irrigation schemes, programmes for pollution control, reuse and recycling of waste water; establishing strategic water catchments and water storage areas in rural and urban areas. Providing technical assistance for exchange programmes and capacity-building on water governance, service standards and regional water partnerships; facilitating EU ESA partnerships, innovations and joint ventures between economic operators and under the 'Water for Life Initiative'; and finally, establishing a regional research centre and other centres of excellence in research and development.[11]

Taken together, these provisions of the EU-ESA Interim EPA span a number of targets under SDG 6, particularly target 6.5, which asks that States implement integrated water resources management at all levels, including through transboundary cooperation as appropriate, by 2030. Given the urgent need to upscale implementation of integrated water resources management,[12] provisions that promote water resources management should

[7] Chinese Taipei-Nicaragua FTA.
[8] EU-ESA Interim EPA, art 49(1).
[9] Ibid, art 50.
[10] Ibid.
[11] Ibid, Annex IV Development Matrix, art 1(d).
[12] Report of the Secretary-General, Special edition: progress towards the Sustainable Development Goals (2019).

be encouraged. Further, the emphasis which the EU-ESA Interim EPA and its annexed Development Matrix place on international cooperation and support provides a strong example of trade provisions that engage target 6.A.

An interesting aspect of the EU-ESA Interim EPA is its reference to partnerships under the EU's Water for Life initiative, which was established in 2002 by the European Commission (EC) as a transnational, multi-actor initiative designed to aid implementation of the Millennium Development Goals and World Summit on Sustainable Development.[13] The initiative focuses on promoting integrated water resources management and providing support for water governance reform.[14] While a recent study of the initiative identifies a number of weaknesses in it, including a lack of resources and shared understanding of its overall purposes,[15] the EU-ESA Interim EPA's practice of linking trade and investment agreement provisions to specific initiatives that facilitate capacity-building with respect to water resource management initiatives such as Water for Life may provide a useful mechanism for States to institutionalize and advance cooperation on water management in furtherance of SDG 6.

One target under SDG 6 that appears to have been overlooked to this point in most agreements is target 6.B, which requires support and strengthening of local community participation in improving water and sanitation management. Cooperative provisions promoting participation are thus an area for advancing SDG 6.

Goal 7. Ensure Access to Affordable, Reliable, Sustainable and Modern Energy for all

Achieving SDG 7 requires that by 2030, countries have ensured universal access to affordable, reliable and modern energy services; increased substantially the share of renewable energy in the global energy mix; and doubled global rates of improvement in energy efficiency. By 2030, international cooperation with respect to facilitating access to clean energy research and technology (including renewable energy, energy efficiency and advanced and cleaner fossil-fuel technology), and promoting investment in energy infrastructure and clean energy technology, should be enhanced. Further, countries should expand infrastructure and upgrade technology for supplying modern and sustainable energy services for all in developing countries.

Trade and investment agreements address energy use from a diverse array of angles, dealing with renewable energy, energy generation and efficiency. Provisions promoting trade in renewable energy and energy efficiency are reasonably common. By way of example, the Japan-Switzerland FTA provides that Parties shall encourage trade and dissemination of environmental products and environment-related services, including 'sustainable promotion of renewable energy and climate-change-related goals'.[16] The CETA goes further, providing that Parties commit to 'consistent with their international obligations, pay special attention to facilitating the removal of obstacles to trade or investment in goods

[13] O Fritsch, C Adelle and D Benson, 'The EU Water Initiative at 15: Origins, Processes and Assessment' (2017) 42(4) Water International 425.

[14] Ibid.

[15] Ibid.

[16] Japan-Switzerland FTA, art 9. See provision in full in discussion of SDG 6.

and services of particular relevance for climate change mitigation and in particular trade or investment in renewable energy goods and related services'.[17] Importantly, this provision recognizes the importance of both trade and investment for promoting renewable energy goods and services. Similarly, the EU-South Korea FTA provides that 'Parties shall strive to facilitate and promote trade and foreign direct investment in environmental goods and services, including environmental technologies, sustainable renewable energy, energy efficient products and services and eco-labelled goods, including through addressing related non-tariff barriers . . .'.[18] While a requirement to strive to facilitate—rather than a requirement to encourage—is a somewhat weak form of wording, the references to both trade and investment, as well as addressing non-tariff barriers, give the provision greater substance.

The CARIFORUM-EU EPA's articles on cooperation on eco-innovation and renewable energy firstly provide that the Parties recognize the importance of fostering forms of innovation that benefit the environment in all sectors of their economy, with such forms of 'eco-innovation' including energy efficiency and renewable forms of energy. Agreed areas of cooperation and support include 'projects related to energy efficiency and renewable energy' and 'promotion of eco-innovation networks and clusters, including through public-private partnerships', as well as various activities relating to information exchange, research and technical assistance.

These provisions directly advance SDG 7 by promoting measures that increase the share of renewable energy in the global energy mix,[19] and promoting improved energy efficiency.[20] As the Report of the Secretary General recognizes, renewable energy measures also link with achievement of SDG 13 on taking urgent action to combat climate change. These will be discussed in more detail in the following chapter. The Report also identifies that expanding the share of renewable energy is a key area needing increased ambition, leaving opening opportunities for trade and investment agreements to facilitate upscaled efforts in this area. The EU-Colombia-Peru FTA's energy provisions evidence the challenge of balancing the need for transitioning to renewable energy sources with respecting the circumstances of developing countries. Thus, in the article titled 'climate change', Parties provided that:

> considering the global objective of a rapid transition to low-carbon economies, the Parties will promote the sustainable use of natural resources and will promote trade and investment measures that promote and facilitate access, dissemination and use of best available technologies for clean energy production and use, and for mitigation of and adaptation to climate change.[21]

Parties thus 'agree to consider actions to contribute to achieving climate change mitigation and adaptation objectives through their trade and investment policies, inter alia by . . . facilitating the removal of trade and investment barriers to access to, innovation, development, and deployment of goods, services and technologies that can contribute to mitigation or adaptation, taking into account the circumstances of developing countries' and

17 CETA, art 24.9.
18 EU-South Korea FTA, art 13.6(2).
19 Target 7.2.
20 Target 7.3.
21 EU-Colombia-Peru FTA, art 275(4). See further discussion at SDG 13.

'promoting measures for energy efficiency and renewable energy that respond to environmental and economic needs and minimise technical obstacles to trade'.[22]

The EU-ESA Interim EPA's provisions on energy highlight the importance of cooperation in the energy sector as a vehicle for supporting the Eastern and South Africa (ESA) economies' regional and global competitiveness.[23] According to the agreement, cooperation in the energy sector seeks to improve ESA States' access to modern, efficient, reliable, diversified and sustainable and renewable sources of clean energy at competitive prices; enhance the production, distribution and management capacity of energy nationally and regionally; and promote regional energy cooperation. Areas for cooperation include enhancing production and distribution capacity of existing energy sources, particularly hydro, petroleum and biomass; expanding and diversifying the energy mix to include other potential sources of energy that are socially and environmentally acceptable and that reduce dependency on oil; and supporting development of energy infrastructure, including for rural areas.

The Development Matrix reinforces these cooperative provisions, establishing energy as a key area for infrastructure development cooperation. Specifically, its development objective with respect to energy is to increase the ESA region's energy generation capacity, regional networks, distribution and transmission. This may be through such activities as expanding energy generation, transmission and distribution infrastructure and networks to facilitate regional energy trade; research and development of alternative environmentally sustainable sources of energy, innovation and technology transfer including improving energy efficiency and reduction of cost; legal and regulatory frameworks for establishment/strengthening and harmonization of regional and national energy institutions to provide frameworks for cross border energy trade; and capacity-building and design of instruments to mobilize resources for investment.[24] This strong focus on supporting energy infrastructure development clearly engages target 7.1, by promoting universal access to affordable, reliable and modern energy services, as well as target 7.B, which calls for expanded infrastructure and upgraded technology for supplying modern and sustainable energy services for all in developing countries.

Aside from structural and infrastructural activities, EU-ESA Parties also agree to cooperate with respect to broader policy, research and educational aspects of energy management: cooperation covers supporting development of appropriate energy regulatory and policy reforms, including commercialization and privatization; promoting regional interconnectivity and cooperation in the production and distribution of energy; building capacity in human resources, and improving management, service standards and institutional structures; and supporting creation of a conducive environment for attracting investment in the sector. Additionally, cooperation also encompasses technology development and transfer, research and development, innovation, information exchange, development of databases and networks and encouraging EU-ESA partnerships, linkages and joint ventures between economic operators.[25] Including these provisions has potential to advance SDG 7 not only by increasing the share of renewable energy in the global energy mix and improving energy efficiency,[26] but also through enhancing 'international cooperation to

[22] EU-Colombia-Peru FTA, art 276(5).
[23] EU-ESA Interim EPA, art 47(1).
[24] Ibid, Annex IV Development Matrix, art 1(a).
[25] Ibid, art 47.
[26] Targets 7.2 and 7.3.

facilitate access to clean energy research and technology, including renewable energy, energy efficiency and advanced and cleaner fossil-fuel technology, and promote investment in energy infrastructure and clean energy technology', as required by target 7.A. All in all, the comprehensive approach taken by the EU-ESA Interim EPA to energy development in the ESA region, dealing with infrastructure as well as broader technology transfer and research concerns, may provide a useful model for future trade negotiations between developed and developing country Parties wishing for their economic agreements to promote advancement of SDG 7.

In addition to the EU-ESA Interim EPA, the CETA and the Chinese Taipei-Nicaragua FTA also contain provisions covering targets relating to renewable energy, energy efficiency and enhancing international cooperation to facilitate access to clean energy research and technology. Firstly, in CETA's article on cooperation on environmental issues in its chapter on trade and environment, Parties 'commit to cooperate on trade-related environmental issues of common interest' in a number of areas, such as:

> trade-related aspects of the current and future international climate change regime, as well as domestic climate policies and programmes relating to mitigation and adaptation, including issues relating to carbon markets, ways to address adverse effects of trade on climate, as well as means to promote energy efficiency and the development and deployment of low-carbon and other climate-friendly technologies.[27]

Second, the programme of work established by the Chinese Taipei-Nicaragua FTA under its Environmental Cooperation Mechanism (the objective of which is to establish a cooperative framework among the Parties), may provide for cooperative activities related to 'facilitating technology development and transfer and training to promote the use, proper operation and maintenance of clean production technologies'.[28]

Goal 8. Promote Sustained, Inclusive and Sustainable Economic Growth, Full and Productive Employment and Decent work for all

SDG 8 rests on the assumption that inclusive, sustainable economic growth can facilitate progress and generate means to realize the SDGs.[29] To this end, it requires that countries 'sustain per capita economic growth in accordance with national circumstances and, in particular, at least 7% gross domestic product growth per annum in the least developed countries',[30] and 'achieve higher levels of economic productivity through diversification, technological upgrading and innovation, including through a focus on high-value added and labour-intensive sectors'.[31] Countries should also strengthen the capacity of domestic financial institutions to encourage access to banking.[32]

[27] CETA, art 24.12. See further in discussion of SDG 13.
[28] Chinese Taipei-Nicaragua FTA, Annex 19.08. Annex 19.08 details the objectives, organization and functions of the Environmental Cooperation Mechanism.
[29] Report of the Secretary General (n 12).
[30] Target 8.1.
[31] Target 8.2.
[32] Target 8.10.

Achieving SDG 8 also requires countries to improve employment prospects and labour conditions: countries should 'promote development-oriented policies that support productive activities, decent job creation, entrepreneurship, creativity and innovation, and encourage the formalization and growth of micro-, small- and medium-sized enterprises, including through access to financial services', and by 2030, 'achieve full and productive employment and decent work for all women and men, including for young people and persons with disabilities, and equal pay for work of equal value'.[33] Earlier, by 2020, the world should substantially reduce the proportion of youth that is not in either employment, education or training.[34] Further, target 8.7 requires 'immediate and effective measures to eradicate forced labour, end modern slavery and human trafficking and secure the prohibition and elimination of the worst forms of child labour'. Labour rights and migrant workers' rights are also dealt with.[35] Operationalizing a global strategy for youth employment, and implementing the Global Jobs Pact of the International Labour Organization, should have been achieved by 2020.[36]

Target 8.4 asks for progressive improvement of 'global resource efficiency in consumption and production and endeavour to decouple economic growth from environmental degradation, in accordance with the 10-year framework of programmes on sustainable consumption and production, with developed countries taking the lead', thereby paying particular regard to the differing circumstances of developed and developing countries. This target links clearly with SDGs 7 on energy and 13 on climate change. Countries are also asked to implement policies that promote sustainable tourism that both creates jobs and promotes local culture and products.[37]

Importantly, SDG 8 calls directly for international trade cooperation, asking for increased 'Aid for Trade support for developing countries, in particular least developed countries, including through the Enhanced Integrated Framework for Trade-Related Technical Assistance to Least Developed Countries'.[38]

The labour-related aspects of SDG 8 are dealt with thoroughly by a number of economic agreements, with designated chapters on trade and labour issues featuring frequently,[39] as well as references to respecting ILO labour standards. These features play an important role in enabling trade and investment agreements to advance SDG8 by protecting labour rights and promoting safe and secure working environments for all workers,[40] and also promoting full and productive employment for all, and equal pay, as required by target 8.5.

CETA is one example of an agreement which includes a specific chapter on trade and labour,[41] and incorporates ILO standards. In article 23.1 setting out the context and objectives of the trade and labour chapter, 'Parties recognise the value of international cooperation and agreements on labour affairs as a response of the international community to economic, employment and social challenges and opportunities resulting from globalisation. They recognise the contribution that international trade could make to full and productive

33 Target 8.5.
34 Target 8.6. This target links with the discussion on SDG 4, on education.
35 Target 8.8.
36 Target 8.B.
37 Target 8.9
38 Target 8.A.
39 See, e.g., CETA.
40 Target 8.8.
41 CETA, chapter 23.

employment and decent work for all and commit to consulting and cooperating as appropriate on trade-related labour and employment issues of mutual interest'. Further, 'affirming the value of greater policy coherence in decent work, encompassing core labour standards, and high levels of labour protection, coupled with their effective enforcement, the Parties recognise the beneficial role that those areas can have on economic efficiency, innovation and productivity, including export performance. In this context, they also recognise the importance of social dialogue on labour matters among workers and employers, and their respective organisations, and governments, and commit to the promotion of such dialogue'.[42]

In the chapter, Parties commit to respecting ILO labour standards and implementing fundamental ILO conventions, whilst protecting each Party's right to regulate on labour matters.[43] Parties agree to ensure their labour laws and practices promote particular objectives of the ILO Decent Work Agenda, and ILO Declaration on Social Justice for a Fair Globalization of 2008.[44] These include commitments to work health and safety, establishing minimum employment standards, and non-discrimination in respect of working conditions, including for migrant workers.[45]

Another feature of the CETA labour chapter is that it requires that Parties not lower their labour standards to encourage trade or investment.[46] Similarly, the Japan-Switzerland FTA also discourages lowering of labour standards, providing that 'Parties recognize that it is inappropriate to encourage investment activities by relaxing domestic health, safety or environmental measures or lowering labour standards. To this effect, each Party should not waive or otherwise derogate from such measures and standards as an encouragement for establishment, acquisition or expansion of investments in its Area'.[47]

The US-Colombia FTA chapter on labour provides a strong example of an agreement that facilitates protection of workers' rights and 'safe and secure working environments for all workers, including migrant workers, in particular women migrants, and those in precarious employment',[48] whilst also promoting measures to eradicate forced measures to eradicate forced labour, end modern slavery and human trafficking and secure the prohibition and elimination of the worst forms of child labour.[49] It does this through explicit references to the requirements of ILO instruments,[50] with the Parties reaffirming their obligations as members of the ILO at the beginning of the chapter.[51] Parties agree to adopt and maintain in their statutes, regulations and practices, rights to freedom of association; effective recognition of the right to collective bargaining; elimination of all forms of compulsory or forced labour; effective abolition of child labour and, for the purposes of the agreement, a prohibition on the worst forms of child labour; and elimination of discrimination in respect of employment and occupation. Parties also agree not to waive or derogate from such measures

[42] Ibid, art 23.1.
[43] Ibid, art 23.2.
[44] Adopted by the International Labour Conference at its Ninety-seventh Session.
[45] CETA, art 23.2. See also arts 23.7 and 23.8 for capacity-building measures linked to labour protection.
[46] Ibid, art 23.4.
[47] Japan-Switzerland FTA, art 101.
[48] Target 8.8.
[49] Target 8.7.
[50] ILO Declaration on Fundamental Principles and Rights at Work and its Follow-Up (1998); ILO Convention 182 on the Prohibition and Immediate Action for the Elimination of the Worst Forms of Child Labor.
[51] US Colombia FTA, art 17.1.

in a manner affecting trade or investment between the Parties, where doing so would be inconsistent with one of these ILO rights.[52]

The US-Colombia FTA also includes a commitment from each Party to enforce its labour laws,[53] and to ensure appropriate access to tribunals for the enforcement of the Party's labour laws.[54] Parties shall ensure that proceedings before such tribunals are fair, equitable and transparent, complying with due process of law, generally open to the public, and not entailing unreasonable charges, time limits or undue delays.[55]

A further noteworthy feature of the US-Colombia FTA is the institutional arrangements that it establishes with respect to labour. First, it establishes a Labor Affairs Council to oversee implementation of the labour chapter (among other things).[56] Second, it establishes a 'Labor Cooperation and Capacity Building Mechanism'.[57] According to article 17.6, the mechanism is established in recognition of the important role of cooperation on labour issues in advancing development for each Party, enhancing opportunities to improve labour standards and further advancing common commitments on labour matters, including ILO principles.[58] Under this mechanism, the Parties' contact points are to develop and pursue bilateral or regional cooperation activities on labour issues, which may include promoting effective implementation of fundamental rights at work; promoting compliance with the ILO Convention on the worst forms of child labour;[59] strengthening institutional capacity of labour administrations and labour tribunals; improving labour law enforcement and compliance; and establishing and strengthening alternative dispute resolution mechanisms for labour disputes.[60] Further areas of priority for cooperation under the mechanism include cooperation on labour relations, occupational health and safety and raising public awareness of working conditions; protecting migrant workers; skills development; technology and information exchange; labour statistics; programmes promoting employment opportunities; programmes which facilitate elimination of gender discrimination in employment; and promotion of best labour practices.[61] The agreement also provides for possible means for carrying out these cooperative activities,[62] and calls for public participation throughout the process.[63]

The Chinese Taipei-Nicaragua FTA, like the US-Colombia FTA, also establishes a Labor Cooperation and Capacity Building Mechanism. It also sets out a number of 'guiding principles' on common areas for concern that Parties commit to promote, including freedom of association and protection of the right to organize, the right to bargain collectively, the right to strike, prohibition of forced labour, labour protections for children and young persons, minimum employment standards, elimination of employment discrimination and equal

[52] US-Colombia FTA, art 17.2. CETA, art 23.2 and EU-Colombia-Peru FTA, art 296 contain similar provisions.

[53] US-Colombia FTA, art 17.3. CETA, art 23.5 contains similar provisions.

[54] US-Colombia FTA, art 17.4.

[55] Ibid, art 17.4.

[56] Ibid, art 17.5.

[57] Ibid, art 17.6 and Annex 17.6. The Chinese Taipei-Nicaragua FTA also establishes a Labor Cooperation and Capacity Building Mechanism, with similar cooperative functions: see Annex 18.05.

[58] US-Colombia FTA, art 17.6.

[59] ILO Convention 182 on the Prohibition and Immediate Action for the Elimination of the Worst Forms of Child Labor.

[60] US-Colombia FTA, Annex 17.6.

[61] Ibid, Annex 17.6.

[62] Ibid, Annex 17.6 art 3.

[63] Ibid, Annex 17.6 art 4. This is also relevant to target 16.7; see discussion below.

pay for women and men. This explicit reference to equal pay engages directly with target 8.5, which calls for equal pay for work of equal value for all by 2030.[64]

In the CARIFORUM-EU EPA, Parties agreed cooperation provisions that relate to exchange of information on social and labour legislation and related policies; formulation of national social and labour legislation and strengthening existing legislation educational and awareness-raising programmes and enforcement of national legislation and work regulation.

Labour cooperation is subject to a memorandum of understanding in the China-Peru FTA, which provides that 'Parties shall enhance their communication and cooperation on labor, social security and environment issues through Memorandum of Understanding on Labor Cooperation between the Government of the People's Republic of China and the Government of the Republic of Peru'.[65]

This survey of labour-related trade provisions reveals a number of useful tools for countries wishing to incorporate SDG 8 considerations into their trade and investment agreements. Key among these are labour chapters, explicit incorporation of ILO declarations and conventions—including those on child labour and decent work—and establishing institutional mechanisms for facilitating cooperation are key advances. Agreements could more fully address the labour-related targets of SDG 8 by requiring implementation of the Global Jobs Pact of the ILO in their cooperation provisions,[66] showing greater regard for the need to protect rights of migrant workers, particularly women migrants, and those in precarious employment[67] and incorporating requirements to facilitate youth employment in their labour chapters.[68] This aligns with the recent Report of the Secretary General, which identified a need for progress with regard to increasing employment opportunities, particularly for young people and reducing informal employment, among other things.[69]

In addition to the targets on labour rights in SDG 8, economic agreements also feature provisions that advance the economic growth aspect of this SDG through promoting 'development-oriented policies that support productive activities, decent job creation, entrepreneurship, creativity and innovation' and encouraging 'formalization and growth of micro-, small- and medium-sized enterprises, including through access to financial services'.[70]

By way of example, in the Peru-Korea FTA, Parties recognize:

> the importance of technological innovation as well as the transfer and dissemination of technological information to the mutual advantage of technology producers and users, particularly in the new digital economy. Accordingly, the Parties will seek to develop and encourage cooperation programs, through collaboration in science, technology, and innovation.

64 Target 8.5.

65 China-Peru FTA, art 161. The Memorandum is not public, thus whether it is a binding agreement is not known. See <https://www.thirdway.org/report/what-do-chinese-rules-mean-for-worker-rights> accessed 16 December 2020.

66 See target 8.B.

67 See target 8.8.

68 See target 8.6.

69 Report of the Secretary General (n 12).

70 Target 8.3.

This provision may encourage development-oriented activities that support productive activities and innovation, as required by target 8.3.

With respect to supporting small and medium-sized enterprises, the China-Peru FTA's chapter on cooperation provides that Parties will 'promote a favourable environment for the development of the small and medium enterprises (SME) on the basis of strengthening of the relevant private and governmental bodies, as well as the exchange of experiences and good practices with the SME'.[71] Cooperation in this area includes designing and developing mechanisms to encourage partnerships and productive chain linkages; developing human resources and management skills to increase knowledge of Chinese and Peruvian markets; defining and developing methods and strategies for clusters development; increasing access to information relevant to SME exporters; instituting programmes focused on transferring technological innovation to SMEs to improve their productivity; increasing SME access to technological promotion, financial support and encouragement programmes; supporting new exporting SMEs through such mechanisms as sponsorship, credits and guarantees, and seed capital; and encouraging partnerships and information exchanges for SME financing institutions.[72] Similarly, one of the objectives of the Canada-Colombia FTA's chapter on trade-related cooperation is to 'promote sustainable economic development, with an emphasis on small and medium sized enterprises, in order to contribute to the reduction of poverty through trade'. Further, the Peru-Korea FTA's provisions on cooperation and technology transfer include an agreement to exchange views and information on intellectual property legal frameworks to 'stimulate the creation and development of intellectual property by persons of each Party, particularly small and medium-sized enterprises'.[73]

Goal 9. Build Resilient Infrastructure, Promote Inclusive and Sustainable Industrialization and Foster Innovation

SDG 9 focuses on developing quality, reliable, sustainable and resilient infrastructure to support economic development and human wellbeing;[74] promoting inclusive and sustainable industrialization, including by doubling the manufacturing industry's share of employment and gross domestic product (GDP) in least developed countries (LDCs);[75] increasing access of small-scale industrial and other enterprises to financial services;[76] upgrading infrastructure and retrofitting industries to make them sustainable by 2030;[77] and enhancing scientific research and technological capabilities of industrial sectors in all countries.[78] The SDG calls for countries to facilitate sustainable, resilient infrastructure development in developing countries; support domestic technology development, research and innovation in developing countries; and significantly increase access to information and communications technology (ICT), with countries asked to strive to provide universal, affordable access to the Internet in LDCs by 2020.[79] Progress towards achieving SDG 9 has been slow to date.

[71] China-Peru FTA, art 155.
[72] Ibid, art 155.
[73] Peru-Korea FTA, art 17.10.
[74] Target 9.1.
[75] Target 9.2.
[76] Target 9.3.
[77] Target 9.4.
[78] Target 9.5.
[79] Targets 9.A–9.C.

Financing for economic infrastructure in developing countries has increased, but many countries—particularly LDCs—face serious challenges with respect to doubling the manufacturing industry's share of GDP by 2030.[80] Further, investment in scientific research and innovation needs to upscale.[81] Key mechanisms through which economic agreements facilitate advancement of SDG 9 include through promoting scientific advancement, research and information exchange, joint initiatives on technological cooperation and technology transfer.

In CETA, Parties agree to 'endeavour to encourage, develop and facilitate cooperative activities on a reciprocal basis in support of, or supplementary to the Agreement for Scientific and Technological Cooperation between the European Community and Canada'.[82] These activities are to be of mutual benefit to the Parties; and the Parties are to agree on their scope and parameters. Further, the activities should take into account 'the important role of the private sector and research institutions in the development of science, technology, research and innovation, and the commercialization of goods and services thereof'.[83] The EFTA-Central America FTA importantly provides that 'sustainable development shall be integrated and reflected in the implementation of cooperation, assistance and technology transfer in the various sectors to which it is relevant'. Means of cooperation and assistance may encompass information exchange; technology transfer and training; implementing joint actions and technical and administrative assistance.

The CARIFORUM-EU EPA goes further, with a number of provisions that seek to foster the participation of the Parties' research and technological development bodies in cooperation activities.[84] These activities may be in the form of joint initiatives that raise awareness of the science and technology capacity-building programmes of the European Community;[85] joint research networks; exchanges of researches and experts; promotion of advanced science and technology studies which contribute to long-term sustainable development; public–private sector links; policy dialogue and exchanges of scientific and technological information and experience; and participation in Knowledge and Innovation Communities.[86] The EPA places special emphasis on building human potential 'as a long-lasting basis of scientific and technological excellence and the creation of sustainable links between the scientific and technological communities of the Parties, at both national and regional levels'.[87] It further calls for broad involvement of research centres, higher education institutions and micro-, small- and medium-sized enterprises, and commits Parties to promoting participation of their respective entities in each other's scientific and technological programmes.[88]

A further example of encouraging joint research is found in the EU-Colombia-Peru FTA, under which Parties commit to encouraging mechanisms for the participation of entities

80 Report of the Secretary General (n 12).
81 Ibid.
82 This was done at Halifax on 17 June 1995.
83 CETA, art 25.5.
84 CARIFORUM-EU EPA, art 136.
85 In particular, these programmes include the international dimension of the seventh Framework Programme for Research and Technological Development, which ran from 2007 to 2013, and possible successor programmes.
86 These communities are initiatives of the European Institute of Innovation and Technology.
87 CARIFORUM-EU EPA, art 136.
88 Ibid, art 136.

and experts in science, technology and innovation in projects and joint research, for the purpose of strengthening capacity through a variety of mechanisms.[89]

These provisions canvassed engage clearly with target 9.5, which asks for countries to:

> enhance scientific research, upgrade the technological capabilities of industrial sectors in all countries, in particular developing countries, including, by 2030, encouraging innovation and substantially increasing the number of research and development workers per 1 million people and public and private research and development spending.

Their long-term capacity-building focus also advances achievement of target 9.B, through facilitating domestic technology development, research and innovation in developing countries, including by ensuring a conducive policy environment for, *inter alia*, industrial diversification and value addition to commodities.

Sustainable and resilient infrastructure development is another perspective of SDG 9 with which economic agreements engage. The EU-ESA Interim EPA includes supporting the development of infrastructure facilities on environmentally friendly products as an area for cooperation in its chapter on natural resources and environment.[90] Its Development Matrix identifies infrastructure development as a key area for cooperation and support between the Parties,[91] with a view to improving existing and priority infrastructural needs, developing new infrastructure (particularly shared infrastructure) and securing financing. Telecommunications is included in the Matrix as one aspect of infrastructure development, with a view to strengthening telecommunication networks and improving ICT infrastructure to foster competitiveness, innovation and the ESA's transition to an information society.[92] Cooperative activities with respect to telecommunications infrastructure include the 'design of instruments to facilitate EU ESA partnerships, innovation and joint ventures to mobilise resources for investment and facilitate private sector investment in ICT infrastructure'.[93] Taken together, these cooperative provisions in the EU-ESA Interim EPA advance SDG 9 by facilitating the process of upgrading infrastructure and retrofitting industries to make them sustainable, with increased resource-use efficiency and greater adoption of clean and environmentally sound technologies and industrial processes, as required by target 9.4, and facilitating sustainable and resilient infrastructure development in developing countries through enhanced financial, technological and technical support to African countries (target 9.A). In addition, the Parties' commitments to support development of ICT infrastructure advances target 9.C, which calls for significantly increased access to ICT and strive to provide universal and affordable internet access.

Goal 10. Reduce Inequality within and among Countries

The targets under SDG 10 address a range of aspects of inequality among countries, from income to political inclusion and representation of developing countries in global

89 EU-Colombia-Peru FTA, art 255.
90 EU-ESA Interim EPA, art 51.
91 Ibid, Annex IV art 1.
92 Ibid, Annex IV art 1(c).
93 Ibid.

institutions. Thus, target 10.1 calls for countries to, by 2030, progressively achieve and sustain income growth of the bottom 40 per cent of the population at a higher rate than the national average, and target 10.2 requires that by 2030, countries empower and promote the social, economic and political inclusion of all, irrespective of age, sex, disability, race, ethnicity, origin, religion or economic or other status. Achieving SDG 10 also requires ensuring equal opportunity and reducing inequalities of outcome;[94] adopting fiscal, wage and social protection policies that improve equality;[95] improving regulation and monitoring of global financial markets and institutions;[96] ensuring enhanced representation and voice for developing countries in decision-making in global international economic and financial institutions;[97] and facilitating orderly, safe, regular and responsible migration and mobility of people.[98]

The importance of trade and investment cooperation for advancing SDG 10 is magnified by means of implementation targets 10.A and 10.B. Target 10.A requires implementation of the principle of special and differential treatment for developing countries, in particular LDCs, in accordance with WTO agreements.[99] Accomplishment of this target is indicated by the proportion of tariff lines applied to imports from LDCs and developing countries with zero-tariff.[100] Further, target 10.B calls for States to:

> encourage official development assistance and financial flows, including foreign direct investment, to States where the need is greatest, in particular least developed countries, African countries, small island developing States and landlocked developing countries, in accordance with their national plans and programmes.

The Secretary General this year called for additional efforts to increase zero-tariff access for exports from LDCs and developing countries, and assistance to LDCs and small island developing States,[101] indicating the potential for trade and investment agreements to upscale ambition in these areas.

Regional integration provisions are one mechanism through which trade and investment agreements between developed and developing countries may address inequalities in a manner that is inclusive and supports development. A strong example of regional integration provisions are found in the EU-ESA Interim EPA and its Development Matrix,[102] which provides for regional integration with respect to regional economic integration, management of transboundary programs, management of the environment and natural resources, regional peace, stability and security and cultural development.

94 Target 10.3.
95 Target 10.4.
96 Target 10.5.
97 Target 10.6.
98 Target 10.7.
99 Target 10.A.
100 Indicator 10.A.1.
101 Report of the Secretary General (n 12).
102 EU-ESA Interim EPA, Annex IV.

Goal 11. Make Cities and Human Settlements Inclusive, Safe, Resilient and Sustainable

SDG 11 focuses on universal access to adequate housing and basic services,[103] providing access to safe, affordable and sustainable transport systems for all,[104] and to safe, green, accessible public spaces;[105] enhancing inclusive and sustainable urbanization and capacity for sustainable human settlement planning and management;[106] and strengthening efforts to protect and safeguard cultural and natural heritage.[107] This SDG also addresses the impact of disasters, calling for significantly reduced economic losses and numbers of deaths and people affected from disasters.[108] In addition, target 11.6 requires that the adverse per capita environmental impact of cities be reduced by 2030, paying special attention to air quality and waste management.[109]

The potential role of trade and investment agreements in facilitating SDG 11 becomes apparent in the means of implementation targets, which ask countries to support positive economic, social and environmental links between urban, peri-urban and rural areas by strengthening national and regional development planning;[110] and to support least developed countries, including through financial and technical assistance, in building sustainable and resilient buildings utilizing local materials.[111] Further, cooperation is required to substantially increase the number of cities and settlements adopting integrated policies towards inclusion, resource efficiency, climate change mitigation and adaptation, and disaster resilience and risk management.[112]

The China-Peru FTA addresses cultural cooperation, with Parties agreeing to encourage and facilitate activities including dialogue on cultural policies and promotion of local culture, exchange of experience in conservation and restoration of national heritage and the protection of archaeological monuments and cultural heritage.[113]

[103] Target 11.1.
[104] Target 11.2.
[105] Target 11.7.
[106] Target 11.3.
[107] Target 11.4.
[108] Target 11.5.
[109] Target 11.6.
[110] Target 11.A.
[111] Target 11.C.
[112] Target 11.B.
[113] China-Peru FTA, art 156.

21

Trade and Investment Accords for Sustainable Development Goals 12–17

Introduction

This chapter focuses on how trade and investment agreements may contribute to international efforts to achieve SDGs 12 to 17, which address responsible consumption and production patterns (SDG 12), combatting climate change (SDG 13), conservation and sustainable use of marine resources (SDG 14), and sustainable use of terrestrial ecosystems (SDG 15). SDG 16, which calls for peace, justice and strong institutions for sustainable development, is also canvassed in its links to securing stability, effective governance and human rights.[1] Finally SDG 17, which calls on all countries to build partnerships towards achieving sustainable development, is discussed as the foundations of all the SDGs in the concluding note to this chapter and section, particularly given its explicit provisions on economic cooperation, trade, investment and finance.

Goal 12. Ensure Sustainable Consumption and Production Patterns

The rapid expansion of worldwide material consumption to date indicates that increased efforts are needed to prevent resource over-extraction and environmental degradation, and to improve resource efficiency, reduce waste and mainstream sustainability practices across all sectors.[2] In SDG 12, governments agreed to implement programmes on sustainable consumption and production, with developed countries taking the lead;[3] achieve the sustainable management and efficient use of natural resources by 2030;[4] halve per capita global food waste;[5] achieve environmentally sound management of chemicals and all wastes throughout their lifecycles by 2020;[6] and substantially reduce waste generation.[7] Countries are also to encourage companies—especially large and transnational companies—to adopt sustainable practices,[8] and promote sustainable public procurement practices.[9] At an individual level, people everywhere should, by 2030, have the relevant information and awareness for sustainable development.[10]

[1] See UNDP, Goal 16, <https://www.undp.org/content/undp/en/home/sustainable-development-goals/goal-16-peace-justice-and-strong-institutions.html> accessed 16 December 2020.
[2] Report of the Secretary-General, Special edition: progress towards the Sustainable Development Goals (2019).
[3] Target 12.1.
[4] Target 12.2.
[5] Target 12.3.
[6] Target 12.4.
[7] Target 12.5.
[8] Target 12.6.
[9] Target 12.7.
[10] Target 12.8.

Crafting Trade and Investment Accords for Sustainable Development. Marie-Claire Cordonier Segger, Oxford University Press. © Marie-Claire Cordonier Segger 2021. DOI: 10.1093/oso/9780198831341.003.0021

Under SDG 12, support is required for developing countries to strengthen their scientific and technological capacities to facilitate their movement towards more sustainable consumption and production patterns.[11] Cooperation is also required with respect to improving sustainable tourism.[12] Of key significance to trade and investment agreements, SDG 12 also addresses fossil-fuel subsidies: target 12.C requires that countries cooperate to:

> rationalize inefficient fossil-fuel subsidies that encourage wasteful consumption by removing market distortions, in accordance with national circumstances, including by restructuring taxation and phasing out those harmful subsidies, where they exist, to reflect their environmental impacts, taking fully into account the specific needs and conditions of developing countries and minimizing the possible adverse impacts on their development in a manner that protects the poor and the affected communities.

Encouraging voluntary schemes is one means to facilitate sustainable management and use of natural resources, in accordance with target 12.2, and also to encourage companies to adopt sustainable practices, as required by target 12.6. In the Comprehensive Economic and Trade Agreement (CETA), Parties affirm that trade should promote sustainable development. 'Accordingly, each Party shall strive to promote trade and economic flows and practices that contribute to enhancing decent work and environmental protection', including by 'encouraging the development and use of voluntary schemes relating to the sustainable production of goods and services, such as eco-labelling and fair-trade schemes'.[13] Similarly, the Chinese Taipei-Nicaragua FTA contains commitments to encourage development and use of flexible and voluntary mechanisms. An example of a mechanism that facilitates voluntary action to protect or enhance the environment is the:

> sharing of information and expertise among authorities, interested parties, and the public concerning methods for achieving high levels of environmental protection, voluntary environmental auditing and reporting, ways to use resources more efficiently or reduce environmental impacts, environmental monitoring, and collection of baseline data; or incentives, including market-based incentives where appropriate, to encourage conservation, restoration, and protection of natural resources and the environment, such as public recognition of facilities or enterprises that are superior environmental performers, or programs for exchanging permits or other instruments to help achieve environmental Goals.[14]

These voluntary information sharing mechanisms, by encouraging efficient resource use, or publicly recognizing enterprises with superior environmental performance, may advance achievement of targets 12.2 and 12.6.

Further examples of economic accords which have the potential to facilitate sustainable management and efficient use of natural resources through promoting trade and investment in environmental goods and services are the EFTA-Central America FTA and Japan-Switzerland FTA. The EFTA-Central America FTA provides that Parties 'shall strive to

[11] Target 12.A.
[12] Target 12.C.
[13] CETA, art 22.3.
[14] Chinese Taipei-Nicaragua FTA, art 19.04.

facilitate and promote foreign investment, trade in and dissemination of goods and services beneficial to sustainable development', including 'environmental technologies, sustainable renewable energy, organic production, energy efficient and eco-labelled goods and services, including through addressing related non-tariff barriers' and 'goods and services that are the subject of schemes such as fair and ethical trade'. Similarly, the Japan-Switzerland FTA includes a commitment to encouraging 'trade and dissemination of environmental products and environment-related services in order to facilitate access to technologies and products that support the environmental protection and development goals, such as improved sanitation, pollution prevention, sustainable promotion of renewable energy and climate-change-related goals'.[15] In the Peru-Korea FTA, Parties agree to identify a list of environmental goods and services and to facilitate their trade.[16] A further example is CETA, which establishes a bilateral dialogue on raw materials. The purposes of this dialogue include to 'contribute to market access for raw material goods and related services and investments and to avoid non-tariff barriers to trade for raw materials'.

The EU-Colombia-Peru FTA goes beyond encouraging trade in environmental goods and services to promoting corporate social responsibility and best business practice, thus going further towards encouraging companies to adopt sustainable practices.[17] The agreement reaffirms the proposition that trade should promote sustainable development. Thus, Parties not only agree to 'strive to facilitate and promote trade and foreign direct investment in environmental goods and services', but also 'agree to promote best business practices related to corporate social responsibility', and 'recognise that flexible, voluntary, and incentive-based mechanisms can contribute to coherence between trade practices and the objectives of sustainable development. In this regard, and in accordance with its respective laws and policies, each Party will encourage the development and use of such mechanisms'. Commitments to cooperate on areas such as 'the environmental dimension of corporate social responsibility and accountability, including the implementation and follow-up of internationally recognised guidelines' also features in CETA.[18] One purpose of the bilateral dialogue on raw materials is to 'encourage activities that support corporate social responsibility in accordance with internationally-recognised standards such as the OECD Guidelines for Multinational Enterprises'.[19]

The Chinese Taipei-Nicaragua FTA promotes corporate responsibility in a different manner, by providing for 'Principles of Corporate Stewardship'. Thus, Parties, explicitly recognise 'the substantial benefits brought by international trade and investment as well as the opportunity for enterprises to implement policies for sustainable development that seek to ensure coherence between social, economic and environmental objectives', and agree that 'each Party should encourage enterprises operating within its territory or jurisdiction to voluntarily incorporate sound principles of corporate stewardship in their internal policies, such as those principles or agreements that have been endorsed by both Parties'.[20]

Regional integration provisions are a further mechanism for trade and investment agreements to facilitate sustainable natural resource use.[21] The EU-ESA Interim EPA's

[15] Japan-Switzerland FTA, art 9.
[16] Peru-Korea FTA, art 19.4.
[17] Target 12.6.
[18] CETA, art 24.12.
[19] Ibid, art 25.4. See further discussion below.
[20] Chinese Taipei-Nicaragua FTA, art 19.05.
[21] See target 12.2.

Development Matrix includes management of the environment and natural resources as an area for cooperation with respect to regional integration.[22] Enhancing protection and sustainable utilization of natural resources and facilitating and encouraging sustainable utilization of shared natural resources are two objectives of cooperation in this area. Cooperative activities relevant to SDG 12 include 'support to strengthen environment policy, strategies, legislation, administration and resource management and sustainable development; and institutional capacity to enforce environment legislations and standards and programmes to involve communities in the management of natural resources'.[23]

Another mechanism for promoting sustainable consumption through trade and investment cooperation is through ensuring enforcement of Parties' environmental laws. By way of example, the US-Colombia FTA includes a commitment by each Party to ensure 'that judicial, quasi-judicial, or administrative proceedings are available under its law to provide sanctions or remedies for violations of its environmental laws', and to ensure that any request to investigate an alleged violation of its environmental laws is given due consideration. The agreement also sets out detailed requirements on each Party's commitments to providing effective access to remedies for violations of environmental laws. A further feature of the US-Colombia FTA is a commitment to promoting public awareness of each Party's environmental laws, 'by ensuring that information is available to the public regarding its environmental laws, enforcement, and compliance procedures, including procedures for interested persons to request a Party's competent authorities to investigate alleged violations of its environmental laws'.

Agreements also engage directly with target 12.5, which calls for substantially reduced waste generation through prevention, reduction, recycling and reuse. In CETA, promoting life-cycle management of goods, 'including carbon accounting and end-of-life management, extended producer-responsibility, recycling and reduction of waste, and other best practices' is an area in which Parties may cooperate.[24] Another example is the Chinese Taipei-Nicaragua FTA: its Environmental Cooperation Mechanism provides for cooperation on capacity-building activities including financial assistance, as appropriate and mutually agreed, for research projects, biodiversity management and monitoring, wildlife species affected by trade, pollution and hazardous and non-hazardous waste treatment. The work programme to be established under the Mechanism may include long-, medium- and short-term activities related to facilitating technology development and transfer and training on hazardous and nonhazardous waste management.[25]

Goal 13. Take Urgent Action to Combat Climate Change and its Impacts

SDG 13 calls for countries to strengthen resilience and adaptive capacity to climate-related hazards and natural disasters,[26] integrate climate change measures into national policies, strategies and planning[27] and improve education, awareness raising and human and

[22] EU-ESA Interim EPA, Annex IV, art 3(c).
[23] Ibid, Annex IV, art 3(c).
[24] CETA, art 24.12.
[25] Chinese Taipei-Nicaragua FTA, Annex 19.08, art 8(m).
[26] Target 13.1.
[27] Target 13.2.

institutional capacity on climate change mitigation, adaptation, impact reduction and early warning.[28] Achieving SDG 13 requires developed country Parties to implement their commitment under the UN Framework Convention on Climate Change (UNFCCC) to mobilize jointly US$ 100 billion annually by 2020 to address the needs of developing countries with respect to mitigation actions and transparency on implementation, and to fully operationalize the Green Climate Fund through its capitalization as soon as possible.[29] Mechanisms for raising capacity for effective climate change-related planning and management in least developed countries and small island developing States are also to be promoted.[30] Recent reports on the progress towards SDG 13 record positive steps with respect to climate finance flows, but calls for upscaled action on mitigation and adaptation, access to finance and capacity-building, particularly for least developed countries and small island developing States.[31]

Economic agreements such as the EU-ESA Interim EPA advance target 13.1, which calls for strengthened resilience and adaptive capacity to climate-related hazards and natural disasters in all countries, by providing for cooperation with respect to natural disasters. The EU-ESA Interim EPA provides that Parties agree to cooperate, including by facilitating support, in mitigating natural disasters, and preventing environmental disasters and biodiversity loss.[32]

The CETA, the EU-Colombia-Peru FTA and the Peru-Korea FTA each provide examples of agreements that advance target 13.2, by promoting integration of climate change measures into national policies, strategies and planning. CETA's provisions on making efforts to facilitate and promote trade and investment in environmental goods and services, including through reducing non-tariff barriers, specifies that the 'Parties shall, consistent with their international obligations, pay special attention to facilitating the removal of obstacles to trade or investment in goods and services of particular relevance for climate change mitigation and in particular trade or investment in renewable energy goods and related services'.[33] Parties also commit to:

> cooperate in areas such as 'trade-related aspects of the current and future international climate change regime, as well as domestic climate policies and programmes relating to mitigation and adaptation, including issues relating to carbon markets, ways to address adverse effects of trade on climate, as well as means to promote energy efficiency and the development and deployment of low-carbon and other climate-friendly technologies.[34]

In the EU-Colombia-Peru FTA, which includes designated climate change provisions, Parties resolved to 'enhance their efforts regarding climate change, which are led by developed countries, including through the promotion of domestic policies and suitable international initiatives to mitigate and to adapt to climate change, on the basis of equity

[28] Target 13.3.
[29] Target 13.A.
[30] Target 13.B.
[31] Report of the Secretary General (n 2).
[32] EU-ESA Interim EPA, art 51(2)(g). See also Development Matrix, Annex IV, art 3(c).
[33] CETA, art 24.9.
[34] Ibid, art 24.12.

and in accordance with their common but differentiated responsibilities and respective capabilities and their social and economic conditions, and taking particularly into account the needs, circumstances, and high vulnerability to the adverse effects of climate change of those Parties which are developing countries'.[35] Further, the Peru-Korea FTA provides that Parties, within their own capacities, shall adopt policies and measures for promoting sustainable development on issues such as measures for improving energy efficiency, 'research, promotion, development and use of new and renewable energy, technologies of carbon dioxide capture, and updated and innovative environmental technologies that do not affect food security or the conservation of biological diversity' and 'measures for evaluating the vulnerability and adaptation to climate change'. The close links between SDG 13 and SDG 7 are apparent in a provision such as this, which facilitates not only advancement of SDG 13 by integrating climate change measures into national policies, but also facilitates efforts towards ensuring universal access to energy services,[36] and promoting renewable energy.[37]

A number of trade and investment agreements also engage with target 13.B, which requires countries to promote mechanisms for raising capacity for effective climate change-related planning and management in least developed countries and small island developing States, including focusing on women, youths and local and marginalized communities. The EU-Colombia-Peru FTA is a key example, exhibiting a strong regard for the circumstances of developing countries. Thus, it explicitly highlights the importance of increasing adaptation efforts, particularly in developing country Parties. It also asserts that:

> Parties are resolved to enhance their efforts regarding climate change, which are led by developed countries, including through the promotion of domestic policies and suitable international initiatives to mitigate and to adapt to climate change, on the basis of equity and in accordance with their common but differentiated responsibilities and respective capabilities and their social and economic conditions, and taking particularly into account the needs, circumstances, and high vulnerability to the adverse effects of climate change of those Parties which are developing countries.

Parties agree to promote trade and investment measures that promote and facilitate access, dissemination and use of best available technologies for clean energy production and use, and for mitigation of and adaptation to climate change.[38] Further, the agreement recognizes the importance of cooperating in activities such as those related to climate change adaptation and mitigation, including activities related to the reduction of emissions from deforestation and forest degradation (REDD) mechanism.[39] These provisions could more directly engage target 13.B if they paid regard to the needs of women, youths and local and marginalized communities.

[35] EU-Colombia-Peru FTA, art 275.
[36] See target 7.1.
[37] See target 7.2.
[38] EU-Colombia-Peru FTA, art 275.
[39] Ibid, art 286.

Goal 14. Conserve and Sustainably use the Oceans, Seas and Marine Resources for Sustainable Development

Achieving sustainable use of ocean and marine resources under SDG 14 requires that countries sustainably manage and protect marine and coastal ecosystems,[40] effectively regulate harvesting and end over-fishing and destructive fishing practices,[41] implement science-based management plans to restore fish stocks,[42] conserve areas of coastal and marine areas[43] and prohibit certain forms of fisheries subsidies which contribute to overcapacity and over-fishing.[44] By 2025, countries should prevent and significantly reduce marine pollution of all kinds.[45] Key means of implementation targets towards achieving SDG 14 include, firstly, increase scientific knowledge, develop research capacity and transfer marine technology, in order to improve ocean health and to enhance the contribution of marine biodiversity to the development of developing countries, in particular small island developing States and least developed countries;[46] secondly, access for small-scale artisanal fishers to marine resources and markets;[47] and third, enhanced conservation and sustainable use of oceans and ocean resources, in accordance with the UN Convention on the Law of the Seas (UNCLOS).[48]

Fisheries provisions in economic agreements demonstrate a number of mechanisms for advancing SDG 14, with some recognizing the importance of fisheries for the achievement of other SDGs such as those that address poverty and food security.[49] Notable provisions include commitments to combat illegal and unregulated fishing,[50] cooperate with Regional Fisheries Management Organisations (RFMO's),[51] and expand marine protected areas.[52]

With respect to illegal fishing, a number of economic agreements engage directly with target 14.4, by promoting effective regulation of harvesting and the end of over-fishing, illegal, unreported and unregulated fishing and destructive fishing practices, as well as providing for implementation of science-based management plans to restore fish stocks. These provisions are commonly linked to promoting conservation and cooperation with RFMOs: these may advance accomplishment of target 14.C, which requires enhanced conservation and sustainable use of oceans and their resources by implementing international law as reflected in UNCLOS.[53]

One example of an FTA that addresses targets 14.4 and 14.C is the EU-Colombia-Peru FTA, which includes a designated provision on trade in fish products. It asserts that 'Parties recognise the need to conserve and manage fish resources in a rational and responsible

40 Target 14.2.
41 Target 14.4.
42 Target 14.4.
43 Target 14.5.
44 Target 14.6.
45 Target 14.1.
46 Target 14.A.
47 Target 14.B.
48 Target 14.C.
49 See, e.g., CARIFORUM-EU EPA.
50 See, e.g., CETA.
51 See, e.g., CETA.
52 See, e.g., EU-Colombia-Peru FTA.
53 As Target 14.C outlines, UNCLOS provides the legal framework for the conservation and sustainable use of oceans and their resources, as recalled in para 158 of 'The Future We Want', Outcome document of the United Nations Conference on Sustainable Development A/RES/66/288 (2012).

manner, in order to ensure their sustainability', and also 'the need to cooperate in the context of Regional Fisheries Management Organisations'.[54] This cooperation seeks to 'revise and adjust the fishing capacity for fishery resources, including those affected by overfishing, to ensure that the fishing practices are commensurate to the fishing possibilities available'; 'adopt effective tools for the monitoring and control, such as observer schemes, vessel monitoring schemes, transhipment control and port state control, in order to ensure full compliance with applicable conservation measures'; and 'adopt actions to combat illegal, unreported and unregulated (IUU) fishing; to this end, the Parties agree to ensure that vessels flying their flags conduct fishing activities in accordance with rules adopted within the RFMO, and to sanction vessels under their domestic legislation, in case of any violation of the said rules'.[55]

CETA's article on trade in fisheries and aquaculture concerns, within its chapter on trade and environment, similarly addresses illegal fishing and the need for cooperation with RFMOs. Parties explicitly 'recognise the importance of the conservation and the sustainable and responsible management of fisheries and aquaculture and their contribution to providing environmental, economic and social opportunities for present and future generations'. As well as monitoring measures and cooperating to combat IUU fishing, the Parties also undertake to 'cooperate with, and where appropriate in, regional fisheries management organisations in which the Parties are either members, observers, or cooperating non-contracting parties, with the aim of achieving good governance, including by advocating for science-based decisions and for compliance with those decisions in these organisations', and to 'promote the development of an environmentally responsible and economically competitive aquaculture industry'.[56]

The CARIFORUM-EU EPA addresses target 14.A, by facilitating increased scientific knowledge, research capacity development and marine technology transfer, and also facilitates sustainable management and protection of marine and coastal ecosystems, as required by target 14.2. Further, the agreement's regard for the needs of fishing communities and those in poverty may serve to promote access for small-scale artisanal fishers to marine resources and markets, as required by target 14.B. It records that Parties:

> recognise that the fisheries and marine ecosystems of the CARIFORUM States are complex, biologically diverse and fragile and that exploitation should take into account these factors through effective conservation and management of fisheries resources and related ecosystems based on sound scientific advice and on the precautionary principle as defined by the FAO Code of Conduct on Responsible Fisheries.

They also recognize 'that ensuring food security and enhancing livelihoods of rural and fishing communities are critical elements of the eradication of poverty, and the pursuit of sustainable development. They consequently recognise the need to avoid major disruption of markets for agricultural, food and fish products in CARIFORUM States'. Parties thus:

54 EU-Colombia-Peru FTA, art 274.
55 Ibid, art 274.
56 CETA, art 24.11.

> acknowledge the economic and social importance of activities relating to fisheries and the utilisation of the living marine resources of CARIFORUM States, and the need to maximise those benefits in relation to such factors as food security, employment, poverty alleviation, foreign exchange earnings and social stability of fishing communities.

Areas of cooperation with respect to fisheries include exchange of information on market developments for fisheries products; promoting investment in the fisheries sectors; exchanging information on fisheries policies, law and regulations; and discussing policy and institutional changes required to underpin transformation of the fisheries sectors, as well as formulation and implementation of regional fisheries policies in pursuit of regional integration.[57]

The EU-ESA Interim EPA also provides a strong example of an FTA that advances SDG 14 on three fronts: by promoting sustainable management and protection of marine and coastal ecosystems;[58] by promoting marine conservation in line with international law;[59] and also by aiding access for small-scale artisanal fishers to marine resources and markets.[60] Protecting and managing coastal and marine resources is included as an area for environmental cooperation and support.[61] The Agreement's designated chapter on fisheries then provides for cooperation in fisheries trade and development with respect to marine and inland fisheries and aquaculture,[62] and outlines a number of guiding principles of cooperation, these encompassing a principle of conformity with existing relevant international instruments including UNCLOS, and a principle of preservation and priority of particular needs of artisanal or subsistence fisheries.[63] Further, the agreement incorporates a specific chapter on marine fisheries, the scope of which is the utilization, conservation and management of marine fisheries resources, to optimize benefits from fisheries for the Eastern and South Africa (ESA) region, through investment, capacity-building and improved market access.[64] The objectives of cooperation with respect to marine fisheries are focused on capacity-building among ESA States, and include strengthening cooperation towards ensuring the sustainable exploitation and management of fisheries resources as a strong basis for regional integration, paying particular regard to the straddling and migratory species which are shared among island and coastal States and the fact that no individual ESA State has the capacity to ensure sustainability of the resource. Other objectives include ensuring equitable sharing of benefits from the fisheries sectors, and promoting 'effective exploitation, conservation and management of the living marine resources in the exclusive economic zone (EEZ) and waters in which ESA States have jurisdiction based on international instruments, including UNCLOS, for the mutual social and economic benefit of the ESA States and the European Communities Party.[65] Following this, the agreement sets out a series of areas of cooperation which aim towards achieving these objectives, with detailed

57 CARIFORUM-EU EPA, arts 31, 41. These provisions also deal with similar concerns in the agricultural and food sectors.
58 Target 14.2.
59 Target 14.C; EU-ESA Interim EPA, arts 27, 28, 31, 32, 51.
60 Target 14.B.
61 EU-ESA Interim EPA, art 51(2).
62 Ibid, art 27.
63 Ibid, art 28.
64 Ibid, chapter III, title II, art 31.
65 Ibid, art 31.

provisions governing cooperation in the areas of fisheries management and conservation issues, vessel management and post-harvest arrangements, and financial and trade measures and development of fisheries and fishery products and marine aquaculture.[66]

An important feature of the EU-Colombia-Peru FTA is that it directly promotes expansion of marine protected areas. This is consistent with target 14.5, which calls for countries to conserve at least 10 per cent of coastal and marine areas, consistent with national and international law and based on the best available scientific information, by 2020. Parties agree to:

> continue to work towards meeting their international targets of establishing and maintaining a comprehensive, effectively managed, and ecologically representative national and regional system of terrestrial and marine protected areas by 2010 and 2012, respectively, as fundamental tools for the conservation and sustainable use of biological diversity.

While these provisions were clearly negotiated well before establishment of the SDGs in 2015, provisions that set out commitments to expanding marine protected areas may be useful for increasing ambition in this area. This is particularly the case in light of the recent Report of the Secretary General, which records that the expansion of protected areas for marine biodiversity to date—as well as current policies and treaties that encourage responsible use of ocean resources—remain insufficient to combat the adverse effects of over-fishing, ocean acidification and coastal eutrophication.[67] Parties to the agreement also 'recognise the importance of protected areas for the welfare of populations settled in those areas and their buffer zones'.

Bilateral, regional and region-to-region economic agreements also contain provisions which may advance target 14.A—increasing scientific knowledge, research capacity and marine technology transfer. An example is the Chinese Taipei-Nicaragua FTA, which includes research projects for coastal zones and ecosystems as a possible activity to be included in the Parties' programme of work.[68]

Goal 15. Protect, Restore and Promote Sustainable use of Terrestrial Ecosystems, Sustainably Manage Forests, Combat Desertification, and Halt and Reverse Land Degradation and Halt Biodiversity Loss

SDG 15 requires that countries ensure the conservation, restoration and sustainable use of terrestrial and inland freshwater ecosystems and their services,[69] reduce degradation of natural habitats and halt biodiversity loss,[70] and integrate ecosystem and biodiversity values into countries' planning and development processes and poverty-reduction strategies,[71] calling on the international community to mobilize and significantly increase financial resources to conserve and sustain use of biodiversity and ecosystems.[72] This goal calls for

[66] Ibid, art 32(1).
[67] Report of the Secretary General (n 2).
[68] Chinese Taipei-Nicaragua FTA, Annex 19.08. See also China-Peru FTA, art 163.
[69] Target 15.1.
[70] Target 15.5.
[71] Target 15.9.
[72] Target 15.A.

urgent action to end poaching and trafficking of protected species,[73] and enhanced global support for efforts to combat this issue, including by increasing the capacity of local communities to pursue sustainable livelihood opportunities.[74] With respect to forests, it asks that countries promote implementation of sustainable management of all forest types, halt deforestation, restore degraded forests and substantially increase afforestation and reforestation globally.[75] Means of implementation targets call for countries to mobilize significant resources from all sources, and at all levels, to finance sustainable forest management and provide adequate incentives to developing countries to advance such management.[76] Mountain ecosystems are also paid special attention,[77] as is combatting desertification.[78] A particularly relevant aspect of SDG 15 for trade and investment agreements is target 15.6, which requires that countries 'promote fair and equitable sharing of the benefits arising from the utilization of genetic resources and promote appropriate access to such resources, as internationally agreed'.

According to 2019 reports, progress on SDG15 has been insufficient, with high rates of land degradation and biodiversity loss, and illicit wildlife trafficking and poaching preventing effective ecosystem and species protection.[79] Encouragingly, however, forest loss is slowing, and financial flows towards biodiversity are increasing.[80] The role of trade in biodiversity conservation and protection of species is well established, with the Convention on International Trade in Endangered Species of Wild Fauna and Flora (CITES) providing for mandatory regulation of trade in species since 1975, and the UN Convention on Biological Diversity (UN CBD) promoting sustainable use of biological diversity since 1992.[81] Economic agreements address a variety of aspects of SDG 15, commonly focusing on biodiversity conservation, sustainable forest management and equitable benefit-sharing.

The EU-ESA Interim EPA provides one example of an agreement that considers diverse aspects of SDG 15, including biodiversity, environmental degradation, forestry management and desertification: the scope of its title on natural resources and environment in the Agreement's chapter on economic and development cooperation,[82] covers biodiversity, enhancing trade-environment linkages and supporting the implementation of international environmental agreements.[83] Environmental cooperation is aimed at protecting, restoring and conserving the environment and biodiversity, including genetic resources and ecosystems; developing new ESA industries related to the environment; and reducing environmental degradation and desertification.[84] Areas of cooperation that are particularly relevant to achieving SDG 15 are 'sustainable utilisation of biodiversity, forestry and wildlife resources'; 'capacity building in human resources and institutional structures to comply

[73] Target 15.7.
[74] Target 15.C.
[75] Target 15.2.
[76] Target 15.B.
[77] Target 15.4.
[78] Target 15.3.
[79] Report of the Secretary General (n 2).
[80] Ibid.
[81] See A Dale, 'Trade and Sustainable Development Goal (SDG) 15: Promoting "Life on Land" through Mandatory and Voluntary Approaches' (2017) ADBI Working Paper Series No 700, <https://www.adb.org/sites/default/files/publication/236001/adbi-wp700.pdf> accessed 16 December 2020.
[82] EU-ESA Interim EPA chapter IV, title IV.
[83] Ibid, art 49.
[84] Ibid, art 51(1).

with environmental and biodiversity requirements'; 'mitigation of natural disasters, prevention of environmental disasters and the loss of biodiversity'; 'integration of local communities in the management of biodiversity, forestry and wildlife resources' and 'sustainable management of forests and similar mechanisms'.[85]

The US-Colombia FTA's provisions on biological diversity facilitate advancement of target 15.5, which asks for 'urgent and significant action to reduce the degradation of natural habitats, halt the loss of biodiversity and, by 2020, protect and prevent the extinction of threatened species'. In this Agreement, Parties commit to promoting and encouraging conservation and sustainable use of biological diversity, including plants, animals and habitat.[86] Provision is also made for Parties to respect and preserve traditional knowledge and practices which contribute to conserving biological diversity. Further, 'Parties also recognize the importance of public participation and consultations, as provided by domestic law, on matters concerning the conservation and sustainable use of biological diversity' and may publicize information about programmes which they undertake relating to such matters.[87] The Chinese Taipei-Nicaragua FTA's Environmental Cooperation Mechanism innovatively provides that 'developing and promoting incentives and other flexible and voluntary mechanisms in order to encourage environmental protection, conservation and the sustainable use of biodiversity, including the development of market-based initiatives and economic incentives for environmental management' is one priority cooperation area which may feature in the Parties' programme of work.[88] This may be one way in which future trade and investment agreements can help to mobilize financial resources to conserve biodiversity and ecosystems, as target 15.A requires.

CETA provides an example of an agreement that facilitates accomplishment of SDG 15 targets on promoting sustainable forest management. It recognizes:

> the importance of the conservation and sustainable management of forests for providing environmental functions and economic and social opportunities for present and future generations, and of market access for forest products harvested in accordance with the law of the country of harvest and from sustainably managed forests.

In light of this, Parties, in a manner consistent with their international obligations, commit to encouraging trade in forest products from sustainably managed forests, exchanging information, and cooperate on initiatives to promote sustainable forest management, promoting effective use of CITES with respect to timber species at risk, and cooperating, where appropriate, in international fora on sustainable management of forests and their conservation.[89] Similarly, the EFTA-Central America FTA contains a commitment to 'work together in the relevant multilateral fora in which they participate to improve forest law enforcement and governance and to promote trade in legal and sustainable forest-based products', through such instruments as CITES (with respect to endangered timber species), certification schemes for sustainably harvested forest products and Forest Law Enforcement Governance and Trade (FLEGT) voluntary partnership agreements.[90] These voluntary

[85] Ibid, art 51(2).
[86] *US-Colombia FTA* art 18.11.
[87] Ibid, art 18.11.
[88] Chinese Taipei-Nicaragua FTA, Annex 19.08, art 8(b).
[89] CETA, art 24.10.
[90] EFTA-Central America FTA, art 9.8.

partnership agreements are legally binding trade and investment agreements established between the EU and a non-EU timber-producing country, with the aim of addressing legality and sustainability in the timber sector.[91] They involve reforming the producing country's legal system, and capacity-building of government agencies, and have been shown to contribute to improved forest governance and reduced demand for illegal timber in the EU.[92]

The *EU-Colombia-Peru FTA*'s cooperative activities on environmental protection in this agreement include activities relating to 'adaptation to, and mitigation of, climate change, including activities related to the reduction of emissions from deforestation and forest degradation ("REDD")', as well as 'activities related to the determination of the legal origin of forest products' and 'voluntary forestry certification schemes and traceability of different forestry products'.[93] This reference to the REDD initiative engages more directly with target 15.B, which calls for international mobilization of significant resources from all sources and at all levels to finance sustainable forest management and provide adequate incentives to developing countries to advance such management, including for conservation and reforestation. In addition, the Parties recognize the importance of practices that improve forest law enforcement and governance, including CITES implementation and developing systems that allow for the legal origin of timber products to be verified.[94]

Two elements of SDG 15 featured in the China-Peru FTA's comprehensive article on cooperation on forestry matters and environmental protection are aspects of target 15.1 which ask that countries ensure conservation, restoration and sustainable use of forest ecosystems (among others) and their services in line with obligations under international agreements, and target 15.2, which calls for countries to promote sustainable management of all types of forests, halt deforestation, restore degraded forests and substantially increase afforestation and reforestation globally.[95] The article defines the aims of cooperation as including 'establishing bilateral cooperation relations in the forestry sector'; 'developing a training program and studies for sustainable management of forests'; 'improving the rehabilitation and sustainable management of forest with the aim of increasing carbon sinks and reduc[ing] the impact of climate change in the Asia-Pacific region' and 'cooperating on the execution of national projects, aimed at: improving the management of forest plantations for its transformation for industrial purposes and environmental protection'.[96] Further aims are elaborating studies on sustainable timber use, developing new technologies for transformation and processing of both timber and non-timber species and improving cooperation with respect to agro-forestry technologies. In addition, Parties are invited to focus on concluding a bilateral agreement on forestry cooperation, with areas for collaboration in this area including exchanges of science, technology, laws and policies relating to sustainable forest resource use; cooperation in training programmes; exchange of experts; advice and technical assistance to public institutions and organizations on sustainable forest resource use; facilitating forest policy dialogue and technical cooperation under the Network of Sustainable

[91] Dale (n 81) 23.
[92] Ibid.
[93] EU-Colombia-Peru FTA, art 273.
[94] Ibid, art 286.
[95] Target 15.2.
[96] China-Peru FTA, art 162(1).

Forest Management and Forest Rehabilitation in Asia-Pacific Region; and encouraging joint studies.

Economic agreements may also utilize provisions that promote fair and equitable sharing of the benefits arising from the utilization of genetic resources and promote appropriate access to such resources, in accordance with target 15.6. One key example is the CARIFORUM-EU EPA's article on genetic resources, traditional knowledge and folklore.[97] This provision asks Parties to, subject to their domestic legislation, encourage the equitable sharing of the benefits arising from the utilization of the knowledge, innovations and practices of indigenous and local communities embodying traditional lifestyles relevant for the conservation and sustainable use of biological diversity.[98] In the Peru-Korea FTA, each Party has authority to determine access to genetic resources according to its domestic legislation, and shall 'endeavor to create conditions to facilitate transparent access to genetic resources for environmentally sound uses'.[99] With respect to intellectual property, Parties 'shall endeavor to seek ways to share information on patent applications based on genetic resources or traditional knowledge', through providing a publicly accessible information database, and opportunities to file prior art.[100] Further, Parties agree to share views and information on discussions in the World Intellectual Property Organization (WIPO) Intergovernmental Committee on Intellectual Property and Genetic Resources, Traditional Knowledge, and Folklore, the World Trade Organization (WTO) Agreement on Trade-Related Aspects of Intellectual Property Rights (TRIPS) Council and any other relevant fora addressing matters related to genetic resources and traditional knowledge.[101] A different approach is taken by the Canada-Colombia FTA, with Parties setting out their mutual obligations relating to conservation and use of biological diversity and protection and preservation of traditional knowledge in a separate agreement.[102] Experts have proposed that a trade facilitation agreement for environmentally sensitive products might serve as a future mechanism for upscaling efforts towards achieving SDG 15 through trade and investment facilitation.[103]

Goal 16. Promote Peaceful and Inclusive Societies for Sustainable Development, Provide Access to Justice for all and Build Effective, Accountable and Inclusive Institutions at all Levels

SDG 16 requires that countries significantly reduce all forms of violence and related death rates;[104] end abuse, exploitation, trafficking and all forms of violence against children;[105] promote the rule of law at national and international levels, ensuring equal access to justice;[106] significantly reduce illicit financial and arms flows;[107] substantially reduce corruption and bribery;[108] and provide legal identities for all.[109] Achieving this SDG will require

[97] CARIFORUM-EU EPA, art 150.
[98] Ibid.
[99] Peru-Korea FTA, art 17.5.
[100] Peru-Korea FTA, art 17.5(4).
[101] Ibid, art 17.5(5).
[102] Agreement on the Environment between Canada and the Republic of Colombia.
[103] Dale (n 81).
[104] Target 16.1.
[105] Target 16.2.
[106] Target 16.3.
[107] Target 16.4.
[108] Target 16.5.
[109] Target 16.9.

countries to develop accountable, transparent institutions,[110] and guarantee responsive, inclusive, participatory and representative decision-making at all levels,[111] as well as ensuring public access to information and protection of fundamental freedoms.[112] With respect to developing countries, countries are asked to broaden and strengthen the participation of developing countries in global governance institutions.[113] Key to achieving SDG 16 is strengthening relevant national institutions, including through international cooperation, for building capacity at all levels to prevent violence and to combat terrorism and crime, particularly in developing countries.[114] Further, countries are to promote and enforce non-discriminatory policies and laws for sustainable development.[115]

Public participation provisions are a key way in which trade and investment agreements may engage target 16.7, which calls for countries to 'ensure responsive, inclusive, participatory and representative decision-making at all levels'. Trade and investment agreements demonstrate consideration of public participation issues across a range of areas. By way of example, CETA's labour provisions require that each Party 'shall promote public awareness of its labour law and standards, as well as enforcement and compliance procedures, including by ensuring the availability of information and by taking steps to further the knowledge and understanding of workers, employers and their representatives'. The EU-South Korea FTA acknowledges the importance of participation with respect to the use of indigenous and local knowledge, by including a commitment by Parties to:

> preserve and maintain knowledge, innovations and practices of indigenous and local communities embodying traditional lifestyles relevant for the conservation and sustainable use of biological diversity and promote their wider application with the involvement and approval of the holders of such knowledge, innovations and practices and encourage the equitable sharing of the benefits arising from the utilisation of such knowledge, innovations and practices.[116]

Beyond facilitating public participation, agreements may also advance SDG 16 by promoting the reduction of corruption and bribery, as required by target 16.5, and facilitating development of effective, accountable and transparent institutions (target 16.6). The transparency chapter of the US-Colombia FTA provides a prime example.[117] In Section B of this chapter, on anti-corruption, Parties 'affirm their commitment to prevent and combat corruption, including bribery, in international trade and investment', and commit to 'promoting, facilitating, and supporting international cooperation in the prevention and fight against corruption'. Article 19.8 specifically provides for cooperation in international fora on the issue of corruption: Parties agree to 'work jointly to encourage and support appropriate initiatives in relevant international fora', recognizing the importance of multilateral and regional initiatives for preventing and combatting corruption and bribery in international trade and investment, and reaffirming their commitment to implementing the 1996

[110] Target 16.6.
[111] Target 16.7.
[112] Target 16.10.
[113] Target 16.8.
[114] Target 16.A.
[115] Target 16.8.
[116] EU-South Korea FTA, art 10.40. See also SDG15; CARIFORUM-EU EPA, art 150.
[117] US-Colombia FTA, arts 19.7, 19.8, 19.9.

Inter-American Convention Against Corruption and 2003 United Nations Convention Against Corruption. Further, under article 19.9, Parties agree to establish that particular acts of corruption in the sphere of trade or investment are criminal offences, including the intentional acceptance of monetary or other benefits by public officials, and bribing public officials.

The EU-ESA Interim EPA's capacity-building and regional integration engage with target 16.A, which calls for States to 'strengthen relevant national institutions, including through international cooperation, for building capacity at all levels, in particular in developing countries, to prevent violence and combat terrorism and crime'. It identifies regional peace, stability and security as a key area for cooperation and regional integration, with Parties agreeing to promote and enhance regional peace and security initiatives.[118] Activities that may facilitate this goal include capacity-building for a range of conflict-prevention actors; promoting appropriate early warning, conflict management and conflict resolution mechanisms; supporting media, civil society and public institutions 'that are the backbone to peace and security'; and enhancing peacekeeping capacities.[119]

Goal 17 and Concluding Remarks

These three chapters have surveyed each of the SDGs and have identified some of the various mechanisms that current economic agreements utilize to engage with particular targets towards achieving each Goal. The final SDG, SDG 17, which calls for countries to strengthen the means of implementation and revitalize the Global Partnership for Sustainable Development, is particularly relevant for trade and investment. SDG17 recognizes that each of the SDGs can only be realized through strong global partnerships and cooperation, in which trade and investment play a vital role. The targets that must be achieved to accomplish this goal span finance, technology, capacity-building, trade and systemic issues. Finance targets deal with strengthened resource mobilization, fulfilment of official development assistance (ODA) commitments by developed countries, mobilizing additional finance for developing countries (including through foreign direct investment) and implementing investment promotion regimes for least developed countries.[120] Among other things, the technology targets relate to enhancing access to science, technology and innovation and knowledge sharing, promoting diffusion of environmentally sound technologies to developing countries on favourable terms. Achieving SDG 17 also requires international support for effective capacity-building in developing countries to support implementation of their SDGs, and will also improve coherence with respect to policies and institutions.[121]

SDG 17 features a number of trade-specific targets, calling on countries, firstly, to 'promote a universal, rules-based, open, non-discriminatory and equitable multilateral trading system under the World Trade Organization, including through the conclusion of negotiations under its Doha Development Agenda';[122] secondly, to 'significantly increase the exports of developing countries, in particular with a view to doubling the least developed

118 EU-ESA Interim EPA, Annex IV, art 3(d).
119 Ibid.
120 Targets 17.1–17.5.
121 See Targets 17.13–17.19.
122 Target 17.10.

countries' share of global exports';[123] and thirdly, to 'realize timely implementation of duty-free and quota-free market access on a lasting basis for all least developed countries, consistent with World Trade Organization decisions, including by ensuring that preferential rules of origin applicable to imports from least developed countries are transparent and simple, and contribute to facilitating market access'.[124] The 2019 Report of the Secretary General identifies that while some progress has been made with respect to international trade on SDG 17—for example, through wider access to goods and a more open trading system which have been facilitated by decreasing tariffs applied worldwide—the share of least developed countries in world merchandise exports remains low.[125] Enhanced international trade cooperation is therefore needed, and trade and investment agreements may need to make specific reference to these targets in SDG17 in order to better facilitate their implementation.

While technology transfer between developed and developing countries has been discussed with respect to a number of other SDGs, the EU-South Korea FTA's provisions on technology transfer in third party developing countries deserves special mention here, in a discussion about creating global partnerships for sustainable development. This FTA, while not a developed–developing country agreement, pays particular regard to the need to facilitate technology transfer in third party developing countries. Thus, it provides that 'Parties agree to exchange views and information on their practices and policies affecting transfer of technology, both within their respective territories and with third countries', with particular efforts to be made with respect to measures that 'facilitate 'information flows, business partnerships, licensing and subcontracting'. The Parties also commit to paying particular attention 'to the conditions necessary to create an adequate enabling environment for technology transfer in the host countries, including, inter alia, issues such as development of human capital and legal framework'.[126] These innovative provisions may advance target 17.6, which calls for enhanced 'North-South, South-South and triangular regional and international cooperation on and access to science, technology and innovation and enhance knowledge sharing on mutually agreed terms', and target 17.7, which asks countries to promote 'development, transfer, dissemination and diffusion of environmentally sound technologies to developing countries on favourable terms, including on concessional and preferential terms, as mutually agreed'.

As has been seen, trade and investment agreements can—and do—engage with each of the SDGs from a multiplicity of perspectives. Agreements between developed and developing countries, with commitments to capacity-building and regional integration,[127] provide particularly useful examples of provisions which can aid achievement of SDG targets. If one thing is clear, however, it is that progress on achieving the SDGs is lagging behind, and increased ambition and international cooperation is needed with respect to all SDGs.[128] By referring to the provisions that have been discussed in the preceding chapters, it is hoped that future negotiators will be empowered to mould trade and investment agreements that facilitate countries' achievement of their SDGs, and thereby move the world closer towards achieving sustainable development.

[123] Target 17.11.
[124] Target 17.12.
[125] Report of the Secretary General (n 2).
[126] EU-South Korea FTA, art 10.3.
[127] See, e.g., EU-ESA Interim EPA.
[128] Report of the Secretary General (n 2).

SECTION SEVEN

A FUTURE TRADE AND INVESTMENT LAW FOR SUSTAINABLE DEVELOPMENT

22

Integrating Social and Environmental Considerations into Trade and Investment Agreements, for Sustainable Development

From the findings discussed in this volume, it can be concluded that States are experimenting with innovative ways to integrate environmental and social considerations into their trade and investment agreements, particularly in regional and bilateral economic treaties, and that through this integration, international trade and investment law gains opportunities to foster rather than frustrate the world's sustainable development goals.

States are adopting sustainable development as part of the 'object and purpose' of trade and investment law, both in the World Trade Organization (WTO) and in many regional and bilateral treaties. The principle of integration for sustainable development, which is based on the 1992 Rio Declaration Principle 4 with customary legal status supported by an increasing body of *opinio juris* and state practice, requires States to integrate environmental and social measures into their economic decision-making in international law. The research identified three key tensions in trade and investment treaties which, interpreted in light of an emerging 'integration' principle, can be considered opportunities to better position trade and investment law to contribute to sustainable development. It is not enough to simply adopt sustainable development as part of the 'purpose' of an economic treaty, though this does have certain interpretive weight. Rather, States are also adopting innovative operational provisions to: (1) prevent trade and investment treaties from constraining legitimate new environmental and social development measures; (2) mitigate economic law impacts through trade- and investment-related cooperation and strengthening of domestic environmental and social development rules; and (3) incentivize trade and investment in more sustainable economic industries and sectors. Given the diversity of economic, social and environmental conditions among Parties to international economic agreements, the existence of two distinct approaches to sustainable development among large trading blocs, and other factors as between Parties to bilateral and regional accords, there is no 'one-size-fits-all' solution for making a trade and investment agreement sustainable. But the third category of measures, whereby trade and investment rules are crafted to enhance growth in key areas, appears best positioned to contribute to development that is more sustainable over the long term among the Parties, development that helps rather than hinders the implementation of other international obligations related to the Sustainable Development Goals (SDGs).

Further, it was found that there is an important procedural aspect to the integration of environmental and social development concerns in trade and investment law and policy. States are undertaking sustainability impact assessments (SIAs) and other procedural techniques in economic treaty-making which can support their efforts to address environment

Crafting Trade and Investment Accords for Sustainable Development. Marie-Claire Cordonier Segger, Oxford University Press.
 DOI: 10.1093/oso/9780198831341.003.0022

and social development priorities in the economic rules of their trade and investment treaties. Global trade negotiations, which remain stymied on these matters, can gain insights from the regional and bilateral innovations and texts.

The volume was structured to explain these findings. Section One introduced this book by setting out the scholarly context, objectives and central ideas of the research, describing the legal research methodology used, and summarizing the structure of the work. With the help of tables in Annex 2 of this volume, the introductory chapters explained the materials analysed in the research, including over 90 SIAs, environmental assessments (EAs) and environmental reviews of actual trade and investment negotiations, key World Trade Organization (WTO) treaties, WTO dispute settlement decisions and Trade Policy Review Mechanism (TPRM) responses, in addition to over 110 texts of bilateral and regional economic treaties which set sustainable development as part of their object or purpose, as well as relevant secondary literature and cases.

As was seen in Section Two, in the last two decades of State-commissioned or conducted impact assessments of trade and investment liberalization negotiations, many social and environmental concerns have been raised about the type of development that is promoted by increased scale and scope of economic activity in key sectors. This volume demonstrated that in recent decades, international economic liberalization has proceeded quickly through the negotiation of global, regional and bilateral economic liberalization disciplines to reduce tariffs and other barriers to market access, and to encourage foreign investment. Today's trade and investment is governed by several imperfectly embedded systems of economic rules, found in the WTO Agreements and over 470 diverse bilateral or regional accords, with further treaties under negotiation or reform.

As recognized by States in the 1992 UN Conference on Environment and Development (UNCED), the 2002 World Summit on Sustainable Development (WSSD), the 2012 UN Conference on Sustainable Development (UNCSD) and the 2015 SDGs, and as noted in the impact assessments and other materials reviewed in this volume, the effects of foreign trade and investment-led economic growth are not automatically positive for the environment, or for the poor. In global, regional and bilateral economic negotiations, States agree to liberalize trade in goods and services, while also committing to ever-tighter disciplines related to technical barriers to trade (TBT) and sanitary and phytosanitary (SPS) measures, government procurement, intellectual property rights and trade-related investment measures. As seen above, the trade and investment liberalization agenda now covers multiple areas of law and policy, and each set of new rules has material and also regulatory implications for efforts to promote the sustainable development goals. Under each regime, depending on the economic relationship between its Parties, the prevailing social and environmental conditions and other factors, changes in trade and investment rules will affect options for sustainability. A survey of nearly three decades of impact assessments of trade and investment negotiations commissioned or conducted by States, carried out as part of this research, has revealed many potential impacts. It is clear that changes in international economic rules are diverse and complex. They can affect sustainable development possibilities for States in both positive and negative ways. In some cases, even positive economic effects can have negative social or environmental repercussions. For instance, as discussed in the second section of this volume, if not carefully regulated, trade and investment-led increases in the scale, structure and scope of economic activity can lead to over-exploitation of natural resources, exacerbated social dislocations including effects on health and human rights, and rising levels of pollution and waste, especially within the developing country Parties. These material and normative impacts are likely to make sustainable development more difficult to achieve for these countries.

Careful regulation to avoid such impacts also has its challenges under new trade and investment treaties. From the actual impact assessment studies, in the context of relevant secondary literature, the potential normative impacts of trade and investment disciplines on a country's ability to regulate for sustainable development were identified as three key tensions. These tensions, it has been argued, affect the State's capacity to regulate effectively domestically and also to implement obligations from other international treaties on sustainable development. Efforts can be made to address them.

22.1 A Principled Rationale for Addressing Key Impacts and Tensions

As noted in Section Three, it is not optimal for States to simply let the material and normative impacts of poorly crafted, unsustainable trade and investment agreements 'roll downhill' onto the most vulnerable groups and onto the global environment, especially in developing country Parties.

There are both international legal and also global public policy reasons to intervene. The legal nature of State commitments to sustainable development remains contested at the global level, it was found. While there is insufficient evidence of *opinio juris* that States have—as yet—accepted a binding customary obligation to 'develop sustainably' in all instances, there is an emerging customary law requirement that States ensure that environmental protection is integrated into economic development decision-making, as emphasized in Principle 4 of the 1992 Rio Declaration.[1] This integration principle is gaining recognition, including from international tribunals in the *Case Concerning the Gabcíkovo-Nagymaros (Hungary v. Slovakia)*, the *Iron Rhine Award*, and the *Case Concerning Pulp Mills on the River Uruguay (Argentina v. Uruguay)*. It is not an impossible principle to understand or respect. For the European Union, the integration principle has been adopted in its legislative order, has been extended to take social development concerns as well, and is being strategically but unevenly implemented across EU trade and investment law and policy. The customary integration principle is not impossible to respect.

However, as also noted in Section Three, even a mature customary 'integration principle' would not bind States to take important environmental and social development concerns into account in their international trade and investment treaty-making. First, it is not yet clear that the customary norm includes a requirement to take social as well as environmental considerations into account. Second, it is well-recognized in international law that in accordance with the maxim *pacta sunct servanda*, Parties to a treaty not desiring to follow a customary norm can simply agree that in the context of their treaty, it does not apply. When countries or regions desire trade and investment agreements that will promote sustainable development, and integrate, they must negotiate for them.

[1] 'Rio Declaration on Environment and Development (Annex 2)', Report of the UN Conference on Environment and Development, 13 June 1992, UN Doc A/CONF.151/26 (Vol I).

There are important public policy reasons to do so, avoiding negative social and environmental impacts of changes in trade and investment flows. Through global and regional policy debates spanning decades, States have repeatedly reaffirmed their commitment to sustainable development. This global commitment to sustainable development is relevant for international economic law and policy, especially trade and investment regimes. Given the weight of soft law on these matters, especially the 2015 commitment to global SDGs and other shared understanding, from an inter-actional perspective[2], the volume argued, States may have a *legitimate expectation* that effort will be made to ensure that new trade and investment accords will promote sustainable development.

Indeed, through a survey of international, European and bilateral developments, this volume identified several ways that the accords could do so, by addressing the key tensions between trade, environmental and social development regulations through the adoption of integration measures for sustainable development in the treaties.

The first tension was that the provisions of a trade and investment treaty should not, at a minimum, constrain legitimate new regulatory efforts to promote sustainable development. As a related opportunity for integration, a tribunal or, more likely in this field, a regulator can interpret tailored exceptions that States are including in trade and investment treaties to address this tension in a balanced way.

The second tension was that trade and investment treaties should not, wherever possible, cause difficulties for ongoing domestic attempts to secure sustainable development by strengthening and enforcing environmental and social laws. As a related second opportunity for integration, States are agreeing to support new cooperation on environmental and social sustainable development matters related to enhanced trade and investment, and the international economic treaties can be interpreted in this light.

The third and most challenging tension was that trade and investment treaties should not actually contribute to unsustainable development, privileging obsolete and environmentally damaging industries that are being phased out through other international treaties. As a third opportunity for integration, States are including diverse provisions in economic treaties to actually promote trade and investment in more sustainable goods and services, supporting efforts to implement other international treaties on sustainable development.

22.2 New Instruments for More Sustainable Regional and Bilateral Economic Treaties

As is shown in the volume, however, States are still crafting integrated approaches, globally and also regionally and bilaterally. In Section Four, given the diverse interests and approaches that WTO member States have revealed in decades of debates and TPRM replies, it is clear that progress in taking up new opportunities for integration through the WTO itself has been weak, leading to deadlocks on these matters in the WTO Doha 'Development' Round and other negotiations.

However, some States are achieving a measure of success in regional and bilateral economic treaties. In this volume, over 110 regional and bilateral trade and investment agreement negotiations (and related impact assessments) were comparatively analysed, focusing

[2] Brunnee J and Toope SJ, *Legality and Legitimacy in International Law* (Cambridge, CUP 2010), 65–76

on eight as illustrative examples that contained more extensive innovations related to sustainable development. The comparisons have revealed distinct approaches to the integration of social and environmental considerations in trade and investment law for sustainable development, whereby in some treaties, Parties once considered sustainable development as a sub-sector of environmental law (keeping provisions for trade, labour and environment essentially separate), while in other newer treaties economic, environmental and social development are integrated throughout the economic cooperation treaty text. The analysis focused on interpreting this emerging body of trade and investment law in light of the customary integration principle, taking a pragmatic approach. It was found that in a growing number of trade agreements, Parties are adopting increasingly detailed commitments on sustainable development. Essentially, although trade law began as a narrow area of rules focused specifically on economic growth through trade liberalization, just as trade rules have been expanded to address investment promotion, and to discipline a broader area of economic development policy and law, States have also increasingly integrated social and environmental considerations into their trade and investment treaties. Through the comparative research, an analytical framework or typology was developed which assists States to identify the types of measures that can be included in a trade or investment treaty to integrate environmental and social concerns related to sustainable development in the future. This framework focuses on three steps that States can adopt:

22.2.1 Sustainable Intentions

First, there is evidence that similar to world peace, the protection of human rights and the conservation of the environment, sustainable development can now be accurately characterized as an 'object and purpose' of certain international treaties, including trade and investment treaties. There are indications that an increasing number of States seek to promote sustainable development through their international economic agreements. As demonstrated in Section Four of this book, while there are still certain WTO members that consider sustainable development to have first and foremost a developmental dimension and others that focus mainly on the trade and environment intersections, the WTO members' firm commitment to 'the objective of sustainable development' in the 2001 Doha Ministerial Declaration, along with the way it is characterized in the negotiation mandates, demonstrate that in Doha and other subsequent practice, States have recognized sustainable development as part of the 'object and purpose' of the WTO Agreements. While the meaning of the concept remains contested, the commitment is now firmly embedded in the WTO legal regime. In the context of the WTO, this is relevant to the interpretation of specific treaty provisions such as the WTO Preamble and article XX of the General Agreement on Tariffs and Trade 1994 (GATT), as shown in the 1998 *US–Shrimp* dispute, and reaffirmed in the 2004 *European Communities–Tariff Preferences* dispute. As part of the WTO purpose, sustainable development is also shaping debates in the Committee on Trade and Environment (CTE) and the Committee on Trade and Development (CTD), as well as other WTO negotiations on, for instance, subsidies and services liberalization. This said, it is not enough to simply agree on a 'sustainable' object and purpose, and leave further integration to the caprices of dispute settlement. Progress in the WTO, especially the 2001 Doha 'Development' Round, has been regrettably limited.

Perhaps in reaction, States are moving beyond the narrow and deadlocked circumstances of WTO negotiations, and are experimenting with new measures to secure more sustainable development through their bilateral and regional economic agreements. In Sections Five and Six of this volume, as noted above, based on a cross-cutting analysis of over 110 such accords, illustrative examples are provided from trade and investment treaties between the EU, the US and other countries of the Americas, in which Parties had explicitly recognized a commitment to sustainable development in one form or another. In most agreements reviewed, the Parties either recognize their intention to promote sustainable development as a joint resolution; or include preambular and other initial statements which commit to implement the accord both in accordance with a principle of sustainable development *and* in order to achieve a sustainable development purpose. In several leading regional economic partnership and association agreements, such as the EU-CARIFORUM EPA[3] and the EU-Central American AA,[4] Parties agreed to frame and craft their international economic treaty as a 'partnership for sustainable development' providing a definition of sustainable development that highlights the principle of integration and underscores several other substantive and procedural elements. Further, the purpose, in light of the customary 'integration' principle is relevant to the interpretation of many further operational treaty provisions. Indeed, as discussed in this volume, the choice of treaty mechanism has implications for its interpretive weight, with the potential to influence future developments in the trade and investment regimes themselves, including dispute settlement decisions.

22.2.2 Sustainable Development Innovations Addressing Key Tensions in RTAs

The research identified innovative trade and investment treaty provisions that can be interpreted, in light of the customary principle, to be integrating environmental and social measures into economic decision-making.[5] While still experimental, many of these provisions hold potential to address the key tensions identified in the first part of this volume, improving the potential of the trade and investment liberalization accords to contribute to more sustainable development. A great deal depends on the specific circumstances of each regional or bilateral relationship, which responds to particular economic, environmental and other conditions existing between the Parties. However, there are discernible attempts by Parties to address important environmental and social concerns that were identified in the impact assessments, in the texts of trade and investment treaties. Tentatively, it can be concluded that the environmental reviews and especially, the sustainability impact assessments are having an impact.

This volume uncovered three key types of tailored measures, each with a different normative effect, that in trade and investment treaties can be interpreted as addressing the key tensions identified in the assessments, allowing negotiators to integrate environmental protection and social development with economic development in their accords.

[3] EU-CARIFORUM EPA (signed 15 October 2008, entered into force 29 December 2008).

[4] EU-Central America AA (signed 29 June 2012, entered into force 1 August 2013).

[5] There are few systemic legal and institutional analyses of this sort. See OECD, *Environment and Regional Trade Agreements* (Paris, 2007); MC Cordonier Segger, 'Sustainable Development in Regional Trade Agreements' in M Gehring and MC Cordonier Segger (eds), *Sustainable Development in World Trade Law* (The Hague, Kluwer Law International 2005).

Addressing the first tension identified in this volume, the bilateral and regional trade and investment agreements can be found to include tailored provisions to create exemptions from trade rules, where economic law obligations might otherwise constrain sustainable development regulators from developing new policies and regulations on sustainable development. These exemptions follow different formulations in distinct trade and investment treaties.[6] But many now include general exceptions for the use of measures related to the conservation of natural resources, or necessary to protect human, animal, or plant life or health which build on article XX of the GATT; specific exceptions in sections of the Agreement where trade rules on, *inter alia*, SPS standards, TBT, intellectual property rights, public procurement, services or investment, might constrain the use of environmental and social measures; explicit notes to declare trade and investment disciplines non-applicable to socially or environmentally sensitive sectors (such as parks and natural resources not covered by investor protections, or health and education sectors not covered by services disciplines); general 'relations with other agreement' statements to guide potential areas where economic rules could otherwise constrain the implementation of economic instruments from other international treaties; and commitments not to lower standards to attract investments. These provisions may prevent trade and investment agreements from frustrating legitimate social and environmental regulations, but only indirectly ensure that the economic treaties can actually promote more sustainable development.

Second, in more than 110 bilateral and regional treaties analysed for this volume, many innovative provisions were identified that can be interpreted as permitting or even prescribing parallel social and environmental cooperation activities among Parties to an economic agreement.[7] These measures aim to strengthen and secure better enforcement of existing domestic social and environmental laws, in the interest of sustainable development. In one set of treaties studied, those similar to the North American Free Trade Agreement (NAFTA) and the subsequent US, the United Mexican States, and Canada Agreement (USMCA), sustainable development is characterized as a subset of environmental cooperation, mentioned in separate annexes, though the treaty does liberalize environmental goods and services, and includes disciplines on investment (for some Parties) with binding dispute settlement tribunals similar to those found in simple bilateral investment treaties (BITs). In the other set of accords which engage the EU, sustainable development is set as an objective of the overall economic relationship, and is secured through cooperation and trade enhancement in diverse sectors such as agriculture, forestry and renewable energy. Commitments to respect environmental and social laws and standards, along with common work programmes, are found among both sets of economic treaties. These work programmes may be accompanied by reliable institutions, capacity-building, technology transfer and financing commitments. While some Parties have also agreed to use 'assessed monetary contributions' and sanctions to penalize the other Parties if environmental and social laws are not enforced to gain trade advantages or attract investment, this punitive approach has not been greatly utilized. However, several of the treaties reviewed, including the US-Chile FTA, establish a factual report or public submissions mechanism to draw attention to violations or lack of enforcement of environmental or social regulations. While these 'parallel' cooperation initiatives do not always work to integrate environmental and social

[6] See Annex 4 of this volume.
[7] See Annex 3 of this volume.

considerations into trade and investment decision-making, the public 'name and shame' mechanisms do appear to provide an additional avenue for civil society actors and others to advance respect for environmental and human rights laws in their countries. These measures address underlying problems which, according to the impact assessment results, might otherwise be exacerbated by new trade and investment liberalization induced by the agreements.

Third and most promising, to address the final tension identified in this volume, Parties are starting to adopt provisions to prescribe constructive sustainable development oriented trade and investment enhancement initiatives, for specific economic sectors where a positive 'triple-win' might be achieved within the context of the economic agreements themselves. Such provisions differ according to the opportunities offered by the specific economic relationship, and the priorities of the Parties. But in many cases, a direct correlation can be discerned between a new initiative in the trade and investment treaty, and specific concerns raised in the impact assessments. Certain provisions use trade and investments liberalization measures to reduce 'disincentives' for sustainable development such as subsidies which encourage obsolete polluting industries or over-fishing, while others use trade and investment liberalization to enhance development of sustainable goods and services. These measures have the potential to support economic growth in important areas, responding not just to trade and investment, but to commitments in the UN Framework Convention on Climate Change (UN FCCC) to develop low-carbon clean energy technologies and carbon markets, or in the UN Convention on Biological Diversity (UN CBD) to develop sustainable use of genetic resources. Measures to secure additional liberalization of environmental goods and services; and to secure reductions in unsustainable fisheries subsidies; are narrowly defined and deadlocked in the WTO. But in regional and bilateral trade and investment agreements, States are experimenting with SPS provisions which promote joint scientific research, cooperation and risk assessment to improve levels of health or environment protection; government procurement provisions which make public purchasing of sustainable development goods or services more affordable; TBT provisions which promote collaboration on non-discriminatory eco-certification processes or even mutual recognition of standards; Intellectual Property rights provisions which support rather than frustrate biodiversity protection and the recognition of traditional knowledge; investment provisions which encourage firms to adopt corporate social responsibility standards; even collaborative inspection measures to promote reductions in illegal trade in forestry products along with increases in market access; or measures to encourage increased trade and investment in renewable energy technologies. These types of provisions are, in the main, embryonic, and a great deal will depend on how they can be applied, and also interpreted, in light of the customary integration principle. But the sheer diversity of innovations that are being adopted, especially in regional and bilateral trade and investment treaties agreed since the 2002 WSSD, suggests that there is a great deal of scope for further progress. These new 'sustainable trade enhancement measures', in particular, appear to offer one of the clearest ways forward for an economic agreement that seeks to achieve sustainable development by integrating social and environmental considerations into the economic laws themselves. They could offer valuable insights, for instance, for the negotiations that were launched in September 2019 for a new Agreement on Climate Change, Trade and Sustainability (ACCTS) between Costa Rica, Fiji, Iceland, New Zealand and Norway, and for other new trade and investment negotiations with the UK and other countries that seek to contribute to their global Sustainable Development Goals, especially in the context of post-COVID-19 pandemic economic recovery measures.[8]

The textual provisions were considered in light of the rules of treaty interpretation laid out in the Vienna Convention on the Law of Treaties (VCLT),[9] which permits interpreters to take into consideration 'other rules of international law relevant between the Parties' that could include the customary norm of integration,[10] and gives greater weight to clearly indicated obligations in the treaty itself, including the Preamble and annexes, versus memorandum of understandings (MoUs) related to the trade and investment treaty that were agreed at the same time, or supplementary means such as *travaux préparatoires*.[11] As was shown in the instance of the WTO, the ability of a tribunal (or in these instances, most likely a regulator with authority over matters related to sustainable development) to access this interpretive flexibility may be key in resolving how the trade and investment treaty can be crafted to address the key tensions that can arise.[12]

22.3 The Importance of Process for Sustainability

The comparative review of negotiations for the surveyed bilateral and regional economic treaties revealed important procedural innovations undertaken by the Parties. The use of new mechanisms to engage experts, counterparts and the public appears to be important in assisting external affairs and trade ministries to identify 'more sustainable' trade and investment policies in new negotiations.

22.3.1 Sustainability Impact Assessments of Trade and Investment Treaties

SIAs, EAs and ERs are increasingly used not only by Europe and North America, but by many States, including certain developing countries. These procedural mechanisms have been linked in scholarly literature and in practice, including in formal statements of WTO members in the WTO TPRM, to a commitment for sustainable development. Often carried out prior to, or during, trade and investment liberalization negotiations, they assist the Parties to identify potential environmental, social and economic impacts of the trade and investment treaties, and to consider mitigating or 'flanking' measures that might address key tensions. This volume has shown that trade and investment impact assessments,

[8] Joint Leaders' Statement on the launch of the 'Agreement on Climate Change, Trade and Sustainability' Initiative (25 Sept 2019); European Commission Communication, 'The European Green Deal' COM/2019/640, n 9 ch 1; UK Parliament Lords Select Committee (21 July 2020) 'International Trade Secretary Discusses Possible Free Trade Agreements', n 10, ch 1; MC Cordonier Segger and others, 'Human Rights, the Sustainable Development Goals and the Law' (Montreal, CISDL 2020) <https://www.cisdl.org/2020/04/19/human-rights-the-sustainable-development-goals-the-law-international-legal-symposium/> accessed 16 December 2020; C Hepburn and others, 'Will COVID-19 Fiscal Recovery Packages Accelerate or Retard Progress on Climate Change?' (4 May 2020) Oxford Smith School of Enterprise and the Environment Working Paper No 20-02, <https://www.smithschool.ox.ac.uk/publications/wpapers/workingpaper20-02.pdf> accessed 16 December 2020.

[9] Signed 23 May 1969, entered into force 27 January 1980, 1155 UNTS 331, arts 30–31.

[10] Ibid, art (3)(c).

[11] See Chapter 3.

[12] See Chapter 4.

though far from perfect, are having an impact. Among the treaties surveyed, there is a direct and almost teleological link between the economic partnership or association agreements for which the most careful and comprehensive SIAs were done, and the accords with the most detailed, effective and integrative provisions on sustainable development. There is also a great deal of as-yet-untapped potential in these assessments. One of the implications of this volume is that SIAs could benefit from a detailed regulatory assessment component. In few SIAs are potential regulatory impacts considered seriously. One pioneer study examines potential impacts on a Party's ability to implement Rio Declaration principles,[13] and on national sustainable development strategies.[14] But efforts are rudimentary and could benefit from considerable improvement.[15] By including annexes or chapters focusing on the three key regulatory tensions identified in this volume, updated SIAs could uncover: (1) which new laws and regulations, including international market based instruments, might be unduly constrained by the new trade and investment agreements, and how these laws or treaties could be accommodated by a form of exception; (2) which existing laws and regulations on sustainable development, including multilateral environmental agreements (MEAs), could be weakened by the new trade and investment agreements, and how they might be strengthened by trade and investment-related cooperation, including citizen submissions and other mechanisms to improve enforcement; and (3) which future laws and regulations might promote development, trade and investment in sustainable goods and services, including for instance carbon negative technologies and industries which assist in securing higher ambition implementation of the Paris Agreement and SDG 13, and how these could benefit from trade and investment incentives. The outcomes of this legal element of the assessment could assist States in their trade and investment negotiations.

22.3.2 Other Innovative Procedural Instruments

Impact assessments are not, however, the only procedural innovations related to sustainable development that are being adopted by the Parties to regional and bilateral trade and investment treaties, or even in global trade negotiations. States are also making increasing efforts to consult more broadly between national environment, development and economic authorities themselves; to engage the civil society and members of the public in trade and investment policy-making; and to ensure that those responsible for resolving trade or investment disputes under new economic treaties are apprised of sustainable development concerns relevant to their cases. Such procedural steps, alongside procedural innovations in the provisions of the trade and investment agreements themselves, carried out in support of a sustainable development objective, provide certain evidence that, as suggested by

[13] IARC, *Trade Sustainability Impact Assessment (SIA) of the Association Agreement under Negotiation between the European Community and Mercosur: Final Overview Report Trade SIA EU-Mercosur* (Manchester, March 2009) [EU-Mercosur SIA].

[14] OECD, 'National Strategies for Sustainable Development: Good Practices in OECD Countries' (8 September 2005) SG/SD(2005) 6.

[15] For a review of methodological issues in SIAs, see Hugo Rojas-Romagosa, 'Overview of the Evolution of the Methodology and Coverage of EU Ex-Ante Trade Sustainability Impact Assessments over Time' (RESPECT mimeo 2018); Patrick Reynaud, 'Sustainable Development and Regional Trade Agreements: Toward Better Practices in Impact Assessments' (2012) 8 McGill International Journal of Sustainable Development Law and Policy 205, 205.

Professor Vaughan Lowe, 'those negotiating treaties ... at the national or the international level, are likely to approach that task within the context of sustainable development. The concept colours the whole approach to this area of international law.'[16] While it is not clear that these innovations are being included because States consider themselves legally bound to do so by a principle of 'integration' (sometimes called 'sustainable development'), there is an observable tendency of States (and others) to refer to their mutual sustainable development objective as a common starting point, or even a persuasive argument for the inclusion of such provisions.[17]

[16] V Lowe, 'The Politics of Law-Making: Are the Method and Character of Norm Creation Changing?' in M Byers (ed), *The Role of Law in International Politics: Essays in International Relations and International Law* (Oxford, OUP 2000).

[17] This tendency may, indeed, suggest that Lowe (n 16) is correct in identifying an 'interstitial influence' of sustainable development in international law.

23

A Future Agenda for Crafting 'Athena's Treaties' on Trade and Investment for Sustainable Development

23.1 Implications of Sustainability for Trade and Investment Treaties

In bilateral and regional economic accords, States are testing many types of provisions related to sustainable development. This volume has classified them into four categories: a general commitment to sustainable development, and three sets of operational provisions, each of which involves the inclusion of diverse measures in the trade and investment treaty to address one of three main normative tensions which arose numerous times in the impact assessment studies carried out on the likely scenarios of outcomes of economic negotiations. It is not yet clear which of the range of sustainability instruments surveyed in this volume will have the most success in helping to integrate social and economic development and environmental protection. It is likely that no one single measure can provide 'the solution' to all trade- and investment-related sustainable development challenges. Rather, many different provisions may be needed throughout the treaty, addressing potential impacts as they arise.

It is also clear that form makes a difference. Several 'safeguards' touted loudly in final environmental reviews and related press statements prove little more that paper tigers when their form is analysed from an international law perspective, compared with other more integrated provisions. The interpretative weight of vague conflict clauses, no-application notes, annexes, memoranda of understanding and other mechanisms, may be less satisfactory for a tribunal or a regulator, compared to the EU's new 'trade partnership for sustainable development' integrated approach. Future research is needed in this area, examining specific regulations or initiatives that could be disciplined or supported by a bilateral or regional economic treaty.

Several substantive instruments, such as the new US-Peru TPA's system of certification to ensure that forestry products traded from Peru to the United States are not obtained through illegal logging, or the provisions to increase market access for sustainable organic agricultural products and to encourage trade and investment in eco-innovation and renewable energy technologies in the EU-Central America AA, are simply new. Such 'integrated' provisions alone will not necessarily ensure that sustainable development priorities are given more weight by the Parties in complying with their obligations, or by dispute settlement bodies in interpreting agreements, as compared to the other relevant objectives of agreements. However, they do appear likely to contribute to more sustainable trade and investment patterns. This is an important first step towards integration for sustainable development.

There is also room for a great deal of further development, especially in terms of 'process' innovations. For instance, sustainability impact assessments (SIAs) are being used more

Crafting Trade and Investment Accords for Sustainable Development. Marie-Claire Cordonier Segger, Oxford University Press.
 DOI: 10.1093/oso/9780198831341.003.0023

and more, and are having an impact. But the normative or regulatory evaluation elements could benefit from more rigorous evaluation and development. Ideally, elements of this volume's findings might offer valuable insights, for instance, for the new Agreement on Climate Change, Trade and Sustainability (ACCTS) between Costa Rica, Fiji, Iceland, New Zealand and Norway, and for trade and investment negotiations that the UK and other countries are leading, while also seeking to contribute to their global Sustainable Development Goals (SDGs), especially in the context of post-COVID-19 pandemic economic recovery measures, and to implement their international obligations for instance in the Paris Agreement of the UN Framework Convention on Climate Change (UNFCCC).[1]

This volume has shown that trade and investment treaties can have significant material and normative impacts on whether development is sustainable, especially in developing countries. It has also shown that States are not ignorant of the potential social and environmental impacts of new economic agreements. By analysing sustainable developed related negotiations and practices of the World Trade Organization (WTO), including recent WTO disputes and responses of WTO members in the Trade Policy Review Mechanism, the volume has demonstrated that sustainable development is now a recognized objective of WTO law, even if its meaning continues to be contested, and this is still inadequate to address the key tensions outlined in impact assessments. In light of the customary principle of integration that is emerging, the volume has argued that both regional economic agreements and even the WTO itself may adopt actual provisions to address key tensions related to the integration of social development and environmental considerations in trade and investment law and policy-making.

In particular, rather than relying only on article XX of the General Agreement on Tariffs and Trade (GATT), WTO members could negotiate waivers that provide many different types of exceptions to economic rules where the rules might otherwise prejudice legitimate social and environmental objectives. Rather than simply allowing multilateral environmental agreement (MEA) Secretariats to participate in the Committee on Trade and Environment (CTE) as observers, they should establish and promote new collaborative work programmes backed by information, capacity-building, financing and monitoring to strengthen domestic regulations for trade-related aspects of environmental protection and social development. The most challenging innovation is for the WTO to facilitate negotiations of new plurilateral trade agreements to reduce barriers and promote increased market access for sustainable goods and services, as has been proposed jointly by the US and the EU for trade in climate-friendly goods and services.

[1] Joint Leaders' Statement on the launch of the 'Agreement on Climate Change, Trade and Sustainability' Initiative (25 September 2019); European Commission Communication, 'The European Green Deal' COM/2019/640, n 9, ch 1; UK Parliament Lords Select Committee (21 July 2020) 'International Trade Secretary Discusses Possible Free Trade Agreements', n 10, ch 1; MC Cordonier Segger and others, 'Human Rights, the Sustainable Development Goals and the Law' (Montreal, CISDL 2020) <https://www.cisdl.org/2020/04/19/human-rights-the-sustainable-development-goals-the-law-international-legal-symposium/> accessed 16 December 2020; C Hepburn and others, 'Will COVID-19 Fiscal Recovery Packages Accelerate or Retard Progress on Climate Change?' (4 May 2020) Oxford Smith School of Enterprise and the Environment Working Paper No 20-02, <https://www.smithschool.ox.ac.uk/publications/wpapers/workingpaper20-02.pdf> accessed 16 December 2020. See 'Pandemic Recovery, the SDGs and the Law', Online lecture and Distinguished experts panel, 4 November 2020, <https://www.cisdl.org/2020/10/17/online-leverhulme-lecture-distinguished-experts-dialogue-pandemic-recovery-the-sdgs-and-the-law/> accessed 04 April 2021. See also 'Natural Resources, the Sustainable Development Goals and the Law', Online Leverhulme lecture and Distinguished experts panel, 17 March 2021, < https://www.cisdl.org/2021/02/20/online-leverhulme-lecture-distinguished-experts-dialogue-natural-resources-the-sustainable-development-goals-and-international-law/ > accessed 04 April 2021.

More broadly, there is still scant evidence of a binding and fully recognized principle that all development, including all trade and investment law and policy-making, must be sustainable. This is partly due to the diversity of conceptions of 'development', rather than simply lack of clarity as to what is meant by sustainability. However, an 'integration' principle is emerging, as *lex ferenda*, which requires States to integrate environment and social considerations into economic development policy, and this principle is being increasingly reflected in economic treaty texts. States are also including sustainable development as a purpose of the WTO, and many bilateral and regional treaties, with few ill effects and many potential benefits for the ecologies, societies and economies of the Parties. Finally, many trade and investment agreements contain provisions which, if implemented effectively, hold the potential to contribute to achievement of the global SDGs.

23.2 Implications for Future Legal Research

With regards to trade and investment treaties, further legal research may be needed to monitor and propose improvements in State attempts to address regulatory elements in SIA and other processes. Future legal research can also focus on investigating the continuing elaboration of the rules governing the diverse forms of exception to trade and investment; the actual implications and effects of new 'sustainable or green growth' initiatives in regional and global trade and investment treaty negotiations, and the ways of ensuring that new cooperative mechanisms, such as regional social and environmental institutions and work programmes, are actually being implemented. Such research might examine, for instance, how regional trade and investment agreements are addressing specific priorities such as sustainable use of biological resources, nature-based solutions to climate change, sustainable development of renewable energy resources and carbon negative technologies. Further legal research may also be carried out, using a similar framework, to further analyse international investment treaties in greater depth, considering how States might address the potential social and environmental impacts of bilateral investment treaties (BITs), and what types of provisions could integrate social and environmental considerations into resulting international investment law, harnessing investment rules for more sustainable development. Finally, there is legal research to be done to explore how other treaties committed to sustainable development are activating trade, investment and other economic instruments to directly achieve their social or environmental goals, and how, at the areas of intersection with related trade rules, integrated outcomes can actually be secured on the ground, as well as in the law.

Certain bilateral and regional economic treaty mechanisms and provisions related to sustainable development have been documented and debated in trade, investment and environment, or trade, investment and labour related literature. However, this book brought them together within a coherent and normative analytical framework, in the context of how States can integrate environmental and social provisions into trade and investment agreements for the realization of sustainable development, and also considered transversal lessons that can be learned for future global and regional trade and investment law and policy. It is hoped that this framework, along with the data collected and analysed in the table of sustainable development measures in regional and bilateral economic agreements annexed in this volume, can serve as a useful tool for more sustainable international economic law and policy-making in the future. It seeks to support open-minded actors from governments, academic experts, civil society and industry in the design, negotiation and implementation of more sustainable trade and investment regimes. More broadly, it is hoped that this research can contribute to a deeper understanding of trade and investment law, and its potential to foster not frustrate sustainable development. Such new economic agreements, if crafted towards justice, wisdom and sustainability, would become *Athena's Treaties*, to be celebrated for their contributions to our common future.

ANNEX 1

Table of Environmental Reviews, Environmental Assessments and Sustainability Impact Assessment Reports

1. Sustainability Impact Assessments of European Economic Agreements

1.1 EU SIA of EU-Chile Trade Agreement

Planistat, 'Sustainable Impact Assessment (SIA) of the Trade Aspects of Negotiations for an Association Agreement between the European Communities and Chile' (Santiago, Planistat 2002)

1.2 EU SIA of EU-ACP Economic Partnership Agreement

PricewaterhouseCoopers, 'Sustainability Impact Assessment of the EU-ACP Economic Partnership Agreements: Key Findings, Recommendations and Lessons Learned' (Paris, PricewaterhouseCoopers May 2007).

PricewaterhouseCoopers, 'Qualified Preliminary EU-ACP SIA of the EPAs: Phase One' (Paris, PricewaterhouseCoopers, February 2004).

EC, 'Sustainability Impact Assessment of EU-ACP Economic Partnership Agreements: Position Paper' (Brussels, EC 16 November 2007).

1.3 EU SIA of EU-Arab Gulf State Trade Agreement

PricewaterhouseCoopers, 'Sustainability Impact Assessment (SIA) of the negotiations of the trade agreement between the European Community and the Countries of the Cooperation Council for the Arab States of the Gulf (GCC): Final Report' (Paris, PricewaterhouseCoopers May 2004).

EC, 'Trade Sustainability Impact Assessment of the Trade Negotiations between the EC and the Gulf Cooperation Council: Position Paper' (Brussels, EC 20 March 2006)

1.4 EU SIA of EU-Mercosur Association Agreement

IARC, 'Trade Sustainability Impact Assessment (SIA) of the Association Agreement under Negotiation between the European Community and Mercosur: Final Overview Report Trade SIA EU-Mercosur' (Manchester, IARC March 2009)

IARC, 'Trade Sustainability Impact Assessment (SIA) of the Association Agreement under Negotiation between the European Community and Mercosur: Forest Sector Study' (Manchester, IARC June 2007)

Institute for Development Policy and Management, 'Update of the Overall Preliminary Trade SIA EU-Mercosur' (2007)

Planistat (2003) Sustainability Impact Assessment (SIA) of the Trade Aspects of Negotiations for an Association Agreement between the European Communities and Mercosur: Global Preliminary SIA EU-Mercosur, Final Report, Planistat, Luxembourg

1.5 EU SIA of EU-Mediterranean Trade Agreement

IARC, 'Sustainability Impact Assessment of the Euro-Mediterranean Free Trade Area: Final Report of the SIA-EMFTA Project (Manchester, IARC November 2007)

George C and Kirkpatrick C, 'Sustainability Impact Assessment Study of the Euro-Mediterranean Free Trade Area: SIA Methodology, Institute for Development Policy and Management' (Manchester, University of Manchester 2004)

EC, 'Trade Sustainability Impact Assessment (SIA) of the Euro-Mediterranean Free Trade Area: Position Paper' (Brussels, EC June 2009)

C George and others, 'Sustainability Impact Assessment of the Euro-Mediterranean Free Trade Area: Final Report' financed by the EU Commission (2007), <http://trade.ec.europa.eu/doclib/html/137777.htm> accessed 16 December 2020

IARC Sustainability Impacts of the Euro-Mediterranean Free Trade Area: Final Report on Phase 2 of the SIA-EMFTA Project, SIA-EMFTA Consortium (IARC, UN ESCWA, CITET, Bocconi University, ODI, Deloitte Touche, CIHEAM), Impact Assessment Research Centre, Institute for Development Policy and Management (Manchester, University of Manchester 2006)

1.6 EU SIA of EU-Ukraine Trade Agreement

ECORYS, 'Trade Sustainability Impact Assessment for the FTA between the EU and Ukraine within the Enhanced Agreement: Final Report' (Rotterdam, ECORYS 17 December 2007)

EC, 'Trade Sustainability Impact Assessment of the Negotiations on a Free Trade Area between the EU and Ukraine: Position Paper' (Brussels, EC April 2009)

1.7 EU SIA of EU-China Partnership & Cooperation Agreement

Emerging Markets Group/Development Solutions, 'Trade Sustainability Impact Assessment of the Negotiations of a Partnership and Cooperation Agreement between the EU and China: Final Report' (Brussels, EMG August 2008)

Emerging Markets Group/Development Solutions, 'Trade Sustainability Impact Assessment of the Negotiations of a Partnership and Cooperation Agreement between the EU and China: Global Analysis Report' (Brussels, EMG August 2008)

M van der Meer, W van der Geest, HD Evans 'Trade Sustainability Impact Assessment of the Negotiations of a Partnership and Cooperation Agreement between the EU and China' financed by EU Commission (2008), <https://trade.ec.europa.eu/doclib/docs/2010/june/tradoc_146246.pdf> accessed 16 December 2020

EC, 'Trade Sustainability Impact Assessment of the Negotiations of a Partnership and Cooperation Agreement between the EU and China: Position Paper' (Brussels, EC February 2009)

1.8 EU SIA of EU-Korea Trade Agreement

IBM Belgium, 'Trade Sustainability Impact Assessment of the EU-Korea FTA: Final Report' (Brussels, IBM June 2008)

IBM Belgium, 'Trade Sustainability Impact Assessment of the EU-Korea FTA: Global Analysis Report' (Brussels, IBM January 2008)

IBM Belgium 'Trade Sustainability Impact Assessment of the EU-Korea FTA: Final Report-(Phase 3)' financed by the EU Commission (2008), <http://trade.ec.europa.eu/doclib/html/141660.htm> accessed 16 December 2020

1.9 EU SIA of EU-India Trade Agreement

ECORYS/CUTS/CENTAD, 'Trade Sustainability Impact Assessment for the FTA between the EU and the Republic of India: Final Report' (Rotterdam, ECORYS May 2009)

ECORYS/CUTS/CENTAD, 'Trade Sustainability Impact Assessment for the FTA between the EU and the Republic of India: Global Analysis Report' (Rotterdam, ECORYS Aug 2008)

K Berden, J Francois, P Wijmenga 'Trade Sustainability Impact Assessment of the FTA between the European Union and the Republic of India-Interim Report (Phase 2)' financed by the EU Commission (2008), <http://trade.ec.europa.eu/doclib/html/141209.htm> accessed 16 December 2020

1.10 EU SIA of EU-ASEAN Trade Agreement

ECORYS, 'Trade Sustainability Impact Assessment of the FTA between the EU and ASEAN: Final Report' (Rotterdam, ECORYS May 2009)

ECORYS, 'Trade Sustainability Impact Assessment of the FTA between the EU and ASEAN: Global Analysis Report' (Rotterdam, ECORYS Nov 2008)

ECORYS, 'Trade Sustainability Impact Assessment of the FTA between the EU and ASEAN: Final Report' (Rotterdam, ECORYS June 2009), <https://trade.ec.europa.eu/doclib/docs/2010/april/tradoc_145989.pdf> accessed 16 December 2020

EC, 'Trade Sustainability Impact Assessment of the Free Trade Agreement between the EU and ASEAN: Singapore Position Paper' (Brussels, EC June 2010), <https://trade.ec.europa.eu/doclib/docs/2010/july/tradoc_146295.pdf> accessed 16 December 2020

EC, 'Trade Sustainability Impact Assessment of the Free Trade Agreement between the EU and ASEAN: Malaysia Position Paper' (Brussels, EC January 2011), <https://trade.ec.europa.eu/doclib/docs/2011/january/tradoc_147337.pdf> accessed 16 December 2020

EC, 'Trade Sustainability Impact Assessment of the Free Trade Agreement between the EU and ASEAN: Vietnam Position Paper' (Brussels, EC May 2013), <https://trade.ec.europa.eu/doclib/docs/2013/may/tradoc_151230.pdf> accessed 16 December 2020

1.11 EU SIA of EU-Libya Trade Agreement

Development Solutions, 'Trade Sustainability Impact Assessment of the EU-Libya Free Trade Agreement: Draft Final Report' (Brussels, Development Solutions July 2009)

1.12 EU SIA of EU-Central America Association Agreement

ECORYS, 'Trade Sustainability Impact Assessment of the Association Agreement to be negotiated between the EU and Central America: Draft Final Report' (Rotterdam, ECORYS July 2009)

1.13 EU SIA of EU-Andean Trade Agreement

Development Solutions, 'EU-Andean Trade Sustainability Impact Assessment: Draft Final Report' (Brussels, Development Solutions July 2009)

1.14 EU SIA of EU-Mexico Global Agreement (Trade Pillar)

LSE Consulting, 'Sustainability Impact Assessment (SIA) in support of the negotiations for the modernisation of the trade part of the Global Agreement with Mexico: Final Report' (Luxembourg, 17 September 2019), <https://trade.ec.europa.eu/doclib/docs/2020/january/tradoc_158558.pdf> accessed 16 December 2020

EC, 'Sustainability Impact Assessment in Support of Negotiations for the Modernisation of the Trade Part of The Global Agreement with Mexico: Position Paper' (Brussels, EC January 2020), <https://trade.ec.europa.eu/doclib/docs/2020/january/tradoc_158559.pdf> accessed 16 December 2020

1.15 EU SIA of EU-USA Partnership (TTIP)

ECORYS, 'SIA in support of the negotiations on a Transatlantic Trade and Investment Partnership (TTIP): Final Report' (Luxembourg, March 2017), <https://trade.ec.europa.eu/doclib/docs/2017/april/tradoc_155464.pdf> accessed 16 December 2020

EC, 'Sustainability Impact Assessment in Support of Negotiations of the Transatlantic Trade & Investment Partnership between the European Union and the United States of America: Position Paper' (Brussels, EC 31 March 2017), <https://trade.ec.europa.eu/doclib/docs/2017/march/tradoc_155462.pdf> accessed 16 December 2020

1.16 EU SIA of EU-Canada Comprehensive Economic and Trade Agreement (CETA)

Development Solutions, 'A Trade SIA Relating to the Negotiations of a Comprehensive Economic and Trade Agreement (CETA) Between the EU and Canada: Final Report' (Brussels, Development Solutions June 2011), <https://trade.ec.europa.eu/doclib/docs/2011/september/tradoc_148201.pdf> accessed 16 December 2020

EC, 'Trade Sustainability Impact Assessment of a Comprehensive Economic & Trade Agreement between the EU and Canada: Position Paper' (Brussels, EC 4 April 2017), <https://trade.ec.europa.eu/doclib/docs/2017/april/tradoc_155471.pdf> accessed 16 December 2020

1.17 EU SIA of EU-Japan Economic Partnership Agreement

LSE Consulting, 'Trade Sustainability Impact Assessment in Support of Negotiations of a Free Trade Agreement between the European Union and Japan: Final Report' (Brussels, April 2016), <https://trade.ec.europa.eu/doclib/docs/2016/may/tradoc_154522.pdf> accessed 16 December 2020

EC, 'Trade Sustainability Impact Assessment in Support of Negotiations of a Free Trade Agreement between the European Union and Japan: Position Paper' (Brussels, EC February 2017), <https://trade.ec.europa.eu/doclib/docs/2017/february/tradoc_155382.PDF> accessed 16 December 2020

1.18 EU SIA of EU-Georgia and EU-Moldova DCFTA

ECORYS, 'Trade Sustainability Impact Assessment in Support of Negotiations of a DCFTA between the EU and Georgia and the Republic of Moldova: Final Report' (Rotterdam, 27 October 2012), <https://trade.ec.europa.eu/doclib/docs/2012/november/tradoc_150105.pdf> accessed 16 December 2020

EC, 'Trade Sustainability Impact Assessment in Support of Negotiations of a Deep and Comprehensive Free Trade Area between the European Union and respectively Georgia and the Republic of Moldova: Position Paper' (Brussels, EC April 2014), <https://trade.ec.europa.eu/doclib/docs/2014/may/tradoc_152461.pdf> accessed 16 December 2020

1.19 EU SIAs of WTO Millennium Round Trade Negotiations

C Kirkpatrick and N Lee, 'Sustainability Impact Assessment Study WTO New Round: Phase Two Report' (Manchester, IDPM 1999) <https://trade.ec.europa.eu/doclib/docs/2006/june/tradoc_128963.pdf> accessed 16 December 2020

C Kirkpatrick, N Lee and O Morrissey, 'Sustainability Impact Assessment Study WTO New Round: Phase One Report' (Manchester, IDPM 1999).

1.20 EU SIAs of WTO Doha Round Trade Negotiations

A Maltais and others, 'Sustainability Impact Assessment of WTO Negotiations in the Major Food Crops Sector: Final Report' (Stockholm, SEI 2002)

O Morrissey and DW te Velde, 'Sustainability Impact Assessment of Proposed WTO Negotiations Sector Study for Market Access: Final Report' (London, IARC and ODI 2003)

O Morrissey, DW te Velde and I Gillson, 'Sustainability Impact Assessment of Proposed WTO Negotiations for the Agriculture Sector Study: Final Report' (London, IARC and ODI 2004)

R Bisset and others, 'Sustainability Impact Assessment of Proposed WTO Negotiations Sector Study for Environmental Services: Final Report' (Manchester, IARC and others, 2003)

JL Clarke, SJ Evenett and KR Gray, 'Sustainability Impact Assessment of Proposed WTO Negotiations Sector Study for Competition: Final Report' (Manchester, IARC and others, 2003)

C George and C Kirkpatrick, 'Sustainability Impact Assessment of Proposed WTO Negotiations: Preliminary Overview of Potential Impacts of the Doha Agenda: Final Report' (Manchester, IARC 2003)

C George and C Kirkpatrick, 'Sustainability Impact Assessment of Proposed Doha Agenda Assessment of Individual Trade Measures: Preliminary Overview' (Manchester, IARC 2003)

J Arkell and M Johnson, 'Sustainability Impact Assessment of Proposed WTO Negotiations for the Distribution Services Study: Mid-Term Report' (London, IARC and ITSP 2004)

M Katila and M Simula, 'Sustainability Impact Assessment of Proposed WTO Negotiations for the Forest Sector Study: Inception Report' (Helsinki, IARC and others, 2004)

C Kirkpatrick, C George and S Scrieciu, 'Sustainability Impact Assessment of Proposed WTO Negotiations Final Global Overview Trade SIA of the Doha Development Agenda: Final Report' (Manchester, IDPM 2006)

U, Kleih, P Greenhalgh and A Marter, 'Sustainability Impact Assessment of Proposed WTO Negotiations for the Fisheries Sector Study: Final Report' (London, IARC and NRI 2006)

EC, 'Sustainability Impact Assessment of DDA Negotiations: Sectoral Study on Market Access for Pharmaceuticals, Non-ferrous metals, Textiles and Clothing: EC Position Paper' (Brussels, EC 2005)

EC, 'Sustainability Impact Assessment of DDA Negotiations Sectoral Study on Environmental Services: EC Position Paper' (Brussels, EC 2005)

EC, 'Sustainability Impact Assessment of DDA Negotiations Sectoral Study on Competition: EC Position Paper' (Brussels, EC 2005)

2. Environmental Reviews of US Trade Agreements

2.1 US Environmental Review of US-Chile Trade Agreement

USTR, Final Environmental Review of the US-Chile FTA (Washington, USTR 2003) <https://ustr.gov/sites/default/files/chilefinal.pdf> accessed 16 December 2020

USTR, Interim Environmental Review of the US-Chile FTA (Washington, USTR 2003)

2.2 US Environmental Review of US-Australia Trade Agreement

USTR, Final Environmental Review of the US-Australia FTA (Washington, USTR 2003)
USTR, Interim Environmental Review of the US-Australia FTA (Washington, USTR 2003)

2.3 US Environmental Review of US-Bahrain Trade Agreement

USTR, 'Final Environmental Review of the United States-Bahrain Free Trade Agreement' (2004), < https://ustr.gov/sites/default/files/final.pdf>
USTR, 'Interim Environmental Review of the United States-Bahrain Free Trade Agreement' (2004), <http://www.ustr.gov/sites/default/files/interm.pdf> accessed 16 December 2020

2.4 US Environmental Review of US-CAFTA-DR Trade Agreement

USTR, 'Final Environmental Review of the United States-CAFTA Free Trade Agreement' (2005), <https://ustr.gov/archive/assets/Trade_Agreements/Regional/CAFTA/Transmittal/asset_upload_file804_7819.pdf> accessed 16 December 2020

2.5 US Environmental Review of US-Andean Trade Agreement

USTR, 'Interim Environmental Review U.S.-Andean Free Trade Agreement' (February 2005) <https://ustr.gov/sites/default/files/perinter.pdf> accessed 16 December 2020

2.6 US Environmental Review of US-Colombia Trade Agreement

USTR, 'Interim Environmental Review U.S.-Colombia Trade Promotion Agreement' (February 2007) <http://www.ustr.gov/sites/default/files/CTPA%20Final%20Environmental%20Review.final_.pdf> accessed 16 December 2020

2.7 US Environmental Review of US-Jordan Trade Agreement

USTR, 'Final Environmental Review of the Agreement on the Establishment of a Free Trade Area Between the Government of the United States and the Government of the Hashemite Kingdom of Jordan' (2000) <http://www.ustr.gov/sites/default/files/jorfinal.pdf> accessed 16 December 2020

2.8 US Environmental Review of US-Korea Trade Agreement

USTR, 'Interim Environmental Review United States-Korea Free Trade Agreement' (2006), <https://ustr.gov/sites/default/files/uploads/Countries%20Regions/africa/agreements/pdfs/FTAs/KOREA%20Final%20Environmental%20Review.pdf> accessed 16 December 2020

2.9 US Environmental Review of US-Morocco Trade Agreement

USTR, 'Interim Environmental Review of the United-States Morocco Free Trade Agreement' (2000) <http://www.ustr.gov/sites/default/files/Morocco%20interim%20review.pdf> accessed 16 December 2020

USTR, 'Interim Environmental Review of the United-States Morocco Free Trade Agreement' (2004) <http://www.ustr.gov/sites/default/files/morofinal.pdf> accessed 16 December 2020

2.10 US Environmental Review of US-Oman Trade Agreement

USTR, 'Interim Environmental Review of the United States-Oman Free Trade Agreement' (April 2005) <http://www.ustr.gov/sites/default/files/Oman%20interim%20review.pdf> accessed 16 December 2020

USTR, 'Final Environmental Review of the United States-Oman Free Trade Agreement' (2006) <https://ustr.gov/sites/default/files/Oman%20final%20review.pdf> accessed 16 December 2020

2.11 US Environmental Review of US-Panama Trade Agreement

USTR, 'Interim Environmental Review of the United States-Panama Free Trade Agreement' (June 2004) <http://www.ustr.gov/sites/default/files/Panama%20interim%20review.pdf> accessed 16 December 2020

2.12 US Environmental Review of US-Peru Trade Agreement

USTR 'Interim Environmental Review United States-Andean Free Trade Agreement' (2005) <http://www.ustr.gov/sites/default/files/Peru%20Enviro%20Review.Final_.pdf> accessed 16 December 2020

2.13 US Environmental Review of US-Singapore Trade Agreement

USTR, 'Final Environmental Review of the U.S.-Singapore Free Trade Agreement' (June 2003) <http://www.ustr.gov/sites/default/files/Singapore%20final%20review.pdf> accessed 16 December 2020

2.14 US Environmental Review of US-Thailand Trade Agreement

USTR 'Interim Environmental Review United States-Thailand Free Trade Agreement' (2005), <https://ustr.gov/archive/assets/Trade_Agreements/Bilateral/Thail_FTA/asset_upload_file463_8410.pdf> accessed 16 December 2020

2.15 US Environmental Review of US-UAE Trade Agreement

USTR, 'US Environmental Review of US-UAE Trade Agreement' (May 2005) <http://www.ustr.gov/sites/default/files/UAE%20interim%20review.pdf> accessed 16 December 2020

2.16 US Environmental Review of the US-Dominican Republic-Central America Free Trade Agreement

USTR, 'Final Environmental Review of the Dominican Republic-Central America-United States Free Trade Agreement' (June 2005), <https://ustr.gov/archive/assets/Trade_Agreements/Regional/CAFTA/Transmittal/asset_upload_file804_7819.pdf> accessed 16 December 2020

2.17 US Employment Impact Review of US Trade Agreements

USTR *Employment Impact Review* pursuant to s 2102(c)(5) of the US Trade Act, *Labor Rights Report* pursuant to s 2102(c)(8) of the US Trade Act, also *Laws Governing Exploitative Child Labor Report* pursuant to s 2102(c)(9) of the US Trade Act. See US Dept of Labor, 'Labor-Related US Free Trade Agreement Reports'

3. Environmental Assessments of Canadian Trade & Investment Agreements

3.1 Canadian EA of Canada-United States-Mexico Agreement

DFAIT, 'Final Environmental Assessment of the Canada-United States-Mexico Agreement (CUSMA)' (July 14, 2020) <https://www.international.gc.ca/trade-commerce/assets/pdfs/agreements-accords/cusma-aceum/final_ea-ee_finale-en.pdf> accessed 16 December 2020

3.2 Canadian EA of Canada-European Union Trade Agreement

DFAIT, 'Final Environmental Assessment of the Canada-European Union Comprehensive Economic and Trade Agreement' (May 2017) <https://www.international.gc.ca/trade-commerce/trade-agreements-accords-commerciaux/agr-acc/ceta-aecg/ea-ee.aspx?lang=eng&_ga=2.129338378.7047089.1596022088-1897083655.1595695899> accessed 16 December 2020

3.3 Canadian EA of Canada-Honduras Free Trade Agreement

DFAIT, 'Final Strategic Environmental Assessment Report of the Canada-Honduras Free Trade Agreement' (October 2013) <https://www.international.gc.ca/trade-agreements-accords-commerciaux/agr-acc/honduras/report-EA-rapport.aspx?lang=eng> accessed 16 December 2020

3.4 Canadian EA of Canada-Ukraine Free Trade Agreement

DFAIT, 'Final Environmental Assessment Report of the Canada-Ukraine Free Trade Agreement' (January 2016) <https://www.international.gc.ca/trade-agreements-accords-commerciaux/env/final_ea_canada-ukraine_ee.aspx?lang=eng> accessed 16 December 2020

3.5 Canadian EA of Canada-Chile Trade Agreement

DFAIT, 'Final Environmental Assessment of the Government Procurement Chapter to be added to the Canada-Chile Free Trade Agreement' (December 2006) <http://www.international.gc.ca/trade-agreements-accords-commerciaux/agr-acc/chile-chili/report-chile-final.aspx?lang=en> accessed 16 December 2020

3.6 Canadian EA of Canada-Kuwait Foreign Investment Promotion & Protection Agreement

DFAIT, 'Initial Environmental Assessment of the Canada-Kuwait Foreign Investment Promotion and Protection Agreement' (30 April 2009) <http://www.international.gc.ca/trade-agreements-accords-commerciaux/agr-acc/fipa-apie/initial-kuwait-koweit-initiale.aspx> accessed 16 December 2020

3.7 Canadian EA of Canada-Madagascar Foreign Investment Promotion & Protection Agreement

DFAIT, 'Final Environmental Assessment of the Canada-Madagascar Foreign Investment Promotion and Protection Agreement' (13 March 2009) <https://www.international.gc.ca/trade-agreements-accords-commerciaux/agr-acc/fipa-apie/initial-madagascar-initiale.aspx?lang=eng> accessed 16 December 2020

3.8 Canadian EA of Canada-Panama Trade Agreement

DFAIT, 'Initial Environmental Assessment of the Canada-Panama Free Trade Agreement' (28 February 2009) <https://www.international.gc.ca/trade-agreements-accords-commerciaux/agr-acc/panama/ea-panama.aspx?lang=eng> accessed 16 December 2020

3.9 Canadian EA of Canada-Dominican Trade Agreement

DFAIT, 'Initial Environmental Assessment of the Canada-Dominican Republic Free Trade Agreement Negotiations' (15 February 2009) <https://www.international.gc.ca/trade-agreements-accords-commerciaux/agr-acc/dominican-dominicaine/initial-initiale.aspx?lang=eng> accessed 16 December 2020

3.10 Canadian EA of Canada-CARICOM Trade Agreement

DFAIT, 'Initial Environmental Assessment of the Canada-CARICOM Free Trade Agreement Negotiations' (15 February 2009) <https://www.international.gc.ca/trade-agreements-accords-commerciaux/agr-acc/caricom/initialEA-CARICOM-EEinitiale.aspx?lang=eng> accessed 16 December 2020

3.11 Canadian EA of Canada-Madagascar Investment Agreement

DFAIT, 'Initial Environmental Assessment of the Canada-Madagascar Foreign Investment Promotion and Protection Agreement' (25 August 2008) <http://www.international.gc.ca/trade-agreements-accords-commerciaux/agr-acc/fipa-apie/initial-madagascar-initiale.aspx> accessed 16 December 2020

3.12 Canadian EA of Canada-Jordan Trade Agreement

DFAIT, 'Initial Environmental Assessment of the Canada-Jordan Free Trade Agreement' (25 July 2008) <https://www.international.gc.ca/trade-agreements-accords-commerciaux/agr-acc/jordan-jordanie/initialEA-FTA-EEinitiale.aspx?lang=eng> accessed 16 December 2020.

3.13 Canadian EA of Canada-Jordan Foreign Investment Promotion and Protection Agreement

DFAIT, 'Initial Environmental Assessment of the Canada-Jordan Foreign Investment Promotion and Protection Agreement' (FIPA) (12 May 2008) <https://www.international.gc.ca/trade-agreements-accords-commerciaux/agr-acc/jordan-jordanie/initialEA-FTA-EEinitiale.aspx?lang=eng> accessed 16 December 2020

3.14 Canadian EA of Canada-China Investment Agreement

DFAIT, 'Initial Environmental Assessment of the Canada-China Foreign Investment Promotion and Protection Agreement' (21 March 2008) <https://www.international.gc.ca/trade-agreements-accords-commerciaux/agr-acc/china-chine/initialEA-china-EEinitiale.aspx?lang=eng> accessed 16 December 2020

3.15 Canadian EA of Canada-Andean Trade Agreement

DFAIT, 'Initial Environmental Assessment of the Canada-Andean Community Free Trade Agreements' (21 February 2008) <https://www.international.gc.ca/trade-agreements-accords-commerciaux/agr-acc/peru-perou/ea-andean-andine.aspx?lang=eng > accessed 16 December 2020

3.16 Canadian EA of Canada-Korea Trade Agreement

DFAIT, 'Initial Environmental Assessment of the Canada-Korea Free Trade Agreement' (16 November 2007) <http://www.international.gc.ca/trade-agreements-accords-commerciaux/agr-acc/korea-coree/ea-korea-coree.aspx> accessed 16 December 2020

3.17 Canadian EA of Canada-Peru Investment Agreement

DFAIT, 'Final Environmental Assessment of the Canada-Peru Foreign Investment Promotion and Protection Agreement' (3 July 2007) <https://www.international.gc.ca/trade-agreements-accords-commerciaux/agr-acc/peru-perou/finalEA-FIPA-EEfinale.aspx?lang=eng> accessed 16 December 2020

3.18 Canadian EA of Canada-India Investment Agreement

DFAIT, 'Initial Environmental Assessment of the Canada-India Foreign Investment Promotion and Protection Agreement' (25 June 2007) <https://www.international.gc.ca/trade-agreements-accords-commerciaux/agr-acc/india-inde/finalEA-FIPA-EEfinale.aspx?lang=eng> accessed 16 December 2020

3.19 Canadian EA of Canada-Colombia & Canada-Peru Trade Agreement

DFAIT, 'Final Environment Assessment of the Canada-Colombia and Canada-Peru Free Trade Agreement' (FTA) Negotiations <https://www.international.gc.ca/trade-agreements-accords-commerciaux/agr-acc/peru-perou/final-ea-colombia-peru-ee-finale-colombie-perou.aspx?lang=eng> accessed 16 December 2020

3.20 Canadian EA of Canada-Singapore Trade Agreement

DFAIT, 'Initial Environmental Assessment of the Canada-Singapore Free Trade Negotiations' (14 May 2004) <https://www.international.gc.ca/trade-agreements-accords-commerciaux/agr-acc/singapore-singapour/singapore-ea-singapour.aspx?lang=eng> accessed 16 December 2020

3.21 Canadian EA of Canada-CA4 Trade Agreement

DFAIT, 'Initial Environmental Assessment of the Canada-CA-4 Free Trade Negotiations' (18 June 2003)

3.22 Canadian EA of Free Trade Agreement of the Americas

DFAIT, 'Environmental Assessment of Free Trade Area of the Americas Negotiations' (5 May 2003)

3.23 Canadian EA of WTO Doha Round Negotiations

DFAIT, 'Initial Environmental Assessment of Negotiations at the World Trade Organization' (22 November 2002) <https://www.international.gc.ca/trade-agreements-accords-commerciaux/wto-omc/EA-init-EE.aspx?lang=eng> accessed 16 December 2020

3.24 Canadian EA of WTO Uruguay Round Trade Negotiations

DFAIT, 'Canadian Environmental Review of the Uruguay Round of Trade Negotiations' (DFAIT, Ottawa November 1994)

4. Impact Assessments of the United Kingdom of Great Britain and Northern Ireland Trade Agreements

4.1 UK Impact Assessment of the UK-Japan Comprehensive Economic Partnership

Department for International Trade, 'Final Impact Assessment of the Agreement between the United Kingdom of Great Britain and Northern Ireland and Japan for a Comprehensive Economic Partnership' (DIT, London, 2020) https://assets.publishing.service.gov.uk/government/uploads/system/uploads/attachment_data/file/965154/UK-Japan-impact-assessment-comprehensive-economic-parternship.pdf accessed 26 March 2021

5. Inter-Governmental Reports on Trade and Investment Impact Assessment

Commission for Environmental Cooperation (1999) Final Analytical Framework for Assessing the Effects of the North American Free Trade Agreement (NAFTA), Montreal Commission for Environmental Cooperation (2005) Proceedings of the Third North American Symposium on Assessing the Environmental Effects of Trade, Montreal 30 November–1 December 2005, CEC, Montreal DG Trade (2003) Sustainability Impact Assessments of Trade Agreements: Towards Joined Up Thinking. Report of Proceedings. Brussels: DG Trade

EC (2005a) Impact Assessment Guidelines. SEC(2005) 791. Brussels: EC

EC (2005a) Presentation of the SIA Process: The Case of Market Access, Environmental Services and Competition in the WTO negotiations.

European Commission (2002a) Sustainability Impact Assessment, Directorate General for Trade, European Commission, Brussels,

European Commission (2002b) Communication from the Commission on Impact Assessment, COM(2002) 276, Commission of the European Communities, Brussels

European Commission (2003) SIA of Trade Agreements-Making Trade Sustainable? DG TRADE Seminar, 6–7 February 2003

European Commission (2005) Impact Assessment Guidelines, SEC(2005)791, Brussels

European Commission (2006a) Handbook for Trade Sustainability Impact Assessment, DG Trade, Brussels

European Commission (2006b) Sustainability Impact Assessment: EU Trade SIA Stocktaking Conference: Agenda and speeches,

European Commission (2006c) Impact Assessment in Practice, Brussels,

OECD (1994) Methodologies for Environmental and Trade Reviews, Paris: OECD.

OECD (1997) The OECD Report on Regulatory Reform: Synthesis, Paris: OECD.

OECD (2007) Environment and Regional Trade Agreements, Paris: OECD.

UNEP/CBD (2003), The Impact of Trade Liberalisation on Agricultural Biological Diversity: A Synthesis of Assessment Frameworks, UNEP/CBD/COP/7/INF/15, United Nations, Kuala Lumpur

United Nations Economic Commission, Application of Environmental Impact Assessment Principles to Policies, Plans and Programmes ECE/ENVWA/27

UNEP (2006) Economics and Trade Branch Bulletin, Issue No 20, Geneva,

UNEP/MAP (2005) Mediterranean Strategy for Sustainable Development, UNEP(DEC)/MED WG. 277/4, United Nations Environment Programme Mediterranean Action Plan, Athens

UNEP/CBD (2003), The Impact of Trade Liberalisation on Agricultural Biological Diversity: A Synthesis of Assessment Frameworks, UNEP/CBD/COP/7/INF/15, United Nations, Kuala Lumpur

UNEP/MAP (2005) Mediterranean Strategy for Sustainable Development, UNEP (DEC)/MED WG. 277/4, United Nations Environment Programme Mediterranean Action Plan, Athens

World Bank-IMF (2005) Global Monitoring Report 2005: Millennium Development Goals: From Consensus to Momentum. Washington DC: IMF and World Bank

TO, WT/CTE/W/227 29 April 2003 (03-2243) Committee on Trade and Environment Paragraph 33 of the Doha Declaration Submission by the United States

WTO, WT/CTE/W/37 23 July 1996 (96-2906) Committee on Trade and Environment Environmental Review Of Trade Agreements At The National Level Communication from the United States

WTO, WT/CTE/W/224 21 February 2003 (03-1115) Committee on Trade and Environment Sustainability Impact Assessment Of Trade Agreements: Making Trade Sustainable? DG Trade Seminar in Brussels, 6–7 February 2003

WTO,WT/COMTD/W/99, WT/CTE/W/208, TN/TE/W/3 3 June 2002 (02-3034) Committee on Trade and Development, Committee on Trade and Environment, Committee on Trade and Environment—Special Session Sustainability Impact Assessment Communication from the European Communities

WTO, C George and C Kirkpatrick, 'Putting the Doha Principles into Practice: The Role of Sustainability Impact Assessment' in H Katrak and R Strange (eds), *The WTO and Developing Countries* (Basingstoke, Palgrave Macmillan, 2004)

WTO, C George and C Kirkpatrick, (2004b) 'Trade and Development: Assessing the Impact of Trade Liberalisation on Sustainable Development' Journal of World Trade, 38(3)

WTO, C George and C Kirkpatrick, (2006) 'Assessing National Sustainable Development Strategies: Strengthening the Links to Operational Policy' Natural Resources Forum, 30,144–154

WTO, C George and C Kirkpatrick, (2006) 'Methodological issues in the impact assessment of trade policy: Experience from the European Commission's SIA programme', Impact Assessment and Project Appraisal, special issue on trade impact assessment, December 2006

WTO, C George and N Lee, (2002) Further Development of the Methodology for the Sustainability Impact Assessment of the Proposed WTO Negotiations. Final Report to DG Trade. Manchester, IDPM (www.sia-trade.org)

WTO, C George and N Lee, (2002) Further Development of the Methodology for a Sustainability Impact Assessment of Proposed WTO Negotiations (Final Report), Manchester, IDPM

WTO, C George and N Lee, (2002) Further Development of the Methodology for a Sustainability Impact Assessment of Proposed WTO Negotiations (Final Report), Manchester, IDPM

WTO, P Lamy (2005) 'Trade Can be a Friend, not a Foe, of Conservation'. Speech at WTO Symposium on Trade and Sustainable Development. 10-11 October 2005 <https://www.wto.org/english/news_e/sppl_e/sppl07_e.htm> accessed 16 December 2020

ANNEX 2

Sustainable Development Measures In Bilateral and Regional Economic Agreements

Partner Countries	Signature	SD Purpose	SD Exceptions	SD Cooperation	SD Enhancement	SD Process	Notes
1. Andean-MERCOSUR http://www.sice.oas.org/Trade/mrcsrac/eca_s.asp	18 October 2004	No (harmonic dev, ec + soc dev, quality life)	No	No-I art 1 harmonic dev, XX art 37, XXI art 38 sci & tech	No	No info	ALADI approach but even more minimal, no mention of enviro, health, SD
2. Bolivia-MERCOSUR http://www.sice.oas.org/Trade/mrcsbo/merbo_s.asp	17 December 1996	No (ec + soc dev, quality life)	No	No-I art 1 harmonic dev, XXVI art 38 s&t	XXI art 28 Enviro Commercial Accords	No info	ALADI approach. Art 23 TBT enviro is barrier, Annex VIII SPS health is barrier
3. Bolivia-Mexico http://www.sice.oas.org/trade/mexbo_s/mbind.asp	17 May 2010	Preamble (harmonic dev, enviro, labour, SD)	Art 14–18 procure; 15–14 not lower env stand invest; art 20 general excepts XX;	No	Art 4-06 Fisheries subsidies phase-out	No info	NAFTA approach. Art 13–11,12,13 TBT health, enviro + toxic waste defers to UN

Partner Countries	Signature	SD Purpose	SD Exceptions	SD Cooperation	SD Enhancement	SD Process	Notes
4. Canada-Chile http://www.sice.oas.org/trade/chican_e/chcatoc.asp	5 December 1996	Preamble (enviro, labour, SD)	Art A-04 relation to MEAs; art G-14,15 not lower env standard invest + energy regs; art O-01 excepts GATT XX;	SD in Env Side Agreemt w Preamble; art 1; art 2.3 consider DPGs; art 10 MBIs, art 8–18 CEC, Factual, JPAC; 40 other MEAs-No SD in Lab Side Agreemt	Env Side Agreemt; art 2 promote use of MBIs for env, but defs env law not NRs	EA, Public Participation, Consultations	NAFTA approach. SD becomes subset of Enviro Agreement
5. Canada-Costa Rica http://www.sice.oas.org/Trade/cancr/English/cancrin.asp	23 April 2001	Preamble (enviro, labour, SD)	Art I.4 relation to MEAs; art XIV.1 excepts GATT XX	SD in Env Side Agreemt w Preamble; art 1; art 8 Cooperation in Annex 1; art 17 other MEAs	Env Side Agreemt; art 19 defs env law not NRs	EA, Public Participation, Consultations	NAFTA approach. A parallel FIPA was signed, with text on not lowering enviro standards
6. Canada-EFTA http://www.sice.oas.org/Trade/CAN_EFTA_FTA/canefta_in.asp	26 January 2008	Preamble (harmonious development, labour, mutual supp t&e for SD)	Art 22 General Exceptions XX GATT	No	No	In Canada EA, public participation period; consults & inter-agency negotiations. In EFTA, usual process used.	EFTA approach. Very simple + economic only, not much beyond WTO.

7. Canada-Peru http://www.sice.oas.org/TPD/AND_CAN/Final_Texts_CAN_PER_e/index_e.asp	29 May 2008	Preamble (enviro, labour, poverty, SD, CSR)	Ch 2201 General Exceptions XX GATT; Ch 6 SPS art 603 except enviro emergencies; 809 Invest not lower standards; ESA art 2.4 t&i not weaken enviro laws	Ch 17 Enviro, 1701 sust use of resources, 1702 Agree on sust use of biodiv; ESA Preamble (promote SD); Ch 16 Labour, no SD; Annex 18-A Cooperative Labour Activities	810 Invest encourage CSR; ESA art 2.6 encourage trade in EGS; ESA art 5 CBD Sust use of biodiv, ESA art 6 CSR; ESA Annex 1 on EGS & clean tech; Labour SA, no SD	In Canada EA, public participation period; consults & inter-agency negotiations. In Peru, consultations & inter-agency review	NAFTA approach. After US-Peru, includes Enviro Chapter w/in FTA text, also Enviro Side Agreement, with SD as sub-set. Further Case Study
8. Canada-Mexico-United States (NAFTA) http://www.sice.oas.org/Trade/NAFTA/NAFTATCE.ASP	17 December 1992	Preamble (env, labour, SD)	Art 104 MEAs; art 1114 Not lower env standards invest; art 2101 GATT art XX	ESA, art 1(b), art 10.2; CEC, Factual Review & JPAC; Current CEC Agenda on Biodiv & Low-Carbon Economy; LSA, No SD	No	EA in US, Public Particip in US/Can, Inter-agency review in US/Can/Mex	NAFTA approach. Obviously. SD as sub-set of Enviro Side Agreement

(Continued)

Partner Countries	Signature	SD Purpose	SD Exceptions	SD Cooperation	SD Enhancement	SD Process	Notes
9. Canada-Ukraine https://www.international.gc.ca/trade-commerce/trade-agreements-accords-commerciaux/agr-acc/ukraine/text-texte/toc-tdm.aspx?lang=eng	11 July 2016	Preamble (env, labour, SD); art 12.2 Context and Objectives	Art 12.3 Levels of Protection; art 12.5 Non-derogation from environmental obligations; art 13.4 Non-derogation from labour obligations; art 18.2 General Exceptions	Annex 1-A MEAs; Ch 12 Environment, art 12.4 Compliance with and Enforcement of Environmental Laws, art 12.6 EIA, 12.14 Party-to-Party Information Exchange, art 12.15 Cooperative Activities, art 12.16 Committee on the Environment; Ch 13 Labour, art 13.11 Labour Cooperation, arts 13.13–14 Consultations, art 13.20 Cooperation with International and Regional Organization, Annex 13-A Cooperative Activities; art 15.1 Trade-Related Cooperation (SD reference)	Art 12.11 Measures to Enhance Environmental Performance; art 13.3 General Labour Commitments	Art 12.7 Public Awareness, art 12.8 Private Access to Remedies, art 12.9 Procedural Guarantees, art 12.10 Corporate Social Responsibility, art 12.12 National Contact Point, art 12.13 Public Information and Accountability, art 12.18 Public Engagement; art 13.8 Public Information and Awareness; Ch 14 Transparency	NAFTA approach. Separate labour and environment chapters

10. Canada-Colombia https://www.international.gc.ca/trade-commerce/trade-agreements-accords-commerciaux/agr-acc/colombia-colombie/fta-ale/index.aspx?lang=eng	21 November 2008	Preamble (enviro, law, SD), art 1801(d) SD with an emphasis on SMEs	Art 1702 Not lower env standards, art 2201 General Exceptions GATT	Ch 17 Enviro Side Agreement, art 1701 MEAs, sust use of resources, 1703 sust use of biodiversity, ESA art 1703 f coop on advancement of enviro issues	Ch 8 art 816 Encourage CSR	In Canada EA, public participation period; consults & inter-agency negotiations. Colombia—No info	NAFTA approach, includes Enviro Side Agreement, with SD in content
11. Canada-Jordan https://www.international.gc.ca/trade-commerce/trade-agreements-accords-commerciaux/agr-acc/jordan-jordanie/fta-ale/index.aspx?lang=eng	28 June 2009	Preamble	Ch 15 Exceptions	Art 1.5 Hierarchy of MEAs; Annex 1.5 MEAs; art 6.3 Cooperation on Trade (no reference to SD)	Ch 10 Environment; Ch 11 Labour	Ch 12 Transparency; in Canada EA, public participation period; consults & inter-agency negotiations resulting in an In-depth EA report	NAFTA approach, with Environment and Labour Chapters

(*Continued*)

Partner Countries	Signature	SD Purpose	SD Exceptions	SD Cooperation	SD Enhancement	SD Process	Notes
12. Canada-Korea https://www.international.gc.ca/trade-commerce/trade-agreements-accords-commerciaux/agr-acc/korea-coree/fta-ale/index.aspx?lang=eng&_ga=2.248606275.516175561.1568928682-646687167.1568928682	11 March 2014	Preamble (enviro, law, labour, SD)	Art 22.1 General Exceptions, GATT, art 8.10 & art 17.5 Non-Derogation from Enviro standards	Art 17.3, art 1.3 & Annex 1A MEAs, Preamble Cooperation on Enviro issues, art 17.10 coop on trade-related aspects of enviro issues	Art 17.4 Promote trade in EGS, art 8.16 Encourage CSR, art 17.3 & Annex 17A EAC established	In Canada EA, public participation period; consults & inter-agency negotiations resulting in an in-depth EA report	NAFTA approach, with Environment Chapter
13. Canada-Honduras https://www.international.gc.ca/trade-commerce/trade-agreements-accords-commerciaux/agr-acc/honduras/fta-ale/index.aspx?lang=eng	5 November 2015	Preamble (enviro, law, labour, SD); art 18.1 Affirmation of environmental conservation and sustainable use of resources	Ch 22 Exceptions, art 22.2 General Exceptions	Ch 18 Environment, arts 18.2–3 Agreement on Environmental Cooperation; Ch 19 Labour, art 19.3 Labour Obligations, art 19.4 Cooperative Activities	Ch 18 Environment; Ch 19 Labour	Ch 20 Transparency (anti-corruption, provision of information)	NAFTA approach, includes Enviro Side Agreement, with SD in content

14. Canada-Panama https://www.international.gc.ca/trade-commerce/trade-agreements-accords-commerciaux/agr-acc/panama/fta-ale/index.aspx?lang=eng	14 May 2010	Preamble; art 17.01 Affirmations (environmental conservation and sustainable use of resources)	Ch 23 Exceptions, art 23.03 General Exceptions (GATT and GATS reference)	Ch 17 Environment, arts 17.02–3 Agreement on the Environment; Ch 18 Labour, art 18.03 Obligations, art 18.04 Cooperative Activities; Ch 19 Trade-related cooperation	Ch 17 Environment, Ch 18 Labour	Ch 20 Transparency and anti-corruption	NAFTA approach, separate Environment and Labour Chapters, includes Enviro Side Agreement, with SD in content
15. CARICOM-Costa Rica http://www.sice.oas.org/trade/crcrcom_e/crcrcomind_e.asp	9 March 2004	Preamble (env, labour, SD)	Article XVI.01 General Exceptions GATT art XX	No	No	Inter-agency review in CARICOM & CR	NAFTA approach. Less deep, no Enviro Chapter or ESA. SD as Preamble only?
16. CARICOM-Dominican Republic http://www.sice.oas.org/Trade/Ccdr/English/Ccdr_in.asp	22 August 1998	No, only econ dev x4	Annex I TBT art I & art IV legitimate objectives (SD); TBT art II.2 affirms other intl treaties; Annex II SPS art I.3 except measures; Annex III Invest Preamble	Art IX econ coop in sectors	No		ALADI approach. Minimalist economic focus.

(*Continued*)

Partner Countries	Signature	SD Purpose	SD Exceptions	SD Cooperation	SD Enhancement	SD Process	Notes
17. CARIFORUM-European Union EPA http://www.sice.oas.org/Trade/CAR_EU_EPA_e/careu_in_e.ASP	15 October 2008	Preamble (SDx4) & Trade Partnership for SD art 1 Objective; art 3 SD;	Ch 4 Enviro 184 Right to Regulate-188 Not lower standards; Ch 5 Social 192 Right to Regulate-193 Not lower standards; Part V art 224 General Exceptions (like GATT)	Arts 31, 41, 43 Cooperation 2(c); art 136(e) sci & tech SD; art 138 eco-innovation & renewable energy; art 150 IPRs Sust use of biodiv, genetic resources, TK; Ch 4 Enviro art 183–190 SD Context	Ch 4 Services art 83.26 Enviro Services; Ch 5 arts 37, 40 Agriculture SD; TBT art 45 Improve Standards; art 115–117 SD in Tourism; Ch 5 Social art 191 Social & SD, art 194 regional co-operation, art 25 Safeguard measures	SIA, public participation; consultations & inter-agency negotiations in Caribbean and in EU.	EU approach, very new and comprehen-sive. Further Case Study of SD measures addressing all 3 tensions
18. CA-Chile http://www.sice.oas.org/trade/chi-cam/chicamin.asp	18 October 1999	Preamble (trade & enviro, SD)	Art 104(3) Relation w MEAs; art 2002 General Exceptions (GATT XX)	No	No	Inter-agency consultations; private sector participation	NAFTA ap-proach. Less deep, no Enviro Chapter or ESA. SD as Preamble only

19. CA-Dominican http://www.sice.oas.org/trade/camdrep/indice.asp	16 April 1998	Preamble (trade & enviro, SD)	Art 9.15 Adopt/maintain enviro standards; art 17.01 General Exceptions (GATT XX); art 10.07 Services Env Exceptions; art 13.13 TBT Hazard Waste & Env Exceptions	No	No	No information	NAFTA approach. Less deep, no Enviro Chapter or ESA. SD as Preamble only
20. CA-Dominican-United States http://www.sice.oas.org/Trade/CAFTA/CAFTADR_e/CAFTADRin_e.asp	5 August 2004	Preamble (labour, enviro + SD)	9.14 Gov Procurement Exceptions; 10.11 Investment & Enviro; 17.2 Relation to MEAs; 21.1 GATT Exceptions	Ch 17 Enviro enviro & SD coop; ECA Annex 17.9 - LCA Capacity Mech Annex 16.4 No SD	ECA Annex 17.9 f, g, h on SD	ER, inter-agency consultations in US. Private sector particip in both	NAFTA approach. SD as sub-set of Enviro Chapter & Enviro Coop Agreement. Case Study
21. CA-Panama http://www.sice.oas.org/Trade/Capan/indice.asp	6 March 2002	Preamble (employment, econo + enviro =SD)	Art 104.3 Relation to MEAs; art 10.15 Investment not lower enviro stands; art 21.02 GATT + GATS Exceptions	Art 8.05-8.07 SPS cooperation;	No	No info	NAFTA approach. Less deep, no Enviro Chapter or ESA. SD as Preamble only

(*Continued*)

Partner Countries	Signature	SD Purpose	SD Exceptions	SD Cooperation	SD Enhancement	SD Process	Notes
22. Chile-Australia http://www.sice.oas.org/Trade/CHL_AUS_Final_e/CHL_AUSind_e.asp	30 July 2008	Preamble (soc + econ benefits, efficient use of resources, enviro conservation + SD)	Art 15.12(6) Gov Procurement not prevent enviro + nat resources tech specs; art 22.1 GATT + GATS Excepts	Art 18 Enviro, Labour and Other Cooperation with Coop Comm	Art 18.2 Brief ref to cooperation for sectors development, labour, enviro	Public particip, consultations, inter-agency collaboration in Chile & Aus	NAFTA approach but more modern. SD mainly sub-set of Enviro
23. Chile-China http://fta.mofcom.gov.cn/chile/xieyi/freetradexieding2.pdf	18 November 2005	Preamble (stand liv, job opps & SD consistent w enviro conservation)	Art 99 GATT XX mutatis; No invest Ch	Art 104–107 Coop on econo + soc dev; art 108 Social & Enviro Coop; 109 SMEs; Chile-China ECA: MOU on Labour + Social Security, No SD	Art 113 Mining Coop	Inter-agency collaboration, consultations in Chile, No info on China	China approach with elements of EU & NAFTA. No copies of ECA available, SD may be sub-set of Enviro
24. Chile-Colombia http://www.sice.oas.org/Trade/CHL_COL_FTA/CHL_COL_ind_s.asp	27 November 2006	Preamble (social capital, SD, enviro+trade SD); Objectives 1.2 t+e mutal sup SD of nat res + ecosystems	Ch 9 Investment, 9.6 exception (GATT), 9.13 not lower env stands; 21.1 General Exception (GATT)	Ch 18 Enviro, 18.1 objective of SD; 18.3 (4) Cooperation on green markets, etc;	Ch 19 Cooperation 19.5 Economic energy dev	IA, public particip, inter-agency, consultations in Chile. Studies & inter-agency in Colombia	NAFTA approach w elements of EU. SD as new form of econ dev

25. Chile-EFTA http://www.sice.oas.org/trade/Chi-EFTA_e/ChiEFTAind_e.asp	26 June 2003	Preamble (enviro + SD, workers, etc)	Art 21 General Excepts (GATT), art 44 Excepts for Services/Est (GATS), art 70 Excepts for Procurement (human, animal, no NR)	No	No	Public particip, inter-agency, consultations in Chile. EFTA usual channels	EFTA approach. Very minimalist, SD in Preamble only
26. Chile-EU http://www.sice.oas.org/Trade/chieu_e/cheuin_e.asp	18 November 2002	Preamble, SD principle, Ch 1 art 1 Principles (principle of SD), Objective too	Art 91 General Exceptions (human/animal, nat res); Invest, art 133 Right to Regulate, art 135 (GATS style); Annexes II + III soc, env + other reservations	Part III, art 16 Objectives of Cooperation; 28 Enviro; arts 43–45 Social Cooperation	Cooperation on 19 SMEs, 22 Energy, 23 Transport, 24 Agriculture, 25 Fisheries MOU; 34 Tourism; 35 Mining	SIA, public particip, inter-agency, consultations in Chile & EU	EU approach. A bit dated, but Case Study of SD measures addressing all 3 tensions
27. Chile-Japan http://www.sice.oas.org/TPD/CHL_JPN/Draft27_03_2007_e/Index_e.asp	27 March 2007	Preamble (econ for SD)	Preamble (Right to regulate); art 151 Procurement Exceptions	No	Impl Agreement Working Group on Fish and Fishery Products	Public particip, inter-agency, consultations in Chile. Japan used usual channels	Japan approach. Very minimal, SD in Preamble only, w a few modern updates

(*Continued*)

Partner Countries	Signature	SD Purpose	SD Exceptions	SD Cooperation	SD Enhancement	SD Process	Notes
28. Chile-Korea http://www.sice.oas.org/Trade/Chi-SKorea_e/ChiKoreaind_e.asp	15 February 2003	Preamble (new work, living standards, SD consistent w enviro)	Art 20.1 General Exceptions (GATT+GATS); art 10.9 Invest exceptions, 10.18 (Not lower env stands for invest); Annex II+III soc, env + other reservations	No	No	Public particip, inter-agency, consultations in Chile	Japan approach. Very minimal, SD in Preambly only, a few modern updates
29. Chile-MERCOSUR http://www.sice.oas.org/Trade/msch/mschind.asp	25 June 1996	No (ec + soc dev, quality life)	Art 49 GATT XX + XXI	Arts 44–45 S + T cooperation	No	Public particip, inter-agency, consultations in Chile	ALADI approach. No mention of SD
30. Chile-Mexico http://www.sice.oas.org/trade/chmefta/indice.asp	17 April 1998	Preamble (trade & enviro, SD)	Art 1-106 Relation w MEAs; arts 9--5 Invest Not lower enviro stands; 19-02 General Excepts GATT XX + GATS; Annex II+III soc, env + other reservations	No	No	Public particip, inter-agency, consultations in Chile	NAFTA approach but more minimal, w no real enviro cooperation or SD.

31. Chile-New Zealand, Singapore and Brunei Darussalam (P4) (Trans-Pacific Strategic Economic Partnership Agreement) http://www.sice.oas.org/Trade/CHL_Asia_e/TransPacific_ind_e.asp	18 July 2005	Preamble (enviro + labour cooperation, integrate soc, env+econ=SD); ECA Preamble (SDx3)	Preamble (right to regulate, flexibility for public); 11.22 Procurement exceptions GATT; Ch 19 General Exceptions 19.1.2 GATT XX and GATS; No invest agree	16 Strategic Partnership; 16.8 Primary industry agriculture + forestry cooperation; ECA cooperate, comply enviro laws, consult; MOU on labour, No SD	No	Public particip, inter-agency, consultations in Chile No info on others.	NAFTA and EU approaches combined, cooperation focus, not too detailed
32. Chile-Peru http://www.sice.oas.org/Trade/CHL_PER_FTA/Index_s.asp	22 August 2006	No (econo dev, enviro, employ); 1.2 Objectives (1a. harmonic + equitable development)	10.6 Tech regs health + env legitimate objective; 11.13 Invest not lower env stands, also Annex 11-D 3b) no indirect expropriation; 17.1 General Exceptions GATT XX and GATS XXI; Annex II + III soc, env + other reservations	Annex 9.2.2 AgroFisheries Accord w biosafety coop; Migratory Workers Rights Accord; No SD	Not on SD, 18.1 Commercial cooperation, inc energy, transport, etc	Public particip, inter-agency, consultations in Chile. Public debates in Peru	NAFTA and ALADI approaches combined, minimalist but includes Investment liberalisation, some innovations

(*Continued*)

Partner Countries	Signature	SD Purpose	SD Exceptions	SD Cooperation	SD Enhancement	SD Process	Notes
33. Chile-Panama http://www.sice.oas.org/Trade/CHL_PAN_FTA/Index_s.asp	27 June 2006	Preamble (enviro, workers, SD)	14 General Exceptions GATT XX and GATS XXI; Annex II + III soc, env + other reservations	No	No	Public particip, inter-agency, consultations in Chile No info on Panama	NAFTA approach. Less, with no Enviro Chapter or ESA, SD only in Preamble
34. Chile-United States http://www.sice.oas.org/Trade/chiusa_e/chiusaind_e.asp	06 June 2003	Preamble (enviro, labour, SD)	1.3 Existing rights in treaties; 9.16 Procurement human, animal, plant Exceptions; 10.12 Invest + enviro, not constrained from env laws; 23.1 General Exceptions GATT XX and GATS	Enviro Chapter w cooperation mechs + env not NR law support; 19.10 CSR Labour; Chapter w no SD; E&L Side Accords	Enviro Side Agreement Annex 19.3 clean fuels, agriculture + mining; art 19.10 CSR Promotion	Public Particip, inter-agency, consultations in Chile Public Particip, inter-agency, consultations in Chile	NAFTA approach. SD as sub-set of Enviro Cooperation, but several provisions to address tensions. Case Study
35. Chile-Turkey http://www.sice.oas.org/Trade/CHL_TUR_Final/Text_FTA_e.pdf	14 July 2009	Preamble	Art 37(7) no prejudice to labour laws; art 56 General Exceptions (art XX GATT reference); art 57 Security Exceptions	Art 37 Cooperation (reference to SD, labour, education, gender issues, SMEs and enviro protection and international enviro and ILO obligations, biodiversity)	No	Art 37 Cooperation on public participation; art 52 Cooperation on Increased Transparency	No SD or environment chapter, but a very extensive cooperation clause envisaging SD, labour and biodiversity issues.

36. China-Korea http://fta.mofcom.gov.cn/korea/annex/xdzw_en.pdf	1 June 2015	Preamble (enviro, SD)	Art 12.16 Non relaxation of environmental measures; art 15.15 Exclusion of patentability if serious prejudice to environment, animal or plant life; art 16.2 Levels of Protection	Ch 16 Environment and Trade, art 16.4 MEAs, art 16.5 Enforcement of Environmental Measures, art 16.6 EIA, art 16.7 Bilateral Cooperation, art 16.8 Institutional and Financial Arrangement; Ch 17 Economic Cooperation, art 17.1 Objective to enhance sustainable trade and investment opportunities, art 17.6 Fisheries Cooperation, art 17.8 Steel Cooperation, art 17.9 SME Cooperation, art 17.10 Information and Tech Cooperation, art 17.11 Cooperation in Textile	Ch 16 Environment and Trade; Ch 17 Economic Cooperation, art 17.5 Food Security, art 17.7 Forestry	Art 17.14 Transparency in Govt Procurement	

(*Continued*)

Partner Countries	Signature	SD Purpose	SD Exceptions	SD Cooperation	SD Enhancement	SD Process	Notes
37. China-Peru http://www.sice.oas.org/TPD/PER_CHN/Texts_28042009_e/FullText_20090422_e.pdf	28 April 2009	Preamble (enviro, SD)	Art 193 General Exceptions GATT	Art 152 (2e) Science & Tech cooperation for SD, art 154 Education Cooperation, art 155 Cooperation for SME development, art 156 Cultural Cooperation, art 161 Labour coop, art 162 Coop on Forestry and Enviro, art 163 Increasing scientific knowledge by research projects, art 164(a) sustainable rural dev, arts 18, 20	Art 16 Elimination of Export Subsidies	No info	No Enviro chapter or ESA
38. Chinese Taipei-Nicaragua http://www.sice.oas.org/Trade/NIC_TWN/NIC_TWN_e/TWN_NIC_full_text_06_16_09.pdf	16 June 2006	Preamble (eco + social dev, enviro, labour, SD)	Art 19.02 Non-Derogation & effective enforcement of enviro laws, art 10.1 Investment & Environment	Art 19.08 & Annex 19.08 Enviro coop, art 19.09 Enviro consultation, art 19.10 MEAs	Art 18.06 & 19.05 encourage Corp stewardship, art 19.04 Voluntary Mechanisms, art 19.06 EAC established, Annex 19.08 8(i) encourage trade in EGS	No Info	

39. Colombia-Mexico (G3 after Venezuela's withdrawal) http://www.sice.oas.org/Trade/go3/G3INDICE.ASP	13 June 1994	Preamble (harmonic dev, employ, SD)	15.19 Procurement Exceptions human, animal, plant; 17.13 Invest not lower env standards; 22.01 General Exceptions GATT XX	Art 14-13 TBT Standards supports cooperation for protection of health	No-Art 4.04 many measures to promote Automotive Sector, art 4.05 w Annex 2 of 4.02 on catalytic converters	No info	NAFTA and ALADI approach combined. Focus on key sectors, but not for SD
40. Colombia-EFTA https://www.efta.int/media/documents/legal-texts/free-trade-relations/colombia/EFTA-Colombia%20Free%20Trade%20Agreement%20EN.pdf	25 November 2008	Preamble	Art 7.3 Exceptions	No	Art 6.5 Measures related to Biodiversity (conservation and sustainable use of biological and genetic resources of indigenous communities); art 6.9 exclusion of patentability for environmental reasons	No	Minimalist, focused on economic agenda

(*Continued*)

Partner Countries	Signature	SD Purpose	SD Exceptions	SD Cooperation	SD Enhancement	SD Process	Notes
41. Costa Rica-Mexico http://www.sice.oas.org/trade/Mexcr_s/mcrind.asp	5 April 1994	Preamble (harmonic, enviro, labour, SD)	Art 9.16 Services Exceptions (GATS, human, animal, plant health, no NR); art 12.8 Procurement (GATS); art 11.5 TBT (defers to Basel Convention); art 13.15 Investment (not lower enviro standards, no constraint); art 18.01 General Exceptions (GATT + GATS)	No	No-art 4.05, 4.06 limit internal/export subsidies for agrofisheries	No info	NAFTA and ALADI approaches combined, w a few exceptions. No ESA and SD mainly in Preamble
42. Costa Rica-China Free Trade Agreement http://www.sice.oas.org/Trade/CRI_CHN_FTA/Texts_Apr2010_e/CRI_CHN_ToC_e.asp	8 April 2011	Preamble (s of living, employ, SD); art 2 Objectives, 2.1(f)	Art 159 General Exceptions (GATT mutatis)	No	No	No info	China approach. Very minimalist trade accord w SD

43. Costa Rica-Singapore http://www.sice.oas.org/Trade/CRI_SGP_FTA/Text_e.asp#Preamble	6 April 2010	Preamble; art 1.2 Objectives	Art 8.21 Exceptions; art 18.2 General Exceptions (GATT and GATS reference)	Art 14.8 Environmental Cooperation, art 14.9 Labour Cooperation	Art 13.3 Sustainable use of Genetic resources and traditional knowledge	Art 8.1 SD in Government Procurement; Transparency (Preamble)	Some SD provisions without a separate chapter
44. The Treaty for the Establishment of the East African Community (EAC) https://www.eacj.org/?page_id=33	30 November 1999	Preamble; art 5 Objectives	No info	Ch 13 Cooperation in Standardisation; Ch 14 Monetary and Financial Cooperation; Ch 19 Cooperation in Environment and Natural Resources Management; Ch 22 Cooperation in Wildlife Management	Ch 18 Agriculture and Food Security; art 112 Management of the Environment; art 114 Management of Natural Resources; art 120 Social Welfare; Ch 22 Enhancing the Role of Women in Socio-Economic Development	Art 127 Creation of Enabling Environment for the Private Sector and the Civil Society	No separate Trade and SD chapter, but sustainable development is referenced throughout the treaty; includes detailed cooperation provisions

(Continued)

Partner Countries	Signature	SD Purpose	SD Exceptions	SD Cooperation	SD Enhancement	SD Process	Notes
45. EFTA-Albania https://www.efta.int/sites/default/files/documents/legal-texts/free-trade-relations/Albania/EFTA-Albania-Free-Trade-Agreement.pdf	7 December 2009	Preamble (SD, enviro, labour); Art 1 Objectives; art 31 Context and Objectives	Art 21 General Exceptions (reference to GATT); art 33 Right to regulate and levels of protection, art 34 Upholding levels of protection	Ch 6 Trade and SD, art 35 International Labour Standards, art 36 MEAs, art 38 Cooperation in International Fora	Art 37 Promotion of trade and investment favouring SD	Art 39 Implementation and Consultations; transparency and good governance (Preamble)	EU approach—includes a Trade and SD Chapter
46. EFTA-Montenegro https://www.efta.int/media/documents/legal-texts/free-trade-relations/montenegro/montenegro-main-agreement.pdf	3 November 2010	Preamble (SD, enviro, labour); art 1 Objectives; art 31 Context and Objectives	Art 22 Exceptions (reference to GATT); art 24 no relaxation of environmental standards (investment); art 33 Right to regulate and levels of protection, art 34 Upholding levels of protection	Ch 6 Trade and SD, art 35 International Labour Standards, Art 36 MEAs, art 38 Cooperation in International Fora	Art 37 Promotion of trade and investment favouring SD	Art 39 Implementation and Consultations; transparency and good governance (Preamble)	EU approach—includes a Trade and SD Chapter
47. EFTA-Peru https://www.efta.int/sites/default/files/documents/legal-texts/free-trade-relations/peru/EFTA-Peru%20Free%20Trade%20Agreement%20EN.pdf	24 June 2010	Preamble (SD, enviro, labour); art 1.2 Objectives	Art 2.19 General Exceptions (reference to GATT)	Ch 6 Protection of IP, art 6.5 International Conventions (to the extent they cover SD)	Ch 6 Protection of IP, art 6.5 Measures related to Biodiversity	Transparency and anti-corruption (Preamble)	Limited SD provisions without a separate Trade and SD Chapter

48. EFTA-Serbia https://www.efta.int/sites/default/files/documents/legal-texts/free-trade-relations/serbia/EFTA-Serbia-Free-Trade-Agreement.pdf	17 December 2009	Preamble (SD, enviro, labour); art 1 Objectives; art 32 Context and Objectives	Art 22 General Exceptions (reference to GATT); art 25 no relaxation of environmental standards (investment); art 34 Right to regulate and levels of protection, art 35 Upholding levels of protection	Ch 6 Trade and SD, art 36 International Labour Standards, art 37 MEAs, art 39 Cooperation in International Fora	Art 38 Promotion of trade and investment favouring SD	Art 40 Implementation and Consultations; transparency and good governance (Preamble)	EU approach—includes a Trade and SD Chapter
49. EFTA-Ukraine https://www.efta.int/sites/default/files/documents/legal-texts/free-trade-relations/ukraine/EFTA-Ukraine%20Free%20Trade%20Agreement.pdf	24 June 2010	Preamble (SD, enviro, labour)	Art 2.17 General Exceptions (reference to GATT); art 4.8 Right to Regulate	Art 10.4 Sustainable Development (review of the agreement in accordance with SD)	No	Transparency and good governance (Preamble; art 4.9)	Very limited SD provisions without a separate Trade and SD Chapter
50. EFTA-Bosnia and Herzegovina https://www.efta.int/media/documents/legal-texts/free-trade-relations/bosnia-and-herzegovina/bosnia-and-herzegovina-fta.pdf	24 June 2013	Preamble (enviro, labour, SD); Art 33 Context and Objectives	Art 26 No relaxation of health, safety or environmental standards; art 35 Right to Regulate, art 36 Upholding Levels of Protection	Ch 6 Trade and SD, art 37 International Labour Standards, art 38 MEAs, art 40 Cooperation in International For a, art 41 Implementation and Consultations	Ch 6 Trade and SD, art 39 Promotion of Trade and Investment Favouring SD	Anti-corruption (Preamble), corporate social responsibility (Preamble)	EU approach—includes a Trade and SD Chapter

(*Continued*)

Partner Countries	Signature	SD Purpose	SD Exceptions	SD Cooperation	SD Enhancement	SD Process	Notes
51. EFTA-Central America https://www.efta.int/media/documents/legal-texts/free-trade-relations/central-america/EFTA-Central-America-free-trade-agreement.pdf	24 June 2013	Preamble (enviro, labour, SD)	Art 2.18 General Exceptions GATT, arts 9.3 & 9.4 Non-Derogation & Right to regulate	Art 9.6 MEAs, art 9.8 Work together to promote sustainable forest-based products	Art 1.2 (g) Trade for SD, art 9.7 Investment for SD, Trade in EGS, art 9.8 Trade in Sust forest products	No info	EU approach—includes a Trade and SD Chapter
52. EFTA-Georgia https://www.efta.int/sites/default/files/documents/legal-texts/free-trade-relations/georgia/EFTA-Georgia-FTA-Main-Agreement.PDF	27 June 2016	Preamble (enviro, labour SD); art 1.1 Objectives; art 10.1 Context and Objectives	Art 2.17 General exceptions (art XX GATT reference); art 6.10 General Exceptions (art XIV GATS reference); art 10.3 Right to Regulate and Levels of Protection, art 10.4 Upholding Levels of Protection	Ch 10 Trade & SD, art 10.5 International Labour Standards, art 10.7 MEAs, art 10.9 Cooperation in International Fora, art 10.10 Implementation and Consultations	Ch 10 Trade & SD, Art 10.8 Promotion of Trade and Investment favouring SD, art 10.6 Forest-based products	No info	EU approach—includes a Trade and SD Chapter
53. El Salvador-Taiwan http://www.sice.oas.org/Trade/SLV_HND_TWN_FTA_e/Index_e.asp	7 May 2007	Preamble (employ, enviro, SD)	Art 10.3.3 Relations to MEAs; art 10.16 Investment (not lower env standards, no constraint); Annex 10B.4b (enviro laws not indirect exprop); 16.02 General Exceptions (GATT, GATS)	Ch 17 Cooperation, art 17.01.2 Objectives (all cooperation, env/NR); 17.06 SMEs	Ch 17, 17.08 SD of Tourism, 17.09 SD of Energy; 17.11 Agri, Forestry, Fish, NRs, also SPS	Public particip, inter-agency, consultations in El Salvador *Check SIA?	EU approach, with innovations. SD measures to address all tensions

54. EU-Albania Stabilization and Association Agreement https://eur-lex.europa.eu/legal-content/EN/TXT/?uri=celex:22009A0428(02)	12 June 2006	No	Art 38 General Safeguard Clause (reference to GATT general exceptions)	Art 86 Cooperation Policy on sustainable economic and social development; art 99 Social cooperation; art 100 Education and training; art 101 Cultural cooperation; art 109 Cooperation in research and technological development	Art 108 Environmental sustainability	Art 4 Anti-corruption; art 111 accountable public administration	No separate Trade and SD chapter, but includes some aspects of SD in various provisions
55. EU-Bosnia and Herzegovina Stabilization and Association Agreement https://eur-lex.europa.eu/legal-content/EN/TXT/?uri=celex:22015A0630(01)	1 January 2008	Preamble	Art 39 General Safeguard clause (reference to art XIX GATT)	Art 86 Cooperation Policies (reference to SD); art 88 Statistical Cooperation; art 108 Environment (reference to cooperation policies centred on SD)	Art 49 Treatment of Workers; art 108 Environment	Art 6 Anti-corruption;	No separate Trade and SD chapter, but includes some aspects of SD in various provisions

(Continued)

Partner Countries	Signature	SD Purpose	SD Exceptions	SD Cooperation	SD Enhancement	SD Process	Notes
56. EU-Montenegro Stabilization and Association Agreement https://eur-lex.europa.eu/legal-content/EN/TXT/?uri=celex:22010A0429(01)	15 October 2007	Preamble	Art 41 Safeguards clause (reference to art XIX GATT)	Art 88 Cooperation Policies (reference to SD); art 90 Statistical Cooperation; art 111 Environment (reference to cooperation policies centred on SD)	Art 49 Treatment of Workers; art 111 Environment	Art 6 Anti-corruption;	No separate Trade and SD chapter, but includes some aspects of SD in various provisions
57. EU-Serbia Stabilization and Association Agreement https://ec.europa.eu/neighbourhood-enlargement/sites/near/files/pdf/serbia/key_document/saa_en.pdf	29 April 2008	Preamble	Art 41 Safeguards clause (reference to art XIX GATT)	Art 88 Cooperation Policies (reference to SD); art 90 Statistical Cooperation; art 111 Environment (reference to cooperation policies centred on SD); art 116 Financial Assistance (reference to SD)	Art 51 Treatment of Workers; art 111 Environment	Art 6 Anti-corruption;	No separate Trade and SD chapter, but includes some aspects of SD in various provisions

58. EU-Canada (CETA) https://ec.europa.eu/trade/policy/in-focus/ceta/ceta-chapter-by-chapter/	30 October 2016	Preamble (enviro, labour, SD)	Art 24.5 Non derogation, art 28.3 General Exceptions GATT, art 23.4 No lowering of employment standards	Art 22.3 Coop on Trade-related SD issues, art 24.4 MEAs, art 24.12 Coop on Enviro issues, art 25.4 Cooperation on Corporate Social Responsibility, art 25.5 art Cooperation on Science and Tech, art 5.11 Notification on Significant Food Safety Issues	Art 22.3 (2a) Encourage Sustainable prod of goods art 22.3 (2b) Encourage CSR, art 22.4 Establishment of CTSD, art 24.9 Trade favouring Enviro protection, art 24.10 Encourage trade in goods from Sustainably managed forests, art 24.11 Sustainable management of fisheries and aquaculture, art 24.12 (f) Trade & Inv in EGS, art 8.15.5(b) National and MFN treatment in cases of environmental disasters, Annex 19-3, note 3 Access to drinking water	SIA, public particip, inter-agency collaboration, consultations in the EU. In Canada EA, public participation period; consults & inter-agency negotiations.	Comprehensive EU approach—contains a Trade and SD chapter, a Trade and Labour chapter, as well as a Trade & Enviro chapter

(Continued)

Partner Countries	Signature	SD Purpose	SD Exceptions	SD Cooperation	SD Enhancement	SD Process	Notes
59. EU-Colombia-Peru FTA https://trade.ec.europa.eu/doclib/docs/2011/march/tradoc_147704.pdf	23 March 2011	Preamble (objective of SD, with econo, labour + enviro, other intl commits), art 4 Objectives 4(j) (contribute to SD objective + work to integrate SD in trade); Title IV, Ch 1 Services, Est, E-Commerce art 107 Objective (SD)	Ch 4 TBT art 81(d) Marking and labelling (if neccessary in view of risk to human, animal, plant, enviro); Ch 7 Trade in Goods Exceptions 106(b) human, animal, plant / (g) enviro measures & NR; Ch 7 Exceptions art 167 (b) human, animal, plant / (c) enviro measures & NR; art 174(b) Procurement Exceptions (human, animal, plant), art 181.6 Tech specs (NR, enviro); Title VII, IPRs Ch 1 art 196.4 Reaffirm rights under UN CBD; art 278 Science (precaution)	Ch 5, SPS art 87.3 animal welfare collaboration; Ch 2 Protect Biodiv & TK art 201 collaborate on ABS & genetic resources; Title IX Trade & SD; art 255 Cooperation in Science and Tech; art 267 SD Cooperation; art 268 Right to regulate & levels of protection; art 269 Labour Agreements, art 270 MEAs; art 280–285 Not fail to enforce Monitoring (Board on T&SD, Panel, Civ Soc Forum); art 324 Trade Capacity Building (SMEs, Fair Trade)	Title IV, Ch 1 Services, Est, E-Commerce art 107 Objective (SD); art 192 SMEs access to procurement; art 271 Trade favour SD; art 272 Biodiversity; art 273 Trade in Forest Products; art 274 Trade in fish products; arts 275, 276 Climate change (renewables, EGS); art 279 SIAs; art 286 Trade & SD Cooperation (REDD, UNFCCC, Biodiv, Forest Certific, Fisheries, CSR, ILA Decent Work)	SIA, public participation, inter-agency collaboration in EU, Colombia & Peru	EU approach, very new and comprehensive. Further Case Study of SD measures addressing all 3 tensions

60. EU-South Africa TDCA https://eur-lex.europa.eu/LexUriServ/LexUriServ.do?uri=OJ:L:1999:311:SOM:EN:HTML	1 January 2000	Preamble soc & econo dev only; but art 1 Objectives 1(c) sust econ & soc dev; Title IV Economic Cooperation, Objectives art 50 (SD) art 51(b) (enviro, SD + econ empower); art 65 Dev Cooperation Aims	Art 27 Exceptions (GATS-style)	Art 83 S&T Cooperation; art 84 Enviro Cooperation; art 86 Social Issues; art 92 Health	Art 53 SMEs; art 57 Energy (renewables, local); art 58 Mining & Minerals (SD, enviro tech); art 60 Tourism (Sd of local tourism); art 61 Agriculture (Sust agri); art 62 Fisheries (sust use)	Inter-agency collaboration, no info as to public participation or SIA	EU approach, with initial SD provisions addressing all 3 tensions.

(Continued)

Partner Countries	Signature	SD Purpose	SD Exceptions	SD Cooperation	SD Enhancement	SD Process	Notes
61. EU-ESA Interim EPA https://eur-lex.europa.eu/legal-content/EN/ALL/?uri=OJ:L:2012:111:TOC	24 August 2009	Preamble (SD 2x, support SD in region); art 2(a) Objectives (consistent w SD); art 36 Cooperation Objectives (sustained growth); art 40 Investment Objective (SD thru investment)	Art 56 General Exceptions	Art 27 Fisheries Cooperation, art 31 Objective of SD, art 32.2.1 precaution; art 36 Econ & Dev Cooperation, 36.1 Objectives (sustained growth); art 38(j) (mainstream enviro, trade, dev); art 49 NR & Enviro (SD, biodiv, climate, cooperation in MEA implementation); art 50 Water (SD); art 51 Enviro (MEAs +) art 52 (Financing); Annex IV Development Matrix (SD cooperation)	Ch 3 Fisheries Trade Enhanced art 25-30 (SD of fisheries), Marine Fishers art 30-32 (SD + benefits); art 33-35 Aquaculture (SD of inland fish); art 40 Investment art 40.2 (invest in SMEs); art 41 Industrial dev (SD econ, enviro, soc); art 43 Mining (enviro); art 44 (SD of tourism); art 46 Transport (sust tranport); art 47 Energy (clean + renewable); Annex IV Development Matrix (T+I enhance), art 21(2) Safeguard measures	SIA, public particip, inter-agency collaboration, consultations in partners & EU	EU approach, with comprehensive SD provisions addressing all 3 tensions.

62. EU-SADC EPA https://trade.ec.europa.eu/doclib/docs/2015/october/tradoc_153915.pdf	10 June 2016	Preamble (SD 2x, employ + invest for SD, agri + SD for poverty alleviation); Trade Partnership for SD Ch 1, art 1 Objectives (eradicate poverty for SD); art 3 SD objective integrated	Ch 13, art 90, General Exceptions (public morals, NR)	Art 4, Cooperation taking SD Strategies into account	Art 94 Joint Council functions 94 art 96.2(f) SIA, T&D Committee functions 96.6(b)5 SIAs;	SIA, public particip, inter-agency collaboration, consultations in partners & EU	EU approach, but minimalist due to interim nature. Article on continued SIAs is innovative.
63. EU-Pacific EPA https://eur-lex.europa.eu/legal-content/EN/TXT/PDF/?uri=OJ:L:2009:272:FULL&from=EN	July 2007 (PNG) 11 December 2009 (Fiji)	Preamble (2x, sus + equit dev, Cotonou); Part 1 Trade Partnership for SD; Objectives art 1(b) (promote SD and world economy); art 3 SD Objective (integration + people centred); art 46 Food Security (exception)	Art 24 General Exceptions (GATT-style); art 10(a) Customs Duties (not higher than internal, except if required for enviro protection); Ch 2 art 21 Bilateral Safeguards 21.5(b) (safeguards ok for productive + sustainable infant industries)	Art 5 Cooperation in intl fora (all where issues discussed); art 34 (cooperate to build capacity for SPS); art 69.2 Continue negotiations on development cooperation.	Art 6.6(a) Fisheries (promote sustainable fisheries management), art 6.6(b) (sustainable tuna purse seine fisheries), 6.6(d) (consultations) + 6.6(e) (combat illegal fishing)	SIA, public particip, inter-agency collaboration, consultations in partners & EU	EU approach, with comprehensive SD provisions addressing all 3 tensions.

(*Continued*)

Partner Countries	Signature	SD Purpose	SD Exceptions	SD Cooperation	SD Enhancement	SD Process	Notes
64. EU-South Korea FTA https://eur-lex.europa.eu/legal-content/EN/ALL/?uri=OJ:L:2011:127:TOC	6 October 2010	Preamble (objective of SD, with econo, soc + env dimensions), art 4 Objectives 4(j) (contribute to SD objective + work to integrate SD in trade)	Art 2.15 Exceptions trade in goods (GATT XX) art 6.1(g) Exceptions (measures facilitate trade); art 7.50 Exceptions (human, animal, plant/enviro measures & NR);	Ch 5, SPS art 5.9 (animal welfare collaboration); art 10.40 Genetic Resources (collaborate on CBD); Ch 13 Trade & SD; art 13.1 SD Cooperation; art 13.3 Right to regulate & levels of protection; art 13.4 Labour Agreements, art 13.5 MEAs; 13.6 Uphold laws; art 13.12-13.16 Not fail to enforce Monitoring (Board on T&SD, Panel, Civ Soc Forum); art 324 Trade Capacity Building (SMEs, Fair Trade) Annex 13 T&SD; 2nd Annex Enviro Regs, Urban Planning, Zoning	Art 13.10 Annex Trade & SD Cooperation; art 13.6 Trade & SD Cooperation (enviro tech, renewables, eco-labels, CSR, ILO Decent Work) art 13.10 SIAs; Annex 13 T&SD; trade enhancement in 1(f) energy efficiency & low-carbon tech, 1(g)biofuels, 1(h)sustainable fishing,1(i) illegal logging, art 10.3 Technology transfer	SIA, public particip, inter-agency collaboration, consultations in partners & EU	EU approach, with comprehensive SD provisions addressing all 3 tensions. Trade & SD Chapter provides useful definitions and focus

65. EU-Central America Association Agreement https://eur-lex.europa.eu/LexUriServ/LexUriServ.do?uri=OJ:L:2012:346:0003:2621:en:PDF	22 March 2011	Preamble (commit 4x to SD as objective, sust economic relations, partnership, NR enviro + dev); Part I Principles art 1.2 (SD as guide principle) art 2 Objectives 2(b) (SD among other objectives), 2(c) (aim of achieving more sustainable and equitable social and economic development in both regions); art 12(a) Political Dialogue Objective of SD; Part V, Title 1, art 78 Objectives art 78(j) T&I for SD; Title VIII art 284 Trade & SD	TBT art 138 Marking & Labelling (eco-labels); art 159 General Exceptions Trade in Goods (GATT XX); art 203 General Exceptions Trade in Services, Establishment, E-Commerce (like GATS but with NR); 216.6 Procurement (tech specs not prevent enviro specs)	Part II Political Dialogue on art 20 Env + SD; art 24(d) Objective econ growth for SD; Title IV social dev + social cohesion art 41.2(b) T&I w SD; art 45 Indigenous ppls; Title 5 Enviro, Nat Disasters & Climate, art 50 Enviro, art 51 DRR; Title 6 Economic & Trade Development; art 75 Info Soc; art 76 S&T; art 156 SPS Sub-Committee cooperate; art 287 MEAs; art 291 Upholding Standards of Protection; art 292 Science (precaution); art 294-301 Not fail to enforce Monitoring (Board on T&SD, Panel, Civ Soc Forum)	Art 59 Fisheries & Aquaculture (SD of fisheries trade); art 60 Artisanal Goods (SD for SMEs); art 61 Organic Goods (SD of organic agriculture); art 64 Trade & SD (SD of trade; art 65 Energy (SD of Renewables); art 66 Mining (enviro tech & SD); art 67 Fair & Sustainable Tourism (SD, local communi, eco-tourism), art 70 SMEs; Section E, art 90 Fisheries, Aquaculture, Artisanal Goods and Organic Products (cooperate); art 288 Trade Favouring SD(enhance trade in SD fish, forests, etc); art 293 SIAs	SIA, public particip, onter-agency collaboration, consultations in partners & EU	EU approach, very new and comprehensive. Further Case Study of SD measures addressing all 3 tensions, many innovations.

(*Continued*)

Partner Countries	Signature	SD Purpose	SD Exceptions	SD Cooperation	SD Enhancement	SD Process	Notes
66. EU-Georgia Association Agreement https://eur-lex.europa.eu/legal-content/EN/TXT/?uri=celex:22014A0830(02)	27 June 2014	Preamble (SD, labour, enviro); art 227 Context and objectives	Arts 33, 134 General Exceptions (GATT reference); art 228 Right to regulate and levels of protection, art 235 Upholding levels of protection	TITLE IV (Trade) – Ch 13 Trade and SD, art 229 Multilateral labour standards, art 230 MEAs, art 238 Review of Sustainability Impacts, art 239 Working together on trade and SD TITLE VI (Other Cooperation Policies)—Ch 2 Energy Coop; Ch 3 Environment; Ch 4 Climate Action; Ch 5 Industrial policy and mining; Ch 10 Agriculture and rural development; Ch 11 Fisheries; Ch 12 Research, Tech Development; Ch 14 Employment, Social Policy; Ch 20 Civil Society Coop	TITLE IV (Trade)—Ch 13 Trade and SD, art 231 Trade and Investment promoting SD, art 232 Biodiversity, art 233 Sustainable Management of Forests, art 234 Trade in fish products	Anti-fraud section, art 237 Transparency, art 241 Joint civil society dialogue, art 242 Government consultations, art 243 Panel of experts	EU approach, detailed provisions, separate Trade and SD chapter

67. EU-Moldova Association Agreement https://eur-lex.europa.eu/legal-content/EN/TXT/?uri=celex:22014A0830(01)	27 June 2014	Preamble (SD, labour, enviro); art 363 Context and objectives	Arts 154, 261 (GATT reference); art 364 Right to regulate and levels of protection, art 371 Upholding levels of protection	TITLE IV (Economic Cooperation)—Ch 4 Employment, Social Policy and Equal Opportunities; Ch 11 Mining and Raw Materials (reference to SD); Ch 12 Agriculture and Rural Development (reference to SD); Ch 13 Fisheries (reference to SD); Ch 16 Environment; Ch 17 Climate Action; Ch 14 Energy Cooperation (reference to SD); Ch 24 Cooperation in research, tech, development; Ch 25 Cooperation on culture; Ch 26 Civil society cooperation; TITLE V (Trade)—Ch 13 Trade and SD, art 365 Multilateral labour standards, art 366 MEAs, art 374 Review of Sustainability Impacts, art 374 Working together on trade and SD	TITLE V—(Trade) Ch 13 Trade and SD, art 367 Trade and Investment promoting SD, art 368 Biodiversity, art 369 Sustainable Management of Forests, art 370 Trade in fish products	Anti-fraud section, art 373 Transparency, art 377 Joint civil society dialogue, art 378 Government consultations, art 379 Panel of experts	EU approach, detailed provisions, separate Trade and SD chapter

(Continued)

Partner Countries	Signature	SD Purpose	SD Exceptions	SD Cooperation	SD Enhancement	SD Process	Notes
68. EU-Ukraine Association Agreement https://trade.ec.europa.eu/doclib/docs/2016/november/tradoc_155103.pdf	27 June 2014	Preamble (SD, labour, enviro); art 289 Context and objectives	Arts 36, 141 General Exceptions (GATT reference); art 290 Right to regulate, art 296 Upholding levels of protection	Ch 13 Trade and SD, art 291 Multilateral labour standards, art 292 MEAs, art 298 Review of Sustainability Impacts, art 302 Cooperation on trade and SD	Ch 13 Trade and SD, art 293 Trade and Investment promoting SD, art 294 Trade in forest products, art 295 Trade in fish products	Art 3 Fight against corruption, art 299 Civil Society Institutions, art 300 Monitoring mechanisms	EU approach, detailed provisions, separate Trade and SD chapter
69. EU-MERCOSUR Association Agreement in principle http://trade.ec.europa.eu/doclib/press/index.cfm?id=2048	28 June 2019	No definitive provisions yet	Right to regulate provisions are envisaged	Information sharing and cooperation in SD, promoting corporate social responsibility, promoting SMEs	Provisions on the conservation and sustainable management of the biological resources, forests and fisheries	Transparency provisions, consultation with civil society	EU approach, with comprehensive Trade & SD Chapter, aims to protect workers' rights, environment and climate, references the Paris Agreement

70. EU – Vietnam Trade and Investment Agreement https://trade.ec.europa.eu/doclib/press/index.cfm?id=1437	30 June 2019	Preamble (enviro, labour, SD), Art. 13.1 Objectives	Art 2.22 General Exceptions (GATT reference); art 13.2 Right to Regulate; art 13.3 Upholding levels of labour and environmental protection	Ch 13 Trade & SD, art 13.1 SD Cooperation; art 13.4 Labour Agreements, art 13.5 MEAs; art 13.10 Trade and Investment Favouring Sustainable Development; art 13.12 Transparency; art 13.13 Review of Sustainability Impact; 13.14 Working Together on SD; arts 13.15–13.17 Committees, Consultations, Panel of Experts; Ch 16 Cooperation and Capacity Building, art 16.2 Cooperation in favour of SMEs and SD	Ch 13 Trade & SD, 13.6 Climate Change (reference to Kyoto Prot); 13.7 Biodiversity; art 13.8 Sustainable Forest Management; art 13.9 Sustainable Living Marine Resources	SIA, public particip, inter-agency collaboration, consultations in the EU	Comprehensive EU approach—contains a Trade and SD chapter

(Continued)

Partner Countries	Signature	SD Purpose	SD Exceptions	SD Cooperation	SD Enhancement	SD Process	Notes
71. EU-Singapore Trade and Investment Protection Agreement https://trade.ec.europa.eu/doclib/press/index.cfm?id=961	19 October 2018	Preamble (enviro, labour, SD), art. 12.1 Context and Objectives	Art 2.14 General Exceptions (GATT reference); art 12.2 Right to Regulate and Levels of Protection	Ch 12 Trade & SD, art 12.1 SD Cooperation; art 12.3 Labour Agreements, art 12.4; art 12.6 MEAs; art 12.10 Environmental Cooperation; art 12.11 Trade and Investment Promoting SD; art 12.13 Transparency; art 12.14 Review of Impact on Sustainable Development; arts 12.15–12.17 Monitoring, Consultations, Panel of Experts	Art 12.7 Trade in timber, art 12.8 Trade in fish	SIA, public particip, inter-agency collaboration, consultations in the EU	Comprehensive EU approach—contains a Trade and SD chapter
72. EU-Japan Economic Partnership Agreement https://trade.ec.europa.eu/doclib/press/index.cfm?id=1684	17 July 2018	Preamble (enviro, labour, SD); Art. 16.1 Context and Objectives	Art 2.22 General Exceptions (GATT reference); art 16.2 Right to Regulate and Levels of Protection	Ch 16 Trade & SD, art 16.3 Labour Agreements, art 16.4 MEAs; art 16.5 Trade and Investment Favouring SD; art 16.10 Transparency; art 6. 11 Review of sustainability impacts; art 16.12 Cooperation (reference to SD); arts 16.13–16.19 Committee, Advisory Group, Joint dialogue with civil society, consultations, panel of experts	Art 16.6 Biodiversity; art 16.7 Sustainable management of forests; art 16.8 Sustainable use of fisheries	SIA, public particip, inter-agency collaboration, consultations in the EU	Comprehensive EU approach—contains a Trade and SD chapter

73. European Union - United Kingdom https://assets.publishing.service.gov.uk/government/uploads/system/uploads/attachment_data/file/948119/EU-UK_Trade_and_Cooperation_Agreement_24.12.2020.pdf	30 December 2020	Preamble (SD, env, social, climate change)	Art 7.2 Non-regression from levels of protection,	Art 8.5 (3) coop on trade-related climate issues; art 8.7 coop on trade-related aspects of sustainable forest management	Art 7.3 Carbon pricing; art 8.3 Multilateral labour standards; art 8.5 Trade & Climate change; art 8.6 (2b) promote CITES; art 8.8 (2b) promote sustainable fisheries; art 8.9 (2b) promote trade & investments in env goods and services; art 8.10 (2a) encourage CSR & responsible bus	SIA	EU and UK approach; new & comprehensive; contains articles on trade & climate change (art 8.5), trade & biological diversity (art 8.6), trade & forests (art 8.7) etc.
74. Eurasian Economic Union (EAEU)-Vietnam http://www.eurasian-commission.org/ru/act/trade/dotp/sogl_torg/Documents/EAEU-VN_FTA.pdf	29 May 2015	Art 12.1 Objectives	Art 1.9 General and Security Exceptions (GATT and GATS reference); art 12.4 Upholding Levels of Protection	Ch 12 Sustainable Development, art 12.3 General Principles (co-operation), art 12.5 Environmental and Labour Cooperation, art 12.6 Environmental and Labour Consultations, art 12.7 International Labour Standards, art 12.8 Review of Sustainability Impacts	No	Transparency (Preamble, procurement, import licensing, quantitative restrictions, customs procedures)	Contains a Trade and SD chapter

(Continued)

Partner Countries	Signature	SD Purpose	SD Exceptions	SD Cooperation	SD Enhancement	SD Process	Notes
75. Guatemala-Taiwan http://www.sice.oas.org/Trade/GTM_TW/Index_s.asp	22 September 2005	Preamble (trade + enviro =SD)	10.15 Investment (not lower enviro stands, not prevent adoption); 19.02 General Exceptions (GATT + GATS)	20.02 Cooperation (econ + env); 20.12 Env & NR, 20.09 SMEs, 20.15 Agriculture SPS	Ch 13 Air Transport, Ch 14 Maritime Transport; 20.11 Tourism, 20.13 Renewable Energy	No info	NAFTA approach. SD as sub-set of Enviro & NR, modern innovations, cooperation on renewables a good model
76. Hong Kong, China-Chile https://www.tid.gov.hk/english/trade_relations/hkclfta/text_agreement.html	7 September 2012	Preamble (SD, enviro)	Ch 18 Exceptions, art 18.1 General Exceptions (GATT and GATS reference)	Ch 14 Environment, art 14.3 Collaborative Framework	Ch 14 Environment, art 14.2 Key Commitments (contribute to SD)	Ch 14 Environment, art 14.4 Institutional Arrangements, art 14.5 Consultations; Ch 15 Transparency	NAFTA approach. SD as sub-set of Enviro
77. Iceland-China https://www.government.is/media/utanrikisraduneyti-media/media/fta-kina/Iceland-China.pdf	15 April 2013	Preamble (enviro, labour, SD)	Art 11 General Exceptions (art XX GATT reference)	Art 96 Labour and Enviro Cooperation	No info	No info	Very minimalist
78. Japan-India https://www.mofa.go.jp/region/asia-paci/india/epa201102/pdfs/ijcepa_ba_e.pdf	February 2011	Preamble (enviro, SD	Art 11 Exceptions; art 99 non relaxation of Environmental Measures (Investment)	Ch 13 Cooperation, art 128 ensuring long-term SD, art 129 Fields of Cooperation (Environment, SMEs)	Art 8 Environmental Protection	Art 4 Transparency, Art 7 Measures against Corruption	Minimalistic, no separate Trade and SD chapter

79. Japan-Switzerland https://www.mofa.go.jp/region/europe/switzerland/epa0902/agreement.pdf	19 February 2009	Preamble (enviro, climate change, SD)	Art 22 General Exceptions GATT, Art 101 Non-Derogation from Enviro & Labour Standards	No	Art 9 Trade in EGS	No info	
80. Japan-Mongolia https://www.mofa.go.jp/files/000067716.pdf	10 February 2015	Preamble (sustainable economic development)	Art 1.10 General Exceptions (GATT and GATS reference); art 10.17 no lowering of Health, Safety and Environmental Measures and Labour Standards	Art 15.1 Cooperation in relation to environment, SMEs, agriculture, forestry and fisheries	No info	Art 1.3 Transparency; art 1.4 Public comment procedures; art 1.6 Review and Appeal; art 1.7 Measures against corruption	No separate Trade and SD chapter, but includes some aspects of SD in various provisions
81. Japan-Brunei Darussalam https://www.mofa.go.jp/region/asia-paci/brunei/epa0706/agreement.pdf	18 June 2007	Preamble	Art 8 General and Security Exceptions	Ch 9 Cooperation, art 101 (reference to promoting SD)	Art 93 Environmental Aspects (reference to international environmental obligations), art 71 Environmental Measures re. investment	Arts 3, 50, 82 Transparency	No separate Trade and SD chapter, but includes some aspects of SD in various provisions

(Continued)

Partner Countries	Signature	SD Purpose	SD Exceptions	SD Cooperation	SD Enhancement	SD Process	Notes
82. Japan-Indonesia https://www.mofa.go.jp/region/asia-paci/indonesia/epa0708/agreement.pdf	20 August 2007	No	Art 11 General and Security Exceptions	Art 104 Cooperation (no reference to SD)	Art 102 Environmental Aspects (reference to SD + international environmental obligations); art 103 Community Development; art 74 Environmental Measures re. investment	Arts 3, 53, 85 Transparency	No separate Trade and SD chapter, but includes some aspects of SD in various provisions
83. Korea-Australia https://www.dfat.gov.au/trade/agreements/in-force/kafta/official-documents/Pages/full-text-of-kafta	8 April 2014	Preamble (SD, enviro, labour); art 17.1 General Principles (Labour); art 18.1 Levels of Protection (Enviro)	Art 22.1 General Exceptions (GATT and GATS reference)	Ch 16 Cooperation, art 16.4 Innovation, Research and Development (Sustainable resource management, biotechnology, food safety, climate change mitigation), art 16.5 Agriculture Coop, art 16.6 Fisheries Coop, art 16.7 Forestry Coop; art 18.2 MEAs, art 18.3 Enforcement of Enviro Laws, art 18.8 Cooperation in Enviro; art 17.5 Cooperation in Labour	Ch 17 Labour; Ch 18 Environment, art 18.4 Trade favouring enviro	Ch 19 Transparency; arts 17.3–17.4 Institutional Mechanism and Consultations (Labour); arts 18.6–18.7 Institutional Mechanism and Consultations (Enviro)	Comprehensive approach. SD as subset of Environment and Labour Chapters.

84. Korea-Turkey http://www.customs.go.kr/download/engportal/han_turkey_02_01.pdf	1 August 2012	Preamble (SD, enviro, labour); art 1.2 Objectives; art 5.1 Context and Objectives	Art 5.3 Right to Regulate and Levels of Protection, art 5.7 Upholding levels of protection	Ch 5 Trade and SD, art 5.4 Multilateral Labour Standards, art 5.5 MEAs, art 5.10 Cooperation	Ch 5 Trade and SD, art 5.6 Trade favouring SD	Art 5.9 Transparency, art 5.12 Institutional Mechanism	Comprehensive approach. Separate Trade and SD Chapter.
85. MERCOSUR-Peru http://www.sice.oas.org/trade/MRCSRPerACE58/ace.asp	30 November 2005	No (harmonic, soc + econ dev)	No	Ch 19, art 36 (S&T Cooperation)	No	No Info	ALADI approach, very basic
86. Mexico-EFTA http://www.sice.oas.org/Trade/mexefta/mexefta.asp	27 November 2000	Preamble (employ, enviro & SD)	Art 17 General Exceptions (GATT style); art 25 Services Right to Regulate (limited by FTA); art 35 Finance (right to regulate); art 44 Investment + Services (GATS style exceptions); art 48 Investment; art 65 Procurement Exceptions;	No	No, but bilateral Agricultural Agreements liberalize on timescales	Inter-agency collaboration in Mexico	EFTA approach. Very minimalist accord

(Continued)

Partner Countries	Signature	SD Purpose	SD Exceptions	SD Cooperation	SD Enhancement	SD Process	Notes
87. Mexico-EU http://www.sice.oas.org/Trade/mex_eu/english/index_e.asp	8 December 1997	Final Act (harmonious + sustainable dev); Preamble (Rio Dec SD principle); Principles	Art 5k (General Exceptions)	Title VI, art 17 SMEs, art 27 Government, art 29 S&T, art 30 Training & Education, art 34 Enviro & NR, art 36 Social Affairs & Poverty, art 37 Regional (women), art 38 Refugees, art 39 Human Rights & Democracy, art 40 Consumer Protection, art 42 Health	Art 21 Agriculture (harmonize health+env stands), art 22 Mining (new tech), art 23 Energy (renewables), art 25 Tourism (local interests)	SIA, public particip, onter-agency collaboration, consultations in Mexico & EU	EU approach. No need for Invest or Gov Procurement exceptions as no provisions on these. Strong collaboration
88. Mexico-EU Trade Agreement in principle https://trade.ec.europa.eu/doclib/press/index.cfm?id=1830	23 April 2018	No definitive provisions yet	Right to regulate provisions are envisaged	Information sharing and cooperation in SD, promoting corporate social responsibility, promoting SMEs	Provisions on the conservation and sustainable management of the biological resources, forests and fisheries	Transparency and anti-corruption provisions, involvement of civil society	EU approach, with comprehensive Trade & SD Chapter, aims to protect workers' rights, environment and climate, references the Paris Agreement

Partner Countries	Signature	SD Purpose	SD Exceptions	SD Cooperation	SD Enhancement	SD Process	Notes
89. Mexico-Israel http://www.sice.oas.org/Trade/meis_e/isr_mexind_e.asp	10 April 2000	No. Preamble employ + living standards only.	Not for art 1-04 Relation to Other Treaties (FTA prevails); 6-18 Procurement (human, animal, plant health); 11-02 General Exceptions (GATT)	No	No	No information	ALADI and Israel approach. Minimalist and focused on economic relations. art 1-104 retrogressive
90. Mexico-Japan http://www.sice.oas.org/Trade/MEX_JPN_e/JPN_MEXind_e.asp	17 September 2004	Preamble econ dev & globalization only, but art 147 recognizes need for enviro to promote SD.	Art 74 Investment (not lower enviro standards, consult); art 126 Procurement (except human, plant, animal health measures); art 168 General Exceptions (GATT, GATS)	Ch 14 Cooperation; art 141 SMEs, art 142 S&T, art 143 Vocational Training; art 147 Environment (strong env laws)	Art 145 Agriculture (SD of agri), art 146 Tourism (SD of tourism), art 147 Environment (Enviro Goods Services, CDM, invest)	Art 161 Public Comments; Inter-agency collaboration, consultations; EA?	Japan approach. Collaboration and exceptions, innovations

(*Continued*)

Partner Countries	Signature	SD Purpose	SD Exceptions	SD Cooperation	SD Enhancement	SD Process	Notes
91. Mexico-Nicaragua http://www.sice.oas.org/trade/menifta/indice.asp	18 December 1997	Preamble (econ dev, labour, employ, enviro, promote SD)	Ch 10 Services arts 10-15 Exceptions (MEAs except); Ch 14 Standards art 14-12 Health, Ch 15 Procurement, art 15-18 Exceptions (human, animal, plant life or health, no NR); 16-14 Invest (no reg chill, not lower env standards); 21-01 General Exceptions (GATT+GATS)	Art 14-14 Enviro & Hazardous Wastes (Basel laws applied);	Not really, Ch 4 art 4-05 & 4-06 Agrofisheries Reduce Internal Subsidies, Reduce Export Subsidies; art 15-21 Procurement SME participation w art 19-01 Annex 2 SME committee	Inter-agency consultations, public debates	NAFTA approach. Few cooperation innovations, not for SD
92. Mexico-Honduras, El Salvador, Guatemala (Northern Triangle) http://www.sice.oas.org/Trade/mextnorte/indice.asp	29 June 2000	Preamble (employ, econo dev w enviro prot=SD)	Art 14-16 Invest (no reg chill, not lower env standards); 20-02 General Exceptions (GATT + GATS)	Art 15-19 Enviro & Hazardous Wastes (Basel laws applied); art 15-07 Risk Eval (intl standards health, enviro, etc)	No. Ch 4 Agrofisheries art 4-06 reduce internal, art 4-08 export subsidies;	No info	NAFTA and ALADI approach. Minimalist, with a few innovations, ie, provisions confirming no regulatory chill

93. Mexico-Uruguay http://www.sice.oas.org/Trade/mexurufta_s/mex-uruind_s.asp	15 November 2003	No. Preamble (soc + econo dev only).	Ch 13 art 13-02(5) Investment (No intention to prevent regs on health + social programs); art 13-07.2 Health + enviro tech not a performance requirement; art 19-02 General Exceptions (GATT, GATS)	No	No. arts 3-12, 3-13 Subsidies (non-agrofisheries eliminated, agrofisheries reduced)	No info	ALADI approach. Minimalist, focused on economic agenda
94. New Zealand-China https://www.mfat.govt.nz/assets/China/Preamble.pdf	7 April 2008	Preamble	Ch 17 Exceptions	Art 96 Regulatory Cooperation; Ch 14 Cooperation, art 176 SMEs, art 177 Labour and Environmental Cooperation	No	Ch 13 Transparency	Minimalist approach with no separate SD, Labour or Environment chapters
95. New Zealand-Hong Kong, China https://www.mfat.govt.nz/assets/FTAs-agreements-in-force/Hong-Kong-FTA/NZ-HK-CEP.pdf	29 March 2010	Preamble (SD, enviro, labour)	Ch 19 Exceptions, art 1 General Exceptions (reference to GATT and GATS)	Art 4 Labour and Environmental Cooperation; art 8 Cooperation for Regulatory Effectiveness	No	Art 9 Transparency	Minimalist approach with no separate SD, Labour or Environment chapters

(Continued)

Partner Countries	Signature	SD Purpose	SD Exceptions	SD Cooperation	SD Enhancement	SD Process	Notes
96. New Zealand-Malaysia https://www.mfat.govt.nz/assets/FTAs-agreements-in-force/Malaysia/mnzfta-text-of-agreement.pdf	26 October 2009	Preamble (SD, enviro, labour)	Art 7.4 Scope of Trade Barriers (no prejudice to animal or plant life or health or the environment); art 10.15 Investment and Environment (no prejudice to environmental concerns); Ch 17 General Exceptions	Art 7.8 Cooperation for Regulatory Effectiveness; Ch 13 Economic Coop	No	No	Minimalist approach with no separate SD, Labour or Environment chapters
97. Panama-Singapore http://www.sice.oas.org/Trade/PAN_SGP/PAN_SGP_e/index_e.asp	1 March 2006	No. Preamble econo + soc benefits only	Annex 9A 4(b) Invest (Enviro + other measures not expropriation)	No SD, Ch 16 Strategic Partnership, 16.02 S&T Cooperation	Annex 16.2 Areas for Cooperation SMEs, Tourism, ICT+E-Commerce, Enviro Services	No information	Collaboration and exceptions, innovations
98. Panama-Taiwan http://www.sice.oas.org/Trade/PanRC/PANRC_e.asp	21 August 2003	Preamble (econ, employ, enviro + SD)	1.03 Relation to other Treaties (MEAs except); Ch 10 Investment, 10.15 Enviro (not prevent enviro measures or lower enviro standards); 20.02 General Exceptions (GATT+GATS); Reservations Annexes	No	No	No information	NAFTA approach, but minimalist, with no cooperation or labour/enviro chapters

99. Peru-Korea http://www.sice.oas.org/TPD/PER_KOR/PER_KOR_Texts_e/PER_KOR_ToC_e.asp	21 March 2011	Preamble (enviro, human rights, SD)	Arts 19.2 & 19.5 Non-Derogation, art 19.6 Biodiversity & Conservation, art 24.1 General Exceptions GATT	Art 19.3 MEAs, art 19.8 Coop on Climate Change Issues, art 19.11 & 19.12 Enviro Coop & consult. Art 20.5 Coop on Fish & Aquaculture, art 20.6 SD of Tourism, art 20.7 Sust forest management, art 17 Cooperation on IP Information	Art 19.1 Trade for SD, art 19.4 Trade in EGS, art 19.9 Clean Tech, art 19.10 EAC, art 19.13 Rev of Enviro impacts	No info	
100. Peru-Singapore http://www.sice.oas.org/TPD/PER_SGP/Final_Texts_PER_SGP_e/index_e.asp	29 May 2008	Preamble not yet available for this treaty	Ch 9 Procurement, 9.20 Exceptions (human, plant, animal life or health); Ch 10 Investment, 10.7 Performance Requirements (health + enviro tech not PRs), 10.8 Invest+Enviro (not constrain enviro measures); Annex 10A.4 Expropriation (health + enviro measures not indirect exp); Ch 17 General Exceptions (GATT + GATS mutatis)	No	No	No information	NAFTA approach, but minimalist, with no cooperation or labour/enviro chapters.

(Continued)

Partner Countries	Signature	SD Purpose	SD Exceptions	SD Cooperation	SD Enhancement	SD Process	Notes
101. Peru-United States http://www.sice.oas.org/Trade/PER_USA/PER_USA_e/Index_e.asp	12 April 2006	Preamble (sust econ alternatives to drugs, labour rights, enviro law + SD)	Ch 9 Procurement 9.6.7 Tech Specs (not preclude tech specs for NR management, enviro or labour rights), 9.1.4 Exceptions (human, plant, animal health or life); Ch 10 Investment 10.9 Performance Reqs (Not preclude enviro, health, NR measures), Annex 10B3(b) enviro regs not indir exprop except rarely; Ch 18 Env Coop, art 18.3.2 Not lower env standards for T&I; 18.13 MEAs; art 22.01 General Exceptions (GATT + GATS)	Ch 17 Labour Cooperation, enforce labour laws, no ref to SD. Ch 18 Enviro Cooperation Objectives (optimal use of resources=SD), 18.1 enviro laws, 18.2 MEAs, 18.3 not fail enforce env laws, 18.4–18.10 Institutions-Enforcement-Capacity, 18.11 Biodiversity, Defs no NR laws	Annex 14.3.4 Forest Sector Governance, establishes system to combat illegal logging, supporting CITES by listing of mahogany + establishing certification + verification mechanism; Understanding Regarding Biodiversity & Traditional Knowledge	ER,Inter-Agency collaboration, Public Participation in USA, Inter-agency collaboration, Public participation in Peru	NAFTA approach, expanded to include Forest & other SD collaboration. Further Case Study

102. Southern African Customs Union (SACU)-European Free Trade Association (EFTA) https://www.efta.int/media/documents/legal-texts/free-trade-relations/southern-african-customs-union-SACU/EFTA-SACU%20Free%20Trade%20Agreement.pdf	26 June 2006	Preamble; art 30 Objectives and Scope	Art 23 General Exceptions (reference to GATT); art 24 Security Exceptions; art 28(3) Non-relaxation of environmental standards	Arts 31–32 Cooperation and Assistance	Art 31(2) Conservation of the environment	No	No separate Trade and SD chapter, but includes some aspects of SD in various provisions
103. Switzerland-China https://www.seco.admin.ch/seco/en/home/Aussenwirtschaftspolitik_Wirtschaftliche_Zusammenarbeit/Wirtschaftsbeziehungen/Freihandelsabkommen/Partner_weltweit/china/Abkommenstexte.html	6 July 2013	Preamble (enviro, SD); art 1.1 Objectives; art 12.1 Context and Objectives (Enviro); art 13.1 Scope and Objectives (Economic and Technical Coop)	Art 2.7 Exceptions (GATT reference), art 8.15 General Exceptions	Ch 12 Environmental Issues, art 12.2 MEAs, art 12.4 Cooperation in International For a, art 12.5 Bilateral Cooperation, art 12.6 Resources and Financial Arrangements, art 12.7 Implementation and Consultations; Ch 13 Economic and Technical Cooperation, art 13.3 Cooperation in SD, art 13.5 Cooperation on Labour and Employment	Art 11.9 Genetic Resources and Traditional Knowledge, art 11.10 Plant Variety Protection, art 12.3 Promotion of the Dissemination of Goods and Services Favouring the Enviro	No info	Separate chapter on Environment and Cooperation

(*Continued*)

Partner Countries	Signature	SD Purpose	SD Exceptions	SD Cooperation	SD Enhancement	SD Process	Notes
104. Turkey-Malaysia https://www.trade.gov.tr/free-trade-agreements/malaysia	17 April 2014	Preamble (enviro + SD)	Art 13.1 General Exceptions	Art 9.5 Cooperation between SMEs; art 9.10 Cooperation in Environment (reference to strategic EIA)	No	Ch 10 Transparency	Minimalist provisions on SD
105. United States-Mexico-Canada (USMCA) https://ustr.gov/trade-agreements/free-trade-agreements/united-states-mexico-canada-agreement/agreement-between	20 November 2018	Preamble (labour standards, SD + enviro protect)	Ch 32 Exceptions, art. 32.1 General Exceptions (GATT and GATS reference)	Art 23.12 Labour Cooperation (no reference to SD); art 24.4 Enforcement of Enviro Laws, art 24.5 Public information and participation, art 24.7 EIA, art 24.8 MEAs, art 24.22 Conservation and Trade, art 24.25 Environmental Cooperation, art 24.26 Environmental Committee, arts 24.29–31 Environment Consultations; art 25.2 Cooperation to increase opportunities for SMEs	Ch 23 Labour; Ch 24 Environment, art 24.9 Protection of the Ozone Layer, arts 24.10, 24.19 Protection of the Marine Enviro and Species, art 24.11 Air Quality, art 24.12 Marine Litter, art 24.15 Biodiversity, art 24.16 Invasive Alien Species, 24.17–18 Fisheries Management, art 24.23 Forest Management; Ch 25 SMEs	Art 24.13 Corporate Social Responsibility; Ch 27 Anticorruption; Ch 28 Good Regulatory Practices	NAFTA approach, expanded to include separate Labour, Environment, SME Chapters

106. United States-Australia http://www.sice.oas.org/Trade/US-AusFTAFinal/USAusind_e.asp	18 May 2004	Preamble (labour standards, SD + enviro protect)	Sec B Forestry + raw log exports not covered; Ch 11 Investment, art 11.9 Perf Requirements 3(b) workers measures; 3(c) enviro measures, 11.11 Not enviro lower standards for invest, Annex 11B4(b) enviro measures not indir expropriation; Ch 15 Procurement, art 15.6(8) Tech Specs disciplines not applied to enviro & NR, art 15.12 Procurement Exceptions (human, plant animal life + health, spec enviro); art 22.1 General Exceptions (GATT, GATS)	Ch 18 Labour, no SD. Ch 19 Enviro; Enviro Cooperation 19.1-2 Enforce domestic laws w high standards; 19.8 Relationship to MEAs (support); United States–Australia Joint Statement on Environmental Cooperation	Ch 16 E-Commerce (encourage by trade) Ch 19 Enviro Cooperation, 19.6(3) May share EIA assessments of trade agreements	ER, inter-agency collaboration, public consultations in US	NAFTA approach, with basic innovations included.

(Continued)

Partner Countries	Signature	SD Purpose	SD Exceptions	SD Cooperation	SD Enhancement	SD Process	Notes
107. United States-Bahrain http://www.sice.oas.org/Trade/US_BHR/USA_BHRind_e.asp	14 September 2004	Preamble (labour rights, econ dev, enviro protect + SD)	Ch 9 Procurement 9.6(7) Tech Specs disciplines not applied to enviro & NR, 9.14 Procurement Exceptions (human, plant animal life + health); 20.1 General Exceptions (GATT GATS)	Ch 15 Labour Cooperation, no SD Ch 16 Enviro Cooperation 16.1–2 Enforce domestic laws w high standards, 16.4(1)b trading permits; 16.9 Relationship to MEAs (support); Memo of Understanding on Enviro Cooperation	Art 2.11 Reduce agricultural export subsidies; Ch 13 E-Commerce (encourage by trade) Ch 16 Enviro Cooperation, 16.7(4) assessment of trade	ER, inter-agency collaboration, public consultations in US	NAFTA approach, with basic innovations included.
108. United States-Colombia http://www.sice.oas.org/Trade/COL_USA_TPA_e/COL_USAind_e.asp	22 November 2006	Preamble (enviro, labour SD)	Art 10.1 Investment & Enviro, art 18.1 & 18.3 Non-derogation, art 22.1 General Exceptions GATT	Art 18.2 & 18.13 MEAs, art 18.19 Enviro Coop	Art 18.5 Mech to enhance Enviro performance, art 18.6 EAC, art 18.11 Sust use of Biodiversity	ER, inter-agency collaboration, public consultations in US, arts 19.7–19.9 reduction of corruption and bribery	NAFTA approach, with some basic innovation, includes a strong labour chapter (art 17, Annex 17)
109. United States-Jordan http://www.sice.oas.org/Trade/us-jrd/USA_JOR_e.asp	24 October 2000	Preamble (labour rights, SD enviro + diff develop levels)	Art 5.1 Enviro, not lower standards; art 12 General Exceptions (GATT XX)	Art 5 Enviro Cooperation, enforce enviro laws; art 13 Econo Cooperation + Tech Assistance art 6 Labour, respect ILO Conventions	Art 7 E-Commerce (encourage by trade)	ER, inter-agency collaboration, public consultations in US	NAFTA approach, with basic innovations included.

110. United States-Korea (KORUS) https://ustr.gov/trade-agreements/free-trade-agreements/korus-fta/final-text	30 June 2007 Text modified as of 1 January 2019	Preamble (labour + enviro laws, workers' rights, SD)	Ch 23 Exceptions	Ch 19 Labour Cooperation, no SD; art 20.8 Environmental Cooperation (reference to promoting SD)	Ch 3 Agriculture; Ch 19 Labour; Ch 20 Environment	Ch 21 Transparency; ER, inter-agency collaboration, public consultations in US	NAFTA approach, with basic innovations included
111. United States-Morocco http://www.sice.oas.org/Trade/US_MAR/US_MAR_E.asp	15 June 2004	Preamble (labour + enviro laws, workers rights, SD)	Ch 9 Procurement 9.7(5) Tech Specs disciplines not applied to enviro & NR, 9.15 Procurement Exceptions (human, plant animal life + health; Ch 10 Investment, 10.8.3(c) Perf Reqs (not prevent enforce env laws, human, plant + animal health + life, NR conserv), 10.10 Invest + Enviro (not prevent env measures); Annex 10B(b) env + health not indirect exprop; 21.1 General Exceptions (GATT GATS)	Ch 16 Labour Cooperation, no SD Ch 17 Enviro Cooperation 17.1–2 Enforce domestic laws w high standards, Joint Statement on Enviro Cooperation, 17.8 Relationship to MEAs (support)	Ch 17 Enviro Cooperation, 17.3(6) Share EIAs of trade agreements, 17.3(7) Enviro Goods + Services liberalisation	ER, inter-agency collaboration, public consultations in US	NAFTA approach, with basic innovations included

(Continued)

Partner Countries	Signature	SD Purpose	SD Exceptions	SD Cooperation	SD Enhancement	SD Process	Notes
112. United States-Panama https://ustr.gov/trade-agreements/free-trade-agreements/panama-tpa/final-text	28 June 2007	Preamble (workers rights + labour law, enviro law + SD)	Art 9.14 Procurement Exceptions (human, plant animal life + health); Ch 10 Investment, art 10.9.3(c) Perf Reqs (not prevent env laws, human, plant + animal health + life, NR conserv), art 10.11 no prevention of environmental measures; Annex 10-B env + health not indirect exprop.; art 21.1 General Exceptions (GATT GATS)	Ch 16 Labour Cooperation, no SD Ch 17 Enviro Cooperation	Ch 17 Environment	Ch 18 Transparency; ER, inter-agency collaboration, public consultations in US	NAFTA approach, with basic innovations included

113. United States-Oman http://www.sice.oas.org/Trade/USA_OMN_FTA_e/USA_OMN_ind_e.asp	19 January 2006	Preamble (workers rights + labour law, enviro law + SD)	Ch 9 Procurement 9.6(7) Tech Specs disciplines not applied to enviro & NR, 9.14 Procurement Exceptions (human, plant animal life + health); Ch 10 Investment, 10.8.3(c) Perf Reqs (not prevent enforce env laws, human, plant + animal health + life, NR conserv), 10.10 Invest + Enviro (not prevent env measures); Annex 10B(b) env + health not indirect exprop; 21.1 General Exceptions (GATT GATS)	Ch 16 Labour Cooperation, no SD Ch 17 Enviro Cooperation 17.1–2 Enforce domestic laws w high standards, Memo of Understanding for Enviro Cooperation, 17.9 Relationship to MEAs (support)	Ch 17 Enviro Cooperation, 17.4(1)b emission trading incentives	ER, inter-agency collaboration, public consultations in US	NAFTA approach, with innovations including cooperation to address SD concerns such as ETS

(Continued)

Partner Countries	Signature	SD Purpose	SD Exceptions	SD Cooperation	SD Enhancement	SD Process	Notes
114. United States-Singapore http://www.sice.oas.org/Trade/USA-Singapore/USASingind_e.asp	6 May 2003	Preamble (employ opps, SD, enviro law + MEAs implement)	Ch 13 Procurement 13.4 Exceptions (human, plant, animal life + health); Ch 15 Investment 15.8 Performance Requirements (enviro measures ok), 15.10 Invest + Enviro (not prevent enviro measures); 18.2.2 Not lower enviro standards; 21.1 General Exceptions, GATT XX and GATS	Ch 17 Labour Cooperation, no SD Ch 18 Enviro Cooperation 18.1–2 Enforce domestic laws w high standards, Memo of Intent for Enviro Cooperation, 18.18 MEAs	Ch 18 Enviro Cooperation, 18.19 CSR for SD, 18.6(3) may share EIA of trade agreement work	ER, inter-agency collaboration, public consultations in US	NAFTA approach, with basic innovations included, useful provisions to share EIA conclusions
115. United Kingdom-Japan https://assets.publishing.service.gov.uk/government/uploads/system/uploads/attachment_data/file/929181/CS_Japan_1.2020_UK_Japan_Agreement_Comprehensive_Economic_Partnership__v1.pdf	23 October 2020	Preamble (enviro + social + econo dimensions, enviro + labour protection)	Ch 2 Art 2.21 General Exceptions, GATT XX	Ch 16 Art 16.12 SD cooperation - coop on trade-related aspects of MEAs, coop on climate change, coop on sust use of Biodiversity, coop on evaluating impacts of trade on env & labour); Ch 19 Art 19.1 Coop on sust agriculture; Ch 21 Art 21.2 coop on enhancing participation of women in economic opportunities as a result of agreement	Ch 16 SD Coop, coop on CSR enhancement; Ch 21 on Trade & Women's economic empowerment	Ch 16 Art 16.11 reviewing & monitoring of sust impacts of agreement	EU approach with enhanced SD provisions

Source: Constructed by author based on information compiled by the OAS Sistema de Informacion sobre Commercio Exterior (SICE), the EU DG Trade Information System, and other databases

ANNEX 3

Perspectives on Trade and Sustainable Development from Wto Members in the Trade Policy Review Mechanism

WTO Members Characterizations of Integration in TPRM Round of Questions on Sustainable Development (2006–2007 Review)		
Country	**Details**	**Status**
Iceland	'Iceland's . . . trade policy is largely intertwined with sustainable development.'	3
UAE	'Sustainable development has been an increasingly important objective of public policy, and sustainable development is now an essential component of government policy.'	2
Uruguay	'El gobierno Uruguayo ha puesto un gran énfasis en una estrategia de crecimiento sostenido con equidad. El concepto de desarrollo sustentable se encuentra inserto en todas las estrategias de desarrollo del Uruguay.'	1
Chinese Taipei	'To enhance the protection of the environment and ecology, guarantee social fairness and justice, promote economic development, and establish us as a 'green silicon island,' the government in August 1997 established the Council for Sustainable Development.'	3
Bangladesh	'Trade Policy has always been regarded as the most important tools to foster development. Conducive trade policy boosts export earning and in turn promotes industrialization and generates employment. The Experience of Bangladesh shows that export has contributed to women empowerment and thus reducing poverty to facilitate sustainable development.'	1
Kyrgyz Republic	The general intent of the Country Development Strategy is the raise of living standards and quality, through sustainable economic growth, creation of terms for full employment, receiving high and stable incomes, the availability of wide spectrum of social services and following the high living standards.	2
China	[China believes] that multilateral environmental agreements (MEAs) have been playing an important role in addressing global and trans-border environmental issues and in promoting the global sustainable development. In the meanwhile, with the increase of trade measures for environmental purpose, the interaction between MEAs and World Trade Organization (WTO) rules is increasingly notable. China supports the principle of 'appropriate and moderate' to deal with the relationship between MEAs and WTO rules.	2
Colombia	The objective [of the National Development Plan] is to deepen the internationalization of the Colombian economy through regional trade agreements and thus create favourable trade conditions for Colombian exports.	2

Japan	[Japan believes] that the sustainable development of developing countries is very important for the stability and prosperity of the world. Japan has been actively supporting the efforts by developing countries to achieve sustainable development through the promotion of trade. Based on this concept and experience, Japan launched the 'Development Initiative for Trade', prior to the WTO Hong Kong Ministerial Conference in 2005, which aims to support these efforts by developing countries in a comprehensive manner through official development assistance (ODA), duty-free and quota-free treatment for LDCs and other related measures.	3
Australia	Australia has established processes to ensure a whole-of-government approach to all policy development and implementation, including in relation to environmental and trade policy.	2
Argentina	En consonancia con los lineamientos establecidos en el preámbulo del Acuerdo por el que se establece la OMC, el logro de un desarrollo sostenible y la protección del medio ambiente ocupan un lugar muy importante en la estrategia de política comercial de Argentina. Unofficial translation: In line with the guidelines established in the preamble of the Agreement establishing the WTO, the achievement of sustainable development and the protection of the environment occupy a very important place in Argentina's trade policy strategy.	2
Macao, China	To emphasize the attention the Government has been paying to nurture sustainable development in the economy, a Research Centre for Sustainable Development Strategies was established in 2005 (formerly as the Center for the Studies of Quality of Life) to, among other functions, analyse and propose strategic options that the Government may take on to support sustainable economic development.	2
Canada	Sustainable development is a cornerstone of Canadian foreign policy. Canada employs trade policy as a strategic tool to help build a world that is more secure, more prosperous, and more sustainable. We apply a coherent and principled approach to trade policy development and implementation, fostering the integration of economic, social and environmental considerations.	2
Costa Rica	Costa Rica promueve diversas actividades innovadoras que buscan lograr un comercio sostenible. En este sentido, el país ha desarrollado un Programa Nacional de Biocomercio y además, incentiva actividades como eco-turismo, pago por servicios ambientales y el desarrollo de investigación de la biodiversidad como servicio. Unofficial translation: Costa Rica promotes various innovative activities that seek to achieve sustainable trade. In this sense, the country has developed a National BioTrade Programme and also encourages activities such as eco-tourism, payment for environmental services and the development of biodiversity research as a service.	3
Indonesia	... some policies have given opportunity and space to conduct such coordination, or to stress environmental issues in sectoral policy, including trade sector.	1

Panama	La estrategia de desarrollo sostenible de Panamá se fundamenta en la necesidad de reforzar la estructura económica del país. Con ello entre otros fines, podremos reducir el impacto social que se deriva del proceso de liberalización comercial, procurando incorporar en este ciclo a los grupos de atención prioritaria de Panamá (como la población rural y la población indígena). [Also Sustainable Development Council]	3
Bahrain	Bahrain has adopted the principle of open-markets as a development philosophy, and believes that sustainable development is based on sound economic policies, an open, transparent and efficient public administration, and that environmental policy should be integrated into the economic development planning.	1
India	The convergence of the trade and development agendas has been important for India for achieving sustainable growth. India seeks to achieve sustainable growth by fostering greater transparency in trade and development of infrastructure which helps to access the global trade. Appropriate amendments to the legislation concerning environment, mining, labour, etc. take care of the issue of sustainable development.	3
Peru	Perú se adscribe a la Declaración de Río de 1992 sobre desarrollo sostenible y subsecuentes instrumentos internacional ... una Política del Estado dentro del Acuerdo Nacional el Desarrollo sostenible y la gestión ambiental ... pretende integrar la política nacional ambiental con las políticas económicas, sociales, culturales y de ordenamiento territorial, para contribuir a superar la pobreza y lograr el desarrollo sostenible; Unoffical translation: Peru subscribes to the 1992 Rio Declaration on Sustainable Development and subsequent international instruments . . a State Policy within the National Agreement on Sustainable Development and Environmental Management ... aims to integrate national environmental policy with economic, social, cultural and land-use planning policies, in order to contribute to overcoming poverty and achieve sustainable development;	3

Classifications: Country supports a relationship between environment and economic development, or integration of environment into economic development (level 1); Country supports complementary social, economic and environmental policy governing trade and investment (level 2); Country aims to promote sustainable development through integration of social and environmental priorities into trade and investment policy and law (level 3).
Source: Compiled by author based on WTO TPRM Reports from Questions on Sustainable Development in Trade Policy from 2006–2009.

Bibliography

1. International Declarations and Reports

(i) United Nations

Havana Charter for an International Trade Organization, UN Conference on Trade and Development, Final Act and Related Documents (24 March 1948) UN Doc E/Conf 2/78.

ILC, Yearbook of the International Law Commission (1950-II) (5 June–29 July 1950) UN Doc A/CN.4/SER.A/1950.

Economic Development and the Conservation of Nature, UNGA Res 1831 (XVII) (18 December 1962) UN Doc A/Res/XVII/1831.

Establishment of the United Nations Conference on Trade and Development as an Organ of the General Assembly, UNGA Res 1995 (XIX) (30 December 1964).

Stockholm Declaration, UN Conference on the Human Environment (16 June 1972) UN Doc A/Conf 48/14/Rev.1, (1972) 11 ILM 1461.

Permanent Sovereignty over Natural Resources of Developing Countries, UNGA Res 3016 (XXVII) (18 December 1972) UN Doc A/Res/3016 (XXVII).

Declaration on the Establishment of a New International Economic Order, UNGA Res 3201 (S-VI) (1 May 1974) UN Doc A/Res/3201(S-VI).

ILC, Yearbook of the International Law Commission (1978-II) (8 May–28 July 1978) UN Doc A/CN.4/SER.A/1978/Add.1 (Part 2).

World Charter for Nature, UNGA Res 37/7 (28 October 1982) UN Doc A/Res/37/7.

Process of Preparation of the Environmental Perspective to the Year 2000 and Beyond, Meeting No 102, UNGA Res 38/161 (19 December 1983) UN Doc A/RES/38/161.

Declaration on the Right to Development, UNGA Res 4/128 (4 December 1986) UN Doc A/Res/41/128.

Report of the World Commission on Environment and Development, UNGA Res 42/187 (11 December 1987) UN Doc A/Res/42/187.

Rio Declaration on Environment and Development (Annex 2), Report of the UN Conference on Environment and Development (13 June 1992) UN Doc A/CONF.151/26 (Vol I).

Agenda 21, Annex 2 Report of the UN Conference on Environment and Development (13 June 1992) UN Doc A/CONF.151/26 (Vol I).

Institutional Arrangements to Follow Up the United Nations Conference on Environment and Development, UNGA Res 47/191 (29 January 1993) UN Doc A/RES/47/191.

Establishment of the Commission on Sustainable Development, UNESC Res 1993/207 (12 February 1993) UN Doc E/1993/207.

UNCSD, 'National Information Report of the Secretary-General' UNSEC Rep (5 March 1996) UN Doc E/CN.17/1996/19.

Programme for the Further Implementation of Agenda 21, UNGA Res S-19/2 (19 September 1997) UN Doc A/Res/S-19/2.

UNCESCR, 'The Substantive Issues Arising in the Implementation of the International Covenant on Economic, Social and Cultural Rights: Statement of the United Nations Committee on Economic, Social and Cultural Rights to the Third Ministerial Conference of the World Trade Organization' (26 November 1999) UN Doc E/C.12/1999/9.

UNCESCR, *General Comment No 12 The Right to Adequate Food (Art. 11)*, UN ESCOR, 1999, UN Doc E/C.12/1999/5.

UNCESCR, *General Comment No 13: The Right to Education (Art. 13)*, UN ESCOR, 1999, UN Doc E/C.12/1999/10.

UNCESCR, *General Comment No 14: The Right to the Highest Attainable Standard of Health*, UNESCOR, 2000, UN Doc E/C.12/2000/4.

United Nations Reform: Measures and Proposals; and Strengthening of the United Nations System, UNGA Res 53/239 (5 September 2000) UN Doc A/Res/53/239.

United Nations Millennium Declaration, UNGA Res 55/2 (8 September 2000) UN Doc A/55/49.

Ten-year Review of Progress Achieved in the Implementation of the Outcome of the United Nations Conference on Environment and Development, UNGA Res 55/199 (20 December 2000) UN Doc A/RES/55/199.

Report of the International Conference on Financing for Development, UNGA Rep 198/11 (18-22 March 2002) UN Doc A/Conf.198/11.

Report of the World Summit on Sustainable Development (4 September 2002) UN Doc A/CONF.199/L20 5.

Draft Plan of Implementation of the World Summit on Sustainable Development (4 September 2002) UN Doc A/CONF.199/L.3/Add.1-13/Corr.2.

Follow-up to the World Summit on Sustainable Development and the Future Role of the Commission on Sustainable Development: The Implementation Track UNESC Rep 2003/2 (21 February 2003) UN Doc E/CN.17/2003/2.

UNCESCR, *General Comment No 15: The Right to Water (Arts. 11 and 12)*, UN ESCOR, 2003, UN Doc E/C.12/2002/11.

UNCESCR, *General Comment No 16: The Equal Right of Men and Women to the Enjoyment of All Economic, Social and Cultural Rights (Art. 3)*, UN ESCOR, 2005, UN Doc E/C.12/2005/3.

(ii) World Trade Organization

Differential and More Favourable Treatment, Reciprocity and Fuller Participation of Developing Countries (28 November 1979) BISD 26S/203 ('Enabling Clause').

Adverse Trade Effects of Environmental Measures, Communication from UNEP (25 November 1988) GATT Document L/6437 <https://docs.wto.org/gattdocs/q/GG/L6599/6437.PDF> accessed 16 December 2020.

Communication from Austria, Finland, Iceland, Norway, Sweden and Switzerland (3 December 1990) GATT Document MTN.TNC/W/47 <http://www.wto.org/gatt_docs/English/SULPDF/92120048.pdf> accessed 16 December 2020.

Minutes of Meeting held in the Centre William Rappard on 6 February 1991 (5 March 1991) C/M/247 <http://www.wto.org/gatt_docs/English/SULPDF/91530241.pdf> accessed 16 December 2020.

Minutes of Meeting held in the Centre William Rappard on 29–30 May 1991 (28 June 1991) C/M/250 <http://www.wto.org/gatt_docs/English/SULPDF/91530724.pdf> accessed 17 December 2020.

Trade and Environment-Statement by the Delegation of Peru (12 June 1991) Spec(91)39 <http://www.wto.org/gatt_docs/English/SULPDF/92270088.pdf> accessed 17 December 2020.

Trade and Environment-Statement by the Delegation of Canada (2 July 1991) Spec(91)38 <http://www.wto.org/gatt_docs/English/SULPDF/92270087.pdf> accessed 17 December 2020

Note on Proceedings of the Seventy-Fifth Session, 26 July 1993 (20 October 1993) GATT Document COM.TD/134 <http://www.wto.org/gatt_docs/English/SULPDF/91730169.pdf> accessed 17 December 2020.

Draft Decision on Trade and Environment (13 December 1993) MTN.TNC/W/123.

Committee on Trade and Development-Report by the Chairman on the Follow-up to UNCED in GATT (11 February 1994) GATT Document COM.TD/W/509 <http://www.wto.org/gatt_docs/English/SULPDF/91760062.pdf> accessed 17 December 2020.

Ireland-Statement by Mr Charles McCreevy-Minister for Tourism and Trade (13 April 1994) MTN.TNC/MIN(94)/ST/52.

Ministerial Decision on Trade and Environment (15 April 1994) LT/UR/D-5/8, 33 ILM 1267.

WTO Council for Trade in Services, Decision on Trade in Services and the Environment (1 March 1995) S/L/4.

Report of the Committee on Trade and Environment (12 November 1996) WT/CTE/1.

Singapore Ministerial Declaration (18 December 1996) WT/MIN(96)/DEC, 36 ILM 218.
Geneva Ministerial Declaration (20 May 1998) WT/MIN(98)/DEC/1.
Preparations for the 1999 Ministerial Conference—Trade and Environment, Communication from Norway (30 April 1999) WT/GC/W/176.
Preparations for the 1999 Ministerial Conference—EC Approach to Trade and Environment in the New WTO Round—Communication from the European Communities (1 June 1999) WT/GC/W/194.
Preparations for the 1999 Ministerial Conference—Trade and Sustainable Development—Communication from the United States (6 August 1999) WT/GC/W/304.
Preparations for the 1999 Ministerial Conference-Canadian Approach to Trade and Environment in the New WTO Round-Communication from Canada (12 October 1999) WT/GC/W/358.
Preparations for the 1999 Ministerial Conference—Trade, Environment and Sustainable Development—Paragraph 9(d) of the Geneva Ministerial Declaration-Communication from Cuba (15 November 1999) WT/GC/W/387.
Trade Policy Review Norway, Minutes of Meeting (26 July 2000) WT/TPR/M/70.
Trade Policy Review Madagascar, Minutes of Meeting (11 June 2001) WT/TPR/M/80.
Draft Doha WTO Ministerial Declaration (27 October 2001) JOB(01)/140/Rev.1.
European Communities—The ACP-EC Partnership Agreement (14 November 2001) WT/MIN(01)/15.
European Communities—Transitional Regime for the EC Autonomous Tariff Rate Quotas on Imports of Bananas (14 November 2001) WT/MIN(01)/16.
Doha Ministerial Declaration (14 November 2001) WT/MIN(01)/DEC/1.
Declaration on the TRIPS Agreement and Public Health (20 November 2001) WT/MIN(01)/DEC/2.
Implementation-Related Issues and Concerns (20 November 2001) WT/MIN(01)/17.
Procedures for Extensions under Art 27.4 for Certain Developing Country Members (20 November 2001) G/SCM/39.
Committee on Trade and Environment—Trade in Used and Re-treaded Tyres—Submission by Brazil (12 July 2005) WT/CTE/W/241.
Committee on Trade and Environment—Report of the Meeting Held on 6 July 2005 (2 September 2005) WT/CTE/M/40.
Doha Work Programme—Ministerial Declaration (21 December 2005) WT/MIN(05)/DEC.
Trade Policy Review China—Minutes of Meetings (6 June 2006–12 June 2007) WT/TPR/M/161 to WT/TPR/M/181.
Committee on Trade and Environment—Committee on Trade and Environment Special Session-Matrix on Trade Measures Pursuant to Selected Multilateral Environmental Agreements (14 March 2007) WT/CTE/W/160/Rev.4.
Committee on Trade and Environment Annotated Bibliography of Selected Literature Concerning the Use of Trade Measures in Multilateral Environmental Agreements (MEAs) Note by the Secretariat (31 January 2000) WT/CTE/W/129.
WT/CTE/8 11 July 2003 (03-3739) Committee on Trade and Environment Report to the 5th Session of the WTO Ministerial Conference in Cancún Paragraphs 32 and 33 of the Doha Ministerial Declaration.
WT/CTE/W/4 Approaches to the relationship between the provisions of the multilateral trading system and trade measures pursuant to Multilateral Environmental Agreements—Note by the Secretariat.
WT/CTE/W/12 Trade measures for environmental purposes taken pursuant to Multilateral Environmental Agreements: recent developments—Note by the Secretariat.
WT/CTE/W/15 Trade measures for environmental purposes taken pursuant to multilateral environmental agreements: recent developments—Note by the Secretariat—FAO Code of Conduct for Responsible Fisheries.
WT/CTE/W/18 Convention on Biological Diversity: recent developments—Note by the Secretariat.
WT/CTE/W/19 Trade measures for environmental purposes taken pursuant to multilateral environmental agreements: recent developments—Seventh meeting of the Parties to the Montreal Protocol—Note by the Secretariat.

WT/CTE/W/20 Item 1: The relationship between the provisions of the multilateral trading system and trade measures for environmental purposes, including those pursuant to multilateral environmental agreements (MEAs)—Submission by New Zealand.

WT/CTE/W/31 The relationship between trade measures pursuant to MEAs and the WTO Agreement—Proposal by Japan.

WT/CTE/W/39 The relationship between the provisions of the multilateral trading system and trade measures for environmental purposes, including those pursuant to multilateral environmental agreements (MEAs)—Proposal by ASEAN.

WT/CTE/W/44 Multilateral environmental agreements: recent developments—Note by the Secretariat.

WT/CTE/W/48 Results of the ad hoc Intergovernmental Panel on Forests—Note by the Secretariat.

WT/CTE/W/55 Recent trade-related developments in the Basel Convention—Communication from the Basel Convention Secretariat.

WT/CTE/W/57 The Montreal Protocol and trade measures—Communication from the Secretariat for the Vienna Convention for the Protection of the Ozone Layer and the Montreal Protocol on Substances that Deplete the Ozone Layer.

WT/CTE/W/58 Nature and extent of GEF projects in assisting in the implementation of Multilateral Environmental Agreements—Communication from the GEF Secretariat.

WT/CTE/W/59 The proposed Prior Informed Consent (PIC) and Persistent Organic Pollutants (POPS) Conventions—Communication from UNEP Chemicals.

WT/CTE/W/60 Nature and extent of projects supported by the Multilateral Fund—Communication from the Multilateral Fund for the implementation of the Montreal Protocol.

WT/CTE/W/61 The United Nations Framework Convention on Climate Change—Communication from the UNFCCC.

WT/CTE/W/62 The 1994 Agreement relating to the implementation of part XI of the 1982 UN Convention on the Law of the Sea—Communication from the United Nations Division for Ocean Affairs and the Law of the Sea, Office of Legal Affairs.

WT/CTE/W/63 The Convention on International Trade in Endangered Species of Wild Fauna and Flora—Communication from the CITES Secretariat.

WT/CTE/W/64 The Convention on Biological Diversity and its relation to trade—Communication from the Executive Secretary of the CBD.

WT/CTE/W/68 The Montreal Protocol on Substances that Deplete the Ozone Layer—recent developments—Note by the Secretariat.

WT/CTE/W/71 Convention on International Trade in Endangered Species of Wild Fauna and Flora—Note by the Secretariat.

WT/CTE/W/74 United Nations Framework Convention on Climate Change—Note by the Secretariat.

WT/CTE/W/84 Communication from the Secretariat of the Intergovernmental Forum on Forests (IFF).

WT/CTE/W/86 Recent developments in Multilateral Environmental Agreements (MEAs)—Note by the Secretariat.

WT/CTE/W/87 Communication from the Secretariat of the International Commission for the Conservation of Atlantic Tunas (ICCAT).

WT/CTE/W/88 Communication from the Secretariat of the UN/ECE Convention on Long-Range Transboundary Air Pollution.

WT/CTE/W/89 Communication from the Secretariat of the International Tropical Timber Organization.

WT/CTE/W/90 Communication from the Secretariat of the Basel Convention.

WT/CTE/W/91 Communication from the Secretariat of UNEP Chemicals (IRPTC).

WT/CTE/W/92 Communication from the Secretariat of the Convention on Biological Diversity (CBD).

WT/CTE/W/95 The International Commission for the Conservation of Atlantic Tunas (ICCAT)—Communication from Brazil.

WT/CTE/W/104 The Montreal Protocol on the Substances that Deplete the Ozone Layer-recent developments—Note by the Secretariat.

WT/CTE/W/112 Draft International Legally Binding Instrument for Implementing International Action on Certain Persistent Organic Pollutants (POPS)—Note by the Secretariat.
WT/CTE/W/113 Communication from The Commission for the Conservation of Antarctic Marine Living Resources.
WT/CTE/W/115 Communication from the Secretariat for the Vienna Convention and the Montreal Protocol, UNEP.
WT/CTE/W/116 Communication from the Secretariat of the Convention on Biological Diversity.
WT/CTE/W/117 Convention on Biological Diversity (CBD), Draft Protocol on Biosafety, Recent Developments —Note by the Secretariat.
WT/CTE/W/119 Communication from the Secretariat of the Convention on International Trade in Endangered Species of Wild Fauna and Flora (CITES).
WT/CTE/W/120 Communication from the Secretariat of the International Tropical Timber Organization (ITTO).
WT/CTE/W/122 Communication from the Secretariat of the Intergovernmental Forum on Forests (IFF).
WT/CTE/W/123 Communication from the Secretariat of the United Nations Framework Convention on Climate Change.
WT/CTE/W/124 Convention on Biological Diversity (CBD)—Draft Protocol on Biosafety-Note by the Secretariat.
WT/CTE/W/128 Recent Developments in Multilateral Environmental Agreements (MEAs)—Note by the Secretariat.

Non-Papers submitted under Items 1 and 5 of the CTE's work programme:

- **Non-paper (19 February 1996) Submission by the European Community on Item 1**
- **Non-paper (20 May 1996) Submission by Switzerland on Item 1**
- **Non-paper (12 June 1996) Submission by Korea on Item 1**
- **Non-paper (23 July 1996) Submission by Hong Kong on Item 1**
- **Non-paper (23 July 1996) Submission by India on Items 1 and 5**
- **Non-paper (11 Sept. 1996) Submission by the United States on Multilateral Environmental Agreements.**

(iii) Other

Council of the European Union, 'Renewed EU Sustainable Development Strategy' (26 June 2006) 10917/06.
EC, 'A Sustainable Europe for a Better World: A European Union Strategy for Sustainable Development' COM(2001) 0264 final, 15 May 2001.
EC, 'Towards a Global Partnership for Sustainable Development' COM(2002) 82 final, 13 February 2002.
ILA, *Report of the Sixty-Second Conference* (ILA, Seoul 1987).
ILA, *Report of the Expert Group on Identification of Principles of International Law for Sustainable Development* (ILA, London 1995).
ILA, 'New Delhi Declaration of Principles of International Law Relating to Sustainable Development' (2002) 2 International Environmental Agreements 209.
ILA, *Sustainable Development and The Green Economy in International Trade Law* (ILA, 2018).
ILA, *Sustainable Development and The Green Economy in International Trade Law* (ILA, 2019).
OECD, 'Trade Facilitation Reforms in the Service of Development' (30 July 2003) TD/TC/WP(2003)11/FINAL.
OECD, 'Trade Measures in the Basel Convention on the Control of Transboundary Movements of Hazardous Wastes and their Disposal' (27 May 1998) COM/ENV/TD(97)41/FINAL.
OECD, 'National Strategies for Sustainable Development: Good Practices in OECD Countries' (8 September 2005) SG/SD(2005)6.
OASGA, 'Declaration of Panama: Energy for Sustainable Development' (5 June 2007) OAS Doc AG/DEC 52.

OASGA (11 September 2001) OAS Doc AG/RES 1 (XXVIII-E/01).
Summit of the Americas on Sustainable Development, *Santa Cruz de la Sierra Declaration* (1996) <http://www.summit-americas.org/summit_sd/summit_sd_dec_en.pdf>.
WTO, *The Trade Situation in 2009-2010* (Geneva, WTO 2010).
WTO, *Annual Report 2011* (Geneva, WTO 2011).

2. Secondary Sources

Agriculture Organization, Legal Office Staff, and Agriculture Organization of the United Nations. Legal Office, *Law and Sustainable Development Since Rio: Legal Trends in Agriculture and Natural Resource Management* (Legislative Study 73, Food and Agriculture Organization of the UN (FAO), Rome 2002).
Asian Development Bank (ADB), 'Environmental Policy' (2002) <https://www.adb.org/sites/default/files/institutional-document/33343/files/environment-policy.pdf> accessed 16 December 2020.
Ades A and Chua HB, 'Thy Neighbours Curse: Regional Instability and Economic Growth' (1997) 2 Journal of Economic Growth 279.
African Development Bank Group (AFDB), 'African Development Bank Group's Policy on the Environment' (2004) <https://www.afdb.org/fileadmin/uploads/afdb/Documents/Policy-Documents/10000027-EN-BANK-GROUP-POLICY-ON-THE-ENVIRONMENT.PDF> accessed 16 December 2020.
Aggarwal KV, Espach RH and Tulchin JS, *The Strategic Dynamics of Latin American Trade* (Stanford, Stanford University Press 2004).
Akehurst M 'Custom as a Source of International Law' (1974–195) 47 British Yearbook of International Law 1.
D'Alfonso, A, 'European Development Fund, Joint Development Cooperation and the EU Budget: Out or In?' (European Parliamentary Research Service. Members' Research Service. PE 542.140, 2014).
Allot P, *The Health of Nations* (Cambridge, CUP 2002).
Anaedu O and Engfeldt L-G, 'Sustainable Development Governance'.
Anand S and Sen A, 'Human Development and Economic Sustainability' (2000) 28 World Development 12, 2029–2049.
Appleton AE, 'Environmental Labelling Schemes Revisited: WTO Law and Developing Country Implications' in Gary P Samson and W Bradnee Chambers (eds), *Trade, Environment and the Millennium* (2nd edn, New York, United Nations University Press 2002) 235.
Arrow K and others, 'Economic Growth, Carrying Capacity, and the Environment' (1996) 1 Environment and Development Economics 104.
Atapattu, S 'Sustainable Development: Myth or Reality?: A Survey of Sustainable Development under International Law and Sri Lankan Law' (2001–2002) 14 Georgetown International Environmental Law Review 265.
Atapattu S, *Emerging Principles of International Environmental Law* (New York, 2006 Transnational).
Ayres J, 'Power Relations under NAFTA: Reassessing the Efficacy of Contentious Transnationalism' (2004) 74 Studies in Political Economy 101.
Ayres RU and Ayres EH, *Crossing the Energy Divide: Moving from Fossil Fuel Dependence to a Clean Energy Future* (USA, First Printing 2009).
Badgley C and others, 'Organic Agriculture and the Global Food Supply' (2007) 22(2) Renewable Agriculture and Food Supply 86.Management 133.
Bahla R, *Modern GATT Law: A Treatise on the General Agreement on Tariffs and Trade* (London, Sweet and Maxwell 2005).
Baibourtian A, 'Statement by the Deputy Minister of Foreign Affairs of the Republic of Armenia at the 14th Session of the Commission on Sustainable Development' (2006) <http://www.un.org/esa/sustdev/csd/csd14/statements/armenia_hls_10may.pdf> accessed 16 December 2020.
Balassa BA, *The Theory of Economic Integration* (London, Allen and Unwin 1961).
Balassa BA, *Economic Development and Integration* (Mexico, Centro de Estudios Monetarios Latinoamericanos 1965).

Baldwin RE, 'Multilateralising Regionalism: Spaghetti Bowls as Building Blocs on the Path to Global Free Trade' (Oct 2006) NBER Working Paper No W12545.

Baldwin RE and Low P, *Multilateralising Regionalism: Challenges for the Global Trading System* (Cambridge, CUP 2009).

Baldwin RE, McLaren J and Panagariya A, *Regulatory Protectionism, Developing Nations, and a Two-Tier World Trade System* (Washington, Brookings Trade Forum 2000).

Barbier EB, 'The Economic Determinants of Land Degradation in Developing Countries' (1997) 352(1356) Philosophical Transactions of the Royal Society B: Biological Sciences 891.

Barry J and Eckersley R (eds), *The State and Global Ecological Crisis* (Cambridge, MA, MIT Press 2005).

Barritt E, 'Global Values, Transnational Expression: From Aarhus to Escazú' Research Handbook on Transnational Environmental Law (Cheltenham, Edward Elgar 2020).

Bartelmus P, *Environment, Growth and Development: The Concepts and Strategies of Sustainability* (Florence, KY, Routledge 1994).

Bartels L and Ortino F (eds), *Regional Trade Agreements and the WTO Legal System* (Oxford, OUP 2006).

Bastiaens I and Postnikov E, 'Greening up: The Effects of Environmental Standards in EU and US Trade Agreements' (2017) 26(5) Environmental Politics 847–869.

Baughen S, *International Trade and the Protection of the Environment* (London, Routledge Cavendish 2007).

Baxter R, 'Treaties and Custom' (1970) 129 Recueil des Cours de l'Académie de Droit International 62.

Bellmann C, Dutfield G and Meléndez-Ortiz R, *Trading in Knowledge: Development Perspectives on TRIPS, Trade and Sustainability* (London, Earthscan/ICTSD 2003).

Bellmann C and Melendez- Ortiz R, *International Legal Protection for Genetic Resources, Traditional Knowledge and Folklore: Challenges for the Intellectual Property System– Weerawit Weeraworawit* (London, Routledge 2013) 174.

Ben-David D, Nordström H and Winters LA (eds), *Trade, Income Disparity and Poverty* (Special Studies 5, Geneva, WTO 1999).

Bernhardt R, 'Evolutive Treaty Interpretation, Especially of the European Convention on Human Rights' (1999) 42 German Yearbook of International Law 11.

Bernstein B and Hannah E, 'Non-State Global Standard Setting and the WTO: Legitimacy and the Need for Regulatory Space' (2008) 11(3) Journal of International Economic Law 575–608.

Bethlehem D and others, *The Oxford Handbook of International Trade Law* (Oxford, OUP 2009).

Bhagwati JN, 'The New International Economic Order: The North-South Debate' (1977) MIT Bicentennial Studies.

Bhagwati JN, Krishna P and Panagariya A (eds), *Trading Blocs: Alternative Approaches to Analyzing Preferential Trade Agreements* (Boston, MIT Press 1999).

Bhala R, 'Clarifying the Trade-Labor Link' (1998) 37(1) Columbia Journal of Transnational Law 30.

Birdsall N and Wheeler D, 'Trade Policy and Industrial Pollution in Latin America: Where are the Pollution Havens?' (1993) 2(1) Journal of Environment and Development 137.

Birnie P, Boyle A and Redgwell C, *International Law & the Environment* (OUP, Oxford 2009).

Blanco H, Araya M and Murillo C, *ALCA y medio ambiente: Ideas desde Latinoamerica* (Santiago, CIPMA/GETS/CINPE 2003).

Blanco H, Togeiro de Almeida L and Gallagher K (eds), *Globalizacion y Medio Ambiente: Lecciones desde las Americas* (Santiago, RIDES- GDAE 2005)

Boas M and Vevatne J, 'Sustainable Development and the World Trade Organisation' in McNeill D and M Boas (eds), *Global Institutions and Development: Framing the World?* (London, Routledge 2004) 98.

Bodiguel L and Cardwell M (eds), *The Regulation of Genetically Modified Organisms: Comparative Approaches* (Oxford, OUP 2010).

Boden TA, Marland G and Andres RJ, *Global, Regional, and National Fossil-Fuel CO2 Emissions* (Tennessee, Carbon Dioxide Information Analysis Center 2009).

Bolle MJ, 'Overview of Labor Enforcement Issues in Free Trade Agreements' (CRS Report prepared for Members and Committees of Congress. Order Code RS22823, 2016).

Bottriel K and Cordonier Segger MC, 'The Principle of Public Participation and Access to Information and Justice', CISDL Legal Working Papers on Recent Developments in International Law Related to Sustainable Development (CISDL, Montreal 2005).

Bottriel K and French D, 'The Duty of States to Ensure Sustainable Use of Natural Resources', CISDL Legal Working Papers on Recent Developments in International Law Related to Sustainable Development (CISDL, Montreal 2005).

Bowman M and Redgwell C, *International Law and the Conservation of Biological Diversity* (The Hague, Kluwer Law International 1995).

Boyle A and Chinkin C, *The Making of International Law* (Oxford, OUP 2007).

Boyle A and Freestone D (eds), *International Law and Sustainable Development: Past Achievements and Future Challenges* (Oxford, OUP 1999).

Brack D, *International Trade and the Montreal Protocol* (London, Earthscan 1996).

Brack D, 'Reconciling the GATT and Multilateral Environmental Agreements with Trade Provisions: The Latest Debate' (1997) 6 Review of European Community and International Environmental Law 112.

Brack D and Gray K, *Multilateral Environmental Agreements and the WTO* (IISD Report, September 2003).

Brack D, Gray K and Hayman G, *Controlling the International Trade in Illegally Logged Timber and Wood Products* (London, RIIA 2002).

Brack D (ed), *Trade and Environment: Conflict or Compatibility?* (London, Earthscan 1998).

Brown Weiss E, Jackson J and Bernasconi-Osterwalder N, *Reconciling Environment and Trade* (Leiden, Martinus Nijhoff 2008).

Brunnée J, 'COPing with Consent: Lawmaking under Multilateral Environmental Agreements' (2002) 15 Leiden Journal of International Law 1.

Brunnee J and Toope SJ, *Legality and Legitimacy in International Law* (Cambridge, CUP 2010)

Brunnée J and Toope SJ, 'The Changing Nile Basin Regime: Does Law Matter?' (2002) 43 Harvard International Law Journal 105.

Brunnée J and Toope SJ, 'Persuasion and Enforcement: Explaining Compliance with International Law' (2002) XIII Finnish Yearbook of International Law 1.

Buffard I and Zemanek K, 'The Object and Purpose of a Treaty: An Enigma?' (1998) 3 Austrian Review of International and European Law 311.

Bugge HC and Voigt C (eds), *Sustainable Development in International and National Law* (Groningen, Europa 2008).

Busch ML and Pelc KJ, 'Words Matter: How WTO Rulings Handle Controversy' (2019) 63(3) International Studies Quarterly 464–476.

Burianski M, Negri C and Ulbrich M, 'Free Trade and Core Labour Rights: Status Quo of a Discussion' (2001) 9(4) Tilburg Foreign Law Review 393–416.

Button C, *The Power to Protect: Trade, Health and Uncertainty in the WTO* (Oxford, Hart Publishing 2004).

Byers M (ed), *The Role of Law in International Politics: Essays in International Relations and International Law* (Oxford, OUP 2000).

Cabrera J, *Propriedad Intelectual, Biodiversidad y Comercio. Opciones para establecer sinergias entre los Acuerdos Ambientales y los Tratados de Comercio* (San Jose, Universidad Nacional Estatal a Distancia, 2009).

Cameron J, 'What Now? Trade and the Environment' in P Geraint, A Qureshi and H Steiner (eds), *The Legal and Moral Aspects of International Trade* (New York, Routledge 1998).

Canadian Government, Department of Foreign Affairs and International Trade, *Retrospective Analysis of the 1994 Canadian Environmental Review: Uruguay Round of Multilateral Trade Negotiations* (DFAIT, Ottawa 1999).

Canadian Government, *The Cabinet Directive on the Environmental Assessment of Policy, Plan and Program Proposals* (Privy Council Office and Canadian Environmental Assessment Agency, Ottawa 2004) <https://www.canada.ca/en/impact-assessment-agency/programs/strategic-environmental-assessment/cabinet-directive-environmental-assessment-policy-plan-program-proposals.html> accessed 16 December 2020.

Caporale GM and others, 'On the Bilateral Trade Effects of Free Trade Agreements between the EU-15 and the CEEC-4 Countries' (2009) 145(2) Review of World Economics 189–206.

Cardoso FH and Faletto E, *Dependency and Development in Latin America* (Berkeley, University of California Press 1979).

Centro de Investigación y Planificación del Medio Ambiente (CIPMA), *Environmental Impacts of Trade Liberalization and Policies for the Sustainable Management of Natural Resources: A Case Study of Chile's Mining Sector* (Geneva, UNEP 1999).

Ceyssens j, 'Towards a Common Foreign Investment Policy? Foreign Investment in the European Constitution' (2005) 32 Legal Issues of Economic Integration 259–291.

Chambers B, 'International Trade Law and the Kyoto Protocol: Potential Incompatibilities' in B Chambers (ed), *Inter-linkages: The Kyoto Protocol and the International Trade and Investment Regimes* (UNU, Tokyo 2001).

Charnovitz S, 'Regional Trade Agreements and the Environment' (1995) 37(5) Environment: Science and Policy for Sustainable Development 95.

Charnovitz S, 'The Labor Dimension of the Emerging Free Trade Area of the Americas' in P Alston (ed), *Labour Rights as Human Rights* (Oxford, OUP 2005).

Chang HF, 'Toward a Greener GATT: Environmental Trade Measures and the Shrimp-Turtle Case' (2000) 74 Southern California Law Review 31.

Cheng B, 'United Nations Resolutions on Outer Space: "Instant" International Customary Law' (1965) 5 Indian Journal of International Law 23.

Cheng B, *General Principles of Law as Applied by International Courts and Tribunals* (Cambridge, CUP 2006).

Chertow MR and Esty DC (eds), *Thinking Ecologically: The next Generation of Environmental Policy* (New Haven, CT, Yale 1997).

Government of Chile/European Union, 'Subsecretario Participó en V Comité De Asociación Chile-Unión Europea' (7 December 2007).

Chinkin C, 'The Challenge of Soft Law: Development and Change in International Law' (1989) 38 International and Comparative Law Quarterly 850.

Cho S, ' The Demise of Development in the Doha Round Negotiations' (2010) 45 Texas International law Journal 573.

Chong S-Y, 'Strengthening Regional Governance to Protect the Marine Environment in Northeast Asia: From a Fragmented to an Integrated Approach' (2010) 34 Marine Policy 549.

Chowdry N and Skarstedt CE, 'The Principle of Good Governance' CISDL Legal Working Papers on Recent Developments in International Law Related to Sustainable Development (CISDL, Montreal 2005).

Christensen S, 'Statement by the Secretary-General of Nordic Council of Ministers at the World Summit for Sustainable Development' (2002) <http://www.un.org/events/wssd/statements/nord-icE.htm> accessed 16 December 2020.

Chumacero RA, Fuentes R and Schmidt-Hebbel K, 'Chile's Free Trade Agreements: How Big is the Deal?' (June 2004) Central Bank of Chile Working Papers No 264.

Cockcroft JD, Frank AG and Johnson DL, *Dependence and Underdevelopment: Latin America's Political Economy* (New York, Anchor Books 1972).

Collier P, *The Bottom Billion: Why the Poorest Countries are Failing and What can be done about it* (Oxford, OUP 2007).

Collier T, 'Why the WTO is Deadlocked: and What can be Done About it' (2006) 29 World Economy 1423.

Collier T and Gunning J, *Trade Shocks in Developing Countries* (Oxford, Clarendon 1999).

Collier T and Dollar D, *Globalization, Growth and Poverty* (New York, OUP 2002).

Commission for Environmental Cooperation, *Potential NAFTA Effects: Claims and Arguments 1991-1994* (CEC, Montreal 1996).

Conrad CR, *Process and Production Methods (PPMs) in WTO Law: Interfacing Trade and Social Goals* (Cambridge, CUP 2011).

Contreras-Hermosilla, A., Doornbosch, R., & Lodge, M. (2008). *The Economics of Illegal Logging and Associated Trade* (Paris, OECD 2007)

Government of Columbia, 'Report on the National Development Plan' (2007).

Commission for Labour Cooperation, *Comparative Guide to Labour and Employment Laws in North America: Labour Relations Law in North America* (Washington, NAALC 2000).

Cooper CA and Massell BF, 'Toward a General Theory of Customs Unions for Developing Countries' (1965) Journal of Political Economy 461.

Cooper HD, 'The International Treaty on Plant and Genetic Resources for Food and Agriculture' (2002) 11 Review of European Community and International Environmental Law 1.

Cooper RN, *Environment and Resource Policies for the World Economy* (Washington, Brookings Institution 1994).

Copeland BR and Scott MS, 'Trade, Growth and the Environment' (July 2003) National Bureau of Economic Research, Working Paper No 9823, <https://www.nber.org/papers/w9823> accessed 16 December 2020.

Corbin H, 'The Proposed United States–Chile Free Trade Agreement: Reconciling Free Trade and Environmental Protection' (2003) 14 Colorado Journal of International Environmental Law and Policy 119.

Cordonier Segger MC, 'Significant Developments in Sustainable Development Law and Governance: A Proposal' (2004) 28 Natural Resources Forum 61.

Cordonier Segger MC, 'Sustainable Development in the Negotiation of the FTAA' (2004) 27(3) Fordham International Law Journal 1118–1206.

Cordonier Segger MC, 'The WTO, Regional Trade Agreements and Sustainable Development' in L Bartels and F Ortino (eds), *Regional Trade Agreements and the WTO Legal System* (Oxford: Oxford University Press, 2006).

Cordonier Segger MC, 'Principles, Practices and Prospects: Sustainable Development through International Treaty Law' in HC Bugge and C Voigt (eds), *Sustainable Development in National and International Law* (Groningen, Europa Law Publishing 2008).

Cordonier Segger MC, 'Intersecting Implementation of Environment, Trade and Social Regimes' in T Komori and K Wellens (eds), *Effectiveness in International Law*, (Lieden, Martinus Nijhoff, 2009).

Cordonier Segger MC, 'The Role of International Forums in the Advancement of Sustainable Development' (2009) X Sustainable Development Law and Policy 4–18.

Cordonier Segger MC, 'Sistemas de inversión y comercio para economías bajas en emisiones de carbono más sustentables' in P Moraga (ed), *Nuevo Marco Legal para el Cambio Climático* (Santiago, LOM 2009).

Cordonier Segger MC, 'Sustainable Development in International Law' in D Armstrong (ed), *Routledge Handbook of International Law* (New York: Routledge, 2009) 355.

Cordonier Segger MC, 'Sustainability, Global Justice and the Law' (2010) 54(4) McGill Law Journal.

Cordonier Segger MC, 'Trade and Investment Implications of the Cartagena Protocol on Biosafety' in MC Cordonier Segger, C Frison and F Perron-Welch (eds), *Legal Aspects of Implementing the Cartagena Protocol on Biosafety* (Cambridge, CUP 2013).

Cordonier Segger MC, 'Innovative Legal Solutions for Investment Law and Sustainable Development Challenges' in Y Levashova and others (eds), *Bridging the Gap Between International Investment Law and the Environment* (Amsterdam, Eleven 2015).

Cordonier Segger MC, 'Advancing the Paris Agreement on Climate Change for Sustainable Development' (2017) 5(2) Cambridge Journal of International and Comparative Law 202.

Cordonier Segger MC, 'Commitments to Sustainable Development through International Law and Policy' in Cordonier Segger MC, Weeramantry CG (eds), *Sustainable Development in International Courts and Tribunals* (London, Routledge 2017).

Cordonier Segger MC, 'Inspiration for Integration: Interpreting International Trade and Investment Accords for Sustainable Development' (2017) 3(1) Canadian Journal of Comparative and Contemporary Law 159.

Cordonier Segger MC, 'Sustainable Development through the 2015 Paris Agreement' (2017) 11(2) Canadian International Lawyer 124.

Cordonier Segger MC, 'Sustainable Developments in International Investment Law and Policy related to Renewable Energy and Climate Change Mitigation and Adaptation' (2019) 7 Hungarian Yearbook of International Law and European Law 29.

Cordonier Segger MC, 'UN Treaties on the Environment and Sustainable Development' in D Malone and others (eds), *Handbook of United Nations Treaties* (Oxford, OUP 2019).

Cordonier Segger MC and French D, 'Promoting Investments through International Treaties on Sustainable Development' in MC Cordonier Segger, M Gehring and A Newcombe (eds), *Sustainable Development in World Investment Law* (The Hague, Wolters Kluwer 2010).

Cordonier Segger MC and Gehring M, 'Precaution, Health and the World Trade Organization: Moving Toward Sustainable Development' (2003) 29 Queen's Law Journal 133.

Cordonier Segger MC and Gehring M, 'Making Progress? Climate Change, Sustainable Development and International Trade and Investment Law' in C Streck and D Freestone (eds), *Legal Aspects of Carbon Trading: Kyoto, Copenhagen and Beyond* (Oxford: Oxford University Press, 2009).

Cordonier Segger MC, Gehring M and Newcombe A, 'Conclusions: Promoting Sustainable Investment through International Law' in MC Cordonier Segger, M Gehring and A Newcombe (eds), *Sustainable Development in World Investment Law* (The Hague, Wolters Kluwer 2010).

Cordonier Segger MC and Gehring M, 'Climate Change and International Trade and Investment Law' in R Rayfuse and SV Scott (eds), *International Law in the Era of Climate Change* (Cheltenham, Edward Elgar 2013).

Cordonier Segger MC and Gehring M, 'Overcoming Obstacles with Opportunities: Trade and Investment Agreements for Sustainable Development' in S Schill, C Tams and R Hofmann (eds), *International Investment Law and Development: Bridging the Gap* (Cheltenham, Edward Elgar 2015).

Cordonier Segger MC, Gehring M and Wardell DA, 'REDD+ Instruments, International Investment Rules and Sustainable Landscapes' in C Voigt (ed), *Research Handbook on REDD+ and International Law* (Cheltenham, Edward Elgar 2016).

Cordonier Segger MC, Gehring M and Wardell DA, 'Analysing CITES Trade Measures' in MC Cordonier Segger and A Wardell (eds), *Implementing CITES on Sustainable Development* (Cambridge, CUP 2020 forthcoming).

Cordonier Segger MC, Holmgren P and Wardell DA 'Financing Sustainable Landscapes through Innovative International Economic Law and Governance Instruments' (2018) 7(1) Global Journal of Comparative Law 169.

Cordonier Segger MC and Khalfan A, *Sustainable Development Law: Principles, Practices and Prospects* (Oxford, OUP 2004).

Cordonier Segger MC and Newcombe A, 'Integrating International Investment, Environmental and Social Law' in MC Cordonier Segger, M Gehring and A Newcombe (eds), *Sustainable Development in World Investment Law*, (The Hague: Wolters Kluwer, 2010).

Cordonier Segger MC and Saito Y, 'Innovative Legal Measures for Climate Change Response in the Green Economy: Integrating Opportunity, Equity and Inclusion' (2013) World Bank Legal Review 5.

Cordonier Segger MC and Wardell DA, 'Global Commodities Governance for Sustainable Development' in MC Cordonier Segger and A Wardell (eds), *Implementing CITES on Sustainable Development* (Cambridge, CUP 2020 forthcoming).

Cordonier Segger MC and others, 'Prospects for Principles of International Sustainable Development Law after the WSSD: Common but Differentiated Responsibilities, Precaution and Participation' (2003) 12(1) Review of European Community and International Environmental Law 54.

Cordonier Segger MC and Weeramantry CG (eds), *Sustainable Justice* (Leiden, Martinus Nijhoff 2004).

Cordonier Segger MC and Leichner Reynal M (eds), *Beyond the Barricades: An Americas Trade and Sustainability Agenda* (Aldershot, Ashgate 2005).

Cordonier Segger MC, Gehring M and Newcombe A (eds), *Sustainable Development in World Investment Law* (The Hague, Kluwer Law International 2010).

Cordonier Segger MC and Perron-Welch F (eds), *Legal Aspects of Implementing the Cartagena Protocol on Biosafety* (Cambridge, CUP 2013).

Cordonier Segger MC with Weeramantry CJ (eds), *Sustainable Development in International Courts and Tribunals* (London, Routledge 2017).

Cortes CJ, *GATT, WTO and the Regulation of International Trade Textiles* (Aldershot, Ashgate 1997).

Cosbey A, 'New Views of Trade and Sustainable Development: Using Sen's Conception of Development to Re-examine the Debates' (2003) Thematic Research Paper, TIPS/IISD Trade Knowledge Network Workshop.

Cosbey A, 'NAFTA's Chapter 11 and the Environment' (2003) Discussion Paper for the CEC's Public Workshop on NAFTA's Chapter 11, <https://www.iisd.org/publications/

naftas-chapter-11-and-environment-discussion-paper-cecs-public-workshop-naftas-chapter> accessed 16 December 2020.

Cosbey A, 'Lessons Learned on Trade and Sustainable Development: Distilling Six Years of Research from the Trade Knowledge Network' (2004) IISD Working Paper <http://www.tradeknowledgenetwork.net/pdf/tkn_lessons_learned_en.pdf> accessed 16 December 2020.

Cottier T, Pauwelyn J and Bürgi E (eds), *Human Rights and International Trade* (Oxford, OUP 2005).

Crawford JA and Fiorentino RV, *The Changing Landscapes of Regional Trade Agreements* (Geneva, WTO 2005).

Creason J and others, 'The Environmental Impacts of Trade Liberalisation: A Quantitative Analysis for the United States using TEAM' (2005) 34 Agricultural and Resource Economics Review 90.

D'Amato A, *The Concept of Custom in International Law* (Ithaca, Cornell University Press 1971).

D'Amato A, 'Agora: What Obligation Does Our Generation Owe to the Next? An Approach to Global Environmental Responsibility' (1990) 84 American Journal of International Law 190.

Dasgupta S and others, 'Agricultural Trade, Development and Toxic Risk.' 30 World Development 1401.

Decleris M, 'The Law of Sustainable Development: General Principles-A Report for the European Commission' (2000) <http://www.pikpotsdam.de/avec/peyresq2003/talks/0917/sillence/background_literature/sustlaw.pdf> accessed 16 December 2020.

Deere C and Esty D (eds), *Greening the Americas: NAFTA's Lessons for Hemispheric Trade* (Boston, MIT Press 2002).

Demaret P, 'The Metamorphoses of the GATT: From the Havana Charter to the World Trade Organisation' (1995) 34 Columbia Journal of Transnational Law 123.

de Mestral A, 'The North American Free Trade Agreement: a comparative analysis' (1998) 275 Recueil des Cours de l'Académie de Droit International 219, 375.

Desker B, 'In Defence of FTAs: From Purity to Pragmatism in East Asia' (2004) 17(1) Pacific Review 3.

Devlin R, 'The Free Trade Area of the Americas and MERCOSUR-European Union Free Trade Processes: Can They Learn Something from Each Other?' (IADB, Washington 2000) Occasional Paper 6 <http://ctrc.sice.oas.org/geograph/westernh/devlin.pdf> accessed 16 December 2020.

Dirección General de Relaciones Económicas Internacionales del Ministerio de Relaciones Exteriores de Chile, 'Evaluación De Las Relaciones Económicas Y De Cooperación Entre Chile Y Los Países De La Unión Europea: A Cuatro Años De Vigencia Del Acuerdo De Asociación' (October 2007) <http://www.sice.oas.org/TPD/CHL_EU/Studies/Evaluacion2007_s.pdf> accessed 16 December 2020.

Dodds F (ed), *Earth Summit 2002: A New Deal* (London, Earthscan 2002).

Dufey A, Claro E and Borregaard N, 'Liberalising Trade in Environmental Goods and Services in the Czech Republic' (2005) OECD Trade and Environment Working Paper, OECD, Paris.

Durbin W, *A Comparison of the Environmental Provisions of the NAFTA, the Canada-Chile Trade Agreement and the Mexican-European Community Trade Agreement* (New Haven, Yale Centre for Environmental Law and Policy 2000).

Dunkley G, *Free Trade: Myth, Reality and Alternatives* (London, Zed Books 2004).

Dudley and others, *Bad Harvest?* (Gland, WWF 1995)

Dworkin R, *Taking Rights Seriously* (London, Duckworth 1977).

Earth Summit, 'Governance for Sustainable Development' (2002) <http://www.earthsummit2002.org/es/issues/Governance/governance.html# Sustainable%20Governance> accessed 16 December 2020.

Echevarria C, Brooks D and Peeling G, 'Mining and Stakeholders' Involvement: Addressing Social Sustainability Changes' in MC Cordonier Segger and M Leichner Reynal (eds), *Beyond the Barricades: The Americas Trade and Sustainable Development Agenda* (Aldershot, Ashgate 2005) 97.

Echols M, *Food Safety and the WTO: The Interplay of Science, Culture and Technology* (The Hague, Kluwer Law International 2001).

Endresen O and Sørgaard E, 'Emission from International Sea Transportation and Environmental Impact' (2003) 108, D17 Journal of Geophysical Research 4560.

Escobar A, *Encountering Development: The Making and Unmaking of the Third World* (Princeton, Princeton University Press 1995).

Eskeland GS and Harrison AE, 'Moving to Greener Pastures? Multinationals and the Pollution Haven Hypothesis' (2003) 70 Journal of Development Economics 1.

Estevadeordal A, Shearer M and Suominen K, 'Multilateralizing RTAs in the Americas: State of Play and Ways Forward' in R Baldwin and P Low (eds), *Multilateralising Regionalism: Challenges for the Global Trading System* (Cambridge, CUP 2009) 427.

Esty D, *Greening the GATT* (Boston, MIT Press 1994).

Esty D, 'Non-Governmental Organizations at the World Trade Organization: Cooperation, Competition, or Exclusion' (1998) 1 Journal of International Economic Law 123.

European Bank for Reconstruction and Development (EBRD), 'Environmental Policy' (2003).

European Commission, *Handbook for Trade Sustainability Impact Assessment* (Brussels, EC 2006).

European Commission, 'Portal on Sustainable Development'.

EU–Canada Summit, 'Joint Summit Statement' (2002).

EU–Chile Association Council, 'First Meeting of the EU-Chile Association Council: Joint Communiqué' (27 March 2003) UE-CL 3903/03 (Press Release 97).

EU–Chile Association Council, 'II EU-Chile Association Council' (26 May 2005) 9352/05 (Press Release 125).

EU–Chile Association Council, 'Third Chile-EU Troika Summit' (17 May 2008) 9540/08 (Press Release 131) <http://www.eu2008.si/si/News_and_Documents/download_docs/May/0516_EU-LAK-Chile.pdf> accessed 16 December 2020.

EU–China Summit, 'Joint Statement' (2005) <http://europa.eu/rapid/pressReleasesAction.do?reference=IP/05/1091> accessed 16 December 2020.

EU@UN, 'EU and Chile Settle WTO/ ITLOS Swordfish Dispute' (24 January 2001) <http://www.eu-un.europa.eu/articles/en/article_2230_en.htm> accessed 16 December 2020.

Evans M (ed), *International Law* (3rd edn, Oxford, OUP 2010).

Evans T, 'Trading Human Rights' in A Taylor and C Thomas (eds), *Global Trade and Global Social Issues* (London, Routledge 1999).

SJ Everett and J Wiley, 'Resist Green Protectionism-or pay the Price at Copenhagen' in R Baldwin and SJ Everett (eds), *The Collapse of Global Trade, Murky Protectionism and the Crisis: Recommendations for the G20* (London, VoxEU.org and Center for Economic and Policy Research 2009) 93.

Experts Group on Environmental Law of the World Commission on Environment and Development, *Environmental Protection and Sustainable Development* (London, Martinus Nijhoff 1987).

Fastenrath U, 'Relative Normativity in International Law' (1993) 4 European Journal of International Law 305.

Francioni F (ed), *Environment, Human Rights and International Trade* (Oxford, Hart 2001).

French D, *International Law and Policy of Sustainable Development* (Manchester, Manchester University Press 2005).

Friedman M, *Capitalism as Freedom* (Chicago, University of Chicago Press 1962).

Fuller LL, *The Morality of Law* (New Haven, Yale University Press 1969).

G8, 'Science and Technology for Sustainable Development' (2003).

Gabriella B-D, 'Statement on behalf of the Council of Europe at the World Summit for Sustainable Development' (2002) <http://www.un.org/events/wssd/statements/ceE.htm>.

Gallagher KP and Blanco H, 'Sustainability Assessments: Tools for Effective Trade Policy in the Hemisphere' (2003) Interhemispheric Resource Center Paper <https://www.iisd.org/system/files/publications/trade_beyond_barricades_draft.pdf> accessed 16 December 2020.

Gantz DA, 'Government to Government Dispute Resolution under NAFTA's Chapter 20: A Commentary on the Process' (2000) 11 American Review of International Arbitration 481.

Gardiner R, *Treaty Interpretation* (Oxford, OUP, 2010).

Gehring M, 'Sustainable Development Angles to the Swordfish Dispute' (2001) 5(7) BRIDGES 13.

Gehring M, *Nachhaltigkeit durch Verfahren im Welthandelsrecht* (Berlin, Duncker and Humbolt 2007).

Gehring M and Cordonier Segger MC (eds), *Sustainable Development in World Trade Law* (London, Kluwer Law International 2005).

Gehring M, Hepburn J and Cordonier Segger MC, *World Trade Law in Practice* (London, Globe Law and Business, 2006).

Gehring, M, Stephenson, S and Cordonier Segger, MC, 'Sustainability Impact Assessments as Inputs and as Interpretative Aids in International Investment Law' (2016) 17 Journal of World Investment and Trade 155.

Gehring T, 'When Arguments Prevail Over Power: The CITES Procedure for the Listing of Endangered Species' (2008) 8 Global Environmental Politics 123.

Geisinger A, 'Sustainable Development and the Domination of Nature: Spreading the Seed of the Western Ideology of Nature' (1999) 27 British Columbia Environmental Affairs Law Review 43.

George C, 'Sustainable Development and Global Governance' (2007) 16 Journal of Environment and Development 102.

George C, 'Developments in Regional Trade Agreements and the Environment: 2012 Update', OECD Trade and Environment Working Papers No 2013/04 (Paris, OECD 2013) <https://doi.org/10.1787/5k43m4nxwm25-en>.

George C and Kirkpatrick C, 'Trade and Development: Assessing the Impact of Trade Liberalization on Sustainable Development' (2004) 38 Journal of World Trade 441.

George C and Kirkpatrick C, 'Assessing National Sustainable Development Strategies: Strengthening the Links to Operational Policy' (2006) 30 Natural Resources Forum 146.

George C and Kirkpatrick C, 'The Influence of the European Union's Sustainability Impact Assessment of Multilateral and Regional Trade Negotiations' (2006) Institute for Development Policy & Management Working Paper No 14.

George C, Kirkpatrick C and Scrieciu S, *Final Global Overview Trade SIA: Inception and Mid-Term Reports* (Manchester, Institute for Development Policy & Management 2006).

Giljum S and Eisenmenger N, 'North-South Trade and the Distribution of Environmental Goods and Burdens: A Biophysical Perspective' (2004) 13 Journal of Environment Development 73.

Ginthers D, Denters M and de Waart P (eds), *Sustainable Development and Good Governance* (Dordrecht, Kluwer Academic Publishers 1995).

Glastra R, *Cut and Run* (Ottawa, IDRC 1999).

Gostin LO, 'Meeting Basic Survival Needs of the World's Least Healthy People: Toward a Framework Convention on Global Health' (Inaugural Lecture for the Investiture of the Linda D and Timothy J O'Neill Professor of Global Health Law, Georgetown University Law Center, Washington, DC, 19 April 2007).

Gray K, 'Accommodating MEAs in Trade Agreements' (Presentation given at the International Environmental Governance Conference in Paris, March 2004).

Gray K, 'Brazil: Measures Affecting Imports of R etreaded Tyres' (2008) 102 American Journal of International Law 610.

Grosz M, *Sustainable Waste Trade under WTO Law* (Leiden, Martinus Nijhoff Publishers 2011).

Gruchalla-Wesierski T, 'A Framework for Understanding Soft Law' (1984–1985) 30 McGill Law Journal 37.

Guangtao W, 'Statement by the Minister of Construction of the People's Republic of China and Head of the Chinese Delegation at the High-level Segment of the 13th Session of the Commission on Sustainable Development' (2005) <http://www.un.org/esa/sustdev/csd/csd13/statements/2104_china.pdf> accessed 16 December 2020.

Hafner-Burton EM, 'Trading Human Rights: How Preferential Trade Agreements Influence Government Repression' (2005) 59 International Organization 593.

Haggard S and Simmons BA, 'Theories of International Regimes' (1987) 41 International Organization 491.

Handl G, 'Environmental Protection and Development in Third World Countries: Common Destiny--Common Responsibility' (1987–1988) 20 New York University Journal of International Law and Politics 603.

Handl G, 'Environmental Security and Global Change: The Challenge to International Law' (1990) 1 Yearbook of International Environmental Law 25.

Handl G, 'The Legal Mandate of Multilateral Development Banks as Agents for Change towards Sustainable Development' (1998) 92 American Journal of International Law 641.

Hayman G and Brack D, *International Environmental Crime: The Nature and Control of Environmental Black Markets* (London, RIIA 2002).

Hepburn J and Ahmad I, 'The Principle of Common but Differentiated Responsibilities' (CISDL, Montreal 2005) CISDL Legal Working Papers on Recent Developments in International Law Related to Sustainable Development <http://cisdl.org/public/docs/news/brief_common.pdf> accessed 16 December 2020.

Hepburn J, Cordonier Segger MC and Gehring M, 'The Principle of the Precautionary Approach to Human Health, Natural Resources and Ecosystems' (CISDL, Montreal 2005) CISDL Legal Working Papers on Recent Developments in International Law Related to Sustainable Development <http://www.worldfuturecouncil.org/fileadmin/user_upload/papers/CISDL_P3_PrecautionaryPrinciple.pdf> accessed 16 December 2020.

Hepburn J and Khalfan A, 'The Principle of Equity and the Eradication of Poverty' (CISDL, Montreal 2005) CISDL Legal Working Papers on Recent Developments in International Law Related to Sustainable Development <http://www.worldfuturecouncil.org/fileadmin/user_upload/papers/CISDL_P2_Equityetc.pdf> accessed 16 December 2020.

Hilf M and Oeter S (eds), *WTO-Recht* (Baden-Baden, Nomos 2005).

Hohfeld WN, *Fundamental Legal Conceptions, As Applied in Judicial Reasoning and Other Legal Essays* (Ashgate, Aldershot 2001).

Holliday C Jr., Schmidheiny S., and Watts P, *Walking the Talk: The Business Case for Sustainable Development* (London, Routledge 2017).

Horn H, 'The Burden of Proof in Trade Disputes and the Environment' (2011) 62 Journal of Environmental Economics and Management 15.

Homeyer I von, 'Experimentalist Environmental Governance in the EU: Complex Challenges, Recursive Policy-Making, International Implications' (Berlin Conference on the Human Dimensions of Global Environmental Change, 22–23 February 2006, Berlin, Germany).

Howse R, 'The Appellate Body Rulings in the Shrimp/Turtle Case: A New Legal Baseline for the Trade and Environment Debate' (2002) 27 Columbia Journal of Environmental Law 491.

Howse R, 'Human Rights in the WTO: Whose Rights, What Humanity?' (2002) 13 European Journal of International Law 651.

Howse R and Mutua M, 'Protecting Human Rights in a Global Economy: Challenges for the World Trade Organization' in ICHRDD, Rights and Democracy (Montreal, ICHRDD 2000).

Huesa Vinaixa R and Wellens K, *L'influence des sources sur l'unité et la fragmentation du droit international*, Travaux du Seminaire tenu a Palma, les 20-21 Mai 2005 (Brussels, Bruylant 2006).

Hufbauer GC and Cimino-Isaacs C, 'How Will TPP and TTIP Change the WTO System?' (2015) 18(3) Journal of International Economic Law 679–696.

Julian RH, 'Statement on behalf of Santa Lucia at the 57th Session of the General Assembly of the United Nations' (2002) <http://www.stlucia.gov.lc/addresses_and_speeches/julian_hunte/statement_at_57th_session_of_the_united_nations_general_assembly_september_18th_2002.htm> accessed 16 December 2020.

Hunter D, Zaelke D and Salzman J, *International Environmental Law and Policy* (New York, Foundation Press 2001).

Institute for Development Policy and Management, 'Development of Criteria to Assess the Effectiveness of National Strategies for Sustainable Development' (IDPM 2001)

Institute for Development Policy and Management, *Update of the Overall Preliminary Trade SIA EU-Mercosur* (IDPM, 2007) <http://trade.ec.europa.eu/doclib/docs/2007/july/tradoc_135275.pdf> accessed 16 December 2020.

Inter-American Development Bank, 'Environment and Safeguards Compliance Policy' (IADB, 2006).

International Centre for Trade and Sustainable Development, 'Ministerial Preparations On A Bumpy Ride To Seattle' *Bridges Weekly Trade News Digest* (ICTSD, 1 November 1999).

International Centre for Trade and Sustainable Development, 'New Issues' *Bridges Weekly Trade News Digest* (ICTSD 24 November 1999) <http://ictsd.net/i/news/bridgesweekly/19194/> accessed 16 December 2020.

International Centre for Trade and Sustainable Development/International Institute for Sustainable Development, *Climate Change, Technology Transfer and Intellectual Property Rights* (Geneva, ICTSD 2008).

International Centre for Trade and Sustainable Development, *Trade, Climate Change and the Sustainable Development* (Geneva, ICTSD 2010).

International Institute for Sustainable Development, 'Earth Negotiations Bulletin' <http://www.iisd.ca/linkages/2002/wssd/> accessed 16 December 2020.

International Institute for Sustainable Development, *A Sustainable Development Roadmap for the WTO* (IISD: Trade and Investment Program, 2009).

International Trade Centre, 'Export Impact for Good' <https://www.intracen.org> accessed 16 December 2020.

International Union for Conservation of Nature and Natural Resources, *World Conservation Strategy* (IUCN 1980).

International Union for Conservation of Nature and Natural Resources, *An Explanatory Guide to the Cartagena Protocol on Biosafety* (Cambridge, IUCN/FIELD 2003).

Jackson JH, 'The Birth of the GATT-MTN System: A Constitutional Appraisal' (1980) 12 Law and Policy in International Business 21.

Jackson JH, *The World Trading System: Law and Policy of International Economic Relations* (2nd edn, Boston, MIT Press 1997).

Jackson JH, Davey W and Sykes A, *Legal Problems of International Economic Relations* (3rd edn, West, St Paul 1995).

Jaffe A, Peterson S and Portney P 'Environmental Regulation and the Competitiveness of US Manufacturing: What Does the Evidence Tell Us?' (1995) 33 Journal of Economic Literature 132.

Jennings R, 'What is International Law and How Do We Tell It When We See It?' (1981) 37 Schweizerisches Jahrbuch für Internationales Recht 59.

Jennings R and Watts A, *Oppenheim's International Law* (9th edn, Harlow, Longman, 1992).

Jinnah S and Morgera E, 'Environmental Provisions in American and EU Free Trade Agreements: A Preliminary Comparison and Research Agenda' (2013) 22(3) Review of European, Comparative & International Environmental Law 324–339.

Johnson B. (ed), *Who Pays the Price?* (Washington, Island Press 1994).

Johnson P-M and Beaulieu A, *The Environment and NAFTA: Understanding and Implementing the New Continental Law* (Washington, Island Press 1996).

Jonas DS and Saunders TN, 'The Object and Purpose of a Treaty: Three Interpretive Methods' (2010) 43(3) Vanderbilt Journal of Transnational Law 565–610; R Gardiner, *Treaty Interpretation* (2nd edn, Oxford, OUP 2015).

Kaniaru D (ed), *The Montreal Protocol: Celebrating 20 Years of Environmental Progress* (London, UNEP 2008).

Kaufmann G, *Globalisation and Labour Rights: The Conflict between Core Labour Rights and International Economic Law* (Oxford, Hart 2002).

Kaye Nijaki L and Worrel G, 'Procurement for Sustainable Local Economic Development' (2012) 25 International Journal of Public Sector Management 133.

Kelsen H, *Theorie Generale des Normes* (Paris, Presses Universitaires de France 1996).

Keohane NO and Olmstead SM, *Markets and the Environment* (Connecticut, Island Press 2007).

Kessie EK, 'Developing Countries in the World Trade Organisation' (1999) 22 World Competition 83.

Kilbert CJ, *Sustainable Construction: Green Building Design and Delivery* (New Jersey, John Wiley and Sons 2008).

Kirkpatrick C and Lee N, *WTO New Round: Sustainability Impact Assessment Study (Phase Two Report)* (Manchester, Institute for Development Policy and Management 1999).

Kirkpatrick C and Lee N, *Further Development of the Methodology for a Sustainability Impact Assessment of Proposed WTO Negotiations* (Manchester, Institute for Development Policy and Management 2002).

Kirkpatrick C and George C, 'Methodological Issues in the Impact Assessment of Trade Policy: Experience from the European Commission's Sustainability Impact Assessment (SIA) Program' (2006) 24 Impact Assessment and Project Appraisal 325.

Kirkpatrick C and Parker D (eds) *Regulatory Impact Assessment: Towards Better Regulation* (Cheltenham, Edward Elgar 2007).

Kirton J, 'The Commission for Environmental Cooperation and Canada-U.S. Environmental Governance in the NAFTA Era' (1997) 27 American Review of Canadian Studies 459.

Kirton J and Maclaren V (eds), *Linking Trade, Environment and Social Cohesion: NAFTA Experiences, Global Challenges* (Ashgate, Aldershot 2002).

Kiss A and Shelton D, *International Environmental Law* (2nd edn, New York, Transnational 1994).

Kiss A, Shelton D and Ishibashi K (eds), *Economic Globalization and Compliance with International Environmental Agreements* (The Hague, International Environmental Law and Policy Series 63, Kluwer Law International 2003).

Kjellen B, *A New Diplomacy for Sustainable Development: The Challenge of Global Change* (New York, Routledge 2008).

Kleiman D, Guinan J and Mavroidis PC, 'The Doha Round: An Obituary' (June 2011) Global Governance Programme Policy Brief.

Kong H and Kinvin Wroth L, *NAFTA and Sustainable Development* (Cambridge University Press, CUP 2015).

Knox, JH 'The Judicial Resolution of Conflicts between Trade and the Environment' (2004) 28 Harvard Environmental Law Review 1.

Krajewski M, 'External Trade Law and the Constitution Treaty: Towards a Federal and More Democratic Common Commercial Policy?' (2005) 42 Common Market Law Review 91–127.

Krasner S (ed), *International Regimes* (Ithaca, Cornell University Press 1983).

Krasner S, *Sovereignty: Organized Hypocrisy* (Princeton, Princeton University Press 1999).

Krieger MJ, 'Intellectual Property Rights and Traditional Knowledge: Biopiracy or Bioprospecting?' (2008) ETH Research Reports Working Paper 15.

Krueger A, 'Free Trade Agreements versus Customs Unions' (1995) NBER Working Paper No 5084 <https://www.nber.org/papers/w5084> accessed 16 December 2020.

Lamy P, 'Trade Can be a Friend, and Not a Foe, of Conservation' (Speech at the WTO Symposium on Trade and Sustainable Development Geneva, 10 October 2005) <http://www.wto.org/english/news_e/sppl_e/sppl07_e.htm> accessed 16 December 2020.

Lang W (ed), *Sustainable Development and International Law* (London, Martinus Nijhoff 1995).

'Latin America and the Caribbean Regional Statement to the Ninth Global Civil Society Forum and the Tenth Special Session of the Governing Council/Global Ministerial Environment Forum' (2007) <https://wedocs.unep.org/bitstream/handle/20.500.11822/13705/ROLACstatement.pdf? sequence=1&amp%3BisAllowed=> accessed 16 December 2020.

Lawson RA, 'Economic Freedom and the Well-Being of Nations' in E Chamlee-Wright (ed), *The Annual Proceedings of the Wealth and Well-Being of Nations* (Wisconsin, Beloit College Press 2010) 65.

Lee SH, 'The Role of WTO in Sustainable Development Governance Revisited' (2018) 10 135, 135.

LePrestre PG (ed), *Governing Global Biodiversity: The Evolution and Implementation of the Convention on Biological Diversity* (Ashgate, Aldershot 2002).

Lester S and Mercurio B (eds), *Bilateral and Regional Trade Agreements: Commentary, Analysis and Case Studies* (Cambridge, CUP 2008).

Lewis BN, 'Biting without Teeth: The Citizen Submission Process and Environmental Protection' (2007) 155 University of Pennsylvania Law Review 1229.

Lexikon der Nachhaltigkeit <https://www.nachhaltigkeit.info/> accessed 16 December 2020.

Li Y and Hewitt CN, 'The Effect of Trade between China and the UK on National and Global Carbon Dioxide Emissions' (2008) 36 Energy Policy 1907.

Lightbourne M, 'The FAO Multilateral System for Plant Genetic Resources for Food and Agriculture: Better than Bilateralism?' (2009) 30 Washington University Journal of Law and Policy 465.

Low P (ed), *International Trade and Environment* (1992) World Bank Discussion Paper No 159.

Low P and Yeats A, 'Do Dirty Industries Migrate?' in Low P (ed), *International Trade and Environment* (World Bank Discussion Paper No 159, 1992)

Low P and Mattoo A, 'Is there a Better Way? Alternative Approaches to Liberalization under the GATS' in P Sauve and RM Stern (eds), *GATS 2000: New Directions in Services Trade Liberalization* (Washington, The Brookings Institute 2000) 449.

Lowe V, 'Sustainable Development and Unsustainable Arguments' in A Boyle and D Freestone (eds), *International Law and Sustainable Development: Past Achievements and Future Challenges* (Oxford, OUP 1999) 27.

Lowe V, 'The Politics of Law-Making: Are the Method and Character of Norm Creation Changing?' in M Byers (ed), *The Role of Law in International Politics: Essays in International Relations and International Law* (Oxford, OUP 2000) 214.

Lowe V, *International Law* (Oxford, OUP 2007).

Lowenfeld A, *International Economic Law* (Oxford, OUP 2002).

Lucas, R. E., Wheeler, D., & Hettige, H. (1992). Economic development, environmental regulation, and the international migration of toxic industrial pollution, 1960–88 (Vol. 1062). World Bank Publications.

Mathews JT, 'Power Shift' (1997) 76 Foreign Affairs 50.

Maresceau M, 'Bilateral Agreements concluded by the European Community' (2004) 309 Recueil des Cours de l'Académie de Droit International 125, 311.

Mathis J, *Regional Trade Agreements in the GATT / WTO* (The Hague, TMC Asser 2002).

Matusz S and Tarr D, 'Adjusting to Trade Policy Reform', World Bank Policy Research Working Paper No 2142 (Washington, DC, World Bank 1999).

Matsushita M, Schoenbaum TJ and Mavroidis PC, *The World Trade Organization: Law, Practice, and Policy* (Oxford, OUP 2006).

Matus M and Rossi E, 'Trade and the Environment in the FTAA: A Chilean Perspective' in C Deere and D Esty (eds), *Greening the Americas: NAFTA's Lessons for Hemispheric Trade* (Boston, MIT Press 2002) 259.

Mavroidis PC, 'Trade and Environment after the Shrimp-Turtles Litigation' (2000) 34 Journal of World Trade 73.

Mayrand K, 'Integrated Assessment of Trade-Related Policies: Agricultural Trade Liberalisation and the Convention to Combat Desertification' (2006) 24 Impact Assessment and Project Appraisal 311.

McConnell VD and Schwab RM, 'The Impact of Environmental Regulation on Industry Location Decisions: The Motor Vehicle Industry' (1990) 66(1) Land Economics 67.

McCoy M and McCully P, *The Road From Rio: An NGO Action Guide to Environment and Development* (Amsterdam, Utrecht International Books 1993).

McCrudden C, 'International Economic Law and Human Rights: A Framework for Discussion of the Legality of "Selective Purchasing" Laws under the WTO Government Procurement Agreement' (1999) 2 Journal of International Economic Law 3.

McCrudden C 'Using Public Procurement to Achieve Social Outcomes' 28(4) Natural Resources Forum 257 (2004).

McCrudden C, 'Social Aspects in Sustainable Public Procurement', Presentation at the Second Expert Meeting on Sustainable Public Procurement, Kifissia, Greece (2003) <http://www.un.org/esa/sustdev/sdissues/consumption/ChristopherMcCrudden.pdf> accessed 16 December 2020.

McCrudden C, *Buying Social Justice* (Oxford, OUP 2007).

McCulloch NA, Winters LA and Cirera X, *Trade Liberalization and Poverty: A Handbook* (London, Centre for Economic and Policy Research 2001).

McGoldrick M, 'Sustainable Development: The Challenge to International Law' (1994) FIELD Review of European Community and International Environmental Law 3.

Meadows DL and others, *Limits to Growth* (Boston, MIT Press 1972).

Mendelson MH, 'The Formation of Customary International Law' (1999) 272 Recueil des Cours de l'Académie de Droit International 9.

Mendes E and Mehmet O, *Global Governance, Economy and Law: Waiting for Justice* (London, Routledge 2003) 67.

Government of Mexico, 'National Development Plan 2007-2012' (2007).

Meyers GD and Muller SC, 'The Ethical Implications, Political Ramifications and Practical Limitations of Adopting Sustainable Development as National and International Policy' (1996) 4 Buffalo Environmental Law Journal 1.

Miller SR, 'NAFTA: A Model for Reconciling the Conflict between Free Trade and International Environmental Protection' (1994-1995) 56 University of Pittsburg Law Review 483.

Mooney H and Hobbs R (eds), *Invasive Species in a Changing World* (Island Press, Washington 2000).

Morgenstern O and others, 'The World Avoided by the Montreal Protocol' (2008) 35 Geophysical Research Letters 1.

Morin J-F and Bialais C, 'Strengthening Multilateral Environmental Governance through Bilateral Trade Deals' Policy Brief No. 123, Centre for International Global Innovation.

Moses RS, 'Statement by the Secretary of External Affairs of the Federated States of Micronesia in the General Debate of the 48th Session of the General Assembly of the United Nations' (1993) <http://www.fsmgov.org/fsmun/48thga.html> accessed 16 December 2020.

Motaal D, 'The Observership of Intergovernmental Organizations in the WTO post-Doha' (2005) 5 Journal of World Intellectual Property 477.

Mukherji I, 'The Bangkok Agreement: A Negative List Approach to Trade Liberalization in Asia and the Pacific' (2005) 1 Asia- Pacific Trade and Investment Review 27.

Muradian R and Martinez-Alier J, 'Trade and the Environment: From a "Southern" Perspective' (2001) 36 Ecological Economics 281.

Murphy L, 'EC and Chile Reach Agreement on 10-Year Swordfish Dispute' (2001) 4 International Fisheries Bulletin, <http://www.intfish.net/igifl/archive/ops/ifb/focus/2001/4.htm> accessed 16 December 2020.

Narlikar A, *Deadlocks in Multilateral Negotiations: Causes and Solutions* (Cambridge, CUP 2010).

Negi A, 'World Trade Organisation and the EC Biotech Case: Procedural and Substantive Issues' (2007) 44 International Studies 1.

Neumayer E, 'Trade Measures in Multilateral Environmental Agreements and WTO Rules: Potential for Conflict, Scope for Reconciliation' (2000) 55 Aussenwirtschaft 1.

Neumayer E, 'Do Countries Fail to Raise Environmental Standards? An Evaluation of Policy Options Addressing 'Regulatory Chill' (2001) 4 International Journal of Sustainable Development 231.

Newcombe A, 'Sustainable Development and Investment Treaty Law' (2007) 8 Journal of World Investment & Trade 357, 65–69.

Newcombe A, *Report on Issues Related to 'General Exceptions' in Future Trade/Investment Agreements*, prepared for Natural Resources Canada (10 August 2007).

Neumayer E, *Greening Trade and Investment: Environmental Protection without Protectionism* (London, Routledge 2017)

Newcombe A and Paradell L, *Law and Practice of Investment Treaties* (Chicago, Kluwer Law International 2009).

Newell P, 'Managing Multinationals: The Governance of Investment for the Environment' (2001) 13 Journal of International Development 907

Newell P and Tussie D, 'Public Participation in Trade Policy-Making in Latin America: Reflections and Lessons' (May 2006) IDS Working Paper No 267.

Newfarmer R, *Trade, Doha and Development: A Window into the Issues* (Washington, The World Bank 2005).

Ngangjoh- Hodu Y, 'Relationship of GATT Article XX Exceptions to other WTO Agreements' (2011) 80 Nordic Journal of International Law 219.

Nizzetto L and others, 'Past. Present, and Future Controls on levels of Persistent Organic Pollutants in the Global Environment' (2010) 44 Environmental Science and Technology 6526.

Nordström H and Vaughan S, *Trade and Environment* (Special Studies 4, WTO Geneva 1999).

North American Agreement on Environmental Cooperation (NACEC), 'Assessing the Environmental Effects of Trade' (2002) <http://www.cec.org/pubs_docs/documents/index.cfm?varlan=english&ID=40> accessed 16 December 2020.

North American Free Trade Agreement Free Trade Commission, 'Notes of Interpretation of Certain Chapter 11 Provisions' (31 July 2001) <http://www.sice.oas.org/TPD/NAFTA/Commission/CH11understanding_e.asp> accessed 16 December 2020.

Oeter S, 'Trade, Agriculture and Sustainability in Land Use' in M Gehring and MC Cordonier Segger, *Sustainable Development in World Trade Law* (Kluwer Law International, The Hague 2005) 327.

Orellana M, 'The EU and Chile Suspend the Swordfish Case Proceedings at the WTO and the International Tribunal of the Law of the Sea' (February 2001) 60 American Society of International Law Insights <http://www.asil.org/insights/insigh60.htm> accessed 16 December 2020.

Orellana M, 'The Swordfish Dispute between the EU and Chile at the ITLOS and the WTO' (2002) 71 Nordic Journal of International Law 55.

Organisation for Economic Co-operation and Development, *Environment and Regional Trade Agreements* (Paris, OECD 2007).

Organisation for Economic Co-operation and Development, *Freight and the Environment: Effects of Trade Liberalization and the Transport Sector Reforms* (Paris, OECD 1997).

Organisation for Economic Co-operation and Development, *Trade Measures in Multilateral Environmental Agreements* (Paris, OECD 1999).

Organization of American States, Department of Sustainable Development <http://www.oas.org/dsd/> accessed 16 December 2020.

Organization of American States, Foreign Trade Information System (SICE) <http://www.sice.oas.org/tpd_e.asp> accessed 16 December 2020.

Pallemaerts M, 'International Law and Sustainable Development: Any Progress in Johannesburg?' (2003) 12 Review of European Community and International Environmental Law 1.

Pallemaerts M, 'The EU and Sustainable Development: An Ambiguous Relationship' in M Pallemaerts and A Azmanova (eds), *The European Union and Sustainable Development: Internal and External Dimensions* (Brussels, VUB Press 2006) 24

Pallemaerts M, Herodes M and Adelle C, 'Does the EU Sustainable Development Strategy contribute to Environmental policy Integration' EPIGOV Paper No 9, Ecologic—Institute for International and European Environmental Policy, Berlin.

Palmeter D and Mavroidis PC, 'The WTO Legal System: Sources of Law' (1998) 92 American Journal of International Law 398.

Panagariya A, 'The Return of Labour Standards in the WTO?' *Economic Times* (6 November 1999) <http://www.columbia.edu/~ap2231/the-return-of-labour-standards-in-the-wto/> accessed 16 December 2020.

PANNA, 'US Muscles Montreal Protocol on MB Limits' (2004) <http://www.panna.org/legacy/panups/panup_20041210.dv.html> accessed 16 December 2020.

Paul JR, 'Free Trade, Regulatory Competition, and the Autonomous Market Fallacy' (1994) 1 Columbia Journal of European Law 29.

Pauwelyn J, *Conflict of Norms in Public International Law: How WTO Law Relates to Other Rules of International Law* (Cambridge, CUP 2003).

Pauwelyn J, 'Human Rights in WTO Dispute Settlement' in T Cottier, J Pauwelyn and E Burgi, *Human Rights and International Trade* (Oxford, OUP 2005) 205.

Pearce DW and Turner RK, *Economics of Natural Resources and the Environment* (Baltimore, John Hopkins University Press 1990).

Perrin M, 'Sustainability Assessments of Trade Liberalisation Agreements', Paper presented at Workshop on *Methodologies for Environemtnal Assessment of Trade Liberalisation Agreements* (Paris, OECD 1999).

Peru, 'State Policies on Sustainable Development and Environment'.

Petersmann EU, 'Taking Human Dignity, Poverty and Empowerment of Individuals More Seriously' (2002) 13 European Journal of International Law 845.

Polanco R, 'Third-Party Rights and Transparency in Foreign Investment International Arbitration' (2010) Revista de Derecho Económico, año XLVII, No 75, Chile.

Polanco R, Mayorga R and J Morales, *Foreign Investment: Legal Regime and Dispute Settlement* (Santiago, LexisNexis 2004).

Polaski S, 'Protecting Labor Rights through Trade Agreements' (2004) 10 University of California Davis Journal of International Law 13.

Polaski S, *Winners and Losers: Impact of the Doha Round on Developing Countries* (Washington, Carnegie Endowment 2006).

Pollack M and Shaffer GC, *When Cooperation Fails: The International Law and Politics of Genetically Modified Foods* (Oxford, OUP 2009).

Price VC, 'GATT's new Trade Policy Review Mechanism' (1991) 14 World Economy 227.

The Public Citizen, 'Global Trade Watch: Promoting Democracy by Challenging Corporate Globalization' <http://www.citizen.org/trade/> accessed 16 December 2020.

Rajamani L, *Differential Treatment in International Environmental Law* (Oxford, OUP 2006).

Ranjan P, 'International Trade and Human Rights: Conflicting Obligations' in T Cottier, J Pauwelyn and E Burgi, *Human Rights and International Trade* (Oxford, OUP 2005).

Ravallion M, 'Looking Beyond Averages in the Trade and Poverty Debate' (2004) World Bank Policy Research Working Paper No 3461 <http://ideas.repec.org/p/wbk/wbrwps/3461.html> accessed 16 December 2020.

Ricardo D, *The Principles of Political Economy and Taxation* (London, Dent 1965).

Richardson S, 'Sovereignty, Trade, and the Environment-The North American Agreement on Environmental Cooperation' (1998) 24 Canada-United States Law Journal 183.

Richardson S, *A 'critique' of the EU's WTO sustainability impact assessment study and recommendations for phase III* (Gland, Switzerland, WWF-European Policy Office 2000).

Redgwell C, 'Universality or Integrity? Some reflections on Reservations to General Multilateral Treaties' 64 (1993) British Yearbook of International Law 245.

Redgwell C, 'The Protection of the Antarctic Environment and the Ecosystem Approach' in M Bowman and C Redgwell (eds), *International Law and the Conservation of Biological Diversity* (The Hague, Kluwer Law International 1996).

Redgwell C, 'Reservations To Treaties and Human Rights Committee General Comment No.24(52)' (1997) 46 International and Comparative Law Quarterly 390.

Reynaud P, 'Sustainable Development and Regional Trade Agreements: Toward Better Practices in Impact Assessments' (2012) 8 McGill International Journal of Sustainable Development Law and Policy 205.

Rodrik D, 'Policy Uncertainty and Private Investment in Developing Countries' (1991) 36 Journal of Development Economics 229.

Robb C, *Trade and Environment* International Environmental Law Reports 2 (Cambridge, CUP 2001).

Robinson NA (ed), 'Agenda 21: Earth's Action Plan' (1993) IUCN Environmental Policy & Law Paper No 27.

Roheim CA and others, 'Evolution and Future of the Sustainable Seafood Market' (2018) 1(8) Nature Sustainability 392–398.

Rojas-Romagosa H, 'Overview of the Evolution of the Methodology and Coverage of EU Ex-Ante Trade Sustainability Impact Assessments over Time' (RESPECT mimeo 2018).

Rolland SE, 'Developing Country Coalitions at the WTO: In Search of Legal Support' (2007) 48 Harvard International Law Journal 483.

Rosales O, 'Chile-U.S Free Trade Agreement: Lessons and Best Practices' (2003) <http://www.sice.oas.org/TPD/CHL_USA/Studies/lessons_e.pdf> accessed 16 December 2020.

Rose-Ackerman S and Tobin J, 'Do BITs Benefit Developing Countries?' in C Rogers and RP Alford (eds), *The Future of Investment Arbitration* (Oxford, OUP 2009).

Ruggie JG, 'International Responses to Technology: Ideas and Trends' (1975) 29 International Organization 557.

Ruggie JG, 'Reconstituting the Global Public Domain: Issues, Actors, and Practices' (2004) 10 European Journal of International Relations 499.

Ruggiero R, 'Defining the Singapore Message' (1996) 12 WTO Focus 7.

Ruggiero R, 'The Road Ahead: International Trade Policy in the Era of the WTO', Address to the fourth Sylvia Ostry Lecture in Ottawa, 28 May 1996, <http://www.wto.org/english/news_e/sprr_e/ottawa_e.htm> accessed 16 December 2020.

Runnalls D, 'Shall We Dance: What the North Needs to do to Fully Engage the South in the Trade and Sustainable Development Debate' (1996) IISD Working Paper (IISD, Winnipeg 1996).

Ruse-Khan HG, 'A Real Partnership for Development? Sustainable Development as Treaty Objective in European Economic Agreement Partnerships and beyond' (2010) 13 Journal of International Economic Law 139.

Sachs W (ed), *The Development Dictionary: A Guide to Knowledge as Power* (London, Zed Press 1992).

Sagar JV, 'The Labor and Environment Chapters of the United States-Chile Free Trade Agreement: An Improvement over the Weak Enforcement Provisions of the NAFTA Side Agreements on LAbor and the Environment?' (2004) 21 Arizona Journal of International & Comparative Law 913.

Salzman J, 'Executive Order 13.141 and the Environmental Review of Trade Agreements' 95 (2001) American Journal of International Law 368.

Salzman J, 'Seattle's Legal Legacy and Environmental Reviews of Trade Agreements' (2001) 31 Environmental Law 501.

Sampson G, *The WTO and Sustainable Development* (Tokyo, United Nations University Press 2005).

Sampson G and others, 'Secure Sustainable Seafood from Developing Countries' (2015) 348(6234) Science 504, 504–506.

Sampson G and Chambers B, *Trade, Environment and the Millennium* (Tokyo, UNU 2000).

Sands P, 'International Law in the Field of Sustainable Development' (1994) 65 British Yearbook of International Law 303.

Sands P, 'Treaty, Custom and Cross- Fertilization of International Law' (1998) 10 Yale Human Rights and Development Law Journal 3, 11–12.

Sands P, 'International Law in the Field of Sustainable Development: Emerging Legal Principles' in W. Lang (ed), *Sustainable Development and International Law* (Oxford, OUP 1999).

Sands P, *Principles of International Environmental Law* (2nd edn, Cambridge, CUP 2003).

Sarkar R, *International Development Law: Rule of Law, Human Rights & Global Finance* (Oxford, OUP 2009).

Sarooshi D, 'The Future of the WTO and its Dispute Settlement System' (2005) 2(1) International Organizations Law Review 129.

Saunders O, 'NAFTA and the North American Agreement on Environmental Cooperation: A New Model for International Collaboration on Trade and the Environment' (1994) 5 Colorado Journal of International Environmental Law and Policy 273.

Schrijver N, *Sovereignty over Natural Resources: Balancing Rights and Duties* (Cambridge, CUP 1996).

Schrijver N and Weiss F, 'Editorial Introduction' (2002) 2 International Environmental Agreements 105.

Schrijver N and Weiss F (eds), *International Law and Sustainable Development: Principles and Practice* (Leiden, Martinus Nijhoff 2004).

Schuurman FJ, *Beyond the Impasse: New Directions in Development Theory* (London, Zed Press 1993).

Schott J (ed), *The WTO after Seattle* (Washington, IIE 2000).

Scott J, 'International Trade and Environmental Governance: Relating Rules (and Standards) in the EU and the WTO' (2004) 15 European Journal of International Law 307.

Scott J, *Commentary on the Sanitary and Phytosanitary Measures Agreement* (Oxford, OUP 2007).

Scott J and de Burca G (eds), *Law and New Approaches to Governance in the EU and US* (Oxford, Hart 2006).

Seely MK and others, 'Creative Problem Solving in Support of Biodiversity Conservation' (2003) 54 Journal of Arid Environments 155.

Selin H, *Global Governance of Hazardous Chemicals: Challenges of Multilevel Management* (Massachussets, MIT Press 2010).

Sell SK, 'Corporations, Seeds, and Intellectual Property Rights Governance' in Jennifer Clapp and Doris A Fuchs (eds), *Corporate Power in Global Agrifood Governance* (Massachusett, MIT Press 2009) 187.

Sen A, *Development as Freedom* (Oxford, OUP 1999).

Shaffer GC and Pollack MA, 'Hard vs. Soft Law: Alternatives, Complements, and Antagonists in International Governance' (2009) 94 Minnesota Law Review 706.

Shaw M, *International Law* (6th edn, Cambridge, CUP 2008).

Shaw S, 'Business and the Environment: Is there more to the Story?' (2005) 40 Business Economics 40.

Shaw S and Schwartz R, 'Trade and Environment in the WTO State of Play' (2002) 36 Journal of World Trade 129.

Shine C, Williams N and Gündling L, 'A Guide to Designing Legal and Institutional Frameworks on Alien Invasive Species', Environmental Policy and Law Paper No 40 (Gland, Switzerland, Cambridge and Bonn, IUCN 2000).

Shone M, 'Social Dimensions of Public Procurement: An ILO Perspective', Presentation at the Second Expert Meeting on Sustainable Public Procurement, Kifissia, Greece (2003) <http://www.un.org/esa/sustdev/sdissues/consumption/MikeShone.pdf> accessed 16 December 2020.

Simpson G, 'The Situation on the International Legal Theory Front: The Power of Rules and the Rule of Power' (2000) 11 European Journal of International Law 439.

Sloan A, 'An Empirical Study on the Impact of the United States Chile Free Trade Agreement on Chilean Employment and Value Added' (Major Paper Presented to the Department of Economics of the University of Ottawa, 2019).

Smith MJ and others, 'Assessing the Impacts of International Trade on CITES-listed Species: Current practices and opportunities for scientific research' (2010) 144 Biological Conservation 82.

Sprinz DL and Wolinsky-Nahmias Y, *Models, Numbers & Cases: Methods for Studying International Relations* (Michigan, University of Michigan Press 2004).

Steinfatt K, 'Preferential and Partial Scope Trade Agreements' in S Xirinachs and M Roberts (eds), *Towards Free Trade in the Americas* (Maryland, Phoenix Colour 2001) 108.

Stenzel PL, 'Free Trade and Sustainability through the Lens of Nicaragua: How CAFTA-DR should be amended to promote the Triple Bottom Line' (2010) 34 William and Mary Environmental Law and Policy Review 653.

Stern DI, 'The Rise and Fall of the Environmental Kuznets Curve,' (2004) 32 World Development 1419.

Stern NH and others, *The Stern Review: The Economics of Climate Change* (2006) HM Treasury, <http://webarchive.nationalarchives.gov.uk/+/http:/www.hm-treasury.gov.uk/sternreview_index.htm> accessed 16 December 2020.

Stiglitz J and Charlton A, *Fair Trade for All: How Trade Can Promote Development* (Oxford, OUP 2006).

Stilwell M, 'Trade and Environment in the Context of Sustainable Development' in Markus Gehring and Marie-Claire Cordonier Segger (eds), *Sustainable Development in World Trade Law* (Kluwer Law International, The Hague 2005) 27.

Stoler AL, 'The Doha Round Negotiations on the MEA-WTO Interface: Shared Perceptions or Ulterior Motives?', International Bar Association Conference, Auckland, New Zealand, 2004.

Streck C and Freestone D, *Legal Aspects of Carbon Trading: Kyoto, Copenhagen and Beyond* (Oxford, OUP 2009).

Subramaniam A and Wei S-J, 'The WTO promotes Trade, Strongly but Unevenly' (2007) 71 Journal of International Economics 151.

Swanson D and others, *National Strategies for Sustainable Development: Challenges, Approaches and Innovations in Strategic and Co-ordinated Action* (Winnipeg, International Institute for Sustainable Development 2004).

Sykes A, *Product Standards for Internationally Integrated Goods Markets* (Washington, Brookings Institution Press 1995).

Tarasofsky R, 'Ensuring Compatibility between Multilateral Environmental Agreements and GATT/WTO' (1996) 7 Yearbook of International Environmental Law 52.

Tarasofsky R, *The Kyoto Protocol and the WTO* (London, Chatham House 2005).

Tarasofsky R and Stilwell M, *Towards Coherent Environmental and Economic Governance: Legal and Practical Approaches to MEA-WTO Linkages* (Gland, WWF/CIEL, 2001).

Taylor A, 'The Trade and Environmental Debate' in A Taylor and C Thomas (eds), *Global Trade and Global Social Issues* (London, Routledge, 1999).

TEEB, *The Economics of Ecosystems and Biodiversity: Mainstreaming the Economics of Nature: A Synthesis of the Approach, Conclusions and Recommendations of TEEB* (TEEB, 2010).

Thirlway H, 'The Law and Procedure of the International Court of Justice' (1990) 60 British Yearbook of International Law 1.

Thomas C and Trachtman JP, *Developing Countries in the WTO System* (Oxford, OUP 2009).

TMC Asser Institute (ed), *International Law and The Grotian Heritage: A Commemorative Colloquium on the Occasion of the Fourth Centenary of the Birth of Hugo Grotius* (The Hague, TMC Asser Institute 1985).

Tobey JA, 'The Effects of Domestic Environmental Policies on Patterns of World Trade: An Empirical Test,' (1990) 43(2) Kyklos 191.

Todd J, 'Trade Treaties, Citizen Submissions, and Environmental Justice' (2017) 44 Ecology Law Quarterly 89.

Toope SJ and Brunnée J, 'International Law and Constructivism: Elements of an Interactional Theory of International Law' (2000) 39 Columbia Journal of Transnational Law 19.

Trebilcock M and Howse R, *The Regulation of International Trade*, (3rd edn, New York, Routledge 2005).

Trionfetti F, 'Discriminatory Public Procurement and International Trade' (2002) 23 World Economy 57.

Trouwborst A, 'The Precautionary Principle in General International Law: Combating the Babylonian Confusion' (2007) 16 Review of European Community and International Environmental Law 185.

Trzyna TC (ed), *A Sustainable World: Defining and Measuring Sustainable Development* (Sacramento, California Institute of Public Affairs 1995).

Turner BL and others (eds), *The Earth as Transformed by Human Action: Global and Regional Changes in the Biosphere over the Past 300 Years.* (CUP, Cambridge 1990).

UK Government, *Securing the Future: Delivering UK Sustainable Development Strategy* (2005) <https://www.gov.uk/government/publications/securing-the-future-delivering-uk-sustainable-development-strategy> accessed 16 December 2020.

UN CBD Secretariat, 'The Impact of Trade Liberalization on Agricultural Biological Diversity' CBD Technical Series No 16 (Montreal, UN CBD 2006).

UNCSD, 'Sustainable Development: The Challenge to International Law. Report of a Consultation held at Windsor 27 to 29 April 1993' (1993) 2(4) Review of European Community and International Environmental Law 1.

UNCSD, 'Report of the Expert Group Meeting on Identification of Principles of International Law for Sustainable Development' (Geneva, September 26–28 1995) <https://digitallibrary.un.org/record/212979/?ln=en> accessed 16 December 2020.

UNCSD, *Indicators of Sustainable Development: Framework and Methodologies* (UNCSD 1999).

UNCSD, 'Latin America and Caribbean Meetings on Sustainable Consumption and Production' (2003) 8(3) UNCSD Update On-Line.

UNCTAD, *Developing Countries in World Trade* UNCTAD Trade and Development Report 2002 (Washington, UNCTAD 2002) 51.

UNCTAD, *World Investment Report 2003* (New York and Geneva, UNCTAD 2003)

UNCTAD, *Policy Coherence, Development Strategies and Integration into the World Economy* UNCTAD Trade and Development Report 2004 (Washington, UNCTAD 2004) 43–69. See UNCTAD Trade and Development Reports.

UNCTAD, *Multilateralism and Regionalism: The New Interface* (New York and Geneva, UNCTAD 2005).

UNCTAD, *Trade and Development Report, 2005* (New York and Geneva, UNCTAD 2005).

UNDESA, 'Financing for Development', <http://www.un.org/esa/ffd> accessed 16 December 2020.

UNDP, *Human Development Reports* <http://hdr.undp.org> accessed 16 December 2020

UNDESA, 'Federated States of Micronesia: National Assessment Report' (June 2006) <http://www.un.org/esa/sustdev/natlinfo/nsds/pacific_sids/fsm_nar.pdf> accessed 16 December 2020.

UNEP, 'Green Procurement Initiative', <http://www.uneptie.org/pc/sustain/policies/green-proc.htm> accessed 16 December 2020.

UNEP, 2011, Towards a Green Economy: Pathways to Sustainable Development and Poverty Eradication, <https://www.unep.org/greeneconomy> accessed 16 December 2020.

UNEP, *Trade Liberalisation and the Environment: Lessons learned from Bangladesh, Chile, India, Philippines, Romania and Uganda*, A Synthesis Report (Geneva, UNEP 1999).

UNEP, *Climate and Trade Policies in a post-2012 World* (Geneva, UNEP 2000).

UNEP, *Reference Manual for the Integrated Assessment of Trade-Related Policies* (Geneva, UNEP 2001).

UNEP and IISD, *Environment and Trade: A Handbook* (2nd edn, Winnipeg, UNEP/IISD 2005).

Usha A (ed), *Environmental Law: Principles and Governance* (Hyderabad, ICFAI University Press 2008).

USAID, 'Strategic Plan: Fiscal Years 2007-2012' (2007) <http://www.state.gov/documents/organization/86291.pdf> accessed 16 December 2020.

United States Trade Representative and Council on Environmental Quality, *Guidelines for Implementation of Executive Order 13141: Environmental Review of Trade Agreements* (December 2000) <http://www.ustr.gov/sites/default/files/guidelines%20for%2013141.pdf> accessed 16 December 2020.

US Department of Labor, 'Labor-Related US Free Trade Agreement Reports'.

USTR, 'USTR Focus on Environment', <https://ustr.gov/archive/Trade_Sectors/Environment/Section_Index.html> accessed 16 December 2020.

USTR, 'Free Trade with Chile: Summary of the U.S.-Chile Free Trade Agreement' (12 November 2002) <https://ustr.gov/trade-agreements/free-trade-agreements/chile-fta> accessed 16 December 2020, 5

Van den Putte L and Orbie J, 'EU Bilateral Trade Agreements and the Surprising Rise of Labour Provisions' (2015) 31 International Journal of Comparative Labour Law and Industrial Relations 263.

Vaughan S, 'Understanding the Environmental Effects of Trade: Some Lessons from NAFTA' in John J Kirton and Virginia W Maclaren (eds), *Linking Trade, Environment, and Social Cohesion* (Aldershot, Ashgate 2002) 225.

Vaughan S, 'World Trade Organization Gridlock and Alternative Regimes to Pursue an International Social Cause' in J Kirton and P Hajnal (eds), *Sustainability, Civil Society and International Governance* (Aldershot, Ashgate 2006) 261.

de Velde DW and Bezemer D, 'Regional Integration and Foreign Direct Investment in Developing Countries' (2006) <http://www.odi.org.uk/iedg/Projects/ec_prep2.pdf> accessed 16 December 2020.

Villiger ME, *Customary International Law and Treaties* (Leiden, Martinus Nijhoff 1985).

Vitousek PM and others, 'Human Appropriation of the Products of Photosynthesis' (1986) 36(6) BioScience 368.

Vogler J, *The Global Commons: Environmental and Technological Governance* (2nd edn, Chichester, John Wiley and Sons 2000).

Wackemagel M and Rees WE, *Our Ecological Footprint: Reducing Human Impact on the Earth* (Canada, New Society Publishers, 1996).

Wacziarg R and Welch KH, 'Trade Liberalization and Growth: New Evidence' (2008) 22 World Bank Economic Review 187.

Ward H, 'Common but Differentiated Debates: Environment, Labor and the WTO' (1996) 45 International Comparative Law Quarterly, 592.

Weber W, 'Competing Political Visions: WTO Governance and Green Politics' (2001) 1 Global Environmental Politics 92.

Weiler JHH and Paulus AL, 'The Structure of Change in International Law or is There a Hierarchy of Norms in International Law?' (1997) 8 European Journal of International Law 545.

Weiss EB, *In Fairness to Future Generations: International Law, Common Patrimony and Intergenerational Equity* (New York, Transnational 1989).

Weiss MS, 'Two Steps forward, One Step back-or vice-versa: Labor Rights under Free Trade Agreements from NAFTA, through Jordan, via Chile, to Latin America, and beyond' (2002–2003) 37 University of San Francisco Law Review 689.

von Weizsacker E and others, 'Factor Five: Transforming the Global Economy through 80% Improvements in Resource Productivity' (London, Earthscan 2009).

Weller C, Claro E and Blanco H, *Sustainable Public Procurement: Where Do We Stand in Chile?* (Winnipeg, IISD 2008).

Wheeler S and Beatley T, *The Sustainable Urban Development Reader* (London, Routledge 2004).

Williams S and Shumway CR, 'Trade Liberalization and Agricultural Chemical Use: United States and Mexico' (2000) 82(1) American Journal of Agricultural Economics 183.

Winters A, 'Trade Liberalization and Economic Performance: An Overview' (2004) 114(493) Economic Journal F4.

World Bank, 'Operational Policy 4.04-Natural Habitats' (2001) <http://www.worldbank.org> accessed 16 December 2020.

World Commission on Environment and Development, *Our Common Future* (Oxford, OUP 1987).

World Commission on the Social Dimension of Globalization, *A Fair Globalization: Creating Opportunities for All* (Geneva, International Labor Organization 2004).

Wrigley EA and Souden D (eds), *The Works of Thomas Robert Malthus Vol 1: An Essay on the Principle of Population* (London, William Pickering 1986).

WTO, 'The Doha Mandate on Multilateral Environmental Agreements (MEAs)' <http://www.wto.org/english/tratop_e/envir_e/envir_neg_mea_e.htm> accessed 16 December 2020.

WTO Secretariat (ed), *Trade, Development and the Environment* (London, Kluwer Law International 2000).

WTO Secretariat, 'The Changing Landscape of RTAs', Paper prepared for a Seminar on Regional Trade Agreements and the WTO (2003) <http://www.wto.org/english/tratop_e/region_e/sem_nov03_e/boonekamp_paper_e.doc> accessed 16 December 2020.

WTO Secretariat, *Trade and Environment at the WTO* (Geneva, WTO 2004).

WTO Committee on Trade and Environment Special Session, 'Matrix on Trade Measures Pursuant to Selected Multilateral Environmental Agreements' WTO Doc. WT/CTE/W/160/Rev.4, TN/TE/S/5/Rev.2 of 14 March 2007 (Note by the Secretariat).

WTO, 'Regional Trade Agreements: Scope of RTAs' <http://www.wto.org/english/tratop_e/region_e/scope_rta_e.htm> accessed 16 December 2020.

WTO and WHO, *WTO Agreements and Public Health: A Joint Study between the WHO and the WTO Secretariat* (Geneva, WHO/WTO 2002).

Young OR, *International Cooperation: Building Regimes for Natural Resources and The Environment* (Ithaca, Cornell University Press 1989).

Young OR (ed), *Global Governance: Drawing Insights from the Environmental Experience* (Boston, MIT Press 1997).

Zaleke D and Higdon T, 'The Role of Compliance in the Rule of Law, Good Governance and Sustainable Development' (2006) 3 Journal for European Environmental and Planning Law 376.

Zhang ZX, 'Liberalizing Climate-Friendly Goods and Technologies in the WTO: Product Coverage, Modalities, Challenges and the Way Forward' (2009) 1 UNCTAD Trade and Environment Review 1.

Ziemele I, (ed), *Reservations to Human Rights Treaties and the Vienna Convention Regime, Conflict, Harmony or Reconciliation* (The Hague, Martinus Nijhoff 2004)

Index

Tables are indicated by *t* following the page number